MEL
WATKINS

SIMON & SCHUSTER

NEW YORK   LONDON   TORONTO

SYDNEY   TOKYO   SINGAPORE

On The Real Side

Laughing, lying,

and signifying—

the underground

tradition of

African-American humor that

transformed American culture,

from slavery to Richard Pryor

SIMON & SCHUSTER
Rockefeller Center
1230 Avenue of the Americas
New York, New York 10020

DESIGNED BY
BARBARA M. BACHMAN

Manufactured in the United States
of America

10 9 8 7 6 5 4 3 2 1

Library of Congress Cataloging-in-
Publication Data

Watkins, Mel
    On the real side : laughing, lying, and
signifying— : the underground tradition
of African-American humor . . . / Mel
Watkins.
        p.   cm.
    Includes bibliographical references
and index.
    1. African-American wit and humor—
History and criticism.   I. Title.
PN6231.N5W38   1994
792.2′3′08996073—
dc20   93-39868   CIP

ISBN: 0-671-68982-7

Frontispiece photo of Bert Williams
courtesy of Frank Driggs Collection.
(Credits continued on page 621.)

FOR MY PARENTS,

KATIE AND

PITTMAN WATKINS,

AND MY

DAUGHTER, KIM.

ACKNOWLEDGMENTS

My fascination with and curiosity about African-American humor began in earnest when I heard Richard Pryor's routines in the early 1970s. By 1979, I had decided to research the subject. I was fortunate enough to receive an Alicia Patterson Fellowship and, during 1979 and 1980, I spent a year in Los Angeles interviewing comedians, comedy writers, and studio executives, and gathering material. I thank the Alicia Patterson Fellowship committee and all those who cooperated with me during that time, especially Matt Robinson, Cecil Brown, comedians Flip Wilson and George Wallace (who was just starting his career), and a host of writers in Los Angeles. I am particularly grateful for the assistance of the late Honi Coles, with whom I spent many hours reminiscing about black performers in bars off and on Broadway in New York City.

I would like to thank all those at the Schomburg Library and the Lincoln Center Library for the Performing Arts for their assistance and advice. They were instrumental in leading me to the books, references, records, films, and other examples of African-American humor without which this study could not have been completed. Many others, like Phil Berger, author of *The Last Laugh,* contributed material and/or ideas for this study, and I thank them for their time and thoughtful contributions.

Lastly, I wish to thank those friends and acquaintances who provided editorial assistance or supported me morally and sometimes financially while this book was being written. George, Nancy, Herb, Cherry, Pat, Russell, and my parents, are among them. They, and others whom I've undoubtedly overlooked, know who they are—more important, they know that I know who they are.

CONTENTS

When asked about the nature of his own work and that of other black comedians, comic actor Godfrey Cambridge replied: "The line that leads to Moms Mabley, Nipsey Russell, Dick Gregory, Bill Cosby and myself can be traced back to the satire of slave humor, back even through minstrelsy . . . " Aside from suggesting that minstrelsy preceded slave satire, Cambridge was correct—up to a point. For African-American humor—like much of black Americans' speech, dance, and music—while most certainly shaped and molded by the initial slavery experience in American, has even more ancient roots. The line that leads to Mabley, Russell, Gregory, Cosby, Cambridge, as well as to Bert Williams, Stepin Fetchit, Mantan Moreland, Pigmeat Markham, Redd Foxx, Flip Wilson, Richard Pryor, and comedians of the eighties and nineties—such as Eddie Murphy, Whoopi Goldberg, Sinbad, Damon Wayans, and Martin Lawrence—actually can be followed all the way back to West Africa, the homeland of an estimated fifty percent of all Africans brought to the Americas.[1]

Still, the complexity of black humor and its impact on America's larger comic tradition has been largely ignored. This avoidance is partially the result of mainstream America's general reluctance to acknowledge black Americans' influence on American culture—particularly on an aspect of that culture that, by its very nature, is primarily cognitive and often critical of mainstream society. For instance, many books on American humor either avoid the contribution of blacks altogether or dismiss it in one or two short paragraphs. Biographies of leading white comedians such Milton Berle, Groucho Marx, and Bob Hope, while often lauding the achievements of their nonblack colleagues, often completely ignore the work of estimable black comics with whom they performed or, at the very least, with whose work they must have been familiar. When one considers that during vaudeville some of these comedic stars worked with black performers who were routinely shuttled from one position to another on Broadway bills because white acts were intimidated by having to follow them or, worse, quite simply fired because they were too good, such deletions seem suspiciously more than mere oversight.

In the late 1950s, in an *Ebony* magazine article Steve Allen—the versatile entertainer, writer, and humorist who hosted NBC television's *Tonight Show* in the early 1950s— argued that "our society would not permit the emergence of black comedians who were the equivalent of Bob Hope, much less any that were the equivalent of Lenny Bruce or Mort Sahl." In a more recent book, Allen amended his earlier remarks, noting that the sixties social revolution created a climate in which more cerebral comedians such as Dick Gregory and Richard Pryor could flourish. But, despite the surfacing of talents such as Gregory and Pryor, mainstream America still does not readily acknowledge the tradition that to a great extent molded the style of these performers. They are usually treated as individual phenomenons, *geniuses*, with no attachment to a rich and viable cultural heritage of their own.[2]

The underestimation of black America's contribution to the American comic style is partially due to black sensitivity regarding its own comic tradition. One of the characteristics of black American humor— as is also the case with Jewish or Irish humor—is a tendency toward self-mockery or self-deprecation. Having been so vehemently maligned and negatively stereotyped by mainstream society, blacks have been understandably wary of adding to the fire by revealing the often denigrating self-appraisals that emerge from their own humor. The furor over the 1950s television show, *Amos 'n' Andy*—a subject that will be treated at length later—is an example of African America's thin-skinned reaction to public performances that disclosed heretofore veiled aspects of their private humor. Despite the show's enormous popularity, complaints from civil rights organizations and the black community about its stereotypical portrayals of black family life and black professionals led to its being lifted from the air.

On the Real Side on one hand attempts to document the growth and development of the black American comic tradition and to demonstrate how that tradition emerged as one of the major shaping forces on American humor in general. In addition it is intended to probe the relationship between black private and public humor, and to explore the reasons for blacks' extreme sensitivity over the rich but, until very recently, closely guarded humorous style that has grown out of their experience as slaves and second-class citizens in America. In so doing, it may provide some valuable insight into the nature of life in the United States generally. For, as we shall see, comedy—what Americans laugh at—has been a telling index of the American character since the beginning of the Republic.[3]

The purpose of this book, then, is to trace African-American humor from its African roots through its development from slavery to the present. The narrative is intended to chart and examine its public expression (as reflected on stage, radio, screen, and television as well as in print) and its less visible and more authentic unfolding within the black community (from slave shanties and street corners to cabarets). The interaction and ultimate merging of these two previously diverse faces have molded African-American humor as we know it today.

This circuitous evolution of African-American humor has also largely determined the structure of *On the Real Side*.

"Antecedents," the first section of the book, examines the African origins of the humor, its early expression by slaves, and its initial distorted presentation on the minstrel stage by first white and then black performers.

Part Two, "The Outside," charts the minstrelsy-inspired image of black-American humor projected by mainstream media. It traces the metamorphosis of the comic Negro from his initial appearance in silent films and on the vaudeville stage to mid-twentieth century movies, radio, and television—chronicling the mostly distorted image of black humor presented to mainstream America before the 1960s and examining early black comedians attempt to change it.

The final section, "The Inside," examines the humor that originated within black communities and flourished not only on the street and in folktales but also (only slightly altered) in "chitlin' circuit" cabarets and theatres, black literature, all-black films, as well as on so-called race records. It concludes with Richard Pryor's rise to stardom and crossover success.

Pryor's emergence in the seventies signaled the end of diffident black comedy and challenged Americans to acknowledge the full range of African America's humorous tradition. Pryor and a few of his sixties predecessors began unveiling the satirical barbs concealed beneath the black jester's clownish attire. In contrast to Pryor's artful diversity, the new breed of in-your-face comics who followed him in the eighties have mostly opted for the rim-shattering approach of the basketball phenom Shaquille O'Neal. And, if some of the subtlety, misdirection, and magic that have previously characterized black American humor have been lost, the most outrageous and impious elements of African-American humor are now being emphasized.

On the Real Side chronicles of the rise of African America's formerly underground humor—tracing the individuals and social currents that expedited its emergence. It is hoped that when appropriate, even as it attempts explaining it, the account may also serve to evoke some of the laughter and pleasure that are ultimately the richest and most memorable issue of African-American humor.

PROLOGUE:

BLACK HUMOR . . . *what it is*

2

3

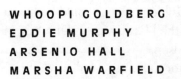

4

5

WHOOPI GOLDBERG
EDDIE MURPHY
ARSENIO HALL
MARSHA WARFIELD

HUMOR IS LAUGHING AT WHAT YOU HAVEN'T GOT WHEN YOU OUGHT TO HAVE IT. OF COURSE,
YOU LAUGH BY PROXY. YOU'RE REALLY LAUGHING AT THE OTHER GUY'S LACKS, NOT YOUR OWN.
THAT'S WHAT MAKES IT FUNNY—THE FACT THAT YOU DON'T KNOW YOU ARE LAUGHING AT
YOURSELF. HUMOR IS WHEN THE JOKE IS ON YOU BUT HITS THE OTHER FELLOW FIRST—BECAUSE
IT BOOMERANGS. HUMOR IS WHAT YOU WISH IN YOUR SECRET HEART WERE NOT FUNNY, BUT IT
IS, AND YOU MUST LAUGH. HUMOR IS YOUR UNCONSCIOUS THERAPY.

—LANGSTON HUGHES

A NAIVE PERSON THINKS HE HAS USED HIS MEANS OF EXPRESSION AND TRAINS OF THOUGHT
NORMALLY AND SIMPLY, AND HE HAS NO *ARRIÈRE PENSÉE* IN MIND. . . . IT WILL NOT SURPRISE
US TO FIND THAT THE NAIVE [IN HUMOR] OCCURS FAR THE MOST OFTEN IN CHILDREN, AND IS
THEN CARRIED OVER TO UNEDUCATED ADULTS, WHOM WE MAY REGARD AS CHILDISH. . . . [BUT]
THERE IS THE POSSIBILITY OF *MISLEADING NAÏVETÉ*. WE MAY ASSUME IN THE CHILD AN
IGNORANCE THAT NO LONGER EXISTS; AND CHILDREN OFTEN REPRESENT THEMSELVES AS
NAIVE, SO AS TO ENJOY A LIBERTY THAT THEY WOULD NOT OTHERWISE BE GRANTED.

—SIGMUND FREUD

THE AMBIVALENCE OF COMEDY REAPPEARS IN ITS SOCIAL MEANING, FOR COMEDY IS BOTH
HATRED AND REVEL, REBELLION AND DEFENSE, ATTACK AND ESCAPE. IT IS REVOLUTIONARY
AND CONSERVATIVE. SOCIALLY, IT IS BOTH SYMPATHY AND PERSECUTION.

—WYLIE SYPHER[1]

I

Humor—as a folksy Southern relative of mine was fond of saying—
is something like a rich man's wallet: it's a hard nut to crack. No one
seems able clearly to define it or explain why we laugh.

African-American laughter, in particular, has been something of a
mystery, a dilemma, or, quite often, a source of irritation for mainstream Americans from the time blacks first arrived in the Colonies in
the seventeenth century. Reports of white Americans' astonishment at
the uninhibited display and heartiness of blacks' "cackling laughter" can
be found throughout early American writings. In the early nineteenth
century, for instance, Washington Irving observed that "the obstreperous peals of the broad-mouthed laughter of the Dutch negroes, who,
like other negroes, are famous for their risible powers," could be heard
at the Battery of New York even though the blacks were celebrating in
a small New Jersey village across the Hudson.[2]

And in the mid-1800s, a Northern visitor to South Carolina wrote:

At midnight I was awakened by loud laughter, and, looking out, saw that the loading gang of negroes [slaves hired out to the railroad] had made a fire, and were enjoying a right merry repast. Suddenly, one raised such a sound as I never heard before; a long, loud, musical shout, rising, and falling, and breaking into falsetto, his voice singing through the woods in the clear, frosty night air, like a bugle call. . . . When there was silence again, one of them cried out, as if bursting with amusement: "did yer see de dog?— when I began echoing, he turn roun' an' look me straight in der face: ha! ha! ha!" and the whole party broke into the loudest peals of laughter, as if it was the very best joke they had ever heard.[3]

At about the same time, James Fenimore Cooper, perhaps summing up the contemporary contempt for black laughter, wrote of a festive gathering of New York blacks "collected in thousands of . . . fields, beating banjoes, singing African songs, drinking, and worst of all, laughing in a way that seemed to set their hearts rattling within their ribs."[4]

Clearly, the accursed laughter of blacks had early on established itself as one of the race's prominent foibles—still minor, of course, when compared to other more blatantly demeaning stereotypes. By the 1940s white disdain for and, ironically, curiosity about Negro laughter were so well confirmed that Gunnar Myrdal in his massive study of black life in America, *An American Dilemma* (1944), would write confidently that the "Negro's cackling laugh," which "amused the white man and often staved off punishment or brought rewards," was an indication of blacks' ignorance and their "accommodation to class."[5]

Now, interestingly, these writers and most other white observers conspicuously neglected defining or commenting on exactly *what* blacks found so humorous or *why* they were laughing. African-American laughter undoubtedly still causes confusion, consternation, and bafflement among whites. In fact, many whites readily admit that they have experienced some anxiety when confronting a group of blacks laughing uninhibitedly, and many more admit to some curiosity over the timbre and intensity of that revelry. Conversely, most black Americans have felt that their laughter has been interpreted as inappropriate or aggressive by whites or, at least, has been greeted with puzzlement and anxiety. As the African-American presence has increased in mainstream corporations, among blacks it has become a standard joke that when two or more of them gather, any display of joviality could bring an office to a virtual halt. As Richard Pryor has quipped: "White folks get upset when they see us laughing. . . . 'Wha'd'ya think they're doing, Martha? Are they laughing at us?' "

Both the depth of whites' obsession with African-American laughter and blacks' often amused reaction to that obsession are evident in the old "laughing barrel" tale, popular among Southern blacks for decades. As the story goes, whites in a small Southern town were so determined to control black expressiveness that they installed large barrels marked FOR COLORED ONLY in the town square. Negroes who felt the urge to laugh were required immediately to thrust their heads into the barrels. The laughing barrels, as Ralph Ellison facetiously explained, not only "saved many a black a sore behind (and the understaffed police force, energy sorely needed in other areas), [but] performed the far more important function of providing whites a means of saving face before the confounding, persistent, and embarrassing mystery of black laughter."[6]

While in junior high school in Ohio, I was once caught snickering and whispering to the only other black student in the class about the teacher's rigidly formal explanation of a spiritual that we knew in a much less formal manner (much better than he, we thought). In short time, we were loudly reprimanded. But despite trying to hold back our laughter, a minute or so afterward we were at it again. At this point, the teacher, scarlet with anger, approached and, menacingly pointing his finger toward me, screamed in his most outraged voice, "You know, you irk me!" The word *irk*, of course, was not a common term in my working-class home. I had never heard it before, and certainly had never heard anyone express rage in such a curiously restrained manner. If he had shouted that he was "pissed off," I might well have understood and responded accordingly with timidity. Instead, I immediately fell into a fit of laughter that overwhelmed any fear that I might have had of the adult authority figure before me. It was only later, when I had been expelled from the class and given a failing grade that I began to understand the perils of black laughter in an integrated setting.

Whites, of course, did not always regard black laughter as a negative trait. In fact, under certain circumstances, jovial, amusing blacks were a source of comfort. Before Emancipation, lighthearted, grinning slaves were usually preferred to more surly or morose types. The popular 1980s musical maxim, "Don't worry," laugh and "be happy," expresses a mode of behavior that most slave masters favored for their chattel. And by the 1990s, with America becoming more sanguine and ostensibly tolerant of *minor* black cultural eccentricities, black laughter has again lost most of the threatening overtones it once had. In fact, when employed by professional entertainers it may even become a comic signature, a source of comfort and instant recognition for the audience, and a critical part of the entertainer's comic arsenal.

Black minstrel performers such as Billy Kersands—whose uproarious broad-mouthed laugh could be sustained even while he clenched two billiard balls in his jaws—discovered this as early as the nineteenth century. Sammy Davis, Jr.'s, thigh-slapping, foot-stomping laughter was, of course, as broad and expansive as his legendary talents and almost as extravagant as his jewelry. By the 1980s, Eddie Murphy's outrageous, cackling laughter was one of his most striking and effective comic devices, as is the robust, no-holds-barred laugh of late-night television host and comic actor Arsenio Hall. The same may be said of Whoopi Goldberg, Flip Wilson, or Bill Cosby; each has a distinctive manner of laughing and associated body language that enhances and complements their humor. They have made black Americans' hearty, much-maligned laughter an important part of their comic stage presence.

Still, black laughter expresses only one aspect of black American humor (a term that should not be confused with literary "black humor," dark satire, or so-called gallows humor, although they sometimes overlap); its essence lies somewhere underneath the screen of uninhibited mirth. For instance, the hip street persona Murphy affects at the beginning of both his popular *Beverly Hills Cop* films is a slick, apparently frenetic, fast-talking black con man engaged in outthinking and outtalking some dangerous, if somewhat inept, white criminals. This situation, as we will see later, harks back to one of the earliest black comic modes —the black slave outwitting a more powerful and presumably more knowledgeable master, or the even more venerable tradition of the black trickster. In the films, Murphy's quips are distinctively black in character.

Responding to one criminal's accusations that he is an undercover cop, which in fact he is, Murphy averts the danger by turning to his accuser's partner and asserting: "Yeah, I have the money and I *do* wanna do business . . . but with *you.* I ain't doing nothing in front of this dude 'cause this dude is a cop. I know when I smell a *pig* inside the room. I used to be a Muslim, man, and I know there's *po'k* over here . . . [sniffing and, eyes closed, rotating his head in imitation of

Stevie Wonder] Yes, *po'k*, man, it's definitely *po'k*. I ain't doing shit around this dude, man. You wanna do business, you know where to find me."

Arsenio Hall's wide-eyed, infectious laugh—sassy one minute, coy the next—helped catapult his late-night show to the top of the television ratings in the 1980s. It also helped take the edge off satirical potshots he aimed at celebrities ranging from Madonna to Jesse Jackson:

> I took my bus fare
> And went to the state fair.
> I had a corn-dog there,
> It was medium rare.
> Now I need Medicare.
>   Keep hope alive!

Similarly, the laughter of comic actress Whoopi Goldberg—whether the subtle, ironic laugh that deepens her portrait of the ingenue or the hip titter that distinguishes her characterization of Fontaine, the intellectual junkie—has become a recognizable staple of her stand-up comedy act. But Goldberg's humor, when focused on racial subjects, incorporates other more fundamental aspects of black America's culture and viewpoint. In her 1988 cable television special *Fontaine . . . Why Am I Straight?*, for instance, the hip laugh conceals an irreverence and social awareness common in black humor: "Now Nancy [Reagan], on the other hand, anorexic bitch that she is . . . I don't like her. . . . This is a woman who probably had nothing to do. You know, all the first ladies are supposed to be together with their President husbands, right. And poor Nancy, she didn't know what to do. So somebody probably said, 'Nancy, shit, do drugs.' And, of course, she misunderstood. She's a woman living in an unreal world. Explain to me how you tell an urban teenager who lives in the streets, in the school systems of the real world, 'Just say fucking no!' How do you justify that to a mother who's maybe got six kids and three hundred sixty five bucks a month from welfare and one of those kids is bringing in fifteen grand a week?"

Flip Wilson, one of the first blacks to host a network television variety show, was known almost as much for his cherubic smile and enthusiastic belly laugh ("What you say?") as he was for his hilarious characterization of Geraldine, the down-to-earth black character that he made famous. Yet Wilson's humorous stories were quite often pointedly black in another, more revealing sense. The imposition of black dialect and black attitudes onto famous historical figures was a hallmark of his comedy style. In his version of the discovery of America, Christopher Columbus approaches Queen Isabelle Johnson and informs her that if he doesn't find America there'll be no Benjamin Franklin, no "Star-Spangled Banner" or home of the free, and no Ray Charles. The frantic Queen responds: "Ray Charles! You gon' fine Ray Charles? He in America?" After the Queen agrees to support his venture, Columbus immediately goes out and buys some items that, while not common in Italian households, are recognizably funny to most blacks: "three used ships, two pair of fatigues, some shades, two chicken sandwiches, three cans of Vienna sausages, five cases of Scotch, a small Seven-Up, and a new rag to tie his head with."

Wilson's "Cowboys and Colored People" bit, which involves a dialogue with an Indian named Henry, offers another example of this wry racial humor: "The biggest thing that happened to you Indians is when they put you on the nickel. They put a buffalo on the other side, Henry. If you guys belonged to the NAACP we'd have you on the quarter. Maybe we'd change the name, Henry. Maybe we'd call it the National Association for the Advancement of Colored People Immediately . . . and the Indians on a Gradual Basis."

Bill Cosby, America's most popular sitcom star during the 1980s, is known for his disarming facial contortions and impish, pursed-lipped, chuckle, which helped establish him as one of television's most effective celebrity pitchmen for products ranging from Jell-O to Kodak film. Here again, black laughter and black humor (or, at least, blacks as humorous individuals) become, in the public mind, intrinsically connected.

Still, black laughter is not the most critical ingredient in black humor. After all, some *thing*, some particular set of circumstances, events, acts, or words must induce that laughter. And it's easy to enumerate examples of what most would consider black humor.

It can be as simple as when Moms Mabley walked out onto the Apollo Theatre stage, scanned the audience with a tired, exasperated look, and said, "Yeah, I know how y'all feel . . . Yes chillun, Moms knows."

It is as readily accessible as a group of black schoolboys standing on a corner playing the dozens:

"Duane, yo momma is like a doorknob, everybody done had a turn."

"I don't play that shit, my man. You better get off my momma . . . cause you know I just left yo house and got off yours."

It can be seen in the comments of two elderly, well-dressed black men who, sitting on a Harlem bench, observed a black teenager hip-hopping by with his baseball cap worn askew, in the nineties' fashion:

"Look at that boy," one said, "ain't he somethin'."

"Yeah," the other offered, "got his hat all turned around on his head. Fool done forgot where his face is."

Or in the cinema exchange between their fictional counterparts, Sweet Dick Willie (played by comic Robin Harris) and his two middle-aged cronies, who rap and trade quips in Spike Lee's *Do the Right Thing* (1989):

"You fool, you thirty cents away from having a quarter. How the fuck you goin' get a boat?"

"Don't worry about it."

"You goddamn right, don't worry about it. Look at you! You raggedy as a roach, eat the hole out a donut . . ."

"I'll be on my feet, soon enough."

"Not in them raggedy-ass shoes. Look at you! Shoes so run over, you got to lay down to put 'em on."

It's also reflected in a remark made by a middle-class businessman upon seeing one of New York City's peripheral, media-anointed "race leaders" pontificating on a television news program. In the time-honored black tradition of naming people with regard to some essential character trait, he immediately dubbed him "Uncle Sharp-Tom."

Or it may be found in the behavior of the bedraggled panhandler who works a corner near Fifth Avenue in lower Manhattan. Speaking with an obsequious black Southern dialect and appearing to have an advanced case of arthritic deformity or cerebral palsy, he never fails to solicit sympathy and a healthy reward with his contortions and slurred pleas for money. The humor surfaces later when, after the rush-hour pedestrians disappear, he reappears with erect posture, precise articulation, and a visibly large wad of bills stuffed into the pocket of his designer jeans.

Certainly, it was apparent in the tales told to me as a child by my next-door neighbor. Known admiringly as the biggest liar in town, he would sit on his front porch or in the local barber shop or nearly anywhere and command an audience with outrageous stories of his war exploits, his battles with the Klan in Mississippi, or his triumphs over his wife (in her absence, of course) or gullible white folks at the bank, his job, the Veterans Administration, and the unemployment office. He was working in a venerable black comic tradition—the tall tale or, simply, *lying*.

The outlandish story or tall tale is a central part of black American comedy (as it is among other ethnic or folk traditions). "I heard most of my early comedy backstage at the Apollo," the late Sammy Davis, Jr., recalled. "We didn't call them jokes at the time, we called them lies. 'That nigger sure can lie' was a common phrase at the time. I would imagine it is still used today." Indeed, it is. If Richard Pryor's down-home raconteur, Mudbone—one of the most eloquent and popular purveyors of the tall tale or big lie in modern comedy—had a real-life prototype, it was surely someone like my irrepressible neighbor. In fact, I believe it was in the mid-fifties when I first heard the line about fighting in World War II at the "battle of Chateaubriand" (used by Pryor, as Mudbone, in the seventies) as my neighbor chronicled his heroic efforts in saving the allies.[7]

By the 1980s, black humor, like black music, had become so much a part of mainstream American culture that it could even be seen on prime-time television sneaker commercials like the popular "Bo [Jackson] Knows" spots or the series of ads that featured the popular young comedian Sinbad. In the Jackson commercial, the superstar athlete demonstrated his skills in various sports (including baseball and football) and representative sports celebrities acknowledged his expertise. Finally, after Jackson was shown flailing away at an electric guitar, blues singer and guitarist Bo Diddley appeared on camera. With a cynical grin on his face, the musician said wryly: "Bo, you don't know diddly!" Sinbad showcased his comic talent in a variety of street corner basketball vignettes. The funniest, which mirrored Eddie Murphy's slick rap in *Beverly Hills Cop*, featured Sinbad introducing a motley crew of playground misfits and castoffs as he tried to talk two foreign television executives into backing televised broadcasts of a schoolyard basketball league.

In short, black humor and its insistent companion black laughter can now be found wherever blacks are found or, in some instances, wherever they might be expected to appear. By the mid-1970s black American humor had come out of the closet or, as it were, the black community. But it continues to provoke some peculiar reactions and curious consequences.

Still, assuming that blacks laugh more or less for the same reasons that others do, we can reasonably expect that some of the classical writings on laughing and comedy might shed some light on black mirth. From Aristophanes to the present, philosophers and pundits have been fascinated by gelogeny, or the study of laughter and humor. Aristotle, having provided an accepted theory of tragedy, went on to suggest that we laugh at the incongruous or antithetical—that is, the contrast between *what* is presented and *the way* it is presented. Whatever its limitations, that definition has stood the test of time; it readily explains such present-day comic personas as the impeccably dressed but obviously inept and bumbling executive or politician. It also accounts for the usually hilarious reception accorded black comedian Robert Townsend when he appears on stage dressed in natty hipster attire and, with an upper-class British accent, delivers lines such as, "I'd like to say tonight that . . . I haven't changed. I'm still that same old black boy from the ghet-*to*. Truly! I am . . . I am . . . I am."

In 1650, Thomas Hobbes wrote: "The passion of laughter is nothing else but sudden glory arising from sudden conception of some eminency in ourselves, by comparison with the infirmity of others." Hobbes then warned against those who laugh too heartily or too often, since laughter, in his view, was most common among those overly conscious of the paucity of their own ability and therefore driven to observe the imperfections of others. A few centuries later, the creator of the *Lil Abner* comic strip, Al Capp, succinctly paraphrased Hobbes: "All comedy is based on man's delight in man's inhumanity to other men."[8]

This is a somewhat narrow and gloomy depiction of the human spirit. But when we consider the usual howls of laughter solicited by the unfortunate victims in the Three Stooges' slapstick routines, Bud Abbott's physical abuse of Lou Costello, or Oliver Hardy's abuse of Stan Laurel, we are forced to admit that Hobbes was onto something. We should all pause before giving vent to uninhibited amusement at someone else's misfortune—particularly if we heed Goethe's suggestion that men show their character most clearly by what they find amusing. Unfortunately, Hobbes's caveat was as readily ignored in the

nineteenth century (when minstrelsy and black-faced entertainers be-
guiled America) as it was in the late twentieth century (when Andrew
Dice Clay substituted phobia and misogyny for jokes). Minstrelsy, with
its buffoonish caricatures of blacks, enthralled an entire nation with its
exaggerated image of the behavior of its underclass victims—behavior
that, to a great extent, it had initially encouraged and often demanded.
And Clay . . . well, his act speaks not only for itself but for those amused
by it. As Wylie Sypher points out, comedy is both "sympathy and persecution," "hatred and revel," attitudes we will see revealed throughout
the history of black American humor.

Sigmund Freud, of course, wrote extensively on the subject of humor
and laughter. He asserted that to adopt a humorous attitude toward
others is to assume "the attitude of an adult toward a child, recognizing
and smiling at the triviality of the interests and sufferings which seem
to the child so big." On another occasion and in a slightly different vein,
he argued that we often laugh because of our awareness of the disparity
between a perceived action (such as that of a clown or bungling comedian) and what we know is possible for us. Such laughter provides an
outlet for sublimated aggression. Charles E. Schutz in his book, *Political
Humor*, comments that the "pleasure of such humor is in the feeling of
release from the tensions of repressing the impulse to be aggressive,
and also in a sense of superiority at the successful exercise of a prohib-
ited aggression."[9]

The theories and definitions of humor and the comic forwarded by
Aristotle, Hobbes, and Freud, among numerous others, have been end-
lessly combined, rearranged, restructured, and reinterpreted during the
past fifty years of this century. At the Second International Conference
on Humor held in Los Angeles in August 1979, a group of scientists,
psychologists, and scholars from other behavioral disciplines upheld the
three principal theories of their noted predecessors: that humor is
"based on a sense of superiority" or on the "juxtaposition of two incongruous ideas," or that it "comes from tension relief or pleasure in the
direct expression of forbidden urges." Even so, those scientists and
other researchers using modern cognitive and social-psychological theories have demonstrated that there are many more variables to humor
than we or previous theorists might have expected.[10]

For instance, according to Norman N. Holland, researchers have
shown that specific groups of people return to their own favorite subjects for joking. "Jews tell Jewish jokes," he writes. "Soldiers joke about
death and army food. Hospital patients tell jokes about being flat on

one's back. Americans' jokes are apparently more aggressive than those of other nationalities. . . . Different cultures choose different subjects for jokes. The Chinese joke about social relationships. Nonliterate cultures joke about the immediate physical environment. The West jokes about sex and aggression." Black Americans, I might add, often joke about the hypocrisy of American society as well as racism and the raft of outrageous stereotypes that racists have concocted.[11]

It is apparent, then, that humor cannot be simply defined. Most theorists agree that, finally, there is an indefinable element—the peculiarities of the individual human psyche. Laughter and the comical ultimately depend on the expectations and assumptions that an individual brings to a situation. One person's idea of superiority may represent inferiority to another, and what is incongruous to one group may be perfectly normal to another. William Shakespeare affirmed the relative nature of humor when, in *Love's Labour Lost*, he wrote:

A jest's prosperity lies in the ear
Of him that hears it, never in the tongue
Of him that makes it.[12]

II
- - - - - - - - - -

In *The Souls of Black Folk*, W. E. B. Du Bois alluded to a perceptual peculiarity that underlies much black behavior and directly influences blacks' view of themselves and others: "It is a peculiar sensation, this double-consciousness, this sense of always looking at one's self through the eyes of others, of measuring one's soul by the tape of a world that looks on in amused contempt and pity. One ever feels his twoness—an American, a Negro; two souls, two thoughts, two unreconciled strivings; two warring ideals in one dark body."[13]

Du Bois, of course, was writing about the grave circumstances facing black Americans at the turn of the century. But what he calls "twoness," viewing reality from dual perspectives—the conventional as well as the unexpected or unconventional—is advanced by many theorists as a crucial aspect of creating humor. As Luigi Pirandello wrote: "Ordinarily the artist concerns himself with only the body. The humorist concerns himself with body and shadow at the same time and sometimes more with the shadow than the body. He notes all the fine turns of that shadow, how it stretches this much or grows that much fatter, as if to make fun of the body, which all this time does not concern itself with the shadow or its size."[14]

Although each writer approached the subject from a different vantage, they were both concerned with the consequences of split vision—the ability (or, for Du Bois, an enforced burden) to see oneself and others from multiple perspectives. And, if we concede, as many modern comedians do, that everyone's behavior—status or position notwithstanding—from an objective outlook can be construed as comical, then in observing his own "shadow" the humorist could be adopting the "double-consciousness" and self-appraisal of "amused contempt and pity" that Du Bois attributes to blacks. Accordingly, Du Bois's eloquent description of African America's psychological predicament provides a salient clue to the source and special tenor of black American humor.

In the 1960s, Ralph Ellison echoed Du Bois's idea and reaffirmed the connection between the Negro situation and Pirandello's notion of humor. Countering Irving Howe's assertion that "Negroness" is a "metaphysical condition, one that is a state of irremediable agony which all but engulfs the mind," Ellison wrote that "It is not skin color which makes a Negro American but cultural heritage as shaped by the American experience, the social and political predicament." It derives from a "special perspective on the national ideals" and a "tragicomic attitude toward the universe. . . . It imposes the uneasy burden and occasional joy of a complex *double vision* [italics added], a fluid, ambivalent response to men and events which represents, at its finest, a profoundly civilized adjustment to the cost of being human in the modern world."[15]

Ellison, then, suggests that African-Americans have adopted a "special perspective" which incorporates the comic vision as a means of coping with America's social and political predicament. Pursuing this theme, in the essay "The Shadow and the Act," he analyzes Hollywood's illusionary portrayals of blacks in films by delineating the differences between "image [shadow] and reality [act]" or "portrayal" and "action." He concludes that, "Obviously these films are not *about* Negroes at all; they are about what whites think and feel about Negroes." As Ellison's essay demonstrates, "twoness" of vision is not exclusive to blacks or humorists, and is not always used for comedic purposes; it can and has been employed to perpetuate perjorative images of others.[16]

So black humor (like Jewish humor, perhaps the most prominent influence on the American humor tradition) is in many ways shaped by the minority status of its creators. The outsider or "shadow" position of Jews and blacks in mainstream American society has given them a unique perspective on themselves as well as on the dominant or majority culture. But this is not to say that black or Jewish humor is primarily forlorn or self-derisive, as some observers would suggest.

In *The Big Book of Jewish Humor*, William Novak and Moshe Waldoks point out that a "prominent misconception about traditional Jewish humor [the humor of the European *shtetl*] is that it is essentially composed of 'laughter through tears.' " They argue convincingly that, although the subjects of many of the jokes emerging from nineteenth-century Polish and Russian ghettoes were "frequently unpleasant—or worse," the "Jew's endless struggle with adversity" did not provide the "dominant theme." Jewish humor, according to Novak and Waldoks, "is optimistic in the long run, but pessimistic about the present and the immediate future."[17]

Similarly, we do not have to search hard for self-effacing jokes or instances of melancholy in black American humor. Slave sayings and proverbs provide some early examples:

Nigger don't sing much plowin' de hillside.

Ef torment was a big icehouse,
heap o' bad niggers would jine de chu'ch.[18]

Later, Bert Williams, America's first black cross-over comic star, wrote the music for the famous dirge "Nobody" and made the touching but mournful routine that accompanied it the showpiece of his act. The song's refrain—repeated after disclosure of a litany of hardships and abuses—insists that since no one has responded to the singer's troubles, "until I get me somethin' from somebody, sometime, I don't intend to do nothin' for nobody, no time."[19]

A more recent example is Richard Pryor's bittersweet tale of two down-and-out blacks, a wino and a junkie, which ends with this exchange:

Junkie: I'm sick, pops. Can you help me? My mind thinkin' about shit I don't wanna think about. I can't stop the mutherfucker, baby. Movin' too fast for the kid. Tell me some ah'them ole lies o' yours and make me stop thinkin' about the truth. . . . Could you help me?

Wino: Yeah. I'm goin' hep you, boy. 'Cause I believe you got *potential*. That's right! You don't know how to deal with the white man, that's yo' problem. I know how to deal with 'em. That's right. That's why I'm in the position I'm in today.[20]

Still, for every authentic African-American joke or humorous tale reflecting an acceptance of the downtrodden condition of the black community, there are numerous others that cleverly suggest transcending that condition. Black humor most often satirizes the demeaning views of non-blacks, celebrates the unique attributes of black community life, or focuses on outwitting the oppressor—as it were, "getting over."

The distinction between jokes *about* blacks (for instance, *What do you call a high-rise in Harlem? A Coon-dominium*; or *What's the favorite game show in the South? Maim that Coon*) and those created *by* blacks is crucial here. As with Jews or several other minorities, confusion about the larger society's humorous conception of blacks and authentic black comedy is largely responsible for the misinterpretation of the character of black humor.

In addition, in humor there is a crucial distinction between purposeful jest or wit (the creative telling of a joke or knowing assumption of a comic posture) and naive comic expression (unwittingly saying or doing something that others find funny). The latter may be just as amusing but, depending on one's knowledge of the source, is funny for an entirely different reason. According to Freud, the childish or naive person does not possess the cultural or intellectual sophistication necessary to produce jokes, which demand a conscious suspension of inhibition and reasonability as well as interaction between at least two people who are "subject to approximately the same inhibitions and internal resistances." Naive humor depends on the observer's possessing inhibitions that the source of the humor lacks and, generally, only the observer "obtains the yield of pleasure which the naive brings about." In much the same way, early estimates of Negroes' humorous attributes by white Americans were little more than confirmation of blacks' supposed childishness and naïveté. Blacks were funny for most white Americans only insofar as they engaged in quaint, foolish, and childlike behavior, or stumbled over a language that they were only halfheartedly taught to speak and forbidden to read. With the introduction of minstrelsy, they were rigidly cast as naive humorists on the stage. It was this distorted mainstream perception of black humor that later led Dick Gregory to insist, "I've got to be a colored funny man, not a funny colored man."[21]

This perception of Negroes, to a great extent, dictated racial relationships, directed and often limited the course of black advancement, and influenced nearly every phase of day-to-day living involving blacks. It also defined the role that black Americans were compelled to play if they were to move unimpeded in society. Out of it, an uneasy pact emerged. Whites presumed that Negroes were still naively adjusting to a superior culture, and blacks ritualistically reenacted the scenario for their own benefit and well-being. White Americans clung to this illusion well into the twentieth century. Moreover, occupying a dominant position, they could and usually did insist that the charade be affirmed. For the majority of non-black Americans, accepting the Negro's humanity would have meant acknowledging their own callousness and barbarity —an admission of venality and hypocrisy belying nearly all the democratic principles on which the nation was founded.

Since slavery, as they were realistically compelled to, blacks have recognized the lowly nature of their position in our society, and their humor has reflected that recognition. The humor of nearly all minorities reveals a tendency toward self-deprecation or, as Novak and Waldoks term it, "masochism." These authors also point out that Sigmund Freud noted the self-critical aspect of Jewish humor when he wrote: "I do not know whether there are many other instances of a people making fun to such a degree of its own character." But Freud's observation was qualified: he noted that Jews also "know their real faults as well as the connection between them and their good qualities." Psychoanalyst Martin Grotjahn reinforces that conclusion. In *Beyond Laughter*, he observes that "No other people on earth, whether in the past or the present time, has taken itself so mercilessly as the butt of its own jokes as the Jewish people." But he also asserts that the "Jewish joke is only a masochistic mask; it is by no means a sign of masochistic perversion. . . . The persecuted Jew who makes himself the butt of the joke deflects his dangerous hostility away from the persecutors onto himself. The result is not defeat or surrender but victory and greatness."[22]

The same tension is evident among African-Americans. In *Harlem Renaissance*, Nathan Irvin Huggins questions whether blacks' humor and character are not, largely, reflections of negative, white-created stereotypes; whether the mask used to appease whites or conceal true sentiments did not, ultimately, become reality. "There is a danger of corrosion of the self in this pretense, and surely a rending of integrity," he writes. "How, and when does one call upon the real self to dispel that make-believe and claim humanity and dignity?" Finally, he asks:

"Who were these black men *really*? It was just possible that the trick had been too perfect; *legerdemain* had undone itself in a disappearance act where the self had vanished, but also the incantation to call it back again."[23]

Just as emphatically, Joseph Boskin, in a 1986 study, strongly suggested that the comic, demeaning image of "Sambo" created by whites "to subordinate a minority group" was so pervasive that it not only determined white America's conception of blacks but markedly influenced the self-estimate and, consequently, the humor of blacks themselves. Although in the latter part of his study Boskin admitted that the Vietnam war and the civil rights movement of the fifties and sixties were "enough to render Sambo totally meaningless," he argued that from slavery until the forties the Sambo image had an overwhelming effect on black character and expression.[24]

And, of course, there are numerous authentic African-American jokes and sayings that support the *masochistic* interpretation. Slavery proverbs such as, "Nigger jes' like a mule, white man like a hoss. Yuh jes' touches the bridle and hoss go. Yuh got tuh beat a mule to get'um out his tracks," and post-slavery tales and jokes such as the following seem to confirm a self-debasing tendency in black humor:

> Soon after Emancipation a Union Army officer encountered Amos, a slave who had reservations about his new freedom. Surprised at his reaction, the officer scolded Amos. "Amos, I don't believe you realize you are a free man. You can go where you please, do as you please, eat what you please."
>
> "I awready bin eatin' ez I please," grumbled Amos.
>
> The officer was taken aback. "I wager, Amos, you never even tasted chicken before," he said.
>
> "I eats chicken ev'ry Sund'y," maintained Amos doggedly. "An' whut's mo', Massa allus save me de tenderes' paht."
>
> "What part is that?"
>
> "De gravy, uv co'se!" said Amos.

Then there is the familiar joke about the elevated status blacks occupied in the hierarchy of white Southern hospitality:

> A New Yorker, born and raised in Harlem, went to visit his relatives in a small Mississippi town. But as soon as he arrived, he noticed the complete absence of any other black people. He

turned to a white man standing nearby. "Where do all the colored folks hang out in this town?"

The stranger pointed to a big oak tree in front of the court house. "See that limb . . . ?"[25]

But viewing these tales and jokes too quickly as evidence that main-stream society's perception of blacks was accepted and reaffirmed in African-American humor ignores the irony of much black comedy. (For instance, the aphorism about black sluggishness reflects not only surface self-ridicule but also obstinate resistance to labor under a system where there were no rewards. The last tale reveals both blacks' recognition of their marginal status in the South and their comic sense of some white southerners' scantly veiled barbarity. Only the Amos tale, which ap-peared in *The Atlanta Constitution* in 1867, is clearly self-denigrative, and there is some doubt about its origin.) A superficial view also disre-gards the effectiveness of one of black Americans' most inventive sur-vival tactics, which from the time of their arrival in the New World fostered a dual mode of behavior and expression—one for whites and another for themselves.

William Schechter, an early commentator on black humor, points out that among slaveholders or other whites a black slave "could, of course, criticize himself openly, without fear of reprisal. But his critical humor, when directed at whites, had to be cloaked in subtlety. . . . [It] had to provide a secondary meaning." So the question of viewpoint becomes crucial in interpreting black humor. The tale of the slave who is con-fronted after appropriating one of his master's turkeys is illustrative:

"You scoundrel, you ate my turkey," the master admonishes.

"Yes, suh, Massa, you got less turkey but you sho nuff got mo' Nigger," the slave replies.[26]

This tale may be interpreted as an example of black self-effacement, a groveling attempt to amuse in order to stave off punishment as well as an affirmation of black masochism and self-emasculation. But, much more realistically, it may be seen as an example of a calculated ploy to acquire a prized treat knowing full well that the acquisition can be achieved with impunity. So who is the butt of the joke? In fact, who is the aggressor? This and numerous similar tales illustrate not only the intricacy of the comic interaction and the importance of the interpretative perspective in assessing black humor but also the multi-faceted nature of the evolving relationship between blacks and whites.

Increasingly African-Americans became the arbiters of a reversed joke in which others' assumption of their ignorance became the source of humor.

The dynamics of the interaction was complex, and varying interpretations lead to vastly different conclusions. Nathan Huggins argued that in the course of this charade blacks internalized the traits ascribed to them and, to a certain extent, became Sambo, the naive stage Negro. Joseph Boskin suggested that although "blacks were able to develop a repertoire of retaliatory humor to partially offset their situation," by dictating blacks' superficial social behavior, white America largely achieved its desired end. "Humor was a weapon of no mean importance for blacks," Boskin wrote, "nevertheless their surface jocularity worked against them. Whites assumed that their performing and laughing were clear signs of their natural and inherent natures." Neither viewpoint fully evaluates or adequately credits the creative resourcefulness involved in reversing an accepted joke and turning it to one's advantage. Therefore each diminishes the import of the underlying assertiveness of what Freud calls "misleading naïveté," the act of representing oneself "as naive, so as to enjoy a liberty that . . . would not otherwise be granted"—an assertiveness that led psychiatrists William Grier and Price Cobbs to suggest that Sambo may have been the first black revolutionary.[27]

The dark side of this "misleading naïveté" is summed up by James Baldwin writing from the perspective of a non-black American: "Aunt Jemima and Uncle Tom, our creations, at the last evaded us; they had a life—their own, perhaps a better life than ours—and they would never tell us what it was." Ralph Ellison, in a speech entitled "American Humor," said, "We couldn't escape, so we developed a style of humor which recognized the basic artificiality, the irrationality, of the actual arrangement."[28]

Of course, what is humorous (who or what is the butt of the joke) depends almost entirely on the perspective taken. Erroneously evaluating humor as naive, for example, may reveal one's own unworldliness in mistaking impudence for innocence, or ironic folk perceptions for simpleminded banter. The slave who, after tripping and falling in the darkness, remarked, "Why de debil do a sun shine all day when nobody want um, and nebber a night, when it's so berry dark gentlum can't see his way," may indeed have been as simple as his eighteenth-century slaveholders contended. But it is just as likely that he was simply engaging in a kind of witty repartee that was common in his African homeland. Almost certainly, however, if the remark had not originated with an African-American (his naïveté an assumed fact) and had not been couched in broken dialect (the written version a creation of an Englishman), the question of whether it was an example of ironic wit would have risen.

Similar assumptions cloud broader definitions of humor and often reflect the astounding egocentricity and biased predispositions of their creators. Freud, for example, argued that people appear comic to us, "in comparison to ourselves," when they make "too great an expenditure on . . . bodily functions and too little on . . . mental ones." We then laugh, expressing our "pleasurable sense of the superiority we feel." In contrast, if others' physical exertion is less and their mental output is greater than our own, "we are filled with astonishment and admiration."[29]

From a Western outlook that places extremely high value on cerebral accomplishment, the conclusion is perfectly reasonable. But it rests on a culture-bound definition that ignores contrasting viewpoints. The epigram, "You study long, you study wrong," for instance, reflects an African-American attitude that places priority on spontaneous action, not studied thought. That attitude is reflected when black Americans ridicule Europeans' inhibited, intellectual approach or joke about Negroes who assume superior attitudes after having "rubbed the hair off their head against some college wall."

But even though African-Americans did not necessarily share all of mainstream America's views and cultural assumptions, they remained scrupulously attentive to them. Economic dependence and basic survival dictated that their awareness *never* lapse.

Describing his rite of passage as a black youth in the South during the 1920s in his autobiography, *Black Boy,* for instance, Richard Wright recounted the advice another black teenager had given him: "When you're in front of white people, *think* before you act, *think* before you speak. Your way of doing things is alright among *our* people, but not for *white* people." This advice is similar to views expressed in Frederick Douglass's autobiography (where he claimed that slaves' seemingly jovial behavior among whites did not reflect their true state of mind) and in numerous slave narratives.[30]

In fact, examples of this guarded and flexible approach to encounters with whites can be found in nearly all black autobiographical writing set in the years before the 1960s civil rights movement. John H. Johnson, who would become the multi-millionaire publisher of *Ebony* and *Jet* magazines, grew up in poverty in Arkansas. The process of altering his behavior had begun by the time he was an adolescent in the 1920s. As he wrote in *Succeeding Against All Odds*, "I always knew I was different, and that I was in danger." For instance, he recalled that after hearing that a black man had been lynched nearby for winking at a white female, "to prevent any misunderstandings we made a conscious effort not to blink our eyes in the presence of a white woman." This cautionary approach was often reflected in jokes that blacks told among themselves. In one, a black man intent on suicide leaps from a skyscraper but just before he hits the ground he sees a white woman coming around the corner. Knowing he had better not fall on her, he turns in the air and sails right back up to the top of the building.[31]

These behavioral adjustments forced many African-Americans to assume dual social roles: one for a hostile white world, the other the natural demeanor they reserved for interactions among themselves. Humor was a crucial factor in dealing with the situation. In interactions with whites, it eased tensions that might otherwise have exploded into violence. The humor many African-Americans displayed in public, however, often affirmed America's vision of blacks as naively funny and fundamentally simpleminded.

In the privacy of completely black settings, black humor was more acerbic and more explicitly revealed that evasive, hidden life to which James Baldwin alluded—a life kept under tight wraps. For a vulnerable black minority, surreptitiousness and trickery were the principal defenses against repression, and humor played a key role in this deviousness. For much of America's past, the two faces of black humor could not be combined without serious risk.

Initially, the racial roles assumed during slavery were, in a perverse way, mutually beneficial. But whether out of compulsion or for their own immediate advantage, blacks often fostered and affirmed the most insidious and demeaning stereotypes. As folklorist and historian Robert E. Hemenway wrote, bondsmen and chattel "were participating in an elaborate ritual of self-delusion. . . . [The slave] had always known what the truth was, and his master had known that [he] did. . . . Both knew that they were participating in a verbal hoax."[32]

Ritual and hoax, however, soon became an entrenched assumption for white America. The deeply embedded illusion first obscured and then distorted most realistic interchanges between the races. Long after the slave-master relationship had ended and free blacks began to demand equality, the phantasm persisted.

The African-American's proclivity for sensing his "twoness" and looking at himself "through the eyes of others"—while it defined and enriched black culture in many ways—also instilled a nagging ambivalence or self-consciousness. No matter how ironic the wit, or aggressive the underlying implication, blacks were simultaneously aware that it was invisible to most whites. Ole John the slave may have indeed tricked his master, Bert Williams may have infused his slow-talking stage darky with intelligence and humanity, Stepin Fetchit may have successfully wheedled his patron out of a few dollars in Hollywood movies, or Kingfish may have conned Andy out of some pittance on television, but to white America they were still little more than minstrel Sambos. During slavery, when the "ritual of self-delusion" was a realistic necessity, the knowledge was acceptable. Small victories, however oblique, were golden. With freedom and increased black expectation and ambition, the satisfaction derived from this indirect humor in integrated settings began to diminish.

Some black writers have argued that this self-consciousness is confined to middle-class blacks. In the essay "Characteristics of Negro Expression," for instance, novelist and folklorist Zora Neale Hurston argued that the "average Negro glories in his ways. The highly educated Negro the same. The self-despisement lies in a middle class who scorns to do or be anything Negro. . . . The Negro 'farthest down' is too busy 'spreading his junk' in his own way to see or care." My own experience as a youth among blacks who were near the bottom rung, however, partially belies that observation. It was not that my peers did not see or feel the intrusive presence of white evaluation; it was simply that many opted not to *care* about it. But even those who flaunted their blackness in the presence of whites still were noticeably more natural, their laughter more hearty, their behavior less tinged with reactionary overtones, when in an exclusively black setting.[33]

Removed from integrated gatherings, the same humorous approach defined by the Pompey and Ole John slave stories, the same indirect wordplay and double-edged wit that had shaped African-American humor from the outset thrived without second-guessing or reservation. During the fifties, for instance, I could and did laugh hilariously at my eccentric next-door neighbor's tales, even though they were couched in heavy dialect and almost always turned on feigned ignorance or helplessness. Among the group of adults and, when the lies were not too low-down, children who gathered to listen there was not the slightest hint of self-consciousness. His lies were outrageous.

One, which as a child I suppose I should not have heard, concerned his alleged prosperity during the Depression. As he told it, he was "the only nigger in Mobile, Alabama, sportin' 'round town in a brand-new Cadillac":

Black folks down there was so close to the po'house some ain't dirtied a plate nor licked a spoon in months, and I was ridin' 'round in the finest automobiles on dah streets. Had different ones ev'ry day if I pleased and use to choose the colors to go 'long with what-so-else-and-ever I was wearing that day. Had mo' women than Goodyear had rubber, you know, and treated 'em like queens—dem girls thought they was Be'sheba's daughter. How? What yo mean, "*how*," fool? If you had as much gumption as I did you wouldn't been beggin' fo' white folks' handouts yo'self. See, I was at Pearl's hospitality house one night and who come sneaking in dere all sheepish and weasel-like but ole Morris Witherspoon, dah most important white man in de city. Always in dah papers wit his wife 'cause he done give some'ah what he stole from us to dis or dat char'ty. Well, when I spies him comin' out one of dem gals' rooms puttin' dah horse back into de barn and tryin' to shiel' his face at dah same time, I steps up and says, "Say, boss, ain't I seen you somewheres befo'?" First, he tried to hightail it on out dah backdoor, but I kinda eased in front of him blocking dat exit and fin'ly he decided to speak to me. We didn't talk but 'bout a minute and I 'splained to him that I was one a de quietest niggers in Alabama and weren't no way his wife was goin find out bout his nighttime appetite fo' choc'late sweets. So he asked me over to his office at dah car lot the next day and I ain't had no trouble wit soup lines and transportation all through dah Depression. After it was over though, when I got up here . . . well, that's another story.

Of course, in those encounters with my neighbor, the listeners were all black, the comic referents understood, and the satire unsullied by the intrusion of an outside viewpoint. Similarly, in the privacy of my own living room, the antics of Kingfish or Calhoun did not seem "slanderous." They were simply funny characters, cartoonishly unreal, who in a wildly exaggerated manner bore some resemblance to folks in the neighborhood—one of which was my neighbor.

In the presence of non-blacks, however, I would have had second thoughts about both situations. In each instance, self-consciousness or "twoness" of vision would have hampered my enjoyment as well as that of the friends with whom I grew up. At the time, it was clear to most blacks that, from a non-black perspective, Negroes were homogeneous, and awareness of that dehumanizing, all-inclusive evaluation was unsettling. In interracial settings it often impeded blacks' enjoyment and appreciation of the fruits of their own cultural heritage—most obviously black ethnic humor and the blues.

Middle-class African-Americans and those who aspired to that position were particularly sensitive to the implied judgment introduced by the white presence, and struggled vainly to disassociate themselves from America's mythical Negro. Like some Jews, as described by Jean-Paul Sartre in *Anti-Semite and Jew*, they often "allowed themselves to be poisoned by stereotypes that others have of them, and they [lived] in fear that their acts [would] correspond to this stereotype." In many instances, they were, as Frantz Fanon wrote, "overdetermined from without"; consequently, the havoc and disorientation of "seeking to satisfy two unreconciled ideals ... seemed about to make them ashamed of themselves."[34]

Within this public, integrated framework, black buffoonery of any sort, like instances of criminal behavior or any hint of indolence, were invariably assumed to implicate and define all blacks. To most Negroes, laughing at Negro idiocy (in real life or the media) was, in effect, to ridicule yourself.

Behind closed doors, however, whether at home, in segregated black theatres, or at social gatherings in an exclusively black setting, most African-Americans reacted differently to authentic black ethnic humor. By the mid-nineteenth century, nearly all of the naïveté that may have initially sparked laughter in slaveholders had disappeared. The contrast between America's egalitarian pretensions and its treatment of slaves was clear; to most blacks the disparity between the social masks they wore and their true identities was also obvious. And while they were embarrassed by and increasingly frowned on displays of exaggerated, coon-like behavior before white audiences after the Civil War, in private they laughed as heartily at the covert trickery involved as whites did at the assumed naïveté and apparent confirmation of Negro imbecility.

The self-deprecatory aspect of early black humor, then, as with Jewish humor, has seemingly been grossly exaggerated. During slavery and on into the first half of the twentieth century—as mainstream America howled at the antics of Sambo and coon figures presented in minstrel shows or by the screen images of performers such as Stepin Fetchit, Willie Best, Mantan Moreland, or countless others who enacted coon stereotypes—the humor that emanated from the black community and emerged at house parties, barber shops, lodge meetings, and other all-black social gatherings or on stage at primarily black cabarets and variety houses was quite often assertive and openly critical of mainstream society. Although some self-deprecatory elements engendered by the slavery experience and codified during the relatively extended and popular run of blackface entertainment endured, black American humor, like other varieties of ethnic comedy, displayed a broad range of outwardly directed satire, as well as in-group ridicule.

And even when it acknowledges despair, black American humor transcends the present situation: it nimbly moves on to a vision of a brighter future or insistently counters the disparaging picture at hand with the image of an underdog (blacks themselves) with superior attributes. More subtly, by its expressive tone it may transform a negative situation or stereotype into a positive one by exposing its essentially ludicrous nature.

"Swapping Dreams," for example, is a slavery tale focused on a conversation between Ike, a witty house servant, and Jim Turner, a good-natured master who had a fondness for telling stories based on what he claimed were his dreams. Like many of the black animal stories such as *The Uncle Remus Tales,* it demonstrates how black slaves cleverly and subtly used humor to gain an edge—even an oblique sense of superiority—over their masters:

One morning, when Ike entered the master's room to clean it, he found the master just preparing to get out of bed. "Ike," he said, "I certainly did have a strange dream last night."

"Sez yuh did, Massa, sez yuh did?" answered Ike. "Lemme hyeah it."

"All right," replied the master. "It was like this: I dreamed I went to Nigger Heaven last night, and saw there a lot of garbage, some old torn-down houses, a few old broken-down, rotten fences, the muddiest, sloppiest streets I ever saw, and a big bunch of ragged, dirty Negroes walking around."

"Umph, umph, Massa," said Ike. "Yuh sho' musta et de same t'ing Ah did las' night, 'cause Ah dreamed Ah went up ter de white man's paradise, an' de streets wuz all ob gol' an' silvah, and dey wuz lots o' milk an' honey dere an' putty pearly gates, but dey wuzn't uh soul in de whole place."[35]

The late Moms Mabley's whimsical, parodical ditty (sung to the tune of "All the Way") about the "deliberate speed" with which freedom was forthcoming from mainstream America offers an excellent example of offsetting the negative aspect of a situation with ridicule:

> But if they gonna free us
> Then why don't they go ahead and free us . . .
>   All the way.
> Let'um keep on sayin', what they sayin'
> And we'll keep on prayin' . . .
>   Come what may.
>
> Who knows what the color under the skin is
> Only a fool can say.
> But if they gonna free us
> Then why not go ahead and free us . . .
>   Right a-w-a-y.
> And I mean, all the way![36]

Another significant component of black humor is its realism. As the critic Saunders Redding wrote of African-American humor:

> It is real. . . . It is sometimes aphoristic—recording the accumulated folk wisdom of the race. It is very often true—and the truth strikes deep into the follies, the paradoxes, the ambiguities, and the pulpy moral fiber of American life.[37]

It may sometimes take on the appearance of the romantic, outrageous or absurd, or it may surface as a subtle facial expression indicating incredulity or dissent—what comic actor Robert Guillaume describes as "mumbling on the face"—but black humor is for the most part based on the actual experiences and attitudes of the black community and is aptly described by Richard Pryor's often used transition line, "on the real side." To ignore this truth is to misunderstand both the nature and the thrust of the humor, even as Joel Chandler Harris—the principal collector of the Uncle Remus tales—did when he failed to recognize that, like many of the work songs and spirituals of the same period, the stories he popularized as the childlike creations of a simple, docile community were in fact veiled protests against the actual circumstances of slavery and discrimination.[38]

Finally, traditional black humor is as much physical as it is verbal. It is almost always intricately connected with physical postures that reflect the style of black common folk and, not surprisingly, the two most accomplished professional African-American comedians (Bert Williams and Richard Pryor) were accomplished mimes. Whether the humorist is on stage at the Apollo Theatre or the Hollywood Bowl or on a street corner in Harlem or Watts, the joke or gag is usually delivered with recognizable expressions and gestures, which, in themselves, are a source of humor among blacks. As an old blues lyric expresses it:

> It ain't what you do,
> It's the way you do it.
> Baby, what you're doing I can plainly see,
> But just how you do it is a mystery to me.[39]

Black American humor is nearly as dependent on a delivery that incorporates black America's generally more expressive and flamboyant style as it is on wit or verbal dexterity.

Still, all this is only to allude to the unifying characteristics of the African-American humor tradition. As Henri Bergson pointed out, "To understand laughter, we must put it back into its natural environment, which is society, and above all we must determine the utility of its function, which is a social one."[40]

On the Real Side views African-American humor in its social setting, chronicling the development from its African antecedents through slavery and on through most of the twentieth century. The present study traces and examines the social functions of two disparate strains of humor: the often distorted *outside* presentation in mainstream media (initially by non-blacks) and the authentic *inside* development of humor in black communities (from slave shanties and street corners to cabarets) as well as in folklore and black literature, films, and race records. In a real sense, this is the story of how these discrepant comic faces gradually converged and, through the efforts of a small group of writers and comedians, merged in the 1970s.

PART ONE:
ANTECEDENTS

1.

SLAVERY . . . "don't nobody know my name but me"

6

WE RAISE THE WHEAT, DEY GIB US DE CORN;

WE BAKE DE BREAD, DEY GIB US DE CRUST;

WE SIF DE MEAL, DEY GIB US DE HUSS;

WE PEAL DE MEAT, DEY GIB US DE SKIN;

AND DAT'S DE WAY DEY TAKES US IN.

WE SKIMS DE POT, DEY GIB US DE LIQUOR,

AN' SAY, "DAT'S GOOD ENOUGH FER A NIGGER."

—ANONYMOUS

NO MASTER COULD BE THOROUGHLY COMFORTABLE AROUND A SULLEN SLAVE; AND, CONVERSELY, A MASTER, UNLESS HE WAS UTTERLY HUMORLESS, COULD NOT OVERWORK OR BRUTALLY TREAT A JOLLY FELLOW, ONE WHO COULD MAKE HIM LAUGH.

—W. D. WEATHERFORD AND CHARLES S. JOHNSON

THE LINE THAT LEADS TO MOMS MABLEY, NIPSEY RUSSELL, BILL COSBY, AND MYSELF CAN BE TRACED BACK TO THE SOCIAL SATIRE OF SLAVE HUMOR, BACK EVEN THROUGH MINSTRELSY, THROUGH COUNTLESS ATTEMPTS TO CAST OFF THAT FANTASY.

—GODFREY CAMBRIDGE[1]

I

Something peculiar happened on the way to the New World—or, at least, very shortly afterward. Somewhere between their departure from West Africa's shores and the early stages of their arrival as human chattel in the Americas, the African captives transported across the Atlantic underwent a subtle but far-reaching and remarkable psychological transformation.

It may have begun aboard one of the large canoes that snaked along the winding Gambia or Senegal rivers, stopping periodically to take on more human cargo and then moving away from the dense interior toward Africa's western coast. It could have been there that it first took form in the minds of some of those captives as, bound and yoked together in coffles, their destiny now almost certain, they were transported from the familiarity of tribal life to an ominous if, to them, yet unknown fate. Or it may have occurred later, when branded and fettered and, no doubt, still baffled and dismayed, they waited in cattlelike stockades or slave pens at ports such as Britain's Cape Coast Castle on the Gold Coast or the infamous Maison des esclaves on Gorée Island off the coast of Senegal. At these and similar sites, "tens of millions of

Africans" were estimated to have last touched their own soil before being forcibly transported overseas.[2]

Or perhaps it happened later, during the Middle Passage (the treacherous three- to twelve-week voyage to the New World), as, surely terrified by now, they lay shackled and longing either for the fraternity of their homelands, or more realistically for a merciful death in the dank, cramped bowels of those typically overcrowded slave vessels; it may have even occurred during the brief daily intervals when male captives were joined with females on the ships' decks to momentarily glimpse daylight, exercise in order to restore their throttled circulation, and ceremoniously entertain their captors. Or it might have surfaced even later, at auction blocks in the West Indies or America, as they were prodded, inspected, and bargained over by prospective buyers, or subsequently when, having been duly purchased and dispatched to their owners, they first began their assigned labor on the farms and plantations to which most would be confined for the rest of their lives.

It is nearly impossible to determine exactly where and when it happened—few confirmed testaments of the thoughts of these African captives were sought or recorded during the three and a half centuries of the trans-Atlantic slave trade. Indeed, initially very few slaves could converse or write in the language of their European captors, and it is doubtful, given the express purpose of the endeavor, that their captors would have heeded any such expressions.

But during their transformation from Africans to African-American slaves, a remarkably resilient and inventive manner of behaving and observing both themselves and the external world began to emerge. It would be nurtured and shaped by their interaction with America's social customs and the "peculiar institution" of slavery, be passed on to subsequent arrivals and, eventually, become a key factor in African America's rich and expansive under- or subculture. As one historian put it: "Herded together with others with whom they shared only a common condition of servitude and some degree of cultural overlap, enslaved Africans were compelled to create a new language, a new religion, and a precarious new lifestyle." Later, that black lifestyle or subculture would become quite probably the most formidable influence on American popular culture.[3]

It is in music, of course, that this impact has been most significant. There is also plentiful evidence of the impact on, among other pursuits, dance, sports, colloquial speech, and fashion. But it is the expressive manner of African-American humor that, second to music, has most influenced mainstream America's popular culture. And although bondage and oppression hardly seem to favor the development of a comic tradition, slavery was, ironically, the primary factor in molding the style and content of both private and public black humor. From the beginning it combined cultural elements of traditional African societies with the new language, social institutions, and behavioral patterns of antebellum America. Since then it has taken a course that is as labyrinthine, ironic, and melodramatic as the work of some of our most darkly inventive Southern Gothic fiction writers.

What might have been going through the minds of those African captives when they arrived in the Americas?

Some, no doubt, still entertained thoughts of escaping or destroying themselves. The recorded instances of suicides, attempted breakaways, and rebellions attest to the numbers who chose death or the slimmest opportunity for freedom over the safety of serfdom. At the height of the transatlantic trade, epidemics, futile escape attempts, and suicides claimed 6 to 25 percent of the captives; the British Privy Council, after examining records of slave ships, concluded that, on the average, of the African captives who began the Atlantic journey, 12.5 percent perished.[4]

Statistics, however, convey little of the reality. The story related by a South Carolina black man who had endured the Middle Passage offers a more vivid description:

Dey been pack in dere wuss dan hog in a car when dey shippin' 'em. An' everyday dem white folks would come in dere an' ef a nigger jest twist his self or move, dey'd cut de hide off him wid a rawhide whip. An' niggers died in de bottom er dat ship wuss dan hogs wid cholera. Dem white folks ain' hab no mercy. Look like dey ain' known wha' mercy mean. Dey drag dem dead niggers out an' throw 'em overboard. An' dat ain' all. Dey th'owed a heap er live ones wha' dey thought ain' guh live into de sea.[5]

In addition, there were numerous reports of insurrections and suicides, sometimes before the slave vessels ever left port. According to the captain of the British ship *Hannibal*:

Negroes are so wilful and loth to leave their own country, that they have often leap'd out of the canoos, boats and ship, into the seas, and kept under water till they were drowned to avoid being taken up and saved by our boats, which pursued them; they having a more dreadful apprehension of Barbadoes than we have of hell. . . ."[6]

Other less obstinate Africans undoubtedly initially consoled themselves with the thought that the servitude they faced in America would be similar to what many of them had seen or experienced directly in tribal Africa. Slavery, after all, had existed in Africa since recorded times, although major slave regimes, especially in the west, were "relatively few and of limited longevity in the period prior to the arrival of the Christian Europeans." As in Europe, domestic servitude was common in most of the early, more complex African societies, and caravan routes across the Sahara Desert had facilitated Africa's commercial export of slaves to the Mediterranean area even before the emergence of the Roman Empire.[7]

After the onset of the trans-Atlantic trade, commercial use of slaves within the African interior increased. And more African states, reacting to the European demand for slaves, resorted to intertribal warfare and detainment of criminals as a means of acquiring the human chattel that was fast becoming Africa's chief export. Still, slaves or "wageless workers" in the inland regions of Africa, which were generally isolated from Muslim and eventual European influences, functioned primarily within a comparatively amiable system. They were "seldom or never men without rights or hope of emancipation" and were not "outcasts in the body politic," writes the British historian Basil Davidson. "On the contrary they were integral members of the community. Household slaves lived with their masters, often as members of the family. They could work themselves free of their obligations. They could marry their master's daughters. They could become traders, leading men in peace and war, governors and sometimes even kings."[8]

So despite the suicides, insurrections, and barbaric conditions of the Middle Passage, some African captives must have clung to the hope that the treatment awaiting them in the Americas would be less hostile and dehumanizing than what they had experienced since their capture. Those who arrived anticipating a system of bondage even remotely resembling the comparatively benevolent form that some had experienced in the interior of their homeland, however, were quickly and bitterly disappointed. What they actually found was what Davidson describes as a "deep soil of arrogant contempt for African humanity." That contempt was quite possibly the most destructive consequence of the transatlantic slave trade.[9]

Africans dispatched to the New World found themselves in a perplexing if not devastating position. The possibility of successfully escaping and returning to their native land was practically nonexistent. And they faced not only a cruel and, for the most part, inflexible system that governed practically every aspect of their lives, but also a community of people who placed little or no value on their humanity. What were they to do?

Some, overwhelmed and sensing the futility of any type of resistance, quite probably succumbed to melancholy and despair and dolefully submitted to the status of mere chattel—becoming, in effect, Uncle Toms, harmless darkies, or Sambos. As the historian Stanley M. Elkins has suggested, these slaves, like many concentration camp victims in the 1940s, accepted their dependent status and internalized the social role demanded of them by their masters. But Sterling Stuckey and numerous other historians have pointed out that many others avoided "being imprisoned altogether by the definitions the larger society sought to impose." They neither desperately sought an immediate, violent solution to their condition nor entirely capitulated psychologically; instead, they chose deception and subterfuge as a primary survival tactic.[10]

"The first line of defense for any vanquished or occupied nation, as for any camp of war-prisoners," writes James Pope-Hennessy, "is calculated cunning and deceit."[11]

Accordingly, many slaves adopted an obsequious *social mask* as an essential survival apparatus. "Slaves who behaved like Sambos," contends Ronald T. Takaki, "might not have actually been Sambos, for they might have been playing the role of the loyal and congenial slave in order to survive. . . . Sambo-like behavior may have been not so much a veil to hide inner emotions of rage and discontent as an effective means of expressing them." In effect, this behavior may have demonstrated "resistance to efficiency, discipline, work, and productivity. Where the master perceived laziness, the slave saw refusal to be exploited . . . the same action held different meanings, depending on whether one was master or slave."[12]

To maintain respect for themselves or preserve any remnants of their native culture, subterfuge and lying were absolutely necessary for the

Africans brought to America's shores. In addition to the primary tasks of tilling the fields of cane, cotton, and tobacco plantations and providing domestic and skilled craft services, survival in the New World depended to a great extent upon appeasing slaveholders' demands for an ingratiating demeanor and the eradication of nearly all vestige of Africanisms.

The response of most blacks to these demands was both rational and effective. As one social historian puts it: "Over many generations the slave developed techniques of deception that were, for the white man, virtually impenetrable." Numerous comments from slaveholders or white observers affirm the existence as well as the effectiveness of black duplicity: "So deceitful is the Negro," one explained, "that as far as my own experience extends I could never in a single instance decipher his character. . . . We planters could never get at the truth." Another claimed: "He is never off guard. He is perfectly skilled at hiding his emotions. . . . His master knows him not."[13]

Obviously, the pragmatically adopted policy of "puttin' on massa" and thereby making deceit part of their lifestyle had negative long-term consequences for slaves and their descendants. But it did solve some immediate problems presented by bondage. Slaves also used subversion and sabotage—work delay, theft, arson, and destruction of crops—as a means of resistance. In addition, they often feigned ineptitude and ignorance to achieve their own ends.

The dynamics of this strained interaction, with its contradictory goals and clandestine motives—a methodically fashioned maze of non-communication and misdirection from the black perspective—are largely responsible for the convoluted interpersonal relationship of black and white Americans to this day. The reaction of one Louisiana physician to slave duplicity and subversiveness not only points out the extent to which slaves duped many of their masters but, in retrospect, is also quite humorous. In the mid-ninetenth century Dr. Samuel Cartwright wrote an essay on diseases peculiar to the Negro, among them, DYS-AESTHESIA AETHIOPICA:

> From the careless movements of the individuals affected with this complaint they are apt to do much mischief, which appears as if intentional, but is mostly owing to the stupidness of mind and insensibility of the nerves induced by the disease. Thus they break, waste, and destroy everything they handle; abuse horses and cattle; tear, burn, or rend their own clothing. . . . When driven to labor by the compulsive power of the white man, he performs the task

assigned to him in a headlong, careless manner, treading down with his feet or cutting with his hoe the plants he is put to cultivate; breaking the tools he works with, and spoiling everything he touches that can be injured by careless handling.[14]

The chicanery and deception established in the initial contacts between black slaves and white masters added a note of comic absurdity and dissemblance that, as one would expect, still surfaces frequently in jokes about interracial confrontations emerging from the African-American community. For instance, there is the tale of a black maid who worked in a home near an Army camp during World War II. Her employer, displeased with her work, asks: "Do you suppose we'll be able to get more work out of you girls now that they've moved all the colored soldiers away from this camp?" Unruffled, the black woman replies: "I don't know, ma'am. They ain't moved none of the white fellows away." A tale popularized by Dick Gregory in the sixties is even more pointed: A black man enters a Southern restaurant and is told, "Sorry, we don't serve colored folks here." His reply, "Fine, I don't eat them, just bring me a medium rare hamburger."[15]

When they adopted subterfuge and the masking of real feelings as the central means of coping with slavery, African-Americans set in motion a social and psychological dynamic that has had far-reaching consequences. Most obviously, it established a split in their social behavior; alternate forms of deportment for integrated settings (public) and in gatherings among trusted blacks (private) became a reality in slave communities. This is reflected with typical folk pointedness in the following slave aphorism:

Got one mind for white folk to see
'Nother for what I know is me.[16]

The deepseated distrust of white America and codification of a deceptive approach to racial interchanges laid the foundation for a culture that the German historian Berndt Ostendorf aptly described as "double-edged, indirect and ambivalent"; one that "will not yield meaningful answers to the positivist who is preoccupied with surface phenomena."[17]

Along with subterfuge, the irony, contradiction, and distortion that are fundamental to the comic spirit became a central element in American racial relations. But the psychosocial dynamics that shaped African-

American humor would, until the second half of the twentieth century, create an almost unassailable barrier to mainstream America's exposure to it in its authentic form.

II

Secrecy and subterfuge molded black American humor's indirect manner and also helped slaves perpetuate the African customs that gave their humor a distinctive cast. As Sterling Stuckey points out, slave deception aggressively "worked against whites acquiring knowledge of slave culture that might have been used to attempt to eradicate that culture."[18]

As incredible as it may seem from the vantage point of the 1990s, for more than three hundred years after the arrival of African slaves in America nearly all historians and sociologists insisted that African-Americans had *no* culture of their own. Early in the twentieth century, the renowned black sociologist W. E. B. Du Bois apparently became the first scholar to suggest that the behavior of black Americans was significantly influenced by African culture. Subsequently Carter G. Woodson, founder of the *Journal of Negro History,* supported those claims. But it was not until Melville J. Herskovits's 1941 book *The Myth of the Negro Past,* in which he reaffirmed the idea of African cultural retentions advanced by Du Bois and Woodson, that the issue was seriously debated in academic circles.[19]

Prior to Herskovits it was presumed that the Middle Passage, restrictive black codes (outlawing practically all African customs except dancing and singing, which were thought to facilitate productivity), and the impact of Western society's more advanced culture had magically eradicated all vestiges of African beliefs. (Or, much less frequently, in a complete reversal, it was argued that blacks' lowly position in America was the consequence of having brought all of their barbaric customs across the Atlantic.) In fact, according to the informed opinion of many historians, Africa—mirroring fictional depictions in Edgar Rice Burroughs's Tarzan novels—was simply a primitive, pagan civilization with little or no culture worth considering.

One can easily disregard the pro-slavery propaganda of such writers as George Fitzhugh, Dr. John H. Van Evrie, and Dr. Josiah C. Nott, whose unsubstantiated and skewed views were instrumental in establishing many of the popular myths about Africa and African-Americans during the nineteenth century. But even the most reputable scholars presented a more or less homogeneous estimate of African savagery and the dearth of African-American culture.[20]

In 1919, for instance, Robert E. Park, the esteemed and influential co-founder of the University of Chicago's School of Sociology, commented: "In fact, there is every reason to believe, it seems to me, that the Negro, when he landed in the United States, left behind almost everything but his dark complexion and his temperament. It is very difficult to find in the South today anything that can be traced directly back to Africa."[21]

Later, Gunnar Myrdal (the Swedish social scientist commissioned by the Carnegie Foundation in 1937 to prepare a study on the Negro problem and American civilization), while admitting that "perhaps" there was "a measure of truth" in some of Herskovits's claims, proceeded to dismiss nearly all of them. In his much-acclaimed *An American Dilemma,* Myrdal argued that "In practically all of its divergences, American Negro culture is not something independent of general American culture. It is a *distorted* development, or a *pathological* condition, of the general American culture [italics added]." According to Myrdal, "In his cultural traits, the Negro is akin to other Americans. . . . True, there has developed recently a glorification of things African, especially in music and art. . . . But this is a reaction to discrimination from white people, on the one hand, and the result of encouragement from white people, on the other hand."[22]

In a different context, Myrdal wrote that

Negro thinking is almost completely determined by white opinion —negatively and positively. . . . [It] seldom moves outside the orbit fixed by the whites' conceptions about the Negro and about caste. . . . This vicious cycle of caste operates upon the finest brains in the Negro people and gives even to the writings of a Du Bois a queer touch of unreality as soon as he leaves *his* problem, which is the American Negro problem, and makes a frustrated effort to view it in a wider setting as an ordinary American and as a human being.[23]

Although Myrdal's book is a virtual goldmine of information—the most exhaustive study of black America ever undertaken—it is also littered throughout with such leaden nuggets of misinterpretation. Of course, Myrdal was not the only scholar to take exception to Herskovits's revised appraisal of the survival of African culture among blacks in

America. Those who initially objected most vociferously included a number of prominent black intellectuals.[24]

One of the most adamant and vocal was the distinguished sociologist E. Franklin Frazier, author of numerous texts, including the prize-winning study *The Negro Family in the United States* (1939). Frazier's chief objection concerned the influence of African customs on the structure of black American family and church life. But he had previously written rather emphatically that the "most conspicuous thing about the Negro is his lack of culture."[25]

The sociologist and civil rights leader Charles S. Johnson—who was president of Fisk University from 1946 to 1956 and whom Langston Hughes and Arna Bontemps considered one of the "nursemaids of [the Harlem] Renaissance"—was another outspoken critic. Johnson, who had studied with Robert E. Park at the University of Chicago, consistently argued that black behavior was the result of blacks' accommodating adjustment to slavery rather than any residual African cultural traits.[26]

How could those early twentieth-century intellectuals and even some modern-day scholars suggest that African slaves' memory of their culture had simply disappeared along with nearly all vestiges of that culture after the trans-Atlantic journey?[27]

The primary reason, asserts Berndt Ostendorf, "is quite clearly politics. Other reasons, though they seem to hinge on questions of method or scholarly accuracy, are equally political." For example, Alain Locke, editor of the highly acclaimed *The New Negro* (1925), contended that if whites acknowledged a strong African heritage, they might conclude that blacks were unassimilable; and Frazier feared that if whites believed that the "Negro's social behavior was rooted in African culture, they would lose whatever guilt they had for keeping the Negro down."[28]

Ostendorf also noted pro-slavery propagandists' justification of slavery by creation of the "Sambo" myth, which fixed the stereotype of the inferior black incapable of being assimilated into whites' "higher" culture; the integrationist aims of many blacks as well as of many whites sympathetic to the black cause; and blacks' reluctance to be associated with an African cultural tradition that had been so insistently portrayed as primitive and inferior.

Yet it is now apparent that blacks preserved many of their African beliefs and practices after arriving in America: among them are religious and burial practices, family structure, interpersonal social behavior, motor habits (walking, speaking, laughing, sitting posture, etc.), music, rhythmic response, folklore, and rhetoric or language. Although there is still some debate over social institutions such as family and church, there are few who seriously or convincingly deny the impact of African culture on artistic and social expression, areas that largely shape our humorous expression. More and more, contemporary scholars are heeding the venerable Ashanti proverb: "Ancient things remain in the ears."[29]

Lorenzo Turner's much-acclaimed book *Africanisms in the Gullah Dialect* (1949), for instance, demonstrates that the accents of blacks living on the coastal Sea Islands of South Carolina and Georgia were derived "from Africa and not, as was once widely held, from archaic dialects of sixteenth-century England." And Sterling Stuckey's *Slave Culture: Nationalist Theory and the Foundation of Black America* (1987) not only demonstrates specific examples of African culture surviving in religion, singing, dancing, and the use of musical instruments, but suggests that circle dances and shouts (a common practice in many West African tribes) allowed Africans of disparate origins and cultural backgrounds to participate in a common ritual that eventually facilitated the integration of various African tribal customs and the formation of a distinct African-American subculture. According to Stuckey, this "cultural convergence" provides "the key to understanding the means by which they achieved oneness in America."[30]

In all probability, dance—along with music and singing—was also an activity that initially allowed slaves to communicate furtively with one another. Forbidden directly to voice any protest about their condition or even to speak in their native languages, slaves used music and dancing not only to establish a symbolic or kinesthetic connection to their homeland and one another but also to convey feelings and thoughts to other slaves. As Stuckey and others have noted, chanting, foot stomping, hand clapping, and dance were central elements in the various rituals and religious ceremonies of most of the West African tribes from which the slaves had been abducted. Moreover, in those tribes, dance was a highly esteemed art and means of communicating. Robert Farris Thompson quotes an elderly member of a Cameroon Ngbe community who, after observing one dancer, commented: "I like him because he uses the conversation with his body. Even an old man can dance conversation."[31]

The argument Charles Keil makes in his *Urban Blues* (1966) about music applies to humor and black culture in general:

The entertainment component of Negro culture is significant in at least four basic respects. First, it is the one area in Negro life that was clearly not stripped away or obliterated by slavery. . . . Second, unlike the immigrant cultural traditions which have been either diluted or dissolved almost completely in the American context, this important cultural legacy linking American Negroes to Africa has not only survived but has thrived on adversity and grown stronger through the years. Third, it is now a full-fledged tradition in its own right. One does not have to be a specialist in African culture ever on the alert for Africanisms or a psychologist of race relations studiously attuned to the marks of oppression in order to understand a performance by B. B. King, a sermon by the Reverend C. L. Franklin, a Moms Mabley comedy routine, or a John Coltrane saxophone solo. Familiarity (preferably intimate) with contemporary Negro culture and some sensitivity to the particular form of expression in question—music, rhetoric, choreography— are the only basic analytic prerequisites. Finally, and most important, the entertainers are masters of sound, movement, timing, the spoken word. One can therefore find in their performances the essentials and defining features—the core in fact—of Negro culture as a whole.[32]

III

At the same time that black slaves were furtively sowing the seeds of their own subculture, they were helping to establish a public image of ever merry, frivolous, happy-go-lucky "Sambos" in the minds of the majority white population. Their music, singing, dancing, and barely distinguishable English were quickly becoming a source of great amusement to American whites and European visitors. A century or so after their arrival in the United States, in the eyes of one noted eighteenth-century English comedian, black slaves had acquired the dubious distinction of being the "greatest humorists in the union." This designation was, of course, quite obviously double-edged since it was seen as further evidence of their "childlike nature" and total dependency on whites, and became another justification for slavery.[33]

Blacks' behavior had long been the object of an ambivalent fascination and curiosity for Europeans. The writings of fifteenth- and sixteenth-century travelers repeatedly reflect the intrigue and sense of foreboding that originally fashioned the "Dark Continent" mystique and their astonishment at what was perceived as the Africans' inexplicably cheerful nature. During slavery, however, at closer range and under circumstances where whites were a majority clearly in control, the European and American view of black slaves was significantly altered. Black behavior that in Africa may have seemed bizarre and somewhat threatening was in antebellum America generally perceived as merely odd and entertaining.

Southern slaveholders often encouraged the slaves' merrymaking. It was a source of entertainment for plantation masters as well as for their Northern American and European guests. Former slave Frederick Douglass wrote: "Slaves are generally expected to sing as well as to work." He also contended that a "silent slave is not liked by masters or overseers. *Make a noise, make a noise*,' and *Bear a hand*,' are the words usually addressed to the slaves when there is silence amongst them." And Solomon Northrup, a freedman who was abducted and forced into slavery, recalled that his master "often received letters, sometimes from a distance of ten miles, requesting him to send me to play at a ball or festival of the whites. He received his compensation, and usually I also returned with many picayunes jingling in my pocket —the extra contribution of those to whose delight I had administered." He also confirmed that musical ability could be a crucial factor in mediating the harshness of slavery: "Alas! Had it not been for my beloved violin, I scarcely can conceive how I could have endured the long years of Bondage."[34]

Slave narratives, journals and diaries of visitors from Europe and North America, and commentaries by journalists and social scientists all offer a more or less identical portrait of the public image of black slaves as clowns and entertainers. Even when they were not required to entertain, their leisure activities—what little leisure they had—were often observed with fascination. Europeans were enthralled by their rhythmic movements and dance, their seemingly nonsensical antics, quaint pulsating music, and overall uninhibited behavior. Even religious and burial ceremonies were watched with amusement by whites when possible.

After Africa, a collection of extracts from British travel accounts and journals of the seventeenth, eighteenth, and nineteenth centuries edited by Roger D. Abrahams and John F. Szwed, provides numerous samples of the impressions Europeans had of antebellum blacks in America. John Finch, for example, wrote in 1833:

In Maryland dancing is fashionable; the slaves frequently dance all night. In Virginia musical parties are more frequent: every negro is a musician from birth. A black boy will make an excellent fiddle out of a gourd and some string. In autumn they play tunes on the dried stalks of Indian corn, when it is still standing in the field. By striking it near the ground or at the top, they make it discourse most excellent music. The banjo is another instrument they are fond of, but the supreme ambition of every negro is to procure a real violin. . . . An instrument of music seems necessary to their existence.[35]

Joseph H. Ingraham, his infatuation barely constrained, waxes almost poetic in the following account of slave revelry published in 1860:

The little Africans danced harder and harder. Their parents caught the spirit of the moment, and this one, dashing his old cap down, sprang into the arena, and that one, uttering a whoop, followed, till fully fifty were engaged at once. I never enjoyed any thing so much! I could fancy myself witnessing some heathen incantation dance in the groves of Africa! The moonlight shining through the trees, the red glare of the torches upon them, their wild move- ments, their strange and not unmusical cries, as they kept time with their voices to their quick tramping feet, their dark forms, their contortions, and perfect *abandon*, constituted a *tout ensem- ble* that must be witnessed to be appreciated.[36]

Overall, the image of black slaves held by Europeans and Americans outside of the South is perhaps best and most revealingly summed up in the following comment by an observer in 1846: "When you hear them, you are half inclined to laugh at their queerness, and yet cannot but be affected at the sincerity."[37]

This image of the merry, mirthful black was also important to white slaveholders, since slaves with musical ability or a knack for entertaining increased in value. Slaveholders commonly supplied musical instru- ments and insisted that slaves develop their "natural" inclinations. In addition to monetary incentives, there was also the propaganda motive of affirming the image of the slave's supposed childlike, dependent nature in order to confound any move to abolish slavery and, however misleading, the psychological reassurance derived from the belief that blacks were content with their status as bondsmen.

Even so, as the historian Joseph Boskin quite accurately observed, "Being mirthful meant the full gamut of humor, the ability to contrive and to be the object of laughter." Consequently, for whites, "the entertainment blacks provided was not limited to performing but encompassed humor itself—not the humor of the child, despite the heavy use of the word by contemporaries and later scholars, but of the fool."[38]

Indeed, while the comic persona blacks established in public functioned as a survival mechanism, it simultaneously made them objects of ridicule and derision. For many Americans, the slaves' comic demeanor was largely based on their exotic behavior—a style of singing and dancing, for example, that was common in African secular customs and religious rituals, but strange and unfamiliar to most Westerners. Those practices, combined with the frequent malapropism and mispronunciation of words issuing from slaves' attempt to learn a foreign language, initially delineated black slaves' comic image for most whites. And, not surprising, it was not far removed from the traditional European image of the Fool, a character that most colonists knew very well.

Punning, for example, was a comic ploy frequently used by European troubadours or fools. In fact, puns—a form of wordplay involving the use of words with the same sound and more than one meaning (*the comedian with hair on his jests* or *the critic who pans for gold*)— are closely related to malapropisms. But while malapropisms can be inadvertent, puns are deliberate. And the pun, although some insist it is the lowest form of humor, has been a key element in European wit, especially British, since classical times. Still, as Walter Redfern points out in his study of puns, "Americans wanted to disassociate themselves from the British, especially in so personal a matter as the sense of humour." Accordingly, early Americans developed what is perhaps an even lower type of comedy, cacography—deliberate misspelling for humorous effect—as a popular comic form.[39]

The use of this comic literary device, probably based on the crude dialect of the yokel or common man, grew out of American folk humor that was widespread by the eighteenth century. The popularizer of one vein of this type of comedy, Yankee humor, is usually acknowledged as Seba Smith, a New England journalist whose fictional tales had a large following and appeared in newspapers throughout the country in the early 1800s. It was James Russell Lowell, however, who established the Yankee type as a cornerstone of American humor. Considered the "most effective political satirist" of the pre–Civil War period, his homely wit was perhaps best demonstrated in *The Biglow Papers*

(1848), in which the characters voice some scathing anti-war attacks in typical dialect fashion:

> They may talk o' freedom's airy
>   Till they're pupple in the face,—
> It's a grand gret cemetary
>   For the barthrights of our race;
> They jest want this Californy
>   So's to lug new slave-states in
> To abuse ye, an' to scorn ye,
>   An' to plunder ye like sin.[40]

American Frontier humor or the humor of the old Southwest was another comic offshoot that accentuated the contrast between the common man and the gentleman or the establishment. Yankee and Frontier characters were usually heroes or, perhaps more precisely, anti-heroes who, through commonsense and a vernacular voice, ridiculed pretension wherever they found it—usually among politicians and the effete elitists who continued to embrace British standards of propriety. Augustus Baldwin Longstreet, whose *Georgia Scenes* (1835) "ushered in the whole movement," was one of the leading practitioners. But it was Johnson Jones Hooper's character Captain Simon Suggs who became the prototype of the colorful, rascally, but witty lout that epitomized the humor and distinct vernacular dialect of the Frontier type in the mid-nineteenth century. The following selection from *Some Adventures of Captain Simon Suggs* (1845) illustrates the comic use of vernacular:

> "My apinion, folks, is this here. We ought to form a company right away, and make some man capting that ain't afeard to fight—mind what I say now—*that-ain't-afeard-to-fight!*—some sober, stiddy feller"—here he sipped a little from the tumbler [filled with whiskey]—"that's a good hand to manage women and keep 'em from hollerin—which they're a-needin' somethin' of the sort most damdibly, and I eech to git holt o' that one a-making that deveilish racket in the corner, that" . . . [41]

One outgrowth of the Yankee and Frontier humorists was the "Misspellers" or so-called "literary comedians" of the late nineteenth century, whom detractors described as "popular funny men whose prime comic stock in trade was the butchery of the English language." A

Cleveland newspaperman, Charles Farrar Browne (writing under the name of Artemus Ward), was the most successful of these writers, and in 1862, at the height of his career, became the editor of *Vanity Fair*, then a New York City comic weekly. By the twentieth century the popularity of this form of literary comedy had waned, although humorists associated with the school continued publishing until the fifties. Humorists such as Harrison Dickson, E. K. Means, Hugh Wiley, and Octavus Roy Cohen wedded this literary approach to portrayals of black characters and often presented themselves as experts on the "Negro." Advertisements for Cohen's *Polished Ebony* (1919) in *Publishers Weekly*, for example, referred to him as "the Negro's O. Henry."[42]

Cacography or comic misspelling is, of course, only an earshot away from malapropism—the comic misuse of words that so tititlated whites when observed in black slaves struggling to learn a new language. The phenomenon was poignantly observed during the 1970s in Richard Pryor's caustic bit about the former heavyweight champion Leon Spinks:

> I hate when white people be calling [Leon] Spinks dumb, too. Right! "Don't you think he's dumb?" My mind immediately says, "What is this motherfucker goin' think about me if I agree with him?" I mean, Spinks may not articulate the language, but it ain't his anyway. . . . Like to see how you do in Zaire. . . .[43]

In the nineteenth century, however, the European minstrel, court jester, or Fool, minus cap and bell, appeared miraculously as the buffoonish black slave, decked out in his master's hand-me-down clothes, displaying a reportedly continuously mirthful countenance, and (at least on stage) pretentiously spewing out multi-syllabic words that were unerringly used incorrectly.[44]

Blacks were, of course, incidental to the social dynamics that cast them in the role of the nation's natural entertainers and humorists. They were merely symbols, since there was no serious thought of extending the social benefits of America's egalitarian precepts to them at that time. Slaves as comic figures were objects of derision—in most instances both the vehicle for and butt of the humor. What better way to fashion a common man's culture than to spotlight a comic type at which the average man could laugh, indeed, recognize some part of himself in veiled form, and at the same time feel superior? And, perceived as comic entertainers and later established as stage symbols of the comic, blacks permitted other Americans safely to transfer some parts of their European cultural background to America in a form that was readily distinguished from the parent country.

At the same time, blacks had brought from Africa certain cultural attributes that hastened their facile adaptation to their role as the nation's principal comics. The wordplay associated with punning, for instance, as Walter Redfern points out, "is at home in so-called 'primitive' groups" as well as in "sophisticated societies." In fact, according to Maurice Charney, author of *Comedy High and Low*, "In an oral culture, the sounds are literally the basic units of meaning, with almost unlimited possibilities of punning. The awareness of spelling tends to restrict the free play of comic imagination." Another scholar has affirmed that "myth can simultaneously speak of serious things and set those who hear it laughing. . . . It is not unusual for these ['primitive'] cultures to entrust their myths with the job of entertaining the people."[45]

There are many examples of wordplay and clever verbal interchange in the oral cultures of the West African societies from which most of America's slaves were taken.[46]

The French commentator Genevieve Fabre writes that "Satire was commonly used in African societies to express grievances against a relative, friend, or superior while avoiding confrontation. It became a powerful means of social control when used to call attention to transgressions or to neglected duties; it provoked laughter, but it also invited the audience to render immediate judgment." An English writer's observation of a Sierra Leone ring dance in 1721 includes a description of a specific instance of this activity: "Men and Women make a Ring in the open part of the Town, and one at a time shews his Skill in antick Motions and Gesticulations . . . the Company making the Musick by clapping their hands together during the time. . . . Sometimes they are all round in a Circle laughing, and with uncouth Notes, blame or praise somebody in the Company."[47]

Elaborating on the nature of the rituals in which satiric African "libelists" performed, William Schechter in his book on Negro humor noted that Ashanti natives "chanted and sang ridicule verses known as *opo*" and that "*Ghanian* chiefs allowed public criticism of their stewardships through this form of witty expressions of protest." And the English writer Geoffrey Gorer, who traveled in Africa in 1934, wrote that the Wolof "have a great admiration for cunning. Many of their ancedotes —and their conversation takes largely that form—are concerned with successful tricks . . . how a cripple—particularly blind men, who are credited with great sharpness—a poor man or a weak man gets the better of his stronger and richer neighbours. . . . They are also very fond of conundrums, of which they have a large repertoire, and of fables. . . . Verbal wit to which the language is well suited is the most highly prized of the lesser social qualities."[48]

Specific word games or verbal contests such as signifying (verbally putting down or berating another person with witty remarks, also called ranking, sounding, or dissin') or the dozens (mocking someone by ridiculing their relatives) can be traced to a number of African tribal groups. Roger D. Abrahams writes that "The practice of mother-rhyming [the dozens] has been observed in various . . . Afro-American communities as well as in a number of groups in Africa, including the Yoruba, Efik, Dogon, and some Bantu tribes." Such play, according to Abrahams, "is one aspect of a special kind of aggressive joking activity calling for verbal quickness and wit. . . . These joking domains, whether in Africa or the New World, are always described in terms of the giving of license because of special relationships or festive occasions. Joking, in this way, is related to the entire scandal-piece tradition and the various practices of playing the fool."[49]

The role of *griots* in African life provides additional evidence. *Griots* are popularly and properly known as the verbal historians of African society. But as the musicologist Samuel Charters found when he traveled through Western Africa seeking to discover a connection between African music and African-American blues, the *griot* combined the talents of the musician with those of the innovative poet (weaving "his own comments, moral judgments and isolated poetic images" into his songs) and the clever trickster-jester to accomplish his ends. Like the European troubadours or jesters, they were consummate performers.[50]

The similarity was recognized as early as 1745, as the following excerpt from notes of an Englishman traveling in Africa demonstrates:

Those who play on the instruments are persons of a very singular character, and seem to be their poets as well as musicians, not unlike the Bards among the Irish and ancient Britons. All the French authors who describe the countries of the Jalofs and the Fulis call them *Guiriots*. . . . The traveler Bardot says the Guiriot in the language of the Negroes toward Sanaga, signifies Buffoon, and that they are a sort of syncophant." The kings and great men in the country keep two or more of these Guiriots to divert them and entertain foreigners on occasion."[51]

The accuracy of the terms "Buffoon" and "syncophant" (sycophant), however, is questionable here. In fact, the impression given by most commentators suggests that *griots* were most often feared by fellow tribesmen because of the great power they were thought to possess. The French writer Mylene Remy, for example, observes:

> The truth is the griot's treasure and weapon. . . . When he is properly paid, he remembers only the pleasant, but the edge of his tongue is always ready for those who earn his anger. The people compensate for his power by pretending to consider him a servant, a tongue for hire . . . behind his back. But the griot knows he is irreplacable [sic].

And Francis Bebey—a contemporary Cameroon musician, composer, and novelist—reports that *griots* were so feared that in some parts of Africa, they were "not allowed the right to a proper burial. . . . When a *griot* died his body was placed inside the hollow trunk of a gigantic baobab tree," where it was permitted to rot. They were thought to be so powerful that, if buried in the normal manner, their spirits "would render the earth perpetually barren."[52]

The evidence of Africans' traditional high esteem for "verbal wit" in discourse and their familiarity with the manner and benefits of "playing the fool" strongly suggest that blacks were not merely imitating whites or acting in a purely reflective manner to divert white enmity when they struggled to acquire verbal acuity in English or took on the guise of Sambo or the Fool. It seems far more likely that they were simply relying on well-established and highly esteemed customs from their own background, both to sustain a connection with their past and to contend with the "arrogant contempt" they faced as human chattel in the New World.

IV

Still, there was little chance that any but a few whites would have noted or recognized the serious underlying intent of slaves' activities, since the surface image of frolicking, irresponsible blacks more readily and conveniently suited white assumptions and purposes. Consequently, misinterpretation of slave behavior was commonplace. As Frederick Douglass wrote: "The remark is not infrequently made, that slaves are the most contented and happy laborers in the world. They dance and sing, and make all manners of joyful noises—so they do: but it is a great mistake to suppose them happy because they sing. The songs of the slave represent the sorrows, rather than the joys, of his heart. . . . In the most boisterous outbursts of rapturous sentiment, there was ever a tinge of deep melancholy."[53]

Moreover, as slaves began to develop rudimentary facility with the language, naive malapropism was slowly but stealthily transformed into double-entendre and self-conscious or willful ambiguity, assuming the more consciously manipulative, goal-directed, and sophisticated cast typical of European and indigenous African wordplay. This *deliberate* linguistic misdirection allowed slaves both to communicate surreptitiously with one another and, without detection, express humorously some of the pent-up outrage resulting from their treatment as bondsmen.[54]

At the same time, maintaining the *appearance* of the naive was crucial as a survival technique, providing the perfect guise for aggressive humor and wit. Whereas a "sullen slave" might merely cause discomfort for a master, an "impudent" slave would most likely force slaveholders to inflict quick and severe punishment. From the opposite perspective, slaveholders clung to their image of the innocent, docile, childlike slave, even though that image was diametrically opposed to another prominent stereotype—that of the brutish, dangerously intractable savage. Now, this tandem of stereotypes may seem irrational, but racist categorizing has seldom been noted for its reasonability. (In fact, the eleventh, twelfth, and thirteenth editions of the *Encyclopedia Britannica,* under the definition "negro" [*sic*], would later submit: "Mentally, the negro is inferior to the white. . . . The mental constitution of the negro is very similar to that of a child, normally good-natured and cheerful, but subject to sudden fits of emotion and passion during which he is capable of performing acts of singular atrocity." An important factor in slaveholders' zealous embrace of the naive, contented-child stereotype was the need to allay concern and anxiety associated with the more insidious fear of violent slave insurrection. Not, to be sure, because rebellion posed any real threat to the Old South or could not have been quickly and summarily thwarted, but because the carnage resulting from such mutiny might have severely curtailed the extremely profitable exploitation of a wageless work force.[55]

Given their mind-set, it is not inconceivable that many slaveholders would interpret the following story of Pompey and his master—related in Peter Randolph's 1855 slave narrative, *From Slave Cabin to Pulpit* —and many similar tales as examples of black naïveté instead of cutting satire:

"Pompey, how do I look?" the master asked.

"O, massa, mighty. You looks mighty."

"What do you mean 'Mighty,' Pompey?"

"Why, massa, you looks noble."

"What do you mean by noble?"

"Why, suh, you looks just like a lion."

"Why, Pompey, where have you ever seen a lion?"

"I saw one down in yonder field the other day, massa."

"Pompey, you foolish fellow, that was a jackass."

"Was it, massa? Well, suh, you looks just like him."[56]

Misdirection, pretense, cryptic speech, in fact, a kind of homespun Socratic irony, as the above example demonstrates, loom prominently as characteristics of early authentic black humor. And in many instances these effects were achieved through the "aberrations" of African-American speech now recognized as resulting from the attempt to conform African patterns of speech to American ones. Specific colloquial terms such as *dig, bad* (meaning "very good"), and *okay*, for instance, have African prototypes that, according to many social scientists and linguists, are linked to their initial use by African-Americans. *Dig* is derived from the Wolof *deg* or *dega*—to understand or appreciate; *bad*, an example of the use of negative terms to describe positive attributes common in African languages, is associated with the Sierra Leone *i gud baad*—"it's very good"; *okay*, although attempts have been made to establish a French or Greek source, is probably derived from the Mandingo *o-ke* or the Western Fula *'eeyi kay*—both meaning "yes, indeed."[57]

It is easy to understand how the slave use of a term such as *bad* to designate something desired might have confirmed, for non-blacks, both the comic status and the ignorance of bondsmen. Comedian Redd Foxx expresses the irony of this miscommunication in a tale of an

African learning to speak English from a white, Southern tutor: " 'Hey, boy. Bring daat dere yonder. Chunk it, nigger, chunk it.' The African responds by saying: 'ooba gooba,' which he and other slaves know to mean: 'Chunk that shit yo'self!' " As one analyst noted, "the American Negro, more than most people, has had subtlety and irony forced upon his art."[58]

But other rhetorical devices were even more significant than the carryover of individual words. In addition to the dozens or mother-rhyming and signifying or dissing, other prominent devices were "call and response," "tonal semantics," and "indirection." Call and response —the extemporaneous interaction between speaker and listener—is most often associated with the black church and musical performances, where the audience's uninhibited reaction to a speaker or musician indicates clear approval or condemnation of the rap or riff being presented. (One visit to an Apollo Theatre "Amateur Night" provides an instant, indelible demonstration of this phenomenon.) For African-Americans and their African ancestors, the device also allowed a form of subtle communication between two parties in which a listener could express awareness of the veiled meaning of an assertion. This device, combined with tonal semantics—the practice of using voice intonation and altered speech rhythm to convey meaning—could (and still does) allow an overt remark or action to be transformed into veiled, unde-tected ridicule and satire, in which often only the participating parties are aware of the intent and purpose. Indirection, which employs sug-gestion and innuendo rather than direct, declarative statement, not only works hand in hand with the traditional African custom of expressing protest without confrontation, but also permits cloaked or disguised conversation that only initiates can decipher. Its use in black humor is evident in the Pompey tale as well as in much of the humor of the classic black comedians of the early twentieth century.[59]

In the presence of slaveholders and other whites, these and other devices were not merely affectations or instruments of disguise used solely to mask the critical intent of slave humor. They were from the outset an integral part of the entire stylistic and substantive nature of black humor. The particular circumstances of slavery—most obviously the adversarial relationship of blacks and whites—undoubtedly influ-enced the frequency with which these devices were used and the often exaggerated manner in which they were displayed; in fact, they were in all probability used more often by slaves who truly succumbed to and identified with the notion that they were Sambos. But they also emerged as conspicuous characteristics of the dual consciousness that African-Americans adopted to maintain a positive self-image while resisting white America's derogatory stereotypes.

The difference between private and public black humor during slavery was not just a matter of style but also of assertive content—and, even then, perhaps often just a matter of degree. Given the scantly inhibited humor openly revealed to whites, it takes no outrageous conjecture to imagine the derision that on occasion must have emerged behind closed doors when no inhibition was required. And if we consider the doggedly subversive nature of black behavior in other areas— the routine sabotage of crops, destruction of tools and animals, work slowdowns, even occasional instances of protective infanticide—the wide scope of that humor is more apparent.[60]

Of course, very little of the original humor of the slave quarters has survived. The African-American inclination toward secrecy, particularly with regard to uncensored expressions about whites, combined with the late entry of folklorists into the field of collecting slave folk humor has left us with relatively few samples. Slave narratives, which have been much more rigorously collected, unfortunately offer few examples of slave humor, since collectors were apparently, and quite justifiably, more interested in the work routines, living conditions, and hardships of the subjects interviewed. But a considerable body of trickster and animal tales is available, and they provide what are perhaps the most revealing examples of the critical and often outer-directed aggression of black humor; although, in customary African fashion, most of these tales are oblique and indirect.

Still, piecing together available samples, a fragmented picture does emerge. Aphorisms and rhymes, most of which are focused on black slaves' day-to-day interests, reflect some of their pragmatic concerns and folk wit:

Fiddlin' nigger say hit's long ways ter de dance.

De proudness un a man don't count w'en his head's cold.

Heap o' people rickerlec' favors by markin' 'em down in the snow.

It don't make much diffunce whar de rain comes fum, jes' so it hits de groun' in de right place.

De mornin'-glories ain't pertickler lubly to a man wid de backache.[61]

These examples reflect slaves' subtle and ironic acknowledgment of the hardships and injustices they faced: the inequity of time allotted for labor and leisure; the fatal consequences of displaying an "uppity" or arrogant attitude and, conversely, the wisdom of feigned humbleness; the worthlessness of promised rewards to slaves; and the eroding, spiritual debilitation that accrues from unrelenting hard labor.

Slave rhymes vary from the nonsensical and playful mocking of pretentiousness,

> The hairy ape, now, chillun see,
> He's lookin' fo' a li'l ole flea.
> If he should tuhn aroun' we'd fine
> He has no hair on his behine[62]

to veiled protests of bondage in which even death is seen as a preferable alternative,

> Ol' King Buzzahd floatin' high,
> Say "Sho do wish dat cow would die."
> Ol' cow died an' li'l calf cried,
> "Oh mou'nah, you shall be free"[63]

to the more incisive ridiculing of white and, as in the following example, even heavenly justice:

> Our Fader which art in heaben,
> White man owe me eleben and pay me seben.
> D'y kingdom come, d'y will be done,
> If I hadn't tuck dat I wouldn't git none.[64]

Trickster tales were among the most popular and commonly expressed varieties of slave folklore and, outside of physical resistance and rebellion, probably represented the most aggressive and cynical view of white America expressed by slaves. The animal variety of these tales was initially popularized in mainstream America by Joel Chandler Harris in the nineteenth century.

Harris was a white journalist and humorist who as a teenager during the 1860s lived on a Georgia plantation and listened attentively to folktales related by slaves. A complex and retiring man—self-conscious and shy—he was also an ambitious writer and an assertive commentator on social issues. His attitude toward African-Americans was equally complex. During the early 1870s, his newspaper humor included jibes such as "A lumpkin negro seriously injured his pocketknife recently by undertaking to stab a colored brother in the head." Yet near the end of his career, he had his pseudonymous rural philosopher, Billy Sanders, criticize the violent suppression of blacks. The retelling of the stories he had heard from elderly black slaves first appeared in *The Atlanta Constitution* and, when published in 1880 as *Uncle Remus, His Songs and His Sayings,* became an immediate success. The tales were rendered nearly authentically; Harris's ear for the slave's "quaint dialect" was finely tuned and, in fact, so phonetically exacting that his version of the stories may be difficult for many modern readers to follow. (The following line from the beginning of *The Wonderful Tar-Baby Story* is illustrative: "Brer Fox went ter wuk en got 'im some tar, en mix it wid some turkentime, en fix up a contrapshun wat he call a Tar-Baby, en he tuk dish yer Tar-baby en sot'er in de big road, en den he lay off in de bushes fer ter see wat de news wuz gwineter be.)[65]

Much of their instant popularity resulted from Harris's creation of the character Uncle Remus, a "faithful darky" type who relates stories to a young white child. In the introduction to these tales, Harris—who wrote that the slaves' "most prominent characteristic" was their "homely humor"—insinuates that the portrayal of weaker animals such as the rabbit as heroes reflected some social awareness on the part of slaves. But he quickly rejected the idea of an allegorical basis for the tales as "unreasonable." The "myth-stories" related by Uncle Remus, for Harris, are examples of the "shrewd observations" and "humorous philosophy of the race of which Uncle Remus was a type," and the fictional Remus character is an example of the slave "who has nothing but pleasant memories of the discipline of slavery." He was, as one critic wrote, "the ventriloquist's dummy on Harris's knee."[66]

Uncle Remus, then, much like the protagonist of Harriet Beecher Stowe's popular novel *Uncle Tom's Cabin* (1852)—subtitled *Life Among the Lowly* in the 1900 Henry Altemus children's edition—is a fictional character who reflects an image of blacks popular among abolitionists during the mid-nineteenth century and among black sympathizers after Emancipation. (Ironically, pro-slavery forces also subscribed to this characterization, since it supported their contention that blacks' dependency necessitated the institution of slavery.) Now, to be sure, there were many docile, childlike, contented blacks who personified the fictional creations of Stowe and Harris. Stowe's character Uncle

Tom, for instance, is said to be partially based on the life of the Reverend Josiah Henson, a slave who after his escape became a minister and an active worker for the Underground Railroad. As a slave, however, Henson, according to his own testament, ostensibly epitomized the faithful servant who had internalized his master's view of blacks.[67]

The intentions of Stowe and Harris as well as other "romantic racialists"—many of whom extolled the so-called "Christian" and "feminine" qualities of the Negro race—were in one sense commendable. But because they emphasized only one aspect of the slavery experience, their writings neither reflected the true nature of blacks' indirect resistance to slavery nor alluded to the vast number of slaves who presented a less obsequious and passive demeanor. In fact, the Uncle Remus character—when one considers the ironic thrust of the trickster theme in the animal stories he relates—seems primarily a fictional fabrication designed to establish a safe context in which the tales could be heard, thereby assuaging white anxiety and making the tales more accessible to and palpable for mainstream readers. Harris's fictional Remus also served to perpetuate the carefully fabricated myth of genteel plantation owners and contented slaves with nothing but fond memories of bondage, which was created by Southern writers after the Civil War.[68]

In themselves, these stories generally provide humorous portraits that are far less accommodating. Like the Aesop fables (whose actual origins have been attributed variously to ancient Chinese, Babylonian, Egyptian, or African sources instead of the Greek slave, Aesop), many of these African-American animal tales depict the triumph of physical weakness, hypocrisy, mischievousness, trickery, and cunning over brute strength and guilelessness.[69]

Since the trickster theme is not exclusive to African culture, at one time there was some controversy over the original source of the tales, and as late as 1968, a critic still insisted that the Negro dialect was but a "supreme ruse." But it is now generally accepted that Harris's tales were based on black American stories firmly based in the West African tradition of storytelling—one in which fables and tall tales provided entertainment but were also used for moral instruction and protest. "The African jackal survived as the American fox," Arna Bontemps wrote, "the African hare as the American rabbit," and the African tortoise as the American dry-land turtle or terrapin." The hyena, a common villain in the African tales, became the wolf in America, although the bear or fox was sometimes given that hapless role. Animals such as tigers, monkeys, and lions maintained their original identities.[70]

It was the rabbit, however, who commanded center stage in this galaxy of animal characters. And although Harris distorts the tales' social purpose and obfuscates their veiled intention by the unlikely circumstance of having them openly and guilelessly related to a white child, there is little doubt that it was this weak but crafty animal's ability to consistently outwit stronger, more powerful foes that accounted for much of the humor and gratification the tales initially provided slaves.

"One of the persistent delusions of the slaveholder, of visitors to the plantations, and of several generations of others," wrote the folklorist and historian Charles Joyner, "was that the trickster tales told by plantation slaves were mere entertainment."[71]

As in Africa, trickster tales in the antebellum period were required to entertain as well as provide moral instruction. But contrary to general belief, these tales did not always idealize the trickster. In animal tales, the rabbit or hare, who could be mischievous, even arrogant and malicious, was occasionally tricked by weaker animals. This counter theme, which Joyner designates as the "trickster out-tricked," accentuated another aspect of slave morality.[72]

For instance, in the traditional Harris version of the "Tar-Baby" story, after Brer Fox succeeds in luring Brer Rabbit into attaching himself to the Tar-Baby, Brer Rabbit escapes by using wit and deception: " 'I don't keer w'at you do wid me, Brer Fox,' sezee, 'so you don't thrown me in dat brier-patch. Roas' me, Brer Fox,' sezee, 'but don't fling me in dat brier-patch!' " And after Brer Fox, convinced that the brier-patch was the worst fate he could inflict on the rabbit, frees Brer Rabbit and tosses him into the brier-patch, Brer Rabbit escapes unharmed. " 'Bred and bawn in a brier-patch, Brer Fox—bred and bawn in a brier-patch,' " Brer Rabbit hollers before scampering off to safety.[73]

Charles Joyner relates another version of the tale culled from testimonies collected in the 1930s from former slaves of the All Saints Parish slave community in South Carolina. In this version, unlike the Harris tale where the Fox is clearly the villain, "Buh Rabbit" emerges as the scoundrel. During a drought, he conceals the whereabouts of a secret well from the other animals. When the rabbit's deception is discovered, the animals lure him to the Tar-Baby. Before releasing him, they scold and reprimand him for his selfishness. Here the moral is that hubris, boastfulness, and lying are traits that can be dangerous—even for the wily trickster.[74]

Other tales repeat this not uncommon subtheme. The most famous is probably the story of the Turtle and the Hare, in which the slow-footed turtle, after wagering that he can beat Brer Rabbit in a fair race, dispatches his look-alike relatives along the race route and at the finish line to convince his rival that he won the contest. In other tales from the All Saints Parish community, Buh Rabbit is outwitted by Buh Partridge on several occasions—in one tale he is tricked into having his wife decapitate him—when he allows arrogance, greed, or lack of concern for fellow animals to dictate his behavior.[75]

In addition to their entertainment and didactic purposes, animal folktales represented one dimension of the slaves' artistic expression. As Joyner put it: "In the animal tales they found the perfect vehicle to express those impulses, those often painful cultural truths, in an indirect, and thus less painful way. Such indirection goes to the heart of African concepts of eloquence."[76]

When related as animal stories, the trickster tales could be shared with slavemasters—as in the Remus tales—but the trickster theme also appears in stories involving interactions between slaves and their masters. These less veiled tales were usually told only among slaves, since, as the following story illustrates, the tale is not symbolic but realistic, the hero is a slave, and the intent is obvious.

Nehemiah, a clever slave who had a reputation for avoiding work with his wit and humor, had been transferred from one master to another because of his ability to outwit his owners. Then David Wharton, known as the most cruel slave master in Southwest Texas, heard about Nehemiah. He bought him and vowed to "make that rascal work." The morning after Nehemiah was purchased, David Wharton approached him and said, "Now you are going to work, you understand. You are going to pick four hundred pounds of cotton today."

"Wal, Massa, dat's aw right," answered Nehemiah, "but ef Ah meks you laff, won' yuh lemme off fo' terday?"

"Well," said David Wharton, who had never been known to laugh, "if you make me laugh, I won't only let you off for today, but I'll give you your freedom."

"Ah decla', Boss," said Nehemiah, "yuh sho' is uh goodlookin' man."

"I am sorry I can't say the same thing about you," retorted David Wharton.

"Oh, yes, Boss, yuh could," Nehemiah laughed out, "yuh could if yuh tole ez big uh lie ez Ah did."

David Wharton could not help laughing at this; he laughed before he thought. Nehemiah got his freedom.[77]

Many examples of this type of trickster tale emerged in the late nineteenth and early twentieth centuries, when former slaves were less concerned with maintaining the cloak of secrecy they had adopted about interactions with slaveholders. In them, John (sometimes Jack, Golias, Pompey, or Nehemiah) often cunningly outsmarted his master —securing access to better food or other rewards, foiling attempts at punishment for various indiscretions, forestalling some imminent calamity, or gaining his freedom.

One story related by former All Saints Parish slaves concerns the master's attempt to kill John because of his cunning and trickery. Massa takes John to the river and, intending to drown him, ties him in a sack. But he decides to eat dinner before killing him. While he is away, John hears a woman passing by and tells her he's going to Heaven today. When she says she would like to go to Heaven herself, John says, "I can go up any old day. I'll let you go in my place." She frees John and takes his place in the sack. Massa returns and throws the sack into the river. Within a few days John strolls back onto the plantation:

"Mornin' Maussa," John says.

"John, I thought I killed you."

"Yes, Cap'n, you kill me! I been all to heaven and come 'round by Hell. The devil have these cows. Say he ain't want 'em. You want 'em?"

"Drive 'em in the stable, John. John, you know where my money?"

"I know where your money [was] 'fore I leave."

"Well, you go get that money and spend it for anything you want."

John became a rich and powerful man, although the price he paid was the sacrifice of an innocent woman.

Another tale relates how Jack, the trickster, wins a swimming race without ever getting into the water:

Jack was a very wise nigger. Cap'n brag on Jack. Cap'n say, "Jack can beat all swimmin' "! Then he come tell Jack, "Jack, tomorrow a man coming here to swim with you. Want you to swim two three miles. Want you to beat him. I bet money on you. You must best him so's we can get all that money."

Now Jack can't swim nary lick. He go get him a stove, grits meal, meat, and lard and ALL and put'em on his back. Man come to swim with Jack he say, "What you got them bundle for and goin' swimmin'?"

Jack tell him, "You think I goin' swim three four miles 'thout any sumptin' t'eat. You must think I a big fool!"

And the man what come think if Jack goin' swim so far he have to stop and cook rations long the way he better back down. Jack's Cap'n got all THAT MONEY.[78]

Trickster stories such as these are excellent examples of slave humor that also mirrored themes that would resurface in black stage humor at the beginning of the late nineteenth century and survive in the acts of turn-of-the-century comedy teams such as Flournoy Miller and Aubrey Lyles, Bert Williams and George Walker, as well as later in the antic television comedy of Kingfish on the *Amos 'n' Andy Show* (1951) and Fred Sanford on *Sanford and Son* (1974).

Another important source of humor, clandestine satire, and protest was the slaves' music and songs. Black sacred music, of course, seldom had any comic intent; such instances occur only when sacred and secular themes are integrated. Spirituals, however, do provide numerous examples of veiled protest—for, as with black secular music, slaveholders tolerated sentiments expressed in song that would have been considered insolent if expressed more directly.

Beginning in the eighteenth century, white missionaries started attempting to change the slaves' "pagan" beliefs. They urged slaves to substitute constrained Christian religious practices for the far less inhibited "heathen" ceremonies they brought from Africa, and to replace the more expressive music associated with African religions with solemn Christian hymns. Black acculturation to Christianity continued throughout the antebellum period: slaveholders variously exhorted slaves to conversion or legally forbade religious gatherings because of fear of slave arousal and insurrections, such as the abortive conspiracy instigated in Charleston by the slave preacher Denmark Vesey in 1822, and the Southampton, Virginia, revolt led by Nat Turner, also a preacher, in 1831. For similar reasons, black religious music was alternately encouraged and repressed.

Slave spirituals, or "sorrow songs," as they were called later, survived, however, and by the Civil War were being seriously collected and studied. By 1873, largely through the efforts of the Fisk Jubilee Singers, who began touring two years earlier, Negro spirituals had provoked international interest. From the outset, black religious practices as well as black sacred music—although greatly modified by European restraint and piety—maintained a distinctive non-European cast.[79]

Some versions of religious songs incorporated humorous, secular material. But humorous lyrics are naturally found much more readily in slave shouts and work songs. An early novel about plantation life in the late eighteenth century describes one variety of the slave shout (the so-called "corn song") as being "natural at expressions of kind and amiable feelings—such as, praise of their master, gratitude for his kindness, thanks for his goodness, praise for one another, and, now and then, a little humorous satire." But these extemporaneous outbursts of song were not always as good-natured as this fictional account suggests. A report from the West Indies in 1804 provides the following description of slaves at work: "Some one takes the lead and breaks out with a song, to which there is always a chorus. In this they all join . . . These songs are not without their jibes; sometimes too levelled at the master, and then they are sung with peculiar vivacity, when the negroes come under his window or near his house."[80]

Although there are differences between the slave cultures that emerged in North America and those in the West Indies, there is no reason to believe that the description of improvised work songs or shouts, which reflects the African use of such songs, did not apply sometimes to the musical expression of slaves in the United States as well. Again, for obvious reasons, few of these impromptu songs—in a real sense, the precursors of the blues—were recorded or documented. But a prominent musicologist submits that black American work songs range in substance "from the ribald to the devout, from the humorous to the sad, from the gentle to the bitter, and from the tolerant to the unforgiving. . . . As throughout Negro singing generally, there is an incidence of social criticism, ridicule, gossip, and protest."[81]

Not surprisingly, among the secular slave songs that survived are some interesting examples of the irony and satiric thrust of slave humor:

Missus in the big house, Mammy in the yard,
Missus holdin' her white hands, Mammy workin' hard.

Old Marse ridin' all time, Niggers workin' round,
Marse sleepin' all day, Niggers diggin' in the ground.

John Morgan came to Danville and cut a mighty dash,
Last time I saw him he was under whip and lash.

I went to Atlanta, Never been dere a fo'.
White folks eat de apple, Nigger wait fo' de co'.

I went to Charleston, Never been dere a fo'.
White folks sleep on feather bed, Nigger on de flo'.

No more driver's lash for me. No more, no more.
No more pit of salt for me. No more, no more.
Many t'ousand go.

No more hundred lash for me. No more, no more.
No more mistress' call for me. No more, no more.
Many t'ousand go.[82]

Lawrence Gellert's *Me and My Captain* (1936) contains examples of African-American folk lyrics that are even more aggressive in their ridicule of whites. Some scholars are suspicious of the songs' origins, but many others readily accept their authenticity. These lyrics sometimes echo assertive jibes purportedly heard among West Indian slaves:

My bossman name was Sammy,
The meanest dog I ever know.
Speak soft, 'cause he got more ear-sights
Than the Devil down below . . .

If I had my sweet way
Graveyard's place my Bossman'd lay.
I even hates to hear his name,
Could kill him like an express train.

All the wrong, Captain, you do to me
Bound to come back to you—wait and see.
When it comes, white folks, shows you I'm a man,
Not a no-tail monkey, what get rattling his chain.

"The frequency with which these are sung, that is, the extent to which they enter into life," wrote one analyst, "is of course unknown." But given the clandestine nature of slave life, it is not far-fetched to assume that such direct lyrics were whispered and sung in closed quarters.[83]

Slave songs—along with all of the folktales, rhymes, animal stories, and aphorisms that survived the antebellum period—can finally reveal only the surface qualities of black bondmen's private humor. They are merely ripples that suggest and sometimes vaguely delineate the ironic playfulness or underlying surge of defiance and outright mockery that would be discovered later in black humor. The vast majority of the authentic humor of the slave quarters, unfortunately, remains hidden. The oral nature of black culture, the secretiveness that became such an important part of slave survival, and the inescapable reality of the consequences of overt satire or unveiled aggression, assured that most slave humor appeared in the guise of misdirection and passivity or was whispered and forever sealed in the dark recesses of slave shanties. But these early examples of slave wit, irony, and satire—however muted they may now seem—established the foundation for a tradition of humor that would survive bondage and emerge as a significant part of American culture and of black Americans' struggle for equality.

After Emancipation, just as the slaves were physically unshackled, their innermost thoughts also found freer expression in a less restrictive and repressive environment, and the authentic character of the more aggressive, undisclosed humor of the slave quarters began to emerge. A clue to the nature and content of this veiled humor may be found in stories such as the following:

Slave Owner: Ah, dear, faithful, loyal Uncle Tom! Lincoln has forced you to accept freedom—against my wishes, and, I am sure, against yours. Dear old friend and servant, you need not leave this plantation. Stay here with us; kindly, gentle, self-sacrificing Uncle Tom!

Uncle Tom: Thank you, deah, kine, lovin', gen'rous Massa. I reckon I'll leave. But befo' I go I wants you ter know I will allus 'membuh you ez de son uv a bitch you is an' allus wuz![84]

2.

MINSTRELSY . . .

the die is cast

JIM CROW.

NEW YORK.

Published by Firth & Hall No 1 Franklin Sq

COME LISTEN ALL YOU GALLS AND BOYS
I'SE JIST FROM TUCKYHOE,
I'M GOIN TO SING A LITTLE SONG,
MY NAME'S JIM CROW.

WEEL ABOUT AND TURN ABOUT
AND DO JIS SO,
EB'RY TIME I WEEL ABOUT
AND JUMP JIM CROW.

—THOMAS DARTMOUTH RICE

A NIGGER COME FROM ARKANSAW,
DE BIGGEST FOOL I EBBER SAW,
AT MORNIN WHEN DIS NIGGER ROSE,
HE PUT HIS MITTENS ON HIS TOES.

HE WENT TO SHELL CORN IN DE SHED,
HE SHELL'D HIS SHINS ALL BARE INSTEAD,
HE WENT TO FEED DE HORSE AT DE BARN,
HE PUT HIMSELF IN DE TROUGH FOR CORN.

—ETHIOPIAN SERENADERS

STEPHEN FOSTER'S PASTORALISM OF "OLD FOLKS AT HOME" AND "MASSA'S IN THE COLD, COLD
GROUND," THOUGH SEEMINGLY INNOCENT, EXPRESSED A SUBCONSCIOUS DESIRE TO SEE
BLACKS "WAY DOWN UPON THE SWANEE RIVER" AND NOT IN PITTSBURGH.

—BERNDT OSTENDORF [1]

I

The distinctive character of authentic African-American humor—
sometimes ironic, evasive, and oblique, sometimes playful and purely
entertaining, and sometimes aggressively militant—was well established by the early nineteenth century. Although this humor was most
often conspicuously quiescent, confined to isolated black gatherings and
concealed by an outer face of passivity and compliance, occasionally it
erupted in pointed satire, directing barbs at the pretentiousness of
whites or other blacks, or at the injustices and dehumanization of bondage. But even as this private humor developed among blacks, mainstream America was about to introduce a form of entertainment that
would codify the public image of blacks as the prototypical Fool or
Sambo.

By the 1840s, a systematized form of blackface stage entertainment —minstrelsy—would emerge as the rage of American popular culture, the first concerted appropriation and commercial exploitation of a black expressive form. African-American humor (along with elements of song and dance) was lifted from its original context, transformed and parodied, then spotlighted for the entertainment and amusement of non-black audiences. The phenomenon, in a less satiric and consciously malicious form, would be repeated over the years; Paul Whiteman would be promoted as the "King of Jazz," Benny Goodman as the "King of Swing," Elvis Presley as the "King of Rock," and a raft of non-blacks would achieve popular success by burlesquing supposed Negro performance and lifestyles. But none of these subsequent mimetic excursions into black cultural life would be as methodically demeaning or as lastingly damaging as minstrelsy.[2]

Theatrical impersonation of blacks, of course, did not begin with minstrelsy. Blacks, like women, were customarily represented by white males in European stage performances long before the mid-nineteenth century. Shakespeare's *Othello*, written in 1604, was regularly performed with white actors playing the lead thereafter. A less accomplished drama, Thomas Southerne's *Oroonoko* (1696)—the tale of an African prince captured by whites—was popularly received on the British stage until the mid-1700s and, later that century, in America. These serious, sympathetic stage portrayals of blacks, however, were rare.

In America, blackness was associated with humor almost from the outset. An early example, although in some important ways an exception, is Andrew Barton's ballad opera *The Disappointment; or The Force of Credulity* (1767), which was "the first native work to present a black character," as well as "the first ballad opera published by an American in America." Although the black character Raccoon speaks in dialect and is a comic figure, he is in stark contrast to the buffoonish image of blacks that emerged on the popular stage in later years. Raccoon—in what was a scandalously revolutionary act for the time—was portrayed as a wealthy, free black man with a white mistress. Not surprisingly, *The Disappointment* was not a popular success; labeled "unfit for the stage," it was quickly withdrawn.[3]

Black characters continued to appear sporadically on the American stage as minor comic figures or sometimes as the tragic noble savage, throughout the eighteenth century; but it was not until the early 1800s that they began to emerge as principal figures in America's comic lexicon. Other regional and ethnic types had already become comic staples, having an enduring appeal in America's culture of the common man. In the 1820s, black-faced caricatures began supplanting white rural comic types. And although only fragmentary, often contradictory, documentation exists about the careers of the pioneer blackface entertainers, it is evident that by this time America was developing a growing interest in blackface mimicry.

In her *American Humor: A Study of the National Character* (1931), Constance Rourke noted that: "In the early '20's ... the southern plantation Negro was drawn on the stage in Cincinnati by young Edwin Forrest." Forrest, who was to become the leading American actor of the period, made himself up as a black man and strolled through the streets mingling with blacks. His impersonation was so authentic, legend has it, that an old black woman mistook him for a friend, and he persuaded her to join him in a performance that evening.[4]

Around the same time (1822–1823) Charles James Mathews, the acclaimed English actor, mimic, and comedian, was making the first of two tours of the United States. During these visits he methodically collected impressions of distinctly American types. Mathews—considered "the paterfamilias of the Yankee theatre and the progenitor of all native American dialect comedy" by some experts—included Negroes among his impressions and, in his one-man stage review, *A Trip to America,* introduced a version of the now familiar song "Possum Up a Gum Tree." Mathews insisted that it was an authentic copy of an "original Negro Melody" and that his impersonation of blacks was based on fact. Most historians and musicologists now reject Mathews's assertions, as well as Rourke's avowal that Forrest's black-faced character was a "faithful drawing" of the Negro. But there is little doubt that the claims of Forrest and Mathews, and their stature as entertainers, whetted the public appetite for black-faced mimicry in both Europe and the United States.[5]

It also prompted others to explore the possibilities of black impersonation. Around 1828, for example, George Washington Dixon introduced "Coal Black Rose," a comic song about a Negro woman and her rival lovers (Sambo and Cuffee), to American audiences. The song ridiculed the lovers' vows of affection and ended with a burlesque confrontation in which love turns to hate. With Dixon's performances of this and other minstrel songs at circuses and variety shows in New York, his popularity increased significantly. Some maintain that he was the first white entertainer to establish a broad reputation as a blackface performer.[6]

George Nichols, another circus clown, began doing blackface impersonations in the 1820s and claims to have written "Zip Coon" (now popularly known as "Turkey in the Straw"), although Dixon and another blackface performer, Bob Farrell, known as "Zip Coon," also claimed authorship of the song. Some show business historians even contend that Nichols originally introduced "Jim Crow"—a tune that, when brought to the stage by another performer, almost singlehandedly catapulted blackface acts into national prominence.[7]

In 1828 or thereabouts, Thomas D. Rice, a minor actor in the dramatic play *The Rifle,* reportedly saw a crippled and deformed black hostler or stable groom singing and performing a striking but peculiar dance as he went about his work. The actor, recognizing the potential appeal of the song—"Weel about and turn about, and do jis so./Eb'ry time I weel about I jump Jim Crow"—and the black man's twisted, antic movements, memorized the lyrics and copied the dance. (The actual year and place of this legendary interaction are still disputed by historians, leading some to question whether it was an actual occurrence or the product of Rice's imagination and knack for self-promotion.) Expanding the verses and, so the story goes, even buying the old man's clothes to assure authenticity, Rice began presenting the impersonation between acts of *The Rifle.*

Rice's performances became an immediate sensation, and he soon incorporated additional "Negro" characters, songs, and dances. Perhaps the most famous was his shadow dance, in which he appeared with a gunny sack slung across his shoulder. After putting the sack down and beginning a song ("Me and My Shadow") and dance, a child actor in blackface would crawl from the sack and begin emulating his every move. (In the mid-twentieth century, Ted Lewis would revive this routine and, using a grown man instead of a child imitator, make it a central part of his act.) Rice also began combining his "Jim Crow" impersonation with an established comic figure of the time when he appeared in the long blue coat and striped pants traditionally associated with the popular Yankee stage character. Whatever the source of his material, Rice's intuition about what would appeal to nineteenth-century white audiences was correct. Subsequently billed as Jim Crow Rice, his popularity continued to grow and, within a decade, he had become one of America's best-known comedians.

By the 1830's, blackfaced white performers were one of the most

popular attractions on the American stage. Rice as well as such performers as Nichols, Farrell, Dixon, Ben Cotton, and J. W. Sweeney, calling
themselves "Ethiopian delineators," toured the country, performing
supposedly authentic Negro songs and dances in traveling shows, circuses, and between acts at variety theatres.

Theatregoers during the decades of the 1820s, 1830s, and 1840s
were usually presented with a hodgepodge of entertainment. A typical
evening included not only a full-length play but an assortment of variety
acts: "dances, popular songs, black-faced acts, jugglers, acrobats,
trained animals, and novelties." The public demand for a common
man's culture had begun to transform American entertainment, and
showmen such as P. T. Barnum responded by offering variety shows
designed to satisfy that demand.[8]

To a great extent, this consciously low-brow entertainment emphasized the spectacular and bizarre. Barnum's American Museum in New
York City, for instance, offered midgets, fat men, bearded ladies, and
trained fleas, in addition to plays, variety acts, and educational displays.
Given the public appetite for the bizarre and unusual, it is not surprising that black-faced performers soon became major attractions. As Constance Rourke pointed out, "to the primitive comic sense, to be black
was to be funny, and many minstrels made the most of this simple
circumstance." For northerners in particular, blacks were still seen as
curiosities; Thomas Rice and many of the other black-faced precursors
of minstrelsy were aware that they presented the perfect foil for burlesque and exaggeration.[9]

"Blackface archetypes fundamentally issued from the imagination of
northern whites," writes the historian Ronald L. Davis. Although they
may have been influenced by slave performances and a few early black
entertainers, most of the first burnt-cork troupers "were either immigrants or showmen from the East and Middle West," who were not
familiar with plantation slavery. "What they brought to their blackface
portrayals was barely a germ of reality indirectly received, but affably
coated with the romantic attitudes and general misconceptions about
the American black. Although incidentals of the caricature may have
been drawn from direct experience, the essence was based on hearsay
and popular lore and projected in overstated, exotic terms."[10]

Rice, for instance, if he is to be believed, was copying the movements
of a cripple—a far cry from a representative example of Negro dance.
And while it is clear that black music provided the inspiration for many
of the songs of the early black-faced impersonators, most of the songs

—including "Jim Crow," "Possum Up a Gum Tree," and "Long Tail Blue" (the song that Rice often performed when donning his Yankee attire)—have been shown to be of European origin, although they were performed in a manner intended to mimic blacks' speech and style. In addition, the sentiments typically expressed, as the lyrics from "Going Ober de Mountain" at the beginning of this chapter demonstrate, indicate that most early minstrel songs were the creation of whites set on ridiculing blacks rather than of blacks themselves.

On the other hand, the raucous, sensational, and often profane atmosphere of popular American entertainment during this period makes it clear why black-faced mimicry was so appealing. Whether enslaved or free, blacks were the outcasts of American society; to many they were no more than freaks, like P. T. Barnum's geeks and bearded ladies. And at a time when the nation was engaged in heated debate about slavery, what better way both to satisfy the public's curiosity about blacks and to influence the overall estimate of the country's racial pariahs than to spotlight them as burlesque figures? By focusing on and exaggerating the supposed earthy peculiarities of blacks, black-faced mimics provided the simple, folksy entertainment white audiences demanded and assured them that, indeed, they were superior to their enslaved brethren.

The formula proved immensely successful. By the late 1830s, through refinement and more determined exploitation of the subject, black-faced characterization had virtually eliminated all other ethnic and regional types. "Jim Crow," the unkempt, ignorant plantation slave, displaced the backwoods or Frontier caricature; and "Zip Coon" or "Jim Dandy," the bombastic, dandified city slicker, replaced the Yankee character as America's central comic figures.

II

As with many events in American cultural history, the establishment of the minstrel show as a separate form of entertainment was accidental. America had experienced a financial panic in 1837, and in the early 1840s the nation still reeled near the brink of financial disaster. Unemployment was rampant, and even among variety performers jobs were hard to find. Seeking a solution to their own professional problems, four out-of-work white performers met in a New York City hotel in 1842—a year that some historians described as the "nadir" of the theatrical scene. The men—Billy Whitlock, Frank Brower, Frank Pelham, and Dan Emmett—all had previous experience as blackface entertainers. (In fact, Emmett's earlier stage act, according to some sources, was borrowed almost in its entirety from Rice.)[11]

Dan Emmett, described as a "backwoodsman of Irish descent who looked like a Yankee deacon," took the lead in suggesting that they form a troupe and concentrate exclusively on blackface mimicry. The idea, while certainly opportunistic, was no more than a pragmatic solution to their immediate problems. They were unaware that they had stumbled upon a notion that would transform American entertainment and firmly establish the image of blacks as happy-go-lucky plantation darkies and outrageously dressed, ignorant dandies in the entertainment media.[12]

In February 1843, Emmett and the others introduced their act, the Virginia Minstrels, on stage at the Bowery Amphitheatre in New York City as part of the Olympic Circus. Shortly afterward, at the Masonic Temple in Boston, they performed for the first time an entire evening of what they originally called the "oddities, peculiarities, eccentricities, and comicalities of the Sable Genus of Humanity." They were an instant sensation. By the end of the year the Virginia Minstrels had begun a successful tour in England, leaving behind a raft of imitators; blackface minstrelsy was well on its way to becoming America's preeminent form of popular entertainment. And, if not quite coincidentally, a grossly distorted public image of black Americans and their humor was being persuasively etched into the American mind.[13]

Still, from the viewpoint of pure entertainment, the reasons for the Virginia Minstrels' popular appeal are readily apparent. This troupe had managed to integrate the raucous and irreverent style of most Yankee and Frontier humor with what audiences were led to believe was authentic black comedy, song, and dance. In fact, the cloak of blackness apparently allowed them to cast most of their own inhibitions to the wind, thereby heightening the excitement and frenetic pace of their performance. And they accomplished this not just in a short skit or single, isolated number, as Thomas D. Rice had, but throughout a complete show. The exuberance and vitality they reportedly brought to these performances is reflected in the following description from Robert C. Toll's *Blacking Up: The Minstrel Show in Nineteenth Century America* (1974):

They burst on stage in makeup which gave the impression of huge eyes and gaping mouths. They dressed in ill-fitting, patchwork clothes, and spoke in heavy "nigger" dialects. Once on stage, they could not stay still for an instant. Even while sitting, they contorted their bodies, cocked their heads, rolled their eyes, and twisted their outstretched legs . . . their wild hollering and their bobbing, seemingly compulsive movements charged the entire performance with excitement.[14]

The original Virginia Minstrels performed together for only a short time; while still abroad, they disbanded as the result of personal differences. Dan Emmett returned to the United States to find that minstrelsy was fast becoming the nation's craze and resumed his career as a blackface performer. He composed, sang, and played the banjo as a solo act, and worked with various minstrel troupes until he retired in the 1890s. Many of the compositions that he claimed as his own (including "I Wish I Was in Dixie Land," the Confederate rallying song) became minstrel standards. The disbanding of his original group, however, had allowed another troupe, the Ethiopian Serenaders, to take center stage. By 1844, this new entertainment genre had so swept the nation that the Serenaders were invited to the White House to perform for the "Especial amusement of the President of the United States."[15]

The Ethiopian Serenaders gradually began to refine their performances, apparently to appeal to a more genteel audience. They introduced romantic, sentimental material as a substitute for some of the raucous, black-inspired humor that had been the basic ingredient of the Virginia Minstrels. They even began performing selections from popular operas on alternate evenings.

When the Serenaders set off for a European tour in 1846, E. P. Christy and the troupe that would become the most famous minstrel act of all time left upstate New York and opened in New York City. Combining the robust, usually rowdy, humor of the earlier minstrel acts with the "refined" approach of the Serenaders, the Christy Minstrels immediately restored the original tenor of the minstrel show and created an entertainment blend that outstripped all of its predecessors in popular appeal. The Ethiopian Serenaders returned in 1847 to find that their more sophisticated approach was no longer in vogue. They continued to perform, but the public obviously wanted to see more of the antic comedy of black impersonators and less of the lyricism and sentimentality that the Serenaders had introduced.[16]

Stephen Foster, who, like the popularizer of black animal tales, Joel Chandler Harris, had become mesmerized by blackface entertainment in his youth, was a major contributor to the Christy Minstrels' musical repertory. His frequently saccharine ballads, which often romanticized Southern plantation life and slavery, were mixed with the rougher, more pointedly satirical older tunes of Rice, Dixon, and Emmett to produce a varied musical array that made E. P. Christy's troupe the most successful minstrel act in antebellum America and established the traditional minstrel format.

By the late 1840s, minstrelsy had reached an unprecedented level of national popularity. Most famous minstrel acts were still based in the northeastern United States, but there was a Southern minstrel circuit that included Baltimore, Charleston, Mobile, Memphis, and New Orleans. Minstrelsy had, in fact, spread throughout the Midwest and as far west as San Francisco, which within a decade would claim several permanent professional troupes. Among the many acts were the African Melodists, the Congo Minstrels, the Buckley Serenaders, the Ethiopian Mountain Singers, and Bryant's Minstrels; there were even a few professional juvenile minstrel troupes. In fact, many famous contributors to American popular culture—including Stephen Foster—began their careers as amateur minstrel performers while still adolescents.

By the late 1850s, nearly all of the most popular troupes followed a standard, formalized three-act presentation. The shows opened with a walk-around during which the entire company, made up in the usual highly exaggerated blackface masks and dressed in flashy clothes, paraded on stage singing some currently popular upbeat song. Then, arranging themselves in a semicircle, they would alternate comic songs and jokes with more serious material such as popular dances or love ballads. The first act ended with a rousing song and dance routine. Throughout this segment, the *interlocutor* or master of ceremonies controlled the tempo and, often, the content of the show.

The action was fast, furious, and most often improvised to suit a specific audience's tastes. The interlocutor, seated in the center of the semicircle, determined how long a skit or comedy routine would continue. More important, he decided how often the comic dialogue between the *endmen*—called "Mr. Bones" and "Mr. Tambo" because of the instruments they played—would be spotlighted. That dialogue was the featured comedy routine in the first segment:

"Sambo, what part ob man was made first, de beef or de bones?"

"Why, de bones first else dar would been nothin' to hang de beef on."

"Say Pomp, you nigger, where you get dat new hat?"

"Why, at de shop, ob course."

"What is de price if such a hat as dat?"

"I don't know, nigger, I don't know—de shopkeeper wasn't dar!"[17]

Although he sometimes wore blackface, the interlocutor dressed with more decorum than the other actors and represented the white presence on stage; he projected a loftier, less frantic and less ignorant image than the rest of the troupe. He commonly spoke with a deep, resonant voice and often used standard English. Typically, his pompous, exaggeratedly elitist demeanor was in direct contrast to the wild antics and preposterous language of the endmen, for whom he functioned as a straightman. According to one contemporary critic, he was "the minstrel mentor to a brace of African Telemachuses . . . always the same genial, gentlemanly, unruffled creature surveying the endmen . . . with the smiling forbearance which comes of innate superiority."[18]

The following is a representative exchange between the interlocutor and one of the endmen:

Mr. Bones: Mr. Interlocutor, sir!

Interlocutor: Yes, Mr. Bones?

Mr. Bones: Mr. Interlocutor, sir. Does us black folks go to hebbin? Does we go through dem golden gates?

Interlocutor: Mr. Bones, you know the golden gates is for white folks.

Mr. Bones: Well, who's gonna be dere to open dem gates for you white folks?[19]

Despite the interlocutor's importance—and that actor was generally among the highest-paid performers—the endmen were the real comedy stars of this first segment. Made up and dressed more outrageously than the other performers, they usually spoke with a more pronounced black accent and were engaged in non-stop activity throughout this part of the show. They continuously mugged and contorted their bodies as they joined in comic songs or played their instruments. For most observers, their frantic behavior and witty repartee with the interlocutor was the high point of the show.

The jokes, which usually had no specific connection to authentic black humor or social circumstances—remember, the general assumption among intellectuals and common folk alike was that blacks had no wit—were of the simplistic, broad-based type that later became popular in burlesque houses. They might jest about blacks' supposed ignorance —an endman, for instance, would explain how he got the best of a railroad company when he bought a cheaper round-trip ticket and never used it to return, or how he asked to be put into the seventh regiment so he could be near his brother who was in the sixth.

The central element in minstrel humor—in addition to nonsensical, malaprop-ridden stump speeches—was quips, riddles, and puns: "The difference between a schoolmaster and an engineer is that one trains the mind and the other minds the train." Barbers were a key source of punning humor: "In about ten minutes in *comb* the barber. He entered all in a *lather*, and said he'd just give his boss a *strapping* . . ." Poems with inane, sometimes clever, wordplay were also extremely popular:

I've seen the *rope-walk* down the lane,
　　The *sheep-run* in the vale;
I've seen the *dog-watch* on the ship,
　　the *cow-slip* in the dale;
I've seen the *sea-foam* at the mouth,
　　the *horse-fly* in the air;
I know the *bul-warks* on the deck,
　　And the *fire-works* many a scare;
I've seen *a-bun-dance* on the plate,
　　A *lamp-light* on the floor.

This type of wordplay had infinite variations. Compared with the more direct, often sophisticated social and political humor of today's comedians, this vein of minstrel comedy now seems childish and strained.[20]

Still, minstrel audiences could laugh *with* the endmen and identify with their lunacy when they ridiculed the interlocutor's pompous airs. And when the interlocutor corrected their ignorant assumptions and their butchery of the English language, the audience could laugh *at* them and feel superior to characters intended to represent simpleminded blacks, who, by this time, had become both a topic of immense concern and a source of dissension for white Americans.

Mr. Bones and Mr. Tambo were the most popular performers in the traditional minstrel show. Their influence was such that they established rapid-fire puns and gags as standard elements in American humor. Many of their frequently used quips—*Why did the chicken cross the road?* or *Why does a fireman wear red suspenders?* for instance— filtered down and remain even today staples of America's adolescent humor. Others—*Who was that lady I saw you with last night? That was no lady, that was my wife!*—are still part of the comic repertoire of some performers. Evan Esar, in *The Comic Encyclopedia*, maintains that the endmen "were chiefly responsible for turning riddle wit in America into gags. . . . They also popularized gag routines and jocular dialogue."[21]

Although there is disagreement on this point, some historians contend that a black theatrical family—John Luca, his wife, and sons— actually created the traditional minstrel show opening segment. In a memoir completed just before his death in 1954, the black entertainer Tom Fletcher wrote that the "presentation of the John Luca family, according to all the information I have ever been able to dig up, was the original appearance of the 'minstrel, first part' format." According to Fletcher, the Lucas (although primarily known for their presentation of serious entertainment) began using the semicircle stage arrangement in the early 1840s. After they had sung their opening song, John took the center seat and functioned as the M.C. or interlocutor; two of his sons took the outside positions and, like minstrel endmen, provided the comedy.[22]

In the second part of the show—the olio, or variety segment—the comedy highlight was the stump speaker, a lone comic who stood and delivered a discourse that ranged from pure nonsense to supposedly serious lectures on some social or philosophical issue. The comic, usually one of the endmen, spoke in a black version of the familiar vernacular dialect of the Yankee or Frontier type. Often he satirized Emancipation, women's suffrage, education, or some other current political or scientific topic. Malaprop reigned supreme; although important issues were often addressed, the focus here was purely on humor. It was double-edged burlesque in which not only were serious issues lampooned, but blacks' ability to understand or interpret sophisticated ideas were ridiculed and mocked. Robert C. Toll offers the following example of a typical stump speech opening: "Feller-fellers and oder fellers, when Joan of Ark and his broder Noah's Ark crossed de Rubicund in search of Decamoran's horn, and meeting dat solitary horseman by de way, de anapulated in de clarion tones of de clamurous rooster, de insignification of de—de—de hop-toad. . . ."[23]

The third and final part of the traditional minstrel show was initially a slapstick plantation skit, featuring song and dance with colorfully costumed Sambo and Mammy types cavorting on stage. After the mid-1850s, however, most minstrel shows began to feature farcical blackface versions of serious dramas such as Shakespeare's *Macbeth*. These parodies maintained the tenor of the earlier plantation skits—malaprop, frenetic action, and slapstick abounded—but the emphasis shifted from the simple glorification of plantation life and the presentation of happy, contented slaves to the more insistent derision of free blacks as bombastic fools or helpless incompetents who are obviously misplaced in any serious context.

In fact, the image of blacks projected by minstrelsy shifted periodically with the current of public opinion and political expediency. Most historians and social critics agree that before the early 1850s, white America was generally content to accept the Southern view that black slaves were a fortunate lot, who basked in the comfort of plantation hospitality and sought nothing more than a continuation of their merry lives as servile chattel, free from the practical responsibilities that burdened whites. Minstrelsy reflected and indeed strengthened this view, with its elaborate plantation extravaganzas featuring carefree, happy-go-lucky darkies who delighted in their station and rarely if ever expressed discontent or sought their freedom. The idyllic portrait of plantation life served Southern pro-slavery interests as well as the interests of northerners who comprised the largest audience for minstrel shows and were none too anxious to have hordes of free blacks migrating to their urban communities. Even those whites who may have been ideologically opposed to slavery but uninformed about the actual condition of slaves were influenced, since the myth of the happy-go-lucky Negro justified adopting a hands-off attitude toward a practice they may have morally condemned.

During this period, some negative views of slavery *were* presented on the minstrel stage. The ordeal of the broken family was occasionally treated; even the problems of runaway slaves and, in a few instances, slave insurrections were engaged. The nagging ambivalence over the moral contradiction between slavery and democracy sometimes prompted minstrel performers to introduce material resembling black trickster tales. In these rare instances, minstrels portrayed blacks who outwitted whites and, as in the Pompey tale in the previous chapter, managed to express discontent while making their masters the butt of the joke.

But despite the seriousness of the issues sometimes addressed, blacks in minstrelsy were nearly always treated as *comic* figures. Performers could and did demonstrate support for such lofty concepts as the right to freedom and equality or the sanctity of the family and, at the same time, through caricature and ridicule, suggest that blacks should be excluded from these ideals. Toll provides a balanced appraisal of this aspect of minstrel acts prior to 1850: "White Americans had gotten a brief glimpse, though itself quite limited, of the complexity and humanity of the black man and a clearer look at the consequences of their own egalitarianism if extended to black Americans."[24]

With the publication of Harriet Beecher Stowe's *Uncle Tom's Cabin, or Life Among the Lowly* in 1852, however, anti-slavery feelings rose dramatically in the northern United States. Called the "ultimate protest novel" by James Baldwin more than a century after its publication, Stowe's melodramatic account of angelic Little Eva, villainous Simon Legree, and the martyrdom of the near-saintly Uncle Tom galvanized abolitionist sentiments in the 1850s. An instant best seller in the North, it was banned in many Southern states. But by this time it had become apparent that the national rift could no longer be easily ignored. Always attentive to the tide of public opinion, minstrel acts reflected the widespread concern over the sanctity of the Union. Confronted with a choice of preserving the Union or supporting black Emancipation, they soon eliminated all but the most servile and disparaging images of blacks from their shows.

From about 1853 to the Civil War, then, nearly all vestiges of black humanity were excised from minstrel performances. During this period the portrait of the plantation was made even more idyllic, and the stereotype of black males as childlike, shiftless, irresponsible dolts was heightened. Freed blacks, in particular, came under pointed attack. They were invariably pictured as inept, hopelessly inadequate souls, who longed for the guidance of white men and the security of the "ole plantation," or, perhaps worse, as arrogant, near-bestial reprobates who, with disastrous consequences, foolishly took on "white" airs and lusted after white women. The comic, degrading image of blacks had almost reached its peak.

America's most popular entertainment form had become a forum in which white performers posing as blacks actively lobbied for the continuation of slavery by presenting degrading, consciously distorted comic stereotypes intended to "prove" that slavery and black subordination were justified or, even more insidiously, to demonstrate that blacks actually preferred serfdom. A verse from one version of a popular minstrel song, "Old Dan Tucker," reflects a commonly expressed minstrel attitude about slavery:

There is some folks called abolition,
Want to mend de nigger condition,
If dey would let the niggers alone,
The niggers will always have a home.[25]

This politicizing is nowhere more evident than in the alterations that surfaced in the third part of minstrel shows after 1853. With the escalation of the anti-slavery movement, minstrels apparently felt a need to be more direct about their position on blacks and slavery. Harriet Beecher Stowe provided the perfect target for minstrel parodies—some in an anti-slavery vein, many more in dramatically altered pro-slavery renditions.[26]

With titles such as *Uncle Dad's Cabin* and *Uncle Tom and His Cabin*, minstrels completely reversed the thrust of Stowe's protest tract. In some versions, Little Eva and Simon Legree were eliminated altogether and, typically, all allusions to any cruel or harsh treatment of slaves were removed. The Christy Minstrels called the final part of their show "Life Among the Happy"; following in their footsteps, many minstrel acts billed their parodies as *Happy Uncle Tom.* Uncle Tom was indelibly cast as a servile, docile sycophant, more worthy of laughter than humanistic concern. In contrast to Stowe's character—who despite his lack of assertiveness was intended as a tragic figure, in fact, a heroic figure in the Christian mold—the minstrel Tom epitomized all the negative attributes that would survive on and off stage into the late twentieth century.

III

Just as it dramatically changed American society, the Civil War also permanently altered minstrelsy. From 1861 through 1865, as the war dragged on and the death toll mounted to heights unimagined at the onset, minstrel shows naturally waned in popularity. Initially, minstrels continued romanticizing plantation life and lampooning Negro slaves and freedmen; they seemed confident that a speedy Northern victory would inevitably result in a return to the prewar black-white predicament. It was literally show business as usual, with blackface Fools and Sambos extolling the virtues of the Old South and lambasting all those forces—Union or Confederate—that seemed intent on separation or Emancipation. Overwhelmingly nationalistic in sentiment, minstrels stressed reunification and avoided taking sides throughout most of the war. But as the conflict continued and the Union first enlisted black soldiers and then reluctantly announced its intention of freeing the slaves, a shift occurred.

Although they still performed primarily in blackface and vigorously showcased the stereotypical images, minstrels increasingly turned their attention to the problems of white northerners. Sentimental skits bemoaning the fate of young white soldiers or widowed mothers were staged, and the comic pillorying of all those seen as obstacles to reunification was heightened. When black soldiers' entry into the fray seemed to have improved the Union position, some performers even began to demonstrate mild support for Emancipation, and the theoretical opposition to the concept of slavery that had appeared in some early minstrel shows resurfaced.

Still, the stage image of blacks remained substantially unchanged. Throughout the war, blacks were portrayed as unquestioned inferiors. Since minstrelsy was primarily a comic form, what was given with one hand could easily be taken away with the other. The black soldier, for instance, although given some credit for his contribution to the Union war effort, was routinely ridiculed in much the same manner as the black freedman or dandy. Farcical skits with black soldiers who (like the later Italian soldiers in World War II) were portrayed as more adept at retreating than fighting were common, and the strutting black soldier who mistakenly thought his uniform made him the equal of whites became a popular slapstick feature. During the war years Northern audiences left theatres assured that, although the ideological scourge of slavery might soon be removed, blacks were perfectly content to accept their second-class status and remain in the South as agrarian serfs.[27]

After the war and Emancipation—during the Reconstruction period when constitutional amendments were passed to assure civil rights and voting rights for former slaves—the minstrel stage often became a platform for ridiculing the newly elected black members of the House and Senate. Minstrel stump speakers frequently aimed their satire at black officials:

> Is yar to vindicate de cullid race, sah, frum de sperhons ob dar enemies—dar enemies sah. W'ats all de moanin and sobbin and whinin in de land about Niggers anyway. W'y sah, it's de manifes ob every colored man ob observation dat de howl is jes jealousness sah, jealousness ob the on coming mutability ob de sable race, suh. . . . Now, sah, as the represetative suh ob de powerful constituency —constituency, sah, ob de sable race. . . . I am proud to declare there's no disagreemen' on this great question of soshul quality, sah am de inference ob pregidies.[28]

Here again, white audiences were assured that Negroes' rise into the nation's seat of power was temporary; their intrinsic ineptness would divert any real threat to white dominance.

Although it would continue as a popular stage attraction until the late nineteenth century, minstrelsy began gradually relinquishing its place after Reconstruction. Variety shows of the type popularized by P. T. Barnum were increasingly coming into vogue and, in many instances, offered a less earthy, more wholesome form of entertainment than minstrelsy, which made them more attractive to family audiences. These shows were also slicker and offered a broader-based form of amusement: they tried to provide something for everyone. While they featured some blackface comedians and included some of the slapstick routines common to minstrelsy, variety shows were not restricted to minstrelsy's rigid format and black subject matter.

In addition, during the late 1860s variety shows began featuring female entertainers, who earlier had been most often confined to dis-reputable saloons. Some historians, in fact, attribute the demise of min-strelsy to women's emergence in popular entertainent. According to Lewis A. Erenberg, "the form of minstrelsy declined because it could not present women and sexuality in its ritual without destroying the form and threatening audiences who had come to expect minstrel Ne-groes to be asexual buffoons."

Minstrel audiences were further depleted by the introduction of vaudeville and silent films in the mid-1890s.[29]

In response to these shifts in public taste, and the competition from other forms of entertainment, minstrels began expanding and varying their programs. After the war, more and more plantation material was excised; in addition, to compete with the emergence of women performers, female impersonation assumed a more important role. George Christy had begun popularizing female impersonation before the war, but now the prima donna became a major specialty act. Women were usually portrayed as giddy sex objects, their behavior burlesqued in much the same way as plantation blacks. Minstrel troupes also increased dramatically in size. More endmen were added; at times as many as nineteen performers were included in the traditional semicircle. They also adapted much of the promotional ballyhoo associated with Barnum and other entrepreneurial showmen. In fact, J. H. Haverly, called "the greatest minstrel entrepreneur" by some critics, had practically remade the face of American minstrelsy by the 1870s.[30]

Submitting that minstrelsy "had not grown with the nation and was not appealing to the country's expansive spirit of large, indeed unbounded growth, development and improvement," he set out to "astonish and satisfy the most exacting amusement seeker in the world." Throughout the seventies and the early eighties, he did exactly that. Haverly—who at the height of his career in 1881 owned six theatres, four minstrel troupes, and numerous other theatrical companies—instituted marketing and advertising techniques that rivaled or exceeded those of Barnum and other showmen. He also so thoroughly glamorized and revamped the minstrel show that by the mid-eighties, except for blackface performers, it bore almost no resemblance to the work pioneered by Dan Emmett and E. P. Christy. Other large companies, adopting Haverly's marketing techniques and lavish productions, gradually forced the smaller, traditional acts out of the picture. It was only a matter of time before minstrelsy disappeared as a major theatrical attraction in America.[31]

In his *Tambo and Bones: A History of the American Minstrel Stage* (1930), Carl Wittke, an unabashed minstrel enthusiast, maintained that "the minstrels themselves were responsible for the collapse of their once successful form of entertainment. . . . From a simple, and fairly truthful imitation of Negro folkmusic and Negro folkways . . . minstrelsy had developed into a mixture of comic opera, burlesque, variety acts and buffoonery" that was indistinguishable from other forms of entertainment.[32]

Various authorities indicate different dates for minstrelsy's final demise. Toll, for instance, suggests that although some individual performers kept white minstrelsy "alive and distinct" until the twentieth century, the traditional show expired in the late 1880s. Others argue that it survived well into the twentieth century.[33]

In 1919, Al G. Field, one of the last of the major white minstrel owners and managers, contended that there were only three first-class minstrel troupes playing in the United States, although inferior companies with few performers still appeared in some areas.

"The days of the American minstrel show, except as a vehicle for amateurs, seemed over," Wittke wrote in 1930. "The end, which might have been forecast at least as early as the 1880s, did not actually come until the second decade of the twentieth century." Admitting that burnt-cork performers were still popular on the vaudeville stage, over the radio, and in musical comedies, Wittke asserted that with the closing of the Al G. Field Minstrels in Cincinnati in the spring of 1928, it could be said that "the final curtain was wrung down on what, at one time, was America's most successful form of entertainment."[34]

But according to Joseph Boskin, "every city, town, and rural community had amateur minstrel groups" at the turn of the century. Citing the distribution of minstrel songs and scripts by the federal government as late as World War II, the release of movies such as *Dixie* (1943) and *Jolson Sings Again* (1949), and even isolated performances by local amateur groups in small towns as late as 1970, Boskin contends that minstrelsy persisted until at least midcentury, when "the minstrel show and blackface theatrics virtually disappeared on the urban stages and in the electronic media."[35]

If the date of white minstrelsy's final demise is arguable, its legacy and impact are more certain. Like Carl Wittke, a few prominent observers viewed the phenomenon positively. Mark Twain, for instance, claimed: "If I could have the nigger show back again in its pristine purity and perfection I should have but little further use for opera." And Constance Rourke contended that the "Negro minstrel joined with the Yankee and the backwoodsman" to create a comic trio embodying the nation's "deep-lying mood of disseverence." For her, "comic triumph appeared in them all."[36]

Others, such as Berndt Ostendorf, offered benign explanations for the popularity of minstrelsy: "Minstrelsy was the staging of *alien* culture as *lower* culture"; its comic appeal was based on the fundamental human tendency to deprecate others in order to transcend one's own deficiencies.[37]

Similarly, the historian Nathan Huggins cited white America's desire to escape the restraints of the prevailing Protestant Ethic, to which most aspired. Whether literally as a performer, or figuratively as an observer, "the white man who put on the black mask modeled himself after a . . . black man of lust and passion and natural freedom." He thereby not only indulged the desire to escape the binds of "civilized" behavior but also affirmed his superiority.[38]

Huggins's assessment brings us back to a venerable old bugaboo—that damnable "cackling laughter" that has so intrigued and disconcerted whites since European missionaries and mercenaries first engaged the African continent. The assumed "natural freedom" of blacks is nowhere reflected or expressed more obviously than in their uninhibited laughter, symbolized so directly by the grotesque, gaping, perpetually smiling mouth that was always part of the blackface mask. The imbecilic stage black man created by white minstrels functioned in part to cast black laughter (and blacks' uninhibited behavior in all forms) permanently in a recognizable, absurd, and non-threatening form. But more than just defusing their lingering anxiety, white Americans indulged their fascination with and attraction to black naturalness.

As Huggins and others have pointed out, the minstrel black man served as a kind of alter ego, providing whites with the vicarious experience of breaking free from the rigid restraints of "civilized" European behavior and expressing their natural or, as they interpreted it, vulgar instincts. Moreover, they did so while allowing white audiences the luxury of remaining aloof from the ludicrous sable figures that pranced before them. To a great extent those minstrelsy-defined stereotypes became the barometer of whites' assessment of black Americans in general. Any other behavior by blacks characterized them as different or, possibly, as *exceptions*—labels that in themselves could be dangerous for those so defined if translated as *uppity*. Knowing one's role or place was essential to surviving, and Southern towns often made this abundantly clear. Tom Fletcher, the black entertainer who began as a minstrel and performed until the mid-twentieth century, recalls that such towns "usually had signs prominently displayed that read 'NIGGER, READ AND RUN.'" Apparently some Southern civic leaders also had an ironic if menacing sense of humor; according to Fletcher, "sometimes there would be added 'and if you can't read, run anyway.'" Although the popularity of minstrelsy induced many Southern whites to relax those proscriptions for black entertainers at times, stepping outside the minstrel role was always risky for blacks.

The need to confirm their stage role was so essential that, according to Fletcher, when his troupe arrived in one of those towns, "we knew we were in for a day of parading." Arriving in their own Pullman car, his entire troupe would march vigorously to the performance site, playing some rousing, upbeat tune—usually "Dixie," since that old Southern favorite placated white audiences. Safety depended on continually projecting the image of the stage black; when the show was over, prudence dictated a hasty departure. "After the show that night all the colored people connected with the show would get together and parade down to the car. If there were no trains leaving that night we would hire an engine and get right out of town without delay."[39]

W. C. Handy, known primarily for his role as a pioneer in formally writing and publishing blues music, was a musician with the Mahara Minstrels years before he wrote "Memphis Blues" in 1912. Like Fletcher, he discovered that the hazards of transgressing one's socially assigned role were so great at the turn of the century that he avoided walking alone or wearing his regular middle-class clothing when playing in Southern towns. Even with these precautions, black minstrels were not safe from harassment. For some of the inhabitants of Orange, Texas, the "conception of wild, he-man fun was to riddle our car with bullets as it sped through their town," he wrote in his autobiography. And when a member of Handy's troupe contracted smallpox in another Texas town, the entire troupe was detained nearby. They were denied medical treatment, food, or water, and were informed that anyone who left the Pullman car would be lynched. Handy recalled that county officers came to inform them that "the appearance of only one more case of smallpox among us would be the signal for them to burn the car and carry out the doctor's lynching threat." The troupe finally escaped by disguising the sick men as women and smuggling them out of the area.[40]

Other performers who risked stepping out of their place or even briefly dropping the minstrel mask were not so fortunate. According to Handy, Louis Wright, an improvidently proud black minstrel, made the error of cursing at a group of Missouri whites who threw snowballs at him and a female companion. The incensed crowd threatened to lynch him on the spot, and he escaped only by firing his gun at them. Later, a mob surrounded the minstrels' Pullman car and demanded that Wright be turned over to them. When the troupe refused, the entire company was arrested. Although no one in the troupe identified Wright —despite some back-room persuasion—a member of the crowd recognized him and he was taken into custody. He was released in the middle of the night. After he had been lynched and his tongue cut out, his mutilated body was sent to his mother in Chicago.[41]

The danger and confusion resulting from defying the minstrel stereotype was, of course, never restricted to black entertainers. For instance, my father reluctantly related an early incident in his life that perfectly mirrors the experiences of Fletcher and Handy.

Born in Mississippi around the turn of the century, he struck out on his own as a teenager. On at least two occasions, groups of white men detained him and insisted that he dance for them. In one instance, his hesitation prompted them to draw their pistols and fire at his feet. When I first heard this story, I associated it only with those Western movies in which villains amused themselves by terrorizing some innocent *white* victim while firing at his feet and yelling, "Dance!" Obviously, however, my father's experiences—occurring in the early twentieth century while minstrelsy still flourished in some form—had much more significance. Beyond the actual embarrasssment he demonstrated while relating the story and the real terror he must have felt, his ordeal—like countless other routine interactions between blacks and whites—reflects how deeply and pervasively minstrelsy's stereotype of the happy-go-lucky, dancing black Sambo had influenced Americans.

So even as minstrelsy waned in popularity during the late nineteenth century, its impact continued to be felt. Blackface comics gradually disappeared from the American stage, but the *stage* black remained indelibly etched into the American mind until well into the twentieth century.

Of course, the Sambo stereotype began long before minstrelsy. It had been disseminated through books, newspaper and magazine articles, song lyrics, song sheet illustrations, cartoons, and word of mouth since early in the nineteenth century. But the popularity of minstrel shows heightened its acceptance and riveted it into the national consciousness. By the 1880s, that image had become public property. Illustrations of gap-mouthed, bug-eyed, nappy-headed blacks—male and female, children and adult—began appearing everywhere: newspaper advertisements, postcards, magazine covers, household goods, knick-knacks, and food packages now displayed the stereotype for its comic effect as well as its effectiveness in hyping sales. The appearance of the Sambo or Mammy image—its female counterpart—usually assured the popularity of any item. (Similar items resurfaced and became immensely popular in the mid-1980s when Japanese manufacturers began producing them in mass quantities; protests by American blacks ultimately prompted these manufacturers to halt production.) Americans who detested flesh-and-blood blacks relished the minstrelsy-inspired caricatures that flooded the country. Minstrelsy had made Sambo as American as apple pie. Few Americans, black or white, escaped its degrading influence.

Minstrelsy had established a fraudulent image of Negro behavior (in both the serious and the comic vein) to which all African-Americans were forced to respond. And early black entertainers—perhaps even more than blacks in less visible occupations—bore the burden of working within the strict confines of that distorted standard. Indeed, they were expected not only to corroborate white minstrels' illusionary specter but, because they were *authentic* examples of the type, to heighten it.

Those expectations assured that the initial efforts of the pioneer black performers who ventured into the world of commercial entertainment would bear little resemblance to the authentic behavior of blacks. If slavery and the slave/master relationship constrained public black humor—forcing ironic misdirection and obliqueness—then minstrelsy very nearly stifled its genuine expression completely. Early professional black entertainers, most of whom debuted as minstrels after white performers deserted the form for more lucrative vaudeville careers, worked within a virtual straitjacket of distortion.

Minstrelsy's blackface humor bore about as much relationship to the authentic, private humor of African-Americans as Pat Boone's late 1950s cover recordings of "Ain't That a Shame" and "Tutti Frutti" bore to the original performances by Fats Domino and Little Richard. But black entertainers were stuck with it—or, more precisely, chained to it. In a sense, the story of the emergence of authentic private black humor in the public arena in the person of such comedians as Redd Foxx, Moms Mabley, Dick Gregory, Flip Wilson, Richard Pryor, Eddie Murphy, Whoopi Goldberg, Robert Townsend, and Martin Lawrence begins with the pioneer black performers' hesitant, sometimes inept efforts to add some dignity, authentic style, and human truth to the minstrel caricature of Sambo—a caricature that for many whites defined black Americans on and off stage for more than a hundred years.

3.

BLACK MINSTRELSY TO

VAUDEVILLE . . .

black on black

BILLY KERSANDS.
CALLENDER'S (GEORGIA) MINSTRELS.

IT GOES WITHOUT SAYING THAT MINSTRELS WERE A DISREPUTABLE LOT IN THE EYES OF A LARGE
SECTION OF THE UPPER-CRUST NEGROES . . . BUT IT IS ALSO TRUE THAT ALL THE BEST TALENT
OF THAT GENERATION CAME DOWN THE SAME DRAIN. THE COMPOSERS, THE SINGERS, THE
MUSICIANS, THE SPEAKERS, THE STAGE PERFORMERS—THE MINSTREL SHOWS GOT THEM ALL.

—W. C. HANDY

"I SAY, CLEM, WHAT AM DE REASON DAT DE PEOPLE OB DE COLORED RACE SMELL SO MUCH
LOUDER DAN DE WHITES?"

"WHY, DE GENUS OB MUSIC AM SO STRONGLY DEVELOPED IN DAR WHOLE SYSTEM DAT DE AIR
COMES OUT THROUGH ALL OB DE PORES!"

—ANONYMOUS MINSTREL SHOW DIALOGUE

"THIS WAS THE PIQUANT FLAVORING TO THE NATIONAL JOKE, IT LAY BEHIND OUR UNEASINESS
AS IT LAY BEHIND OUR BENEVOLENCE: AUNT JEMIMA AND UNCLE TOM, OUR CREATIONS, AT THE
LAST HAD EVADED US; THEY HAD A LIFE—THEIR OWN, PERHAPS A BETTER LIFE THAN OURS—
AND THEY WOULD NEVER TELL US WHAT IT WAS.

—JAMES BALDWIN [1]

I

Despite their reputed natural ability at entertaining, few blacks emerged as professional performers before the Civil War. As slaves, of course, many had been required to perform for their masters' amusement and profit, and there were scattered instances of freedmen and slaves performing on the commercial stage before Emancipation. The few who made this leap into professional show business, however, faced staunch resistance and, most often, overwhelming restrictions.

Among the early non-comic entertainers was John Hewlett, one of the original members of the African Company—the first notable black American drama group. Performing before primarily black audiences, this small, novice group "managed to give performances of Shakespeare and other classics in Manhattan with a fair degree of regularity" in the early 1820s. After the theatre, located at Bleecker and Mercer streets, closed because of harassment from "white hoodlums," Hewlett emigrated to England and continued his acting career. In similar fashion, Ira Aldridge, perhaps the most critically acclaimed nineteenth-century black actor, reportedly began his acting career in New York City, then left for Europe, where a less biased reception allowed for greater freedom of expression; he became a celebrated tragic actor, and performed in the most prestigious concert halls on the continent. The Shakespeare Theatre at Stratford-on-Avon honored him with the Ira Aldridge Memorial Chair after his death in 1867.[2]

Black antebellum performers with aspirations to "serious" musical expression included the soprano Elizabeth Taylor Greenfield (admiringly called the "Black Swan"), who, like Hewlett and Aldridge, found her greatest success in Europe during the early 1850s, and Thomas Bowers, a tenor, known as "the Colored Mario," because he sounded like the Italian opera tenor Giovanni Mario. Then there was John Luca and his family—credited with inspiring the minstrel circle arrangement by Tom Fletcher—who, in addition to their minstrel performances, traveled throughout the Northern United States in the mid-1800s performing classical music for small audiences of cultivated blacks. Thomas Greene Bethune ("Blind Tom"), a young slave who demonstrated signs of being a musical prodigy as early as age five, is the most noted and best known of these early musicians. He performed at concert halls throughout the United States as well as in Europe and South America from 1857 to the mid-1880s, and was recognized as a gifted concert pianist.[3]

But few antebellum blacks were allowed exposure to the European classics, and even fewer were given the time, training, or opportunity to study or familiarize themselves with so-called "high art." As Berndt Ostendorf points out in *Black Literature in White America,* by "keeping blacks barred from middle class literate culture [whites] forced them back upon the resources of their folk tradition." Despite its travesty and distortion, minstrelsy was the door that opened American popular culture to the "influence and influx of black American culture." A few black entertainers had even established local reputations as popular songsters and clowns in a style that anticipated the minstrel tradition.[4]

In New Orleans, a street vendor and singer known as Signor Cornmeali, or "Old Corn Meal," traveled about the area with cart and horse performing as he sold Indian corn meal. With his fine baritone voice, "which he easily transformed into a ringing falsetto," he performed songs such as "My Long Tail Blue" and "Old Rosin the Beau," as well as his own tune, "Fresh Corn Meal." His popularity was such that in 1837 he was asked to perform on the stage of New Orleans's St. Charles Theatre. Signor Cornmeali influenced the famed white minstrels George Nichols and Thomas "Jim Crow" Rice (who, after seeing Cornmeali in 1837, added a skit called "Corn Meal" to his act), as well as another local black entertainer, John "Picayune" Butler. Described as a "French darky banjo player" by one minstrel historian, Butler established a reputation as a musician and clown traveling through the Mississippi Valley region as early as the 1820s. By the 1850s, his banjo playing and odd ditties were known from New Orleans to Cincinnati. Neither Butler nor Cornmeali performed in blackface, but along with a raft of unknown slave performers of the era, they had tremendous influence on early white minstrels.[5]

A select few black performers had even appeared with white minstrel troupes before the Civil War. The most famous was William Henry "Juba" Lane, who began performing in urban saloons as a teenager in the early 1840s, and by 1845 had appeared as a featured act with various minstrel troupes. In 1848 he traveled to England and performed as a member of the Ethiopian Serenaders.[6]

As the sobriquet "Juba" suggests, Lane was most acclaimed for his achievements in dance. The *juba*, like the jig as performed by black slaves, was a dance whose roots could be traced back to West Africa. Similar to African stick dances, in which sticks are slapped against dancers' bodies or against the ground to complement drums and heighten rhythmic accompaniment, the juba involved hand clapping, foot stomping, and slapping the hands against the body.[7]

While the juba is universally attributed to African sources, some confusion arises over the use of the term *jig*—not, to be sure, in its pejorative ethnic sense, but with reference to dance. Both white and black minstrels frequently presented some variation of jigs based on folk dances popular in England and Ireland. And in contemporary writings, the term seems to have been applied indiscriminately to a number of popular folk dances, including African secular dances and African-American slaves' sacred ring shouts. Despite the confusion, from eighteenth- and nineteenth-century reports of Europeans observing black dancers, it seems clear that the jig as danced by African slaves was quite distinct from English or Irish jigs.[8]

William Henry Lane combined European and African jigs with the juba to produce a dance form that was new to the minstrel stage: from available descriptions, it resembled a combination of what we now know as the hand jive and an early form of tap dance. Many authorities consider him the father of tap dancing. Whatever its exact components, Lane's dancing was a fresh and spectacular addition to the minstrel stage; contrary to the claims of nineteenth-century critics, it also quite probably represented the first appearance of authentic black dance on the American stage. Like the great John Bubbles of the dance-comedy team Buck and Bubbles, who debuted about a century later, Lane was most praised for innovations in "the manner in which he beats time with his feet." According to Robert C. Toll, "He had learned a European dance, blended it with African tradition, and produced a new form."[9]

Lane's unique style, as well as the distinctly African-based rhythms of juba patting, were recognized and extolled by contemporary entertainment critics, as well as by such literary luminaries as Edgar Allan Poe, Mark Twain, and Charles Dickens. Indeed, Dickens called him "the greatest dancer known." In his *American Notes* (1842), Dickens described Lane's performance:

> **Single shuffle, double shuffle, cut and cross-cut: snapping his fingers, rolling his eyes, turning in his knees, presenting the backs of his legs in front, spinning about on his toes and heels like nothing but the man's fingers on the tambourine . . . all sorts of legs and no legs—what is this to him?[10]**

At the height of his career in the late 1840s, Lane competed in a series of challenge dances with John Diamond, the greatest white minstrel dancer of the time, and consistently won. Lane died in 1852 at the age of twenty-seven, but during his short career he established himself as one of minstrelsy's most talented and innovative performers.

The only other black known to have performed with a white minstrel troupe before the war was Thomas Dilward, a dwarf said to have been about two or three feet tall. Known as "Japanese Tommy," apparently to obscure his African ancestry, Dilward was recognized as a talented dancer, singer, and musician; however, his size probably accounted for his appeal and access to the white minstrel stage. From 1853 to the late 1860s, he performed with numerous white troupes; by the end of his career, he was appearing with several of the growing number of black minstrel troupes that had begun performing just before the Civil War.[11]

Lane and Dilward were among the first black performers to break into America's white entertainment world and probably deserve recognition as the first entertainers to present close approximations of *real* African-American song, dance, or comedy on stage. Certainly, the impression made by Lane, or "Master Juba," as he was sometimes called, indicates that—at least in dance—something new and distinctly African-American had been added to the repertoire of blackface theatrics.

It is doubtful whether either Lane or Dilward introduced any similarly significant elements of authentic African-American song or comedy to the white troupes with which they worked. While they may have brought some genuine nuances of movement and intonation, overall they no doubt adhered to accepted minstrel routines. The long transformation of public black humor from the debased distortions of the early minstrels to anything resembling authentic private black humor did not begin in earnest until the appearance of all-black minstrel troupes.

The first of those troupes debuted around 1855. Most did not survive long, but as Toll points out, they understood that "their principal appeal was their authenticity as black men." One group that toured in New York and Massachusetts, for instance, billed itself as "SEVEN SLAVES just from Alabama, who are EARNING THEIR FREEDOM by giving concerts under the guidance of their Northern friends."[12]

More black troupes emerged during the Civil War, making appearances from New York to San Francisco, but none had real impact or staying power until Brooker and Clayton's Georgia Minstrels began touring in the Northeast around 1865. Not coincidentally, Charles "Barney" Hicks—destined to become one of black minstrelsy's most energetic and creative proponents and performers—managed this troupe. The next year, perhaps spurred on by the success of Brooker and Clayton's troupe, Sam Hague, a British minstrel dancer, took a company of black minstrels to England. This group, called Sam Hague's Slave Troupe of Georgia Minstrels, toured successfully for years and helped establish the legitimacy of black minstrel performers.

In that same year, Charles Hicks organized his own troupe of black performers (also called Georgia Minstrels). Although this was a short-lived venture, his entry into the minstrel field as a black owner and operator was significant. Hicks was one of the few black owners who had any success competing with the larger, better-funded, white-owned companies. In the 1860s, a number of black-owned minstrel troupes surfaced, but by the mid-seventies most of these had either disappeared or been taken over by whites. Black minstrel troupes were quickly becoming profitable business ventures; foreshadowing a trend that would characterize black entertainment until after the mid-1900s, both the management and the profit derived from black stage acts were controlled by whites.

Charles Callender, a white tavern owner, was among the first to realize the immense business potential of black minstrels: in 1872, when Sam Hague's Georgia Minstrels returned to America, he purchased the company and renamed it Callender's Georgia Minstrels. Among the performers were Charles Hicks and two of the most talented black comedians to emerge from minstrelsy, Bob Height and Billy Kersands. Using promotional and advertising techniques similar to those employed for white troupes by the minstrel entrepreneur J. H. Haverly, Callender quickly catapulted this troupe to the top of the heap, and for about five years they reigned as the number-one black minstrel act in America. In fact, their popularity was such that Callender's name—along with "Georgia" and "Colored"—became synonymous with black minstrelsy. In 1877, they were the lone black troupe listed among the leading American minstrel companies.[13]

In 1878, Haverly—perhaps the most flamboyant of the minstrel showmen—bought Callender's Georgia Minstrels and immediately applied the same promotional hype that had kept his white companies ahead of their competitors. The size of the troupe was increased and the shows were advertised as plantation extravaganzas. In Haverly's hands, the troupe emphasized "THE DARKY AS HE IS AT HOME, DARKY LIFE IN THE CORNFIELD, CANEBRAKE, BARNYARD, AND ON THE LEVEE AND FLATBOAT." Perhaps more significant, Haverly's Colored Minstrels strove for the spectacular: in a field near a Boston theatre in 1880 he built a replica of a Southern plantation, which included "overseers, bloodhounds, and darkies at work." More than one hundred blacks were employed, supposedly presenting songs, dances, and "antics peculiar to their people."[14]

In 1881, Haverly's immensely successful Colored Minstrels embarked on an extended European tour. In their absence, theatrical producers Gustave and Charles Frohman purchased the new Callender minstrel company and set out to exceed Haverly in staging the spectacular.

Keeping the extremely marketable Callender name (the troupe was called Callender's Consolidated Colored Minstrels), the Frohmans' company presented even more lavish plantation fantasies, advertising themselves as "THE PICK OF THE EARTH'S COLORED TALENT." By 1882 this troupe was so successful that the Frohmans were able to purchase Haverly's minstrels and merge the two troupes. In so doing, they established a virtual monopoly. For the remainder of the decade the Frohmans' Callender company (split into three separate groups) dominated the field of black minstrelsy. It prospered throughout the 1880s, and other white-owned troupes mimicked the Frohman brothers' approach—presenting extensively advertised, lavishly produced plantation extravaganzas—well into the 1890s.[15]

Numerous other smaller black troupes also toured during this period, of course. Among them were white-owned companies such as Sprague and Blodgett's Georgia Minstrels, W. S. Cleveland's Big Colored Minstrels, and Richard and Pringle's Minstrels. And despite their marginal success, a number of small black-owned companies toured. Lew Johnson organized his first company in the mid-1860s (many contend that this was the first black minstrel troupe) and was a manager and owner for nearly three decades; some consider him the most successful black owner of the period. Although they played primarily in the Western states, outside the more competitive big-city markets, his troupes reportedly had a dedicated following and headlined some of the most prominent black minstrel stars. In addition to Johnson's Plantation Minstrels (also billed as the Black Baby Boy Minstrels and Lew Johnson's Original Tennessee Jubilee Singers), there were companies organized by minstrel performers such as Billy Kersands, Bob Height, James Bland, and Ernest Hogan, the last a transition performer who starred in minstrel and vaudeville shows as well as musical comedies.[16]

Early in the twentieth century, after minstrelsy had declined in the Northeast and in most urban areas, two other notable black-owned and -managed troupes emerged. In 1900, William McCabe organized the Georgia Troubadours. This traveling show toured the Western states (primarily the Dakotas, Iowa, Michigan, and Minnesota) for about ten years and was considered one of the best troupes of the time. Also in 1900, Pat Chappelle formed his Rabbit Foot Company, which was based in Florida but traveled throughout the South and, according to the black entertainment expert Henry T. Sampson, was "perhaps the best" of the black-owned companies. After Chappelle's death in 1911, the troupe was sold to F. S. Wolcott, a white promoter. In addition to standard minstrel fare, the show featured future blues and stage stars such as "Ma" Rainey, Ida Cox, Ethel Waters, Bessie Smith, and the comedy team of Butterbeans and Susie. Walcott's Rabbit Foot Minstrels traveled and performed into the middle of the century.[17]

Most interesting of the black owner-managers was Charles Hicks, himself a performer, whose name figured prominently in black minstrelsy from the outset. Hicks, the original manager of Brooker and Clayton's Georgia Minstrels, had organized a troupe of his own as early as 1866. In 1870, he took a company to Germany, and when that venture failed, he starred in Sam Hague's integrated European troupe. When Charles Callender purchased the Hague troupe, Hicks was the business manager. Soon afterward, he again attempted to stage his own minstrel shows, briefly fielding the African Minstrels and yet another Georgia Minstrel troupe. In the early 1880s, he joined with black minstrel stars A. D. Sawyer and Tom McIntosh in another attempt to organize a black minstrel company, and when Billy Kersands formed his own company, Hicks was the manager. During his career as a performer, manager, and owner, he took black minstrel troupes to Canada, Europe, Australia, New Zealand, and Java. Hicks died in Java in 1902, still pursuing the dream of establishing his own permanent minstrel company.[18]

By the end of the century, then, even as the minstrel craze neared its end, black performers had made an indelible mark on America's popular culture. Ironically, although the narrowly defined, primarily demeaning images of blacks that they commonly fostered were no different in most respects from those projected by white minstrels, as professional entertainers they brought a small measure of dignity to themselves and therefore, indirectly, to other blacks.

II

The most important consequence of black minstrelsy was that it provided a vehicle for the emergence of America's first professional black musical and comic artists. "The canny Negro," writes Rudi Blesh in *They All Played Ragtime,* "turned his version of the burnt-cork divertissement into a subtle but devastating caricature of the white Ubermensch, employing the blackface like an African ceremonial mask, and through the whole thing insinuated his way onto the white stage."[19]

Although these men developed from the anonymity of blackface masks and ritualized performances, some were nevertheless able to establish themselves as unique talents among a host of look-alike, homogenized entertainers. At the outset some black minstrel troupes had used burnt-cork makeup only for the endmen; the other performers wore none. As black minstrelsy grew and prospered, however, like their white counterparts they began performing almost exclusively in blackface. The elaborate makeup and similarity of most minstrel entertainment fare no doubt contributed to the relative obscurity of these performers, whether white or black. Those few who did achieve star status usually had some outstanding talent that set them apart.

The most acclaimed or, depending on one's viewpoint, the most notorious black minstrel performer was the exuberant dancer and comedian Billy Kersands. Born around 1842, he began his career about the time of the Civil War and was an active performer until two years before his death in 1915. He performed with nearly every top minstrel group, his own as well as the Haverly and Callender troupes. At the peak of his career, according to Tom Fletcher, he was so popular that, in the South, "a minstrel show without Billy Kersands was like a circus without elephants." He was the consummate minstrel performer in the traditional sense; indeed, from all reports, he probably re-created the white minstrel's caricature of the slow-witted, slow-moving Sambo type with more gusto and authenticity than any other black minstrel.[20]

Kersands's greatest asset as a performer was his agility at acrobatics and dancing. Although he weighed more than two hundred pounds, he was a stylish, innovative dancer. His showcase routines were the Virginia Essence or Essence of Old Virginia (a forerunner of the soft shoe) and the Buck and Wing; some credit him with creating both dances. Certainly, Kersands was recognized as one of the era's master performers. He was influential in establishing the dances as show business staples that are still performed in Broadway and Las Vegas shows as well as Hollywood musicals.[21]

Kersands's immense popularity, however, accrued primarily from his comedy routines: he was celebrated for his comic dancing, drumming, and singing. And central to those routines were the facial contortions that highlighted his depiction of the ignorant coon character which was his comic mainstay. He had an arresting physical anomaly—his exceedingly large mouth—which he exploited for all its comic value. While performing a lightfooted, slick, soft shoe dance to a song like Stephen Foster's "Swanee River," Kersands, to the audience's amazement, might fill his mouth with billiard balls without interrupting his dance. Or he might break into a song like "Mary Gone with a Coon"— "De chile dat I bore, should tink oh me no more/Den to run away wid a big black coon"—and emphasize the lyrics with outrageous distortions of his face and huge mouth. "The slightest curl of his lip or opening of that yawning chasm termed his mouth was of itself sufficient to convulse the audience," one commentator remarked. W. C. Handy described Kersands as "a man who could make a mule laugh," and insisted that he saw the comic put a coffee cup and saucer into his mouth. It was rumored that after a performance in London, Kersands quipped to

Queen Victoria, "If God ever wanted my mouth any bigger, he would have to move my ears."[22]

Mocking or making light of some aspect of one's own anatomy, of course, is not unusual among comedians: Bob Hope's elongated, sloped nose serves as a constant source of one-liners in his stage act, and the late Marty Feldman used his saucerlike eyes as a central element in his comic repertoire. Comedians, after all, are clowns, and for a clown physical abnormalities are just another means of eliciting a laugh.

For Kersands, however, the rub was that the traits he exaggerated and burlesqued were features that white minstrels had established as a central element in their caricature of blacks. Some blacks objected to Kersands's act, although in general he was more popular among blacks than with white audiences. Still, he was probably the first prominent black entertainer to confront a dilemma that would plague a succession of black show business people, especially comedians—the conflict between satirizing social images of blacks and contributing to whites' negative stereotypes of blacks in general. Ernest Hogan, "Pigmeat" Markham, Stepin Fetchit, Willie Best, Mantan Moreland, nearly the entire cast of the *Amos 'n' Andy* television show, and, more recently, Richard Pryor, Eddie Murphy, and the TV variety show *In Living Color*, have faced a similar dilemma.

At the peak of his career, Kersands was the most sought-after and popular black minstrel in America. He was also reportedly among the highest paid—his salary just below that of featured white minstrels. According to Tom Fletcher, "when his name appeared on the billboards, the whole town would get ready for the show, taking on a holiday air."

Apparently impervious to criticism from detractors, Kersands relished the popularity and success his act brought him. Late in his career, in 1904—at a time when most top-billed black entertainers had successfully dropped the minstrel format and moved on to urban shows that had abandoned plantation themes—Kersands was asked to star in a black-produced show in the East. After a brief stint, he returned to minstrelsy, again formed his own troupe, and, although he played some towns in the Northeast, resumed traveling through his beloved South, presenting traditional minstrel fare. When asked why he didn't leave minstrelsy and venture into vaudeville, Kersands responded simply: "All of my money came from the people of the South, the white and the colored, while playing down there. Whether they meant it or not, the way I was treated by them, and still am, I feel at home. I also make a good living with no worries."[23]

James Bland was another outstanding performer whose talents lifted him above the obscurity of blackface minstrel ritual. Although known primarily as a songwriter, his popularity on stage was probably exceeded only by Kersands's. Born of middle-class parents in 1854, Bland grew up in Flushing, New York, and (when his father was given a federal political appointment during Reconstruction) Washington, D.C. Bland had tinkered with the banjo since childhood, but while studying arranging and composing at Howard University in 1874, he saw George Primrose—a well-known white minstrel—at the Ford Theatre. Fascinated by minstrelsy and performing, Bland left Howard for the stage.

In little more than a year he was managing and starring in his own minstrel troupe. By 1875, he had written "In the Morning by the Bright Light" and "Carry Me Back to Old Virginny," and the next year he starred in Sprague's Georgia Minstrels—a troupe that included superstars Billy Kersands and Sam Lucas. In 1880 he joined Haverly's Colored Minstrels, where, with typical minstrel hyperbole, he was billed as "the world's greatest minstrel man." He accompanied the Haverly troupe on its European tour in 1881 and remained there when the troupe returned to America the following year. In Europe, Bland reached his peak as a performer. He starred in both his own troupe and companies managed by others. Well educated, handsome, a talented composer, singer, and comedian, Bland became something of a matinée idol in England and Germany, and is said to have earned as much as $10,000 a year. By 1890 he was back in America. As his career waned during the decade, he performed with W. C. Cleveland's Colored Minstrel Carnival, as well as with other all-black troupes. Bland died in 1911 and was buried in an anonymous pauper's grave in a black cemetery near Philadelphia.

Bland's songwriting talent and singing so overshadowed his comic abilities that there are few remaining references to the latter. It seems apparent, however, that his comic demeanor was more low-key than that of Billy Kersands. Tom Fletcher, his contemporary, recalled that Bland was "a great comedian as well as a composer. When he walked on-stage to do his specialty no one knew just what he was going to say. He followed no set routine and could convulse an audience with . . . his handling of whatever crossed his mind." Others refer to him as a "refined comedian." One can only surmise that Bland's education and desire to be recognized as a "serious" composer and matinée idol led him to avoid most of the blatant coon antics.[24]

Still, Bland remains a controversial figure in black entertainment history. He wrote as many as seven hundred songs during his lifetime and was known among his peers as the "black Stephen Foster." At the time, it was common practice for writers to sell songs outright to publishing companies and other entertainers; consequently, many of his songs were attributed to other composers. Although the music historian Eileen Southern contends that Bland's "unpretentious sentimental songs were lightly syncopated and reflected the influence of the folksongs he heard sung by ex-slaves in Washington, D.C.," many musicologists argue that Bland's music reflects little or no influence from genuine black folksong. Generally, their form and content are indistinguishable from the raft of degrading, stereotype-ridden minstrel songs that were turned out by white composers. The familiar "Carry Me Back to Old Virginny" (which was adopted as Virginia's official state song in 1940), for instance, is a paean to a mythical antebellum South where Massa and Missus awaited their loyal servant and, even after their deaths, "the old darky's heart am long to go." "In the Evening by the Moonlight" reiterates the theme of darkies hoping to be reunited with Massa and Missus since "Eb'rything was den so merry, gay and bright."

Ironically, Bland, like many composers of this genre of songs, had never witnessed or experienced the reality of slavery. Tom Fletcher, along with Eileen Southern, suggests that Bland "absorbed" his knowledge of slavery from ex-slaves who lived and worked in Washington after Emancipation. But more likely Bland was mimicking the sentiments and working within a musical form that was inspired primarily by the mythology of the minstrel stage; not, as Fletcher suggests, by the "beautiful melodies" of his own people. As the musicologist Sam Dennison aptly puts it: "What is indisputable is Bland's genius in imitating white song types." And he did so with amazing regularity and consistency; among the hundreds of minstrel and parlor tunes he composed are favorites such as "In the Morning by the Bright Light," "Listen to the Silver Trumpet," and "Oh, Dem Golden Slippers."[25]

The demeaning character of his songs aside, Bland was the most prolific and famous black composer of the minstrel period, as well as one of its most successful and influential performers. Still, his education and ambition suggest that his quest for recognition and stardom accounts for the character of his work. To a great extent, the music industry itself dictated the type of songs that would be published. Faced with the dilemma of succeeding personally at the expense of publicly denigrating blacks or not being published at all, he opted for success.

Ultimately, the choice cost him in ways he perhaps had not foreseen. Bland's career seems to have caused some of the same inner turmoil that, years later, would plague the black vaudeville comedian Bert Williams—who is recognized by many as America's first comedy star. Bland's compositions had become minstrel staples, but many whites were unaware that he or any other black man had written them. And although he was idolized in Europe, he was restricted to performing with all-black troupes in the United States. Then, in the late 1890s, when work in minstrel shows declined and most black minstrels turned to black-produced shows with urban settings, Bland was left out—he was too closely associated with the plantation themes of traditional minstrelsy. Racism had both restricted his opportunities and denied him the recognition he thought he deserved.

Toward the end, both his life and his career seem to have fallen apart, and he apparently turned to alcohol. Eubie Blake, reminiscing about a meeting in Atlantic City during the early 1900s when Bland left him holding the check, suggested that despair played a key role in Bland's death. "I never saw him again," Blake said. "But I guess he didn't live too long after that. Poor Jimmy was another drinkin' man. I guess that's why he was so unreliable."[26]

When he died, penniless, in Philadelphia, authorities did not know who Bland was or what he had accomplished. The circumstances of his death stand as a melancholy footnote to the career of America's first successful black popular songwriter.

Although not as popular as Kersands in America or Bland in Europe, Sam Lucas still looms as one of the most beloved and respected black minstrel performers. He was, in fact, a transitional figure between minstrelsy and the more glamorous, lavishly produced shows with urban settings that ushered in the era of black show business at the turn of the century. Moreover, as an entertainer, Lucas was celebrated for his comic and dramatic roles, as well as for his performances on the minstrel stage, the Broadway stage, and, at the very end of his career, in motion pictures. His impact on black entertainment was such that James Weldon Johnson—a civil rights leader as well as a dramatist, songwriter, poet, and novelist—called him the "Grand Old Man of the Negro Stage."[27]

Lucas was born in Ohio of free parents in 1850. He began singing and playing the guitar as a teenager; while working as a barber, he established a local reputation as a performer. After the Civil War, when black minstrel troupes gained in popularity, he joined a few of the traveling black companies and played and sang on boats on the Ohio River. "Eventually, colored shows began to catch on with the public," he told Tom Fletcher. "By that time I had built myself up to the point where I was one of the best all-around entertainers in the business and I could pick my own shows." Subsequently, he starred with most of the successful black minstrel companies as a comedian and singer. But Lucas was not content with such limited roles, and throughout his career he attempted to establish himself as a serious actor. He had short stints in dramatic roles with the Hyers Sisters (a "refined" operatic and dramatic company that presented serious plays based on black history as well as musical comedies) during the 1870s. And when the Frohman brothers staged a serious production of *Uncle Tom's Cabin* in 1878, Lucas became the first black man to play the leading role. After the touring play closed, however, there were few opportunities for dramatic expression and Lucas returned to minstrelsy.[28]

In 1890, he took the part of an endman in Sam T. Jack's *The Creole Show*—the production that most historians credit with being the first black show to abandon the straight minstrel format. Although *The Creole Show* maintained an overall minstrel structure, it introduced a chorus line of sixteen female dancers and foreshadowed productions like *The Octoroons* and *Oriental America,* variety shows that debuted in 1895 and further departed from the minstrel tradition. Lucas met his wife during his stint with *The Creole Show;* afterward, they traveled throughout the country, appearing at museums, variety houses, and vaudeville theatres. Then, in 1898, Lucas went to Boston, where he joined Bob Cole's *A Trip to Coontown*, a production that set several precedents: it was the first show to be written, directed, and produced by blacks, as well as the first black show to make a complete break with minstrel tradition.

Lucas's career was capped in 1915 when he became the first black man to star in a film version of *Uncle Tom's Cabin.* Shortly afterward, on January 15, 1916, he died of an illness contracted during production of that film.[29]

Lucas made many significant strides and was associated with several milestone productions during his career. Yet, like most black entertainers of the period, he was forced to return repeatedly to stereotypical minstrel roles in order to support himself. He had neither the comic talent of Billy Kersands nor the songwriting ability of James Bland, but throughout his career he balanced his buffoonish role as minstrel comic with serious roles in which blacks were depicted with dignity.

Unlike Bland, Lucas occasionally successfully inserted lyrics that countered some of the prevailing stage images of blacks—particularly concerning slaves' supposed nostalgia for the comfort and safety of their former masters' plantation. His "My Dear Old Southern Home" proclaims: "But bress de Lord de good times come;/ I'se freed by dose Northern men." And in "De Day I Was Sot Free," Lucas joyously celebrates Emancipation. Lucas's act also regularly included songs by other composers, such as C. A. White's "Old Uncle Jasper," which belied the romanticized image of the helpless darky hopelessly connected to the ole plantation: "And de 'mancipation day,/ I hab lived to see that too,/ De happiest day de colored man e'er knew."[30]

Bob Height was another standout black minstrel. By the 1870s, he had established himself as a star with Charles Hicks in Sam Hague's integrated Slave Troupe of Georgia Minstrels in England. In 1872, when Hague's troupe returned to America and was bought by Charles Callender, Height (a proud man whose talents as a comedian were later compared to those of the great Bert Williams) along with Hicks, Kersands, and others demanded more money and recognition. Their demands were ignored, so they quit and tried to start their own troupe —a move that prompted considerable controversy and racial tension, particularly after Callender asserted that they had been "stolen" from him. Their newly founded black troupe failed, however, and most of the performers returned to Callender's company. But Height, despite the general assumption that he was destined for stardom, refused to rejoin. He emigrated to Europe and performed there for years.

Other prominent black minstrel performers included Tom McIntosh, who, along with Charles Hicks and A. D. Sawyer, organized several all-black troupes and was said to rival Billy Kersands at low comedy, particularly mugging and outrageous facial distortions. Horace Weston established his reputation as an extraordinary dancer and, according to some historians, ranked with "Juba" Lane as one of the most inventive early black dancers. Tom Fletcher began in minstrelsy as a teenager in 1888 and, in addition to performing on stage until the mid-1900s, was among the first black performers to appear in motion pictures. He was also the author of *100 Years of the Negro in Show Business,* which remains an indispensable firsthand guide to the early development of black entertainment in America.

Billy McClain debuted as a minstrel performer at age seventeen with

Lew Johnson's Minstrels in 1883. Considered "one of the most talented and versatile performers on the American stage," he worked with numerous minstrel troupes (among them Blythe's Georgia Minstrels, Cleveland's Minstrels, and Callender's Minstrels) before establishing himself as a performer, writer, and producer in early twentieth-century black shows and vaudeville. He received sensational reviews for his performance with Ernest Hogan during the Afro-American Minstrel company's tour of Australia and Honolulu. The *Pacific Commercial Advertiser* of Honolulu commented: "McClain is an actor. He is not only a dancer, the best Negro minstrel that has been here in years but in fact he has made some strides along the way and his poise, his quiet demeanor and his command of a situation show real dramatic instinct." Later, with Hogan, McClain wrote and organized the original *Smart Set* company, one of the most successful black road shows produced in the early twentieth century. He also claimed that he introduced the cakewalk (an 1890s dance fad) to the American stage.[31]

Ernest Hogan, best known for the song "All Coons Look Alike to Me" (1896) and for his vaudeville appearances as a comedian, also began his career in minstrelsy. He joined Pringle's Georgia Minstrels as a teenager, starred in *Black Patti's Troubadours* in the mid-1890s, and in 1899—after a successful stint as a headliner at Hammerstein's Victoria in New York City—was featured with the Afro-American Minstrels as "the unbleached American." Hogan created the character George Washington Bullion for *Smart Set* and was immediately acclaimed as an exceptional comedian. His comic talent, similar to but slightly more refined than that of Kersands and McIntosh, was also featured in the 1905 production of *Rufus Rastus*. He died in 1909 while working on a new production, *The Oyster Man*.[32]

These early performers were the stars of black minstrelsy. At a time when almost no blacks were allowed access to high-paying or highly esteemed occupations, they carved a niche for themselves in the world of popular entertainment. Although few of them were able to introduce much of their own authentic folk heritage into the stilted presentation of the minstrel Negro, they did manage to open doors for the scores of black performers who followed. Some, outlasting minstrelsy, went on to lead efforts to eliminate the minstrel image. Despite their achievements, they have been vigorously attacked by observers who justifiably criticize their active part in helping to reinforce black Sambo and coon stereotypes. But serious questions remain about the charge that they were ever anything more to blacks than theatrical caricature.

III

Overall, black minstrelsy introduced an ironic new component to America's popular entertainment. If the sight of whites disguising themselves as blacks and distorting their own music, dance, and humor was bizarre, the phenomenon of non-white performers blackening their already dark faces and imitating the grotesque antics of their white impersonators was even more outlandish. But the travesty did not end there.

From the outset, troupes with black performers were advertised and promoted as "the real thing." Frank Queen, editor of *The Clipper,* a contemporary entertainment newspaper, bluntly referred to them as "real nigs." Black troupes also emphasized their link to plantation life and often referred to their companies as Slave Troupes. They were so successful at this that critics and journalists frequently praised their authenticity. A New York newspaper called the Brooker and Clayton troupe "genuine plantation darkies from the South" and hailed them as "great delineators of darky life," who vigorously showcased the "peculiar music and characteristics of plantation life." Black minstrel shows were seen as real-life scenarios in which the participants engaged in their normal behavior, revealed their childlike, irresponsible natures, and unleashed their natural inclination toward song, dance, and comedy, as well as their primitive passions. Black minstrelsy was regarded not as performance but as a kind of peep show that offered an unobscured view of Negroes in their natural and preferred environment— servitude and the Southern plantation. Insistent advertising and promotion as well as long-standing stereotypes of blacks enhanced the illusion. Moreover, the political and social circumstances of the time reinforced white audiences' quick and generally unquestioned acceptance of the fantasy.[33]

Black minstrelsy emerged as a viable and profitable entertainment venture near the end of the Reconstruction period (1867–77), when America grappled with the question of how to treat thousands of newly freed blacks. The period began on a positive note when the Civil Rights Act of 1866 made blacks full citizens and promised them equal treatment under the law. The Reconstruction Act (1867) and its three subsequent refinements sought to ensure protection for the political rights of black citizens. For a brief period, the United States Army was used in former Confederate states to guarantee that freedmen's rights were upheld.

Most blacks responded to the challenge of full citizenship in a positive manner. With their newly granted voting right, ex-slaves were the decisive factor in the election of many progressive lawmakers, including the first African-American public officials. Several black Americans became lieutenant governors of Southern states; others served as treasurers, speakers of the house, state and U.S. representatives; two (Hiram R. Revels and Blanche K. Bruce, both of Mississippi) were elected to the U.S. Senate. Despite strident claims about the mongrelization of government and determined resistance by white officials, these black lawmakers and officials helped initiate progressive social and educational programs intended to benefit both black and white citizens. From the start, however, most white southerners resented the idea of equal rights for their former slaves. Active resistance to nearly all black participation in government and society began immediately.

Black Codes (later known as "Jim Crow" laws) were enacted in many Confederate states soon after the Civil War. These ordinances, aimed specifically at blacks, were supposedly intended to "guard them [freedmen] and the state against any evils that might arise from their sudden emancipation." In reality they not only segregated blacks socially (public facilities, education, etc.) but also limited their right to vote and seek protection under the law (when whites were involved) and prescribed where they could live and work, and in some instances, when and if they could leave certain areas without the written consent of whites.[34]

In addition, to further guard against black upstarts who believed that Emancipation meant freedom in any true sense or equality in any sense whatsoever, America's most infamous vigilante group emerged in the South.

The Ku Klux Klan began innocently enough when six former Confederate soldiers in Pulaski, Tennessee, decided that they needed some activity to replace the excitement and adventure they had experienced during the war. In May 1866, they formed a social club. The name of the club was taken from *Kuklos Adelphōn*, a Greek letter fraternity on college campuses. The phrase means "circle of brothers" in Greek, hence the organization was called Ku Klux Klan. Initially, the secret rituals and strange hooded costumes were innocuous incidentals intended to add mystery and allure to a frivolous social club. As the club grew, however, it quickly shed its harmless image.

Enraged about the establishment of schools to educate blacks, members of the Athens, Alabama, faction of the Klan took matters into their own hands and "disciplined" one of the students. Soon afterward, they announced that "maintaining white supremacy" was one of their primary aims. The Klan had stumbled upon a goal that had instant appeal for many southerners. Klan membership burgeoned, and the "club" spread to all of the former Confederate states. An organization of thrill-seeking pranksters had been transformed into a terrorist group, dedicated to keeping blacks and other minorities in their place.[35]

In April 1868, an unsigned letter from one of six original Klan members appeared in *The Citizen,* the Pulaski newspaper. "The simple object of the original Ku-Kluxes," it read, had become "perverted. Better the Ku Klux had never been heard of."[36]

Faced with legislative and vigilante opposition, ex-slaves found themselves in a bewildering if not impossible situation. Generally without physical resources or education, most found it difficult to sustain themselves at even a bare sustenance level. A few, through either their own almost Herculean individual efforts or the generosity of their former masters, managed to secure property and establish lives as independent landowners. Some—the forerunners of the vast migration that would occur near the end of the century—left their rural homes and set out for urban areas. Most of them were less prepared for poverty in urban ghettos than they had been for destitution in the rural South; many fell victim to the degradation of slum living and a white Northern populace that resented their presence. Others remained in the South and—determined to exercise their freedom but unprepared and unable legitimately to provide for themselves—took to theft and debauchery as a way of life. Most settled into lives as sharecroppers on plantations and farms owned by their previous masters, where they found that bondage was not limited to chattel slavery.

With Emancipation, discrimination in America had shifted from an ostensible class or caste basis (master/slave) to a frankly racial basis (white/black). Blacks were free, technically, but very few white Americans seriously contemplated a society in which they would live and work side by side with their former slaves. Perhaps even more than during slavery, white America needed justification for the subordination and repression of an ethnic group that had become its supposed social and legal equal.

It was against this social backdrop that blacks emerged as comic entertainers on America's popular stage. Unfortunately, a distorted black spectre already dominated the stage and, initially, blacks had no choice but to reaffirm it. In so doing they also helped provide superficial justification for the racial repression that marked late nineteenth-century America.

It is easy to understand why white audiences continued to flock to minstrel shows during this period. Freed blacks posed a substantial threat to most whites—not so much a physical as a psychological menace, and as competition in the labor market. Both white and black minstrels provided a source of comfort and reassurance to white audiences. On the other hand, the black audience's positive response to minstrelsy has always prompted debate.

Many commentators insist that black participation in the minstrel phenomenon (both as audience and performer) suggests a conspiratorial connection, a kind of guilt by association. For instance, Nathan Huggins writes that "to watch a slow-witted blackface incompetent on stage, or a Negro who stumbles through foolish predicaments, is at once to recognize an identity and to assume a superiority as viewer and critic." Comparing blacks who laugh at black ineptitude on the minstrel stage with Jews who were amused by the antics of the traditional green-horn on the Yiddish stage, Huggins concludes: "It is all a kind of masochism which converts self-hatred—through its indulgence—into gratification and the pleasure of self-esteem . . . but the rub is that the contempt for self and race on which such humor turns must be ever-present to make it work."[37]

His interpretation is a turn on the familiar "laughter through tears" assessment of ethnic humor. But even though there is some validity to the catchy street axiom, "You have to be one to know one," identifying with the ethnic group being satirized is not a prerequisite for being amused and made to feel superior by ethnic humor. In fact, those most amused are usually clearly outside the target group.

After all, as spectators rather than participants, blacks had virtually no impact on the popularity of minstrelsy as performed by white entertainers. Minstrelsy was created by white performers for the entertainment of white audiences. In antebellum America, most blacks were still in bondage and few freedmen could have afforded such entertainment if they were welcomed or, indeed, if they had been so disposed. When black performers ventured into minstrelsy, however, black audiences became a central factor in the success or failure of a troupe. In fact, blacks became the primary audiences for most black minstrel shows.

Initially, the large white-owned troupes that provided plantation extravaganzas usually played in urban areas before mostly white audiences. These lavish shows were originally intended for whites, although the lure of seeing real black performers attracted many blacks and occasionally caused theatre owners to modify the practice of barring blacks or seating them only in a small roped-off section of the gallery, which was dubbed "Nigger Heaven."

In 1873, for instance, a *Clipper* correspondent in New Orleans reported that Callender's Minstrels were viewed by a substantial audience "largely composed of colored people who were attracted by the novelty of a corps of 'real nigger' performers." In Cleveland, the Callender troupe attracted a black audience that "took possession of dress circle and galleries." There were similar reports about black attendance at other performances by the white-owned troupes. In the South, Billy Kersands was so popular that, according to Tom Fletcher, owners "often would split accommodations in half. Prejudice was half forgotten as owners arranged for colored customers to occupy a full half of the theater from the ground floor or orchestra section right up to the gallery, with whites filling the other side."[38]

From the outset, blacks comprised the majority audience for the smaller, black-owned minstrel troupes. Hicks and Height's Georgia Minstrels were characterized as being very popular among Washington, D.C., blacks as early as 1869, and a few years later in Pittsburgh the "colored element of the city" reportedly "turned out en masse" to see Hicks's Georgia Slave Troupe. And for the duration of minstrelsy small companies operated by blacks such as Lew Johnson, William McCabe, Pat Chappelle, and, of course, Hicks, Kersands, and Hogan (before his rise to stardom as a vaudeville entertainer), performed before largely black audiences. Robert Toll concludes, "it seems that black minstrels drew primarily black common people," and the scant evidence available suggests that he is correct.[39]

In the nineteenth century, middle-class blacks as well as black intellectuals either ignored or actively criticized black minstrels. As W. C. Handy observed, they generally saw black minstrels as a "disreputable lot." Their estimate of minstrelsy foreshadowed an attitude implicit in W. E. B. Du Bois's concept of "the talented tenth," advanced at the turn of the century. Like Du Bois, they believed that to overcome segregation and racism, they should emphasize the accomplishments of the small, educated, and polite segment of the black community. Even legitimate aspects of black folk culture—work songs, spiritual music as sung by the masses, nearly all dances assumed to be related to African sources—were denounced and labeled vulgar; minstrelsy, a consciously distorted white caricature of black behavior, was treated more con-temptuously since it pointedly lampooned behavior that was intended to characterize *all* blacks. Du Bois put it quite simply: "The more highly trained we become, the less we can laugh at Negro comedy."

The black middle class, perhaps even more zealously than most white Americans, accepted and aspired to European standards of taste and behavior. More important, these blacks urgently sought to disassociate themselves from the stereotypical image of common black folks, think-ing this would hasten their acceptance in mainstream society.

Conversely, the black masses (primarily recently freed slaves) appar-ently saw no reason to fashion either their behavior or their choice of entertainment on the basis of what whites might think. In all probability they attended minstrel shows for many of the same reasons and were amused by the same things as whites. Politics of race aside, minstrel shows, despite their decidedly low order of humor, were the period's most popular form of entertainment. Moreover, the audiences they attracted—whether black or white—were drawn primarily from the lower levels of society. Minstrelsy never had much appeal among the polite or intellectual segment of society, despite such well-known ex-ceptions as Mark Twain and Charles Dickens.

Of course, minstrelsy's primary attraction for black audiences was the opportunity to see other blacks perform. Billy Kersands, Sam Lucas, Tom McIntosh, Tom Fletcher, and other black minstrels were celebri-ties in black communities. Like the athletes and politicians who rose to prominence in the late nineteenth century (black jockeys and trainers, for instance, excelled in racing until after 1894, when the newly formed Jockey Club began systematically eliminating them from the sport), they were living reminders that it was possible to escape at least par-tially the poverty and degradation that was so common among blacks.[40]

Moreover, blacks who attended minstrel shows apparently laughed as much or even more heartily at the performers' antics than did whites. This reaction did and, in fact, still does confound some observers. In 1891, for instance, a white reporter criticized a performance by Tom McIntosh because the comic, in the manner of Billy Kersands, centered his act on "facial contortions and mouthings," which were "neither funny nor pleasing." Still, "a goodly number of colored people" in the New York City audience "seemed to vastly enjoy the ludicrous portion of the program." The writer's reaction reflects not only his estimate of McIntosh's act but also his puzzlement over blacks *not* being offended.

This reaction to some black comedy persisted from minstrelsy through the *Amos 'n' Andy Show* and many present-day sitcoms.[41]

The criticism is largely unfounded since the blacks attending the performance, unlike the white reviewer or many intellectual blacks who usually avoided those shows, were not concerned with the effect of the comic act on white society's estimate of black people. Most likely, like the crowd of people with whom I gathered in the privacy of a neighbor's house to watch eagerly the adventures of Amos, Sapphire, and Kingfish in the late 1950s, they took the performance at face value. They did not view it with one eye focused on white opinion. And from that perspective, black minstrelsy—despite its original intent, and however inept and distorted its portrayal of authentic black humor—may well have been entertaining to black audiences.

Comic performances are partially dependent on the comedian establishing a rapport with the audience. And for the mostly downtrodden black audiences who flocked to see Kersands, Lucas, and others, there was an immediate bond. Minstrelsy may have been far-fetched, but it did feature black performers who, despite the political or social implications of their stage routines, provided a rare vision of legitimate celebrities with whom they could identify.

The black masses' enthusiastic endorsement of minstrelsy is often construed as evidence of wholesale black capitulation to the derogatory mainstream image of themselves and, consequently, of blacks having a self-denigrating outlook that is reflected in their humor. And in fact, the question of how deeply or pervasively demeaning minstrel stereotypes affected African-Americans' character remains a complex and troubling matter.

Stereotypes, after all, are not created from mere air. Many of the customs and behavioral traits that, after being exaggerated and burlesqued, were attributed to blacks, did have their roots in the West African territories where most slaves were seized. It is no secret, for instance, that in many African societies religious ceremonies encouraged more demonstrative behavior than was acceptable in the Catholic and Protestant rituals of America's European settlers. In addition, the emphasis on rhythm in African music, which is commonly believed to elicit a physical response from listeners, educed more effusive responses than most European music, which emphasized melody and harmony.

Similarly, climate and ritual dictated that Africans dress in a manner that no doubt shocked Europeans, whose religion and customs demanded that they shun any public bodily display. The Protestant Ethic as defined and extolled in Europe—the rigid insistence that hard work and personal restraint were the keys to individual success and happiness —was not as highly regarded in African communities. Although no less demanding, the work ethic in most African societies had a tribal, communal basis. Behavioral traits stemming from these and other cultural and environmental differences provided the grist for white America's propaganda and parodic mill. Therefore, while some are loath to admit it, many characteristics attributed to blacks, although grossly distorted by white Americans, had some basis in black Americans' African heritage.

At the same time, unlike most whites, black audiences *knew* that black life was much richer and more diverse than the one-dimensional portrayal of happy-go-lucky simpletons that minstrelsy presented. This is not surprising, since incongruity is the central element in nearly all humor: we laugh because of our awareness of the disparity between a perceived action and what we know is possible for us. A joke focused on a black comic's ravenous consumption of a watermelon or on his assertive misuse of multi-syllabic words loses most of its humorous overtones if the listener is incapable of recognizing that one may eat in a less demonstrative manner or speak properly.

In fact, one might reasonably argue that educated blacks' *inability* to laugh at minstrel exaggeration reflected some paranoia and self-doubt among themselves. Normally, the ability to laugh even when the joke is at one's own expense is a sign of assurance and confidence. Of course, the racist environment of late nineteenth-century America was far from reasonable or normal. And contrary to the maxim made famous by Flip Wilson's female stage persona—the ebullient commonwoman, Geraldine—during that time what you saw was *not* necessarily what you got.

Educated blacks responded to minstrelsy by reacting as much to what they knew whites saw in it as to what was presented on stage. They denounced it because they understood that mainstream America saw the stage Negro as *the* essential black person. They wanted no part of that equation; their adamant denial was partly a personal matter, but it was also politically and socially motivated. Although in the privacy of their own homes they probably did find some humor in minstrelsy's outlandish farce, publicly they felt compelled to condemn it. And in so doing, they broadened the rift between blacks' public and private reaction to black stage humor.

But the black masses' enjoyment of minstrelsy did not imply any internalization of the stereotypes presented. In fact, their response may be seen as an affirmation of cultural values that, while deprecated by the larger society, had been covertly extolled by blacks since arriving in America; many, no doubt, looked upon mainstream society's restrained behavior with amused irreverence. Without education or the indoctrination in mainstream values that would begin surfacing in second- and third-generation freedmen, the ex-slaves and first-generation freedmen who enjoyed minstrelsy seemingly took it for what it was—comic exaggeration of behavioral traits that they esteemed. A more flamboyantly overt reemergence of the identification with these behavioral traits would be seen in the twentieth century during the twenties' Harlem Renaissance, the seventies' black power movement, and to some extent in the insistently ghettoized style of the nineties' rap music and assertive, in-your-face comedy. Moreover, as the historian Paul Oliver suggests, black entertainers, "by adopting the burnt cork or soot and flour make-up" of minstrel shows, may have clearly shown that minstrelsy was "a vehicle for satire" and helped defuse charges of African-American inferiority.[42]

Without doubt, minstrelsy did establish a set of derogatory racial stereotypes in American humor. These not only became standard elements in popular stage humor (and later, radio, film, and television humor) but also common referents in the everyday humor of nearly all Americans—blacks included. Just as some popular minstrel songs (originally inspired by black style but composed in a European idiom) were adopted by blacks and subjected to a folk reinterpretation, many stereotypes introduced in anti-black jokes were incorporated into black humor. Watermelon jokes, coon jokes, jokes about blacks' odor, appearance (big lips, wide noses, dark skin, nappy hair, etc.), simplemindedness, trickiness, brutishness, cowardice, ungainliness, carnality, and laziness—although not all exclusively created by minstrels—were indelibly etched into the American psyche by minstrel performers.

But just as many saccharine minstrel tunes were altered and revitalized when subjected to a black folk interpretation, many racist jokes and gags from the minstrel stage were subtly transformed when adopted by the black community in the late nineteenth century.

Still, documentation of the *private* humor of blacks during any period before the mid-twentieth century is scant, particularly from the Civil War to the 1920s. Slave narratives and folklore collections afford adequate examples of antebellum black humor. And beginning with the

Harlem Renaissance, the increased publication of fiction and biographies by blacks, as well as newspaper accounts and interviews with blacks of the period, provide ample illustrations of private black humor. From Reconstruction to the early twentieth century, however, with the exception of scattered and limited folklore collections, few examples of the everyday thoughts or humor of blacks exist. Historians, for the most part, were not interested in the private diversions and amusements of common black folks. And even if they had been, as we've seen, distrust of whites had made secrecy, deception, and a guarded attitude about nearly all authentic details of life fundamental tenets in the black community.

The social condition of blacks—their travails under the yoke of Southern repression and racism—dominated the works of the few black writers published during the period. Although Charles W. Chesnutt is a prominent exception, there is little or no humor in the writing of "talented tenth" authors such as Sutton Griggs, W. E. B. Du Bois, and James Weldon Johnson; their works may be fairly characterized as overwhelmingly serious and polemical. And Paul Laurence Dunbar's fiction, although humorous, most often reflected the stereotypical minstrel image of Negroes and the prevailing plantation literary tradition of the time more than an authentic portrait of black life. The folklorist and poet Saunders Redding suggested that Dunbar's popularity was based more on his portrayal of the charming, lighthearted darky than on literary merit.

Still, one can only assume that, like the slavery humor that preceded the period and the Harlem Renaissance humor that followed it, private black humor of the late nineteenth and early twentieth century displayed an ironic, double-edged attitude toward white society and blacks' position in it.

Gilbert Osofsky suggests as much, in the introduction to *Puttin' on Ole Massa*, a collection of slave narratives, when he writes: "I have been impressed by the way in which so much of the *tone* of late nineteenth- and twentieth-century black folk stories and jokes about slavery simply repeat the substance of recorded slave humor of the 1830s, 1840s, and 1850s. . . . Perhaps we have the continuation of an oral tradition whose roots are centuries old."[43]

One can safely assume that the same oral tradition that permitted aspects of African humor to survive in America during the eighteenth and early nineteenth century was sustained through the years following the war until the 1920s. It is quite probable that in everyday verbal games such as signifying, those nineteenth-century freedmen—like slaves before them, the teenagers with whom I grew up in the 1950s and, no doubt, much of today's youth—used derogatory racial epithets and jokes that might have been seen in the most anti-black minstrel routine. (Given the borrowing that characterized minstrelsy, some of those jokes may even have originated among blacks.) When used by blacks, however, the intent and often the meaning of the gag or epithet would likely have been altered.

In minstrelsy, for example, disparaging jokes about blacks most often had a general target, that is, the comic reproach was markedly racist and aimed at all blacks. For instance:

Nigger's hair am very short,
White folks hair am longer,
White folks dey smell very strong,
Niggers dey smell stronger.

But when privately engaging in this type of ridicule, blacks typically refer to a specific person. In fact, the speaker usually clearly distinguishes him- or herself from the traits or characteristics being mocked —even though the speaker may more obviously display the physical traits being ridiculed than the target does. A common turn on the above rib might simply be: "White folks may smell strong, but nigger, *you* smell stronger."

Moreover, as those familiar with black street language know, the meanings of most words or phrases depend on the speaker's intonation and the context in which a remark occurs. Again, in black culture what you see is usually not what you get. Although blacks adopted many of the epithets and referents of minstrel humor, they did not necessarily accept the general racist connotations.

This common alteration of the meaning of racial epithets and jokes within the black community is also largely responsible for the typical misunderstanding of blacks' private humor. On the simplest level it may be seen in outsiders' bewilderment at blacks casually referring to one another as "nigger" but being outraged if the term is used by non-blacks. The term "nigger" (although presently out of favor) may denote anything from a close, respected friend to a despised reprobate—from the positive, "That's a *bad* nigger," to the negative, "What is that nigger doin'?" While the term is almost always used in a negative manner by whites, its use in a joke or (apparent) racial slur by blacks needs a subtler analysis. On a more complex level, this private alteration of public stereotypes results in the erroneous and perverse assumption by social scientists and commentators that blacks embrace the derogatory mainstream meaning of the epithets they use.

The misinterpretation results partly from the fact that black culture and humor have generally been officially interpreted by non-blacks or the black middle class—groups who for different reasons insist upon a literal, mainstream interpretation of black behavior.

Folktales and jokes collected in the late nineteenth century, however, reveal that despite the influence of minstrelsy, private black humor maintained its ironic edge and assertiveness. As Osofsky points out, stories told by freedmen of this period often harked back to slavery and emphasized a common theme: the ascendancy of the trickster or the slave's ability to outwit his master. As we saw earlier, the "Old John" tales collected during this period repeatedly demonstrate the theme of blacks using deception, wit, and guile to dupe their masters and avoid calamity.

In one, Old John the trickster is told by his master that he must fight the most powerful black man on a nearby plantation; a few thousand dollars have been wagered on him. At the battleground John finds that his opponent is a massive man who, chained to a stake, is growling and pawing at the ground like a wild animal. Instead of approaching his opponent, John approaches his master's wife and slaps her in the face. Witnessing this, his opponent quickly pulls up the stake and, terrified, runs away. The bet is forfeited. Still, John's master is furious and demands that John justify his actions. "Well," John replies, "Jim knowed if I slapped a white woman I'd kill him, so he ran." His master won the bet and rewarded John.

In another, John has a passion for onions and, each night, sneaks into his master's garden and steals some. The master discovers that his vegetables are being stolen and tells John to catch the thief. A few days later John brings in a skunk who, he insists, is the culprit. When his master reacts with disbelief, John says that if he doesn't believe the creature was the crook, "he could smell the skunk's breath" himself.[44]

Minstrel comic referents were almost surely subjected to the same double-edged interpretation that characterized the humor of black slaves. Deception, irony, and an irreverent estimate of white affectation and pretense no doubt continued as essential elements in the private humor of blacks at the turn of the century, even as minstrel shows began to decline in popularity.

On stage, however, the public ridicule of blacks continued. Even after vaudeville supplanted minstrelsy as mainstream America's favorite form of popular entertainment, white performers still "corked up" and impersonated blacks. Such luminaries as Buster Keaton, Eddie Cantor, Eddie Leonard, Mack and Moran, Freeman Gosden and Charles Correll, and Al Jolson all performed in blackface in vaudeville theatres and reworked some of the old minstrel bits. Black performers like Bert Williams, George Walker, Irvin C. Miller, Flournoy E. Miller, Ernest Hogan, and Butterbeans and Susie also worked in blackface in vaudeville.

And decades after B. F. Keith had opened what is considered the first authentic vaudeville house in Boston in 1882, when minstrelsy had vanished as a premiere stage phenomenon, black performers toured with traveling minstrel acts throughout the South, Midwest, and West, presenting shows that might have been performed at the height of the minstrel craze.

Blackface entertainment, in fact, would survive well into the twentieth century. Even when it was not required by promoters and theatre owners, some black comedians continued to use it. It was as if black performers felt that comedy and burnt cork were inseparable. Pigmeat Markham, for example, worked in blackface until after World War II. When audiences and critics demanded that the burnt-cork performances end, they were astonished to find that he was actually darker than the makeup he had used.[45]

Black minstrelsy is a paradoxical element in black entertainment history. Stigmatized by critics, its performers considered disreputable or, worse, racial turncoats, it remains a cornerstone in the development of the black performing arts. As W. C. Handy points out, it was the conduit for the passage of black entertainers into the spotlight of the American stage; for more than half a century it was practically the only way a black performer could achieve recognition. And for nearly all of the illustrious black performers who emerged in the early twentieth century —from musicians and singers such as Handy, Bessie Smith, Ma Rainey, and Eubie Blake to dancers and comics such as Bert Williams, Pigmeat Markham, Moms Mabley, Mantan Moreland, Bill "Bojangles" Robinson, Josephine Baker, and Stepin Fetchit—it was the proving ground on which their reputations were earned and from which their careers were launched.

PART TWO:
THE OUTSIDE

···

AFRICAN-

AMERICAN

COMEDY

ON STAGE,

SCREEN,

AND

RADIO

4.

··

VAUDEVILLE AND EARLY

TWENTIETH-CENTURY

BLACK HUMOR . . .

the blackening of America

9

FLOURNOY MILLER AND AUBREY LYLES
IN *SHUFFLE ALONG*

EV'RY CAFE NOW HAS THE DANCING COON.
PRETTY CHOC'LATE BABIES
SHAKE AND SHIMMIE EV'RYWHERE
REAL DARKTOWN ENTERTAINERS HOLD THE STAGE.
YOU MUST BLACK UP TO BE THE LATEST RAGE.
YES, THE GREAT WHITE WAY IS WHITE NO MORE,
IT'S JUST LIKE A STREET ON THE SWANEE SHORE;
IT'S GETTING VERY DARK ON OLD BROADWAY.

—ZIEGFELD FOLLIES (1922)

EAVESDROPPING ON HUMAN NATURE IS ONE OF THE MOST IMPORTANT PARTS OF A
COMEDIAN'S WORK.

—BERT WILLIAMS

IN HIS STYLE OF COMEDY AND DANCING, OR IN HIS DELIVERY OF A SONG, BERT WILLIAMS WAS
INIMITABLE. NO AMERICAN COMEDIAN HAS EVER REACHED HIS HEIGHTS. HIS FACIAL
EXPRESSION AND PANTOMIME SURPASSED THE GREATEST CLOWNS. THE GREAT CHAPLIN COULD
HOLD AN AUDIENCE NO BETTER.

—HENRY T. SAMPSON[1]

I

By the turn of the century, most blackface performers (white and black) had modified their stage routines to find acceptance in tent shows, road shows, circuses, carnivals, variety shows, even vaudeville— the more polite form of entertainment that had supplanted minstrelsy.

It was a transitional period in American history, the so-called "Age of Reform." Between 1890 and World War I, American industry, technology, demography, and popular culture underwent a revision that was more thorough and sweeping than any the nation had previously experienced. Increasingly, America was becoming more an urban nation than a rural one. In 1860, there were only 141 cities with populations of more than eight thousand; by 1910, there were 778. Pundits speculated about the loss of "deeply-rooted values and traditions" and viewed the consequences with pessimism. "In the future," an *Atlantic Monthly* article warned, "as never heretofore, our cities with their multiplying wealth and lavish luxury are likely to need the country for that steady renewal of their better life which shall keep them from relaxing into sensuality and sinking into decay."[2]

In 1877, Thomas Alva Edison filed a patent for the tin-foil cylinder phonograph. Although his recording device would be superseded by Emile Berliner's gramophone (invented in 1887) with its disc recordings, Edison's invention helped usher in the era of commercial recording at the turn of the century. Phonograph records would eventually revolutionize the music industry, bringing isolated strains of folk music to a national audience and thereby expanding the nation's popular musical taste.

Edison's flickering silent images—which had first appeared in Kinetoscope Parlors in major cities in 1894—began as featured presentations at Koster and Bial's Music Hall in New York City in 1897, and by 1900 had become a regular feature on most variety bills. Subsequently, silent film stars such as Charlie Chaplin, D. W. Griffith, Clara Bow, Douglas Fairbanks, Greta Garbo, Buster Keaton, and Rudolph Valentino would mesmerize Americans until the late 1920s, when a black-faced Al Jolson introduced "talkies."

It was also a time of transition and adaptation for America's recently freed black population. Reconstruction had failed or succumbed to a combination of neglect and exploitation by Northern whites and sabotage by Southern whites. In 1888, Benjamin Harrison, the twenty-third U.S. President, had asserted optimistically: "My colored friends . . . all men are now free. You are thrown upon your own resources. The avenues of intelligence and of business success are open to all." Without adequate preparation for freedom, however, these "avenues" were virtually meaningless. Blacks had been left not only to their own devices but at the mercy of their former masters. Outside of farm work, which usually meant a deadend sharecropping arrangement that was nearly as repressive as slavery, jobs were scarce. Jim Crow laws and Black Codes restricted practically every public facet of their lives. And those who resisted the South's new order or, in many cases, even mildly complained, were faced with harassment, intimidation, and the Ku Klux Klan's ultimate deterrent for uncooperative or "uppity" blacks: lynching. It was, as the humorist Dave Barry later wrote, "a period during which the South was transformed, through a series of congressional acts, from a totally segregated region where blacks had no rights into a totally segregated region where blacks were supposed to have rights but did not."[3]

Not surprisingly, then, blacks from the rural South looked to the urban areas of the North as a haven from repression and unemployment, and their mass migration to the North would have a profound

effect on virtually every aspect of American life—particularly its popular culture. In many Northern cities the black population had actually
decreased for several decades prior to the Civil War, but after Emancipation the black presence increased steadily. Between 1870 and 1890,
over 80,000 blacks left the South, and over 200,000 more moved to the
North and West between 1890 and 1910, most of them settling in large
cities. The black populations of the states of New Jersey, Pennsylvania,
and Illinois increased some two and a half times; in New York, the
black population tripled. This migratory trend was only a prelude to the
so-called "Great Migration," which began with World War I and involved millions of blacks moving from the South to industrial centers in
the North.

In the South, planters became alarmed, praising "before-the-war
negroes" for their faithfulness and work habits while characterizing the
new generation of emigrants as "hopelessly degenerate" wanderers. A
fresh barrage of pseudoscientific theories documenting blacks' depravity, laziness, and inability to survive outside a paternalistic rural setting
emerged. Mainstream newspapers and magazines routinely lampooned
former slaves, mocking their rural background and, ultimately, giving
credence to stereotypes about blacks' trifling natures while intimating
that they were unfit for urban life.

Before all the news was truly fit to print, *The New York Times,* in
addition to casually using derogatory references in news stories, regularly published "negro" jokes in its "Nuggets" column. "Chicken-stealing negro" and "razor-totin' negro" were common descriptive terms for
blacks, as were epithets such as "coon" and "darky." An oddly fractured
"Negro dialect" was also frequently used in news articles—sometimes
apparently in a haphazard or arbitrary manner. In July 1910, for instance, a response by heavyweight champion Jack Johnson to questions
about how he would use his fight earnings appeared in different forms.
In an editorial, Johnson was quoted as saying he would invest the money
in "Gov'munt bonds; they don't bring so much, but they's gilt edged."
A news article about the same incident reported that Johnson said,
"They do not pay as much interest as some stocks, but they sure pay."
Another "news story" offered an example of a black preacher's sermon
that could have been lifted from the Christy Minstrels:

Gibe dis pore brudder de eye of de eagle, dat he spy out sin afar
off. Glue his hands to de gospel plow. Tie his tongue to de line of
truf. . . . Oh lord, and fix his knees way down in some lonely, dark,

and narrow valley, where prayer is much wanted to be made. Noint him with de kerosine of salvation and set him afire.

The "Nuggets" column, which often used items from other newspapers, featured jokes such as:

Parson Jackson: In de mattah of watahmelon, I s'pose yo' b'liebe stolen fruits am always sweetest?

Sam Johnson: I dunno, I ain't nebah eat any but de one kind.

Or:

It was a Maysville negro preacher who needing the money said: "Brethren, we will now staht de box, an' fo' de glory of heaven, which ebber of you stole Mr. Jones' turkey, will please not put anything in hit." And every man in the congregation contributed.[4]

In this atmosphere, it was difficult for African-Americans to gain respect or be taken seriously. As Edgar A. Toppin points out, blacks "were particularly sensitive to Negro jokes, stereotypes, and epithets in the early years of the twentieth century because they had not at that time gotten far enough away from the conditions pictured . . . not to be harmed by them." Moreover, these derogatory depictions intensified the disdain and antipathy with which many whites already regarded blacks.[5]

Whites in the South were faced with a peculiar dilemma: they abhorred the presence of free blacks in their midst but, disinclined to assume the burden of manual labor that for generations had been assigned to black menials, they fought desperately to keep them there. Numerous Southern states passed laws limiting the free movement of blacks.

White northerners, disturbed by the rapid influx of Southern blacks, avoided the newcomers, and pockets of poor black southerners sprang up in the most undesirable sections of Northern cities.

In New York City, for instance, migrating blacks initially settled in lower Manhattan, in the presently gentrified area of Greenwich Village. Alternately called "Coontown" or "Nigger Alley," this area differed little from "Stagg Town"—the district at the southern tip of the island in which most blacks had lived during the mid-nineteenth century and which Charles Dickens had described as a place where "dogs would howl to lie." The district was known for its "black and tan saloons" and "all kinds of underworld and salacious activities could supposedly be bought for the right price." By 1900, the primary concentration of blacks in Manhattan was found in what is now midtown, but conditions remained basically the same; at the turn of the century the communities that most blacks were herded into were still characterized by their poverty, crime, and vice.[6]

Inevitably, tensions arose between blacks and whites in Northern cities. African-Americans were clearly not welcomed. Civil disorders, often motivated by competition for jobs between blacks and whites but usually sparked by some fleeting racial encounter, broke out in urban areas throughout the nation.

In New York City on August 15, 1900, after a black man killed a plainclothes policeman who he thought was harassing his girlfriend, white mobs took to the street, invading saloons and tenements, dragging blacks from streetcars and beating whomever they could find.

The mob, focusing their wrath on the city's prominent black entertainers, was said to have screamed: "Get Ernest Hogan and Williams and Walker and Cole and Johnson." Hogan, who was appearing at the Winter Garden, hid in the theatre for safety, and George Walker narrowly escaped serious injury. According to The New York Times, "The police made little or no attempt to arrest any of the assailants." The violence continued for two days. Afterward, although there were hundreds of complaints by blacks who insisted they had been attacked by the mob and by police, none of the rioters was charged. Still, on August 24, in answer to charges of race hatred in the city, The New York Times reported that "There are no signs that the citizen of African descent is distrusted or disliked. . . . His crude melodies and childlike antics are more than tolerated in the music halls of the best class."[7]

The worst racial riot of this period occurred in Springfield, Illinois, Abraham Lincoln's hometown. The use of black miners as strikebreakers had increased racial tension in the area, and when a black handyman was falsely accused of the rape of a white woman, whites decided to take matters into their own hands. As one rioter later admitted, "the niggers came to think they were as good as we were." On August 14, 1908, mobs began gathering. Before the militia arrived two days later, rioters had destroyed the black neighborhood. Eight blacks were killed and more than two thousand fled the city. The community organized an economic boycott to drive out any remaining blacks.[8]

Yet despite the social conflicts and upheavals that ensued, the mass movement of blacks from the South to the North gave black musicians and entertainers the opportunity to break away from minstrel routines, absorb many show business techniques not associated with minstrelsy, and find audiences receptive to forms of black entertainment that were more and more frequently defined outside the narrow plantation tradition.

More than just tolerated, as the *Times* suggested, black America's "crude melodies and childlike antics" were quickly becoming a rage. By the early 1910s, the cakewalk, "coon" songs, and ragtime music—all with inspiration or origin in black communities—had begun dominating America's popular entertainment. The transformation probably occurred first in New York City's elite ballrooms and cabarets, but it soon spread throughout the nation.

The cakewalk had its roots in West African festive dances. It was reportedly a common activity during harvest festivals on Southern plantations, where slaves competed for prizes, generally a cake. They formed a circle: in the center one couple after another promenaded and pranced, often with a bucket of water on their heads, sashaying and high kicking to the accompaniment of banjos and hand clapping. The dance had many variations, and in some was apparently a slightly veiled comic parody of their masters' pretentious posturing and highfalutin attitudes.

This spirited, improvisatory black dance had been seen in minstrel shows and in stage shows such as *Walking for Dat Cake* (1877), but its appearance in Sam T. Jack's *Creole Show* in 1890 and, later, in the act of Bert Williams and George Walker catapulted it to nationwide popularity.

In *The Creole Show*, the dance was spotlighted—and performed with showgirls instead of men dressed as women, as it was in minstrelsy. Interpreted by the comedy-dance team of Williams and Walker, it reached new heights of popularity. A March 3, 1897, article in the *Indianapolis Freeman* called their cakewalk finale "the best feature of the bill" and gave the following description of the routine:

There are but two couples and as the cake is now in evidence the walkers get down to business. One pair holds the floor at a time and the men's manners are in strong contrast. One chap [Williams] is clownish, though his grotesque paces are elaborate, practiced, and exactly timed, while the other [Walker] is all airiness. It is a revolution to see such jauntiness in one human being. . . . Away up stage he and his partner meet and curtsey, she with utmost grace, he with exaggerated courtliness. Then down they trip, his elbow squared, his hat held upright by the brim, and with a mincing gait that would be ridiculous were it not absolute in its harmony with the general scheme of airiness. With every step his body sways from side to side and the outstretched elbows see-saw but the woman clings to his arm, and this grandest of entities is prolonged till the footlights are reached. . . . Here he faces the audience, and no lack of grace comes from his unusual position in walking. The smile is thus in view throughout the promenade, and, if one could doubt that this chap is a dandy of dandies, it should be dispelled. . . . The other chap's rig is rusty, and his joints work jerkily, but he has his own ideas about high stepping, and carries them out in a walk that starts like his companion's but that ends at the other side of the stage. Then the first fellow takes both women, one on each arm, and, leaving the other man grimacing vengefully, starts on a second tour of grace. Even then he walks across the front of the stage with that huge smile wide and open, and goes off, leaving the impression that he'd had a pretty good time himself.[9]

By the turn of the century, the cakewalk had become one of America's most popular dances. According to Tom Fletcher, "when playing in the large cities, the big colored companies would set a night aside and . . . offer a prize to the best local couple. . . . As a result the Cake Walk craze spread like wildfire." Mainstream fascination with the dance was reflected early on by its adoption as an alternative to the waltz and its appearance in stage reviews and in many of the earliest motion pictures.[10]

The dance spread so quickly that it soon fanned out from black communities, stage shows, exhibitions, contests, and the ballrooms and exclusive cabarets of the wealthy to middle- and lower-class white communities. Through the popularized cakewalk songs of John Philip Sousa, it even spread to Europe.

The acceptance of the cakewalk by white Americans marked a major change in manners. Prior to the late nineteenth century, mainstream social dances in America were characterized by "control, regularity, and patterned movements," Lewis A. Erenberg writes in *Steppin' Out: New York Night Life and the Transformation of American Culture.* Even the waltz—which created an uproar when first introduced to

America in about 1812 because it required men and women to embrace each other at the waist—adhered to a patterned, formal approach that limited the amount of body movement and contact. According to Erenberg, "the challenge to this formalism in the dance began in the 1890s, burst into flower in the 1910s, and continued with a good deal of creativity into the 1920s." The Texas Tommy and cakewalk, and subsequent dance rages such as the Turkey Trot, Charleston, and Black Bottom (all with black origins) spurred the shift in white America's dance habits. The impact of black dance on American behavior was such that by 1927, H. L. Mencken would write: "No dance invented by white men has been danced at any genuinely high-toned shindig in America since the far-off days of the Wilson Administration; the debutantes and their mothers now revolve their hips to coon steps and coon steps only."[11]

And as whites increasingly copied black dance steps, black music with its emphasis on rhythm and syncopation also increased in popularity. By 1910, when the cakewalk had been accepted throughout society, black-inspired music, although highly diluted, dominated the popular scene. Generally, this music emphasized rhythm instead of lyrics; its ascent altered the traditional Tin Pan Alley approach, which had focused on romantic waltzes and tearjerker ballads, making danceability the key to a song's potential.

Cakewalk songs "had the distinction of being the first syncopated style of music to become popular in [mainstream] America," according to one musicologist. And Kerry Mills (who made the dubious assertion that he was the originator of the "characteristic cake walk march") is credited with composing the first "truly syncopated cakewalk," *Rastus on Parade* (1895): "When he is walking 'taint no bluff/ He puts 'em in de shade,/ No use in talking, he's hot stuff,/ Is Rastus when on parade." Most experts agree, however, that as a Tin Pan Alley product, the cakewalk was essentially different from the music blacks used to accompany their own cakewalks.[12]

"Coon" songs, the lyrics of which had minstrel origins, appeared shortly after cakewalks and, as the name suggests, were characterized as much by their derogatory, supposedly comical references to blacks as by their slightly syncopated rhythm. Black males were the chief target of coon songs' nearly libelous lyrics. The men were typically portrayed as lazy, cowardly, licentious, lawless, and covetous of being white. One song, foreshadowing the sentiments of the outspoken Springfield, Illinois, rioter, asserted: "And when dey learn how to read and write/ Why most of dem niggers think they're white." The titles of hit songs such as "I've Got a White Man Running My Automobile," "I'm the Luckiest Coon in Town," and "Those Chicken Stealing Coons" speak for themselves. If there was any doubt about the underlying intent of the lyrics, the cover illustrations for the sheet music—featuring grotesque caricatures of black dandies, shrews, and reprobates—made an even more emphatic statement.[13]

Ironically, one of the first and probably the most famous of these songs—"All Coons Look Alike to Me" (1896)—was "written" by the black comedian and composer Ernest Hogan. According to Tom Fletcher, however, Hogan apparently did not so much compose the song as appropriate it. Out on the town in Chicago one night, Hogan overheard a despondent piano player playing a tune in an after-hours joint. "The tune sounded good," Hogan allegedly said, so he went over to the piano, offered the pianist a drink, and asked him to play it again. "Each night found me in that same house asking 'im to play and sing that song.

"It seemed that his girl friend had put him out . . . telling him, 'all pimps look alike to me.' There was no protection for songs in those days, so when I left Chicago that song went with me." Hogan changed elements of both the words and music of the song and, with a little help from the pianist's ex-girlfriend, provided the contemptuously commercial title.[14]

With the publication of "All Coons Look Alike to Me," the popularity of coon songs soared. Their condescending lyrics notwithstanding, the gay melodies and upbeat rhythms created a light, happy-go-lucky quality perfectly suited for dancing. So-called "coon shouters," black and white, immediately appropriated the style, and for the next three decades, hundreds of these tunes were turned out by Tin Pan Alley publishers. The songs dominated sheet music sales as well as the selections played by bands in traveling variety shows, vaudeville houses, and ballrooms for years. A few titles ("Won't You Come Home, Bill Bailey," for instance), with all coon references deleted, remain popular standards today.

America's enthusiastic response to coon songs opened the gates for another, more complicated, form of syncopated music. Ragtime was introduced in the late 1890s and was popular for more than twenty years. Then, after being disregarded for decades by nearly all except aficionados, the music underwent a resurgence through release of the hit movie, *The Sting* (1973), in which six Scott Joplin rags were used as the background score. Joplin, in fact, is credited by most musicologists as the composer of the first "classic" ragtime tune ("The Maple Leaf Rag") in 1909, although so-called "folk rags" were published as early as the mid-1890s. Most of these early songs, had more in common with cakewalks and coon songs than what was later recognized as classic rag, according to music purists. Tin Pan Alley publishers as well as many composers quickly exploited the connection between these musical forms. Tom Fletcher, for instance, claimed that Ernest Hogan's "All Coons Look Alike to Me" was "America's first published ragtime song"; the song was also advertised as such by its publisher. And coon song composer Benjamin R. Harney billed himself as "Originator of Ragtime" while appearing at Tony Pastor's Music Hall in 1896.[15]

Today's musicologists, defining ragtime in a much narrower sense than artists and composers at the turn of the century, deny such claims. And since ragtime as popularized by Scott Joplin was basically an instrumental rather than a vocal form, their denial has merits.

Still, the inspiration for ragtime, as it was for the cakewalk and coon songs, seems clearly to lie in black folk dance and the music that accompanied it. In *Yesterdays: Popular Song in America* (1979)—a book that strains to show that there was little black influence in America's popular music until the 1960s—Charles Hamm, then professor of music at Dartmouth College, writes that "Ragtime is syncopated piano music, developing out of a dance known as the cakewalk," and submits that "there is difficulty in separating songs now thought of as ragtime from 'coon' songs." In fact, as early as the turn of the century, musicians and critics suggested other connections between ragtime and black folk sources. The music was described derisively as "jig piano" by some, and others claimed it originated with blacks ridiculing sentimental aspects of mainstream music and culture. In a 1909 article, J. Rosamond Johnson suggested that, "since there is no record or definition in the dictionaries of music of 'ragtime,' we must then consider the appellation 'ragtime' simply a slang name for that peculiarly distinctive, syncopated rhythm originated by the American Negro." Earlier, in the late-nineteenth century, another critic wrote:

Negroes call their clog dancing "ragging" and the dance a "rag," a dance largely shuffling. The dance is a sort of frenzy with frequent yelps of delight from the dancer and spectators and accompanied

by the latter with hand clapping and stomping of feet. Banjo figu-
ration is very noticeable in ragtime music and division of one of
the beats into two short notes is traceable to the hand clapping.[16]

The tangled origins of the era's music are reflected in Amiri Baraka's
description. "Northern Negro pre-jazz music [African-American music
before 1920]," he writes in *Blues People* (1963),

> was almost like the picture within a picture within a picture, and
> so on, on the cereal package. Ragtime was a Negro music, resulting
> from the Negro's appropriation of white piano techniques used in
> show music. Popularized ragtime ... was a dilution of the Negro
> style. And, finally, the show and "society" music the Negroes in
> the pre-blues North made was a bouncy, essentially vapid appro-
> priation of the popularized imitations of Negro imitations of white
> minstrel music, which ... came from white parodies of Negro life
> and music.[17]

The consequence of this continued appropriation and reappropria-
tion by both black and white musicians and composers was that syncopation—however diluted from its black folk roots—became a key
element in America's popular music during the "Gay Nineties." White
musicians and composers such as John Philip Sousa and Paul
Whiteman, sheet music publishers, and, a few years later, record publishers would reap most of the profits from the phenomenon. But black
musicians and entertainers also benefited. The acceptance of black
music and dance precipitated a golden era for black entertainment in
America during the 1890s, which, although it diminished during the
first two decades of the twentieth century, would pick up again in the
twenties. It extended not just to the musicians who were changing
America's musical taste but also to the comedians and clowns who
began slowly altering the minstrel image of Sambo and Jim Dandy.

II

Traveling black minstrel shows still had their followings, and troupes
such as the Georgia Troubadours, the Rabbit Foot Company, Richard
and Pringle's Georgia Minstrels, and Curtis's Afro-American Minstrel
Company continued touring rural towns in the South and Midwest with

great success. By the turn of the century, however, these companies had begun to combine other forms of entertainment with the basic minstrel routines.

Increasingly, road shows that offered more variation in their entertainment format came to the forefront, even in rural areas. Blues singer Ma Rainey began singing in tent shows around 1902 and, along with Bessie Smith, was performing with Walcott's Rabbit Foot Minstrels by 1915. New Orleans jazzman Bunk Johnson worked with Holcamp's Georgia Smart Set from the early 1900s through the twenties, and in 1910, pianist Jelly Roll Morton played with the McCabe and Young Minstrels. Other shows moved even further afield from standard minstrelsy.

Black road shows offering non-minstrel entertainment had surfaced as early as the 1870s; the Hyers Sisters, for instance, traveled throughout the South presenting serious dramas as well as operatic shows and musical comedies featuring such performers as Billy McClain and Sam Lucas. Emerging at the height of minstrel popularity, they struggled to find enthusiastic supporters and financial backers. By the 1890s, tastes had changed enough that non-minstrel entertainment was welcomed. When white promoter Sam T. Jack introduced his Creole Burlesque Company in New England in 1890, the troupe became an instant favorite.

Although it maintained the three-part format of minstrelsy, *The Creole Show* was more a variety than a minstrel show. Its black cast featured a chorus line of beautiful showgirls; toning down some of the familiar plantation humor and reflecting black migration patterns, the acts assumed an urban ambience. The success of *The Creole Show* opened new avenues for black entertainers, and within a few years musical comedies with black casts began to appear more regularly.

In 1895 the black promoter John W. Isham, who had worked as an advance man for *The Creole Show*, organized his own company, Isham's Octoroons, which "not only presented a series of high class musical entertainment, but performed well in grand opera and comic opera." Minstrel star Tom McIntosh was one of the feature comedians, and his performance with his wife elicited high praise from critics: "Both have an intelligent idea of low comedy," one wrote, "and their act is full of new and original humor."[18]

The following year Isham opened a more elaborate production called *Oriental America*, which according to *The Morning Times*, a Washington newspaper, was "one of the strongest [shows] on the road." In the same year *Black Patti's Troubadours,* starring the acclaimed black soprano Sissieretta Jones, opened to rave reviews. The *Indianapolis Freeman* described the show as "vaudeville, comedy, burlesque, and opera interpreted by fifty of the best artists ever organized for this style of entertainment." And Jones is said to have had "most of the qualities essential in a great singer: the natural voice, the physical figure, the grand air."[19]

The road show that first made a complete break with minstrel tradition was *A Trip to Coontown,* written by Bob Cole. The show opened in 1896 and toured until 1898, when it debuted in a small theatre near Broadway and was hailed as the first musical comedy written and produced by blacks to succeed in New York City. Cole, along with his partner Billy Johnson, also starred in the show. Cole's portrayal of his most famous comic character, the tramp Willie Wayside, brought him instant acclaim.

Despite their break with minstrel structure, each of these early shows featured comedy acts that basically adhered to the old minstrel routines. Black-faced comedians such as Tom McIntosh, who appeared at one time or another in the Sam T. Jack and John W. Isham shows, and Bob Cole, stuck with the coon humor that had originated in minstrelsy. So, although all-black-cast shows were developing and expanding, leaving behind some remnants of minstrelsy and adding more authentically black music, the comic image of Sambo remained virtually unchanged.

King Rastus, a show developed by the Octoroon Company under the direction of John Isham's brother, Will, in 1900, is a case in point. The show toured briefly with Billy Kersands before it failed. Its biggest drawback was the humor, which apparently offended even those black audiences weaned on minstrelsy's low comedy. In one bit a character says, "Every nation has a flag but a coon," then unveils a rag with a chicken and watermelon imprinted on it along with the inscription: "Our Rag." The bit was probably based on a song by Will Heelan and J. Fred Helf ("Every Race Has a Flag But the Coon"), which was published in the same year, and featured such lines as:

Now I'll suggest a flag that ought to win a prize,
  Just take a flannel shirt and paint it red,
Then draw a chicken on it, with two poker dice for eyes,
  An' have it wavin' razors 'round its head;
To make it quaint, you've got to paint,
  A possum, with a pork chop in its teeth,

> To give it tone, a big ham-bone
> You sketch upon a banjo underneath . . .

A black critic who saw the show in Memphis, while admitting that whites might enjoy the production, wrote: "As a whole the show was one that citizens of this place care not to see repeated. It is a slander on the Negro of America."[20]

Smart Set, organized and written by Billy McClain and Ernest Hogan in 1902 (the producer, Gus Hill, was white), was another milestone black production, although it offered few glimpses of private black folk humor in its comedy routines. A traveling musical comedy more than a road show, *Smart Set* toured successfully for years; after Hogan and McClain left, it starred such performers as Tom McIntosh and S. H. Dudley, a competent musician and comedian who later made his mark by forming the first successful booking organization for black performers.

During this same period blacks became more extensively involved in carnivals, tent shows, and circuses, which, largely through the efforts of P. T. Barnum, had become an American institution by the turn of the century. The big carnivals and circuses performed principally for white audiences, but some featured sideshows (called "dirty shows" or "jig shows") that presented black performers playing for black audiences.

The cornetist Perry J. Lowery is usually credited with introducing black vaudeville acts into the circus in 1899. Subsequently, he toured with his own traveling bands and with P. G. Lowery's Vaudeville Company, before permanently associating himself with the circus in 1901. He toured with Barnum & Bailey, Ringling Brothers, and Cole Brothers for the next three decades.[21]

It was out of the circus and carnival circuit that the most enduring and famous black tent show emerged. According to the black producer and composer J. Homer Tutt, around 1902 Eph Williams, a pioneer black showman, ran into trouble with his dog and pony circus, losing everything except his animals. He met Tutt's brother, Salem Tutt Whitney (who was traveling with his own tent show, Whitney and Bernard's Troubadours), and Whitney incorporated the animals into his show. Shortly afterward, these two showmen organized *Silas Green from New Orleans,* the legendary tent show that would provide a stage for black performers (neophytes and proven stars) for decades. From 1905 until just before his death in 1921, Williams ran the show independently.

Subsequently it was purchased by white promoters and toured the South and Midwest until the early 1950s.

In an essay on the avant-garde saxophonist Ornette Coleman, who toured with a *Silas Green* troupe during the forties as a blues musician, the jazz critic A. B. Spellman provided a description of the famous tent show during its decline. "As an adolescent in Elizabeth, North Carolina," he wrote,

> I recall crawling under the canvas tents of "Silas Green from New Orleans" to watch the semi-naked women do their dances and to hear the comedians' crude but, I thought then, hilariously funny jokes. . . . By 1950 the company was seedy, its canvas tent was ragged, its dancers somewhat shopworn . . . the Negroes who lived in [Elizabeth City] seldom attended Silas Green shows; the group drew its biggest revenue from the "country people" who lined the city streets on weekends. We had radio, and most of the country people did not; we also had a movie house. Fights were frequent, gambling always took place behind the tents.

"Every big actor of Harlem has at some time or another played with 'Silas Green,' " Tutt wrote in 1936.[22]

In fact, from 1890 through World War I, black road shows provided the primary proving ground for the host of comedians who surfaced in black theatres and in films during the twenties. These road shows, playing before primarily black audiences, were like a rich underground spring that nurtured a form of black stage comedy more closely aligned to the authentic humor of black folks. Removed from the expectations of white audiences and, often, from the pressure of white promoters, black comedians working in traveling shows before black patrons could and gradually did alter the image of depravity, venality, and ignorance that characterized minstrel humor, as well as much of the humor seen in mainstream arenas such as vaudeville and Broadway musicals. Although many still worked in blackface, these comics, performing in tents and so-called "dark" houses, before dark audiences, were among the first black professional comedians subtly to alter the minstrel stage presentation of black humor.

One of the areas where slight alterations appeared first was in song lyrics. Black minstrel and medicine show road companies initially offered the same stereotypical images found in the coon songs prevalent in white shows. Gradually, however, black composers (nearly all of them also performers) began altering the lyrics, "using the popular song idiom to get in a barb or two." During this period it was common practice to accommodate the specific taste of a given audience. Just as white companies no doubt increased the intensity of ridicule directed at blacks when they appeared before rural Southern white crowds, black performers changed their own songs and those written by others when they played to black audiences.[23]

Moreover, black composers such as Irving Jones occasionally produced humorous songs that belied the fashionable stereotypes and did have sardonic bite. Jones's "When a Coon Sits in the President's Chair," "St. Patrick's Day Is a Bad Day for Coons," and "You Needn't Think I'm a Regular Fool" (all published around the turn of the century), although they adhered to some coon song clichés, provided alternatives to the persistent chicken-stealing, razor-toting images proffered in most of the era's popular songs. As Paul Oliver noted, "Songsters could trade on white fears and fantasies and mock them."

Even more directly, "on the minstrel and medicine show stage, points could be made that arose out of both content and situation." The sociologist Arthur F. Raper's report of a minstrel show in Oglethorpe, Georgia, for instance, affirms the practice. "The whole troupe was doing a twisting, jiggling dance which was followed by a dialogue in which a black boy pleaded for the attention of a mulatto girl, only to be refused with: 'Who me? Why you don't know who I am; my daddy's the biggest planter in Georgia.' " Later, during a sketch in which a performer sang, "I'll Leave My Gun at Home," according to Raper, "it seemed quite accidental that he was . . . pointing straight to a white man when he came to the line, 'I'll leave my gun at home, if you'll leave my wife alone.' " While this kind of assertive redirection of minstrelsy's racially demeaning humor was by no means revolutionary, it does demonstrate the shifts that performers gradually insinuated into their acts.[24]

These road shows were the forerunners of the Theatre Owners Booking Association and, as we shall see, it was on that black theatrical circuit that the changes begun in tent shows came to fruition.

Many of the comedians who worked the early road shows emerged later as black entertainment superstars. For instance, Tim Moore, the veteran comic who starred in vaudeville and Broadway musical comedies before taking on the role of Kingfish in the Amos 'n' Andy television show in the 1950s, began his career in Dr. Mick's traveling medicine show in 1900; Pigmeat Markham joined a minstrel company in 1917 and performed in tent shows and carnivals before his "Here

come de Judge" routine made him famous; Jackie "Moms" Mabley
debuted as a blackface comedienne in tent shows in the early 1900s
prior to her success in musical comedies and as a stand-up comic;
Mantan Moreland—who starred in more than three hundred films
and, on stage, often teamed with Nipsey Russell and Redd Foxx, comedians whose careers extended well into the television era—began his
career with a traveling circus in 1915; Jodie Edwards—"Butterbeans"
of Butterbeans and Susie, one of the first and most famous black hus-
band-and-wife comedy teams—began in a pickaninny bit in the Moss
Brothers Carnival in 1910; Bill "Bojangles" Robinson began performing
on street corners as a teenager in the 1890s before graduating to tent
shows, traveling black musical comedies, and, finally, becoming Hollywood sidekick to Shirley Temple and the toast of Broadway in the
1930s; and Stepin Fetchit, Hollywood's most successful Sambo figure,
started his show business career as a comic in the "plantation show" of
a traveling carnival in 1913.

Just as black road shows in the rural South benefited from the increased popularity of syncopated music, black musicians and entertainers in urban areas advanced their careers. Southern black musicians
flocked to the North, finding jobs in urban cafés, cabarets, and restaurants whose clientele lusted for the new dance music. Although, as
Amiri Baraka points out, they basically played light, diluted versions of
authentic black music (ignoring more serious jazz-oriented forms such
as Scott Joplin's classic rags), these were preferred to the string orchestras that previously held sway.

In 1910, for instance, James R. Europe was instrumental in organiz-
ing the Clef Club, a New York City–based black musicians' association
that, besides forming its own extremely successful symphony orchestra,
helped provide bookings for its members and assisted them when they
were unemployed. The Clef Club was so effective that a few years
after its inception black orchestras were playing in many of the private
ballrooms of first-class restaurants and hotels, as well as in most of the
dance halls along Broadway. Europe, in fact, was the musical arranger
for Irene and Vernon Castle (the white dance team who popularized
black dances such as the Turkey Trot in the teens) and directed the
orchestra at their dance salon. Shortly before Europe was killed by a
knife-wielding drummer in 1919, violinist and bandleader Will Marion
Cook, another Clef Club member, had formed the New York Syncopated Orchestra and was performing at large music halls in major cities

throughout the North as well as overseas. And in 1920, when broadcast radio debuted, Clef Club bands were featured on early programs. Musically, black performers were making great strides in the mainstream entertainment world.

In comedy, however, vaudeville houses and Broadway theatres presented a dilemma for black performers. The white audiences there were accustomed to seeing the familiar minstrel image, and white owners and producers ensured that they were not disappointed. So the performers who initially broke the color line here were forced to reflect the old stereotypes if they wanted to work. Yet, as "crossover" entertainers, their ascent was crucial to the evolution of black comedy and entertainment. Their capitulation to minstrel images should be weighed against the gains they made for black performers in the long run.

During the 1890s, vaudeville supplanted minstrelsy as America's major popular entertainment form. B. F. Keith opened the prototype for the new, respectable vaudeville theatre in Boston in 1882. In 1893, he leased the Union Square Theatre and established himself in New York City. Soon, he had developed a network of theatres from the East Coast to Chicago. The Keith Circuit worked in association with Martin Beck's Orpheum Circuit, which controlled major vaudeville houses west and south of Chicago. These well-organized circuits dominated vaudeville, although some independent theatres did book vaudeville acts.

From their inception the Keith and Orpheum circuits sought to define vaudeville in contrast to the rowdy, sometimes vulgar and salacious entertainment offered in minstrelsy and in variety houses. Keith demanded that the acts playing at his theatres conform to rigid controls. According to one contemporary journalist, "Every word that is spoken or sung, gestures, pantomime, costumes, everything that goes to make up an act, undergoes a censorship infinitely more rigid than exercised in any high priced 'legitimate' theatre." In fact, Keith's censuring of remarks and gestures that were even slightly off-color and his insistence upon consistently pristine humor lead some old variety comics to label vaudeville comedy "Keith's anemia."[25]

Keith had set out to create comfortable, spacious theatres, offering polite entertainment that would attract family audiences, and initially he did so. The Keith and Orpheum circuits offered popular music, comedy, and variety acts that drew an across-the-board audience which included women and children. Some independents strayed from this strict code, but by and large vaudeville theatres conformed to the ideal of polite entertainment and bright, clean accommodations that contrasted with the earthy atmosphere of most variety houses.

Under the control of the Keith and Orpheum circuits, big-time vaudeville flourished from the late 1890s through the early 1920s. In about 1935, however, succumbing to competition from network radio (1926) and sound films (1929), and the sale of the Keith-Orpheum Circuit to the Radio Corporation of America (the merger produced RKO) in the thirties, the vaudeville era came to an end.

Before its demise, vaudeville produced an illustrious group of entertainers: among them are Sarah Bernhardt, Charlie Chaplin, Will Rogers, Al Jolson, Ed Wynn, Eddie Cantor, Sophie Tucker, Jimmy Durante, W. C. Fields, Fred Allen, Mae West, Buster Keaton, Joe E. Brown, the Marx Brothers, James Cagney, Milton Berle, Jack Benny, Fred Astaire, and Bob Hope. Many of these performers would dominate show business until the second half of the twentieth century.

As the preponderance of comedians on this list suggests, comedy was one of the mainstays of vaudeville theatre. Comic routines that became classics of film, radio, and stage in the mid-twentieth century were developed there; they ranged from Charlie Chaplin's bizarre penguinlike strut and Groucho Marx's inimitable cigar-chomping leer to Milton Berle's quick-paced one-liners:

Girl: Why don't you kiss me the way you used to?

Berle: Why don't you wash your neck the way you used to? You have a face like a saint.

Girl: Like a saint?

Berle: Like a Saint Bernard!

But only the most celebrated and talented black performers initially had access to the big-time vaudeville circuits. Bert Williams, whom many consider the best comedian of all time, was one of the first. His talent and genius was recognized almost from the instant he and his partner George Walker arrived in New York. Walker's contribution was his radiant personality and exuberant interpretation of a new urban black style. His high-stepping dance routine was, according to critics, unmatched in its energy and flourish. And his portrayal of the conniving, fun-loving dandy—always tempting his partner with some outrageous get-rich-quick scheme—was perfect. He thrived on the part, bringing to it all of the nuance and flamboyance he observed in the black community that he so relished.

Williams had met Walker in San Francisco in 1893. They performed in traveling shows in the Midwest for a time, then one of the producers of Victor Herbert's *The Gold Bug* saw them at a small hotel in Indiana. He asked them to return to New York and join the show as a specialty act. Billing themselves as the "Two Real Coons," the team opened on Broadway in 1896. The show closed shortly afterward, so they turned to vaudeville and quickly became one of the most sought-after and popular acts on the circuit. It was in their vaudeville act at Koster and Bial's independent theatre that they popularized the cakewalk. By 1898, the team had left vaudeville for the legitimate theatre and musical comedy. But during their two years of vaudeville appearances Williams and Walker established themselves as one of the foremost comedy-dance acts in show business. Later, after George Walker's death, Williams would return to vaudeville briefly before becoming the star of the Ziegfeld *Follies*.

Late in his career, veteran minstrel performer Ernest Hogan also became a headline attraction on the vaudeville stage. After years of minstrelsy and appearances in such traveling shows as *Smart Set, Black Patti's Troubadours,* and his own independently produced shows, Hogan had convinced producers and critics that he was an exceptional comedian. He debuted on the Keith Circuit in the early 1900s. His most successful stint was in *Rufus Rastus,* which was produced in 1905.

Bill "Bojangles" Robinson also moved from minstrelsy and variety houses to independent vaudeville theatres and then to Keith's Union Square Theatre in the early 1900s. By the early twenties he had become a headliner at New York's Palace Theatre, where he is said to have introduced his trademark Staircase Dance routine.

The team of Bob Cole and J. Rosamond Johnson was also a headline act in vaudeville. Cole is justifiably better known for his work as a musician and composer than as a comedian, but he did establish himself as a formidable actor and comic. Early in his career he had developed an act that featured a comic monologue—rare for black comics until Bert Williams—in addition to his singing and guitar accompaniment. And by the late nineteenth century he had developed the tramp character that would become famous as Willie Wayside in *A Trip to Coontown* (1898), written and produced with his partner, Billy Johnson. After dissolving his partnership with Johnson in 1901, Cole teamed up with

J. R. Johnson, a talented pianist, singer, and composer. J. R. Johnson (not related to former partner Billy) was the brother of James Weldon Johnson, the lyricist, poet, author, and civil rights leader who became the head of the National Association for the Advancement of Colored People (NAACP).

By 1905, Cole and Johnson had become "the most popular song writing team in America." In 1906 they produced A Shoo-Fly Regiment, which opened in Washington, D.C., and, after touring the South, had a brief but undistinguished engagement at the Bijou Theatre on Broadway in 1907. A year later they produced The Red Moon, which ran successfully for one season on Broadway and another on the road. Neither of these shows was noted for their original comedy; instead, critics praised the rousing dancing and scintillating music. The two men wrote for many successful white musical comedies of the period and had an impressive list of hits: among them, "Under the Bamboo Tree" (which was based on the old spiritual "Nobody Knows the Trouble I've Seen"), "Didn't He Ramble," and "The Maiden with the Dreamy Eyes." Their popularity as songwriters led to vaudeville appearances on the Keith Circuit in which their music and Cole's comedy made them headline attractions. They left vaudeville to write and produce musical comedies in 1906, but after the closing of The Red Moon in 1910, returned for another successful tour. Cole's show business career ended shortly afterward when he had a nervous breakdown while performing in New York; months later (August 1911) he drowned while convalescing in the Catskills.[26]

These performers were among a few select black acts that headlined big-time vaudeville during its early years. Others were booked by smaller vaudeville circuits and independents, but bookings were scarce on the Keith-Orpheum bills. When they did occur, only one black act was permitted in a show. Managers feared that their white, family clientele, already anxious about the influx of blacks into urban areas, would react negatively. White performers complained about having to work with blacks, and if the black act was extraordinary—as was certainly the case with Williams and Walker—whites objected to following it on the bill. White blackface comedians also balked at appearing with traditional black minstrels such as Ernest Hogan and Tom McIntosh.

Despite this resistance, many headline black acts became established as vaudeville performers in later years—among them the former Our Gang child star Ernie "Sunshine" Morrison, and the teams of Flournoy Miller and Aubrey Lyles, and Eubie Blake and Noble Sissle.

After appearing in silent films from 1922 to 1924, Morrison at age ten left the *Our Gang* series when he was offered a three-year vaudeville contract. Billed as "Sunshine Sammy," he performed on stage into the 1930s. In the forties, he returned to the screen as Scruno in the *East Side Kids* series.

The most influential black comedy team early in the century was without doubt Flournoy Miller and Aubrey Lyles. Miller and Lyles began their careers as playwrights in Chicago in 1905, but by 1908 had created their own act. They starred in their own productions at Robert T. Motts's Pekin Theatre on Chicago's South Side and played so-called "black vaudeville" houses in the Midwest before coming to New York where, in 1910, they opened at the Hammerstein Victoria Theatre, an independent vaudeville house. They continued as vaudeville performers until they moved on to musical comedy in the 1915 production *Darkydom* and, later, as performer-producers in the ground-breaking 1921 black production, *Shuffle Along*.

Ragtime pianist Eubie Blake and singer-lyricist Noble Sissle worked the Keith-Orpheum Circuit in the late teens, then, in 1920, joined Miller and Lyles to write the music for *Shuffle Along*. While in vaudeville, they billed themselves as "the Dixie Duo"; they were one of the most acclaimed acts on the circuit. Their act featured Blake's superb ragtime piano playing and Sissle's singing; unlike almost all other black vaudeville performers, they did not work in blackface. Along with Cole and Miller, they were also immensely successful as songwriters, producing tunes for such vaudeville stars as Sophie Tucker. Eubie Blake's career extended until the 1970s, when he was "rediscovered" and through television talk shows was introduced to a generation that was largely unfamiliar with ragtime or the hit black musical *Shuffle Along*.

Black shows broke the color line on Broadway a few years after Bert Williams's debut in vaudeville. Three months after *A Trip to Coontown* debuted off Broadway in 1898, another black show, *Clorindy; or, the Origin of the Cakewalk*, opened at the Casino Roof Garden—on Broadway.

The show was written by Will Marion Cook (an outstanding composer as well as an acclaimed violinist and bandleader) and the famed black poet Paul Laurence Dunbar. It was hailed for its ragtime rhythms and powerful chorale works, but, predictably, also featured comic songs like "Who Dat Say Chicken in Dis Crowd?" delivered by the show's star comedian, Ernest Hogan. Later, Cook would write of the success of the show: "Negroes were at last on Broadway, and there to stay.

Gone was the uff-dah of the minstrel! Gone the Massa Linkum stuff! . . . Nothing could stop us, and nothing did for a decade."[27]

In fact, although the "Massa Linkum" stuff was far from gone, black musical comedies were to have immense influence on the Broadway stage for more than a decade. The primary reason for that impact was the entry of Bert Williams and George Walker into the musical comedy field.

After the success of Bob Cole and Will Marion Cook in 1898, Williams and Walker formed a black production company and made their first musical comedy appearances in *A Lucky Coon* and *Senegambian Carnival*. Those shows and their next effort—*The Policy Players* (1900) —were only mildly successful.

But in 1902 they produced *In Dahomey*, which opened at the New York Theatre on Broadway after receiving outstanding reviews on the road. The show set out to celebrate African aspects of black American culture. In reality, it was a simple farce about African recolonization in which Williams (Shylock Homestead) is duped into posing as a detective and helping Walker (Rareback Pinkerton) attempt to con a rich southerner into financing the back-to-Africa scheme. New York critics raved. After a European tour in 1903, the show was taken on the road in the United States and toured successfully for two more years.

In 1906, Williams and Walker produced their most extravagant show, *Abyssinia*, which had an elaborately staged African setting that included live camels. Following their usual pattern, Walker was featured as a flashy dandy and Williams as a bedraggled, inept bumpkin. It was here that Williams introduced the hit song, "Nobody" (music by Williams and lyrics by Alex Rogers). The show opened at the Majestic Theatre and was greeted with critical acclaim.

Bandana Land, their next venture, opened in 1908 and was their biggest hit, despite a controversial storyline: it was one of the first major theatrical productions in which a black trickster engaged a white adversary and won out. "For the most part, white managers have kept their hands off this time," a critic for the *Brooklyn Eagle* observed; "it is genuine and honest and—what matters most for the audience—it is so funny that you will laugh yourself tired. . . . Anyone who loves laughter but stays away from 'Bandana Land' in fear that it is an ordinary rough and tumble 'darky show' will make an unfortunate mistake."[28]

Like the two previous works, the book was written by the actor and playwright Jesse Shipp. It was a satire on black life in the South that revolved around the adventures of a black couple who form a corporation and buy land in a white neighborhood; after moving in, the pair throw wild parties so that whites will buy the property back at inflated prices. The highlights were Will Marion Cook's syncopated music, Walker's inimitable cakewalk, and the introduction of Williams's classic poker game routine, in which he mimes a lone individual playing poker with a group of imaginary friends. That routine, along with his forlorn rendition of "Nobody," would become Williams's comic staples. The success of the Williams and Walker productions significantly influenced black performers' acceptance on Broadway and the vaudeville stage.

But the deaths of Bob Cole and George Walker in 1911, along with the loss of Ernest Hogan (who had died in 1909 after collapsing during a performance of his new show *The Oyster Man*), contributed heavily to the decline of black musical comedies during the next decade.

The years from 1890 to 1921 were a roller-coaster era for black performers: a golden age from 1890 to 1910, a virtual washout from 1911 to 1920, and a revival in 1921. Yet throughout these vacillations, diluted forms of black dance and music made significant inroads into popular entertainment. After 1921, black-inspired dances would again become the dominant force at social gatherings as well as in most popular musical reviews. Although black musical comedies disappeared from Broadway stages for more than a decade after the closing of *Mr. Lode of Koal* (1909) and *The Red Moon* (1910), black producers were visibly active beyond "the Great White Way." For instance, J. Homer Tutt and his brother Salem Tutt Whitney (who helped create the *Silas Green from New Orleans* road show) produced, directed, and wrote sixteen musical comedies during that period. In 1915, *Darkydom* (produced by Lester Walton and written by Jesse Shipp and James R. Europe) opened at the Howard Theatre in Washington, D.C., and later that year, played at Harlem's Lafayette Theatre; the show starred the fast-rising comedy team of Flournoy Miller and Aubrey Lyles, and was touted as the best black musical comedy since *Bandana Land* by some critics. That same year, Flournoy's brother Irvin C. Miller produced *Broadway Rastus*, which opened in Atlantic City and featured the music of W. C. Handy. These shows, like numerous other all-black-cast musicals produced during the period, played primarily at black-owned theatres such as Robert T. Motts's Pekin in Chicago, or in houses like the Lafayette and Lincoln in Harlem, which welcomed black patrons.

It was not until 1921 that black musical comedy returned to Broadway. The show that ended the hiatus was based on *The Mayor of Dixie*, a successful comedy that Flournoy Miller and Aubrey Lyles had created and starred in at Motts's Pekin Theatre in 1907. As *Shuffle Along*, the show opened at the Sixty-Third Street Theatre on May 23, 1921. Within weeks it was the sensation of New York, ushering in a new era of successful black musicals on Broadway and establishing the prototype for the shows that would follow.

Raising money had been difficult since most whites doubted that a new black musical could attract white audiences. So at the outset, Lyles and Miller were forced to underwrite most of the expenses themselves. The show worked on a shoestring budget as it previewed in black areas outside New York. Although this was a hardship for the creative team, it paid off in other ways. Lacking the backing and consequent interference of white financiers during the formative stages, few concessions were made to white tastes in either music or dance.

In order to expand their original show, Miller and Lyles had sought out Eubie Blake and Noble Sissle. In addition they expanded the chorus line, presenting a group of glamorous women who, unlike the chorus girls in white shows, actually danced instead of simply standing on display. In fact, Josephine Baker's comic antics (clowning, stumbling, rolling her eyes) on the end of the chorus line not only made her a featured attraction and instant star but set the precedent for end-line humor in chorus lines. The music and dance, heavily steeped in the tradition of black variety houses, astounded Broadway audiences, and critics raved. Langston Hughes described it as "Swift, bright, funny, rollicking, and gay, with a dozen danceable, singable tunes." [29]

Blake's ragtime-oriented rhythms, less diluted than most Tin Pan Alley rags, provided a lively, pulsating beat that consistently fired the musical numbers and, along with Sissle's lyrics, produced a score of memorable hit tunes, among them "Shuffle Along," "If You've Never Vamped a Brownskin Vamp, Then You've Never Vamped at All," "Love Will Find a Way," "In Honeysuckle Time," "Gypsy Blues," "Bandana Days," and "I'm Just Wild About Harry," which resurfaced as a hit tune when Harry Truman used it as a campaign song during the 1948 presidential elections.

The dance numbers featured routines that, although familiar on the black variety theatre circuit, were new to most white patrons. The soft shoe, acrobatics, time steps, rapid-fire tap dancing, shimmies, the Buck and Wing, and the Texas Tommy were all performed with an energy and style that had seldom, if ever, been seen on Broadway.

"Every sinew in their bodies danced," one critic wrote. "Every tendon in their frames responded to their extreme energy. They revelled in their work; they simply pulsed with it, and there was no let-up at all." *The New York Herald Tribune* critic echoed those sentiments in even more hyperbolic fashion:

> It is when the chorus and the principals of a company that is said to contain the best negro troupers in these parts gets going in the dances that the world seems a brighter place to live in. They wriggle and shimmy in a fashion to outdo a congress of eels, and they fling their limbs about without stopping to make sure that they are securely fastened on.
>
> They plead justification for their wild, Corybantic revellings, for Noble Sissle wrote music that is an aggravation for sore feet. . . .[30]

It was clearly the energy and fresh style of the dancing and music that made *Shuffle Along* such a successful and extraordinary show. The plot remained essentially the same as the original *Mayor of Dixie*, involving two friends who are running for mayor of a small town. The humor—as was common in most Miller and Lyles shows—was closely associated with traditional minstrel comedy. Inept, stereotyped black-faced characters presented the familiar verbal misuses and performed familiar coon antics. For instance, one mayoral candidate is told that the other has stopped stealing chickens. "Oh yeah," he replies. "When did he die?" The brightest comedy spot was the introduction of a blackboard math routine ("mulsifying" and "revision"), in which Miller attempts to prove to Lyles that seven goes into thirteen twenty-eight times. This bit became a comic staple and variants would be seen later in the acts of mainstream comedians such as Abbott and Costello and of black impersonators Gosden and Correll as Amos and Andy.

Despite the overall routine comedy, *Shuffle Along* was a milestone production. Its unprecedented success opened the gates for the raft of black musicals that were produced during the twenties and thirties. Moreover, it presented songs and dance routines that are still being copied on the Broadway stage. And not least of its accomplishments, it featured performers such as Florence Mills and Josephine Baker, who became entertainment legends.

During the "Roaring Twenties," the Charleston and other new dances rooted in black culture—along with those introduced in *Shuffle Along*—swept the country and dominated Broadway theatre. By 1921, syncopated music and ragtime were the accepted staples of Tin Pan Alley; in the "Jazz Age," blues and jazz seized an even more steadfast grasp on America's popular musical tastes. As the 1922 song intoned, in terms of music and dance it was, indeed, "getting very dark on old Broadway" and, for that matter, in most other areas of the popular entertainment world.

By contrast, the authentic folk humor of blacks—much, much too revealing about real attitudes toward American bigotry to be accepted by whites at the turn of the century—would remain far from the public eye. Despite the triumphs of early black comics, the private humor of blacks, like the hero of Ralph Ellison's novel *Invisible Man,* would thrive underground, as it were, ensconced in all-black barber shops, honky-tonks, house parties, and, in a less assertive form, in the acts of comedians performing before all-black audiences on the black theatre circuit for more than forty years.

III

The comedy that surfaced in black road and tent shows, variety shows, vaudeville acts, and musical comedies during the 1890s and early twentieth century was generally indistinguishable from the minstrel comedy that preceded it—at least with regard to its *spoken* component. Nearly all the eminent comics of the period began their careers in minstrelsy, and that training, combined with pressure from producers and mostly white audiences to stick with the familiar, undoubtedly dictated the verbal thrust of their humor. But a careful reading of descriptions of their work suggests that—despite the blackface makeup, splintered dialect, and ludicrous costumes—a subtle change *was* occurring. Ernest Hogan, Bob Cole, Flournoy Miller and Aubrey Lyles, and Bert Williams and George Walker, the leading black comics of the time, in varying degrees seem to have added an almost imperceptible nuance to their acts: a distinctly black physical style that set them apart from vaudeville's white minstrels and blackface imitators. Gradually they began moving away from the antic, wildly exaggerated caricature of black physical movement typical of white blackface acts, to a less frenetic form of bodily expression that, while not losing its flair, was by comparison "cooler" and, at the same time, more realistically mirrored actual black behavior. Not coincidentally, it was in the routines of Williams and Walker that this change was most dramatically seen.

Unfortunately, only the routines of Williams and Flournoy Miller were filmed—and Williams's original routines are only available in two short vignettes, *Fish* and *A Natural Born Gambler.* Still, Williams's partner, George Walker, alluded to the emerging stylistic difference between black and white performers a few years before his death in 1911. "The one hope of the colored performer must be in making a radical departure from the old 'darky' *style* [italics mine] of singing and dancing," he said. "There is an artistic side to the black race, and if it could be properly developed on stage, I believe the theatregoing public would profit much by it. . . . My idea was always to impersonate my race just as they are. The colored man has never successfully taken off his own humorous characteristics, and the white impersonator often overdoes the matter."[31]

Despite Walker's tacit reaffirmation of an old stereotype—blacks as naturally humorous—his remarks pinpoint the physical style of black culture as a key ingredient in African-American humor. Style, however, is an elusive concept. Some regard it simply as flair or embellishment, as in, say, the spectacular manner in which Julius Erving (Dr. J) or Michael "Air" Jordan have performed on the basketball court. But, in fact, an austere, unadorned approach also represents a definite style, although not a highly esteemed one in black communities. For example, as a basketball player, Boston Celtic Larry Bird was not without style; the style he reflected was simply less consciously elegant. It was exemplary of a mainstream no-frills attitude that—until the 1980s, at least—typically decried excess and panache for its own sake.

Conversely, in black communities, assertiveness, flamboyance, and grace are extolled. From Willie Mays's basket catches, Muhammad Ali's shuffle and ringside theatrics, and the swooping slam dunks of Dr. J and Michael Jordan, to Duke Ellington's cool, elegant understatement, Miles Davis's cantankerous aloofness, soul singer James Brown's earthy exuberance, or nineties' rappers' in-your-face gesticulations, black performers have usually displayed a practiced self-assurance and stylishness that reflects the community's regard for *high* style.

In *Black and White Styles in Conflict*, Thomas Kochman defines style as an "attitude that individuals within a culture express through their choice of cultural forms . . . and the way they choose to express themselves within a form." Loosely, then, it is the external manifestation of an inner attitude that shapes what individuals do and how they do it. Moreover, it determines the manner in which they perform everything from such ordinary tasks as talking, walking, or eating, to more elaborate endeavors such as athletics and the performing arts.[32]

Among most urban blacks, establishing a distinctive personal style was a central part of their daily lives. The crippled stable groom from whom Thomas D. Rice appropriated his famous Jim Crow song and dance was *working*—not entertaining an audience. Then as now, one's walk and "rap," one's manner of moving and dressing, often determined status in black communities. Black teenagers do not simply walk down the street, they move rhythmically—bopping, swaggering, strutting. Their stride is a signature, a syncopated choreography in which head, shoulders, and limbs work in fluid harmony with one another. As Kochman points out: "black style is more self-conscious, more expressive, more expansive, more colorful, more intense, more assertive, more aggressive, and more focused on the individual than is the style of the larger society in which blacks are part."[33]

For black entertainers, the element of style was and remains even more important. In a community where practically everyone consciously cultivates flair in some form, any pretense to eminence requires that one demonstrate at least a minimal amount of individual flourish. Talent alone is usually not enough; that intangible element, stylistic flair, is demanded. *It ain't what you do; it's the way you do it* is not merely an old blues lyric, it is an axiom in the black community.

But minstrelsy established a parody of African-American style. Black entertainers had to excise this comic exaggeration and restore grace and elegance. And that is precisely what Williams and Walker and, to some extent, other black entertainers achieved during the early twentieth century.

Compare, for instance, Charles Dickens's description of the dancing of "Juba" Lane (page 108) with the description of Walker's cakewalk on pages 143–44. Despite his agility and the innovative nature of some of his steps, Lane, according to Dickens's report, moved with the same wild, frenetic verve that characterized nearly all minstrel dance. Humor and ridicule was the desired effect; therefore Lane aimed at giving the impression of being out of control and looking foolish even as he demonstrated the most difficult dance steps.

Walker, on the other hand, was intent on displaying black style even as he worked for laughs. His cakewalk is described in terms of "airiness," "jauntiness," and "grace," despite the humorous intent. The effect, aside from Walker's individual talent, was due largely to the imposition of black style onto the act. Few would argue that Walker was Lane's equal as a dancer, yet Walker had added an intangible quality of style and flourish that set his routine apart.

In addition, black comedians turned to their own folk roots to add another dimension to their stage humor. They clearly began investing their acts with motifs derived from the trickster tales that dominated slave humor. Not that the trickster theme was exclusive to Africans or African-Americans. Occasionally, it was even used in minstrelsy, when black-faced actors portraying illiterate black characters were seen pontificating on weighty subjects such as politics or philosophy.

But the traditional trickster theme—an essential ingredient in both the slaves' animal stories and the John and Ole Massa tales—was usually avoided in minstrel humor. In minstrelsy, as we have seen, the black-faced trickster was both the vehicle for the humor and the butt of the joke. A new, denigrative twist had been added. The black trickster as portrayed by whites did not demonstrate commonsense and homespun wisdom to satirize the pretenses of the elite as did the Yankee and Frontier types. Instead, he was himself the object of derision —that is, the humor was derived from the trickster's untutored and unerringly abortive attempts to understand or explain some platitude considered beyond his conception or, more pointedly, to outsmart a presumed white character. (The interchange between Moran and Mack on page 170 is an example of the reversal of the trickster motif as used by whites in minstrel comedy.)

Around the turn of the century, however, black comedians began portraying a type that more validly reflected the intent of traditional black tricksters. Once recast in an image reflecting more authentic black style and less blatant buffoonery and ineptitude, the stage dandy took on many traditional characteristics. Initially, however, the comic stage version seldom approached the pointed satire found in the Brer Rabbit stories and hardly ever reflected the cynicism and obvious disdain for white authority found in trickster folktales. There were exceptions, such as Williams and Walker's *Bandana Land*, but mainstream audiences would have to wait nearly half a century before that aspect of the black comic sensibility was fully unleashed in the routines of Redd Foxx, Moms Mabley, Dick Gregory, Flip Wilson, and Richard Pryor.

Instead, in the early appearances, the black stage trickster's adversary was usually another black character. Sometimes the schemes were successful; most often they failed—reflecting what folklorist Charles Joyner calls the "trickster out-tricked" motif.

Williams and Walker and Miller and Lyles introduced comedy acts based on the interaction between a conniving, unscrupulous, and fast-talking trickster and his gullible, apparently slow-witted friend. In their routines, the trickster-dandy's schemes occasionally worked out so that the pair successfully duped an adversary. But, since both comedy teams worked primarily before white audiences, more often the scheme back-fired, and the trickster and his friend were discovered and reprimanded. Even more frequently—in an obvious turn on the trickster out-tricked gambit—the trickster's attempt to inveigle his gullible sidekick back-fired and he was embarrassed or humiliated.

Of the leading comedians, Ernest Hogan altered his comic routine less than others. A venerable minstrel performer, Hogan often seemed more intent on exploiting the minstrel coon image than changing it. As a composer, he defended calling his most popular song "All Coons Look Alike to Me" until just before his death, when he admitted that he regretted the "Coon" reference. Even though he moved from min-strelsy to road shows and, finally, to black musicals and vaudeville, his comic routines remained consistently mired in the Southern plantation buffoonery on which his popularity was originally established.

Still, the Harlem Renaissance novelist Jessie Fauset credits Hogan with a subtle alteration of minstrelsy's stage Negro. Hogan "changed the tradition of the merely funny, rather silly 'end-man' into a character with a definite plot in a rather loosely constructed but none the less well-outlined story," she wrote in 1925. "A little of the hard luck of the Negro began to creep in. If he was a buffoon, he was a buffoon wearing his rue. A slight, very slight quality of the Harlequin began to attach to him. He was the clown making light of his troubles, but he was a wounded, a sorely beset clown." Perhaps—but if so, the transition was slight indeed. A bit in which he pantomimed eating a watermelon with slavering delight while the band played "Watermelon Time" was fea-tured in his act to the end of his career. As one critic noted, too harshly perhaps, Hogan "pushed the darky characterization to the limits of unction and denigration."[34]

As a comedian, Hogan compares with minstrel performers such as Billy Kersands and Tom McIntosh more than with Bob Cole and Bert Williams. Hogan's greatest comic success was in the musical *Rufus Rastus*, but even there it was the first-act minstrel routine that critics praised. Like Kersands and McIntosh, Hogan seems to have reacted to the minstrel parody of blacks by exaggerating and satirizing it; he made the white minstrel parody even more ridiculous and, thereby, in an ironic way, confirmed its absolute idiocy. But this subtle twist went unnoticed by most; for mainstream America, Hogan's act only con-firmed blacks' presumed connection with the stage Negro. Hogan did, however, help establish the prototype for the kind of broad, quintessentially low humor that—when stripped of its plantation overtones and given an urban, trickster flavor by comics such as Flournoy Miller and Tim Moore—became a staple of the black theatre circuit after 1920.

Bob Cole's character, Willie Wayside, like other tramp and drunken characters created by black comics of the period, slyly shifted the emphasis from the character's ethnic background to a conspicuous social problem. (Tom McIntosh, generally a traditional black-faced minstrel comic, also did a drunk routine in red-nosed makeup that occasionally allowed him to escape the confines of coonism.) Cole—whose father was a prominent local politician in Atlanta, Georgia, during the Reconstruction era—had attended college before striking out on his own as a musician, and his education partially accounts for the absence of the standard coon humor in his early comedy routines and his vaudeville act. As a monologist, he often toned down the fractured English that characterized much low comedy. In *Black Manhattan* (1930), James Weldon Johnson reaffirmed Cole's status among early black performers, calling him "the greatest single force in the middle period of the development of the Negro in the American theatre. . . . He was the most versatile theatrical man the Negro has yet produced: a good singer and an excellent dancer, and able to play several musical instruments. He could write a dramatic or musical play—dialogue, lyrics, and music—stage the play, and act a part. In his role as a tramp he received the highest praise of the critics." Cole died in 1931, and none of his work is currently available on film; but he remains one of the first black comedians who significantly, if subtly, altered traditional plantation humor on stage.[35]

As writers and performers, Flournoy Miller and Aubrey Lyles were primary forces in shaping the new urban black comic style. This new style was perhaps best typified later by the broad, audacious humor and flamboyance of Kingfish as portrayed by Tim Moore on the *Amos 'n' Andy* television show in the fifties—a show for which Flournoy Miller wrote. With Hollywood's Sambo-servant, popularized through the performances of Stepin Fetchit in the twenties and thirties, and the perennial black maid-cum-earth mammy, this urban black common man would dominate black public humor until the 1960s.

In 1908, Miller and Lyles began experimenting with two characters who, although similar to the familiar minstrel stereotype, had an assertiveness, an urban flair, and just enough trickster's cunning to set them apart. The pair appeared in several of Miller and Lyles's early musicals and were popularized when they appeared as comic leads in *Shuffle*

Along. In that show, however, perhaps as a concession to the largely white audience expected on Broadway, they were played primarily as stereotypical minstrel buffoons.

Shortly afterward, two white minstrel performers, Moran and Mack, billing themselves as "The Two Black Crows," became immensely popular. They were stars of vaudeville in the twenties and thirties, and were also featured in films and on radio. Both the characters and the dialect in their act were remarkably similar to the Miller and Lyles routine.

> *Moran:* Dat's a fine pair o' shoes youse wearin' dere, my frien'.
>
> *Mack:* Yeh, I done cheated the store man out of dem.
>
> *Moran:* How come? I seen you give him de check. Ain't the check no good, nohow?
>
> *Mack:* Sure de check is got money behind it in de bank, but dat man he can't cash it.
>
> *Moran:* He can, too, I saw you sign it.
>
> *Mack:* Sure I signed it, big boy, but wait till dat man git to de bank. I didn't fill in the amount.

In fact, the similarity between the two sets of characters has led to claims and counterclaims as to who created them first. The controversy deepens because early twentieth-century literary humorists used similar dialect comedy, and the popular twenties radio show, *Amos 'n' Andy*, also featured lines such as, "I'se regusted," and, "It all repends on de sitchi-ation yo is in," which were common in the routines of both teams.

What is clear is that Miller and Lyles were experimenting with an urban black persona that differed ever so slightly—although not nearly enough for most middle-class black critics—from the familiar plantation coon figure in both style, assertiveness, and its authentic connection to black folklore. Their presentation of the type, if not assuredly their creation of it, influenced comedy on the black theatre circuit for decades. Unfortunately, the proliferation of this comic figure on stage, screen, radio, and television provoked a dispute between black spokesmen and white producers, as well as among blacks themselves, that would simmer for years before erupting into the public controversy that saw the *Amos 'n' Andy* television show withdrawn from network airing in the fifties.

Neither Miller nor Lyles sang or danced, so their stage act consisted primarily of conversation between the two characters: Lyles, as the smaller, feistier, but more gullible one; Miller, as the scheming city slicker who towered over his partner. In their vaudeville act, unlike *Shuffle Along*, they often avoided exaggerated minstrel coonery, using these characters to introduce routines that quickly became comic staples among black and white performers.

Their usual stage interaction involved Lyles's character getting himself into situations that required courage and action far beyond his capabilities. His portrayal of the fiery, boastful little man who inevitably gets in over his head was the team's comic mainstay. From that they evolved one of their most acclaimed routines: an acrobatic prizefighting bit in which Lyles takes the challenge of facing down his much larger partner as far as he dares before wisely fleeing. This "pugilistic travesty," according to Henry Sampson, "became a classic on the American stage."[36]

Their most famous and most imitated routine was the "Indefinite Talk" bit, introduced into their vaudeville act in the mid-twenties. The setup is simple: Two characters begin talking to one another, but before either can finish a sentence, he is interrupted by the other. Variations on this routine are infinite, since the content of the dialogue is secondary to the comedians' timing and facial expressions. But performed with accurate timing, the routine remains a hilarious comic set piece; among black audiences it is as famous as Abbott and Costello's "Who's on First?" bit. The following examples are from live performances by Nipsey Russell and Mantan Moreland (a former partner of Miller's who made the routine a specialty in his own act) at the Apollo Theatre in the fifties, so the language is not as fractured as it may have been when Miller and Lyles first performed the skit in the twenties:

NR: Who he goin marry?

MM: He goin marry the daughter of Mr. . . .

NR: That's a nice girl. Lemme tell you, I heard once . . .

MM: Naw, that was her sister. I'm keepin company with her.

NR: You are?

MM: Oh yeah, I been with her now every since . . .

NR: I didn't know you knew her that long.

MM:　Sure!

NR:　And I thought all the time she was . . .

MM:　She was! But she cut him out.

NR:　Well, you know, I was talkin to her father the other day and the first thing . . .

MM:　That was yo fault. What you shoulda done was . . .

NR:　I did!

Or again:

MM:　How come you can't pay me now?

NR:　Horse races.

MM:　What track you play at?

NR:　I play over there at . . .

MM:　That track's crooked. Why don't you play over here around . . .

NR:　That's where I lost my money!

MM:　Yeah! How much did you lose?

NR:　I lost about . . .

MM:　You didn't have that much!

NR:　Naw?

MM:　No. All you had was about . . .

NR:　I had more than that.

MM:　Really!

NR:　Yeah, and you know what, I bet on a horse and that rascal didn't come in until . . .

MM:　Was he that far behind?

NR:　Yeah!

MM:　Who was the jockey ridin' him?

NR: A jockey by the name of . . .

MM: He can't ride! I thought he went out there to ride for . . .

NR: He did! But they fired him. He came on back . . .

MM: Oh yeah.

In their writing as well as their performance of the prizefighting routine, the "Indefinite Talk" bit, and perhaps above all in what they called "mutilatin' " the language ("You gotta be repaired for that," or, "I's regusted"), Miller and Lyles exacted more influence on the transition of black American stage humor than any other performers in the early twentieth century.

Their so-called "mutilatin' " of standard English replaced the imbecilic minstrel patter that previously had been the accepted comic imitation of black speech. It did not assuage middle-class critics like W. E. B. Du Bois, but it was more closely aligned with the way the average uneducated black person spoke, and it represented a gigantic step toward a more respectable comic image. Miller's portrait of the city slicker added nuances of authenticity to minstrelsy's old Jim Dandy caricature by placing him in the context of the traditional black trickster and altering his physical presentation in terms of gestures, attire, and manner of speech. In fact, Miller's intonation, which was closely replicated by Tim Moore as Kingfish, became the accepted way of affecting black dialect by white and black comedians until the sixties. And many white comedians—Robin Williams, for instance—still use an approximation of Miller's intonation when imitating blacks.

Miller and Lyles continued writing and appearing in musical comedies and vaudeville throughout the twenties. When Aubrey Lyles died in 1932, Miller alternately teamed with Mantan Moreland (best known as the chauffeur and sidekick in the Charlie Chan film series) and Johnny Lee (who played Calhoun on the *Amos 'n' Andy Show*) and continued his stage career. In the late thirties, he moved to the West Coast, where he wrote and starred in numerous Hollywood and independently produced black films. In the forties, he worked as a writer for the *Amos 'n' Andy Show;* when the television version was produced in 1951, he was instrumental in placing Tim Moore and his former partner, Johnny Lee, in key roles.

Miller died in 1971, but his seminal position in the evolution of black American stage humor is assured and his contributions are still being felt. He not only fought for and insisted upon dignified treatment of black performers but created "some of the funniest comedy sketches ever written or spoken."[37]

The character portrayed by George Walker was similar to Flournoy Miller's trickster character and Tim Moore's portrayal of Kingfish on the *Amos 'n' Andy* television show in the 1950s. Although Walker could not match the pure comic talent of Miller or Moore, he exceeded both in other ways. To conceive of Walker's effect, one must imagine Flournoy Miller or Kingfish with an added dimension—the silken smoothness of a Fred Astaire or, more precisely, the grace and elegance of John Bubbles, the unparalleled black dancer who played the role of Sportin' Life in George Gershwin's *Porgy and Bess* (1935).

The enthusiasm and flashy demeanor that Walker displayed on stage apparently reflected his personality away from the theatre. Although he was the business mind behind the success of the Williams and Walker team, as well as a serious proponent of equal rights for blacks, Walker demonstrated the same zest and fun-loving nature in his personal life as he projected on stage. He enjoyed the wealth and acclaim to the full —often to the point of ostentation. He lived with the same verve with which he performed, relishing the adoration of the black community and generally ignoring the cold reception he experienced in the white world when the footlights dimmed.

Bert Williams's portrayal of the ignorant darky on stage, on the other hand, was in complete contrast to his personal life. Williams was born in the Bahamas in 1876; his parents moved to the United States shortly afterward and he grew up in Riverside, California, where he graduated from high school. The African-American slave dialect that he used in his act was methodically practiced ("Don't loaf 'round de corners an' pend on de Lord fuh yo' daily bread. De Lord ain't running no bakery"), as was the shuffling, slow-witted demeanor that his darky character projected. "I must study his movements," Williams said of the character. "He is not me."[38]

In fact, Williams was a shy, almost obsessively sensitive man, who spent his spare time reading Nietzsche and Mark Twain. The shiftless, black-faced darky he portrayed with such perfection was entirely a stage creation. And the contradiction between the character he was forced to play in the theatre and his true nature largely accounts for the torment and aura of tragedy that marked his life.

W. C. Fields, a vaudeville contemporary of Williams, called him a "super-sensitive soul," and, summing up the relationship between

Williams's art and his life, said, "Bert Williams . . . is the funniest man I ever saw and the saddest man I ever knew."[39]

Much of that sadness derived from Williams's inability to adjust to the bias and consequent humiliations he faced as a black man in America despite his stature as an entertainer. He occasionally told a story about two black comedians traveling in the South who were confronted by a group of less than hospitable whites in a small town. The local inhabitants took exception to the dapper manner in which the entertainers were dressed; after a short interrogation, they decided to relieve the performers of their expensive attire. Forcing them to strip and giving them burlap sacks, they ran them out of town. The unfortunate comedians, it turns out, were Williams and his partner George Walker, who were on their way to New York.

The contradiction between being idolized on stage and scorned outside the theatre nagged Williams throughout his life. The despair was such that toward the end of his career he noticeably soured and began drinking heavily. But the agony of his personal life apparently did not affect his performances on stage. In his later years he became an even more consummate comedian.

Initially, Williams was confined to the role of a shiftless darky playing against Walker's prancing dandy. The tension and humor of their act flowed from the contrast—Williams's slow, cumbersome movement and speech set against Walker's radiance, agility, and silver-tongued connivance. With Walker on stage, every move Williams made was magnified and intensified; his dim-witted darky literally wrenched laughter from the audience by the force of his inertia. In essence, he was playing a character that Stepin Fetchit, with much less finesse and insight, would mythify through his broader exposure in films during the twenties and thirties. It was a standard caricature, distinguished only by the nuance and depth that Williams brought to the portrayal.

Williams would come onto the stage in tattered clothes, shambling, ill at ease, a forlorn, wide-eyed expression on his face, which was corked to appear much darker than Walker's. Playing energy and intensity against laggardness, they would usually begin some routine patter in a dialect that was noticeably less fractured than that of Miller and Lyles or white minstrels such as Moran and Mack. Inevitably, Walker preyed on Williams's naïveté and supposed ignorance:

Walker: I tells you I'm lettin' you in on this 'cause you're a friend
             of mine. I could do this alone . . . but I wants you to

share in it 'cause we's friends. Now after you gets into the bank you fill the satchel with money.

Williams: Whose money?

Walker: That ain't the point. We don't know who put the money in there, and we don't know why they got it. And they won't know why we got it. All you have to do is put the money in the satchel. I'll get you the satchel—ain't nothin' to bother 'bout—that's 'cause you're a friend of mine, see.

Williams: And what do I do with dis satchel?

Walker: All you got to do is bring it to me at the place where I tells you.

Williams: When they come to count up the cash and finds it short, then what?

Walker: By that time we'll be far, far away—where the birds is singin' and the flowers is in bloom.

Williams: And if they catch us they'll put us so far, far away we never will hear no birds singin'. Everybody knows you can't smell no flowers through a stone wall.[40]

This type of interchange might be followed by Williams singing one of the songs that made him famous, "Nobody" or "Jonah Man": "My luck started when I was born/ Leas' so the old folks say./ Dat same hard luck's been my best friend/ To dis very day." Invariably, the act would end with the cakewalk, in which Walker's grace and vitality was the perfect foil for Williams's dawdling, hesitant maneuvers. In content, the act was not innovative. But Walker's flourish and Williams's genius for understatement and for projecting the feelings of the perennial underdog gave their routine a dimension that no other comedy team working similar material could match.

Bandana Land was the last of the Williams and Walker musicals. George Walker became seriously ill during the run and was forced to seek convalescence at a health resort. He died in 1911 at the age of thirty-seven.

Williams sought no permanent replacement for his partner. He produced one more Broadway show, *Mr. Lode of Koal*, which opened in

1909 and closed in December of the same year. For the remainder of his career he performed primarily as a single act in vaudeville and the Ziegfeld *Follies*.

Without Walker, Williams was forced to dig even deeper to project the pathos and humor of his character. "All the jokes in the world are based on a few elemental ideas, and this is one of them. The sight of other people in trouble is nearly always funny," he wrote in 1918. "I am the 'Jonah Man,' the man who, even if it rained soup, would be found with a fork in his hand and no spoon in sight, the man whose fighting relatives come to visit him and whose head is always dented by the furniture they throw at each other." Williams took this elemental aspect of humor and studied it, polishing and molding it until he was able to transcend the shiftless caricature through which his humor emerged.[41]

Being black in America, as Williams said, was inconvenient. So much so that when Florenz Ziegfeld first proposed that Williams join the *Follies*, most of the white performers threatened to quit or boycott the show. Ziegfeld resisted their demands and, out of loyalty, Williams remained even though he could have made twice as much money in vaudeville. Still, in his contract with Ziegfeld, he insisted on a clause stipulating that no female performers would appear on stage with him. He did not want to incite audiences with even the hint of fraternization with a white female entertainer. In return, Ziegfeld agreed that the *Follies* would make no Southern tour when Williams was performing.

On one occasion, in 1919, Williams went to the theatre and began his usual routine of dressing and applying makeup. When he left his dressing room, however, he found the stage dim and the theatre empty. A strike had been called by Actors' Equity but no one had bothered to tell him; even though he was the star of the Ziegfeld *Follies*, he was barred from the union.

Williams's act consisted of songs, stories, and, most importantly, pantomime. Most of the songs, like "Nobody" and "Jonah Man," had been part of his routine with Walker; but many of the stories and the pantomime routines were created for his single act.

His ghost stories were particularly poignant because they frequently incorporated a subtle common-sense factor that was missing in most "scary nigger" tales. In one he told of having to cross a graveyard to get home one night. Seeing a ghost, he started running; when he got to the street, he looked around and, not seeing anything following him, sat down on the curb. But a moment later he sees something out of the corner of his eye and turns to find the ghost sitting next to him. "The ghost says: 'That was a fine run we had. It was the best running I ever saw.' I says: 'Yes, and soon as I get my breath you're going to see some more.'"

Williams's anecdotes sometimes echoed standard vaudeville humor or turned on the stage Negro's ignorance:

When an old lady is unjured in a railway accident, someone urges her to sue for damages.

"Lord knows I done got enough damages," she said. "What I'm gwine sue fuh is repairs."

Or:

After looking up and down the bill of fare without enthusiasm, a guest finally decides on a dozen fried oysters.

The colored waiter became all apologies.

"I'se ve'y sorry, suh, ve'y sorry, but we's all out uv *all* shell fish —'ceptin' aiges."

More often, however, he transcended those limitations, venturing into the kind of wit for which Will Rogers was best known. "The character I try to portray," Williams said, "is the shiftless darky to the fullest extent, his fun, his philosophy. Show this artless darky a book and he won't know what it is all about. He can't read. He cannot write. But ask him a question and he'll answer it with a philosophy that's got something."[42]

Scattered throughout his monologues were sage tidbits that mirrored not only his view of the world but the viewpoint of the blacks that he so methodically observed. Williams's dim-witted character could observe that "Mankind ain't neethur as good as he says he is nur as bad as dey makes out to be," or, "Some folks shows de mos' liberal'ty when dey ain't got nothin'," and warn that "Anytime you commences to git de big head, you oughter stop an' think 'bout all de grate men whut's died an' 'bout how well de worl' got long widout 'em." He could also be assertive or defiant, as when he sang: "You all heard about the straw that broke the camel's back./ Well, a bubble added to my load,/ Would surely make mine crack./ But believe me, woe be to he or she-e./ Who tries to ease me that bubble. Believe you me."[43]

But it was through pantomime that Williams truly released his comic genius. After Walker's death, mime became a more important part of his routine, and it was largely because of this shift in emphasis that he emerged as an even greater comedian. He studied with the French mime Pietro while Walker was ill, and that experience, he said, "taught me that the entire aim of art in the theatre was to achieve simplicity." Throughout the second half of his career, understatement and simplicity were key elements in his performances.[44]

Through pantomime Williams was able completely to eliminate minstrel dialect and the low comedy associated with it in much of his act. This freed him to focus his creative energy on nuances of movement and facial expression that belied the darky caricature he presented—to employ the subtle facial work that the comic actor Robert Guillaume has called "mumbling on the face." According to most critics, among performers on the popular stage he was matchless. His "poker game" pantomime (which according to Tom Fletcher was inspired by observing a psychotic patient in a hospital) is considered a classic stage routine, as were the mime bits he interspersed with his vocal rendition of "Nobody."

There is enough evidence to suggest that Bert Williams was one of the best comedians of all time, and certainly the best of his own time. Critics and peers, despite the flagrant bias of the era, readily recognized his ascendency. For instance, in a review of *Bandana Land*, a mainstream New York critic wrote that Williams and Walker stood in "the very forefront of the American stage . . . if not all alone in the forefront," and asserted that "it is single justice to say that our stage has no white comedian as good as Bert Williams." Flo Ziegfeld, after Williams's death, wrote that he "was one of the greatest comedians I ever employed. In fact, he was one of the greatest in the world." Eddie Cantor (who, like W. C. Fields, played on the same bill with Williams) said, "Whatever sense of timing I have, I learned from him." And in an article published after Williams's death, Cantor wrote: "He knew each mental attitude of his own race and its humorous reaction to every situation . . . he was far superior to any of us who put on burnt cork."[45]

Williams's achievements were such that Booker T. Washington commented that he had done more for the Negro race than any other black of the period. He was instrumental in breaking down barriers for blacks in vaudeville and on the Broadway stage. He was the first black performer to star in a motion picture. The 1901 recordings that he and George Walker made of songs from popular black musicals are the earliest documented instance of blacks on phonograph records. And when he died, at the height of his career in March 1922, he was the highest-paid performer in the Ziegfeld *Follies*.

Perhaps more important, Williams demonstrated that even the most denigrative stereotype could be invested with dignity. His comic genius permitted him to humanize the debased caricature that white minstrels had created and black minstrels had perpetuated. Surpassing the efforts of Bob Cole, Flournoy Miller, and George Walker, he did not merely cover the stereotype with a veneer of black style—he turned it inside out to reveal the humanity beneath the cynical distortion. In so doing, he achieved a goal that black comedians would struggle to repeat for decades. For Williams's genius made the path he took almost impossible to follow.

The years between 1890 and 1921 saw many advances for black entertainers in the acceptance of black folk or syncopated music, in the wider acceptance of blacks in vaudeville and on Broadway, and in the growth of independently produced black shows; but in comedy the changes were more cosmetic than meaningful. Blackface still thrived and, although elements of black style and restricted aspects of the trickster motif had been added to the comic stage caricature, the face of Sambo persisted.

Given the circumstances at the turn of the century, however, Hogan, Cole, Miller, Lyles, and Walker had done nearly as much as was possible to invest the stage Sambo with elements of black style and authentic folkways. Williams's genius was noted. But during the early twentieth century Hollywood would nearly eradicate all the advances made by introducing a host of celluloid stereotypes. In the public domain, humanizing minstrel stereotypes would be confined to black theatres—the Theatre Owners Booking Association and the so-called "chitlin' circuit." And the private humor of blacks would begin to shift dramatically from its Southern folk base to a hipper, more assertive and caustic urban style.

5.

HOLLYWOOD'S SILENT

YEARS . . . *the curse*

of a nation

10

SCENE FROM *THE BIRTH OF A NATION*

I

Although he had numerous European predecessors in the field, Thomas Alva Edison assumed the lead in the development of motion pictures in the United States when he patented his "optical photograph," a type of moving film strip, in 1888. Historians now insist that Edison "had an influence on the moving picture out of all proportion to his real contribution." But despite the documented contributions of others, because of his stature as an inventor (he had already produced the telephone transmitter, phonograph, and incandescent lamp), advances pioneered by others were often funneled through Edison's laboratory. It was Edison who opened the world's first motion picture studio at West Orange, New Jersey, in February 1893. A year later he opened one of the first movie theatres, a peep show that featured his boxlike Kinetoscope, an apparatus into which customers dropped a penny to briefly view moving images of scenes such as Buffalo Bill mounting and dismounting his horse. And in April 1896, at the Koster and Bial Music Hall in New York City, he unveiled the Vitascope (a system actually developed by Thomas Armat), which projected moving photo images onto a large screen. Shortly afterward, America's fascination with the movies began in earnest.[2]

The Edison Film Company and its chief rival, Biograph Studios (which had developed an alternate moving picture device, the Mutoscope), were initially based in the New York City area and dominated the early years of filmmaking. Those companies also produced two of the silent era's most influential directors: Edwin S. Porter (Edison) and D. W. Griffith (Biograph), who would surpass their American contemporaries in nearly every aspect of their fledgling craft. Porter's *The Great Train Robbery* and his adaptation of Harriet Beecher Stowe's *Uncle Tom's Cabin* (both made in 1903), in addition to introducing the first successful close-ups, were instrumental in elevating motion pictures from mere amusements to a respectable entertainment capable of attracting middle-class patrons.

Griffith, of course, was by far the most famous silent filmmaker, and his brilliantly executed propaganda film, *The Birth of a Nation* (1915), would establish motion pictures as an estimable art form, attracting an even more expansive audience. The son of a Southern Civil War veteran, Griffith was born in Louisville, Kentucky, in 1875. When he initially came to Biograph in 1908, he was an actor and writer, pursuits that despite his ambition had left him nearly destitute; months later he more or less stumbled into the role of director and found his niche.

During 1908 and 1909 he made numerous comedies for Biograph Studios and counted among his protégés Mack Sennett, who later produced the Keystone Kops series at his own studio. (Sennett was unable to convince Griffith that cops could be funny.) Two of Griffith's comedies, *Balked at the Altar* and *The Curtain Pole*, were released in 1908 and featured Sennett as an actor. Griffith's use and refinement of techniques pioneered by others (most notably Georges Meliès, the French experimental filmmaker, who explored slow motion, fade-ins, and fade-outs) as well as those that he and cameraman Billy Bitzer introduced would revolutionize the film industry. He was hailed primarily for his lavish spectaculars, his moody, moralistic melodramas, and his visionary technical approach; but, almost incidentally, he was to become cinema's most influential molder of the comic image of African-Americans.[3]

Humor was the mainstay of the budding motion picture industry. More than a third of the movies produced before 1912 were comedies and the mid-teens ushered in the golden years of screen comedy, the silent era's most enduring contribution. The films of Charlie Chaplin, Roscoe "Fatty" Arbuckle, Buster Keaton, Harold Lloyd, and comedy producers Mack Sennett and Hal Roach, among others, comprise the majority of the most memorable works from Hollywood's silent era.

Negroes were also comically represented during the formative years. But, despite their reputation as the nation's foremost comedians, African-American actors were curiously scarce in early silent films— comedy or otherwise. Negroes were nearly always portrayed by white actors in burnt cork. The use of white actors for these roles was, in part, a concession to southerners who claimed to have been affronted by the appearance of genuine blacks. To appease white patrons, films playing in the South were preceded by advertisements assuring patrons that blackface whites actually played black roles.[4]

The insistent use of white actors in burnt cork assured that no hint of either the characters' genuine humanity or humor would reach the screen. The Negro characters represented were most often portrayed as thieves, reprobates, servants, or amoral brutes; they were usually no more than incidental comic foils. Most of these films, embarrassments even to those who produced them, have been lost, forgotten, or suppressed; but the images they presented set the tone for much that followed.

During the early years of motion pictures, before scripted, fictive stories were filmed, movie makers shot basic real-life scenes: children playing, sports events such as heavyweight champion Jack Johnson's knockout of Tommy Burns (1908), vaudeville and animal acts, crowd scenes—anything that might demonstrate the potential of the new medium. Among these films was a series of short documentaries produced by Edison Kinetoscope in 1895 featuring a group of West Indians dancing, bathing, and working aboard ships. Edison's *Watermelon Contest*, a film predictably offering four toothy, wide-mouthed, apparently ecstatic blacks ingenuously slurping watermelons and spitting seeds, was released at about the same time. Biograph also ventured into this area when, in 1896, they shot *Watermelon Feast* and two other films (*Hard Wash* and *Dancing Darkies*) featuring black performers. Still, despite these offensive stereotypes, before 1905—when editing advances allowed filmmakers more control of the images presented—real African-Americans were employed and, although the activities filmed were selective, they were usually shown in a comparatively guileless manner.

Tom Fletcher, for example, recalled that around 1900 in New York, he and his partner Al Bailey "got leading comedy parts" in motion pictures. According to him, there was little direction involved; performers were simply required to act out a comic scene as they saw fit. "You never heard the words 'lights, action, camera, roll 'em' or 'cut,' " he wrote. "There were no script writers, no make-up artists, wardrobe mistresses or anything like that. There was just one man, everybody called him Mr. Porter." (Fletcher was probably referring to Edwin Porter.)[5]

With more editorial control, however, directors imposed their own imagination on screen images and the cinema presentation of blacks moved away from realistic depiction. It began to more closely reflect the image of Negroes etched in the white mind, the Negro portrayed in minstrelsy and conjured up or fabricated by Southern mythology.

By 1910, the fledgling motion picture industry had already produced a body of films that enumerated and heightened nearly all of white America's stereotypes of blacks, among whose traits were malingering, philandering, crapshooting, chicken stealing, and, lest audiences forget, the ravenous consumption of watermelons. Biograph released *Nigger in the Woodpile* (1904), a "comedy" about two Negroes who steal some wood from a farmyard. The harassed white farmer, however, has placed a stick of dynamite in one of the cords. When the thieves put it into their stove, it explodes. The film ends as the farmer searches the debris for the remains of the culprits. In addition to Edison and Biograph, other companies made substantial contributions to this genre.

William Selig, for example, had released *Interrupted Crap Game* (1905), a comedy short about a group of "darkies" torn between their crap game and the irresistible urge to chase a chicken. The Essanay company offered *The Dancing Nig* (1907), which depicted Sambo-like blacks who, at the merest hint of music, are compelled to roll back the rug, and *C-H-I-C-K-E-N Spells Chicken* (1910), an exploration of Negro addiction to fowl play. The Pathé company initiated its Rastus series, which followed the farcical exploits of a minstrelsy-inspired buffoon who would become Hollywood's most offensive black stereotype —the ignorant, shiftless coon—in films with such titles as *How Rastus Got His Turkey* and *Pickaninnies and Watermelons*. Harrison Dickson, the white Southern writer whose stories about the irrepressible dandy Virgil Custard appeared regularly in the *Saturday Evening Post*, also adapted his characters for a cinema series.[6]

Another film depicted "the catching, taring [sic] and feathering and burning of a negro for the assault of a white woman." Lynching, in fact, seems to have been a popular theme in early Hollywood films. In 1909, Lester Walton of *The New York Age* criticized promotional copy distributed for the midtown Manhattan showing of a film, which read: "Hear His Moans and Groans, Price One Cent." For its Bowery showing, this film was hyped as "educational." Perhaps even more alarming, as Thomas Cripps writes, some of these films "burlesqued racial violence, reducing it to comic surrealism, as if this would make acts such as lynching somewhat more acceptable."[7]

Heavily influenced by the South's vision of its former slaves, the motion picture industry would eventually settle on a central black image that satisfied white audiences in both North and South. Coons, Sambos, pickaninnies, crapshooting and chicken-stealing reprobates persisted, of course, but a slightly more subtle and diverting stereotype emerged, one that had not only been popularized in the works of regional writers such as Joel Chandler Harris and Thomas Nelson Page but also accurately reflected the most common relationship between West Coast blacks and Hollywood's elite.

It was no more than an amalgam of the lazy, inept coon and faithful Tom, or a facsimile of the Southern humorist's handkerchief-headed, feisty Mammy caricature. But the loyal, docile servant—nearly always smiling or dancing or singing—would slowly and indisputably eclipse other stereotypical portraits to become Hollywood's premier black figure, both in dramatic roles and as a comic foil. By 1910, when most filmmakers had discovered that Southern California's scenic variety and balmy weather provided an excellent setting for cranking out silent one-reelers and left the New York area, the comic caricature of blacks had nearly been codified. African-Americans had gained access to the novel world of cinema comedy in a scandalously perverse manner. Unfortunately, the social vision that defined their entry would not be significantly altered for more than half a century.

II

In the early twentieth century, Los Angeles, very much as it is today, was not so much a city as a sprawling complex of suburban enclaves connected by a network of roadways. To a great extent its pastoral setting isolated its inhabitants from the social upheaval drastically affecting other urban areas and gave it a distinctively Southern aura. Even as late as the twenties, when he first visited Los Angeles as a teen-aged musician, the bandleader Lionel Hampton wrote that "Hollywood was a pretty town, but I didn't think much of the attitude toward blacks there. It was my first real experience with discrimination . . . out in Hollywood, it was like the South in some ways. You had to sit in the back of the bus, go into the white nightclubs by the back door. Taxis wouldn't stop for you." Stepin Fetchit put it more succinctly when he quipped that "Hollywood is more segregated than Georgia under the skin."[8]

Although debates raged throughout most of the country over the conflict between rural and urban lifestyles, and "Lost Generation" intellectuals railed against repression and genteel middle-class values, the film colony basked in an idyllic setting where such conflicts seemed insignificant. African-Americans had settled primarily in the Los Angeles basin area now known as Watts, while whites occupied the surrounding hills; except for servant-employee encounters (a relationship that would be insistently and comically magnified in films), they rarely interacted. And later, despite a veneer of liberalism and sophistication, the film colony knew less of Alain Locke's "New Negro" than did the average white city dweller in the East. Although some whites ventured into Watts and the Central Avenue nightclubs that emerged in the twenties, fascination with black night life on the West Coast never reached the frenetic heights it achieved in Harlem.

For their part, most African-Americans seemed satisfied simply by virtue of living on the periphery of the nation's movie capital. Even after organized protests against Griffith's *Birth of a Nation* in 1915 by groups such as the recently formed National Association for the Advancement of Colored People, few blacks in Hollywood—within the film community or without—actively complained about derogatory depictions of Negroes on the screen or discrimination within the industry itself. Hollywood was quickly becoming the nation's most popular and revered illusionist, and for the most part, those most impugned by its phantasm observed with awe, impotence, and silence.

The film industry, of course, was not devoid of some minor inklings of social concern. In a 1912 article entitled "The Social Uses of the Moving Picture," W. Stephen Bush, an early commentator on the new medium, asserted that "some of the best known film makers of our country have given us pictures dealing with social evils and making a strong appeal for redress and reform. The Biograph, Selig, Vitagraph and notably the Edison studios deserve credit for their efforts along these lines." But those efforts focused on issues such as temperance and child labor and almost never touched on African-Americans' struggle for equal rights. The basic concern of early filmmakers, and, eventually, the studio executives who controlled the industry, was to attract white middle-class patrons to movie houses. They had little interest in rectifying the slavery or minstrel images of Negroes or in reflecting controversial social questions—not as long as box office receipts increased and their desired audience was content.[9]

Filmmakers, like radio and television pioneers decades later, had no desire to rock the boat. As business people, they were concerned with providing a product—entertainment—despite the work of socially conscious directors such as Edwin Porter, Erich von Stroheim, and Griffith (however questionable the latter's motives). The social consequences of the entertainment presented (at least for blacks) were nearly always incidental.

In this regard, the release of and reaction to Griffith's *The Birth of a Nation* (1915)—a blatant condemnation of Emancipation and homage to the Ku Klux Klan—is illuminating.

The movie was based on Thomas Dixon's notorious novel, *The Clansman* (1905), which depicts the experiences of two families—the Camerons, a South Carolina family representing Southern gentry, and the Stonemans, a Northern family headed by a radical Republican patriarch —during the Civil War and the Reconstruction era. As a novel it was a thin, melodramatic propaganda tract that built to its climax (the intervention of the Ku Klux Klan) through invidious juxtaposition of saintly Aryan types and docile, contented slaves with unscrupulous white Northern Carpetbaggers and ignorant or venal Negro freedmen. Its night-riding Klan members who, much like the cavalry in Hollywood Westerns, gallop in to save the day are presented as knightly defenders of decency and the genteel, Southern way of life.

Dixon, whom Griffith greatly admired and who acted as a consultant on *The Birth of a Nation,* had previously aired his white supremacist views in his novel *The Leopard's Spots* (1902), where he described how the Civil War had changed blacks from "chattel to be bought and sold into a possible beast to be feared and guarded." For him, Negroes were subhuman, a menace "throwing the blight of its shadow over future generations, a veritable Black Death for the land and its people." (The stage adaptation of that novel became a hit Broadway play in 1903.) Dixon often employed comic parodies of black speech and culture to enhance the crude stereotypes that served his polemical needs. His rigid portrayals of blacks as either evil reprobates or benign toadies flowed from an equally fixed, almost fanatical supremacist viewpoint. In *The Clansman,* for example, dialect humor and racial caricature were used to dramatize a confrontation between Aleck (an uppity black who has had the temerity to assume a position as supervisor of voter registration during Reconstruction) and Jake (a loyal servant who happily accepts his inferior status and impuissance):

"Tryin' to vote, is yer?"

"Lowed I would."

"You hear 'bout the great sassieties de Gubment's fomentin' in dis country?"

"Yas, I hear erbout 'em."

"Is yer er member er de Union League?"

"Na-sah. I'd rudder steal by myself. I doan' lak too many in de party!"

"En yer ain't er No'f Ca'liny gemmen, is yer—yer ain't er member er de 'Red Strings'?"

"Na-sah, I come when I'se called—dey doan' hatter put er string on me—ner er block, ner er collar, ner er chain, ner er muzzle—"

"Will yer 'splain to ter dis cote—" railed Aleck.

"What cote? Dat ole army cote?" Jake laughed in loud peals that ran over the square.

Aleck recovered his dignity and demanded angrily:

"Does yer belong ter de Heroes ob Ameriky?"

"Na-sah. I ain't burnt nobody's house ner barn yet, ner hamstrung no stock, ner waylaid nobody atter night—honey, I ain't fit ter jine. Heroes ob Americky! Is you er hero?"

"Ef yer doan' b'long ter no s'iety," said Aleck with judicial deliberation, "what is you?"

"Des er ole-fashun all-wool-en-er-yard-wide nigger dat stan's by his ole marster 'cause he's his bes' frien', stays at home, en tends ter his own business."[10]

Although both slaves are characterized as ignorant and childish, Dixon ensured that Jake, the faithful sycophant, would outwit and embarrass his insolent adversary.

Griffith's film, perhaps because of the absence of sound and the inability to reproduce the long racist diatribes featured in *The Clansman*, avoided some of the novel's shrillness. It did, however, include inflammatory sequences in which a white woman, assuming that she is about to be raped by a Negro, leaps from a cliff; a group of black radicals kidnap the film's heroine; and illiterate, drunken, and depraved blacks, many of them newly elected officials, harass and threaten whites at every turn. Dixon was obviously not displeased with the message projected by the movie; when *The Birth of a Nation* was greeted by protests from blacks and white liberals, he arranged to have President Woodrow Wilson—a college friend who in many ways shared his ideological outlook—view it in what was probably the first screening of a motion picture in the White House. As expected, Wilson heartily endorsed it, thereby blunting "growing agitation against the film." The President said, "It is like writing history with lightning. And my only regret is that it is all true."[11]

Still, protests and legal actions by the NAACP and other groups were mounted throughout the country, and they were joined by intellectuals such as the president of Harvard University, the novelist Upton Sinclair, and the socialist leader Eugene Debs. African-American leaders from the accommodationist Booker T. Washington to militants such as William Monroe Trotter spoke out against the film. Trotter, whose protests and insistence on being admitted to a showing at a Boston theatre precipitated a violent disturbance, charged that the film was "an incentive to great racial hatred," labeled Dixon as, among other things, "an unasylumed maniac," and challenged Boston's mayor with the quip, "If this was an attack on the Irish race he would find a way pretty quick to stop it."[12]

But even though such protests often delayed an opening, they seldom halted the ultimate showing. Riots were reported in some cities when the film premiered, but the controversy only heightened its appeal. Audiences multiplied. Ironically, the furor primarily kept black audiences away, barred from many theatres because owners felt their presence would incite confrontations. Yet, despite the overall ineffectiveness of the protest, it did momentarily galvanize black leadership; and, for the first time, the need to monitor mass media images of African-Americans was seen as a crucial element in the struggle for equality.

Throughout this tempest, Griffith maintained a guileless astonishment. Anita Loos, then a writer in his employment, later said that the movie "created a racist problem in the United States that exploded and caused any number of theatres to cancel the film, and this horrified D. W. Griffith who was raised in the South and saw nothing wrong in it at all." Until his death, Griffith adamantly insisted that neither he nor the film was racist, maintaining that "I am one who cherishes a great affection and a profound admiration for the negro. . . . *The Birth of a Nation* presents many lovable negroes who win hearty applause from the audiences. It presents also some exceedingly hateful negroes." Most of the Hollywood community agreed with him. They saw little distortion or pernicious intent—even though former members of the Ku Klux Klan burned down a major street in Atlanta in celebration of the film's opening in June 1915, and the modern Klan was revived in November of the same year. By the twenties, the Ku Klux Klan had again risen to national prominence. Finally, the protest and uproar elevated Griffith to the status of a national celebrity and "had the long-range effect of driving all but the most comic black roles from the screen."[13]

Despite the furor, Griffith's film was lauded by most critics. One contemporary journalist described it as "beyond question the most extraordinary picture that has been made—or seen—in America so far." An anonymous critic at *The New York Times* noted that it was "a film version of some of the melodramatic and inflammatory material" from Dixon's novel, then applauded the "impressive new illustration of the scope of the motion picture camera." Most other mainstream critics ignored the film's overt racism and historical distortion while extolling its innovative technical achievements. It is still considered one of the "key films of motion picture history" by film historians, and many contend that it has been viewed by more people than any film ever made.[14]

The Birth of a Nation was the most popular film affirming regional writers' portraits of an idyllic Southern agrarian society. But there were many others. Scores of them featured massive plantations, columned mansions, high-strung Southern belles, courtly masters, and contented well-kept slaves toiling happily in picturesque cotton fields. Soon, along with such exotic locale films as the Tarzan series and adventure films depicting the eradication of Native Americans and the winning of the West, plantation tales and Southern romances would dominate the works of early filmmakers. In fact, the South's ideological viewpoint had a disproportionate influence on the neophyte film industry that reflected neither its importance as a potential audience nor the more exploitative reality of slavery.

Before the release of *The Birth of a Nation* (between 1909 and 1911), for example, D. W. Griffith himself had produced more than a half dozen Civil War dramas that magnified the virtues of Southern life and generally presented a picture of Southern purity unmarred by anything except Northern interlopers or uppity, rowdy blacks gloating over their status as freedmen. As Thomas Cripps notes, "More than any other director Griffith gave future moviemakers a model, a cinematic language, and a rich romantic tradition that would define an Afro-American stereotype." Other film companies drew heavily on the myths portrayed in Southern writing because, as one commentator suggested, that "body of writing provided just the right touch of romance, splendor, and diversion [audiences] craved and was in the tradition of the minstrel shows and tunes with which the many lower-class viewers were so familiar."[15]

Harking back to the black minstrel performers just after the Civil War, comic images and stereotypes of stage blacks were presented as dramatic reality in early films. Most producers and directors, perhaps reflecting their own bias, believed that audiences expected blacks to be depicted in these familiar comic or servile roles. Even Africans in their own homeland, awestruck as they inevitably succumbed to Tarzan's mastery, took on the appearance of Uncle Toms and minstrel-stage Sambos. The depiction of black characters was generally restricted to two categories: the "Yassah Boss" and "Ooga Booga Bwana" varieties.

Of course, black Americans—unlike Jewish, Irish, or most other ethnic groups that had been lampooned on the American stage—had no input in creating their own screen image. They had no representatives among the producers and directors who determined the course of early cinema. And, as the black critic Lester Walton pointed out in *The New York Age*, they had no history visible to whites other than slavery and minstrel portraits. The film community, like most of white America, knew little or nothing about the actual day-to-day nature of black American life, let alone life in Africa. (As late as 1931, *Variety* magazine reported that a movie producer, responding to a writer's irate query about a script, "What do you want, *Black Beauty*?", curtly replied, "There ain't no market for them Nigger Operas.")[16]

For instance, William Selig, who is credited with initiating film production in Los Angeles in 1907, had managed a black stage show in the South and, before he switched to film, had met Bert Williams. Yet, despite the acclaimed performer's imposing good looks and impeccable behavior, Selig later remembered merely a "yellow boy" with a "deep, wide, open watermelon expanse of a mouth"—who affirmed the filmmaker's illusory view of blacks.[17]

Although Williams was a Ziegfeld *Follies* star and the nation's premier stage comedian, efforts to film his comedy routines met with formidable resistance. Williams reportedly wrote and directed some films himself and, in 1914, appeared in the independently produced *Darktown Jubilee,* which some contend was the "first all-Negro"-cast movie. It was certainly the first film in which an established black star played a leading role, and Williams's appearance in top hat and zoot suit (instead of the raggedy outfit he usually donned on stage), without blackface makeup, apparently was too much for the mixed audience at its Brooklyn opening. The film was greeted with catcalls from whites and nearly precipitated a race riot. Subsequently it was boycotted by most distributors.[18]

Some Hollywood companies also professed interest in Williams, but somehow the proposed movies never materialized. Difficulty in raising funds or fear of white audience reaction was cited. Ironically, it was Biograph, the pioneer company that Griffith had made famous, which finally contacted Williams. After Griffith's departure in 1913, the studio had fallen on bad times; desperately seeking rejuvenation, it consented to shoot two one-reel films starring Williams.

The two silent shorts, *Fish* and *A Natural Born Gambler* (both 1916), were not innovative; in fact, largely because of the producer's anxiety over offending white audiences, they were merely watered-down versions of the comedian's stage routines worked into thin scenarios. Still, a spark of Williams's personality and comic genius filters through, as well as something that had heretofore been absent in motion pictures: the appearance of a self-reliant, willful, and intelligent, if larcenous, black man being portrayed by a black actor.

In *Fish*, Williams plays a country bumpkin, a character close to the darky he usually portrayed on stage. He is lazy and unsophisticated, but he has enough guile and ambition to attempt pawning off spoiled fish on some unsuspecting white customers. Working in blackface, Williams manages to elicit humor and pathos as his ragged character slips away from the farm on which he is employed (the owners, also in blackface, are equally shabby) and begins his slapstick commercial venture. At the end, Williams fails and returns to the farm where, obviously disenchanted, he is last seen once again chopping wood for his employers. But the audience is left with the impression that his spirit is unbroken; before long, he will be off on another adventure.

In *A Natural Born Gambler,* he runs a continuous poker game in the back room of a black lodge. His efforts to conceal the illegal game from a police informant and maintain his position at the lodge provide some dated but surprisingly nuanced humor. Here, Williams's ability as a mime is expansively shown, and on several occasions it is easy to see why some consider him one of the greatest mimes of all time. Despite his efforts, Williams and his cohorts are arrested when the card game is discovered. At the hearing, the others are released but Williams is sent to jail. Alone in his cell, he performs one of his most famous stage bits—the classic poker routine in which he mimes all the players. This is the highlight and, by itself, makes the movie worthwhile. In this film, as Thomas Cripps points out, Williams "is leader of blacks, enemy of convention, the 'good-bad-nigger' for all who could see through his darky makeup." He was also a black performer appearing in a starring role that clearly deviated from Hollywood's standard caricature of blacks.

These two short films demonstrate the direction that Hollywood films featuring blacks might have taken if black performers had been allowed to participate freely as actors and creators. Williams, much like Sennett in his Keystone Kops series and Chaplin in his Little Tramp roles, sets up a contrast between his rebel character and the prevailing social norm. Sennett's wild farces lampooned established social order by subjecting it to a comic chaos, reducing its pretense to the absurdity of a pie in the face. Chaplin was more subtle, allowing his alienated tramp to wring pathos from his audiences, thereby suggesting the moral ambiguity and absurdity of many conventional attitudes. Williams's films also comically suggested an alternative to accepted attitudes, but what he gently twits is the perception of blacks as contented servants and ignorant roustabouts. Both films were destined for oblivion. Neither Hollywood nor the primarily white audiences of the time were prepared for a black comic playing parts that despite burnt cork and darky attributes projected such unconventional traits as cunning and resourcefulness.[19]

III

By the twenties, a more or less defined stable of Negro caricatures had been established in silent films. The title of Donald Bogle's history of blacks in film, *Toms, Coons, Mulattoes, Mammies, and Bucks* (which mirrors a list of literary stereotypes of blacks enumerated by Sterling Brown in *The Negro in American Fiction*), pointedly reflects the essential types, although, as Bogle points out, each of these categories had subtle variations.[20]

The earliest appearance of the Uncle Tom character was probably in Edwin Porter's *Uncle Tom's Cabin* in 1903; this short film distinguished itself from most later versions by including some of the abolitionist sentiment in Harriet Beecher Stowe's novel. Numerous remakes followed, among them Sam Lucas's precedent-setting portrayal of Tom in

1914, and the 1927 version, which starred another black actor, James B. Lowe. From the earliest silent movies through later Griffith films such as *One Exciting Night* (1922), with its combination Tom-coon character Romeo Washington (played by the white actor Porter Strong), this neutered, docile, faithful slave would make his self-effacing, phlegmatic appearance in practically every Hollywood movie set in the antebellum South. The tradition would continue after the arrival of talkies with Bill Robinson's mawkish debacles with Shirley Temple in the mid-thirties, and such later films as *Gone With the Wind* (1939); Walt Disney's adaptation of the Uncle Remus tales, *Song of the South* (1946); and the exploitative slavery drama *Mandingo* (1975).

Bucks or "bad niggers" also made an early appearance in silent films. The first was probably in the surrealistic fantasy *Off to Bloomingdale Asylum* (1903). According to its creator, the French magician and fil-mmaker Georges Meliès, four blacks (again, blackface white actors) pulling a mechanical horse and omnibus are thrown to the ground when the horse rears up. While engaging in some frantic slapstick antics, they alternately change from black minstrels to white clowns. "Suddenly they emerge into one gigantic Negro. When he refuses to pay carfare, the conductor sets fire to the omnibus and the Negro bursts into smith-ereens." Both the bus and the menacing black buck are obliterated.[21]

This odd, impressionistic romp offered a rare comical portrait of the black buck that perhaps only a foreigner could have filmed. Typically bucks were villains who, although sometimes ridiculed and shown as loudmouthed cowards, were never treated whimsically. Their unswerv-ingly menacing presence on the screen reflected America's anxiety over the depiction of black manhood in an aggressive guise and, ultimately, was used to vindicate racial repression.

The most controversial and infamous depiction of the buck occurred in *The Birth of a Nation*. There a leering black soldier (comical only in that the white actor's makeup barely conceals his true skin color and, in fact, gives him the ghostly appearance of a mutant) approaches and proposes to a terrified Southern belle; traumatized by his impertinent advances, she flees. When he pursues her, she leaps from a cliff, killing herself. The scene graphically punctuated Griffith's caveat about the perils posed by free black men who assumed they were the equals of whites, and also helped justify the movie's climax, which depicts the "heroic" intervention of a gang of hooded Ku Klux Klan vigilantes. This kind of violent, often gratuitously vicious, black character appeared in motion pictures from the silent era (most often in Griffith's films) right through—some would contend—the exploitative films of the seventies and eighties.

Like brutal bucks and obsequious Toms, ill-fated, inevitably tragic mulattoes were not usually truly comic characters. Toms sometimes *told* humorous stories, but generally they were harmless, guileless folks, who faithfully fulfilled white fantasies about respectful, docile blacks. The humor (usually only perceptible to non-black audiences) derived most often from the degree of obsequiousness shown. Typically, Toms were devoid of the surface sarcasm and irony that would eventually define many Hollywood depictions of post-slavery servants.

The primary burden of soliciting laughter was left to a more irreverent or slothful servant breed: the hallowed, robust black mammy, who was either drolly independent or assertively outspoken; and the inept, ever present coon, who alternately amused by his shuffling, dim-witted incompetence or by his clever shirking of any and all responsibility.

Donald Bogle argues that the screen mammy made her debut around 1914 in a blackface version of Aristophanes' *Lysistrata* entitled *Coon Town Suffragettes*. The film dealt with "a group of bossy mammy washerwomen who organize a militant movement to keep their good-for-nothing husbands at home." This mammy variant (the derisive, domineering shrew) appeared infrequently in early Hollywood movies since black family life was seldom portrayed. But the caricature persisted and could occasionally be seen in silent films such as *Manslaughter* (1922), a Cecil B. DeMille production. Later sound film examples were *Framing of the Shrew* (1929), a black-cast film that featured Evelyn Preer as a castigating, bullying wife; *Judge Priest* (1934), in which Hattie McDaniel offers a forceful interpretation of the hot-tempered, emasculating female opposite Stepin Fetchit; and *Bubbling Over* (1934), in which Ethel Waters as a Harlem housewife reacts to her shiftless husband's malingering with anger mediated by despair. Her curiously blasé version of the mournful "Darkies Never Cry"—delivered over a washboard with a bandana tied about her head—is as ironic as it is poignant. The most vivid comic presentation of the domineering mammy, however, would not occur until the appearance of the legendary Sapphire on the *Amos 'n' Andy* radio and television series.[22]

Another mammy type, slavery's strong, fiercely loyal Aunt Jemima variety, appeared in silent Civil War spectaculars and became a familiar part of Griffith's lexicon of black characters. The humor associated with Aunt Jemima types usually arose from their absolute dedication to their white mistresses (even in the face of threats from their masters); the broadly drawn contrast between their own nearly always overweight and mannishly tough appearance and their mistresses' markedly more refined, "feminine," and demure appearance; their suspicious and demeaning treatment of any black male who might stray into the film; and their legendary facility with spatula and flapjacks, which apparently accounts for the enduring role assigned them as the nation's most revered apostles of breakfast foods. Like Uncle Tom, this slave character was a fixture in silent Civil War films, perhaps reaching its zenith with Hattie McDaniel's performance in *Gone With the Wind*, for which she won an Oscar as best supporting actress.

The variant of the mammy character that emerged as most popular —the female domestic servant—commanded only incidental attention and cameo appearances until the advent of talkies in the late twenties and early thirties. And their status as true cultural icons would not be attained until the radio debut of Beulah (initially played by the white actor Marlin Hurt) as a maid on the *Fibber McGee and Molly* show in 1944.

Coon characters had been introduced in films with the appearance of Edison's ravenous pickaninnies in *Watermelon Contest;* subsequently, they not only flourished but achieved select status in Hollywood's hierarchy of black screen imagery. Mimicking minstrelsy and the popular Negro caricatures peddled in song lyrics and the covers of Tin Pan Alley song sheets, Hollywood movies advanced the stereotypical portrait of the no-account, lazy "Nigra" more zealously than any other black image.

Topsy, Little Eva's slave companion in *Uncle Tom's Cabin,* initially appeared on the screen in 1903 and was among the first fictional coon figures; she was also among the few female characters who truly deserved the coon designation. Her frantic, madcap misadventures provided the comic relief in a score of Hollywood remakes of Harriet Beecher Stowe's novel. So great was her popularity that in 1927, at about the same time Universal released yet another version of *Uncle Tom's Cabin,* a rival company released *Topsy and Eva,* which starred the white actress Mona Ray as Topsy.

In one scene, Ray's Topsy—her mouth stretching from ear to ear in hideous blackface makeup and hair bedecked with ribbons that look, to all the world, like bones—literally stumbles out of the house. Obviously ill at ease in her mistress's "civilized" attire (a white dress, stockings, and shoes), she finds her way to the chicken coop. Unable, as coons are wont, to pass up such an inviting feast, after a moment of salivating, lip-smacking indecision, she breaks in. Her entrance precipitates a slapstick, knockdown interlude in which she finally secures two of the embattled fowl. As she skulks away, muddied and in tatters, the audience is left with the graphically etched impression that Topsy's camouflage could never disguise her inherent barbarity and ignorance.

Perhaps even more demeaning were two unpardonably venal and ignorant male coon caricatures who debuted in early silent films. Sigmund "Pop" Lubin, a somewhat rough and unsavory filmmaker who among other things was known as "a notorious duper" ("he had duped, or copied, successful films and put them out under his own trade mark since the earliest days"), produced two all-black comedy series between 1908 and 1911. The first featured Sambo, "a comic black man who 'knows his place' and gets hell beat out of him by a variety of laughing whites." During the same period, Lubin introduced his Rastus series (which competed with Pathé's Rastus series). For several years these two hapless characters fulfilled the promise of their names, which resonated with derisive slavery and minstrel overtones, and stumbled through a series of inane, slapstick adventures. Blackface white actors portrayed these feckless clowns in *Rastus and Chicken*, *Chicken Thief*, and *Rastus in Zululand*. The plots, as these titles suggest, were unwaveringly offensive. In *Rastus in Zululand*, for instance, the bumbling hero goes to Africa, where his buffoonish behavior is matched only by that of the chief whose daughter he pursues. This interaction sets the stage for the crude, tasteless ridiculing of both African-Americans and Africans that follows. Rarely has America's contempt for African humanity been more candidly reflected. As one historian noted, "The series presented a fumbling, conniving, lazy, greedy individual whose very fictional existence revealed the animosity of whites."[23]

Along with crude comedies such as *The Wooing and Wedding of a Coon* (1905), the Sambo and Rastus comedy series established minstrelsy's coon figure in motion pictures and probably represented the nadir of ethnic burlesque in the medium. The stereotype, however, would remain a Hollywood staple throughout the silent film era. Although few movies matched the earlier exaggerated obtuseness and depravity, filmmakers continued promulgating the image of the witless, lazy, rural black buffoon. This grotesquery only began to diminish after 1915, when black protest organizations started to monitor movies and voice their dissent. Gradually, blackface whites were replaced by black performers. With the change, cinema Negroes—most noticeably women and children—began being depicted in a slightly less demeaning manner.

Ultimately, the stridently exaggerated coon would be replaced by another caricature—the male domestic servant or houseboy. This character combined elements of the coon stereotype with more "humane" traits of the venerable Tom caricature. The popularity of the type was foreshadowed by the appearance of D. W. Griffith's fearful toady Romeo Washington, in *One Exciting Night,* considered "the first film to boast the quickly stereotyped figure of the terrified Negro manservant." Washington was "afraid of the dark, of thunderstorms, of firearms, of animals, of police and above all—of white folks." Later, films like *California Straight Ahead* (1926), in which a blackface actor plays Sambo, a dedicated valet, amplified the character and by the name revealed the source of the satire. But like that most popular mammy figure, the maid, male domestic servants would not emerge as Hollywood's primary black presence until the introduction of sound films.[24]

Still, by the mid-twenties, with black music assuming a more significant role in America's popular culture and a kind of bizarre Negrophilia emerging in Eastern cities, there was hope for a reversal of the trend toward disparaging stereotypes. And, indeed, before the decade ended, Hollywood would introduce the first black comedian to star in feature films. The debut of Stepin Fetchit would establish a new era in the slow evolution of black humor in the mass media.

6.

THE NEW NEGRO: HARLEM AND HOLLYWOOD . . .

exotics, imposters, and other misshapen identities

11

STEPIN FETCHIT IN *HEARTS IN DIXIE*

A NEW NEGRO IS EVOLVING—A CITY NEGRO. . . . AND THIS IS A FACT OVERLOOKED BY THOSE STUDENTS OF BEHAVIOR. . . . IN TEN YEARS, NEGROES HAVE BEEN ACTUALLY TRANSPLANTED FROM ONE CULTURE TO ANOTHER.

—CHARLES S. JOHNSON

THEY'VE MADE THE CHARACTER PART OF STEPIN FETCHIT STAND FOR BEING LAZY AND STUPID AND BEING A WHITE MAN'S FOOL. . . . MAYBE BECAUSE THEY DON'T REALLY KNOW WHAT IT WAS THEN. HOLLYWOOD WAS MORE SEGREGATED THAN GEORGIA UNDER THE SKIN. A NEGRO COULDN'T DO NOTHING STRAIGHT, ONLY COMEDY. . . . YOU MADE AN IMAGE IN YOUR MIND THAT I WAS LAZY, GOOD-FOR-NOTHING, FROM A CHARACTER THAT YOU SEEN ME DOIN' WHEN I WAS DOIN' A HIGH-CLASS JOB OF ENTERTAINMENT.

—STEPIN FETCHIT

NAWSAH, I AIN'T AFRAID, BUT MY FEETS AIN' GOIN' STAND AROUND AND WATCH MY BODY GET ABUSED.

—WILLIE BEST[1]

I

•••••••••

When Lincoln Theodore Monroe Andrew Perry (his father was fond of naming his children after U.S. presidents) was born on May 30, 1902, in Key West, Florida, most black entertainers worked in the tradition established by early minstrels. For years to come, road shows and circuses would pass through his hometown. And, as an adolescent, young Perry, a practical joker and irrepressible clown, studied the blackface comedians—many of whom, by then, were actually black under the burnt cork—who continued acting out the charade of the slapstick, rowdy, Sambo-inspired comedy that mainstream America loved and demanded. Prior to World War I, when Perry joined a traveling plantation show and began his show business career, although black entertainers had integrated Broadway and vaudeville, very little had changed in the presentation of comedy by blacks on stage. So when Perry and his partner—originally billed as "Skeeter and Rastus: The Two Dancing Crows from Dixie"—decided to change their name to "Step 'n' Fetchit: The Two Dancing Fools from Dixie" and to introduce a song that Perry had written and a dance he had created, no one suspected that it would develop into anything more than just another catchy Sambo act and coon song: "The Stepin Fetchit! Stepin Fetchit! Turn around, stop and catch it."

And even in the twenties, when his partner occasionally did not show up or owners would insist they could not afford two performers and Perry would respond, "No, it's not two of us, it's just one of us, the Step and Fetchit," or rhetorically ask, "What you need him for?", no one paid inordinate attention to the lean, slack-faced comedian who diligently went out and worked solo. Even after he began billing himself as Stepin Fetchit while performing on the Theatre Owners Booking Association (TOBA) tour, no one imagined that this gangling comic, who by now had brought the art of indolence and insouciance to a new level of inertia, would cause any stir in the entertainment world. After all, he himself had said that he didn't think people would pay very much to see someone do nothing. Moreover, as he freely admitted, he didn't even create the routine that became his specialty; the inspiration came from his partner, who "was so lazy, he used to call a cab to get across the street."[2]

In the mid-twenties Stepin Fetchit was just one of hundreds of acts touring black theatres in the South and Midwest on the TOBA circuit. There was no reason to pay much attention to yet another comedian working the traditional plantation version of the shiftless darky gambit, even if his billing was a little out of the ordinary. More important things were happening. A more assertive urban style was emerging in centers like New York, where blacks had taken the Broadway stage by storm and where the mystique of the New Negro was growing in Harlem.

The mood and expectations of blacks had undergone a dramatic shift following World War I. In part, this was directly related to the thousands of black servicemen who returned from Europe in 1919. (Over 200,000 blacks were sent to France, with 30,000 serving as combat soldiers on the front lines.) In Harlem and throughout the country black leaders hailed the performance of these soldiers and predicted that their contribution to the fight for democracy would help advance the cause of freedom at home. Black soldiers, after risking their lives in a foreign country, felt even more strongly about the matter. A new aggressiveness was immediately apparent, particularly in Northern cities, even though many whites outspokenly resisted any concessions that might be made in racial matters. As one New Orleans white man put it: "You niggers are wondering how you're going to be treated after the war. Well, I'll tell you, You're going to be treated exactly like you were before the war."[3]

He was correct: little or nothing changed. In fact, America's immediate response to peace was an upsurge in racial repression, as well as in religious and political intolerance and moral conservatism, which led H. L. Mencken to label the new America as simply an "ignominious goosestepper." Evaluating America's victory in 1922, Mencken insisted that the results were "government by usurpation and tyranny, a complete collapse of national decency . . . the bitter and senseless persecutions of minorities, Know-Nothingness, Ku Kluxism, terrorism and espionage." The appointment of J. Edgar Hoover as the director of the newly created anti-radical division of the Justice Department (1919), the Sacco and Vanzetti case (1920–21), and Prohibition (1920) were merely signs of the time. Involvement in a foreign war had intensified America's desire to solidify and preserve the traditional, rural ideals that were threatened by increased industrialization and migration to the cities, and the country struggled desperately to reaffirm its puritan traditions. "The genteel middle class cultural structure, which had ruled over American values and ideals for nearly two centuries, raised itself to new heights of rhetoric, energy, repression, and control," one historian has noted.[4]

Reaffirming the old values, of course, meant assuring that blacks stayed in their place. Throughout the country, blacks, seeking to secure their rights as citizens, were quickly lumped with anarchists, immigrants, union organizers, and other dissenters who did not conform to traditional rural values; they too became prime targets of the new puritanism. And, in the spring of 1919, less than a year after the war ended, black Americans' new militancy and increased expectations clashed violently with mainstream intransigence. Beginning with the "disturbance" in Charleston, South Carolina, on May 10, riots broke out in twenty-six American cities; throughout the nation violent racial encounters were responsible for hundreds of deaths during the year.

The worst of these clashes occurred in and around Elaine, Arkansas, in early 1919, after a group of black sharecroppers united to protest the prices their landlords paid them for cotton. The protesters were attacked while holding a meeting one night, and in the ensuing melee a white deputy sheriff was killed. In the subsequent "reign of terror," more than two hundred blacks were "hunted down in the fields and swamps to which they had fled, and shot down like animals." Twelve

more blacks were executed and sixty-seven sentenced to life imprisonment after a "farcical" trial in which an all-white jury deliberated five
minutes before delivering its verdict. "What they were actually guilty
of," wrote James Weldon Johnson, "was attempted assault on the peon-
age system—the system by which the Negro in the agricultural South
is as effectively robbed of his labor as ever he was under slavery."[5]

But America's mood was shifting, and the conservative push did not
go unchallenged. Even moderate members of the middle class resented
the intensity of traditionalists' demands for conformity. Mainstream
intellectuals were among the first to protest. Writers, artists, scholars,
and bohemians of various persuasions began openly criticizing postwar
repression and, more significantly, the ideals on which it was based.
H. L. Mencken, whose *Prejudice: First Series,* a collection of essays
that ridiculed American materialism and cultural pretensions, was published in 1919, became the leading intellectual dissenter. Along with
"Lost Generation" writers such as Ernest Hemingway and F. Scott
Fitzgerald, Mencken was instrumental in establishing a postwar attitude
that countered the vehement parochialism of American traditionalists.
The result was a literary culture that produced such writers as John
Dos Passos, Hart Crane, Wallace Stevens, William Carlos Williams, and
William Faulkner.

The designations "Jazz Age" and "Roaring Twenties" aptly reflect
the enthusiastic way in which much of America gravitated toward an
urban lifestyle that zealously defied staid tradition and rejoiced in rebellion. Out of that upheaval came the prominent social symbols of the
decade: speakeasies, the Charleston, bathtub gin, flappers, and the acceptance and glorification of the gangsters who controlled bootlegging
and urban night life. This open defiance of traditional values (largely an
urban versus rural affair) also sparked a renewed interest in black life
by many liberal and intellectual whites.

Nowhere was that interest more evident than in Harlem.

In March 1924, the sociologist Charles S. Johnson—who had come
to New York as the Urban League's national director of research and
investigations and editor of its monthly magazine, *Opportunity*—organized a dinner at the Civic Club in lower Manhattan to which Jean
Toomer, Jessie Fauset, Langston Hughes, Countee Cullen, Alain
Locke, and other young literary luminaries were invited. This dinner
was later recognized as the birth of the Harlem Renaissance.[6]

Both Johnson and Locke, the jaunty former Howard University professor who had been the first black Rhodes Scholar, believed that the

arts and literature offered a relatively unimpaired means of combating racism. While white society had geared itself to resist advances by blacks in employment, voting, housing, and union affiliation, there were fewer obstacles to blacks in publishing and entertainment. There, they felt, the battle for racial equality could best be fought by presenting a more complete view of black life and by demonstrating that blacks could make worthwhile contributions to higher culture. "The interest in the cultural expression of Negro life," Locke wrote, "heralds an almost revolutionary revaluation of the Negro." The idea had been suggested earlier when William Pickens published a collection of essays entitled The New Negro (1916), and wrote of the transition "from the patient, unquestioning, devoted semi-slave to the self-conscious, aspiring, proud young man."[7]

Locke, in an essay in a book of the same title, The New Negro (1925) —an anthology of stories, articles, and poems, which he collected and edited—argued that the mass migration of blacks to urban centers in the North and Mideast had eradicated the simplistic, outworn concepts of black mammies, Sambos, and Uncle Toms. The complexity of city living had created a community of Negroes who were forced to deal with an urban, industrialized environment. Their task was to redefine Negro life and culture, to place it in a broader context than that imposed by whites who had defined Negroes in a manner that justified repression. Working with Johnson on Opportunity, Locke guided the careers of a significant number of young black writers (some of whom had been his students at Howard). Langston Hughes, Claude McKay, Zora Neale Hurston, Rudolph Fisher, Jessie Fauset, Wallace Thurman, E. Franklin Frazier, and George S. Schuyler were among the writers he helped bring to the attention of the American public.

Renaissance novels and stories provided a welcome alternative to the skewed caricatures presented in the fiction of popular white writers such as Thomas Dixon, Hugh Wiley, and Octavus Roy Cohen (who was hyped as the Negro's O. Henry). But, from a literary viewpoint, it was the poetry of writers like Claude McKay, Countee Cullen, and, especially, Langston Hughes that made the Renaissance remarkable; the fiction, while sound, was seldom outstanding. Still, this was a period of tremendous expansion of black artistic expression, which produced some notable literary figures as well as a raft of lesser lights whose charisma far exceeded their contributions ("Niggerati," as Zora Neale Hurston dubbed them).

Despite Locke's efforts and the support of white intellectuals and such figures as Melville J. Herskovits, Carl Van Vechten, and H. L. Mencken, who took an inordinate interest in black life ("Negrotarians," in Hurston's colorful terminology), mainstream America was only mildly concerned with black literary expression. Just as whites generally ignored blacks' efforts to enact anti-lynching legislation, A. Philip Randolph's diligent attempt to organize the Brotherhood of Sleeping Car Porters and Maids, and Marcus Garvey's grass-roots-based Universal Negro Improvement Association (which was also ridiculed by the black middle class), the literary thrust of the Harlem Renaissance was generally dismissed or regarded frivolously by mainstream America in the twenties.

The period's mainstream humor is particularly revealing. Minstrel joke books abounded and Sambo routines and gags were extremely popular among the masses. Better-educated whites were amused by the presumably more imaginative racial jokes that appeared in magazines such as *Judge, Life,* or *College Humor.* And, indeed, some were relatively benign. For instance, a cartoon picturing a little black girl walking in the rain with an umbrella was captioned "Just a shade under the weather" (*Judge,* 1920).

Typically, however, the jokes focused on blacks' physical appearance, appetites, or supposed laziness and ignorance:

"Madame," said the conductor politely to the colored lady, "you must remove that suitcase from the aisle."

"Fo' de lawd sake, conducto', dat ain't no suitcase. Dat's mah foot." (*Judge,* 1918)

"Seems to me," said Mammy Chloe, "dat sometimes you'd rather sleep than eat."

"Speck I would," answered Pickaninny Jim. " 'Cause when I'se asleep I'se liable to dream about fried chicken an' spare ribs an' watermelon—an' I ain't seen no such dinner as dat in a long time." (*Judge,* Darkeyisms column, 1919)

"Rastus, what you doin' wid dat mustache?"

"Dat ain't no mustache, boy. Mah gal uses lipstick." (*College Humor,* 1923, credited to *The University of Texas Ranger*)

"Wot you doin', chile?"

"Nothin', mammy."

"My, but you is gittin' like yoh father." (*Judge,* 1921, credited to *The Boston Transcript*)

Doctor (noticing a squalling black child on the floor): Missus Johnson, that baby is spoiled, isn't he?

Mrs. Johnson:　No sah, doctah, all nigger babies smell dat way.
(*Judge,* 1922)

The most insidious jested about the revival of the Ku Klux Klan and
the upsurge of anti-black violence and lynching:

"More throat trouble in the South."
　"How's that?"
"They just hung another coon." (*College Humor,* 1921, credited
to *Harvard Lampoon*)

Teacher:　Percival, you are half an hour late. What's the matter?

KKK Percy:　I went out with papa to a lynching party and we
stayed until the last man was hung.

Teacher (severely): Was *hanged,* Percival. (*College Humor,* 1923,
credited to *Harvard Lampoon*)

Cartoon picturing a black man (carrying a hatchet and an opossum)
cowering behind a house as a Ku Klux Klan parade goes by is
captioned: "Now I know why dey calls it a white Christmas." (*Life,*
1923)

Still, Americans continued their ambivalent and ironic fascination
with black life. They rushed to see and hear African-American musicians, mimicked black dances, and glorified black style while, in private,
they retained their disdainful view of Negroes. Even as they violently
suppressed black efforts to advance in education and employment, and
exercise their lawful rights, whites turned to the black community as a
model for their rebellion against puritanical rural values. They flocked
to black communities—Chicago's South Side, Watts's Central Avenue,
Beale Street in Memphis, and, of course, Harlem, the "mecca of the
New Negro."
　Harlem had become a major attraction for the adventurous of every
level of white society—working class, middle class, socialites, and intellectuals, even European visitors, including royalty. A cab ride from

midtown, through Central Park, opened up an exotic world of dark, uninhibited revelry and uncharted dissipation.

Speakeasies and nightclubs, the most lavish of which were generally mob-controlled and strictly segregated, dotted Lenox and Seventh avenues. "Duke" Ellington, "Fats" Waller, Fletcher Henderson, Ethel Waters, Noble Sissle, Bill "Bojangles" Robinson, Lena Horne, Earl "Snakehips" Tucker, Cab Calloway, Louis Armstrong, and other entertainers of their stature held sway on stage at Harlem night spots. At the Bamboo Inn, the Lenox Club, the Exclusive Club, Small's Paradise, and many other smaller clubs, white visitors who truly wished to submerge themselves in black exoticism could rub shoulders with real Harlemites in the audience. For those who preferred tempering their indulgence with a dash of social reality and could afford the luxury, the Cotton Club, run by the notorious gangster and bootlegger Owen Madden, and Connie's Inn catered exclusively to whites. Black presence was limited to service roles, stage fantasy, and the few who passed for white.

These clubs generally indulged the white stereotype of blacks as natural primitives. Waiters danced the Charleston in the aisles as they served food and drink; beautiful black women (always of light complexion) slithered about in scanty costumes on stage; and at the Cotton Club, Duke Ellington played so-called "jungle music" in a sumptuous African setting. On a given night, the audience for this exotic display might include such downtown luminaries as Sophie Tucker, Eddie Duchin, Helen Morgan, Gene Tunney, Joan Crawford, William Powell, Mae West, Jack Dempsey, Tallulah Bankhead, Benny Goodman, Gertrude Vanderbilt, Hoagy Carmichael, or George Raft, who frequented the Cotton Club and, according to rag pianist Willie "the Lion" Smith, was "a sharpie in those days and about the best dancer in New York."[8]

The profligate nature of Harlem night life was glamorized in two of the period's most controversial novels: *Home to Harlem* (1928), by the black writer Claude McKay, and *Nigger Heaven* (1926), by Negrotarian Carl Van Vechten. The latter had long been an advocate of black exoticism and, in an earlier book, had demonstrated his ardor as well as his often myopic and paternalistic viewpoint in a skewed estimate of Williams and Walker's act: "How the darkies danced and sang and cavorted! Real nigger stuff. . . . They're delightful niggers, these unexhaustible Ethiopians, those husky, lanky blacks!" Harlem had become a fantasy land, an exotic attraction that fascinated blacks and whites. Renaissance writer Arna Bontemps wrote of the "foretaste of paradise" he experienced at initially seeing Lenox Avenue; Cab Calloway was "awestruck by the whole scene"; and Duke Ellington gushed, "Why, it is just like the Arabian nights." For whites it provided a haven where, in the words of a contemporary journalist, one could assuage "the asperities of a Puritan conscience" or, quite simply, "go on moral vacation." The influx of whites to Harlem led James Weldon Johnson to write: "At these times, the Negro drags his captors captive. On occasions, I have been amazed and amused watching white people dancing to a Negro band in a Harlem cabaret; attempting to throw off the crusts and layers of inhibitions laid on by sophisticated civilization; striving to yield to the feel and experience of abandon; seeking to recapture a taste of primitive joy in life and living; trying to work their way back into that jungle which was the original Garden of Eden; in a word, doing their best to pass for colored."[9]

But America's infatuation with black style and night life was not restricted solely to visiting Harlem or other black communities. In a blatant throwback to minstrel times, Lew Leslie, who would later produce *Blackbirds of 1926* (a show that opened at the Alhambra in Harlem, then played Paris and London before going to Broadway), opened his Plantation Club on Broadway in 1923. The club's decor replicated a Southern plantation: upon entering, patrons would find themselves surrounded by log cabins, picket fences, and servants dressed as traditional mammies and bucks. In one cabin, Aunt Jemima could be seen happily flipping flapjacks. Although the noted star of *Shuffle Along*, Florence Mills, was a headline attraction, the entertainment generally reflected the dubious taste of the decor.[10]

Broadway theatres also began to take note of mainstream fascination with black life. Just as Florenz Ziegfeld had bought the rights to the 1913 Lafayette Theatre production *Darktown Follies* (which introduced an early dance sensation, the Texas Tommy) and brought it downtown for his Ziegfeld *Follies*, some theatre owners simply moved successful shows or revues from Harlem to midtown. With the increased presence of blacks in Harlem and the integration of theatres like the Lafayette and the Lincoln, such relocations became an expedient and profitable way of serving white audiences who, while curious about the "New Negro," preferred satisfying that curiosity on their own turf. Among these transplanted shows was Fats Waller's *Hot Chocolates* (1929), which began as a musical revue at Connie's Inn.

Some of the best of the new black Broadway musicals of the period were *Dinah* (1923), which featured a new dance sensation, the Black Bottom; Miller and Lyles's *Runnin' Wild* (1923), which introduced the

Charleston to the stage; *Chocolate Dandies* (1924), featuring the future internationally known star Josephine Baker; *Dixie to Broadway* (1924), starring Florence Mills; *Africana* (1927), which starred Ethel Waters; *Blackbirds of 1928*, in which Bill Robinson performed the Stair Dance routine that became his signature; *Weather Clear—Track Fast* (1927), notable primarily because it starred Buck and Bubbles; *Blackbirds of 1930*; and *Shuffle Along of 1932*.

Despite the ferment, the comedy was usually patterned after routines introduced by Miller and Lyles in the original *Shuffle Along*. Harlem nightclubs and theatres as well as Broadway theatres focused basically on music and dance. Mainstream interest had simply shifted from the Reconstruction era's obsession with ex-slaves as childish, inept darkies to viewing them as carefree, stylish exotics.

But as the hardship of the Depression began subverting fantasies of earthy Harlem cabarets and free-and-easy urban lifestyles, as economic deprivation forced nearly all Americans to focus on essentials and embrace traditional values, the more comforting image of blacks as inept simpletons or faithful servants began to reappear. Those images, insistently established in the formative years of motion pictures, would be emphatically reinforced in Hollywood sound films beginning in the late twenties.

II

The debut of sound movies, in fact, temporarily heightened enthusiasm for a variety of black performers and film projects in Hollywood. Based partially on the claims of Bill Foster—an energetic black promoter and filmmaker who had vainly attempted to carve a niche in the Hollywood film hierarchy since early silent films—the speculation that black voices "recorded with better fidelity than white" and were better suited for sound pictures began circulating within the industry. Bolstered, no doubt, by the impact of black musicians and vocalists on society at large and the discovery that the voices of many silent film stars were too weak for talkies, the rumor gained credence. Hollywood responded with a rash of black-oriented movies.[11]

Even as the industry turned to black themes, however, old bugaboos persisted. Whether out of fear of annoying its mainstream audience or as a simple reflex, Hollywood's heightened interest in blacks was accompanied by an upsurge of blackface films. *The Jazz Singer* (1927), which starred Al Jolson (a minstrel and vaudeville singer who was fasci-

nated by the "new rhythm" and "primitive appeal" of Negro voices),
was the most famous of these sentimental retreads and is credited
with ushering in the sound era. Jolson would continue making corked
appearances in films until the forties, proving more popular and resilient than such white minstrel comics and black impersonators as Eddie
Leonard, Mack and Moran ("The Two Black Crows"), and Freeman
Gosden and Charles Correll, who abortively brought their popular radio
characters Amos and Andy to the screen in *Check and Double Check*
(1930).[12]

Nonetheless, more than two decades after syncopated music (coon
songs and ragtime) began dominating America's popular musical taste
and altering its social dances, nearly a decade after *Shuffle Along* had
first captivated New York audiences, and several years after the "New
Negro" was introduced in Harlem, the film industry finally took notice
of urban blacks and their music. The most dramatic shift was seen in
all-black musical shorts or feature productions in which black musical
stars made cameo appearances. But two notable full-length, all-black
movies were produced in the late twenties.

The first was *Hearts in Dixie* (1929), a plantation musical that, although steeped in a mythological Southern setting featuring requisite
dancing pickaninnies, contented field hands, and mournful spirituals,
broke ranks with previous Hollywood films by depicting African-Americans who displayed a measure of self-reliance and struggled to better
themselves. The movie starred Clarence Muse as a tenant farmer and
Stepin Fetchit, the fast-rising comic star, in the role of a shiftless coon
that he would soon patent. The Fox Studio advertisements were blatant:
"Hear those hearts beat the cadences of their race . . . along the levees
and in the cotton fields. . . . All the happy-go-lucky joy of living, laughter, and all-embracing gusto of plantation life." But Muse's dignified
performance and Fetchit's unusual comic presence kept the film from
sinking completely into the category of hackneyed stereotype.[13]

Fetchit, cast as the traditional languorous buffoon, occasionally transcended his role, surprising with some nimble patter and dance steps.
Moreover, in contrast to the lachrymose, hardworking farmhands surrounding him, his behavior suggests that, at least in the plantation
setting, play, malingering, and frivolity were much to be preferred over
dedicated toil without reward.

Hallelujah! (1929) was greeted with even more anticipation than
Hearts. Director King Vidor had pursued the project with a zealousness
bordering on fanaticism, finally offering part of his salary to defray

production costs and ensure that Fox Studios completed the film. His stated goal was to depict Southern Negroes realistically. Ultimately, however, his undoubtedly sincere attempt was limited by some familiar, biased perceptions. *Hallelujah!* is basically a morality play that contrasts black rural life (benevolent, innocent, God-fearing) with urban life (corrupt, evil, violent), a dichotomy that had been suggested in D. W. Griffith's films years before. The result is a steamy melodrama focused on the obsession of Zeke, a naive farmhand and preacher, for a sexy city vixen. What distinguishes the movie is Vidor's focus on the emotional aspects of this doomed infatuation. Few previous films had earnestly treated black passion or, for that matter, delved into black familial or love relationships without reverting to ridicule or lampoon. Here, although the plot is clichéd, the plight of the characters is handled soberly. Daniel Hayes and Nina Mae McKinney give taut performances as the star-crossed lovers, and their ill-fated entanglement is treated as a serious human dilemma.

Still, in the words of the critic Peter Noble, *Hallelujah!* was "swamped, inevitably perhaps, by the forty or so singing sequences of folk songs, spirituals, baptism wails, work songs and blues." And Haynes's interpretation of a Southern preacher's sermon—centered on the train-to-glory motif and enhanced by Haynes's audible and physical imitation of a locomotive—inadvertently foreshadowed the satiric portrait of black preachers that Flip Wilson and Richard Pryor would present in the sixties and seventies. But, except for the pickaninnies—whose comical dance routines include tap, twirls, the Buck and Wing, itch, and cakewalk—the film avoids intentionally broad comedy. It is a moody, riveting movie; most of its humorous touches grow naturally out of the warm rapport between the members of Zeke's family. It may even be, as Donald Bogle suggests, "an authentic American classic."[14]

Ultimately, the major studios did not follow through on even the faint promise suggested by *Hearts in Dixie* and *Hallelujah!* Seven years passed before the release of the next black-cast feature film, *The Green Pastures* (1936). This was an adaptation of Marc Connelly's successful Broadway play, which, in turn, had been influenced by Roark Bradford's collection of biblical tales *Ol' Man Adam an' His Chillun* (1928). These stories, although set in the rural South and narrated by an Uncle Remus–like character, featured a mixed cast of Southern characters. Connelly, a successful playwright and member of the Algonquin Round Table group, blackened all of Bradford's biblical characters for commercial reasons. At the time, the film represented the major studios' most ambitious attempt to capture black folk life in an expansive, full-length setting.

Its highlights were excellent performances by Rex Ingram and Eddie "Rochester" Anderson (each in multiple roles that included "De Lawd" and a Tomming Noah in high hat and raincoat), the music of the Hall Johnson Choir, and a concluding scene featuring Ingram as an embattled soldier pitted against an obscure but diabolical enemy who one film historian suggests may be seen as a symbol for racism. Overall, however, the film was little more than an extended one-theme gag with musical accompaniment. It treads heavily on the insistent incongruity between the earthiness of black folkways and the hallowed concept of Paradise. After Ingram, as De Lawd, decides to "rare back and pass a miracle," for instance, his flock's intransigence leads him to complain: "Bein' De Lawd ain't no bed of roses." As one critic pointed out, although the movie was "well intentioned, it merely gave filmgoers once more the happy, religious, hymn-singing black man whose idea of heaven seems to consist mainly of long white nightgowns, hymn-shouting and fish-fries."[15]

Humor in *The Green Pastures* is derived from the underlying premise that a black Heaven is a cosmic absurdity. In many ways the movie is comparable to nineteenth-century blackface parodies of politicians, preachers, and pundits, or minstrel satires of classic Elizabethan dramas, which contrasted the stage Negro's ignorance, fractured language, and foolish behavior with "serious" white predicaments. *Pastures* simply played upon the mainstream vision of blacks as untutored children who were quaintly ineffective in an adult, *white* world—certainly in the devoted atmosphere of Paradise.

Hearts in Dixie, *Hallelujah!*, and *The Green Pastures* were the only full-length black-cast features produced by the major studios until 1943, when MGM's *Cabin in the Sky* and Paramount's *Stormy Weather* were released. Both these movies were lavish productions that, as we shall see later, did offer a few vivid examples of black humor. Lukewarm audience response combined with criticism from black pressure groups and studio timidity deflected other projects. In the interim, black writers such as Langston Hughes were occasionally asked to contribute to mixed-cast features like Sol Lesser's *Way Down South* (1939)—a film sadly characterized by its maudlin plantation theme, anachronistic dialect humor, and glorification of Stephen Foster's pseudoslave songs. In a letter to a fellow Harlem Renaissance writer, Arna Bontemps, Hughes wrote of his contribution to the film: "The bad things I do are the only things that ever make me any money." Years later, he would write more pointedly of the movie industry: "Hollywood is our *bête noir*. It is America (and the world's) most popular art. . . . Yet, shamelessly and to all the world since its inception, Hollywood has spread in exaggerated form every ugly and ridiculous stereotype of the deep South's conception of Negro character." He warned Bontemps: "Never take a Hollywood job."[16]

The numerous all-black musical shorts and frequent appearances of black entertainers in feature films during this period are largely peripheral—although the extravagant, sometimes ludicrous costumes, sets, and situations in which otherwise serious musicians, dancers, and singers were required to work are worth noting. In the 1932 short *Pie Pie Blackbird*, for instance, the Noble Sissle and Eubie Blake band, wearing bizarre chef hats, emerged through the top of a gigantic pie crust to perform as the Nicholas Brothers went through an energetic tap routine along the perimeter of the huge confection. *Rhapsody in Black and Blue* (Paramount, 1932), although it features Louis Armstrong singing and playing some of his popular jazz tunes, casts the trumpeter as king of a pseudo-African community and has him perform in leopard skin and Hollywood-inspired "native" headdress.

Rufus Jones for President (1933), a one-reel musical farce, featured jazz vocalist Ethel Waters and seven-year-old Sammy Davis, Jr., as a pint-sized candidate for president of a black lodge. After entering beneath a banner that reads, "VOTE HERE FOR RUFUS JONES, TWO PORK CHOPS EVERY TIME YOU VOTE," the impish Davis is confronted by an irate lodge member. "Wait a minute here! I objects," he shouts. "When we elects a president, we elects him to do somethin'. Dis president jes sits in de chair and don't do nothin'." Immediately Davis stands and, in top hat and tails, breaks into a facile vaudeville song and dance routine. When he stops, Waters announces, "There he is, you ain't never had a president what could do that." Davis, in his first movie role, is charming and effervescent, despite the heavy-handed satirizing of black fraternal orders.

The gratuitous appearance of Duke Ellington and his band in RKO's embarrassingly inept *Check and Double Check* (1930), which starred Freeman Gosden and Charles Correll as Amos and Andy, is a representative example of Hollywood's using black entertainers to enliven lackluster movies. The brief appearance of Ellington and a few establishing shots in Harlem are the only authentic elements in this hackneyed attempt to bring radio's popular but controversial imitation Negroes to the screen. Otherwise the film flounders as its blackface performers present a jaundiced panorama of standard racial gags.

There was the expected fractured language ("I's regusted," "monetary rejuvejation," or "dis is mo reportant"), questionable when delivered by more adept comedians such as Flournoy Miller and Aubrey Lyles, piteously inappropriate when voiced by mediocre black imitators. (On radio, a purely aural medium, Gosden and Correll were much more convincing.) Among the film's blackface actors, only Gosden (Amos), who had studied the accents of blacks in Virginia and other parts of the South, demonstrated any talent as a comedian or believable black man. In addition, there is an enervated facsimile of Miller and Lyles's vaudeville mathematics routine; the obligatory haunted-house scene; and, although the film is set in New York, a mawkish homage to Southern mythology involving the son of the Southern patriarch for whom Amos and Andy had worked:

Richards: What in the world are you boys doing up here? Do you work for Mr. Blair?

Andy: No, we done dreve de band up here. We in business for ourselves.

Amos: Ah, yassar, we's in the taxi cab business in New York City.

Richards: Amos and Andy! You know, boys, I often wondered what became of you after you left Georgia.

Amos: Oh, Mr. Richards, we certainly do miss that ole place too, you know it. Me and Andy talk about it all duh time.

Andy: Yeah . . . dat was duh besty home we eber had.

Amos: Y'all certainly was good to us down dere. Yo papa treated us like we was his own chillun. . . . We sho would like to see him again.

Richards: Well, Amos, I'm afraid that none of us will ever see Dad again.

Andy: What you mean, Mr. Richards?

Richards: Well . . . Dad's gone.

Amos: Gone . . . You don't mean dat. . . . Oh, Mr. Richards, I certainly is sorry to hear that.

Andy: So is I, Mr. Richards.

Amos: (Tearfully) Yo dad was the best family dat we ever had, ever since we worked for him. He raised us and we loved him. And when he was tellin us good-bye, he said to us, "Boys" . . . he said, "if you ever need anything or anything ever go wrong, remember that you can always write home." And he made us feel like we had a home. And I know dat if he didn't have but one loaf o' bread, dat he would give us half of it. And you say he's gone. . . .

Inexplicably, although he is barely recognizable in a brief appearance, Duke Ellington claimed that this film was among the "crowning points" of his career.[17]

Black musicians, singers, and dancers, however, frequently worked in less controversial and less demeaning circumstances. Stars such as Lena Horne, Eubie Blake and Noble Sissle, Ethel Waters, Louis Armstrong, the Nicholas Brothers, Buck and Bubbles, Dorothy Dandridge, Nat King Cole, and Ellington continued making notable brief appearances in full-length Hollywood movies—some until the 1970s.

In addition, these performers and others—Don Redman, Chick Webb, the Mills Brothers, Billie Holiday, Jimmie Lunceford, and Bessie Smith, for example—appeared in the raft of all-black musical shorts that debuted in the late twenties. Despite minor drawbacks, many of these one- and two-reelers transcended their basic formats as showcases for musicians and entertainers. Some, because they showcased black performers in a more or less realistic fashion, remain classics: among them are *St. Louis Blues* (1929), which featured Bessie Smith, Jimmy Mordecai, the dancer, and the music of W. C. Handy and J. Rosamond Johnson; *Black and Tan* (1929), with Fredi Washington and Duke Ellington; *Barbershop Blues* (1933), featuring the dancing Nicholas Brothers; *Yamacraw* (1930), with Jimmy Mordecai and the music of James P. Johnson; *Symphony in Black* (1935), with Earl "Snakehips" Tucker, Billie Holiday, and, again, Duke Ellington; and *Boogie Woogie Dream* (1944), with Lena Horne and Teddy Wilson. Finally, these short films and cameo appearances represent some of the most creative and least distorted presentations of African-Americans offered by the major studios during the period.

A relatively undistorted and unoffensive example of blacks in a comedy series at this time can be found in Hal Roach's successful and enduring *Our Gang* shorts. Beginning with two-reel silents in 1922, the series was produced until 1944 (six years after MGM took over production); a total of 222 *Our Gang* comedies were filmed with an integrated cast of juvenile performers. From its silent film debut to sound movies and on to the currently popular reissues for television as *The Little Rascals*, Roach's Rascals have maintained a loyal audience despite their slightly tainted image.

Four black children were featured as regular members of the gang. The first was Rascal, Ernie Morrison, a proven seven-year-old actor who had performed in films with such comedians as Harold Lloyd and starred in his own *Sunshine Sammy* short before *Our Gang* began. Variously billed as "Booker T.," "Sorghum," and "Sunshine Sammy," he appeared in twenty-eight silent films from 1922 through 1924. Later, he starred in vaudeville, and in the 1940s, he was cast as one of the *East Side Kids*, the teenage comedy series.

In the second *Gang* two-reeler, *Fire Fighters* (October 1922), Morrison was joined by one-year-old Allen "Farina" Hoskins, who reportedly was discovered by Morrison's father in Watts and was enlisted immediately for the role of Sunshine's "sister." Subsequently, Hoskins easily made the transition to sound movies, and he appeared in 105 *Our Gang* comedies, "more than anyone else in the series." After *Fly My Kite* (June 1931), his last regular *Gang* short, he appeared in several feature films.[18]

The next black Rascal was Matthew "Stymie" Beard, who debuted at age five as Hercules in *Teacher's Pet* (October 1930). Noted for his well-timed double-takes and facility with dialogue, Beard made more than thirty-six of the Roach movies. After his last Rascal role in 1935, he continued working in films, appearing as a teenage villain in the independently produced race movie *Broken Strings* (1940) with Clarence Muse. Later, after he survived a serious bout with drug addiction, his acting career was revived in the 1960s.

Like Farina, William "Buckwheat" Thomas, Jr.'s, first appearance in *Our Gang* was as the sister of an older Rascal, Stymie, and for a time the question of his real gender caused national speculation. He debuted in *For Pete's Sake!* (April 1934) and went on to appear in ninety-eight *Gang* movies, including the last—*Tale of a Dog* (April 1944).[19]

Despite the intended similarity between Farina and Buckwheat (they dressed alike and wore similarly restless pigtails), each of the black Rascals had distinct characteristics and personalities.

Ernie Morrison is probably the least familiar of the black actors now, since he only appeared in silent *Gang* films that are rarely aired on television. He was, however, a consummate professional entertainer (the only black Rascal to have begun his acting career before the series), whose staple comic maneuvers—huge rolling eyes, anxiety-ridden mugging, and rapid-fire speech—can be seen on television in the still syndicated *East Side Kids* series.

Allen "Farina" Hoskins, according to Hal Roach, was "one of the finest natural actors we had in the Gang." Early on, his ability to cry on cue was noted by the producers; subsequently, Farina (named, like Buckwheat, after a breakfast cereal) was used as a comic and sentimental foil, consistently getting into trouble, then wringing pathos from the situation with his tears. He was also noted for his oddly husky voice, which contrasted with Alfalfa's squeaky soprano, for his prudence with regard to anything resembling a ghost or spook, and for his seemingly electrified pigtails, which stood straight up every time he was frightened.

Matthew Beard's Stymie, although not immune to intimidation from ghosts, was a much cooler, more self-composed character. With his signature bald head, derby, and air of adult imperturbability, Stymie often projected a maturity, shrewdness, and lack of gullibility that set him apart from the rest of the Gang. In *Free Eats* (February 1932), for instance, Stymie spots two midget thieves dressed as children when everyone else is duped by them. His warning about the two mob "fridgets" goes unheeded until it is nearly too late. In other episodes, Stymie, who more than any other Rascal lived by his wits, was featured in plots centered on his efforts to outsmart his friends. *Dogs Is Dogs* (November 1931), for example, focuses on his attempt to con Sherwood out of his breakfast with an elaborately concocted story about talking ham and eggs. Overall, Stymie's humor flowed from the contrast between his independence and guile and the others' childish naïveté.[20]

Buckwheat, as played by William Thomas, Jr., dressed and acted much like his urchin predecessor, Farina. His understated humor, however, was distinct. He frequently stole scenes even when he had no dialogue; the sight of his wide, bashful eyes and deadpan expression, particularly in the context of the utter chaos that normally surrounded the Gang, was often enough to elicit laughter. Buckwheat and the white character, Porky, formed a team within the group: their innocent, dawdling presence usually worked in counterpoint to the others' mischievous antics. As the film historian Donald Bogle puts it, Buckwheat "came across as a quiet, odd-ball type, the perfect little dum-dum tagalong."[21]

Our Gang, of course, was not always benign; the series was also peppered with standard racial gags. Haunted houses and graveyard scenes with spooks and ghosts abounded, and the black Rascals were most often the terrified victims of pranks that invariably sent them into headlong flight. The derisively titled *Spook Spoofing* (July 1923) and *Spooky Hooky* (December 1936) are examples. Crapshooting blacks also played a large part in the humor on several occasions. In the silent *Lodge Night* (July 1923), Ernie Morrison's real-life father is seen as a college professor who, in the middle of a nonsensical "philosophy" lecture patterned on the old minstrel lampoons of black intellectuals, suddenly realizes that he would rather be gambling; in *Bargain Day* (May 1931), Stymie, after responding to another child's query about his father's occupation with, "Uh-uh, my daddy ain't no chauffeur. . . . My daddy is just a crap-shootin' fool!" advances the stereotype by getting involved in a crap game himself.[22]

Other instances of denigrative stereotypes are found in *Saturday Morning* (December 1922), in which Sorghum (a.k.a. Sunshine Sammy) serves his infant sister a watermelon breakfast in one of the initial examples of the series' running gags about black children's passion for succulent foods; *Little Daddy* (March 1931), which opens in a church where a black congregation fills the collection plate with buttons instead of coins; *Spanky* (March 1932), which features a blackface adaptation of *Uncle Tom's Cabin; General Spanky* (December 1936)—the only full-length Rascal film—in which Buckwheat and Louise Beavers portray slaves in a traditional Old South setting; and *Three Smart Boys* (May 1937), whose plot centers on Buckwheat being mistaken for a monkey.[23]

Despite these and other examples, criticism of the series often seems a bit self-conscious and overblown. Most of the other Gang members were subjected to similar pranks and, on balance, it is difficult to substantiate much focused victimization of the black Rascals. Roach's series actually marked a substantial advance in the presentation of black children on the screen.

Earlier *Gang*-type films had been more explicitly offensive in singling out black kids as buffoons and ne'er-do-wells: David Fleischer's *Busting the Show* (1920), for example, focused on a backyard presentation of "The Grate Nigger Bucking Wing Dancer," and featured a blackface comic whose minstrel-like mugging stole the show; and before becoming one of Roach's Rascals, Ernie Morrison had appeared as Sunshine Sammy in a film bluntly entitled *The Pickaninny* (1921). Moreover, during the more than two decades that the series was produced, other films continued presenting black children in a far more grossly demeaning manner. The character Topsy, as we have seen, in both the 1927 version of *Uncle Tom's Cabin* and *Topsy and Eva*, makes Roach's Rascals look like models of equitable treatment.[24]

Many critics agree. Bogle wrote that despite their dialect speech and episodes in which they are the butt of ghost, food, and color gags—elements that "conformed to the accepted notions and attitudes of the day"—the black Rascals were generally treated "as if there were no such thing as race at all . . . the charming sense of *Our Gang* was that all the children were buffoons . . . everyone had his turn at being outwitted." And Allen Hoskins, in a 1975 interview, pointed out: "There was a certain degree of stereotyping and there was quite a bit of dialect used. [But] thirty or forty years ago, a lot of people were talking in dialect and a lot of them are still doing it. . . . Even the white kids were stereotyped. There was the classic fat boy, the freckled-face boy, the little blonde angel—all the usual stereotypes. But they related to each other as a bunch of kids, doing all the things that kids do."[25]

At its best, *Our Gang* simply offered the kind of cute, light entertainment we expect of kid comedy. At worst, it tripped not so lightly over ethnic gags that made the black Rascals as well as their playmates the butt of jokes. But many of those jokes are harmless reverse color gags relying on difference in complexion. In *Ye Olde Minstrel* (March 1944), for example, after an adult hoofer is transformed to blackface, Buckwheat suddenly appears in whiteface; in *Cousin Wilbur* (April 1939), when Buckwheat attempts to sell a black playmate insurance against black eyes, he is told, "Go way, Buckwheat. How's anybody gonna tell if I has a black eye?"

Yet the series elicited protests from black lobbyists. The groundswell of negative sentiment grew to such proportions that, by the early seventies, the television revival of the films (for legal reasons renamed *The Little Rascals*) faced a major hurdle. To avoid blatant racial stereotypes some episodes were withdrawn from television syndication (among them, *Little Daddy*); others were severely edited. Ultimately, the NAACP approved the abridged prints.

III

But Hollywood's screen image of adult blacks showed fewer signs of improvement. In the late twenties, Paramount was the first studio to produce an adult black comedy series for sound movies. Headed by Al Christie, it became known as the Christie Comedies and set out to adapt Octavus Roy Cohen's coarse comic tales of black life in urban Alabama. And for the first time, a black adviser would have significant input: the comedian Spencer Williams was retained as a consultant, continuity writer, and performer.

Word of the impending project was greeted with elation and optimism by the black community. But if Cohen's track record in films or his reputation as a Southern regionalist writer committed to derisive, minstrel-like dialect humor had been closely examined, their enthusiasm might have been tempered.

Advertised as "the negro's O. Henry," Cohen had staked an early claim as one of the premier white expositors of black life and culture. Although he first published in the early twentieth century, his fiction was a pedestrian derivative of the works of the nineteenth-century "misspellers" such as Artemus Ward. Cohen, however, like Hugh Wiley, opportunistically created an insular fictional world where blacks were the sole focus of his crude satire. "The plots of his stories are derived from jokes—jokes that rely for their effect on the comic caricature of the Negro," wrote the literary critic Sylvia Wallace Holton. "In his work black characters are presented as pretentious and impressed by bourgeois material values; their greatest pleasure in their pursuit of material riches is to outwit one another. Ultimately, the characters are rendered ridiculous by their names, their values, and their misuse of language. All of them come off badly."[26]

By the mid-twenties, he and other literary "Ethiopian Delineators" had secured an inflated reputation as the Negro's realistic chroniclers, just as their minstrel predecessors had done in the mid-nineteenth century. Belatedly and ironically, Carl Van Vechten warned of such a situation in his novel *Nigger Heaven* (1926), when one character says, "If you young Negro intellectuals don't get busy, a new crop of Nordics is going to spring up who will take the trouble to become better informed and will exploit this material before the Negro gets around to it." Someone should have issued that caveat earlier.[27]

At the height of his career, E. K. Means, much like Cohen, was hailed as "THE writer of negro stories." Publishers' advertisements extolled Means's ability accurately to capture blacks' "picturesque idiom of speech," and his "perfect comprehension of the negro's turn of thought, his love of laughter, his shiftlessness, his love of music, his superstition." Collected stories by Means—a rural Louisiana pastor—were considered so unique and authentically black that they needed no title other than the author's name. His comic tales about quaint, superstitious rural blacks were published simply as *E. K. Means* (1918) and *Further E. K. Means* (1920).[28]

Cohen and other Southern humorists specializing in black caricature were not new to the Hollywood scene. At least one Dickson movie, *The Custard Nine* (1911), was shot on location in Vicksburg, Mississippi, and, unlike most films of the time, used black performers. Tom Fletcher, as an actor in Dickson's company, recalled that residents were not pleased when the Pullman car loaded with black actors arrived in Vicksburg. "See those niggers," a local reportedly said. "They came down here in a Pullman car just like white folks, but you can bet a fat penny they won't go back in one." The easy camaraderie of the mixed company infuriated locals, and Dickson, while entertaining at his country club, was reportedly rebuffed by another member who told him that he "didn't shake hands with any white man who called a nigger mister."[29]

But for all his apparent sympathy, Dickson's *The Custard Nine* was just another invidious farce that wrung laughter from its dialect jokes and portrait of a conniving, bumbling Southern black dandy, Virgil Custard (a member of "Darktown's four hundred"), who leads a traveling baseball team through a series of slapstick misadventures.[30]

Hugh Wiley, like Dickson and Cohen, initially published many of his short stories in the *Saturday Evening Post*. The collected tales—*Wildcat* (1920) and *Fo' Meals a Day* (1927)—centered on a black coon figure, J. Vitus Marsden, who was the "Wildcat" of the title. Expectedly, pretentious malaprop and dialect speech, crapshooting and carousing, and outrageous, ill-advised schemes were the prominent comic ingredients. Wiley's stories became so popular during the twenties that J. Vitus Marsden, along with Cohen's character, Florian Slappey, became household names, ranking with Sambo, Uncle Tom, Aunt Jemima, Rastus, Snowflake, and Topsy as the most visible and familiar symbols of blacks to most mainstream Americans.[31]

Consequently, around 1929, when Pathé Studios initiated a series of films intended to compete with Paramount's Christie Comedies, they turned to Wiley's tales. They, too, enlisted black assistants: the ubiquitous black filmmaker and promoter Bill Foster, who had produced a number of silent films, including *The Railroad Porter* (1912) and the controversial *Florida Crackers* (circa 1915), "which contained a graphic lynching scene"; and the black vaudeville song and dance team Buck and Bubbles (Ford Lee Washington and John Sublett). Pathé cranked out black-cast comedy shorts such as *In and Out, Foul Play, Darktown Blues,* and *Honest Crooks.* Most of these two-reelers have not survived; but according to Thomas Cripps, "The plots hung on threats of jail, 'high-yaller mamas,' and other stock situations." Still, Buck and Bubbles occasionally managed to introduce some less brazenly stereotyped material. In addition to their considerable talent as performers, they had by their very presence, Cripps suggested, "imposed black themes and situations on the white man's screen."[32]

Spencer Williams, a witty writer and comedian who would later produce his own films and star as Andy in the television version of *Amos 'n' Andy,* faced a similar task as a performer and writer for the Christie Comedies series.

As a humorist, Cohen had built a considerable reputation exploiting the image of the minstrel stage Negro and burlesquing urban Alabama blacks. Among other projects, from 1926 to 1927 he had produced a silent comedy series based on his stories, which featured the derisive coon character Florian Slappey. Except for the new sound technology and the presence of Spencer Williams, the Christie Comedies would offer more of the same low, racial buffoonery offered in the Florian Slappey series.

The following exchange between a black couple, Anopheles Ricketts and his wife Clarissy, from "Auto-Intoxication," a short story that peared in the 1921 collection *Highly Colored,* is representative of Cohen's least offensive dialect humor:

"I 'clare to goodness gracious, Clarissy," he remarked irritably, "automobiles is the on'y thing you don't talk about nothin' else but."

Clarissy pouted. "We is got money enough to buy us a car, honey. Lots of folks which ain't got as much as what we is got is got automobiles."

"Yeh—reckon they is. An' lots of folks is got bills which ain't paid, but we ain't. You jes' quit talkin' with yo' mouth bouten automobiles. 'Twain gwine git you nowheres, an'—"

"I could of had a automobile," flared Clarissy suddenly. "I sho' could of had a ninety-hawss-power Conley-Detroit if'n I had of chose."[33]

Transferred to the screen, this type of material was perfectly suited to Hollywood's knee-jerk, one-dimensional projection of conniving, un-tutored, inept darkies futilely attempting to mimic "white" manners and mores. The plots of most Cohen stories intensified the insult by focusing on Birmingham's middle-class ("sassietie") blacks, and de-picting them as pretentious, rural buffoons.

Brown Gravy (1929), for instance, opens with a traditional scene: a black choir sings "Every Time I Feel de Spirit" and "Joshua Fit de Battle of Jericho" as they practice for a choral contest. The film then moves through a threadbare plot that ridicules black matriarchal rela-tionships, religion, con men, and fraternal organizations ("the Knights and Ladies of a Better Worl' "). In one scene, a black pastor has the following conversation with the leader of a choir:

Leader: We is the singingest choir in de whole country.

Pastor: I sorry to have to move you downstairs in my piano parlor when I has my big spirita-lipstick meeting up here tonight.

Leader: That's all right, Professor Clemmens, the place what you have downstairs is plenty big enouf for de choir to practice in.

Pastor: Well now, I'se only gon' move you down dere just for duh night. Dat dere parlor is the biggest piano parlor in duh country. Come and look at it.

Leader: I was wantin' to see it.[34]

Other Christie Comedies were equally disparaging. *Framing of the Shrew* featured Evelyn Preer as an obstreperous, nagging black woman who ultimately gets her comeuppance from her timid husband. The part is that of the classic domineering mammy. Set in the same cabaret, *Music Hath Charms* and *Melancholy Dame* both deal with petty jeal-ousies and mistaken rivalries among the owner, his employees, and their paramours. Slapstick, broken English, and egregious portraits of inept blacks prevail in each of these 1929 two-reelers. Contributions by Spencer Williams were relegated to moderating Cohen's minstrel caricatures. As he continued to do throughout most of his career with the Christie Comedies, Williams struggled to "squeeze honest black roles into the crevices of white movies."[35]

Still, Hollywood was using black actors (some, like Evelyn Preer, from the Lafayette Players) instead of corked-up whites. And by the early thirties, a raft of prominent black stage comedians, like their musician counterparts, were allowed access to Hollywood films. For some of the old guard—among them Spencer Williams, Buck and Bubbles, Stepin Fetchit, Miller and Lyles, Mantan Moreland, and Bill Robinson—as well as a host of newcomers, it was a godsend, albeit in many instances a double-edged one. But conspicuously absent from the list were three giants of black comedy: Moms Mabley, Pigmeat Markham, and Tim Moore.

After a career that began in tent and variety shows, Moms Mabley did appear on stage in several musical comedies in the twenties and thirties. Among them were *Miss Bandana* (1927), produced by Clarence Muse, and *Fast and Furious* (1931), which also starred Tim Moore, Dusty Fletcher (a black circuit comic whose "Open the Door Richard" routine was famous in black theatres and became a hit novelty recording in the thirties), and Zora Neale Hurston, the ubiquitous Harlem Renaissance writer, humorist, and folklore collector.

But Mabley was shunned by film producers until the forties. Even then, her initial film credits were confined to several race movies—independently produced films intended for black audiences—such as *Big Timers* (circa 1945), with Stepin Fetchit; *Killer Diller* (1948), with Butterfly McQueen and Dusty Fletcher; and *Boarding House Blues* (1948), with Dusty Fletcher and Johnny Lee. In April 1967, she appeared on the Harry Belafonte television special *A Time for Laughter* (ABC) with, among others, Pigmeat Markham. She did not appear in a Hollywood film until 1974, when she starred in *Amazing Grace*. This film (the creation of black producer/writer Matt Robinson and director Sam Lathum) also starred Stepin Fetchit, Butterfly McQueen, and Slappy White, and was released by United Artists. Moms's homespun humor, as we shall see, was aggressively irreverent before impious or disdainful African-American comedy was considered either fashionable or tolerable; her brand of humor was therefore probably too risky, perhaps even risqué, for Hollywood's early sound films.

Dewey "Pigmeat" Markham, although his typically broad, low comedy seems in retrospect perfectly suited for the type of films produced in Hollywood at the time, was also mysteriously ignored by the major studios. Instead, he became something of a legend on the black stage circuit, seldom veering from the burnt-cork makeup and burlesque humor that had become his trademark by the twenties and thirties. During this time he also appeared with the Andrews Sisters as Alamo, a cook, in their stage and radio shows. In the forties he starred in a series of independent black films with such performers as Noble Sissle, Nina Mae McKinney, and his frequent screen partner John "Rastus" Murray. His "scared darky" routine and numerous burlesque blackout skits predominated. Among those films were *Mr. Smith Goes Ghost, Shut My Big Mouth, One Big Mistake, House Rent Party,* and *Fight That Ghost.* With the advent of television in the late forties, he had several guest shots on Ed Sullivan's *Toast of the Town* variety show. In 1968, after Sammy Davis, Jr., used his classic "Here come de Judge" bit on *Rowan and Martin's Laugh In,* Pigmeat was "discovered" and gained belated recognition as a master comic of the old school.[36]

At age twelve, Tim Moore ran away from home and joined a medicine show as a singer and dancer. Then, teaming up with Romeo Washburn, he appeared as one of the original "gold dust twins" in a traveling pickaninny act. He quit the stage for a time, experimenting with careers in boxing and horse racing while in his teens, but returned to unveil a one-man version of *Uncle Tom's Cabin,* performing with half his face made up with white chalk (as Simon Legree) and the other half with burnt cork (as Uncle Tom). Later, after retiring from boxing, he developed a vaudeville act and, by the early twenties, had become a star attraction on the TOBA circuit. He also appeared in one of the early black-cast silent Hollywood movies, Ben Strasser's *His Great Chance.*

Moore had a featured comic role in Lew Leslie's Broadway hit *Blackbirds of 1928,* which debuted at about the time sound films were initially released, but was still ignored in Hollywood. Instead, during the thirties and forties, he continued working the black theatre circuit, starred in some independently produced black films, appeared occasionally in Broadway shows such as *Fast and Furious, Blackberries,* and *Harlem Scandals,* and, like Pigmeat Markham, was sometimes seen on Ed Sullivan's television variety show. It was not until 1951, however, that Moore's comic genuis was fully revealed. In the role of "Kingfish" Stevens on the *Amos 'n' Andy* show, he vaulted from relative obscurity in the black theatre underground to become one of the best-known entertainers in America. He soon found that celebrity as a black comedian had mixed blessings.

Stepin Fetchit, who was among the first of the seasoned variety show and black circuit comedians to receive feature billing in sound films, had discovered this much earlier. His first film was *In Old Kentucky* (1927), and immediately, his dilatory style captivated mainstream movie audiences. *Variety* reported that "the MGM finish and a colored comedian hold up the picture. He's just a lazy, no good roustabout, wheedling money out of colored help but he's no mean pantomimist." Fetchit's performance as a malingering stable hand and the romantic interest for former Cotton Club chorus line beauty Carolynne Snowden established him as a legitimate film personality. (The serious treatment of their romance, incidentally, was a breakthrough in Hollywood's representation of blacks in film.) Although many blacks had appeared in films before him, Fetchit may have been the first black actor in a non-musical performance who indelibly stamped his own unique stage routine onto an essentially dramatic movie role.[37]

According to a relative, Fetchit, who was appearing on stage in Los Angeles when MGM announced they were looking for a "colored boy" for a film role, may have won the part because he took his stage act directly to the audition.

He said he just stood there looking like he didn't know where he was or why he was there and he was scratching his head, which he had shaved clean, and he was just looking around like he was lost. I guess he looked so sad and lost and everything that he got their attention.

So, one of the directors, he pointed at Step and he said, "Say, You!" And Step, he looked all around the place acting like he thought they couldn't have been talking to him, but knowing all the time that they were, and they called him again. He turned around all slow and wide-eyed and pointed to himself and said, "Is you talkin' to me?" And the dumber he acted, the more they laughed, because nobody had ever seen anybody *that* slow and ignorant. So they told him that he had the part.[38]

Fetchit got the part and a six-month contract; after moving to Fox Studios, he became the first black actor to sign an extended contract with a Hollywood studio. As he insistently claimed, he *was* the first black movie star. In addition to riches and fame, however, history would capriciously cast him as the symbol of Hollywood's perverse manipulation of the black image on screen. By the thirties, when Negro servants became the screen's predominant black stereotype, Stepin Fetchit (the man as well as the name and character) would emerge as the personification of that caricature for many.

Shortly after Stepin Fetchit moved on to such sound films as *Salute* (1929) and the ground-breaking *Hearts in Dixie* for Fox, musical comedy stars Flournoy Miller and Aubrey Lyles were introduced in movies.

Their two first films, *Jimtown Speakeasy* and *The Mayor of Jimtown* (both released around 1929), were musical shorts loosely based on their Broadway hit, *Shuffle Along*. As in that show, the comedy was based largely on ridiculing urban black behavior, and left much to be desired. According to Thomas Cripps, *Jimtown Speakeasy* opened on a boy dancing in a black club with accompanying dialogue describing a "pickaninny" doing the Charleston. The movie includes the team's famous "mulsifying and revision" bit, and is peppered with mispronunciations like "condiculous," "ignorancer," and "dat lady renounced dinner." Similarly, *The Mayor of Jimtown,* although it does include the team's signature boxing routine, bristles with the kind of inane caricature that had depicted the mayoral candidates as chicken-stealing scalawags, one of whom was unable to spell the word "cat."[39]

After Vitagraph released the equally unimpressive *Midnight Lodge* (1930), in which the pair weaved comedy and music around a plot centered on a lodge officer's attempt to conceal his theft of the organization's funds, Aubrey Lyles became seriously ill. He died in 1932, as the team was about to begin rehearsals for a Broadway revival of *Shuffle Along*. In that same year, Miller (as we saw earlier) appeared with Mantan Moreland in *That's the Spirit*—a musical comedy short that cast them as incompetent security guards who are petrified by ghosts. Subsequently, Miller teamed up with comedians such as Moreland and Johnny Lee both on stage and in a series of independent films primarily intended for black theatres and black audiences.

The debut of Miller and Lyles as comic performers in Hollywood films had been, at best, disappointing. When this talented team introduced what they called "mutilatin' " the language in the early 1900s, it was a fresh and, in some quarters, welcome addition to the black comic idiom. But times had changed and what had been innovative was becoming hackneyed, familiar, and offensive, as literary humorists such as Cohen, Means, and Wiley, as well as white theatrical impersonators, began using similar styles.

By the beginning of the thirties, not only had the Cohen and Wiley stories been adapted for the screen, but movies such as *Check and Double Check* and Moran and Mack's *Why Bring That Up* (1929) and

Anybody's War (1930) had been released, and Amos and Andy were popular fixtures on radio. Mutilatin' the language had, quite simply, become an accepted mainstream idiom used to satirize and ridicule black life. Similarly, many of the gags originated by Miller and Lyles and performed before black audiences had been transformed when introduced into the larger culture. What had seemed comparatively innocent jabs at the behavior of uneducated urban blacks struggling to overcome their rural backgrounds, through overexposure, shifts in emphasis, and invidious juxtaposition with "proper" mainstream values and mores had now changed, for most of white society, to racial slurs confirming the incompetence of blacks.

In this atmosphere, the humor of these pioneer funnymen, despite any nuances they may have added, must have seemed compromised. In fact, it can reasonably be assumed that Miller and Lyles, at some point, began being influenced by their imitators. The satirizing of urban black life had become so popular, its origins so convoluted, that pinpointing the original source today proves almost impossible. While contending that Gosden and Correll borrowed their Amos and Andy routine from Miller and Lyles, for instance, Redd Foxx and Norma Miller confirm that the routines were practically identical. They quote Mark Hellinger of the *Chicago Daily Mirror,* who in 1930 wrote of Gosden and Correll, "They're two boys who are cashing in heavily on something Miller and Lyles originated years ago. . . . If Miller and Lyles were substituted for Amos and Andy one night, I would defy anyone could tell the difference." And, in an article on black theatre, Langston Hughes wrote, "Miller and Lyles imitated the white performers Moran and Mack so well that the white actors who played Amos and Andy in turn imitated Miller and Lyles. Then Rochester imitated all of them put together." But, while it is unlikely that Miller and Lyles copied Moran and Mack ("The Two Black Crows" surfaced after Miller and Lyles created their earliest stage comedies), it is quite possible that Gosden and Correll imitated Moran and Mack, who, given the racial priorities of the time, were far better known than Miller and Lyles.[40]

Although Mantan Moreland often teamed with Flournoy Miller on stage and screen, and was undoubtedly influenced by him, he quickly developed his own distinct comic presence.

Born in Louisiana around 1900, he joined a circus at age fourteen and later toured briefly with a minstrel troupe. According to Henry T. Sampson, his comic genius "began to surface when he played second comedian to Tim Moore and Flournoy Miller" in such shows as *Con-*

nie's Inn Frolics of 1927 and *Blackbirds of 1928, 1930,* and *1932.* After his film debut with Miller and Noble Sissle in *That's the Spirit,* however, Moreland went on to appear in over three hundred movies—more than any other black entertainer, comic or otherwise. By the time he played a supporting role in *The Spirit of Youth* (1937)—a black-cast film about the ascent of a poor boxer, which was written and produced by whites and starred heavyweight champion Joe Louis—Moreland had apparently molded the comic persona that made him one of the most durable and arresting black entertainers of his time.[41]

Like Ernie Morrison of *Our Gang* and the *East Side Kids,* Moreland was noted for his accelerated double-takes, gigantic rolling eyes, and the boyish elasticity of his face. But he surpassed Morrison and most others in the subtle use of these devices; he was a masterful actor. His facial expressions, in fact, were so vivid and striking—instantly registering fear or joy, lechery or consternation—that even without a word of dialogue he invariably stole scenes from the most charismatic performers. He also developed signature lines ("Feets, don't fail me now!") and demanding physical routines and gestures (running full-gait while standing in place, or conveying utter bafflement by simply shrugging his shoulders) that perfectly complemented his comic expressions. Even in the most inane, insignificant roles, which he usually got, while he was on camera it was nearly impossible to watch anyone else.

This talent quickly made Moreland a Hollywood bulwark as a comic foil and supportive attraction in a host of otherwise forgettable movies. He appeared in minor roles in the late thirties with stars such as Lucille Ball but, after appearing as Frankie Darro's sidekick in a comic Monogram Pictures series about an inept sleuth, his screen fate was apparently sealed. Although his roles occasionally varied, the specific niche that he carved out was in light, comic mystery films. His most famous role was as Birmingham Brown, Charlie Chan's chauffeur and valet, in the Monogram mystery series that starred Sydney Toler and, later, Roland Winters. During the forties, Moreland was a ubiquitous presence on the screen, portraying the frightened coon retainer more frequently and, one might add, with more panache than any other actor.

Bill "Bojangles" Robinson had entered show business before Stepin Fetchit or Mantan Moreland, although recognition in films came more slowly. Still, prior to his early major studio film appearance in Radio Pictures' Old South melodrama *Dixiana* (1930), where he had a minor role as a dancer, he had established himself as a premier stage performer.

Born in 1878 in Richmond, Virginia, he was forced to support himself at an early age. During his teens he danced on street corners in Richmond and, by the mid-1890s, was performing in bars, carnivals, and traveling tent shows, including the *South Before the War* minstrel company. But, according to Tom Fletcher, Robinson's dancing had not stirred any real attention until about 1900, when he entered a dance contest at the Bijou Theatre in Brooklyn and won in a competitive field that included some of the best white dancers of the era. Later, teamed with George Cooper, Robinson went on to become a headliner on the TOBA tour as well as the Keith vaudeville circuit.[42]

Although he did not drink or smoke, from the time he arrived in New York Robinson was an habitué of the city's numerous professional or sporting clubs—after-hours spots that became hangouts where performers and celebrities gathered for entertainment, libation, and gambling. In these arenas, Robinson was known as something of a raconteur; his humorous stories and colorful language delighted his peers. (For instance, he is credited with coining terms like "copacetic" —meaning excellent, first rate, or, in nineties vernacular, "chill"— which became popular during the twenties.) Gradually, his stories became part of his stage act, inserted between numbers or after the finale. One of his favorites concerned a private named Simpson whose superior officer tells him to prepare for a hike. "Hey Simpson, I want you to pack up all this gear, pick up your rifle, get all those knapsacks and canteens to carry on this fifty-mile hike." The private answers in a disbelieving, quivering voice: "Lieutenant, Sir, did you call me? Do you know my name?" The lieutenant answers, "Simpson, I said Simpson." The private responds, "Oh, I thought you said Sampson." Although the story seems only mildly humorous today, it illustrates the kind of comedy that Robinson combined with his dance routines. Moreover, it is an example of stage comedy by a black performer that contrasts markedly with the mainstream entertainment usually offered.[43]

By the early twenties, billed as the "World's Greatest Tap Dancer," Robinson was performing as a single at the mecca of vaudeville theatres, New York's Palace. Despite appearances in several black-cast musical shorts—*Hello Bill* (1929), *Harlem Is Heaven* (1932) with the Eubie Blake orchestra and veteran comedian John Mason (a.k.a. Spider Bruce), and *King for a Day* (1934) with Dusty Fletcher—he did not blossom as a major studio commodity until he was teamed with Shirley Temple in *The Little Colonel* (1935). That was the first of a series of films that cast Robinson as a loyal, self-effacing Tom dutifully serving his masters and employers.

Even when restricted by stock roles, however, Robinson brought aspects of his stage panache to the parts. In *The Little Colonel,* for example, as Walker the houseboy, he is regularly insulted and berated by Lionel Barrymore, the Southern patriarch. Robinson stoically accepts the abuse, but he does display some of the savoir faire and charm that made him a stage legend in other scenes. He is chipper and effervescent as he playfully jibes with Hattie McDaniel, and when he entices Shirley Temple to go upstairs to bed by demonstrating his famous Stair Dance, he is the lively, lightfooted performer we expect to see.

The comedy in the film, however, is generally as embarrassing as Robinson's scenes with Barrymore. Although Robinson usually speaks without dialect, he is asked to corrupt "coincidence" to "co-in-*side*-dence." In a scene with McDaniel, when the pair attempts to conceal some bad news from Shirley by spelling instead of speaking, they manage to misspell every word. Money becomes "m-o-n-i-e," food becomes "f-u-d-e," and loan "l-o-n-e." When McDaniel spells "p-o-h-o-s," even Robinson is perplexed, and she scolds, "Ain't you got no education? De poo'house." Only once in the movie is the spark of resistance that dances behind Robinson's eyes affirmed through dialogue with Barrymore. That occurs after the patriarch admits that he is "an old fool"; instead of delivering his stoic "yassur," Robinson flashes a broad smile and, walking away, intones, "Yes . . . sir!"[44]

Robinson, although one of the most beloved black entertainers, is still something of an enigma in the history of black comedy and entertainment. While he was noted for his charitable work and efforts to advance black participation in the entertainment world, there was a darker, less engaging side to his personality. Some, for example, maintain that the nickname "Bojangles" was acquired because of Robinson's belligerent temperament—his knack for bringing an element of discord and tension to encounters with other performers. His clashes with black entertainers are legendary. According to Lena Horne's daughter, Gail Lumet Buckley, he was in real life "one of the biggest Uncle Toms in show business." Of her mother's experiences with Robinson on the set of *Stormy Weather,* Buckley wrote: "As far as Lena was concerned, nothing . . . could make up for Bill Robinson. He carried a revolver, was poisonous to other blacks, and truly believed in the wit and wisdom of little Shirley Temple."[45]

Honi Coles, the talented tap dancer and all-around entertainer who in the fifties and sixties was stage manager of the Apollo Theatre before his career was rejuvenated when tap was "rediscovered" in the seventies, came to New York in the early thirties. He knew Robinson from about the time of his Hollywood successes until his death. An ardent admirer both as a friend and artist, even he confirmed Robinson's sometimes puzzling and erratic nature.

"Bo was a very complex person," Coles recalled, "proud, the soul of generosity, but a card player . . . a poolroom man. He'd give you anything, anything under the sun, but he'd have to tell everybody. . . . He had that kind of ego. It's too bad that nobody knew him who could dig into him psychologically and find out what made him tick."

Coles related a few anecdotes illustrating Robinson's conflicting personality. At a benefit show in Louisville, Kentucky, during World War II, Robinson saw one of the white stage hands annoying a black showgirl. After the performance, Robinson forced the crew to remain and "read the riot act" to them, pointing out that if a black performer had touched a white woman, someone would have tried to lynch him. On the other hand, Robinson was fiercely possessive about the Stair Dance he claimed he originated. At the Lafayette Theatre, on one occasion, "he walked right down the aisle and stopped a dance team in the middle of their performance. 'That's my dance,' he shouted. 'You don't have the right to perform it.' He stopped everybody from doing it," Coles said.

And when the Harlem-based black newspaper *The New York Age* ran a story calling him an Uncle Tom, he was quick to react. "The whole thing was derogatory and he was furious," Coles recalled. "He called me late that evening saying, 'Come on with me.' At the time *The Age* was on 135th Street between 7th and 8th Avenues, and he went down there ready to kill somebody. Luckily, nobody was there except a little frightened man running the presses, so nothing happened. . . . His pride was intense. He was just a misunderstood man most of his life."[46]

Robinson's childhood hardships combined with Hollywood's second-class treatment of even the most brilliant black entertainers offer a partial explanation for his irascible nature. The rigid limitations faced by black performers are highlighted when Robinson's film roles are compared with those of Fred Astaire, who shared vaudeville bills with

Robinson in the early twenties. Astaire, who admired Robinson, was usually cast as a debonair bon vivant, while Robinson, equally stylish and polished on stage, was shunted into humble, Old South servant roles in which his renowned dancing was most often overshadowed by insistent Uncle Tom characterizations. The difference in roles can be partly justified by the difference in their ages. Robinson was twenty-one years older than Astaire; when he appeared opposite Lena Horne in *Stormy Weather,* he was sixty-five. Still, despite public silence on his film image, Robinson was, as Coles affirms, a proud, even arrogant man, and the inherent degradation of the roles he played must have gnawed at him. Although blacks found his screen image somewhat less offensive than that of Fetchit, Moreland, and·others, the parts he usually played perfectly fit the obsequious niche that Hollywood had reserved for African-Americans in films.

IV

There was immense variation in the style with which they played the roles, yet nearly every one of the performers who benefited from the rush to enlist black performers into sound films ultimately was cast as a servant. It was a role with a venerable tradition in Hollywood—both on the screen and off. In its formative years, with few exceptions, blacks had found the Hollywood community virtually impenetrable except by way of service jobs.

By the early twenties, only a few professional actors—among them, Noble M. Johnson, George Reed, Madame Sul-te-Wan, and child actors such as Ernie Morrison—were appearing regularly in films. Johnson's light complexion and sculpted features enabled him to find exotic parts as Mexicans, half-breeds, and Indians in a host of movies from the twenties to the forties; he braced his numerous supportive roles in Hollywood B-movies with a career with the Lincoln Company. The equally exotic Madame Sul-te-Wan made her debut in *The Birth of a Nation,* appeared in a 1920 L-Ko Studio black-cast comedy series, then went on to appear sporadically as a voodoo priestess or maid in a number of films. Reed also appeared in *Birth* and played "Nigger Jim" in the 1920 version of *Huckleberry Finn* before being typecast as a porter, stable hand, or butler in a series of films during the years that followed. Morrison was a featured child star before departing for vaudeville. Later, he returned to Hollywood as a comic sidekick in teenage gang movies.

Even these accepted performers had difficulty supporting themselves. Morrison left Hollywood for vaudeville because of inadequate wages, and Madame Sul-te-Wan would complain that "I get bitter sometimes because I don't work long enough to buy a handkerchief."[47]

Most blacks appearing in early Hollywood movies had more precarious and unsettled relationships with the industry. Many had entered through the accepted route of service positions, as porter, bootblack, elevator operator, valet, or maid. Often, since genuine acting was considered beyond the capacity of blacks, aspirants for parts were considered interchangeable and, in a throwback to slavery, favors or parts were bestowed on the most accommodating types.

According to Thomas Cripps, until the late 1920s, when studios turned to the Central Casting Corporation and its black agent Charles Butler, "studio Negroes" such as Jimmie Smith, Harold Garrison, and Oscar Smith functioned as liaisons between the film industry and the black community. They were charged with scanning Watts's Central Avenue for any potential talent, a quality that included the proper "unctuousness."[48]

In addition to his role as a talent scout, Smith appeared in several Paramount feature films in the late twenties. Among them were *Beau Sabreur* (1927), in which Gary Cooper starred, and *Thunderbolt* (1929). Smith, like so many blacks who gained a foothold in the industry during this period, broke in as a retainer. He came to Paramount after World War I as Wallace Reed's valet. In gratitude for his services, and apparently with no disdainful or sardonic intent, Reed stipulated in his will that Smith "be given a shoeshine stand in perpetuity." Garrison—who worked with King Vidor on *Hallelujah!* and, in releases to the black press, was identified as an "assistant director"—was known to whites at the studio as "Kid Slickem," due to his facility as a bootblack. Both Smith and Garrison made optimum use of their back-door entry, extracting as much power, influence, and exposure as possible from the situation.[49]

African-Americans' apparently eager acceptance of servant positions and use of servile attitudes as a means of advancement, of course, was not confined to Hollywood or the film community. Performers were following a well-trodden path. Throughout the nation, from legitimate race leaders such as Booker T. Washington ("Cast down your bucket where you are") to con men and hustlers who milked whites' egos and pocketbooks with ingratiating postures and affirmations of satisfaction with their inferior positions, outward accommodation of bigotry was a common means of circumventing restricted opportunities.

For most ordinary people, although the rewards were not so readily apparent, such accommodation (as it had been during slavery) was often required for survival. Those employed as domestics almost universally adhered to a pragmatic philosophy of deceit that reaffirmed employers' views of blacks as an unambitious, simple (if not simpleminded), and contented lot. The facade not only elicited small favors but brought some measure of status in the black community; there the domestics' access to white society's material comforts was envied, and tales of employers' gullibility and arrogance were cherished as a source of private humor.

Rufus Thomas, the black disc jockey and rhythm and blues singer, mirrored a common attitude among blacks when he recalled his tactics as a waiter in Nashville during the twenties. "During that time, the white fellow was quite boastful . . . he'd say all these things. But he'd pay well, pay well. At the end of the night, I had the money. I won't say that he was broke, but he'd splurged and I had the money. And so you ask yourself: 'Hell, who's the fool or who's stupid?' Because I had the money at the end of the night and that was what I was working for."[50]

The film capital was in the business of selling fantasy and glamour, and movie stars were often urged to flaunt their wealth. Servants were part of the paraphernalia of stardom, symbols of success, so nearly every successful star had a houseboy, valet, or maid. When Stepin Fetchit, as the first black movie star, toured Central Avenue in a pink Rolls-Royce with his name emblazoned in neon on its side and bragged of having fourteen Filipino servants, he was simply mimicking (in his own outlandish manner) a lifestyle common in the film community.

Positions as Hollywood domestics were coveted because of the peripheral rewards. Occasionally, as with Oscar Smith, black retainers were allowed to duplicate the roles on the screen. Libby Taylor, Mae West's maid in real life, was also cast as a servant in several movies, including her employer's *Belle of the Nineties* (1934). The line between screen fantasy and reality for the Hollywood community was thin indeed. As blacks were at the bottom of the social hierarchy, along with exotics like Filipinos and Chinese, they were preferred for real-life roles as domestics. And since blacks were assumed to be *natural* servants, they were acceptable in movie roles as domestics—parts in which, like black minstrels who were advertised as the real thing, they were required only to be themselves.[51]

"From 1915 to 1920 roughly half the Negro roles reviewed in *Variety* were maids and butlers," writes Thomas Cripps, "and 74 percent of them were known in the credits by some demeaning first name. In the 1920s servile roles reached 80 percent of all black roles." But with the advent of sound films and the recruitment of more professional black entertainers in the thirties, the percentage diminished. This move did not represent any shift in social consciousness or racial attitudes, but rather an increase in parts for blacks as natives in films set in Africa and other exotic locales, or for performers such as Duke Ellington, Lena Horne, or Hazel Scott, who portrayed themselves.[52]

Among portrayals of black females, the hefty, bandana-clad black maid—the Hollywood mammy—predominated. There were, of course, a host of black actresses who at one time or another played servants in studio movies, although not all complied with the mammy stereotype. From Madame Sul-te-Wan through Gertrude Howard, Teresa Harris, Libby Taylor, Marietta Canty, Evelyn Preer, on to Ethel Waters, and, yes, even jazz immortal Billie Holiday and stunning Dorothy Dandridge and Lena Horne, black women routinely donned apron and/or bandana and made brief, supporting appearances in Hollywood's illusory, nearly all-white screen world.

Hattie McDaniel, by virtue of her charisma, massive stature, and even more immense talent as a comic actress, set the standard for the mammy caricature; although Louise Beavers and Butterfly McQueen were close contenders, she emerged as the diva of domestics. Early in Hollywood films, as we saw, female servants had been given license to deliver acerbic one-liners and display an aggression and independence usually denied black males. Assertive, fiery, witty, and cantankerous, McDaniel added a patina of belligerence and surliness that, in real life, was usually carefully concealed. That element, although it ultimately upset both blacks and whites, revealed the relationship between servant and employer as far more complex, ironic, and humorous than the Uncle Tom or Aunt Jemima stereotypes might suggest. It was also more pointedly realistic—providing a glimpse of the underside of the docile, contented servant myth.

McDaniel was born in Wichita in 1898; she began in show business as a teenager, singing in tent shows in the South and Midwest before breaking into vaudeville and appearing on the Orpheum Circuit in the twenties. Around 1930 she moved to Los Angeles and, shortly afterward, got her first movie role. After her film debut in relatively unobtrusive, minor roles as a domestic in *The Gold West* (1931), *Blonde Venus*

(1932), and *The Story of Temple Drake* (1933), she quickly developed the wisecracking, irreverent image of a domestic that made her famous. By the mid-thirties she was one of the most sought-after black actresses in Hollywood.

Although she occasionally sang in movies such as *Saratoga* (1937) or appeared in variety films such as *Thank Your Lucky Stars* (1943), in which she joined Willie Best for a song and dance number, McDaniel was primarily a comic actress. And, although she sometimes appeared as the domineering mate of malingering coon figures in such movies as *Judge Priest* (1934) or *Maryland* (1940), her forceful screen presence was almost exclusively in roles as an acerbic, somewhat eccentric domestic.

In a series of films during the thirties and forties she functioned as a comic foil for glamorous actresses, including Jean Harlow, Marlene Dietrich, Claudette Colbert, and Vivian Leigh. As her more refined and demure but usually less assured female bosses waffled in the face of male advances and incursions or (in the case of Civil War films) Northern interlopers, she remained steadfast and unshakable. Her size (over two hundred pounds), commanding voice, and lacerating rejoinders and asides established an indomitable presence on the screen, and the line between boss and servant was often obscured.

In *Alice Adams* (1935), McDaniel plays an unkempt domestic who, during the course of a dinner party, haughtily advises her employer on the proper menu, ignores rude commands from guests, and, with nimble facial expressions, displays obvious contempt as the pretentious hostess (Katharine Hepburn) attempts to impress her guests and disguise critical remarks about the service by speaking in French. *The New York Times* singled out McDaniel's performance as "hilarious," and in 1989, on the *16th Annual Black Filmmakers Hall of Fame* awards program, Gregory Hines called this comedic performance "one of the most brilliant strokes of social commentary in American film." In *The Mad Miss Manton* (1938), her irascibility and fussiness are heightened as she comments on Barbara Stanwyck's suitors ("Seems like a pipsqueak to me"), snaps at a caller at the door ("I ain't deaf"), or, told to discourage one of Stanwyck's admirers, hits him with a water pitcher. "Orders is orders," she comments, "but I used distilled water."[53]

In *Affectionately Yours* (1941), her role was contrasted with Butterfly McQueen's fumbling, whimpering domestic and assumed even greater comic impact. In one scene, after Merle Oberon gives instructions about where guests are to be seated for dinner and leaves the room,

McDaniel, who disapproves of both the arrangements and her employer's new beau, turns to the equally unhappy McQueen and says, "We gwine take dem plates over dere and put 'em over here and I'm gon' break 'em one by one over his head." In this film and several others, McDaniel behaves like the actual mistress of the household. She is the irrespressible arbiter of taste and, when her often naive or shortsighted employers are endangered, the guardian of their rights— a bastion against male aggressiveness. Humor was derived from her assertive, almost mannish behavior, as well as her candidness about racial bias, male-female relationships, and the alleged superiority of her employers. Added to this overtly assertive humor was the visual comedy associated with the contrast between the hefty McDaniel and her svelte, more "feminine" employers; here McDaniel's "illusions" about her femininity often became the object of the satire.

In *China Seas* (1935), for example, a distressed Jean Harlow asks if her maid thinks she looks like a lady. "Nawsuh Miss Dolly," McDaniel replies, "I been with you too long to insult you dat way." Then Harlow asks, "What's that snooty English dame got that I ain't got?" After pausing for a second, McDaniel says, "She's mo' refined like. . . . She would never wear that dress with all them shiny beads you got. That dress is mo' my type." Harlow consents to give up her dress, even though she is aware that she's being conned. Afterward, McDaniel holds the sleek garment against her body and mumbles: "I got to let this out a smidgen." The scene illustrates the underlying irony of McDaniel's irreverent domestic: What was given in assertiveness was quickly canceled by personal ridicule. Although she is allowed to outsmart her dizzy but beautiful employer, simultaneously she is lampooned because of her appearance and size—elements that were a continual source of amusement during a period that one newspaper derisively labeled the "fat, black, and ugly" era of black representation in movies.[54]

But even when she is unwittingly the butt of the joke, McDaniel's screen image is usually without the slightest hint of inferiority. In fact, as she played the part, the assumption is that she is preeminent. And while writers and producers no doubt intended that her imperious attitude would be deflected by the visual contrast between the two women, for many in the audience the weight of McDaniel's personality often counterbalanced her physical heft and negated the slanted implications.

McDaniel's characterization was so realistic and, apparently, galling that many white southerners protested her mammy portrayals. Perhaps as a result, after she won an Oscar as best supporting actress in *Gone With the Wind* in 1939, her roles became less assertive and lost much of their edge.

In the late forties, she starred as Beulah in the radio series of that title and briefly assumed the same role on television in the fifties; but the energy and cutting irreverency of her mid-thirties movies was never quite repeated. She was stricken while playing Beulah on television, and died in 1952. McDaniel, like every black entertainer who gained fame portraying menials and servants, was criticized by many blacks. In films such as *Since You Went Away* (1944), in which she plays Fidelia, a fiercely dedicated maid whose loyalty to her beloved "white folks" supersedes concern for her own welfare, her screen characters could slip hopelessly into a quagmire of Southern romanticism. Nevertheless, until the emergence of black television comics in the seventies, no one —not even her male counterpart, Eddie Anderson, who portrayed the valet Rochester on Jack Benny's radio and television shows as well as in his movies—brought nearly as much vigor, flamboyance, and impious wit to the role of a domestic as did Hattie McDaniel.

Louise Beavers offered a more traditional but less threatening and humorous portrayal of the part. Faithful, warm, and endearing, her screen interpretations more closely mirrored the reassuring image displayed on Aunt Jemima pancake products; they were, no doubt, also closer to the image retained by many Southern gentlemen raised in the doting arms of black mammies. In fact, Beavers played Aunt Delilah, a maid who gives her secret pancake flour mix to her employer (Claudette Colbert) and makes her wealthy, in *Imitation of Life* (1934). On screen she repeatedly portrayed the imperturbable, stalwart retainer whose dedication and loyalty were beyond question. Her film image was that of Uncle Tom's opposite number; she was the female version of the cheerful, loving, self-sacrificing, somewhat naive servant whose mere presence gave credence to the status quo.

Beavers's film career began after she left her native Cleveland and moved to Los Angeles around the advent of talkies. In 1929, at age twenty-two, she had several bit parts as maids in such films as *Coquette, Barnum Was Right,* and the *Our Gang* comedy *Election Day.* By the thirties, her career accelerated. As Clementine, Petulia, Niagara, Willamay, Cassie, or just plain Mammy, she reenacted the role of contented servant/friend in scores of Hollywood movies. Although she occasionally appeared in parts that veered from the stereotype—for example, *Bul-*

lets or Ballots (1936), in which she played a Harlem numbers queen; *Follow the Boys* (1944), a Universal variety showcase that also featured W. C. Fields and Nicodemus Stewart; and *The Jackie Robinson Story* (1950), in which she had a dramatic part as Robinson's mother—she was used almost exclusively in supporting roles as a domestic.

During her five decades in films, Beavers established a reputation as a fine actress. Her repetitive parts never seemed to fatigue her and she managed to bring a sincerity and authenticity to each role. Surprisingly, unlike the characters portrayed by Stepin Fetchit or even Hattie Mc-Daniel, Beavers's domestics elicited few critical outcries from the black community. She was as well loved by blacks as by whites. The reason may be that Beavers, despite the stereotype, played the parts with more sincerity and genuine warmth than anyone else, projecting a deeply felt sense of the value of commitment, perseverance, and concern for others, no matter what position one happened to occupy. While they provided little opportunity for comedy or satirical edge, those attributes helped make Beavers one of Hollywood's most frequently employed and enduring black actresses.

In the early fifties, Beavers—following Hattie McDaniel—starred as Beulah on radio and, later, played the part on television (Ethel Waters initially played the role when the series debuted in 1950). Her career continued into the sixties when, in her last film, she appeared as Bob Hope's maid in *The Facts of Life* (1961). When she died, a year later, she was remembered fondly as the comforting earth-mother figure she had so vividly projected on the screen.

Butterfly McQueen was light-years away from the mammy figures etched by Beavers and McDaniel. As a domestic servant, she was even quirkier than McDaniel, whose belligerent outbursts seem pragmatic and utterly sane in comparison, and her fragile, otherworldly demeanor was in total contrast to the cheerful practicality of Louise Beavers.

Born in 1911, in Tampa, Florida, McQueen displayed an early interest in acting; so, when she and her mother moved to New York City, she joined an amateur stage company. By the thirties she had won bit parts in *Brown Sugar* and *Brother Rat*. Her cinema career began with her being selected for the role of Prissy in *Gone With the Wind.*

McQueen brought her own unique comic spirit to her few Hollywood domestic roles; ultimately, the whimsical characters she portrayed seemed to float not only above the scenes in which she appeared, but above the movie itself. In a sense her comic persona was the female counterpart to Stepin Fetchit's mumbling, frightened, malingering coon; like Fetchit, she could become totally self-engrossed, incoherently drifting off into a somnolent sphere of her own. Yet her lethargy was not so much physical as mental. She seemed perpetually detached from the reality of her films.

In *Affectionately Yours,* appearing with McDaniel, she played a teary-eyed maid who quaked at the slightest mishap, real or imagined. Skittish and fragile, her presence served to exaggerate McDaniel's bombast and aggressivenesss. And in *Gone With the Wind,* as Prissy, a house servant or, as Rhett laughingly refers to her, the "simpleminded darkie," McQueen fancifully meanders through the film as if the brutal Civil War background were a carnival. Here, again, her quixotic insouciance contrasts with McDaniel's portrayal of Mammy, who, with her fierce concern for propriety, decorum, and perpetuation of the South's social hierarchy, often took her white masters more seriously than they took themselves. Although McDaniel won the Oscar, it was McQueen whom *Time* magazine cited for her "sly humor."[55]

In essence, McQueen brought the comic guise that she had established on stage to her screen roles. Her wide-eyed innocence, confused, undirected speech, shrill, high-pitched voice, and little-girl demeanor were part of a comic arsenal that was not unlike that of Gracie Allen, George Burns's wife and stage foil. Ultimately, however, the line between McQueen's stage or film persona and real life seems to have become increasingly obscure. After the forties, she disappeared from the scene, appearing briefly with Ethel Waters on the *Beulah* television show (as Oriole) in the early fifties, and then working at odd jobs as a laborer and servant before taking on a local radio show in Georgia.

Her career revived in the sixties when she appeared in *Curly McDimple* (1968), an Off Broadway production, but sputtered again with infrequent appearances on television during the seventies. Although McQueen did resurface in movies—*The Phynx* (1970) and *Amazing Grace* (1974), with the venerable Moms Mabley and Stepin Fetchit—and made a few television appearances in the eighties, her career had come to a virtual halt.

McQueen was enigmatic and evanescent both on and off stage. In some ways, her life and career rival the kind of shocking tales found in that cult compendium of filmland misfortunes, *Hollywood Babylon.* Observed from outside, there is an eccentric, tragicomic cast to her life, just as there was to the characters she played in films. Yet Butterfly McQueen always seemed buoyed by access to a private inner sanctum. It provided an indelible, subjective edge to her comic performances and, perhaps, offered a sanctuary from the vicissitudes of her off-screen life.

V

The careers of the actors who portrayed the male version of the black servant were often as fickle and bizarre as McQueen's, and the stereotyped characters they played ultimately became even more controversial.

Mantan Moreland and, of course, the now-infamous Stepin Fetchit were Hollywood's foremost comic coon figures, but a host of lesser-known talents also toiled in that much-demanded but thankless role. Among them were Willie Best, Sam "Deacon" McDaniel, Dudley Dickerson, Ben Carter, Fred "Snowflake" Toones, and Nicodemus Stewart.

After Fetchit debuted in Fox's *In Old Kentucky* in 1927, other studios began searching for blacks to emulate him. At least one, Willie Best, came directly from the streets of Watts.

Best recalled walking along Central Avenue and noticing that a white man in a car was following and watching him. Thinking it was a policeman, he turned and ran. Fortunately, he was unable to elude his pursuer and was eventually signed to a studio contract. His initial discovery was based largely on his remarkable likeness to Stepin Fetchit; billing him as "Sleep 'n' Eat" in such films as *Up Pops the Devil* (1931), *The Monster Walks* (1932), and *Kentucky Kernal* (1934), the studios' intent was transparent. Almost immediately, Best revealed a marked talent for reworking Fetchit's shuffling, head-scratching coon caricature.

During the thirties and forties, he played "Eph," "Sambo," "Catfish," "Joshua," "Pompey," "Mo," and "Drowsy" in a series of comic films. The cartoonlike names of the servants, menials, and sidekicks were appropriate since, with few exceptions, they could have been created by riffling through the pages of a standard minstrel joke book. Not that those parts did not require considerable comic ability or that Best did not resist the insistently degrading stereotyping. "I often think about these roles I have to play," he said. "Most of them are pretty broad. Sometimes I tell the director and he cuts out the real bad parts. . . . But what's an actor going to do? Either you do it or you get out."[56]

Best stayed and, for more than twenty years, etched his version of the frightened coon servant into the annals of screen history.

The tall, lean, and gangling Mississippi-born actor projected an almost schizophrenic timidity. On screen he was normally either so languid that he appeared comatose or, conversely, so nervous and ill at ease that he was prone to continually glancing over his shoulder as if something or someone was always after him. Here he showed none of the artful dodging reflected in the Satchel Paige caveat: "Don't look back, something may be gaining on you."

Best's lanky, stoop-shouldered frame usually seemed coiled in readiness for flight, and his dark, slack-jawed face emitted a sense of perpetual awe. When he was frightened, the intensity was heightened. Best's characters would literally quiver with alarm. As his wide eyes dilated, his pupils would dart about frenetically, flashing in pools of white; his lower lip drooped, and sweat popped from his face. Shaken and drawn, when an actual villain or specter appeared, he would bolt: his high-stepping, slew-foot gait sending him into haphazard, headlong flight. The bit had become a cliché by the forties—reenacted countless times by black comedians as well as such mainstream white comics as Stan Laurel and Lou Costello—but few, if any, matched the exaggerated intensity Best brought to his comic portrayal.

In *Thank You, Jeeves* (1936) and *Cabin in the Sky* (1943), with an all-black cast, he was the epitome of the sluggardly coon. In the former, according to one commentator, he "plays (and looks) Drowsy" throughout the film. During a comic scene in *Cabin* where (along with Louis Armstrong, Rex Ingram, and Mantan Moreland) he plays an ideas man for Lucifer, he literally dozes through the proceedings before arising to whine, "Ideas like dat only come once in a million years, junior," then, exhausted, reclines again. In *The Smiling Ghost* (1941), a routine comedy whodunit that starred Wayne Morris and Alexis Smith, he played the familiar petrified coon valet and chauffeur. When Morris asks if he's afraid, Best replies, "I ain't afraid but my feets ain't goin' stand around and see my body get abused." Later, when Morris and Smith tell him they intend to find a body in the graveyard, Best declines their invitation, saying, "When folks stop breathin' and walkin', I'm through wit' em." Finally, after he reluctantly enters the cemetery, Best expresses concern about "tramplin'" around on top of the dead. Smith assures him that "there's six feet between you and them."

"Yessum," he replies, "but it's goin' be six miles between us any minute now."[57]

Contrasted with the restraint and temerity of his white employers, Best's exaggerated responses were hilarious. Although most often Best and other scared servants were frightened by figments of their own imagination, sometimes their timidity was justified. (That circumstance probably prompted Richard Pryor's quip about blacks in horror films like *The Exorcist:* "See, there wouldn't been no movie had there been niggers in it. The movie would've been about seven minutes long. Soon as the devil spoke: 'Hello-o-o-o-o' . . . 'Goodbye!' ")

After his last film was released in 1947, Best moved on to television and, during the fifties, played minor roles on *The Stu Erwin Show* and *My Little Margie.* He died in 1962.

Sam McDaniel (Hattie's brother), Fred Toones, Ben Carter, Dudley Dickerson, and Nicodemus Stewart did not work as consistently or become as popular as Willie Best, but they were all frequently seen portraying servants in the thirties and forties. McDaniel appeared in a glut of servant parts in such films as *Polo Joe* (1934) and *The Great Lie* (1941), in which he was primarily a comic foil, but he was not always pigeonholed. *Bad Men of Missouri* (1941), and *All Through the Night* (1942), with Humphrey Bogart, provided more variety and sharper dialogue than his typical Tom roles permitted. In *Pride of the Bluegrass* (1937), although he suffers the indignity of having to pretend to be a blind horse and mouths standard malapropisms ("Well, you see we's havin' a meetin' of The Order of the White Doves. We's inebriatin' some new members . . ."), he is allowed to rebuke a haughty French-man with the curt remark: "Ah, don't gimme dat, big boy. You ain' been here dat long." And in *Louisiana Purchase* (1941), his pointed comment about a white woman ("Boy, if she was black she'd be beautiful!") resounds with a double meaning that was rare for the time. It was probably intended as a joke by screenwriters who assumed that blacks unequivocally accepted mainstream standards of beauty, and it may have played that way for whites. For many black audiences, however, McDaniel's delivery of the line, besides anticipating the race pride of the sixties, no doubt echoed their private sentiments. Overall, although he was a fine character actor, McDaniel remained a minor figure in black film humor.[58]

Fred "Snowflake" Toones, as his screen name suggests, portrayed more typical coon figures. During the thirties and into the forties, he had Fetchit-like parts in a score of movies and, most often, was billed as Snowflake, although in *The Biscuit Eaters* (1940) he was burdened with the even stranger "1st and 2nd Thessalonians." From the thirties to the early fifties, Ben Carter was cast in numerous servant roles, including a small part in *Gone With the Wind,* several appearances with Mantan Moreland in Monogram's Charlie Chan series, and the role of Hattie McDaniel's besieged husband in *Maryland.* Carter's hapless coon caricatures led Donald Bogle to label him "one of the most rigidly stereotyped and at times most embarrassing black actors to work in American movies."[59]

Dudley Dickerson—whom Whoopi Goldberg has called a "comic genius" and "master of physical comedy"—was seen in frightened coon roles in a score of films. He appeared in *The Green Pastures,* but more typical was his part in *Ready, Willing, and Unable* (1941), in which he ran through doors, outran automobiles, and, when hit on the head by an anvil, quipped: "Sho' glad it didn't hit my feet."[60]

Nicodemus Stewart, while he appeared in a few servant roles in the forties as well as in the 1943 black-cast features *Stormy Weather* and *Cabin in the Sky,* would not gain wide recognition for his interpretation of the coon figure until his role as Lightnin' on the *Amos 'n' Andy* television show in the early fifties.

The undisputed king of the coon servant roles was Mantan Moreland. As valet, chauffeur, porter, or simply sidekick for a series of Hollywood stars, Moreland brought his vaudeville and variety house techniques to films, stamping his own unique brand of humor on them despite lean, demeaning parts and atrocious B-movie scripts.

While Fetchit personified lethargy and Best exuded cautious intensity, the jittery, chubby, moon-faced Moreland, even when motionless, projected boundless energy and excitement. His lines were delivered at a quicksilver pace and his seemingly elastic features shifted expressions nearly as quickly; he could punctuate a joke or upstage a co-actor with devices as broad as rolling his pop-eyes or as subtle as lifting an eyebrow or pursing his lips. The array of gestures and expressions Moreland brought to the screen was unsurpassed by any film comedian of his time.

As Charlie Chan's chauffeur, Birmingham, for instance, he helped to raise an often offensive second-rate mystery series to cult status among movie buffs. Fetchit and Best also played the part, but for many, Moreland defined the role. Interchanges between Moreland and Chan's enthusiastic but naive sons, although they predictably mirrored the frightened coon stereotype, afford a sense of the series' humor as well as its obvious limitations:

#1 son: Confucius remind us, Birmingham, that he who fights and runs away . . .

Mantan: I know . . . will live to run another day!

#1 Son: If you're scared, Birmingham, just keep saying to yourself, "I'm not afraid . . . I'm not afraid."

Mantan: I'm not afraid. *I'm* not afraid. I'm *not* afraid.

#1 Son: How do you feel now?

Mantan: I feel like a liar!

A highlight of Moreland's Birmingham role was the several occasions when he and Ben Carter offered hilarious renditions of Miller and Lyles's old "Indefinite Talk" routine.

Of course, these roles were often interchangeable. Craven, faint-hearted Negroes were popular, so Hollywood producers and writers created endless scenarios for them. To his credit, Moreland was often able to overcome the repetition and banality. In addition to his timing and signature lines such as "Feets, don't fail me now!" it was his vast repertoire of facial intonations and gestures, his body language, that permitted Moreland to transcend the stunted dialogue and give his parts a distinctive comic flavor. His appearance in over three hundred movies attests to his versatility.

Stepin Fetchit—like Moreland, Best, and others who followed him —was also burdened with rigid restrictions and limited character range in his movie roles. But although a host of nearly identical black male servant types were routinely ridiculed in Hollywood films during the twenties, thirties, and early forties, no one else would encounter the radical roller-coaster shift in public esteem—from frantic adulation to mass vilification—that Fetchit was to experience.

The frightened servant stereotype, loosely based on remnants of African religious beliefs retained by slaves and exploited by slaveowners, was primarily the exaggerated creation of minstrelsy and Hollywood. Conversely, Fetchit's shuffling, apparently inept and inarticulate character had clearly defined folk roots: slaves had used these tactics to avoid barbarous work regimens and, while assuring masters that they were indeed superior, to achieve their own ends. Fetchit, like others before him, had adapted this slavery ruse, amplified its comic overtones to reveal the underlying deceit, and brought it to the stage.

Most black comedians had worked this caricature within the confines of black theatres, before all-black audiences, where it was an accepted comic portrayal—one that was usually greeted with knowing, uninhibited laughter. A few, most notably Bert Williams, had ingeniously brought it to mainstream theatres. But, although a gifted comic, Fetchit was no genius. He had simply transferred his version of a standard black stage character (which, in turn, was based on an effective bit of slave deceit) to the screen more or less intact. This caricature was more intricately connected to the behavior of ordinary blacks than many are prone to admit.

From the outset, however, Fetchit's portrayal of the ignorant darky differed from most other interpretations. While Bert Williams, for instance, readily admitted that the character he portrayed was "to the fullest extent" the "shiftless darky," he limited his portrayal to the surface elements of slow movement and speech that, although rendered in dialect, was nevertheless coherent and in fact usually quite clever. His jokes depended "either on word play or lampooning usually solemn institutions," and were delivered, as one critic noted, in the persona of "a wise fool or more often the fool's upstairs neighbor, the common sense philosopher." Underneath the slumped shoulders, dim-witted visage, broken speech, and torpid movement the character had, in Williams's words, "a philosophy that has got something."[61]

Fetchit's stage character, for the most part, eschewed such homely wit and concealed any underlying or contrasting cerebral quality. In effect, Fetchit had made his character's physical movement and meandering speech the primary focus of his humor. He had isolated those elements and honed them to near perfection before coming to Hollywood. Although he sang, spicing his stage act with nonsensical doggerel ("The Stepin Fetchit! Stepin Fetchit! Turn around, stop and catch it"), his humor derived primarily from the contrast between his uncannily slow movements and his lightfooted dance steps, or between his woeful, downcast expression and the lively patter or subtly ironic grin that occasionally infused his lethargy.

Every movement was meticulously controlled. In much the same way that some overweight comedians play their seemingly ponderous size against their ability to dance, moving with finesse and style to garner laughs, Fetchit skillfully played off his slow-moving, dim-witted coon against his considerable skill as a dancer. On stage, he would come shuffling out, scratching his head, looking for all the world as if he were utterly confused and lost. Mouth agape, eyes half closed, shoulders slumped, he would embark on his practically incoherent monologue— usually in a whining monotone that had little meaning beyond the visual impression of confusion that it conveyed. Then, suddenly, he would begin a controlled dance routine that amazed his audience; as he danced, his facial expression changed subtly, the half-closed lids lifting, the eyes widening momentarily to reveal the spark of enthusiasm and arrogance that his simpleton mask concealed. Without this contrast, Fetchit frequently moved beyond that thin line that separates the humorous from the pathetic. On the screen, the contrast was often absent.

By the time he appeared as Gummy in *Hearts in Dixie* in 1929, Fetchit's version of the shiftless, malingering darky was quickly becoming a comic staple in Hollywood. But, despite the many imitators, no one could quite duplicate his languorous charisma. Most certainly, no other black celebrity except the flamboyant heavyweight champion Jack Johnson (to whom Fetchit often compared himself) had even approached the promotional extravagance that he mounted off the screen. This flair for self-promotion also probably accounted for what appeared to be a curious friendship between Fetchit and the militantly outspoken Muhammad Ali in the sixties. The former champion, after all, was no stranger to publicity, hype, and put-on.

Although, even off camera, Fetchit never completely abandoned the darky disguise, he flaunted a lifestyle replete with servants, luxurious cars, and other accouterments of Hollywood's sporting life. His prodigal ways eventually led to bankruptcy; by the forties, he had squandered the more than $1 million made in films from 1928 to 1937. Even while he reveled in ostentatious display of a material sort, however, Fetchit diligently masked the ambition, demanding nature, and behind-the-scenes aggression that fired his climb to stardom. Consenting to the studio's strategy of convincing mainstream audiences that he actually *was* a malingering darky, for public consumption he selectively nurtured the stereotype in personal appearances. Accommodating studio publicists, he posed for ludicrous photographs that affirmed his innate obtuseness and, in interviews, insisted that reporters amend his remarks so that they reflected the meandering, broken speech that had become his screen signature. His moderate education at St. Joseph's College (actually a Catholic boarding school), as well as such cerebral interests as classical music, were methodically concealed from the public.

Fetchit was following a course of action that had worked effectively for blacks throughout their American experience. The same tactic had prompted antebellum southerners to admit that "so deceitful is the Negro . . . I could never in a single instance decipher his character." It was, quite simply, the practice of withholding information about the actual motives for their behavior, pretending to accept and accommodate white prejudice while surreptitiously undermining it and pursuing one's own ends. At the time, nearly all African-Americans understood, respected, and encouraged this commonly accepted ploy. Lincoln Theodore Monroe Andrew Perry was a past master at it. Not only did he use it as the basis of his comedy act but, apparently, made it a central element in all of his real-life dealings with whites.

The actor, comedian, and former Apollo Theatre M.C. Ralph Cooper, for instance, wrote that when both he and Fetchit were on the Fox lot in the thirties, Fetchit concocted an effective ruse for dealing with the often-overbearing Darryl Zanuck. Whenever Zanuck wanted Fetchit to do something, he would take him aside and "patiently explain what was needed." Fetchit would listen attentively, then say, "It sounds good to me, Mr. Zanuck, but I'll have to talk it over with my manager, Mr. Goldberg, and get back to you." Later, Fetchit would tell Zanuck that Mr. Goldberg either agreed or disagreed with the suggestion. There was, of course, no Mr. Goldberg. But for a while the guise worked perfectly: Fetchit was able to conceal the extent to which he controlled his own career—an unacceptable posture for black actors in Hollywood—and buy time to decide how he wanted to respond to Zanuck. Finally, Zanuck, fed up with the delays, demanded to have the phone number of the mythical Mr. Goldberg and Fetchit was forced to admit the duplicity. "I guess you had to find out one day," he said. "I'm Mr. Goldberg."[62]

Similarly, Fetchit encouraged the myth that he was unable to read or write. Even directors and producers initially assumed that Fetchit could not read, so he was not given scripts. He was told what to do and say. This situation allowed him to exercise his sly aggressiveness in still another manner. With no written lines, he could—and did—extend his scenes by pretending ignorance and adding his own ad-libs and pantomime bits. "Directors shrugged and figured it wasn't worth the effort to correct an illiterate . . . the scene was funny anyway so why not use the extended comedy." Fetchit employed the old slavery ruse off camera. "He improvised and padded his part and stole every movie he was in, so much so that for a time many big stars refused to work with him."[63]

The experiences of the writer and producer Matt Robinson on the set of *Amazing Grace* (1974) affirm both Fetchit's aggression and his persistence. "When Slappy White introduced me to him," Robinson said, "I didn't even know he was alive. I talked to him and one day I suddenly decided that it would be a piece of history if I put him in this film. I told him, 'Step, you got this one line . . . you do this.' Afterwards

Step would come in with a long sheet of paper and start talking: 'I see where we could do some more. . . . I could say this, or . . . ' Every day it was something else! I began to understand how he got as far as he did . . . he worried people to death. Finally, like myself, they must have said, 'All right, I surrender. Just do it, we'll see how it works.' He just kept on agitating until people gave in. . . . He had to be aggressive to play that lazy role because, when he started, that's all there was and everybody wanted to do it. Finally, he just out-lazied everyone else."[64]

Fetchit's comedy appearances on stage and radio added to the total effect. The following example demonstrates the fabrication involved in becoming "the World's Laziest Man." "This the way I get lazy . . . the way I get into character," he said on a 1967 radio show in Clinton, Iowa, humorously describing his ascent to movie stardom.

I'm so lazy, even when I walked in my sleep I used to hitchhike. My head was so bald I used to comb it with a spoon. People say, "How'd you get in pictures?" I say, "Well . . . when I was a kid I always wanted to be somethin, course I didn't want to do nothin to be it. I used to go 'round trying to get a job doing nothin, but everywhere I went they either wanted me to do somethin or else they didn't wanna give you nothin for it. So I kept trying til I growed up, then I seen this man in California makin a picture, and I say, 'Mr., you want somebody to do nothin,' and they say, 'Yeah.' So I been busy working every since. Yeah, and I work up to the place where the less I have to do, the mo' I make. Tryin to make as much as I can, so when I get old I can rest."[65]

The press affirmed his absentmindedness and obtuseness in gossip columns, "news" items, and articles. Describing how he "lost several distinguished positions as a shoe-black," as well as his studio contract, one writer labeled him "the world's champion job loser." Another wrote: "Nothing educated or emancipated. He typifies his race. . . . He has their joyous, child-like charm, their gaudy tastes, their superstitions. . . . And would probably steal chickens if he hadn't promised the Lord never to do anything illegal again." Fetchit not only endured such descriptions but fostered them. The promotional conspiracy catapulted him into the position of Hollywood's first black star, but ultimately cast him in the role of the film capital's most castigated villain. Few black celebrities, in the words of Ray Charles, would be "buked and scorned" with such intensity.[66]

As a veteran of variety shows and the black theatre circuit, Fetchit brought an arsenal of performing skills to the screen. In addition to comedy, like many entertainers of the period, he was experienced as a hoofer and could sing as well as dabble with the banjo. His early films put some of that versatility on display. In *Hearts in Dixie*, as we saw earlier, he not only danced and indulged in some clever repartee but added a serious dimension to his comic portrayal. The critic Robert Benchley called him "the best actor that the talking movies have produced. . . . His voice, his manner, his timing, everything that he does, is as near to perfection as one could hope to get . . . one of the great comedians of the screen." And Thomas Cripps noted that Fetchit's Gummy "approached the outskirts of tragedy." Of course, not everyone agreed. Peter Noble, the author of *The Negro in Films* (1948), thought that the Gummy role was one of Fetchit's "more nauseating 'lazy but lovable vagabond' parts."[67]

Those roles continued into the thirties as Fetchit developed a close friendship with the humorist Will Rogers, whom he had known and worked with in vaudeville. Rogers had been a premier stage comedian before beginning his film career in 1918. On the vaudeville stage and with the Ziegfeld *Follies* he had relied on an unassuming Western image and droll monologue that, like nineteenth-century Frontier humor, delivered pungent comments on American politics and society with homespun guilelessness. His simple charm and homely wit, however, did not project well without dialogue, and by 1922 his future in silent films looked bleak. After starring in a series of Hal Roach two-reel comedies, Rogers, unhappy with the slapstick shorts, went back to the stage. When sound films came in, he returned to Hollywood. During the Depression years the country responded more favorably to his rural, cracker-barrel style, and Rogers established himself as one of America's most popular movie stars. Fond of working with friends, he enlisted Fetchit for four films. Perhaps because of their easy rapport, Fetchit's career peaked when he was paired with Rogers in *David Harum* (1934), *Judge Priest* (1934), *The Country Chairman* (1935), and *Steamboat Round the Bend* (1935).[68]

Rogers, whose parents were Cherokee, openly discussed his heritage and often commented ironically about the treatment of Indians: "It's going to make us might proud of it in the future when our children of ten or more generations read of what we did to them. Every man in our history that killed the most Indians had got a statue built for him." Still, because of the iconoclastic roles he played, one reviewer called him the "cowboy Nietzsche." Typically, he portrayed a simple, honest man whose basic kindness and humanitarianism were contrasted with the scheming and corruption of those around him. Paraphrasing George Bernard Shaw, he said of his humor: "I don't have to make up jokes; I just tell the truth." He represented the agrarian ideals and longing for the good old days that characterized America's heartland. Through his penetrating rural wit—"shrewd, homespun comments" on world affairs, politics, and such new-fangled inventions as the automobile— he was invariably opposed to moral decay or malfeasance and usually emerged triumphant. Fetchit, cast as his friend, was therefore aligned with Rogers against wrongdoing and the chaos that accompanied a rapidly changing social order. This curious pairing boosted Fetchit's popularity even while, according to some, it reaffirmed the stereotypical image of black dependence and inferiority, suggesting that Fetchit's shuffling, accommodating role was the proper social posture for blacks.[69]

Moreover, the dynamics of this comic tandem required that Rogers assume responsibility for the clever, verbal aspect of the humor while Fetchit's character—devoid of the philosophical commonsense that elevated Bert Williams's shiftless darky—was reduced to a static, almost entirely physical, comic pose. Fetchit was scolded, pushed, shoved, even kicked in the seat of his pants by Rogers; as one observer later wrote, "It was perfectly acceptable for [Rogers] to talk to Fetchit in much the same manner that one would address a not too bright house pet." Still, a genuine sense of camaraderie surfaced between the two actors. Rogers projected such a relaxed, warm presence on screen that his treatment of Fetchit never seemed punitive or even serious; it was as though two adolescent buddies were engaging in some frivolous play or, in this instance, tomfoolery. For his part, Fetchit often reacted to this hokum by flashing a devilish grin or winking knowingly. More often, mirroring a practice common to nearly all black retainers in film, Fetchit would wander off by himself, mumbling incoherent protests or objections beneath his breath, or delivering comic rejoinders that traditionally were permitted only when white actors were supposedly unaware of them.[70]

From 1927 to 1936, Fetchit's career prospered. He made nearly thirty Hollywood movies, including several with Shirley Temple— *Stand Up and Cheer* (1934), *The Littlest Rebel* (1935), and *Dimples* (1936)—and an unfortunate appearance as Charlie Chan's retainer in *Charlie Chan in Egypt* (1935). By the mid-thirties, his patented version of the Negro houseboy, bootblack, stable hand, comic sidekick, or plain, old-fashioned unemployed toady was indelibly imprinted on the screen. The caricature was so vividly fixed that "every shoeshine boy in the country began copying his lazy drawl and shuffling walk," and cartoon representations of black male characters invariably mimicked him— just as female servants in animated shorts were patterned after Hattie McDaniel.

In fact, whereas in the early roles there had been subtle variations in Fetchit's performances, by 1935 he was becoming a caricature of himself. Even John Ford, a director who admired Fetchit's work and used him in five films, admitted that the star had become "undirectable." His success and absolute faith in the caricature prompted him to pursue a singleminded course that made him even more of a minimalist. Movement that had been deliberate and methodical was further tempered and stylized, becoming so hesitant and controlled that it approached immobility. Speech that had been merely slurred moved beyond obscurity, drifting into incoherence.[71]

Fetchit's description of his stage act during the twilight of his career illustrates his obsessional attachment to "the Laziest Man in the World" image that always dominated his humor but, toward the end, defined it completely. "The first fifteen minutes of my act is getting to the middle of the stage," he joked. "And when I leave I am wheeled off in my chair. I even had a fellow come out and wave my hand good-bye to the crowd."[72]

Finally, his film performances became predictable, dull, embarrassing. In *Stand Up and Cheer,* for example, one bizarre scene has a baffled Fetchit believing that a talking penguin is the comedian Jimmy Durante. They carry on a conversation as Fetchit shuffles about the room in pursuit of the creature or, dropping to his knees, implores: "Mr. Durante! Is dat you? . . . Yessuh, but my goodness how you done shrunk up. . . . Last time I seen you, you was jes as wholesome and standard size as you could be. . . . Don't do nothin rash, now." When Fetchit picks up the animal, he is ridiculed: "in the hands of a slavey . . . a black. . . ." Still, Fetchit ends up diving into an aquarium to help the insolent penguin catch a fish.

A more typical scene in the same movie has Fetchit approaching an executive, played by Warner Baxter, in search of a job. After Baxter learns that Fetchit's name is George Bernard Shaw, he quips, "You're a little sunburned, aren't you?" Cowering, scratching his head, and whining, Fetchit attempts to ingratiate himself by cleaning Baxter's desk and, pulling a whisk broom from his pocket, brushing his suit. Finally, he mumbles, "You need someone can do the shim-sham shammy with words and feet?" Amused by Fetchit's deadpan, slow-motion tap routine, juba patting, and scarcely audible singing, Baxter consents to giving him the job of watching his office to make sure that no one gets in while the secretary is away. Fetchit (with a sly reference to the Depression woes, which the movie was intended to combat) mutters, "Yessuh, nobody can get by now no how 'cause . . . last few years I . . . I jes been barely gettin by myself."[73]

In this scene Fetchit demonstrated many of the characteristics that had become his trademark: the shuffling, head-scratching entrance and obsequious demeanor; the fractured language and incoherent, whining delivery; the precisely controlled, sluggish, indolent movement, and nearly somnolent, deadpan expressions. Fetchit would insist until his death that his film roles presented a "finished character . . . a soul" that projected an "innocence" and contradicted all the negative "qualities of colored people—lack of morals and all that." But the missing element in his performance in Stand Up and most other Hollywood films was any tangible indication of his character's humanity. He had polished and perfected the comic exterior of his character; but, unlike Bert Williams's lazy darky, there was little hint of a "soul" within Fetchit's beleaguered caricature. (Ironically, on the eve of an attempted film comeback in 1952, Fetchit argued that his "imitators were doing the outside of [his] act. They didn't work from the soul like I do." But the stammering darky that he created—when juxtaposed with white mainstream characters—usually came through as a pathetic, cartoonlike figure whose inept comic makeup invited ridicule. In molding him to the exigencies of the white screen world, Fetchit had gradually wrung all of the humanity and much of the humor from the character.)[74]

By the late thirties, his popularity was quickly declining. Both movie audiences and film executives were becoming disenchanted. Blacks began more actively voicing protests over Fetchit's image on screen, and the increasingly more influential civil rights organizations began lobbying to eliminate demeaning stereotypes in movies. Moreover, with the death of his friend and mentor, Will Rogers, in an airplane crash in 1935, Fetchit's off-camera high jinks were not so quickly excused by Fox; lacking leverage inside the studio, his flamboyant lifestyle, brawls, and frequent clashes with the law became less tolerable to executives. With the release of *Zenobia* (1939), his decade-long stint as a major movie attraction came to a virtual halt.

Still, Fetchit forged ahead on the stage and in independently produced race movies in the forties. He replaced Bill Robinson as Louis Armstrong's co-star in the downtown Cotton Club show that opened in November 1939, and, with stars such as Moms Mabley, appeared regularly on the black theatrical circuit as a headline comedian during the next few years. Gradually, even these sources evaporated. Although, at this point, he contended that he had been forced out of Hollywood because he refused to play any more demeaning roles, Fetchit's name was already irrevocably linked to the degrading stereotypes that had dominated mainstream show business in the twenties and thirties. Post–World War II audiences, while many had never even seen his films, had come to resent the old school of entertainers; critics reflected their views. In 1952, his much-ballyhooed return to films in *Bend of the River* was dismissed by *The New York Times* in a one-line notice: "We are sorry to note that Stepin Fetchit is back to play a clownish stereotype." After an equally negative response to his minor role in *The Sun Shines Bright* (1953)—a remake of the Will Rogers vehicle *Judge Priest* —Fetchit would disappear from Hollywood films until the seventies. His career had seemingly hit rock bottom.[75]

The worst, however, was yet to come.

Fetchit struggled during the fifties and early sixties, working the "chitlin' circuit" as well as small Midwestern clubs. By this time the flashy lifestyle had long since gone and, during lean times, he found it necessary to accept the hospitality of friends like the venerable comedy team Butterbeans and Susie, in whose modest Chicago home a visiting entertainer "could always find a plate with greens and cornbread." Responding to the growing criticism about roles he and others had played in Hollywood films, Fetchit began to attack leaders of the rights movement. "Me and the civil rights movement don't get along," he said on an Iowa radio talk show. "I call all of the civil rights leaders—*all* of them—nothin but, ah, playin both ends *and* the middle. . . . And half of them, ah, a majority of 'em has foreign interests—un-American interests."[76]

Although seemingly encouraged by the interviewer, Warren Bolt, Fetchit obviously needed little inducement. He was desperately attempting to save his career by defending a comic characterization that, thirty years earlier, had been totally acceptable. Still, even as he railed, Fetchit began altering his stage act slightly. He still billed himself as "the Laziest Man in the World" and sometimes delivered his mono- logue sitting in an easy chair. But he radically modified the mumbling dialect, and—reflecting the aggressive mood surfacing among comedi- ans like Moms Mabley and Dick Gregory—occasionally added more biting commentary to his routine: "My wife and I were just voted the good-neighbor award, we even went out and burned our own cross."[77]

For a time during the mid-sixties, it seemed that Fetchit's career might be on the upswing. He had resurfaced as part of the entourage of Muhammad Ali and rumors circulated about a television series in which he would play Flip Wilson's father. He insisted that he was on the brink of a comeback, which included "television specials, feature pictures, a book—my life story—and lectures."

But on July 2, 1968, CBS television broadcast a segment of their documentary series *Of Black America* that, in the course of pointedly revealing the gross distortion of African-Americans' image in the media, focused on Stepin Fetchit's film roles as an example of Hollywood's degrading stereotypes. The script of "Black History—Lost, Stolen or Strayed," Fetchit would later contend, had narrator Bill Cosby say: "The tradition of lazy, stupid, crap-shooting, chicken-stealing idiot was popularized by an actor named Lincoln Theodore Monroe Andrew Perry." Perry's more resonant stage name, if for no other reason than its metaphorical aptness to the character he portrayed, was already notorious among blacks who—in the midst of the Civil Rights movement—were determined to eradicate old mannerisms and symbols. Henceforth, Stepin Fetchit became anathema for many blacks.[78]

Three years later, Fetchit would file a suit against CBS, claiming that the program "pretended to relieve racial tension through education and understanding by slurring an entire generation of Negro Americans as inept." He sought punitive damages of nearly $3 million for "malice, invasion of privacy, and defamation of character." Ultimately the suit was blocked, and Fetchit, although he was to make last film appear- ances in *Amazing Grace* and *Won Ton Ton, the Wonder Dog Who Saved Hollywood* (1976), began to show signs of the struggle to salvage his image. At age seventy-four, he suffered a debilitating stroke that seriously impaired his speech and left him partially paralyzed. Reportedly the stroke occurred while Fetchit was reading an article that, typically, blamed him for the negative image of blacks in the mass media. He spent his last years as a resident patient at the Motion Picture Country Home and Hospital in Woodland Hills, California, where he died in 1985. Although he was nearly forgotten by the eighties, astute visitors still trickled in to see this screen legend. Until his death, he continued protesting what he considered the sabotaging of his career.[79]

VI
- - - - - - - - -

Stepin Fetchit remains a seminal figure in the history of black American comedy, both as performer and as symbol of the distorted caricatures of blacks promoted by movies. But when his screen performances are compared with portrayals of servants by other blacks during the thirties and early forties, it is difficult to hold that his roles were any more demeaning or degrading than those of his contemporaries.

Hattie McDaniel, for instance, despite acerbic one-liners and the dominant personality projected in many of her roles, primarily represented a typical Aunt Jemima figure. In her obsessional commitment to her employers, her usually scathing treatment of black men, and quaint pancake package appearance, she mirrored—or, some would argue, established—many of the era's prominent stereotypes of black women. Finally her screen characters were seemingly always more concerned with the welfare of whites than with other blacks.

Chosen because of his resemblance to Stepin Fetchit, initially Willie Best was merely a clone whose somnolent demeanor was carefully molded by the studio. Often billed as "Eat 'n' Sleep," he shuffled through a score of movies, outrunning an even greater number of spooks; some of his roles reached levels of banality that Fetchit could not have imagined.

Butterfly McQueen was also as otherworldly, obtuse, and inept as Fetchit in films. In fact, her whimpering, distraught maid caricature was the distaff side of his whining, befuddled houseboy. The roles played by Fred "Snowflake" Toones are probably best indicated by the sobriquet with which he was identified in film credits. Numerous other prominent performers (including Bill Robinson and Mantan Moreland) who struggled to gain a foothold in the film industry might easily have been cast as the symbol of demeaning black stereotypes in Hollywood films. After all, as Ralph Cooper wrote, "If you didn't want to mug wide-eyed and scared and act the fool, there was no room for you in the big studios."[80]

Still, Fetchit's selection as the most reprehensible symbol was not entirely gratuitous. His drive, ambition, and aggression—not to mention his ego and flair for publicity—had made him the most recognizable and widely discussed of all the black performers who had played coon and Tom roles during the twenties and thirties. Although many of the claims he made when later striking out against his critics were grossly exaggerated, as he insistently professed, he had been the *first* black film star. By his mere presence he did open up doors for future performers. Moreover, he firmly believed in his ascendancy. During the first half of the twentieth century movie stars were larger-than-life figures. They were more than mere idols, having been elevated almost to the status of royalty by a fawning public desperate for heroes. Fetchit basked in his celebrity, demanding and generally receiving the special treatment accorded cultural icons. Given the nature of black roles in Hollywood films during the period, however, that position brought as much notoriety as glamour and celebrity. Ultimately, it made him the natural choice as symbol of the reprehensible images of blacks that mainstream films projected.

What Fetchit's critics ignore is that he was also among the era's most talented actors and comedians. The denigrative aspects of his performances accrued more from context than from content. Fetchit's stage darky was never as articulate or "philosophical" as Williams's comic Negro, that is, he seldom overtly revealed the ironic thrust or underlying impetus for the character's laggardness. But among black audiences in all-black settings, the running inside gag was instantly recognized and was a continual source of humor.

In the independently produced black-cast film *Miracle in Harlem* (1948), for instance, Fetchit plays a role that, although more subtly rendered, is identical in nearly every external gesture to the parts he had played in studio projects the previous decade. The most obvious and notable difference is the absence of whites; but that difference is crucial.

As Swifty, an employee of the black owners of a candy store, he displays all of the usual comic ineptitude. He stumbles through his chores, removes his hat to deliberately massage his head, or mumbles incoherently as he attempts to unravel the simplest equation or complete the most ordinary tasks. This shuffling, stammering incompetent is played for all its comic worth. But in an entirely black setting, Fetchit comes across *purely* as a comedian. The cryptic, often ominous, racial overtones of his graphic interpretation of the malingering black have almost disappeared.

Instead, we see the clown and actor starkly, as he intends, unsullied by condescension or defensiveness. We focus on the precisely controlled exaggeration and carefully orchestrated buffoonery, and, if we look closely, recognize that the humor flows from the disparity between Fetchit's awkward, dense behavior and our own sense of normal behavior in the situation—the skillfully created sense of incongruity. He is a comedian, not an ethnic symbol; we laugh at his ineptitude, even feel a sense of superiority. But we also glimpse that, well, total dedication to work may not be all it's put up to be. The shadowy influence of race is removed and, with it, nearly all the unwarranted overtones of denigrative stereotypes.

In one scene, Fetchit has the following exchange with a black detective.

Fetchit:	This the place that I'm looking for, headquarters man?
Lieutenant:	What do you want?
Fetchit:	Well, you see . . . I, uh, I suppose to know what I want . . . uh . . .
Lieutenant:	Sit down!
Fetchit:	I'll put my hat here (to himself). Uh . . . I was supposed to . . . (searching clothes)
Lieutenant:	What are you nervous about?
Fetchit:	I ain't exactly nervous. I just generally falls to pieces 'round polices. It's much more worst than nervous, Captain yo' honor.
Lieutenant:	Lieutenant, not your honor.
Fetchit:	Well, Lieutenant Not Your Honor, uh . . . the law generally is and I usually ain't.

Later, when the detective questions Fetchit about a murder, he deftly avoids the inquiry and we see how his supposed obtuseness was often used as a diversion:

Lieutenant: What do you know about handling a knife?

Fetchit: I knows lots about a knife but I ain't goin' tell you. But I know I cain't eat my mash potatoes without a knife . . .

Lieutenant: Stop the foolishness!

Fetchit: I ain't foolin' Mr., cause I have to have a fork for everything I eat. If I cain't fork it, I cain't . . . uh, I just don't bother with it myself.[81]

This type of manipulative diversion and deceit, revealed as wit by the allusion to a time-worn, off-color rejoinder at the end, was central to Fetchit's humor. And in black films or on stage before black audiences, it appeared regularly. Although it never quite duplicated the satiric edge seen in some of the Pompey or Old John stories, it was a derivative of traditional slave humor in which the victim or underdog outwits or, at least, confuses his adversary and escapes punishment.

Finally, Stepin Fetchit was a much better actor and comedian and a far more complicated person than his Hollywood persona and the negative dismissal by latter-day critics suggest. He had clawed his way to the top using the few tactics at the disposal of blacks in the early twentieth century: subterfuge, deceit, and the appearance of accommodation to mainstream America's rigid conception of African-Americans' true nature. His achievement as a performer, however, was ultimately his undoing. Somewhere along the way, cinema fantasy and social reality merged, and because of the indelible nature of his portrayal, Fetchit established a cinema type as his own. For most people, he *became* the obsequious clown that he portrayed. In many ways, Fetchit's career—his ascent and demise—was a microcosm of the black experience in general during the first half of the twentieth century.

In most mainstream movies, black performers served merely as stooges, the dark contrast that illuminated what was otherwise a rather dull existence. As in the satiric paint factory scene in Ralph Ellison's *Invisible Man,* where the nameless hero discovers that the addition of a few drops of black liquid to cans containing "a milky brown substance" is used to create a perfect "Optic white . . . the purest white that can be found," blacks were often used to delineate the ideal image of the white world in muddled, second-rate films. Fetchit, and other black performers who were restricted to distorted, stereotyped roles, finally provided the downside to the American dream, the essential contrast that gave it form.[82]

Without doubt, the image of blacks during this period was distorted and demeaning—in many instances, irredeemably so. But subterfuge and playing the fool were indispensable tactics for blacks before the mid-twentieth century. To ignore this point is a questionable attempt to conceal a rich and ingenious part of the African-American heritage. "Shrewd humility," as pundits have pointed out, can be as effective as vainglorious confrontation. To disclaim this facet of black expression, in effect, is to deny the tears, laughter, and ultimate transcendence of many generations. Moreover, by the seventies, psychiatrists would point out that the "foot-shuffling, head-scratching, slow-moving" tactic had "struck at the heart of the system," and that "Sambo may well have been the first militant."[83]

Fetchit's comedy, Flip Wilson shrewdly observed, "was funny, it was good. Everything is right for its time. . . . His humor would only be insulting if you were uptight. For whatever degree of insult you might see in it, it is still a very, very vital part of our history. . . . You have to accept it as a fact."[84]

Genuine African-American humor derived from blacks' simultaneous perception of themselves from both positive (black) and negative (non-black) viewpoints. But with the exception of some irreverent wisecracks, almost none of the former reached the screen. Instead, motion pictures focused on the self-denunciation implicit in the latter. Hollywood ignored not only most overt examples of genuine folk humor but also the psychological framework from which it may have sprung.

As protests over the demeaning public image of blacks by civil rights organizations and newspapers increased in the forties, questions about Hollywood's ignominious comic portraits of African-Americans subsided. Black actors such as Spencer Williams and Clarence Muse, and leaders such as the NAACP's Walter White (who, with Wendell Willkie, the defeated Republican presidential candidate of 1940, met with studio heads in 1942), pressed for more serious, liberalized depictions of blacks in motion pictures. An accord was reached, and studios began gradually phasing out the more obviously disparaging comic stereotypes.

Although the apparent accord did not spawn overnight changes and, in fact, gave rise to many disputes over exactly what the proper black image was, a tangible benefit was the production of two black-cast musicals that enlisted the talents of some of African America's best performers. MGM's *Cabin in the Sky* and Twentieth Century Fox's *Stormy Weather* were both released in 1943. These two movies spotlighted an array of music and comedy stars seldom seen in motion pictures and, more surprisingly, placed them squarely in twentieth-century environments.

Cabin in the Sky, like *The Green Pastures*, is based on a successful Broadway play and places ordinary black life in a thoroughly make-believe setting; here, the forces of Heaven and Hell are out to claim the soul of Joe Jackson, an average workingman. But, unlike its more serious, pious forerunner, *Cabin* is concerned with secular entertainment rather than with biblical allegory. The plot—which has Lucifer's henchmen (Louis Armstrong, Rex Ingram, Mantan Moreland, and Willie Best) devising a scheme to lure black Everyman, Little Joe (Eddie Anderson), away from his dedicated wife (Ethel Waters) with the temptation of money and a sexy enchantress (Lena Horne)—is little more than a scaffold for a series of dazzling dance and musical sequences. Anderson and Waters are the only characters who rise above obvious caricature; in addition to some affecting and exciting song and dance numbers, they invest their dramatic scenes with a touch of reality and display a convincing, if limited, range of emotions despite the corny dialogue. But this motion picture is finally about entertainment, and the all-star cast delivers it non-stop throughout the film.

Among highlights too numerous to enumerate, show-stopping ballads by Waters and Horne, dances by Anderson, Waters, and the inimitable John Bubbles (whom Honi Coles and many others consider the "absolute master" of tap dance), and music by Duke Ellington and the Hall Johnson Choir, all contribute to what amounts to a dream-sequence variety show featuring much of the best black talent available in the forties. Although set in a rural community, the movie usually avoids the maudlin nostalgia and grosser stereotypes ordinarily associated with major studios' portrayal of black country folk. Strangely, however, comedy is muted in this film. Except for a few scenes—one in which the Devil's puckish disciples muse about their part in turning the apple into man's first temptation and the invention of such enduring human nemeses as "flies," another in which Waters outwits would-be hustlers Nicodemus Stewart and Ernest Whitman in a crap game—the movie avoids straight-out comedy. Instead, it is propelled by high spirits and an infectious energy that generally elicits smiles rather than laughter.

Stormy Weather, on the other hand, is embellished throughout by a type of comedy that was rarely seen outside black honky-tonks, variety shows, theatres, and the occasional race movie. Although supposedly based on the lives of black entertainers Jim Europe and Noble Sissle, the story barely touches on them, centering instead on a romance between Bill Robinson, essentially portraying himself, and Lena Horne. No matter. The storyline and ersatz romance are not really important here. As in *Cabin*, the film's real attraction is the parade of black entertainers who literally light up the screen: Horne, Robinson, the Nicholas Brothers, Ada Brown, the Katherine Dunham Troupe, Cab Calloway, and Fats Waller all contribute sparkling musical or dance performances. But the movie is also notable for its hip, urban ambiance and the humor that flows from that overriding spirit.

Nicodemus Stewart contributes a controlled, urbane version of his slow-talking darky character, which, without the usual rural dialect and broad gestures, has a tame, muted quality. Flournoy Miller does his famous "Indefinite Talk" routine with sidekick Johnny Lee; although their blackface makeup may offend some, the bit offers a genuine example of black stage humor rarely presented in mainstream movies.

But the funniest and most genuine instances of true black humor arise out of the attitudes and casual patter that flow effortlessly from the cast. Fats Waller's brief appearances provide some of the film's most hilarious moments. The ad-libs with which he punctuates Ada Brown's version of the blues song "Ain't That Right," for instance, are priceless. "Baby, baby, what's the matter with you?" Brown asks, and Waller shoots back his famous reprise, "One never knows, do one." And to Brown's refrain, "You got the world in a jug," Waller responds, "Yeah, but where's the stopper." The quips continue throughout the song, with Waller topping each of the singer's complaints: "Ah, tell them fools anything but tell me the truth"; "Baby, I was *born* ballin' and I'm gon ball the rest of my life"; "Ah, beef to me woman, beef to me . . . I don't like no pork no-how"; or, finally, "Suffer, suffer, excess baggage, suffer."[85]

Waller and others were able to project a more realistic sense of black humor in *Stormy Weather* because the film had a contemporary setting and most of the characters (unhampered by rural masks) were actually playing themselves. In essence, the "New Negro," or at least a hip comic version of that transplanted city dweller, had finally come to the screen. The arrival made for some delightful entertainment and revealing humor.

In addition to black-cast films, the forties saw the release of *Casablanca* (in which Arthur "Dooley" Wilson, who appeared in *Stormy*

Weather, co-starred with Humphrey Bogart in the now-legendary role of Sam, pianist and nightclub co-owner), as well as such notable issue-oriented films as *In This Our Life, Home of the Brave, Intruder in the Dust, Lost Boundaries,* and *Pinky.*

In Hollywood, then, the end of an era had been reached. But breaking old habits was not easy, either before or behind the cameras. While filming *Cabin,* for instance, the cast was forced to eat in Louis B. Mayer's private dining room "to avoid challenging the color bar in the MGM commissary." Still, an attempt to present blacks in a more equitable light was being made. Yet whether out of timidity or white directors' and producers' unfamiliarity with black life, the characters portrayed in most forties films would function more as symbols of social problems than fully realized people. Later, Ralph Ellison wrote that, "as an antidote to sentimentality," these films should be seen with "predominantly Negro audiences," since, "when the action goes phony, one will hear derisive laughter, not sobs. . . . *Intruder in the Dust* is the only film that could be shown in Harlem without arousing unintended laughter." For a time, however, intentional comic portraits of blacks and black comedians would virtually disappear from mainstream motion pictures.[86]

Of course, motion pictures were not the whole story. On radio—a less visible but arguably more intimate public arena, and the early twentieth century's other influential new medium—traditional comic caricatures of Negroes would not only survive but reach new heights of popularity and, often, distortion.

7.

•••

RADIO AND

EARLY TELEVISION . . .

racial ventriloquy, black

soaps and servants

13
ROCHESTER

12
AMOS AND ANDY

I

With little or no fanfare, commercially licensed radio was introduced in America on November 2, 1920, replacing the amateur broadcasts that had been received on crystal sets since the late teens. Initially, its impact was slight. Low budgets and inadequate facilities restricted programming, so that information or news shows and music provided by local bands predominated. But it soon became apparent that the potential of the new electronic medium was virtually unlimited. By the end of 1922, there were 576 licensed stations, and radio sales increased from $1 million in 1920 to $400 million in 1925. With the National Broadcasting Company's premiere network broadcast on November 15, 1926, and Columbia Broadcasting System's debut in September 1928, radio had arrived as a formidable influence in the nation's cultural life. By 1929, one of every three homes in America had a radio; a decade later, there was at least one radio in every home and one in most cars.

Among the new electronic medium's most exciting and appealing qualities was that listeners could hear concerts or comic monologues, sports events or political speeches, as they happened. Live broadcasts transported audiences from their living rooms or parlors to the site of actual events, establishing a bond between listeners and disseminating a broad-based popular culture that all Americans could enjoy. In addition, radio could reach a much larger audience than movies, and it was more intimate. Listeners who could not afford to take their families to a theatre or auditorium could sit in the privacy of their own homes, with friends, and enjoy a wide range of entertainment. Moreover, lacking visual images, radio forced listeners to use their imaginations. It required a level of participation that was unnecessary when watching motion pictures or, later, television, and thereby produced a subjective intensity that was often missing from other entertainment media.

Although it is difficult in our age of multi-media assault to imagine radio as anything more than an outlet for top-ten recordings and slick, rabble-rousing talk show hosts, during its peak in the thirties and forties it was the nation's most influential popular entertainment and cultural medium. The impact of the live account of the *Hindenburg*'s explosion in Lakehurst, New Jersey, in 1937, and the general panic that swept the Eastern seaboard and parts of the Midwest and South in October 1938 when Orson Welles's Mercury Theatre on the Air presentation of H. G. Wells's *The War of the Worlds* was mistaken for an actual report of a Martian invasion demonstrated radio's persuasive power and its intense dramatic possibilities.

Comedy, however, did not immediately emerge as a key ingredient in radio. Many stage comics, accustomed to live audiences and the use of visual gags and props, were skeptical about performing for silent, unseen, and unknown listeners. As late as 1932, seasoned comedians like Bob Hope still reacted anxiously to radio appearances. "It all seemed strange," Hope said of an engagement on Rudy Vallee's *Fleischmann Hour*, "talking into a microphone in a studio instead of playing in front of a real audience. I was nervous on those first radio shows and the Vallee engineers couldn't figure why they heard a thumping noise when I did my routines until they found out I was kicking the mike after each joke." Others avoided the new medium because variety show and vaudeville producers objected to having their acts appearing on radio or in movies; in fact, many Broadway performers initially displayed the same snobbish attitude toward radio that they had to motion pictures.[2]

Gradually, however, casual humorous patter became a part of most radio programming. "Certain members of radio orchestras on local stations, in order to enliven their programs, started to toss impromptu jokes back and forth," Arthur Frank Wertheim writes in *Radio Comedy*.

"These musicians were among the airwaves' first jesters." Station announcers facilitated the use of humor on the air by pirating jokes from popular magazines such as *Judge, College Humor,* and *Whiz Bang.* Quips and gags were also lifted from *Madison's Budget* (a compilation of gags, routines, and monologues published annually from 1898 to 1921 by the former vaudeville star James Madison). These gags, used to pad or fill out program schedules, were generally standard vaudeville fare, such as:

—I heard your mother-in-law was dangerously sick.
—Yes, but now she's dangerously well again.

—I quit because the boss used repulsive language.
—What did he say?
—He said, "You're fired."

—Sir, I didn't think I deserved a zero on this exam.
—You didn't, but it's the lowest grade I can give.

—Am I tired! I've been running around all day trying to get something for my wife.
—Had any offer yet?

But the humor most frequently heard on early radio was provided by "song and comedy patter" teams. Through the mid-twenties these teams—usually small-time vaudeville acts—provided a steady flow of popular song and amiable chatter. Entertainment on early radio, then, lacked its own distinct character; it depended largely on humorous patter mainly comprised of tired, one-line vaudeville gags and either live broadcasts of dance bands or the innocuous music created by local musicians.[3]

For African-Americans, radio followed the well-trodden course established by mainstream theatres and motion pictures. Again, there was almost no acknowledgment of the ferment in urban centers, of the Harlem Renaissance, of blacks' struggle for equality, or of the repressive measures amassed against that struggle. Radio, like the movies, largely projected an anachronistic, nineteenth-century portrait of black life. With the exception of guest appearances by musicians, blacks were initially ignored. Later, they were burlesqued, imitated, and finally allocated supportive comedy roles as domestics. Little else changed until after World War II.

Since the earliest radio stations concentrated on news and information broadcasts—serious pursuits assumed to be beyond the interest or comprehension of former slaves—it was not surprising that black Americans were not initially enlisted. (African-Americans would be generally excluded from mainstream journalism until the sixties' civil rights disturbances.) Still, since music was integral to the success of the new medium, black musicians were included in broadcasts from clubs and theatres on local stations in the mid-twenties, and continued to appear sporadically as guest artists on variety shows in subsequent years.

The acclaimed jazz pianist and composer Fats Waller, for instance, was first heard on a broadcast from Newark's Fox Terminal Theatre in 1923. By the thirties he had made occasional appearances on other local shows and had been featured on network programs such as *Paramount on Parade* and *Radio Roundup*, where he played, sang, and inserted "sassy jibes at the lyrics." His own show had a short run on CBS. Also in 1923, Kid Ory was "broadcasting classic New Orleans jazz from Los Angeles and Trixie Smith and Fletcher Henderson were broadcasting the blues from New York." During the mid-twenties, according to Louis Armstrong's biographer, James Lincoln Collier, "Clarence Williams, Henderson, Ellington, and others were broadcasting regularly, sometimes every night or even twice a night, from major nightclubs, hotels, and dance halls . . . there was more *good* jazz on radio in New York during the twenties than there is today." Jazz was not the only black music provided; in 1924, "the Hampton Institute Choir was appearing on stations in New York City," and in the late 1920s, "black musical performers like Noble Sissle, Fess Williams, and the Pace Jubilee Negro Singers were heard on the air."[4]

Still, appearances by Waller, Henderson, Ellington, Armstrong, and other legendary black musicians (such as Count Basie, Chick Webb, Will Vodery, Don Redman, Earl "Fatha" Hines, and Cab Calloway) were minuscule when compared with the enormous amount of time allotted to music on early radio. Swing or big-band dance music was in demand and jazz popularizers such as Paul Whiteman, Guy Lombardo, and Al Goodman, along with swing bands led by Ozzie Nelson, Benny Goodman, Glenn Miller, and Kay Kyser, would become radio's best-known orchestra leaders.

By the thirties, Art Tatum, Duke Ellington, Noble Sissle, Louis Armstrong, Bob Howard, Adelaide Hall, the Mills Brothers, and the Ink Spots had all had brief runs at their own series, and stars such as Paul

Robeson, Ethel Waters, Nina Mae McKinney, Cab Calloway, and Bill Robinson were among the guests on network programs. In the forties, black musicians and singers made further inroads on radio and, in addition to numerous guest appearances by stars like Billie Holiday, performers such as Louis Jordan and His Tymphany Five, Cab Calloway, and Nat King Cole would host their own shows. Still, whenever possible, performers' ethnic origins went unrevealed; "radio editors had a tacit agreement not to publish pictures of black radio artists, no matter how successful or popular they became."[5]

Indeed, following a pattern established by minstrelsy and blackface actors on the stage and screen, whites played Negro roles in nearly all of the early radio shows. In the beginning, when programs were not broadcast before a live audience, this new electronic medium made the pretense much easier. The deception depended entirely on mimicking black dialect and intonation. Thus radio had introduced a new phenomenon: racial ventriloquy.

Since early radio generally eschewed drama in favor of light, "wholesome" entertainment for family audiences, mimicry of blacks was most often put to comic use. Consequently, for a time, radio extended the careers of many minstrel comedians whose popularity on stage had nearly reached its nadir.

During the mid-twenties, minstrel-style shows were common on both local and network stations. *The Eveready Hour,* which premiered on New York's WEAF in 1923 and moved to NBC in 1926, often featured Mack and Moran; this blackface team also appeared on the 1928 CBS *Majestic Theatre Hour.* In 1926, *The Burnt Cork Review* was broadcast in Cincinnati on WLW. Later, NBC aired the *Sealy Air Minstrels* (1927–28) and the *Dutch Master Minstrels* (1928–32). In 1928, Tess Gardella brought her blackface Aunt Jemima impersonation to radio and, the next year, *George and Rufus* appeared on WOV (Brooklyn).

In the thirties—besides *Show Boat,* which featured two blackface acts (Honey Boy and Sassafras, and Molasses 'n' January) and became the nation's top variety program in 1932—the NBC schedule featured the *Sinclair Weiner Minstrels, Plantation Party, Molle Minstrels,* and *Minstrel Show.* Among the other thirties' black imitators on radio in the thirties were Moonshine and Sawdust (*The Gulf Show*); Buck and Wheat (*Aunt Jemima*); Sugarfoot and Sassafrass, and Anaesthetic and Cerebelum (both on Portland's KGW); Watermelon and Cantaloupe (*Corn Cob Pipe Club,* WEAF, New York); Pick and Pat (portrayed by Pat Padgett and Pick Malone, who also were Molasses 'n' January, on

Dill's Best Show); and such male-female teams as Conjur and Carolina, and Emmaline and Easy (both on Schenectady's WGY). Even Gosden and Correll took time out from *Amos 'n' Andy* in the late thirties to broadcast a *Mystic Knights of the Sea Friday Night Minstrel Show* on WMAQ, Chicago. (Some are more memorable for their bizarre names than for their humor.)[6]

Racial ventriloquy, like the antics of blackface actors on stage and in silent movies, was crucial in establishing burlesque images that black performers would later be expected to emulate. They would linger for decades and, when authentic black comedians were finally allowed access to the medium, would continue to add an absurd and hauntingly ironic footnote to black radio comedy.

II

In 1925, Freeman F. Gosden and Charles J. Correll, an unheralded, small-time harmony duo, debuted as musicians on WQGA radio in Chicago. Both had been working as talent show directors for a company that staged amateur shows around the country; they also experimented with a musical routine in which they sang and played piano and ukulele. Within the year they had moved to WGN, a station owned by the *Chicago Tribune,* and, according to Arthur Wertheim and Correll's son, Rich, when management began looking for comedians to create a broadcast adaptation of the comic strip serial *The Gumps,* Gosden and Correll were approached. They declined the station's idea but suggested an alternative, black-dialect show.

At this point, the origin of the characters that would become Amos and Andy grows murky. As we have seen, Flournoy Miller and Aubrey Lyles had introduced similar characters after they left Fisk University and began performing in Chicago in the early teens. Shortly afterward, the pair had incorporated their characters in a musical comedy, *The Mayor of Dixie,* which was the source of the 1921 Broadway hit *Shuffle Along.* Even before they left for Broadway, Miller and Lyles had become a popular comedy team in the Chicago area; they performed for society soirées as well as at the downtown Majestic Theatre and were praised by critics such as Ashton Stevens. In 1925, after their Broadway successes in *Shuffle Along* and *Runnin' Wild* (1923), according to Redd Foxx and Norma Miller, they were recruited by radio station WGN and the proposed sponsors of a new show to bring their now-famous comedy characters to radio. A contract was negotiated by their agent, Harry

Bestry; but when the sponsors realized that the comedy team was black and not simply a blackface act, the deal was canceled. "Blackface was acceptable, but black skin was not."[7]

The official version, however, is that Gosden and Correll suggested the idea to WGN: "They had a more exciting idea for a program and presented it to the station. Gosden and Correll wanted to broadcast a serial based on two blacks named Sam and Henry." After some hesitation on the part of station management, their idea was accepted; *Sam 'n' Henry* debuted on January 12, 1926. Like the black characters that Octavus Roy Cohen satirized in his Florian Slappey stories, Sam and Henry were from Birmingham, Alabama. The initial episode "depicted them riding on the buckboard of a mule-driven wagon en route to a train depot" where they would take a train to Chicago. When they arrived in Chicago, again as in Cohen's stories, much of the humor revolved around their membership in "The Jewels of the Crown," a black fraternal organization (the black lodge in Cohen's tales was called "Sons and Daughters of I Will Arise"). Six days a week for nearly two years, the misadventures of Sam and Henry would be heard on WGN in Chicago.[8]

Gosden and Correll's "creation" of Sam and Henry, their pioneer effort in bringing what amounted to a black situation comedy to radio, would become a hotly disputed topic among blacks in the entertainment world. There is, of course, no doubt that Gosden and Correll absorbed or borrowed much of their material from black acts; and the Miller and Lyles team was probably among them, since they were not only the most prominent and best-known black comics in the Chicago area during the early twenties but had also written and starred in a hit Broadway musical. It is likely that Gosden and Correll also incorporated material and ideas from writers like Octavus Roy Cohen (who would later write briefly for the *Amos 'n' Andy Show*), as well as from blackface or minstrel acts such as Mack and Moran or any of the numerous performers who used burnt cork and Negro dialect at the time.

Borrowing from other acts was not a new or unusual occurrence in show business. The song and dance that helped establish Thomas "Jim Crow" Rice in the 1830s, as we have seen, was borrowed from a crippled black stable hand. Ernest Hogan allegedly acquired his most famous song, "All Coons Look Alike to Me," from another musician at the turn of the century. And in the twenties and thirties, many of Fats Waller's riffs, ideas, and original compositions were borrowed or sold for a meal, a few drinks (or less) to various record producers and musicians, including, some contend, George Gershwin and Fletcher Henderson.

In any event, jokes cannot be copyrighted. Some comedians' reputations for appropriating others' material reached the level of a standing joke within the industry. Milton Berle, for example, assumed that "all jokes were public property" and "freely borrowed gags and routines from other comedians," prompting Walter Winchell to dub him "The Thief of Bad Gags." Pigmeat Markham said of Berle: "I'd only been at the Apollo or maybe the Alhambra a week for the first time, when this little white cat hardly out of knee pants showed up with his scratch pad and pencil and started copying down every word I said. . . . " And during the thirties Bob Hope and another comedian set up a good-natured practical joke to chide Berle for his alleged penchant for stealing gags. They arranged to appear before Berle at several benefit shows and perform his entire act before he went on stage. More recently, Richard Pryor, who initially was criticized for emulating Bill Cosby, has admitted: "I did everybody's act for a while . . . it took me a long time to find my own direction, to stop using other people's stuff." Eddie Murphy, one of the most innovative comedians in the eighties, in turn rehashed some familiar Pryor bits in his early concerts; later, Martin Lawrence, one of the nineties' most popular comics, reprised material from Pryor, Murphy, and Flip Wilson.[9]

In comedy, gags, jokes, and routines are regularly exchanged and repeated by various comedians; the originator or inventor is often not as important as the comic who popularizes the routine. And that usually depends on opportunity. Given the racist climate and black entertainers' limited access to mass media outlets in the mid-twenties, there was little chance that Miller and Lyles would have been permitted to star on their own radio show. So Gosden and Correll's presentation of black characters whose prototypes had been brought to the stage years before by minstrels, then refined by black comedians, was not really surprising; it was simply another instance of show business as usual.

In some ways, Gosden and Correll were perfectly suited for the task. Charles Correll's family had moved from the South to Peoria, Illinois, after the Civil War. Born in 1890, Correll displayed a gift for music and mimicry at an early age. He played piano, danced, sang, and told Negro-dialect jokes in amateur minstrel shows before becoming a talent show director. Gosden, a more persuasive comic actor and Negro impersonator, was born in Richmond, Virginia, in 1899. He too demonstrated an early knack for music and comedy. Besides singing and playing an instrument, he dallied in magic, clog dancing, and had performed as an endman in amateur minstrel shows. In addition, although the claim that he was raised by a black "mammy" was a press fabrication, he did have a black childhood friend who worked for his family. He met Garrett Brown (who was nicknamed "Snowball") when he was five, and they often played together, sometimes staging "impromptu minstrel shows." Gosden once claimed that Amos was "partly based on his childhood friend," and a few of the phrases that later appeared on the *Amos 'n' Andy Show* ("Ain't dat sumpin'," for example) were reportedly based on Brown's "amusing jargon." Gosden and Correll "felt they knew enough about the South and Negro life" to write a successful comedy series on blacks.[10]

From the outset, the show depended on stereotyped caricatures of blacks that had been seen on the minstrel stage for nearly a century. Sam, although sincere and industrious, was superstitious, naive, and easily duped. Henry, on the other hand, was lazy, ignorant, conniving, and drawn to the usual Sambo diversions—crapshooting, womanizing, and liquor. Humor was basically provided by the characters' ignorance and the contrast of caricatured minstrel and black Southern folkways with the demands of urban living. But Sam and Henry also reflected the subtle humanizing changes that black performers like Miller and Lyles had insinuated into these stage Negroes. Essentially, what Gosden and Correll added was a more emphatic underscoring of voice distinctions (they did nearly a hundred separate voice impersonations) and a continuous storyline, attributes necessitated by the demands of the medium.

Although it was not an immediate hit, *Sam 'n' Henry* gradually gained a loyal following. Before Gosden and Correll left WGN when their two-year contract expired, their characters had inspired a comic strip and recordings, which were released by Victor.

On March 19, 1928, about three months after the last *Sam 'n' Henry* show, *Amos 'n' Andy* debuted on WMAQ, a rival station in Chicago. Due to legal entanglements, the characters had been renamed, but Sam (Gosden) and Henry (Correll) were virtually unaltered when they resurfaced as Amos Jones and Andrew H. Brown, and the show was even more successful. Recorded and leased to forty other stations, it was an immediate hit in Chicago as well as other parts of the country. Network executives took notice, and in August 1929, with Pepsodent toothpaste as sponsor, the show switched to NBC. Immediately, its popularity soared, and by 1930 it had become a nationwide rage. Until 1943, it was broadcast nightly as a fifteen-minute serial.

If *Sam 'n' Henry* had been radio's first situation comedy, *Amos 'n' Andy* was the first great radio show. Many maintain that, at its peak, it may have been the most popular show ever broadcast, and it also represented the most widespread dissemination of *public* black humor until its time. It was, in effect, a comic, black-voice soap opera that, like minstrelsy, allowed America obliquely to scrutinize and laugh at its own problems. Gosden and Correll spotlighted two Georgia Negroes whose migration first to Chicago and then to Harlem humorously mirrored the plight of the nation's common man, caught in the transformation from an agrarian society to a complex urban one.[11]

The comic currency remained thick dialect speech, malapropisms, and the standard Negro stereotypes: naïveté, imprudence, venality, and ignorance. But the show's enduring success probably rested as much on Gosden and Correll's creation of a dramatic setting that typically reflected non-racial issues and embodied the concerns of a larger segment of society. Unlike minstrelsy, in which the foolish antics of the endmen, Tambo and Bones, were continually contrasted with a staid, often pompous, interlocutor (representing proper mainstream values), the characters in *Amos 'n' Andy* functioned in an entirely black setting, where their behavior was not continually contrasted with the norms of the larger society. (The difference is instantly apparent when the radio show is compared with motion pictures such as *Check and Double Check*, where Amos and Andy were placed in an integrated setting and played against straight, mainstream characters.) Whereas Tambo and Bones were portrayed as unassimilable fools, whose feral antics and uncurbed instincts placed them beyond the bonds of even marginally polite society, Amos and Andy were presented as bona fide Americans (albeit second-class ones), struggling to open their own business—a taxi service—and secure a place in a rapidly changing society that, in a limited manner, was realistically presented.

Less than a year after the show debuted on NBC, as the country grappled with the stock market crash, Andy attempted to explain the financial crisis to Lightnin', a minor character who was seeking a job with the Fresh Air Taxi Company. "Well, Lightnin', 'course I would like to give you a job but de bizness repression is on right now," Andy said. When Lightnin' asked if anybody got hurt in the crash, Andy continued: "Well, 'course, Lightnin', when de stock market crashes, it hurts us bizness men. Dat's what puts de repression on things." A few days later, Andy and George Stevens (Kingfish) offered a comically inspired explanation of the market's intricacies. "Yo' see," Kingfish asserted, "a week ago Thursday, de big crash started. De bulls an' de bears was fightin' it out an' de bears chased de bulls." The plight of the small investor and the value of inside tips were also discussed. "Ev'ybody's got a tip," Kingfish pontificated. "Ev'ybody knows the inside on de stocks, yo' see—dat's whut dey tell yo', so den you buy it an' it just look like dey waitin' fo' you to buy it, 'cause de minute you buy it, it goes down." This kind of folksy interpretation of the "repression" and other social issues helped inform laymen and immensely broadened the show's popularity.

Throughout the thirties and into the early forties, the combination of topical themes, a serial format, and folksy dialect humor kept *Amos 'n' Andy* among the most popular radio programs on the air. In fact, during its peak years in the early thirties the program seemed to have created a kind of national frenzy. Like popular movie serials of the thirties and forties and today's television soap operas, episodes dovetailed and crucial dramatic situations were frequently left unresolved from one broadcast to the next. A sequence aired in October 1931, for example, had Amos falsely accused of murder and brought to trial. The trial went on for several episodes and when it seemed that he was about to be convicted, listeners were outraged. The president of the advertising firm representing Pepsodent warned Gosden and Correll: "The country's mad! The Parent-Teacher Association is going to boycott the program if Amos is convicted." One commentator contends that "no trial in fact or fiction ever interested the people more." On another occasion, in 1939, a series of programs focused on Andy's impending marriage. At the wedding, however, before Andy could utter the final "I do," a shot was heard and Andy collapsed. The next day, "controversy erupted in the press. . . . Lawyers jumped into the fray, bickering over fine points of law." Attorneys, citing statutes from various states, offered contradictory assessments of Andy's marital status and *Time* magazine collected "opinions from jurists in New York, Iowa, and California." When the ballyhoo abated, it was discovered that no one had been shot. The wedding was called off; Andy remained single and continued his philandering ways.[12]

Amos 'n' Andy was the number-one show in the country and, from all reports, was nearly addictive. Newspapers often carried accounts of the previous night's developments. Listeners discussed the characters' problems as if they were real-life events. The daily routines of a group of ersatz black folks had never received such exposure and scrutiny in the national media. (The phenomenon would not be repeated until the debut of Bill Cosby's more realistic but ironically less representative television chronicle of the Huxtables in the eighties.)

By 1935, 70 percent of American homes had radios and, according to some estimates, 40 million listeners were tuned in to the program each night. "No matter what movie house you attended," Eubie Blake recalled, "the show would come to a sudden stop at seven o'clock and loudspeakers would bring to the audience the fifteen-minute Amos 'n' Andy show." During the 1932 presidential campaign, radio spots had to be scheduled so that they did not compete with *Amos 'n' Andy*. "A large part of the American people," some complained, "are more interested in the Kingfish and the Fresh Air Taxi Company than they are in the affairs of their own country." Others claim that telephone calls diminished from 7:00 to 7:15 P.M., and the use of utilities decreased. "Bus lines and taxis had no passengers; if records can be believed, people didn't run water or flush toilets at *Amos 'n' Andy* time." Atlantic City shopkeepers "found it necessary to install loudspeakers at street corners so the tourists wouldn't have to stay in their hotel rooms to keep up with the Kingfish." One newspaper suggested that the show was changing the nation's speech patterns. Throughout the country jokes, gags, the characters' favorite sayings ("Ain't dat sumptin'," " 'Splain dat to me," or "Holy mackerel") were rehashed and repeated the next day. The audience varied from the poor and middle class to celebrities and the nation's wealthiest class, from middle brows to high brows. Avid fans included J. Edgar Hoover, Herbert Hoover, Vincent Astor, Henry Ford, Huey Long (who would appropriate George Stevens's name, the Kingfish), and the British playwright George Bernard Shaw, who submitted that "There are three things which I shall never forget about America—the Rocky Mountains, Niagara Falls, and *Amos 'n' Andy*."[13]

Although the original comic, fifteen-minute soap opera approach was basically unaltered until 1943, subtle changes in emphasis were made along the way. At the outset, most episodes revolved around the close friendship and extreme contrast between Amos (loyal, diligent, but slow) and Andy (improvident, scheming, and idle). Gosden and Correll were essentially presenting two stock black stage characters, but they had added a slight twist. They moderated their main characters, giving them a veil of propriety that partially obscured the patently mean or fatuous traits that had previously defined these comic types.

Amos was neither as dense and gullible as the prototypical stage or screen Sambo portrayed by Aubrey Lyles or Charlie Mack, nor as much the quintessential darky as portrayed by Bert Williams. Although Amos was often duped by Andy's dim-witted schemes and was inevitably the straightman in their comic exchanges, in contrast to Andy's trickster image, he projected a mainstream, almost bourgeois, sensibility. And although Andy was cast in the familiar image of the conniving stage dandy, he seldom displayed the rapacious venality and malevolence that quite often defined the type.

The moderation with which Amos and Andy were initially portrayed probably accounts for their huge following. Amos, after all, was such a beloved and trustworthy character that he became a national symbol of thrift and responsibility during the Depression. One newspaper editorial cited him as a model of a sensible response to the nation's economic woes and suggested there were too many Andy Brown types. As the media historian Arthur Wertheim pointed out, "Through Amos, Gosden and Correll reasserted the values of generosity, diligence, and unpretentiousness, mores that many Americans wanted to return to at the time." And while his prodigal ways and aversion to work were chastened, Andy never moved beyond the point where audiences could react with amused affection. He was a gentle, almost childlike trickster, and listeners responded with overwhelming concern and empathy when he was apparently shot at his wedding or when he was sued by Madame Queen for breach of promise.

Generally, then, Amos and Andy were laughed with, not at. Listeners identified with them, and a columnist could write (without intentional irony in the choice of the word "shades"). "The average radio listener recognizes in the day-to-day affairs of *Amos 'n' Andy* shades of his own triumphs and defeats, joys and sorrows, reactions and reasonings."[14]

Responsibility for the bulk of the program's humor was left to the supporting cast; not coincidentally, their roles embodied nearly all of the derisively humorous attributes of minstrel caricature. Freeman Gosden was far and away his partner's superior as a black mimic; therefore, he assumed the voices of the most prominent comic characters— Lightnin' and George (Kingfish) Stevens. Lightnin' was Sambo without palliation; while Amos's earnestness, industriousness, and commonsense compensated for his naïveté and ignorance, the slothful, simpleminded Lightnin' was a one-dimensional character who mirrored the image projected by Molasses (of Molasses 'n' January) and Stepin Fetchit. Kingfish was an unscrupulous, conniving dandy who seldom displayed the thoughtfulness or self-appraisal that often tempered Andy's scheming, rakish nature. As the program evolved, Kingfish and Lightnin' would gradually assume more and more comic importance.

When the nation's economy strengthened or, at least, slowed its downward spiral, the show's emphasis switched from plots centered on the financial problems of Andy and the hardworking Amos, to focus more and more on scams perpetrated by Kingfish, the exalted ruler of the Mystic Knights of the Sea, who first appeared on the show in May 1928. (The members were called "sardines"; other officers included "de Whale," "de Mackerel," "de Catfish," and "de Shad.") Audiences, apparently tiring of Amos's quiet sincerity, thirsted for more comic action, and with his indefatigable pursuit of easy money, Kingfish supplied it. Amos was gradually reduced to walk-ons in which he attempted to steer Andy away from Kingfish's absurd schemes, which included selling motorless cars or deeds to the Washington Monument and the Brooklyn Bridge. But, as the comedy was heightened by Kingfish's broad, exaggerated ethnic humor and Amos was phased out of the central action, *Amos 'n' Andy* lost some of its realistic dramatic appeal and moved closer to familiar minstrel stereotypes and blackface burlesque. Initially, the changes were effective and slumping ratings were revitalized. By the early forties, however, radio comedy itself had undergone broad changes, in the process radically influencing America's popular entertainment.

Encouraged by the success of Gosden and Correll and Will Rogers —who appeared on a host of variety shows beginning in the twenties and whose monologues were featured weekly on *The Gulf Show* from 1933 until his death in 1935—a number of talented vaudeville performers began testing the radio market. Recognizing its appeal and potential, well-known stage comedians who had initially spurned the new medium began rushing in to capitalize on what was perceived, by the thirties, as a lucrative and comparatively undemanding market. Eddie Cantor, Ed Wynn, Fred Allen, Jack Benny, and George Burns and Gracie Allen had begun radio series by the early thirties; a decade later, W. C. Fields, Fanny Brice, Bob Hope, and Red Skelton (among others) had joined them.

Radio networks had modernized their broadcast methods, so comedians were no longer forced to work without an audience in deathly silence and cramped studios. Increasingly, vaudeville clowns who had molded their routines for live shows and the rigid censorship exercised on the Keith and Orpheum circuits (where salacious material was diligently excised) were finding that their acts were perfectly suited for a medium seeking innocuous humor and family-oriented entertainment. Consequently, radio was "invaded by a host of slick vaudevillians, who came equipped with bands, announcers with charisma, and studio audiences that laughed out loud over the air." This new breed of radio comedian—many of whom flaunted years of experience in movies as well as on the stage—also came with a behind-the-scenes brigade, a corps of writers and pundits who supplied endless new gags for a medium whose weekly regimen voraciously devoured ideas.[15]

By the late thirties, the slow-paced, basically sentimental *Amos 'n' Andy Show* was outmatched by these sophisticated new comedy programs. Pepsodent abandoned the program in 1937 and began sponsoring Bob Hope's show the following year. Gosden and Correll, who still wrote their scripts and portrayed nearly all of the characters themselves, realized that a change was necessary. Early in 1943, the familiar fifteen-minute format was dropped and, in October, a thoroughly revamped half-hour version of *Amos 'n' Andy* returned to the air. The show was performed before a live audience and featured Jeff Alexander's orchestra and chorus, Harlow Wilcox (a lively announcer who established a reputation on the *Fibber McGee and Molly* show), and new supporting characters portrayed by such performers as Eddie Green, Lou Lubin, Harriet Widmer, Ernestine Wade, and Amanda Randolph. Additional writers were employed, celebrity guests appeared, and each show focused on a single comic situation. This new, slicker version of *Amos 'n' Andy*, although it lost much of the intimacy of the original, was well received. Again the show climbed in ratings and, for a time, was among radio's top-ten programs.

Although it never regained the fanatical following of the thirties, the new *Amos 'n' Andy* did represent a breakthrough. For the first time, it moved away from strict adherence to the concept of verbal minstrelsy and introduced black performers. Veteran TOBA comedian Eddie Green, who starred in several race films in the thirties and forties and had a supporting part as a comic waiter on the *Duffy's Tavern* radio show (1941–51), was cast as the lawyer, Stonewall. Amanda Randolph, another featured player in black-cast movies—she co-starred with Green in Sepia Arts' *Comes Midnight* (1940)—played Kingfish's ever-menacing mother-in-law. Ernestine Wade's portrayal of the now-infamous Sapphire, Kingfish's shrill, domineering wife, had more impact than any of the parts assigned to blacks. Her unerring performance was so indelible that her character became synonymous with caricatures of the castigating and cantankerous black female; to this day, the name "Sapphire" defines the stereotype. (Wade, Amanda Randolph, Johnny Lee, who joined the cast later, and Lillian Randolph, who had replaced the white actress, Harriet Widmer, as Madame Queen, were the only performers who would make the transition from radio to television.) James Baskette, who was a favorite at the Apollo Theatre and would later star as Uncle Remus in Disney's *Song of the South* (1946), also appeared on the radio show.

Overshadowing the emergence of black performers on the show was the expanded role assigned to Kingfish. With the new format, he virtually dominated the action. (In the early fifties, when I listened to the program as a child, audiences wondered why it was called *Amos 'n' Andy*.) Amos seldom appeared, and most plots centered either on Kingfish's abortive attempts to bamboozle Andy and Lightnin' or his domestic misadventures with Sapphire and her mother. Although it was no longer the national rage it once had been, and had shed much of its homely mainstream morality, in my working-class black neighborhood the program was still must listening on Friday nights.

In these later shows, the slick, fast-talking Kingfish set the pace, and the program depended almost entirely on his trickster ploys for its humor and appeal. The following exchange illustrates Kingfish's insistent indolence and the source of his friction with Sapphire, as well as the general nature of the show's humor:

Sapphire: George Stevens, I done made up my mind that I'm gonna have a husband that dresses good, knows nice people, and is got a steady job.

Kingfish: Sapphire, you mean to say that you is gonna leave me.

Sapphire: George, I know why you're a no-good bum. It's on account of your association with Andy Brown. Why don't you try to meet a nicer class of men?

Kingfish: Well, I ain't got da opportunity to meet 'em, they's all workin'.

Sapphire: Well, that Andy Brown is the cause of it all. What has he ever accomplished?

Kingfish: Well, yesterday he had a run of thirteen balls in da
              side pocket without leanin' on da table.

Sapphire: Now, that's exactly what I mean: Andy hangin' around
              a pool table all day. Why don't he go to a cultured
              place like a public library?

Kingfish: They ain't got no pool table there.[16]

Kingfish—through the voice of Freeman Gosden—would emerge as one of the electronic media's more memorable and outlandish rogues. For many people, he would become—along with Sapphire—one of the most recognizably opprobrious black characters in the history of radio and, later, television.

Gosden and Correll abandoned the familiar radio rendering of *Amos 'n' Andy* in 1954, and for the next six years hosted a sanitized version of the program, *The Amos and Andy Music Hall*, on which they played records and presented brief comic skits. That show was canceled on November 25, 1960. Except for bootleg films, which were readily available, and, later, video tapes, the original *Amos 'n' Andy* characters— clearly embarrassments for most middle-class blacks—had been banished from earshot and public view.

III

In many ways, the evolution and demise of *Sam 'n' Henry* and *Amos 'n' Andy* paralleled the fate of radio comedy in general. Although *Amos 'n' Andy* mainly avoided minstrelsy of the broadest, most puerile type, Gosden and Correll's characters reflected the Negro mimicry of early radio shows. Originally, like Will Rogers's homespun humor, the show also mirrored the medium's emphasis on traditional, rural values. Revamped and broadcast from the West Coast in the forties, it had adopted the slick, fast-paced Hollywood format that characterized the Bob Hope and Jack Benny shows. Like most radio comedy, it declined with the advent of television and, in the fifties, left the air.

Amos 'n' Andy, however, was one of the few situation comedies that did not cast blacks exclusively as comic servants—a role that otherwise defined the black comic presence on radio.

In 1932, Ernest Whitman showed up as Awful, a butler, on *The Gibson Family*, and teamed with Eddie Green for guest appearances on *Show Boat* in a Sambo-like minstrel routine; Hattie McDaniel did guest spots in her mammy guise on the *Optimistic Doughnut Hour* and *Show Boat* in the same year. Lillian Randolph began her succession of radio maid roles on *Lula and Leander*, a comedy show broadcast by Detroit's WXYZ in the early thirties. Also in 1932, Johnny Lee could be heard on *Slick and Slim*, a black-cast comedy series from New York's WHN.[17]

Although numerous white impersonators had played black maids before, and Georgia Burke had appeared in the thirties as Gardenia, a maid in the soap opera *Betty and Bob*, Lillian Randolph was the first black performer to portray a prominent maid character. In 1941, she took the role of Birdie on *The Great Gildersleeve*—a spin-off of *Fibber McGee and Molly* (after *Amos 'n' Andy*, the second most popular show in radio history). She was less acerbic and irreverent than the character of Beulah, but Birdie was still a no-nonsense type who managed to deflate her obstreperous employer with wit and charm. She would occasionally match Gildersleeve's stentorian outbursts in kind; but usually Birdie projected a stoic unflappability, parrying her employer's boisterousness with discretion and understatement. According to one critic, she was "the best of all the stereotyped maids of old-time radio." Randolph, a seasoned entertainer who also appeared in films and television from the thirties to the seventies, played the part until the fifties.[18]

Birdie's success as a regular character on radio opened the door for a number of black performers who appeared as maids or cooks. Ruby Dandridge, for example, was Geranium on *The Judy Canova Show* (1943); Butterfly McQueen appeared as a maid on several programs; and Randolph also appeared as Daisy on *The Billie Burke Show* (1943).

Beulah, however, was radio's best-known black female servant, and that character evolved in much the same way as the *Amos 'n' Andy* gang. Although the name "Beulah" had often been assigned to stereotypical black maids in motion pictures, the radio version was created by Marlin Hurt, a white actor. Hurt had grown up with a black nursemaid and, as a youngster, developed an interest in minstrelsy. By the time he broke into radio as a singer on such shows as NBC's *Plantation Party* in the twenties, he had developed some humorous black impersonations, which included a high-pitched female voice that he often used in his act. In 1940 on *Show Boat*, he introduced Beulah Brown to radio; later, while performing on *The Fred Brady Show*, Hurt was spotted by an associate of the *Fibber McGee and Molly* show, and in January 1944 his irrepressible black alter ego became the McGees' maid. The show was broadcast before a live audience, so Hurt's performance required more than just verbal minstrelsy; audiences were usually shocked when the white actor faced them and unleashed his piercing soprano intonations. The program had introduced another comic black menial earlier —Silly Watson, a Sambo-like handyman, portrayed by a white actor, Hugh Studebaker—but he was quickly forgotten. Beulah's patented laugh and catchphrases such as "Somebody bawl fo' Beulah" or "Love dat man" immediately caught on with radio listeners; and, soon, it was apparent that the character was too popular simply to play a supporting role.

In 1945, Hurt left *Fibber McGee and Molly* to create his own show featuring the Beulah character. He also did other roles on the new show, including Beulah's trifling boyfriend, Bill Jackson. But Beulah was the jewel of his impersonations. Hurt died in 1946, and the show went off the air. The following year, it was revived when another white actor, Bob Corley, assumed the role. Later that year the format was changed: Hattie McDaniel was given the part and the program was aired as a fifteen-minute serial. McDaniel thereby became the first black non-musical performer to star in her own radio comedy series. After she left, Louise Beavers and Lillian Randolph played the part. The veteran Ernest Whitman was among those who played Beulah's boyfriend, Bill Jackson. The show ran on CBS until 1954, outlasting the television version; but, like *Amos 'n' Andy*, it finally succumbed to the heated controversy about its stereotyped characters.

The most recognizable and enduring black comic character who appeared on early radio was Jack Benny's valet and sidekick, Rochester. Benny was among the first radio stars to use black actors on his program, but before June 1937, when, as Rochester, Eddie Anderson became a permanent member of the cast, they usually made one-shot appearances. "Racial taboos" made it nearly impossible for blacks to get regular acting jobs in the radio industry. Anderson was the first black performer to acquire a regular part on radio, and the cocky, irreverent valet was soon one of the medium's most popular characters.[19]

Unlike most other top bananas on stage and radio, as well as in film, Benny set himself up as the butt of jokes. He was vain, stingy, and pompous; although he did not project the frenetic or bombastic rudeness of the Great Gildersleeve, he did portray a character whose prissy, eccentric nature and stubbornness readily elicited barbs from those around him. Benny's show was among the first to offer major roles to its supporting cast members. Aside from his own impeccable sense of timing, the primary source of humor was the cast's continual deflation of the star's ego. Don Wilson, as the beefy, ebullient announcer; Phil Harris, the effervescent bandleader who joined the show in 1936; and Benny's wife, who played Mary Livingston, were among his most outspoken comic adversaries. They traded quips and insults with the star, and Benny regularly set himself up as straightman for their antic comedy. Soon after joining the show, Eddie Anderson as Rochester was quietly slipped into this reversed comedy format. His involvement, although it may seem routine now, was a revolutionary advance when it occurred: in the thirties, black *males* who challenged white authority were simply not seen in mainstream media—either in dramatic or comedic situations.

Born in 1906, Anderson was a stage brat; his mother and father were circus and minstrel performers. He entered the business as a teenager, playing the black theatre circuit where his contagious smile, deep, rasping voice (said to have been acquired by hawking newspapers on the street as an adolescent), and energetic dance routines made him a favorite. Later, he and his brother formed a song and dance team, working the small-time vaudeville theatres. In the thirties, he settled in Los Angeles and appeared briefly in several studio films before being featured as Noah in *The Green Pastures*. His lively performance in that biblical fantasy led to other offers, and in March 1937, he won a minor part as a dense but jovial Pullman porter on Benny's program.

The role echoed the standard stereotype of black menials seen in Hollywood films; in fact, the script specifically indicated the popular cinema prototype. At one point, Anderson, who during his early appearances on the program spoke with a heavy Southern black accent (not always reflected in the dialogue as printed in the scripts), responds to Benny's query about a garment that was supposed to be pressed by saying, "Gee I'm lazy, don't I remind you of Stepin Fetchit?" Though his early radio appearances were undistinguished, Anderson had one distinctive attribute that made him particularly suitable for the new medium: his unique, gravelly voice. Benny and his associates quickly recognized this, and Anderson was enlisted as part of the gang.[20]

As Rochester, Benny's valet, Anderson gradually evolved into one of the more sardonic and outspoken black comic servants in motion pictures or radio—a male retainer the likes of which would not be heard again until the debut of Robert Guillaume as Benson on television in the seventies.

At the outset, however, Rochester was more or less a carbon copy of the Fetchit-like porter. Although permitted a few sarcastic jibes, he was presented as a comically inept worker, who on his own time was a trifling, carefree, crapshooting philanderer. On a 1938 show, for example, the following exchange occurs after Benny complains about Rochester getting off and delaying the train on a trip from New York to Los Angeles:

Rochester: I thought I'se back in Harlem.

Benny: Harlem? I told you before, all those people at the station were Indians.

Rochester: Indians?

Benny: Yes.

Rochester: Well, just the same, I saw a papoose eatin' a pork chop.

Benny: Well, what of it? He can be an Indian and still eat a pork chop.

Rochester: I know, but he had it between two slices of watermelon.

Benny: Alright, you win. But I want to tell you something, Rochester. This is the last time I'm going to take you to New York. You're supposed to help me. The only time I saw you was when you needed money. Why, you spent more than I did.

Rochester: That ain't no record.

Benny: Never mind that. And another thing, you lied to me. You told me you needed the money for a new suit. Now, where is it?

Rochester: You mean the one I had my heart set on?

Benny: Yeah, where is the suit I gave you the money for?

Rochester: Well, I'll tell ya boss. I was on my way to the store and got mixed up in a game of African badminton.

Benny: Oh, so you lost your suit in a crap game, huh?

Rochester: Yes, sir. I rolled myself right out of the Easter parade.

On another occasion, after admonishing Rochester for losing his bicycle in a crap game, Benny demands that the valet get it back:

Benny: . . . I want you to go to that garage, and tell your friend to give you back my bicycle.

Rochester: Without payin' for it?

Benny: Yes, without payin' for it. . . . Just grab it.

Rochester: Now wait a minute, boss. . . . That boy's got a razor that does everything but run out and get the mail.

Benny: Well Rochester, what are you scared of? . . . *You* carry a razor yourself.

Rochester: Yeah, but it's only a *Gillette* and I'm out of blades.

As late as 1950, Rochester was depicted carousing and shooting craps in Harlem; that broadcast, actually a rerun, elicited calls and letters from scores of blacks, as well as protests from the NAACP and editorials deploring "clichés and horseplay that we had supposed had died a quiet and unmourned death a generation ago." Surprised and distressed, Benny apologized.[21]

But Rochester's character gradually began reflecting the critical attitude assumed by other cast members toward the "boss." Rochester started to show an independence, irreverence, and knack for witty rejoinders usually reserved for non-blacks or black female servants such as Hattie McDaniel in film. It was in this guise that those of us more familiar with the Benny show aired on radio and television in the fifties remember Rochester. A clever, resourceful servant who, like the rest of the cast, was also an accepted friend, Rochester was aware of Benny's foibles and frequently pointed them out. Anderson brought a brash, impudent edge to his role that was similar to traits displayed by radio's Birdie and, later, Beulah. It seemed perfectly natural and good-natured, however, since after the forties Rochester was portrayed more as a companion to Benny, a respected part of the household, than as a grossly stereotyped servant whose role and place were strictly prescribed.

Besides joining the rest of the cast in running gags about Benny's pettiness and parsimony, his vanity, pomposity, inept performance on the violin, and stubborn insistence that he was still thirty-nine, Rochester's twitting was often based on attitudes about recreation and style that were common among the majority of African-Americans. In an early episode in which he assists Benny in preparing to go out for the evening, for example, Rochester lays out a dress suit and a pair of casual shoes:

Jack:	*Those are my sports shoes.* Where did you ever see sports shoes with a full dress suit?
Rochester:	In the Harlem *Esquire.*
Jack:	Well, run over to my dressing room and get my plain *black* ones and hurry.
Rochester:	Black coat, black shoes, black pants . . . you is de most *monotonous* man I ever worked for.

This trend was extended to television, where one episode found Benny waiting for Rochester to return home at 4:00 A.M. When Benny questions him about his nocturnal habits, Rochester responds: "Well, last night the club I belong to had a social gathering, and the president had intentions of breaking it up at 10:00 o'clock. . . . At 9:30 we elected a new president." Frequently, Rochester countered Benny's comically exaggerated emphasis of such middle-class values as moderation, surface decorum, and thriftiness with quips reflecting legitimate options that existed in the black community. In these instances he mirrored comic ploys that were more typically confined to the stages of black theatres.[22]

But, as we have seen, the tendency to contrast Benny's exaggerated middle-class behavior with grass-roots black attitudes could, and often did, slip easily into minstrelsy-derived burlesque. In this reverse form, a fun-loving, carefree attitude could be seen as excess and debauchery, against which Benny's rigidity and fastidiousness were portrayed as normal and preferable. And since most blacks, unlike middle-class whites, were reluctant to have their idiosyncrasies publicly satirized, those comic episodes in which Rochester was portrayed as overly spirited and sensual (licentious) or fun-loving (irresponsible) called forth quick responses from the black community.

Conversely, Rochester's assertiveness and witty deflation of Benny's haughty stage persona precipitated protests from another source. Rochester was quite simply far too uppity for many white listeners, particularly southerners. His cavalier attitude and prickly rejoinders, like those of Hattie McDaniel in her typical roles, frequently annoyed audiences below the Mason-Dixon line. The episode that reportedly caused the "largest deluge of mail in the program's history" was one in which Rochester, helping Benny prepare for a boxing match with Fred Allen, accidentally hits his boss too hard and knocks him out. Comically portraying a Negro hitting a white man, even if it was unintentional and even though Joe Louis was heavyweight champion at the time, was considered a transgression of major proportions.[23]

But despite its mildly controversial aspects, *The Jack Benny Show* survived the purge that discredited and finally eliminated most comedy shows that featured black characters during the forties and fifties. In the early fifties, Benny began a regularly scheduled television program with the same ensemble he employed on radio. In May 1955, dwindling ratings prompted him to drop the radio show, but the bi-weekly television version lasted until the mid-sixties. Rochester remained until the end.

The success of the Jack Benny program and Anderson's long tenure as perhaps the most popular member of the supporting cast on radio and television made Rochester a household name. The character's popularity, in fact, so overshadowed Anderson's accomplishments in other areas that the actor is remembered by many only for that role. Anderson, however, was a gifted entertainer and comic actor, whose talents far exceeded his portrayal of Benny's witty valet. His performances in the black-cast films *The Green Pastures* and *Cabin in the Sky* demonstrated a range of comedic ability that was seldom called upon in his role as Rochester. In *Green Pastures,* he is rousing as an energetic Old South preacher and appropriately dictatorial as Noah. And in *Cabin,* as Little Joe Jackson, an average black man whose soul is sought by the forces of Heaven and Hell, Anderson is equally at ease in the dramatic sequences and the musical comedy routines. Even in some of the more narrowly conceived supporting roles he played in motion pictures from the thirties to the sixties, he projected a self-assurance and independence that set his portrayal of the male comic servant apart. These comic characters (including Rochester) were usually bolstered by a reflective quality and indication of depth even when they mouthed the most inane lines.

Mantan Moreland was the contemporary black comedian with whom Anderson had most in common. In appearance, both were small men, with wide, expressive eyes; each had an impish or devilish quality that lurked just beneath the surface. Moreland was more typically the stage clown or buffoon, however; his humor was broader, more clearly associated with the low, slapstick comedy common in burlesque houses and tent shows, and his frenzied demeanor and wide arsenal of grimaces and comic expressions usually made him a caricature rather than a believable character. Although their specific roles in *Cabin in the Sky* partially account for their divergent styles, that film does offer a clear comparison of the two comedic approaches. The fidgety, nervous movements, high-pitched voice, and rapid delivery that Moreland displays as the Devil's henchman were typical accouterments of the stage clown. Anderson, by contrast, was relaxed, almost serenely understated, as the pawn in a battle of the forces of good and evil. Compared to Moreland, his comedic devices were much less obvious.

Finally, Anderson was a dancer and comic actor rather than a comedian. He relied on an air of restraint and more self-contained mannerisms. Perhaps more than any of the old-time black comics, Anderson had mastered the art of subtly projecting ambiguity or cynicism, disbelief or disdain, through his facial expressions. Whereas Stepin Fetchit and Willie Best amused through exaggerated sluggishness and a mask of stupefaction or cowardice, Anderson's humor usually flowed from his relaxed deportment, his grating but infectious voice, and an underlying sense of confidence and studied reflection.

From the mid-thirties to the sixties, Eddie Anderson flourished as a premier comic presence. By the forties, he had become one of Hollywood's highest-paid black actors. His motion picture roles varied from relatively innocuous appearances as comic menials or sidekicks in *Three Men on a Horse* (1936) and *Brewster's Millions* (1945) to disastrously stereotyped parts such as the unscrupulous, fast-talking preacher in *Tales of Manhattan* (1942) and the familiar coonlike chauffeur in *Topper Returns* (1941). As Rochester in three Jack Benny films—*Man About Town* (1939), *Buck Benny Rides Again* (1940), and *The Meanest Man in the World* (1943)—he brought the sardonic wit that he had popularized on radio to the screen. *The New York Times* asserted that, in *Man About Town,* "a sly little gentleman's gentleman—or comedian's comedian—called Rochester has restored Jack Benny to the comic map and cleared a sizeable place there for himself." Through refinement of the male servant image, Anderson emerged as a key transitional figure in the evolution of public black comedy.[24]

IV
————————

During the forties, other programs gradually introduced black players in sustained supporting roles. Eddie Green, for example, appeared on *Duffy's Tavern*; Nicodemus Stewart, a comedian who played traditional servant roles in numerous Hollywood films, joined the cast of *The Alan Young Show* and appeared on *The Great Gildersleeve*; Wonderful Smith, who like Stewart would join the *Amos 'n' Andy* television cast, appeared often on *The Red Skelton Show*. Mantan Moreland and Ben Carter brought their stage act to Bob Burns's folksy variety show during 1944 and 1945. At about the same time, Pigmeat Markham, by then a legend in burlesque and on the TOBA circuit as a comic with *Gonzelle White and Her Jazz Band,* joined the *Andrews Sisters Eight-to-the-Bar Ranch* program as a loudmouthed cook who continually got into quarrels with the foreman. "Every week," Markham wrote, "me and Gabby [Hayes] would stage a funny fight in the kitchen about somethin' or another—and I'd wind up threatenin' to shave him with the meat cleaver and stuff like that." [25]

Ironically, African-Americans' entry into radio required that black performers, who had been imitated by whites, once again copy their imitators in order to work. When they began auditioning for parts, "networks chose them for servant roles rather than use a white performer as a mimic, but only if the black sounded 'Negro' enough on the air." The established caricature was rigidly maintained. Johnny Lee, who had entered radio as a cast member of *Slick and Slim* in the thirties, admitted that "he had to learn to talk as white people believed Negroes talked." Actress Maidie Norman said she had been told repeatedly that "I don't sound like a Negro." In order to be convincing as Beulah and Madame Queen, Lillian Randolph "studied with a white vocal coach before developing her dialect." And Wonderful Smith, who had been hailed as the "Negro comedy find of the year" in 1941 when he joined *The Red Skelton Show* in the role of a cook, admitted that he was later dropped from the series because he "had difficulty sounding as Negroid as they expected." [26]

The absurd distortion of the media's "white Negro," of course, was not confined to the airwaves. In *Yes I Can,* Sammy Davis, Jr., wrote of an insight that changed his career and helped him hurdle the "wall of anonymity" that restricted black performers. Watching a black comedy act at the Strand Theatre in the forties, Davis realized for the first time that "it sounded wrong." Although "they were pros, funny as hell," he was struck by their insistent stereotyped dialect. " 'Ladies and Gen'men, we's gwine git our laigs movin', heah.' They were talking 'colored' as Negro acts always did. . . . It was the way people expected Negro acts to be so that's the way we were." For Davis, that realization and a subsequent change in his stage persona ultimately catapulted him into a category of cross-over popular entertainers previously attained only by Bert Williams and, possibly, Bill Robinson. Davis, however, was not at the time working in radio, a medium that had an entrenched tradition of comic racial ventriloquy.[27]

Despite advances in radio, verbal minstrelsy continued throughout the forties and into the early fifties. In addition to Gosden and Correll's *Amos 'n' Andy,* for example, Harriet Widmer and Vera Lane followed Tess Gardella as *Aunt Jemima;* the veteran black imitator Jimmy Scribner followed his NBC *Folks from Dixie* charade by portraying an Uncle Remus-type character on *Sleepy Joe* (a children's program); and the white actor Brooks Read inaugurated another Uncle Remus-type show on the Liberty Network in 1951.[28]

Only a handful of those comedians firmly associated with black ethnic stage humor—most notably Flournoy Miller, Mantan Moreland, Ben Carter, Johnny Lee, Wonderful Smith, Stepin Fetchit, Eddie Green, and Pigmeat Markham—appeared on radio, and usually they were limited to brief or infrequent appearances on variety shows in which only their most blatantly coonlike routines were aired.

Unfortunately, mainstream radio, which began as a wasteland for black performers other than musicians, was opening its doors to the wealth of black comic talent just as the medium started to decline. Through the late forties and early fifties, television garnered an increasingly larger segment of the entertainment market, and network radio's big-production variety shows and popular comedians slowly but inevitably fell in the ratings or moved to the more fashionable visual medium. For many, the move was not without unease and trepidation. "In most of the comedians' minds," one observer wrote, "there was no easier way of making a living than to be top banana of one's own radio show." There were usually no lines to be memorized, few rehearsals, and little acting was required. "At the broadcast they'd simply read off lines that a dozen gag writers had slaved over."[29]

Television had stiffer requirements. Whereas radio shows could be taped, television was live. According to CBS founder and chairman William S. Paley, that difference was crucial: "One couldn't cover mistakes by retakes. . . . From any performer's point of view, live telecasts were akin to walking on a high wire without a net." As a result, many of television's top comedians initially came from nightclubs and the stage. Sid Caesar and Imogene Coca (*Your Show of Shows*), for instance, were obscure Off-Broadway entertainers, and Jackie Gleason as well as Dean Martin and Jerry Lewis (*The Colgate Comedy Hour*) had been fairly well-known nightclub performers before their television successes. By 1952, however, when it was apparent that radio could no longer forestall the challenge of the new visual medium, even the most stubborn radio traditionalists began testing the waters.[30]

Some fell flat. Fred Allen, a rather cerebral comedian, whose sardonic wit and mastery of the satiric ad-lib had made him a radio innovator, found the new medium intolerable. He was bluntly critical of television, and audience reaction to him was only slightly more favorable. In 1952, after two seasons as a rotating star on *The Colgate Comedy Hour*, he restricted his appearances primarily to guest spots. Others flourished. Red Skelton, who had overcome the limitations radio placed on his talent as a pantomimist, found television perfectly suited for his routines. Ed Wynn and Milton Berle, both of whom had struggled with radio, also basked in the visual medium's brighter light; by the mid-fifties, Berle was known as "Uncle Miltie" or "Mr. Television." And as Bob Hope, George Burns and Gracie Allen, Jack Benny, and the stars of such situation comedies as *Father Knows Best* and *Ozzie and Harriet* abandoned radio, it relinquished its claim as the fount of media comedy. By 1956, *The Charlie McCarthy Show* would be the sole major evening comedy show on the air.[31]

But even as television gradually eclipsed network radio, station managers began to look more closely at local audiences as their advertising market. The black community would become one of their primary targets, and radio programs expressly aimed at it began cropping up across the nation. Soon, on small, local radio stations, another less polished but even more authentic form of black verbal wit was asserting itself.

"Sponsors, starting in the 1930s," writes Nelson George in *The Death of Rhythm and Blues*, "bought blocks of air time, day or night, to promote pork chops, chitlins, secondhand furniture, patent medicine, and anything else thought to appeal to blacks." As a result, by the forties, new shows premiered, hosted by such established musical stars as Cab Calloway, Duke Ellington, and Nat King Cole, whose NBC show was sponsored by Wildroot hair products. But less assimilated black music such as rural or urban blues and, in the forties, rhythm and blues (all of which was lumped together and commonly referred to as "race music") increasingly became the central attraction on radio shows. And many programs featured black artists who not only performed but also served as deejays and pitchmen for the sponsors. Black pitchmen represented a crucial advance, since earlier many stations and sponsors had avoided having blacks appear, ostensibly out of fear of white reaction and the belief that products would be labeled "nigger" items and suffer on the market.

One of the first of these shows originated at KLCN in Blytheville, Arkansas, in the thirties, and featured blues artists promoting mainstream products. On at least one occasion it resulted in some unexpected cross-cultural humor. According to bluesman Houston Stackhouse, another singer, Peck Curtis, asked the station manager if he could appear on the program:

> "Peck say he asked him to let him sing this song where it was about Good Gulf gasoline, you know.
> *"The monkey and baboon playin' in the grass,"* so instead of he sayin',
> *"And stickin' his finger in the Good Gulf gas,"* he made a mistake and said,
> *"The monkey stuck his finger—,"* you know, and he said "Uh oh!" It was too late then, so the red light come on. There was polices there, all the polices. . . .

Despite this mishap, by the early forties Sonny Boy Williamson's "King Biscuit Time" was being broadcast from KFFA in Helena, Arkansas, and later, B. B. King's Pepticon show debuted on WDIA in Memphis. Although neither Williamson nor King qualified as an apostle of black humor, they helped establish the commercial viability and popularity of radio shows featuring music and patter specifically directed at black audiences.[32]

By the late forties, local disc jockeys playing so-called "race records" began emerging as popular radio personalities. Alan Freed, a white announcer from Cleveland's WJW, who claims to have invented the term "rock 'n' roll," is normally credited with originating the format and popularizing the music. And indeed, in the early fifties Freed was responsible for bringing this underground music to a larger segment of the mainstream population. Once unveiled, its popularity inspired another form of racial ventriloquy. Sun Records owner Sam Phillips's search for a "white man who had the Negro sound and feeling" led to Elvis Presley's note-for-note copy of Arthur "Big Boy" Crudup's "That's All Right (Mama)" in 1954. That song, and subsequent Presley covers of blues tunes by Wynonie Harris ("Good Rockin' Tonight"), Arthur Gunter ("Baby, Let's Play House"), and Big Mama Thornton ("Hound Dog"), were instrumental in helping Presley outdistance other white "interpreters" of black music and establish himself as the "King of Rock 'n' Roll."[33]

But years before, black deejays had begun spinning records on the airwaves and, simultaneously, introducing a form of hip, often comical, patter to radio broadcasts. In 1947, *Ebony* magazine ran a feature story on black disc jockeys, noting that there were only sixteen among the three thousand heard nationwide on radio. That number increased rapidly—and so did the input of streetwise black voices echoing grassroots humor heretofore rarely revealed to the public. On *Ebony*'s list was Al Benson, a Chicago deejay who, although he regularly "killed the King's English," became one of the area's most popular and commercially effective radio voices. Another prominent deejay during this period was Nat D. Williams, who debuted on WDIA in Memphis in 1948, billed as the "Mid-South's first Negro disc jockey." Benson, Williams, and other early deejays were criticized by middle- and upper-class blacks for their clowning and decidedly black styles, but they were pioneers in exposing black music to a wider, racially mixed audience.[34]

"A listener up on his black history," Nelson George suggested, "might have realized that these nighttime motor mouths were very much the inheritors of the black oral tradition that spawned Br'er Rabbit, Mr. Mojo, and the other rural black tricksters created by Afro-Americans during their forced vacation in the 'New World.' " Perhaps, but FCC restrictions and the conservative or assimilationist segment of the black audience usually kept them from spinning humorous but risqué recordings such as the itinerant bluesman Speckled Red's "The Dirty Dozens" ("Now she's a running mistreater, / a robber and a cheater / . . . Yonder go your mama going out across the field, / running and a-shaking like an automobile"). In fact, by the mid-fifties, when it was apparent that rhythm and blues was becoming increasingly popular among mainstream youth, both black music and the behavior of the deejays who played it (black or white) came under intense scrutiny. In the South, circulars were distributed warning listeners about the dangers of "negro records," with their "screaming idiotic words and savage music." Communist conspiracies were alleged and high-minded local leaders such as the executive director of the Alabama White Citizens Council bluntly asserted that "the obscenity and vulgarity of the rock 'n' roll music is obviously a means by which the white man and his children can be driven to the level with [sic] the niggers."[35]

Still, despite objections to their style and the music they played, in a slightly diluted form early black disc jockeys did echo street vibrations. And, without doubt, their efforts spawned generations of slick, charismatic announcers who foreshadowed the nineties' fascination with "rap" and provided an early public glimpse of genuine black humor. In their wake would come figures such as Lavada Durst of KVET in Austin, Texas, spouting: "If you want to hip to the tip and bop to the top, you get some made threads that just won't stop." Or New York's inimitable Jocko Henderson, with his cry of "Great gugga mugga shooga booga" and his catchy sign-on rap:

Be bebop, this is your Jock.
Back on the scene with a record machine,
Saying "hoo-popsie-doo, How do you do?"
When you up, you up, and when you down, you down.
And when you mess with Jock, you upside down.[36]

They were the prototypes for superstar black deejays of the sixties and seventies such as Hal Jackson, the Magnificent Montague, Eddie O'Jay, and Frankie "Holly-*wood*" Crocker, whose smooth deliveries and clever use of black patois were as much an attraction as the music they played. Crocker, in fact, became something of a New York radio legend through his extemporaneous use of rhyme, braggadocio, folk sayings, and sexual innuendo:

This *is* the Frankie Crocker show. Stay with me, baby, 'cause it's bound to put more dips in your hips, more cut in your strut, more glide in your stride. If you don't dig it you know you got a hole in your soul; don't eat chicken on Sunday. Push, girl, push! While other cats be laughin' and jokin', Frankie's steady takin' care of bizness—cookin' and smokin'. For there is no other like this soul brother. Tall, tan, young, and fly . . . anytime you want me baby, I'm your guy! Young and single and love to mingle—can I mingle with you, baby? Closer than white's on rice; closer than cold's on ice; closer than the collar's on a hog; closer than a ham is on a country hog. Truly the eighth wonder of the world—before me there was no other, after me there shall be no more. Aren't you glad you live in this town—you can dig Frankie when the sun goes down. How can you lose with the stuff I use? Lemme rap to you, momma. If I'm all you got, I'm all you need. And remember, if your radio is not on the Frankie Crocker show, your radio is not on. . . .

As network radio became less dominant on a national level, local stations and community-oriented programs assumed more importance. In addition, during and shortly after the war, the country experienced a wave of liberalism, what NAACP director Walter White called a "rising wind" of social change. Radio responded with a rash of new programs, "portraying blacks as it never had attempted to do in the past. Special programs and series extolled black culture, achievement, and heroism." Among them were Kate Smith's impassioned plea for brotherhood and racial tolerance in 1945 on *We the People,* and *New World A-Coming,* a series based on Roi Ottley's book that beginning in 1944 dramatized black achievement and spotlighted racial injustices. Entertainers profited also, as WSM in Memphis produced *Freedom Theater,* the first racially mixed program broadcast from a major Southern station, New York's WNEW broadcast *American Negro Theater,* and in Chicago WJJD featured *Here Comes Tomorrow,* an African-American soap opera written by the prolific black television writer Richard Durham. These shows and many similar ones, along with the new programs hosted by stars such as Cab Calloway and Nat Cole, made the mid- to late forties a progressive era in the development of black radio. Although the Communist scare of the early fifties would dampen or, in some instances, thwart this rush toward social reform, and the traditional servile images of blacks would survive, as the media analyst J. Fred MacDonald points out, "new roles and new images of Afro-Americans entered radio to stay. For every comic type, intelligent, mature characterizations could be found. For every program that slurred blacks, there were programs now that rightfully praised their contributions to American society." By the mid-fifties, there were over five hundred black deejays on the air.[37]

For a brief period before black music effectively crossed over, listeners were offered a relatively unadulterated dose of black culture via music and even had a preview of the humor that black standup comedians would more fully unveil in the sixties and seventies. Although some among their primarily black audience railed against the impiety, mild racial chauvinism, and intentional use of idiomatic language, most delighted in hearing radio voices that echoed sentiments, jargon, and humor they both knew and shared.

VI

Just when local radio stations began featuring black music and presenting scattered instances of genuine black humor, however, a much more powerful and appealing mass medium began its rapid expansion. Television emerged as a viable commercial phenomenon shortly after World War II; during the ensuing decade it would eclipse radio to become America's most popular entertainment outlet. At the outset it appeared that the visual medium would be a boon to African-American entertainers and comedians.

Even as commercially licensed radio was introduced in 1920, crude television broadcasts had been initiated in England and the United States. But technology did not permit significant advances until 1930. An experimental station began broadcasting in New York City on July 30, and, a year later, "one of the first scheduled television shows . . . introduced Kate Smith singing 'When the Moon Comes Over the Mountain.'" By 1940, twenty-three stations were operating; after a lull during the war, the rapid expansion of television began in earnest. In 1946, there were only about six thousand television sets in the country, and CBS, which consisted of one station broadcasting less than ten hours a week, "gave the air time away free." By 1947, there were a quarter of a million sets, and New York City had been linked with Washington, D.C., and Philadelphia by coaxial cable. Between 1948 and 1952, network links were expanded throughout the country.[38]

Still, as late as 1949, over 40 percent of the nation's approximately 1 million television sets were in New York City, and another 40 percent were clustered in urban centers such as Los Angeles, Philadelphia, Chicago, and Washington, D.C. But over 6 million sets were sold the following year, and it was apparent that those futuristic boxes with their flickering black and white images, although still found chiefly in the living rooms of the well-to-do, would not remain playthings for the rich and urbane for long.

Only about one in ten American families had television sets at the beginning of the decade, but people gathered at the homes of friends, went to local bars, or stood outside appliance or department store windows to catch a glimpse of the boxing and wrestling matches, base-

ball games, variety shows, and crude sitcoms that dominated early programming.[39]

In 1946 and 1947, although a few variety and comedy shows had
debuted, live broadcasts of sporting events dominated network programming. But by 1948—"the true beginning of television as we know
it," according to William S. Paley—the networks had begun producing
their own comedy, variety, and dramatic programs. Those shows were
greatly influenced by the media's regional audience and the moral tenor
of the times.[40]

As television successfully expanded, it sought to attract a wider audience, and humor appealing primarily to regional interests simply did
not play well. It had to appeal to rural and suburban types, the Midwest
and South as well as Eastern city dwellers. But because urban, Eastern
areas were more liberal, black entertainers fared better in some ways in
the forties, during television's infancy, than they did when TV became a
national phenomenon in the mid-fifties.

The premiere *Texaco Star Theater* broadcast of June 8, 1948, for
instance, featured Pearl Bailey and Bill "Bojangles" Robinson as guests,
and Milton Berle showcased black performers throughout his show's
peak years. Ed Sullivan, who had liberally featured black entertainers
on his radio show, continued the practice when his *Toast of the Town*
variety show began on CBS television in 1948. In addition to billboard
performers such as Bailey, Robinson, Eartha Kitt, Duke Ellington, Ella
Fitzgerald, Nat King Cole, Louis Jordan, and Sammy Davis, Jr., Sullivan was responsible for the rare prime-time appearances of black
vaudeville performers like the dancer Peg Leg Bates (who Sullivan,
according to Pigmeat Markham, once called the "greatest Negro act of
all time") and comedians such as Markham and Tim Moore in the late
forties and early fifties.[41]

Sullivan, in fact, was an outspoken advocate of black entertainers
when they were spurned by many of his colleagues. The frequent appearances of black performers on his show and his uninhibited display
of friendship and admiration for performers elicited numerous irate
letters from white viewers, many of whom labeled him a "nigger lover."
But Sullivan never backed away from his liberal approach; his comments in a 1951 *Ebony* magazine article reflect his view of the role
blacks played in early television: "If there has been a generosity, television has received it from the Negro. In the first place, you just can't
have great programs unless you integrate the Negro performer into the
show. In the second place, it has never been pointed out that the Negro

performer has been a great friend to television. I personally know that, without his generous help, the early TV days would have been a nightmare."[42]

Compared to what followed in the fifties and sixties, the late forties were banner years for blacks on television. In 1948, Scatman Crothers appeared in the TV version of *Show Boat*, a variety show that had been aired on radio since the thirties. "It was the typical Stepin Fetchit-type role," he later recalled, "with me making wisecracks to the skipper." That same year, CBS introduced the first network show starring a black performer. Although he is scarcely remembered now, Bob Howard, a pianist and vocalist whose ebullient style and spontaneity were reminiscent of Fats Waller, was one of the hosts and regular performers on *Sing It Again*, a nightly fifteen-minute variety show, which ran until 1950. In 1949, CBS also aired *Uptown Jubilee*, probably the first all-black variety show on network TV. The program was hosted by Willie Bryant (a dancer, comedian, and master of ceremonies at the Apollo Theatre, where he was a perennial favorite), and featured as regulars the relatively unknown Harry Belafonte and comedians Timmie Rogers and Leonard Reed (Bryant's partner in a comedy and dance team). In 1950, the jazz pianist Hazel Scott had her own show on the Dumont network.[43]

In addition, numerous black entertainers appeared on local television shows such as *Happy Pappy* (WENR, Chicago), a variety program billed as "the first all-black television show" in April 1949. *The Hadda Brooks Show*, which featured blues singer Brooks and guest performers, debuted on KLAC-TV in Los Angeles in 1950 and was later seen on KGO-TV in San Francisco. And Ray Charles (at a time when he was admittedly doing Nat Cole/Charles Brown routines) became "the first Black act to get its own sponsored television show in the Pacific Northwest" when he appeared with his McSon Trio for five or six weeks on a Seattle station in 1953.[44]

The initial lack of racial controversy over those programs is in marked contrast to the ballyhoo that ensued when *The Nat King Cole Show* appeared on NBC in 1956. At the time, Cole was a major stage and nightclub attraction; his recordings had risen to the top of the popular charts; and he had successfully hosted radio shows on two separate occasions. Moreover, the production costs were minimal since not only had he agreed to accept a meager sum for his own appearances but most of his guests (major Hollywood and Broadway stars such as Sammy Davis, Jr., Bing Crosby, Julius LaRosa, Peggy Lee, Harry Belafonte, and Frank Sinatra) agreed to appear for minimal union scale. Still, the show floundered and was finally canceled when it became apparent that sponsors were unwilling to be identified with a program hosted by a black star.

Hazel Scott, an assertive civil rights advocate and at one time the wife of the flamboyant Harlem congressman Adam Clayton Powell, became involved as a victim of the Red scare in the fifties when her name was listed in *Red Channels* among a host of performers thought to be Communist sympathizers. Her show was terminated after a season and she moved to Europe. Scott's banishment reflected both the growing conservative sentiment in the nation and the increased difficulty that black performers would encounter in sustaining their own shows.

By the mid-fifties, black comedians also found the reception less hospitable. For example, Redd Foxx, whose reputation as a "blue" comedian was an added impediment, commented sarcastically about an abortive audition for the Sullivan show: "It's hard enough trying to be funny in a bare room with just two guys looking at you. But even before I started, they told me to stay off the South, white women, the Congo, and the President. I asked them if I could do the Lord's Prayer." Foxx's experience probably explains why top black comics who were occasionally racy (Moms Mabley or Butterbeans and Susie, for example) seldom saw the lights of TV during the period.[45]

The fifties are often remembered as "the good old days," nostalgically portrayed as an innocent, contented era in which simple pleasures and high morality predominated. But beneath its serene exterior the period was nearly as repressive and intolerant as the twenties. "Both postwar periods were relatively prosperous and highly conservative. In both decades radicalism was singularly suspect and nearly driven out of existence by Red scares and witch hunts," Douglas T. Miller and Marion Nowak maintain in *The Fifties: The Way We Really Were.* "Such fears put a premium on conformity. Bourgeois values reasserted themselves in a manner which would have pleased a twenties fundamentalist." America had moved through the Great Depression, the New Deal, and World War II to convene in an era of Cold War anxiety, surface uniformity, and intolerance of dissent. In the late forties and early fifties, the Alger Hiss espionage case, the Communist takeover in China, and the Soviet Union's development of an atomic bomb spurred a paranoia and xenophobia that paved the way for Wisconsin Senator Joseph McCarthy's theatrical Red hunts, and helped make conformity a national obsession.[46]

Naturally, the behavior of minorities and immigrants came under close scrutiny. Although at first the violent repression that marked the twenties was absent, African-Americans, who had been encouraged by their contribution to the Nazis' defeat, saw their more insistent lobbying for an end to segregation and racism at home met by official stonewalling. The chorus of counsel suggested moving "deliberately," a sly euphemism for "staying in their place." The placid aura of contentment was little more than a rigidly maintained veneer, shielding a complex of underlying fears and injustices. The fifties may not have been, as Norman Mailer has suggested, "one of the worst decades in the history of man," but the serenity of the so-called "good old days" was a mask concealing many entrenched inequities. By the end of the decade, these would lead to an explosion of protests centered on the treatment of blacks and women.[47]

Even earlier, beneath the homogeneous veneer, as in the twenties, there were stirrings of dissent. For instance, "Beat Generation" writers like Allen Ginsberg and Jack Kerouac sparked a new bohemian movement in the mid-fifties with their criticism of the country's rampant materialism, sexual repression, and adherence to middle-class values. Although the era did not produce the kind of mass infatuation with black lifestyle that had occurred during the Harlem Renaissance, there were hints of a reluctant, underlying Negrophilia in phenomena as dissimilar as the resurgent popularity of black music (Freed's "rock 'n' roll") and the publication of works such as Norman Mailer's controversial 1957 essay, "The White Negro." After blithely defining much of Negro life as a kind of reactive psychopathy, a youthful Mailer mused about the emergence of a new breed, the white hipster who—rebelling against the condition of living with the threat of "instant death by atomic war" or "slow death by conformity"—had "absorbed the existential synapses of the Negro."[48]

Moreover, dissatisfied with the deliberate speed with which fundamental rights were being dispensed, blacks had begun taking matters into their own hands. In 1954, Rosa Parks's refusal to stay in her place —the back of a Montgomery, Alabama, bus—precipitated a local boycott that would catapult Martin Luther King, Jr., to national prominence and, later, would be regarded as the beginning of the Civil Rights movement, which escalated into the incendiary black-white confrontations predicted by James Baldwin in *The Fire Next Time* (1963).

At the outset, however, the fledgling television industry generally ignored America's intensifying social ferment. Although landmark programs such as CBS's *See It Now* (1950) and pioneer news journalists such as Edward R. Murrow did address some key social issues as well as contribute to the downfall of Wisconsin's belligerent junior senator, television executives sought to provide shows that appealed to the majority of their audience. When affiliate stations and revenues increased in the fifties, that commercial approach led mostly to sanguine situation comedies and variety shows that reaffirmed the nation's self-righteous perception of a prosperous society that, except for the threat of communism, had only minor flaws and few serious antagonisms. And since television, like radio, was instrumental in creating a national culture and, in fact, "served to reinforce the trend toward sameness" that characterized the fifties, it not only reflected but also helped create the period's prominent social attitudes about everything from family life and sex to race relations and politics.[49]

Black community leaders and the black press—both well aware of radio's attempt to court black audiences in the late forties and optimistic about advances in combating negative images in motion pictures— initially perceived TV as an unsullied medium in which African-Americans might be presented free of previous stereotypes. Before World War II, *The Amsterdam News,* for instance, had portrayed television as "Our New Hope" and, anticipating the medium's more equitable treatment of blacks, had asserted that "it would be suicide to put a show like [*Amos 'n' Andy*] on television." Later, *Ebony* magazine called TV "an amazing new weapon which can be all-powerful in blasting America's bigots." In 1950, *Variety* announced, "Negro Talent Coming on TV Without Using Stereotypes: A Sure Sign That Television Is Free of Racial Barriers." By the end of that year, however, television settled comfortably into the familiar, stereotyped depictions of blacks.[50]

The first situation comedy starring a black performer premiered on ABC in October 1950, when Ethel Waters took the lead in the television version of *Beulah*. With first Percy Harris, and then Arthur "Dooley" Wilson, as her boyfriend Bill Jackson, and Butterfly McQueen as Oriole, Waters brought the role of the Hendersons' cheerful but outspoken maid to television. *Beulah*, like many of the early TV sitcoms, differed minimally from the radio show on which it was based. If there was any change, it was in the more insistent accord seen between the black characters and the Hendersons. All instances of real strife were excised and, unlike the radio show, even Beulah's patented sardonic rejoinders were usually toned down. Despite Waters's spicy presence, the show depicted an ideal suburban world in which whites and black *servants* lived in harmonious acceptance of the status quo. Its humor usually sprang from minor domestic disputes between the Hendersons and their children, the misdirected antics of the show's only truly comic character, Oriole (zany but cheerful), and the basic comic setup of contrasting a more perceptive, if less convention-bound, character of lower social status with apparently more advanced characters. The program depended on comic situations and cultural assumptions common to the glut of suburban sitcoms that later dominated the airwaves— many of which spotlighted the formula interaction between a white housekeeper or maid and families who were just as exemplary, pristine, and cordial as the Hendersons. Except for Beulah's race, one might have been watching *Hazel* or *My Three Sons*.

During its three-year stint on the air, the cast changed often. Hattie McDaniel assumed the part of Beulah briefly during the 1951–52 season, and was succeeded by Louise Beavers; Ernest Whitman followed Dooley Wilson as Bill, and Ruby Dandridge arrived to outdo McQueen as the simpleminded Oriole. Throughout the cast changes, however, little was added that disrupted the show's determined "see no evil, hear no evil" philosophy. If anything, with the switch to McDaniel and Beavers, the show became even more insistently saccharine. Beavers, of course, had long since established herself as the personification of the sanguine, ever jovial housekeeper in countless Hollywood movies. But McDaniel's edgeless portrait may have astounded those familiar with her work in such films as *Alice Adams* and *Affectionately Yours*. As Donald Bogle points out, she "gives a merely perfunctory performance, without any of her characteristic spunk and feistiness."[51]

In one representative episode an enervated McDaniel, after one of her customary opening homilies ("Don't let nobody tell you that I'm in the market for a husband. 'Course, I would be but they don't sell husbands in a market"), intervenes when the Hendersons' girl-shy son Donnie hedges on attending a dance. Beulah and Bill teach Donnie how to dance and, when his date backs out, arrange a blind date for him. Although, through Oriole's incompetence, Donnie ends up with a girl nearly twice his age and minor contretemps ensue, by the end of the show Beulah has set everything right. Donnie has passed his prepubescent anxiety with flying colors and the Hendersons' domestic "crisis" is resolved. As the camera fades, Beulah, forever in pursuit of matrimony, echoes the show's continuing refrain during an interchange with Bill:

Beulah: Miss Alice didn't have no cause to worry about Donnie. All she had to do was let nature take its course.

Bill: I agree with you one hundred percent, pigeon-pie.

Beulah: Then why don't you let nature take its course when it come to us, instead of swimmin' upstream like a salmon.

Bill: That don't sound very romantic, baby. Why come you think of me as a fish?

Beulah: Because, someday . . . I'm gonna hook you.[52]

Beulah was so sanitized, so much a mirror image of the cosmeticized decade, that today most viewers would be hard-pressed to specify exactly what ignited all the fuss. Certainly it was not due to any offensiveness in the warmed-over humor. And despite Beulah's obsessive attentiveness and concern about the welfare of her employers, in its depiction of ordinary black folks who maintained jobs, spoke reasonable English, and had warm, cordial relationships with one another, the show was a singular presence on early television. But *Beulah*, along with a host of other shows that featured black servants in more peripheral roles, became a target of the agitation to upgrade the image of African-Americans in the media.

Among the other eventual casualties were Lillian Randolph, who had reprised her radio role as Birdie on *The Great Gildersleeve* (1955), and Willie Best, who played traditional coon roles as an elevator boy on *My Little Margie* (1952–55) and Willie on *The Stu Erwin Show* (1950–55). Despite protests, Amanda Randolph as Louise on *Make Room for Daddy*, Ruby Dandridge as Delilah on *Father of the Bride*, and, of course, Eddie Anderson as Rochester on *The Jack Benny Show*, survived until the sixties.

If the host of comic servant roles on early TV emerged as a thorny issue for middle-class blacks who were determined to eradicate negative images in the new medium, then the television version of the *Amos 'n' Andy Show* (1951–53) could only be considered a full-scale disaster. Ironically, it was also the only prime-time TV program that consistently offered a realistic sampling of occasionally undiluted and authentic African-American humor.

As we have seen, for many blacks *Amos 'n' Andy* had been tainted by its connection with radio's racial ventriloquy. *Check and Double Check*,

Gosden and Correll's commercially successful blackface film adaptation, had fueled the resentment. In contrast to radio performances in which their imitation of blacks sounded authentic enough to convince even some African-American listeners, on screen the body language of whites belied their slim connection to the physical style that is crucial to most genuine black comedy, and made their thinly disguised minstrel buffoonery embarrassingly obvious. Still, before wiser counsel prevailed, Gosden and Correll initially considered playing the TV roles of Amos and Andy themselves.

Ultimately, that idea was dropped and, in 1948, CBS announced that a search for black performers had begun. Ignoring protests from rights groups, who represented the growing black middle class, CBS promoted this search with typical show business fanfare. According to *Ebony* magazine, even President Harry S. Truman and General Dwight D. Eisenhower joined the hunt. During a White House visit, Truman reportedly suggested that Gosden try a comedian at Texas State University as Kingfish, and Eisenhower told Gosden that he had met a soldier who would be perfect for the role. True or not, the rumors and incessant publicity demonstrated that CBS and Gosden and Correll had no intention of heeding the middle-class black community's strong resistance to a visual adaptation of the popular radio show. But this was a mistake, since black rights groups led by Walter White and the NAACP were forming a coalition that would soon become the spearhead for a formidable social movement. *Amos 'n' Andy,* a "comic anachronism," as Thomas Cripps labeled the show, provided the chance "for blacks to debate, both with CBS and among themselves, the precise nature of racial prejudice."[53]

Nonetheless, CBS unblinkingly proceeded with plans to bring the program to national television. Behind the scene, Gosden and Correll, as executives and writers, were joined by Charles Barton (a veteran director, whose credits included the Abbott and Costello comedies) and, ironically, comedian Flournoy Miller (who, many contend, invented the prototypes for the characters) as a racial consultant and writer. Together they assembled a cast of black actors and comedians who were featured in the premiere broadcast in June 1951. It was, in the words of William S. Paley, "an immediate hit," although five days after the first broadcast, the NAACP "denounced the show as insulting to blacks."[54]

Still, it is fair to say that few mainstream entertainment packages have assembled a more talented group of comic performers presenting (within the limits of its medium and time) essentially unmodified black ethnic humor.

Yes, there were forties films such as *Cabin in the Sky* and *Stormy Weather,* but comedy was subordinated to music and dance in each. Later motion pictures—Matt Robinson's *Amazing Grace* (1974), for example, or Eddie Murphy's *Harlem Nights* (1989)—would come closer. But neither would provide as vast an array of comic personalities or, in fact, any characters as memorable as the Kingfish or Sapphire.

Individual comic stars would surface and shine later on such TV sitcoms as *Sanford and Son* (1972–77), *Good Times* (1974–79), or *The Jeffersons* (1975–85). But even *The Richard Pryor Show* (1977), the legendary comedian's short-lived but blistering TV series, although funkier and much more controversial in terms of the subjects satirized, would frequently abandon the insular black world where the Kingfish and company abided. And Keenan Ivory Wayans's *In Living Color* (1989–93), while it would include nineties' updates of traditional African-American humor couched in hip-hop, Home Boy paraphernalia, and would feature one of the period's most talented young comedians (Damon Wayans), drifted between ethnically inspired comedy and a satirical approach that had its roots in the anti-establishment humor of improvisational groups such as the sixties' Second City and TV shows like *Saturday Night Live.*

For better or worse, *Amos 'n' Andy* displayed no such vacillations. It was determinedly focused on black life and, though liberally sprinkled with familiar vaudeville bits and slapstick or sight gags that could be seen on many TV sitcoms or variety shows of the period, its humor flowed primarily from recognizable attitudes common to lower-stratum blacks. It repeatedly contrasted the harebrained schemes of Kingfish and his cohorts against the day-to-day lives of a more or less sane and respectable group of ordinary Harlem black folks. Kingfish's connivances typically involved the assistance of willing co-conspirators: Algonquin J. Calhoun, a bogus, disbarred lawyer; and Lightnin', the dim-witted, docile handyman at the Mystic Knights of the Sea Lodge. Usually, the schemes depended on Andy Brown's gullible nature and naïveté, qualities that sometimes strained the most willing imaginations.

Although Flournoy Miller and Spencer Williams (who played Andy) occasionally contributed, the scripts were written by Gosden and Correll, and a team of white writers. Wisely, they "left the blocking, shot selection, movement and business, and other fragments of characterization entirely to the director and the actors on the set." This gave the splendid comic cast some scope and direct say in presenting and shaping the comedy. In addition, the veteran cast brought a crucial ingredient that had been missing in the film version of the show and unnecessary on radio—an unerring sense of physical style and timing that indelibly etched their farcical caricatures in viewers' minds.[55]

Selecting the actor for the role of Kingfish was probably the key casting decision since, after the early forties, he had become the series' central comic character. And the choice of Tim Moore, even according to many who opposed the show, was perfect. Moore had established himself as one of the black circuit's top comedians by the late forties; further, as early as the turn of the century, when ambitious blacks faced much stiffer odds, he had demonstrated a flair for some of the ingenious survival tactics that the fictional Kingfish flaunted in a more larcenous vein.

Born in 1888, at age eleven Moore was buckdancing on street corners for money. A year later he had become a "traveling vaudeville star" with *Cora Misket and Her Gold Dust Twins*, an act that toured the United States and England. During his teens and twenties he juggled careers as a jockey and boxer with various fringe show business stints. He appeared as a geek in a carnival (pretending "to bite off the head of a snake every half hour to satisfy a thirst for snake poison"); worked as a medicine show huckster, selling Dr. Mick's cure-all potion to gullible customers ("We sold two bottles for Dr. Mick and one for us"); masqueraded as a native Hawaiian who "took carloads of tourists around Oahu manufacturing ancient Hawaiian legends from his imagination"; and, during his boxing career as Young Klondike, found time to work up his one-man *Uncle Tom's Cabin* act. By the thirties he had worked the TOBA circuit and Broadway, earning as much as $350 a week during the Depression. In the forties, besides performing in black stage shows, he made infrequent guest appearances on television and appeared in race movies, the last of which was *Boy! What a Girl* in 1947. When the search for Kingfish and the other *Amos 'n' Andy* characters began, Moore had retired to his home in Rock Island, Illinois. Flournoy Miller suggested him for the role; once he had auditioned, there was little doubt that they had found the right man.

During the course of the two years that *Amos 'n' Andy* appeared on prime-time television, Moore made Kingfish his signature characterization. The malapropisms that, since minstrelsy, had become a central element in black stage caricature and had received even wider exposure through Gosden and Correll's radio show, took on new comic meaning when delivered with Moore's flamboyant style. Even familiar misuses such as "Excuse me for pertrudin'" or "I'se regusted" were enlivened, and his solicitous flimflam could transcend the basic inanity of lines such as "You is on yo' way to Rio de Geromimo," "Put your John Hamhock on dere," "Don't hurt yo' sacco-crackerjack," or "There was a proxy vote in dere, and you just got peroxided into dah job" into moments of sheer hilarity. He was brilliantly outlandish as the conniving potentate of the Mystic Knights of the Sea and, amid a truly illustrious cast of comic actors and actresses, stole practically every scene in which he appeared. As Sammy Davis, Jr., said, "He had the unique ability in comedy to vault a lot of the build up in a funny situation with a facial expression or a gesture that told more than a hundred words in the mouth of another comedian."[56]

In addition to Moore, other regular cast members included Spencer Williams as Andy, Alvin Childress as Amos, Nick Stewart (billed as Nick O'Demus) as Lightnin', Ernestine Wade as Sapphire, Amanda Randolph as Kingfish's mother-in-law, Johnny Lee as Calhoun, and Lillian Randolph, who frequently appeared as Madame Queen. Performers such as Sam McDaniel and Ruby Dandridge were also often seen in minor parts. Each member of the cast—including Childress, who, although he played the resolutely conscientious Amos, had been auditioned for the Kingfish role—was a seasoned entertainer who had risen from the black theatre circuit where some expertise was required in all facets of performing (acting, music, dance, and comedy). Nearly all had previously performed in motion pictures, radio, and television. Together, these entertainers created the most eccentric, vivid, and authentic example of African-American humor that had ever been brought before an integrated mass audience.

Kingfish was larger than life, more obstreperous, indefatigable, and unrepentant than any con artist (black or white) who had emerged in a radio or TV sitcom, and Moore played the role with an enthusiasm and relish that seemed fired by an inner connection to the character. In fact, given his experiences in early twentieth-century America, it is likely that there was considerable identification with Kingfish's exuberant rascality. If Stepin Fetchit's humor mirrored the acceptable route for Negroes to finagle their way through mainstream society's racial obstacle course, one that was condoned by both perpetrators and victims, then Moore's portrait of Kingfish reflected a comic version of the opposite impulse—the black man as nemesis and unredeemable outsider. Since Kingfish was ensconced in an all-black setting, Moore suffered no adulteration of his trickster role. Although comically exaggerated, he was an unmitigated flimflam artist, who was bilking strangers and friends years before the irrepressible chicanery of Sergeant Bilko came to television on *The Phil Silvers Show* (1955–59, CBS). In different guises this impertinent TV anti-hero would later be approximated by Sherman Hemsley as George Jefferson and Carroll O'Connor as Archie Bunker, the latter a "comic figure of epic proportions" who would be described as "a seething mass of prejudice, half-truths, and malapropisms. In [his] family, father *never* knew best." Like Kingfish, Archie would be destined to weekly frustration as his outrageous schemes and wrongheaded obsessions were deflated and rendered humorous by ridicule and ironic defeat.[57]

Kingfish's behavior and practically all of his problems stemmed from one simple trait: a loathing of manual labor. That trait was emphasized in nearly every show. In a scene from "Door to Door Salesman," for instance, he and Andy pause in front of his apartment to muse about what a tough day they have had: "Kingfish, if it's anything I hate, it's to lay down in de park when they ain't cut the grass." Kingfish responds: "Yeah, dem long blades keep punchin' you in duh ear and wakin' you up. Ahhh, it's a mess all right." Usually, he and Andy treated the thought of work casually, since it was never really a serious consideration; but when confronted with the threat of actual employment, Kingfish became nearly inconsolable:

Sapphire: Well, George, did'ya have any luck finding a job today?

Kingfish: No, honey, it just seem like dere ain't no employment around for mens. I hunted high and low, but I ain't give up. I gonna try again in three-four months.

Sapphire: Well, George, you don't have to look no more. I got some wonderful news for'ya.

Kingfish: Ahhh . . . what's that?

Sapphire: I got a job for'ya at Superfine Brush Company as a door-to-door salesman.

Kingfish: You done what! Now look here, Sapphire, you can't do that. It's a violation of the Atlantic Charter, the

Constitution, the Monroe Doctrine, and not only dat,
it's a violation of one of dah four freedoms, de freedom of speech!

Sapphire: Freedom of speech?

Kingfish: Yeah, you didn't give me a chance to say no.[58]

Kingfish's aversion to work (an attitude that he shared with Stepin
Fetchit's coon figure and most other stereotypical Negro stage characters, as well as with maverick non-black characters such as Sergeant
Bilko) meant that he was always strapped for funds and usually under
siege from his upwardly mobile wife and mother-in-law. That, in turn,
set the stage for the ill-fated schemes that dominated the scripts. Nearly
every week, Kingfish—cigar in hand, and dressed in characteristic swal-
low-tailed coat, vest, string tie, and wide-brimmed plantation hat—set
out to hoodwink one of the other characters.

In one of the series' funniest episodes, after being harangued by
Sapphire about a worthless lot he has purchased in upstate New York,
he decides to sell the property. Naturally, Andy is chosen as the prospective buyer. And, since the land once had been used as a movie set
and still has the imposing facade of a suburban mansion on it, Kingfish
decides to sell both the "house" and the lot. When Andy, aided by
Lightnin', arrives with his belongings, there is an uproarious pantomime
bit in which the two dupes struggle to reconcile their expectations of a
real house with the reality of a nearly empty lot. After moving the
furniture in and commenting on the "good old fresh air," Andy observes
that "we done walked right through the house out into duh yard."
Retracing their steps, they return to the other side of the facade and,
after moments of utter bafflement and careful consideration, conclude
that, as Lightnin' says, "dis sure is a thin house."

When the irate Andy confronts Kingfish about the deception, asserting that "for twenty years you'se been bamboozling me, but I'm
tellin' you right now . . . this is yo' last boozle," the flamboyant con man
is undaunted. He arranges to meet Andy at the property and, aided by
Calhoun pumping oil through an underground hose, convinces him
that, although there is no house on the property, the land is oil-rich.
Finally, Kingfish gets his comeuppance when Andy, through his own
scam, tricks Kingfish into buying the land back. The episode ends with
Kingfish's greed sabotaging his own ploy—another instance of the trick-
ster-outsmarted theme.

Kingfish's audacity had few limitations and during the program's two-year run he attempted nearly every imaginable scam. As a matter of course he kept deeds to Central Park, the Brooklyn Bridge, and the Empire State Building in the desk of his lodge office. On various occasions he posed as a travel agent, director of an employment agency, member of the armed forces, doctor, matrimonial counselor, or car salesman, all in the pursuit of quick money. In one instance he even convinces Andy that, due to a case of mistaken identity at birth, he is actually Andrew H. Brown and that he, instead of Andy, is the recipient of a letter promising a lucrative job in South America. He is so persuasive that, as a befuddled Andy leaves the lodge office, he asks: "Ah, say, tell me somethin' befo' I goes. When we was young fellas and you was takin' all dem good lookin' gals out to parties all dah time, dey was actual goin' out wit, ahh, Andy Brown, huh?" "Das right," Kingfish assures him. "What kind of time was I havin'?" Andy asks. Without a hitch, Kingfish responds, "Those was dah best years of yo' life."

Inevitably, the schemes end disastrously with Kingfish being discovered or, worse, becoming the victim of his own avarice, as when he ends up on a freighter destined for Brazil and a non-existent job, or finds himself working as a laborer in Saudi Arabia after arranging to have Andy win a "pleasure cruise to de glorious beeches of gay Arabia."

Throughout these episodes, Tim Moore's outrageous portrayal of Kingfish was the prime source of comedy. Bombastic, irreverent, stylized beyond belief, Moore's Kingfish was an unbridled example of the ethnic humor that blacks regularly flocked to see in race films and on the stages of black theatres. It usually transcended Gosden and Correll's original conception of the character, which, with Gosden as the voice on radio, most often ridiculed the Kingfish's jaundiced traits (his obvious improvidence, insincerity, and greed), contrasting him with the more respectable Andy and Amos. By virtue of authentic style and the exuberance with which he portrayed Kingfish, Moore projected a character whose jubilant flouting of convention struck a resonant chord with a large section of the black underclass. Moore's Kingfish was not simply the trifling, scheming parasite that he is often made out to be; for many African-Americans, he mirrored an iconoclastic impulse that had lingered since slavery. In many ways he personified the irreverent trickster who refused to be contained or thwarted by a society that merely tolerated his existence. On television, as with his real-life prototypes, he almost never won his battles; but he also never succumbed. His theatrical style, irrepressible nature, and constant twitting of the social

norm made him the show's most humorous character and in all likeli-
hood the most beloved by the majority of black folks.

Kingfish's antics were complemented and embellished by two other
prominent comedic characters: Algonquin J. Calhoun and Lightnin'.
Calhoun, in fact, was crucial in creating the aura of distinct ethnicity
that characterized the show. His involvement in Kingfish's schemes
heightened the comedy and introduced another traditional black stage
figure to television. Although he was presented as a bogus lawyer,
Calhoun, in fact, introduced an outrageous send-up of the black
preacher. His portrayal had roots in the popular minstrel stump
speeches that flourished during the nineteenth century, but it also mirrored the hyperbolic caricature of rural Southern preachers that by the
twenties and thirties had become a staple in black stage comedy and
would persist through the routines of stand-up comedians to the present. Protests by clergy and attorneys notwithstanding, Johnny Lee's
portrayal of Calhoun was always among the program's comic highlights.

In one of the earlier episodes, for example, after discovering that
Andy has an 1877 nickel worth $500, Kingfish pretends to be a doctor
—"I think I'se about to preform a nickelectomy"—and slips the coin
from Andy's pants pocket when Andy undresses for his medical examination. On the way to the coin collector, however, Kingfish accidentally
uses the coin for a telephone call and, naturally, enlists Andy to help
retrieve it. As they mangle the public telephone, they are discovered
and arrested. The hilarious courtroom scene that follows provides the
occasion for one of Calhoun's typical histrionic appearances:

> *Calhoun:* I'd like to enter a plea of not guilty for these two
> crooks.
>
> *Judge:* On what grounds? According to the report these men
> were caught trying to break into a telephone coin box
> in the presence of a witness, who also is a police officer
> of this city.
>
> *Calhoun:* Well, ahhh . . . Yes sir, your honor! But they done
> learned they lesson. They ain't never gone break into
> nothin' in front of a cop no mo'.
>
> *Judge:* . . . . This is an arraignment, not a trial. It's obvious
> from the evidence before me that these men should
> be bound over for trial.

Calhoun:	Just a minute, yo' honor!
Judge:	Do you have something further to say?
Calhoun:	I'll say I is! This may be only an arraignment, but I *demands* justice for these two innocent mens. Yo' honor, let me tell you that you *aaaainnn'* gone put these men behind bars! I happen to know mo' about the law than you think I does. And another thing . . . I'm gonna see to it that you . . .
Judge:	Wait a minute, counselor. Isn't your name Calhoun?
Calhoun:	That's right, yo' honor, Algonquin J. Calhoun.
Judge:	And didn't I disbar you three years ago!
Calhoun:	Ahhhh . . . so long, boys.
Kingfish:	Excuse me, yo' honor, but how much ground did we lose while our lawyer was in defendin' us?

In another episode, Calhoun is called when Sapphire leaves home with her mother and Kingfish mistakenly assumes that she has been the victim of foul play. Accompanied by Lightnin', Calhoun arrives at the police precinct in typical overwrought fashion:

Calhoun:	Uh-um, uh-a-ummm-uh-um. Officer!
Officer:	Do you want something?
Calhoun:	Does I want something? Young man I come *doown* here . . . I rushed *dooown* here, uh-uh-um, 'cause I wanted you to know . . . uh, [looking at Lightnin'] what *did* we come down here for anyhow?
Lightnin':	Kingfish's wife.
Calhoun:	I'se here on behalf of my client, George Stevens. And, as an attorney and a taxpayer of this city, I demands action. My client feels that a dastardly deed has been perpetrated. And my client *feeeels* that his wife, one Sapphire Stevens, has been a victim of foul play. And my client *demaaands* that the police department of New York City take action immediately. . . .

[Meanwhile, the officer has found Calhoun's photo and rap sheet in their files.]

Calhoun: . . . I demands that the foul fiend who is responsible for this heinous crime be apprehended and brought to justice without further delay. My client further demands that the resources of this *en-tirrre* department be . . .

[Calhoun is dragged away by two officers as he continues his speech.]

Johnny Lee was a small man, whose portrayal of Calhoun was marked by a fidgety energy not unlike that of stage and screen comedian Mantan Moreland, with whom Lee had frequently worked. Bespectacled, antsy and nervous, bristling with adrenaline, Calhoun brought an electricity to his frequent appearances on the show; his rapid speech was edged with a vibrato common among black rural preachers and his jerky, near-spasmodic, movements were in stark contrast to Kingfish's protracted pronouncements, deviously studied rhythms, and uncanny projection of the conniving mind at work behind his heavily wrinkled but elastic face. Calhoun—a kind of mischievous sprite, as it were Puck to Kingfish's Falstaff—was an agitator and provoker as well as an abettor in the scams:

Kingfish: Calhoun, I got dah angle of dah year. You know, Andy was a pipe welder in a factory during World War II. Now if I could place Andy in dat job, then dis company would give me $200.

Calhoun: Ohhh . . . I see. But, wait a minute Kingfish, *wait-a-minute*. Andy ain' goin' take no job like dat neither—out dere in the desert, working in the hot sun in Arabia.

Kingfish: Well, Calhoun, I been thinkin' 'bout dat. Now if I can make Andy believe dat dis was a pleasure cruise or sump'tin', then once on de boat and I gets my dough.

Calhoun: Yessah, just get 'im on de boat . . . huh, huh. Kingfish, yo' warped mind is warpin' better ever day . . . ha-ha-ha-haa!

Kingfish's subsequent meeting with Andy, during which he convinces him that Arabia is a vacation paradise, offers an excellent example of the wily double-talk for which Kingfish was famous:

Andy: I done told the clerk where I was goin', and he said he ain't never heard a'nobody goin' to Arabia on vacation cause it's too hot over there. Does he know what he's talkin' bout?

Kingfish: Well, ahhh . . . yes, and no, Andy.

Andy: What'cha mean?

Kingfish: Well, I'll explain dat to you. At one time Arabia was the hottest country in de world. But dats all changed now in the past few years.

Andy: What'cha mean, done changed?

Kingfish: Well, Andy, they opened up the Suez Canal and let the breeze blow into Arabia . . .

Andy: How could it do dat?

Kingfish: Andy Brown, I'm surprised at you, a man a your intelligence asking a crazy question like dat. I'll explain dat to you. . . . Now on one end of Arabia, they got dah Suez Canal wit de gates open. And, den, on the other end, is dah Polish corridor.

Andy: Well, what about it?

Kingfish: Well, dere you is. Arabia is de only country in de world wit cross ventilation.

Andy: I don't guess dah clerk knowed nothin' bout dat.

Lightnin', the show's other leading comic character, was neither as articulate nor, finally, as funny as Kingfish and Calhoun. The character was essentially a thinly veiled version of the shiftless darky or ignorant Sambo type seen on stage since minstrelsy and made infamous by Stepin Fetchit. Lightnin', "a cotton-mouthed, cretinous janitor who eclipsed the excesses of Stepin Fetchit," as one critic observed, was "especially odious." Portrayed by Nicodemus Stewart (or Nick O'Demus, as he was billed here), the character was stripped of almost all verbal wit on the series; overshadowed by the frantic physical action that dominated the plots, there was little opportunity for Stewart to project the subtle resourcefulness that had frequently salvaged the caricature on stage and in Fetchit's portrayals.

Lightnin' was therefore reduced to a static presence, an imbecilic prop, probably only recognizably funny to those viewers familiar with more textured portrayals of the type on stage and in some motion pictures. Slow-moving, continually stupefied and confounded, incapable of performing any task that required thought, he served little purpose on the show beyond looking dumb. The Lightnin' character on *Amos 'n' Andy*, like many of Willie Best's roles on television, gave some credence to Stepin Fetchit's complaint that his imitators were doing only the "outside of his act" and ignoring the "soul." The insistently one-dimensional characterization of Lightnin' would emerge as one of the principal objections to the program.

There were, of course, numerous other reasons for discontent among African-Americans. High on the list of complaints were the questionable characterizations of black women and the accompanying attitudes about women expressed by the male characters.

Kingfish, for instance, comically disparaged women whenever possible. "What was all dem old hens doing here," he asked Sapphire in one episode, "a man's house is supposed to be his castle, not a chicken coop." He regularly referred to Sapphire as "the battle ax" and his combative relationship with her, a continual source of conflict and humor, prompted some of the show's most cutting remarks. On one occasion, when Sapphire disappears and Andy suggests that she may have left with another man, Kingfish quips, "Don't be silly, Andy, anybody dat would run off with her is under lock and key." When Andy considers getting married, Kingfish chides him with, "Welcome to the ranks of dah livin' dead," then muses: "You got a eye for beauty, all right. I wish my eyesight had been dat good when I got married, then I never would have stigmatized myself into what I got." And when Kingfish hires a secretary for the lodge and Sapphire questions his motives, he consoles her with, "You know I wouldn't look at another woman. Don't forget, honey, I been married to you for twenty-two years, and you done soured me on the whole female thing."

Even Andy, a confirmed philanderer, joined the verbal bashing when he echoed Kingfish's view with lines such as, "Dere ain't nothin' like comin' home and hearin' de pitter patter of yo' wife's knees on de kitchen floor."

Sapphire, her mother, and the host of women that Andy courted were nearly always subjected to a kind of snickering, demeaning treatment by Kingfish, Calhoun, and Andy. They were objects of derision as well as frequent victims of the schemes that the trio concocted. Only Amos among the principal male characters displayed any real concern for women or the institution of marriage.

Faced with Kingfish's bumbling connivances and anti-work ethic, the upwardly mobile Sapphire was nearly always at odds with her husband. And although the source of irritation was sometimes imagined or inspired by her fiercely homophobic mother, most often Sapphire had sound reason for nagging or reprimanding Kingfish. Sapphire, as played by Ernestine Wade, was usually an attractive and ostensibly rather prim and proper housewife, who could even be stiffly affectionate; but when provoked, she easily made the transition to dominating and irrepressible harpy. When she did, her deafening outbursts and often violent physical onslaughts were unmatched by any marital spats that one saw in non-black TV sitcoms. Her shoulders straightened, her hands went to her hips, her eyes flared and, as she began shaking and bobbing her head, all hell would break loose. At minimum, Kingfish could count on a shrill, rapid-fire, and unstoppable tongue-lashing. In one episode, she finds out that Kingfish has hired a female secretary, and responds with typical fury:

Sapphire: You done got a secretary?

Kingfish: Well . . . er . . . ah, ahhh, since we got the extra we gone run the lodge efficient. Eery lodge got to have a secretary.

Sapphire: Oh, that's different. Then it's a male secretary, huh? What's his name?

Kingfish: Daphanie Jackson.

Sapphire: Ah, then it's a female! George Stevens, you gonna fire her. I ain't having you working in no office with no woman. You . . . huh, with a secretary! And here I have to rent out our spare bedroom every chance I can to get house money. . . . George Stevens I ain't having you work in no office with a woman. And that's final. She's got to go!

Often the hostilities did not end there. Kingfish, although bold and undaunted when it came to devising outlandish deceptions, collapsed in the face of Sapphire's physical aggression. Inevitably, he sheepishly backed off and scrambled for cover; although often banished from the apartment, he usually managed to avoid physical punishment. But sometimes as Sapphire menacingly approached her cowering husband, the camera cut away; seconds later, Kingfish would reappear, bandaged from head to foot, an expression of mock contrition on his face.

It was a ritual encounter that went far beyond the henpecked husband scenarios in other sitcoms. Disputes between Sapphire and Kingfish made the later battle of the sexes between Ralph and Alice on *The Honeymooners* seem child's play; despite Audrey Meadows's unflinching resolve and Jackie Gleason's bombast, their confrontations nearly always ended with rapprochement and an apology by Ralph. No tidy resolutions occurred in the Stevens household. Like everything else on *Amos 'n' Andy*, these marital spats were played for broad comedy; the underlying philosophy seemed to be, the more outrageous, the funnier.

Although it was indeed funny, the show presented a skewed, unflattering portrait of black women as tough, overbearing females who seldom displayed any hint of feminine charm. Sapphire did occasionally show a softer side, but Kingfish's schemes and intransigence brought out the harpy in her. Her mother, played by Amanda Randolph, however, was completely one-dimensional; meddlesome, badgering, and unrelentingly critical of her son-in-law, she was the epitome of the castigating shrew. Despite the appearance of some attractive, sensible women as Andy's love interests, most other women on the show turned out to be either simpleminded or mirror images of Sapphire and her mother. Madame Queen, played by Lillian Randolph, was an example of the latter.

Still, compared to the passivity and dull predictability of the housewives who appeared on TV's suburban sitcoms (*Father Knows Best, The Donna Reed Show, Leave It to Beaver*), the women of *Amos 'n' Andy* offered a welcome change; they were both livelier and funnier. They had more in common with the "scatterbrain" humor of Lucille Ball and Joan Davis, who, as Linda Martin and Kerry Segrave argue in *Women in Comedy*, "represented an improvement of sorts" over the suburban types. The problem was that they were not just feisty but outright belligerent. Moreover, since, along with Beulah, Oriole, and a few other maids, they were the only black women who regularly appeared on prime-time TV, there were no other examples to counter these shrill comic images.[59]

Ultimately, despite the authentic presentation of some elements of black humor, the usually brilliant comic acting of the main characters, and the simple fact that the program showcased an entire cast of talented black performers, much of the black community objected to the obvious stereotyping of *Amos 'n' Andy*. In private, as in my household, the show was relished. But the comic exaggeration was a *public* embarrassment for many African-Americans—particularly those who had struggled to positions of middle-class respectability. In the fifties, a larger percentage of the black community had begun to acquire stable, secure jobs and optimistically anticipated the fulfillment of the liberal promises of the forties. Sensitivity was at a high point, and many objected to what could be seen as archaic reminders of downtrodden, irresponsible black folks from another era. *Amos 'n' Andy* had entered the TV stakes at the wrong time; in a sense, it was doomed before it ever began.

Even the fact that the main characters were generally contrasted only with staid, well-spoken, middle-class blacks (including children, judges, policemen, salesmen, and *real* lawyers) who were paragons of bourgeois virtue was irrelevant. Kingfish, Calhoun, Lightnin', and Sapphire were such indelible, larger-than-life characters that they obscured any impression the others may have made. This element of comic exaggeration was forgotten by many, and *Amos 'n' Andy* was judged as a wholly inappropriate presentation of African-Americans.

In 1951, shortly after the program's debut, the NAACP launched a vigorous campaign to cancel both the TV and radio versions, claiming they were insulting to black Americans. An article published by the National Association for the Advancement of Colored People early in the 1950s entitled "Why the Amos 'n' Andy Show Should Be Taken Off the Air" listed the following reasons:

1. The show tends to strengthen the conclusion among uninformed and prejudiced people that Negroes are inferior, lazy, dumb, and dishonest.
2. Every Negro is a clown or a crook.
3. Negro doctors are shown as quacks and thieves.
4. Negro lawyers are shown as slippery cowards, ignorant of their profession, and without ethics.

5. Negro women are seen as cackling screaming shrews in big-mouth close-ups, using street language just short of vulgarity.
6. All Negroes are shown as dodging work of any kind.
7. An entire race of 15,000,000 Americans are being slandered each week by this one-sided caricature.[60]

Although there was obvious disagreement within the black community about the program's relative merits (one poll taken during its run indicated that 77 percent of black New Yorkers favored the show), at the end of the 1953 season *Amos 'n' Andy* was canceled. Ironically, it was both a victory for those stressing the necessity of positive middle-class media images for blacks and a setback in terms of the presentation of genuine black humor in mass media.

More than two decades later, in a televised interview, Redd Foxx would say of the show: "It was comedy, man, it was laughs. That's what it's all about . . . get some laughs and you're not hurting anyone. Some people say, 'Hey man, they shouldn't be doin' that,' but if they look at their mothers and fathers around the house sometimes they'd see the same things happening." And Jesse Jackson would contend: "Black people had enough sense to appreciate them as funny people playing roles. Their roles were so limited that we laughed at them and laughed at their roles. But, after all, in the same period where all that was on the radio and TV, out came Martin Luther King, out came Malcolm X, out came Adam Powell. . . . There was a tradition in our community of funny people. [But] it did not dominate black life to the extent that it has been projected. Even to this day, our struggle is to show the breadth and depth of the black experience."[61]

Foxx and Jackson touched on two essential points: First, that there were some actual people who were not too far removed from the caricatures presented on *Amos 'n' Andy;* second, the chief objection to the program was that, except for the ubiquitous comic servants and guest appearances by entertainers, it represented the only depiction of blacks on television. This point outweighed the comic fidelity. Although seen in syndication until the sixties, the departure of the show left a huge vacuum in the presentation of black comedy on television that would not be filled until the late sixties. As one habitué of a Harlem bar commented: "In the fifties, you didn't see no parts of blacks on TV. . . . Me, I used to get up and turn on the radio, listen to *The Shadow*, that's 'bout the closes thing to a spade they had on the air at the time."[62]

As the remainder of the servant characters were gradually eliminated from sitcoms, black appearances were limited basically to infrequent serious roles and guest appearances by musical performers. Perhaps frustrated by resistance to their conception of humorous blacks or tired of the controversy, television executives apparently took the path of least resistance and generally ignored black life. After the mid-fifties, African-Americans made their next significant screen appearances "during the sixties civil rights movement—not in sitcoms, but during sit-ins and on national news broadcasts." It was not until after race riots in numerous major American cities that *I Spy* (1965–68, NBC), the first prime-time adventure series starring a black actor, appeared in 1965, and Bill Cosby emerged as a sort of Jackie Robinson of network TV. Other roles in dramatic series followed; by 1968, Diahann Carroll was appearing in the mildly humorous *Julia* (1968–71, NBC), the first sitcom to star a black woman since *Beulah*. A year later, Cosby appeared in another relatively staid sitcom, *The Bill Cosby Show* (1969–71, NBC), in which he played a high school gym teacher. Cosby, who began his career as a stand-up comedian, was funny, and occasionally introduced guests such as Moms Mabley, but neither his show nor *Julia* added much in the way of black humor. Both programs seemed determined to present only middle-class black perspectives and, compared with the intensity of racial relationships in the real world, seemed antiseptic and far-fetched.[63]

The reappearance of authentic black ethnic humor or anything remotely resembling it on television would not occur until 1970, when NBC introduced *The Flip Wilson Show*, the first successful black-hosted variety show in television history. Wilson—who had been a favorite on the so-called "chitlin circuit" and at the Apollo Theatre—much as the comedians on the *Amos 'n' Andy Show* had done, brought his personal brand of black comedy to television virtually unaltered. Unburdened by a narrowly focused situation comedy format, he was able to avoid rigid stereotypes. Wilson moved in and out of familiar ethnic types with ease, moderating his presentation with his own radiant, upbeat personality. Two years later, Redd Foxx, a more controversial black comedian, would come to television in *Sanford and Son* (1972–77, NBC), a show that was even more insistently ethnic in character.

By the seventies, however, the humor presented on these shows was neither new to the mass media nor shocking to its audience. The sixties had been one of the most cataclysmic decades in American history, and one of the many changes that had occurred was the abrupt ending of the black community's silent perseverance in the face of racial inequity. Accompanying that change was the surfacing of genuine black American humor. A host of new comic voices, as well as more seasoned performers, had been introduced in integrated nightclubs and as guests on television variety shows. And many of these comedians had shed their masks to present a brand of irreverent, emphatically black comedy that was new to mainstream America. Authentic black American humor had been unleashed on an initially unsuspecting public and, in the coming years, would assume even more importance. *The Flip Wilson Show* and *Sanford and Son* were but the tip of a humorous tradition that had been developing in black movies, nightclub acts, the literature, and on the stages of black theatres for decades.

PART THREE:
THE REAL SIDE

••••••••••••••••••••••••••••••

INVISIBLE LIVES

AND

CLANDESTINE

HUMOR

8.

··

RACE RECORDS AND BLACK

FILMS . . . *sounds and*

visions in black and blue

14

BUTTERBEANS AND SUSIE

I

Around the turn of the century, it became more and more apparent that whites and blacks in America's race-conscious society often preferred different types of entertainment and responded differently to what was presented on the stage and, later, in motion pictures. Since public facilities were usually segregated, this disparity was generally not a problem. Performers in the theatres and road shows of the period most often played before audiences of their own race. When shows or movies were presented before mixed crowds, however, some conflicts ensued. John Johnson, for instance, echoed the old laughing barrel tale when he recalled that during the twenties, blacks seated in the balcony of a movie theatre were often warned about laughing ("You niggers, cut out that laughing!") unless whites, seated in the orchestra, laughed first.[2]

If merely for the sake of a more harmonious audience response, the idea of distinctly separate entertainment fare for blacks and whites began to loom as a plausible alternative in the minds of both races.

African-Americans had an additional incentive—the opportunity to correct some of the distorted images of themselves. As early as 1909, efforts to effect an entertainment policy reflecting the nation's separate but "equal" racial agenda had begun. The first organized theatrical circuit for black performers was formed that year. Soon, before swarthy crowds at traveling tent shows, carnivals, and circuses, the tacitly held but rigidly enforced restrictions on blacks' performances were starting to be relaxed. Performers could more easily be themselves, and the dynamic created between audience and entertainer allowed for a change in attitude and expressive focus. Although the alteration may have been imperceptible to non-blacks or even to the few middle-class Negroes who may have errantly wandered into these shows, the pauses, sly winks, and shifts in emphasis insinuated into ritual minstrel buffoonery at those times represented the rudimentary phase of a more genuine form of black entertainment on stage.

A few years later, Bill Foster is said to have made the first black-produced movie. And in 1916, largely in response to Griffith's *The Birth of a Nation,* the first film company dedicated to producing films for blacks was founded in Los Angeles. In 1921, a line of phonograph records featuring music thought to appeal primarily to African-Americans was introduced by Okeh Records. The next year, the Black Swan Company (named after America's first black concert singer, Elizabeth Taylor Greenfield) was founded by Harry Pace, who had previously started a music publishing company with W. C. Handy; it was the first black-owned recording company in America.

Each of these enterprises provided entertainment that could be viewed or listened to in an all-black setting (whether in a theatre or at home) where the distorting shadow of white interpretation was not a significant influence. Moreover, these outlets for humorous expression were more pointedly aimed at the black sensibility. Still, for various reasons (among them the overriding fact that the production process nearly always involved non-blacks) race records and black films had less direct influence on the evolution of African-American humor than did stage performances.

Comedy, of course, was never the central focus of the record industry; it was always something of a novelty, an adjunct to music. Perhaps as a reaction to the saccharine ballads and waltzes that flourished prior to the "Gay Nineties," however, the popular musical lyrics of the early twentieth century often took a humorous turn. Most cakewalks and coon songs, for instance, were characterized as much by their intended humorous lyrics as by their slightly syncopated beats. But the coon songs discussed earlier presented the most uninhibited display of derisive racial humor ever seen in America's popular music. In sheet music and some early recordings, according to Sam Dennison, these songs traded on stereotypes that were "the culminating point in the development of types known to songwriters for years," and represented a "point beyond which songwriters could not go without sinking to a level of invective known only to radical hate-mongers."[3]

With rare exceptions—such as songs from black musicals by Bert Williams and George Walker, spirituals by the Fisk Jubilee Quartet, popular songs and rags by Noble Sissle and Eubie Blake, or the bands of W. C. Handy and James Europe—African-Americans were excluded from the record publishing field until the twenties. At that point, coon songs had diminished in popularity; still, some songs of the genre were released on race labels. As late as 1927, for instance, bluesman Luke Jordan recorded "Traveling Coon" for Victor:

> Folks, let me tell you about a Travelin' Coon,
> His home was down in Tennessee,
> He made his livin' stealin' people's chickens
> And everything he seen.
> Policeman got [straight] behind this coon
> And certainly made him take the road.
> There was never a passenger train so fast,
> That shine didn't get on board.

This song was not typical of race label releases, however; generally, although many coon-like tunes were recorded, they appeared with slightly altered lyrics and reflected the performers' knack of transforming material to suit the tastes of their audiences. Record company owners were perceptive enough to realize that most of the blatantly insulting songs that had been marketed for white consumption would not prove particularly appealing to black patrons. Even so, some of the records released were considered offensive as late as the sixties.[4]

The first company to release recordings explicitly aimed at black audiences was Okeh, which formally instituted its "Original Race Records" in 1921. Largely through the persuasive efforts of Perry Bradford, a young, black musician who was convinced that blues songs were marketable, Okeh had also released the "first documented recording of a black female singer [Mamie Smith]" in 1920 and, the same year, had released Smith's "Crazy Blues," the first blues song recorded. Smith's success opened the way for other black musical performers. Popular stage entertainers of the period were the first to be recorded and, with Bradford's assistance as musical director, many blues and jazz artists were recruited. Mamie Smith was joined by singers and musicians such as Louis Armstrong, King Oliver, Lonnie Johnson, and Sippie Wallace on the Okeh label. The success of the Okeh series prompted others to test the race record market and, within the next few years, Columbia, Paramount, Emerson, Pathé, Victor, and Black Swan initiated race labels. These labels introduced stars such as Bessie Smith, Fletcher Henderson, Ethel Waters, Alberta Hunter, "Blind" Lemon Jefferson, and Ida Cox. At first, "vaudeville blues songs formed the largest class of race records issued," but the industry quickly expanded and by the mid-twenties offered a wide variety of entertainment. Music, of course, predominated but, as one historian noted, "the diversity of singers, entertainers, jazz bands, preachers and other black artists represented on these labels was remarkable." Such divisions as Vocal Blues, Hot Dance, Sermons, and Novelties were established and included in catalogues. Black Swan attempted upgrading its releases by including "numbers of higher standing," and announced the "First Grand Opera Record Ever Made by a Colored Singer" in 1922. This wide variety of recordings also included a rich sampling of the humor of the period.[5]

Some vaudeville performers recorded humorous songs from their stage repertoires. Butterbeans and Susie, a duo that combined song and dance with comedy, for example, released a number of tunes based on routines that burlesqued marital relationships and combined biting quips from the spouses with standard blues lyrics. Their Okeh recordings, now collector's items, included "Construction Gang" and "A Married Man's a Fool If He Thinks His Wife Don't Love Nobody but Him." Other blues and novelty performers contributed tunes that reflected the merger of coon songs, which had been recorded by white artists prior to race records, with the newly "discovered" urban and rural blues. Many of these songs ridiculed the popular denigrative images of blacks in the former by either altering the textural meaning of established myths such as the love of chicken or furtively inserting complaints about inequality in seemingly innocuous comic references. For instance, in "A Chicken Can Waltz the Gravy Around" (Okeh, 1927) by Sam Jones—or Stovepipe No. 1, as he called himself—the appetite for chicken was changed metaphorically to a lust for women:

Oh chicken, oh chicken, you can fry 'em nice and brown,
Oh chicken, oh chicken, you can waltz that gravy around

Oh chicken, oh chicken, I don't mean no fault in that,
Fine chickens grow in this town
And they wings can't get too fat.
   Oh when I come to this neighborhood,
   Chickens knows just what I mean;
   Chickens skippin' and dodgin',
   No chicken can be seen.

And Bo Chatman's "Good Old Turnip Greens" (Brunswick, 1928) manages to add a touch of social realism to a comic ditty about soul food:

White man goes to college
And the Negro to the fields,
The white man will learn to read and write,
And the Negro will learn to steal.
Oh the white folks in their parlors,
Just eatin' their cake and cream,
But the darkey's back in the kitchen,
Just a-scratchin' on the turnip greens.

As Paul Oliver points out in *Songsters and Saints: Vocal Traditions on Race Records,* "Overt comments on relations between the races were rare, and if there were many such songs they scarcely got on record." Black musicians and singers might " 'play the nigger' and satisfy [the audience's] delight in the chicken-stealing black simpleton" while performing for white crowds, but "to a black audience he could lay more emphasis on the harassment by police or the successful duping of white people."[6]

There is little doubt that black listeners who purchased the above recordings (particularly those who had seen the songs performed in person) were aware of their covert implications. Race records provided numerous examples of this type of hedged wit and indirect protest, much of it centered on animal allegory in which the monkey and rabbit were cast as wily black heroes facing white adversaries such as the baboon or mule. Still, simply by virtue of being removed from the immediacy of subtle physical gestures that inevitably altered the meaning of live performances on stage, race records could not fully capture the intended spirit and oblique humor of black songs. In the early stages, besides providing outlets for jazz and blues artists, they most emphatically conveyed the suggestive sexual innuendo or "blue" overtones of the comic element in black song. More satirical social humor, which surfaced when road show performers were faced with all-black audiences, was largely avoided.

This is not to suggest that blues lyrics were obsessively or exclusively concerned with social strictures initiated by whites, even when they were performed before all-black audiences. "The blues are immortal," as one critic suggests, "not because their lyric content sometimes reflects problems produced by a social-cultural order out of tune with the universe," but because their "portrayal of life without facade enables an audience to identify with content and mood, on an honest, personal level." Although the raft of blues tunes released on race records often expressed disenchantment with social conditions in a humorous vein, to a large extent the activities of whites were incidental; the songs most often focused on the intraracial, day-to-day lives of blacks. And while the blues was never specifically a comic form, it was no stranger to irony and satire. The expressive focus was usually financial or marital woes, social injustices, or the perfidies of sexual relationships and friendships, but woven throughout the typically earthy, candid lyrics were examples of wit and amusing observations lifted directly from the underground reservoir of black folk humor. As Albert Murray writes in *Stomping the Blues*, "Even when blues lyrics are about the most harrowing anxieties, hardships, and misfortunes (as they so often but by no means always are), blues music is no less appropriate to good-time situations. . . . And besides, sometimes the lyrics mock and signify even as they pretend to weep."[7]

Indeed, the blues is not only an expression of anguish and misfortune but also a vehicle for transcending and overcoming despair. The spurned lover who is treated so coldly in "Goin' to Chicago," for instance, finally announces: "Goin' to Chicago / Sorry but I can't take you. / S'nothin' in Chicago / That a monkey woman can do." Blues songs often commented just as ironically on mainstream bigotry: "They arrest me for murder / I ain't never harmed a man. / Woman hollered murder / And I ain't raise my hand. . . . Judge, the people all hollerin' / 'bout what in the world they will do, / Lots of people had justice, / They'd be in the penitentiary too." Or sometimes, directly mirroring the African practice of ridiculing in song, they would get down and dirty and zero in on another's heritage, behavior, or appearance: "I like your mama, I like your sister too, / I did like your daddy, but your daddy wouldn't do, / I met your daddy on the corner the other day, / You know about that he was funny that way." Or "Now, now, boys say you ain't actin' fair, / You know about that you got real bad hair, / Your face is all hid now your back's all bare, / If you ain't doin' the bobo, what's your head doin' down there?"[8]

In terms of humor, then, these records represented a kind of twilight zone between blacks' private and public postures. Knowing that their audience would be primarily black, performers could and did loosen many of their inhibitions. At least partially, they were able to abandon the pretense of "coming dark" or acting out white fantasy and, occasionally, display some of the bawdier comic references to sex. Consequently, the recordings presented examples of authentic black humor that were seldom found in Hollywood films or on Broadway and radio. The blues and novelty songs that came from the road shows to race records, as Paul Oliver observes, "were comments on life" and their "fantasy heroes, 'coon' figures, animal parallels, and oblique satirical references" both amused and helped build racial confidence.[9]

The sale of Harry Pace's Black Swan company to Paramount Records in 1924 probably altered the course of race records more than historians care to admit. With Black Swan's demise, despite the continued presence of influential blacks such as Perry Bradford, the race record industry was almost exclusively controlled by whites. Internal censorship through selection of artists recorded and songs released undoubtedly reflected the biases of the owners. Moreover, despite the sense of freedom black artists may have felt knowing the records were destined for a black audience, the reluctance to uninhibitedly air incendiary lyrics in such a public forum obviously deterred expression of the full range of humorous sentiments in African-American song.

Overall, however, race recordings marked the beginning of a black recording tradition featuring comic lyrics and routines that lasted through the fifties, when the genre was renamed rhythm and blues, and on to the nineties and the emergence of rap. During that time, in addition to the raft of recordings made by blues singers and musicians, comedians such as Scatman Crothers, Pigmeat Markham, Dusty Fletcher, and Redd Foxx have recorded comic songs steeped in the blues or rhythm and blues tradition.

During the thirties Cab Calloway's effervescent style and combination of scatting and humorous lyrics dominated with such songs as "Minnie the Moocher." Fats Waller, who had written "Flat Tire Papa, Mama's Gonna Give Him Air" in the twenties, also recorded "Your Feets Too Big" ("She likes your lovin', she likes your rig, / But, oh man, them things is too big") in 1939. The recording ended with Waller's famous quip, "Your pedal extremities really are obnoxious. One never knows, do one?"

By the forties, Louis Jordan had become America's most popular black recording artist largely due to the release of a long list of humorous rhythm and blues songs, such as "Caldonia," "Is You Is, or Is You Ain't My Baby?" and "Ain't Nobody Here but Us Chickens." In another of his hits, "Honey Chile," his amorous interest is described as having "One brown eye, the other blue, / She got false hair, and a teeth or two." And "Beware," which enumerated ploys used by women intent on matrimony, warned, "If she's used to caviar and fine silk / And when she's out with you she wants a hotdog and a malted milk . . . Watch out! Beware, brother, beware."

The ballyhoo created by the release of "Open the Door, Richard" in the late forties was a sure sign of the growing popularity of comic rhythm and blues songs. In 1946, Jack McVea took a comedy routine popularized by Dusty Fletcher, set it to music, and released the first recording of the song. By the time Fletcher released his own version in 1947, according to Jim O'Neal, editor of *Living Blues* magazine, "the Richard craze [had] swept the nation" and the title had become a "catch phrase for national radio personalities," including Bob Hope, Jimmy Durante, Bing Crosby, and Phil Harris. In 1986, an English publication, *Blues & Rhythm,* "published a list of over two dozen recorded versions of *Open the Door, Richard,* ranging from 1947 covers by Count Basie and Louis Jordan to '50s rock 'n' roll renditions cut at Sun Records in Memphis." The recording's success marked one of the first times that a black comic stage routine was catapulted to national prominence.[10]

Publicity arising from disputes over creative rights—McVea was finally assigned rights to the music and along with John "Spider Bruce" Mason, the originator of the routine, Fletcher was credited with the lyrics—increased the song's popularity. It also opened the door for Fletcher's stalled stage career and subsequently allowed him to record other novelty songs.

On the "Richard" release, Fletcher, portraying a drunk who has been locked out of his apartment, delivers his comic monologue over a bluesy track featuring jazzmen George Treadwell, Dickie Wells, Big Nick Nicholas, Jimmy Jones, and Al McKibbon, and trades quips with an irate neighbor and a policeman:

He don't wanna open the door for me! And I owes just as much rent up here as he do. . . . I don't care, I'mah move Saturday anyway. Dis old woman, she chargin' too much rent, three dollars a month. And got the nerve to be mad because we's eleven months in the rear. Why, she come asking me dis morning, she say, "When you boys gwanna give me some'ah my back rent?" So just told her she lucky if she get any front rent outta me. . . .

Fletcher followed the "Open the Door, Richard" single with several other comic releases in 1947. "Mad Hour," for instance, finds Fletcher still inebriated but stirring up comic havoc inside a bar. On this cut, he is accompanied by a jazz group that includes Dickie Wells, Budd Johnson, and Hot Lips Page. In addition to the comic patter, Fletcher belts out some gravel-voiced blues lyrics and makes impromptu comments about the band. Comedy, however, was the focus.

"Hey, Bartender!" Fletcher shouts. "Ah, who is dem pretty little girls over dere? Give dem pretty little girls a drink. What you want to drink over dere, baby?"

When the women request a scotch and soda, Fletcher quips, "They must'a rehershed that. A scotch an soda! Ain't dis a shame! Give dem old chicks a glass o' beer and put two straws in the glass."[11]

The forties produced a raft of tunes with comic overtones by such groups as the Treniers ("Go, Go, Go" and "Rag Mop") and such performers as Slim Gilliard, whose jazzy vocals were heard on "Cement Mixer" and other songs. Even Redd Foxx, who before turning exclusively to humor was a musician and vocalist, released some comic blues recordings with Kenny Watts and His Jumpin' Buddies on the Savoy label. And by the beginning of the next decade, Foxx recorded his first comedy albums for Dooto Records.

During the early fifties, as rhythm and blues began invading the popular charts, Lloyd Price released, among other tunes, "Lawdy, Miss Clawdy" and, later, "Stagger Lee," which was based on a popular black folk ballad. In addition, the Coasters had emerged as the premier novelty artists in black music. They were best known for later songs such as "Searchin'," "Charlie Brown," and "Yakety Yak," which made the top ten on the R & B charts. But they were even funnier on tunes such as "Smokey Joe's Café," "Down in Mexico," and "Shopping for Clothes," which received scant notice outside the black community. The last featured a slow blues riff (King Curtis on tenor sax) and doo-wop background over which a dialect exchange between a salesman and prospective customer was heard:

Them buttons are solid gold.
You made a deal, sold.
That collar's pure camel hair.
And you can just set dat right dere on that chair.

After a credit check, the deal falls through; the customer leaves, groaning, "Pure, pure herringbone," as the clerk chides, "But that's a suit you'll never own."[12]

Race records seldom explored the aggressively ironic side of African-American humor, but because of prevailing assumptions about the nature of black life, more license was given to expression of suggestive erotic metaphors and other subjects that were taboo on mainstream records. The recordings therefore gained a reputation as being somewhat unsavory or low-down and, to that extent, reaffirmed an impression of black humor and music shared by whites and middle-class Negroes.

Race records flourished during the twenties and, after a decline during the Depression, reemerged as a significant musical force in the forties and fifties with the ascendancy of rhythm and blues. The process, however, was long and protracted. Even instrumental music, an abstract, non-verbial idiom, encountered considerable resistance. Critics denounced both the music and the "hot" dances that accompanied it, claiming that the uninhibited revelry it encouraged would undermine mainstream morality. The implicit sexual overtones of the dances associated with syncopated music were always in conflict with the central tenets of the Protestant Ethic. Yet as the Harlem Renaissance and upsurge of Negrophilia during the twenties indicate, that erotic component is precisely what drew whites to Harlem and other black urban centers.

In *Music: Black, White and Blue*, the musician and sociologist Ortiz M. Walton notes that whites attracted to black music are "somewhat like the child who yearns to experience what is tabooed by [his own] culture," and offers a passage from Hermann Hesse's *Steppenwolf* as an example:

From a dance-hall there met me as I passed by the strains of lively jazz music, *hot and raw as the steam of raw flesh*. I stopped a moment. This kind of music, *much as I detested it, had always had a secret charm for me.* It was repugnant to me, and yet ten times preferable to all the academic music of the day [italics Walton's].

Hesse's European narrator-hero goes on to equate the music with a *"savage gaiety,"* "honest *sensuality,"* and *"childlike happiness"* that he felt was "unblushingly negroid. . . . There was *something of the nigger in it."*[13]

But despite the allure of black music, its influence on the lives of white Americans was initially considered an ephemeral diversion, one from which the addicted could easily withdraw without changing their view of blacks or segregated society. Usually music did little to change societal images or established social identities and—particularly since the lyrics of most popular tunes were written by whites and reflected the sentiments of the dominant culture—the symbiotic process of borrowing, absorption, feedback, and alteration went on virtually unabated. Grittier, more down-to-earth lyrics written by blacks (rural and urban blues, for example) were usually confined to race records, which were often banned from radio and ignored in respectable mainstream outlets before the mid-twentieth century.

Concern over black music's effect on society was usually confined to disputes about the relative merits of rhythm versus harmony and melody or questions of good and bad taste. On occasion, racial and social issues were brought to the forefront. In 1954, for instance, an article in *Variety* proposed that "The most astonishing thing about the current craze for ryhthm and blues records and their accompanying leer-ics is that it was ever permitted to happen. Their leerical concoctions belong in the dimlit honkytonks and should never be heard on the air." And in 1956, a *Newsweek* story about the "self-appointed leader of the North Alabama Citizens Council" reported:

"Individual councils have formed action committees to call on owners of establishments with rock and roll music on their juke boxes," he said. "We also intend to see the people who sponsor the music, and the people who promote the Negro bands for teenagers." Rock and roll music, he said, "is the basic beat of Negroes. It appeals to the very base of man, brings out the base in man, brings out the animalism and vulgarity."

Despite the criticisms, however, black music (jazz, blues, and rhythm and blues) continued its gradual ascent.[14]

Ultimately, these records had an incredible impact on America's mainstream popular music. By the late fifties, white performers were commonly making so-called "cover" releases and, as pointed out in chapter 5, by the sixties the rhythms of former race records had been appropriated as rock 'n' roll and were quickly beginning to define America's popular music.

Authentic African-American comedy was not as easily assimilated. When black music was altered for consumption in America's mainstream culture, its so-called primitive aspects were toned down—in effect, giving it a more polite, European veneer. The adaptations of black music popularized by mainstream interpreters from Stephen Foster, John Philip Sousa, Paul Whiteman, and George Gershwin, to Pat Boone, Chubby Checker, Elvis Presley, and Vanilla Ice, were essentially more sanitized or whitewashed versions of the source material. Once the music was accepted, black musicians worked at reversing the process of gentrification, replacing and reaffirming the music's earthier, funkier, or more rhythmical folk elements.

In comedy, mainstream distortion functioned in an opposite manner. Although its sexual overtones and graphic language were eliminated, popular adaptations of African-American humor often involved broadening the comedy or amplifying and ridiculing the assumed primitive characteristics of Negroes. The task of black comedians was to replace derisive comic stereotypes with authentic comic modes that, while reaffirming folk origins, revealed the double-edged meanings and subtle, ironic twists of the humor.

Moreover, unlike music, comedy is seldom neutral; it nearly always involves either the belittling or extolling of the humor's subject (and simultaneously a corresponding detracting or commending of the comic source). For turn-of-the-century black performers, comedy entailed the introduction of reasoned perceptions and satirical overtones that, instead of reaffirming minstrelsy's abjectly self-effacing projection of black life, mirrored often concealed, less accommodating black attitudes. Essentially, it meant replacing minstrelsy's externally imposed stage image of naive ineptitude or buffoonery with a comic presence that reflected deliberate humor created within the black community.

This shift in the humorous presentation of the stage Negro was considered a threat, an attack on America's underlying belief in white supremacy. In fact, it did touch on the very center of white-black relationships in America, for it challenged an assumption America had made about blacks that was as old as slavery. Obviously, the emergence of more assertive black comedy presented a dilemma that would not be quickly or painlessly resolved.

II

Initially, films made primarily for African-American audiences purposefully avoided humorous depictions of blacks. Although Bill Foster produced *The Railroad Porter* around 1912 and Bert Williams filmed *Darktown Jubilee* in 1914, the effective impetus for the production of black films was the controversy surrounding D. W. Griffith's *The Birth of a Nation* (1915). The furor forced black leaders to look more closely at the effect Hollywood's depiction of blacks had on the larger society's perception of racial differences, and it roused enough interest to initiate plans for a film that would counter Griffith's scandalous portrait of black Americans.

Emmet J. Scott, a former journalist and Booker T. Washington's secretary at Tuskegee Institute until the educator's death in 1915, led the attempt to form a black film company and produce a movie that rectified the distortions of *The Birth of a Nation*. With the backing of the NAACP and Universal Pictures, which matched funds derived from selling stock in the project to black businessmen, Scott put together a coalition that included scholars and a veteran screenwriter and set out to produce *Lincoln's Dream*, initially conceived as a short that might be appended to Griffith's film. Aspirations expanded, however, and eventually Scott's group decided to produce a feature movie. Internal disagreements and the defection of Universal as a backer impeded the project but, after three years, Scott managed to release *Birth of a Race* (1918 or 1919). Unfortunately, it was an unfocused, rambling film that bore little resemblance to its creators' original conception. A financial and critical failure, the movie dropped out of sight shortly after a widely ballyhooed Chicago premiere.

During the time that Scott's movie was being filmed, several more successful black companies were founded. Actor Noble Johnson and his brother, George, formed the Lincoln Motion Picture Company in 1916 and, during the next six or seven years, produced about ten films. Like Scott, the Johnsons were intent upon making motion pictures that countered the prevailing image of blacks as laggards and comic buffoons. Their films were largely devoid of humor. Instead, echoing America's popular Horatio Alger myth, the Lincoln company turned out a series of movies that focused on African-American achievement and consciously depicted black men and women who might be seen as heroes or heroines in the community. Among the titles were *The Realization of a Negro's Ambition* (1917), *Trooper K* (1920), and *By Birth Right* (1921). With Noble Johnson starring in many of the Lincoln films, they were a distinct improvement over Scott's effort, although still substandard by Hollywood criteria. Ultimately, distribution problems and pressure from Universal Pictures, where Noble Johnson was maintained as a supporting player until the late forties, doomed the company.

Traverse Spriggins also began his Douglass Film Company in the late teens and, like the Johnsons, set out to produce uplifting films that depicted the Negro in a less demeaning manner than Hollywood had. Their releases included Paul Laurence Dunbar's *The Scapegoat* (1920). The Harlem-based Reol Motion Picture Company followed the same pattern. Backed by Robert Levy, the company employed performers from the Lafayette Players and included among their titles Dunbar's *Sport of the Gods* (1923). There was also Ebony Films, a Chicago-based company presumedly headed by J. Luther Pollard. But Pollard didn't share the others' dedication to serious black films; his company turned out standard blackface comedies such as *Spying the Spy* (1917) and *Black Sherlock Holmes* (undated), both of which presented comic Negro adaptations of mainstream storylines in which the humor turned on basic coon antics.

By the time Lincoln folded in the early twenties, these and many other smaller black companies were struggling to compete in a rapidly expanding industry. Race films were being viewed as viable commercial products not only by blacks but also by independent white filmmakers and Hollywood. Black films, like race records, which emerged at about the same time, were slowly but inevitably falling under the control of non-black interests. Independent white-owned companies soon began dominating the market. By the late twenties, "at least thirty black film production companies were operating," many of them controlled by whites. With more than seven hundred movie houses in black communities and black audiences starved for representation on the screen, race films had been transformed from a minority operation inspired by a desire to rectify distorted images of African-Americans to a largely commercial endeavor that often exploited the same stereotypes established in Hollywood movies.[15]

Remarkably, one independent black filmmaker survived the takeover of race movies and continued to produce motion pictures until the forties. Oscar Micheaux—who was born in Illinois in 1894 and drifted to South Dakota, where he was a porter, farmer, rancher, and novelist before turning to motion pictures—came to the film business with an inventiveness, determination, and con man's spirit that set him apart and sustained him when most other blacks succumbed to its harsh realities. Lorenzo Tucker, the leading man that Micheaux dubbed "the black Valentino," submitted that "he was so impressive and charming that he could talk the shirt right off your back." The historian Thomas Cripps notes that Micheaux attempted to join the Lincoln company in 1919, but the Johnsons "considered him an upstart, a mountebank, and an untrustworthy hustler." Undeterred, Micheaux released his first feature film, *The Homesteader,* that same year and used his unconventional approach and knack for self-promotion to produce over thirty films during the next three decades.[16]

As dancer Honi Coles recalled, Micheaux "would walk into a place and take his camera out and start rolling—without asking anybody. Next thing you knew, you were in a picture somewhere, but nobody seemed to mind. . . . He was his own writer, his own choreographer, his own cameraman, I can't think of anything he didn't do." Notwithstanding his impromptu techniques, shoestring budgets, and frequent use of amateur actors along with professionals from Hollywood, Broadway, and groups like Harlem's Lafayette Players, Micheaux was able to produce a formidable list of surprisingly adept movies. Much of his success can be attributed to a distributing and marketing tack that was as unorthodox as his filmmaking techniques. Using the grass-roots approach he had developed while promoting and distributing novels that he wrote and published, Micheaux traveled throughout the country, meeting prominent people in the black community and lecturing at schools and churches, where he also met the working class. Carrying stills from a new movie, he would visit white- and black-owned theatres in the Black Belt and convince owners to book his films or, in some instances, persuade them to finance projects that were not yet completed. Flamboyant, irrepressible, and endowed with not just a little of the trickster's instinct, Micheaux was the only independent black filmmaker who (generally without the backing and consequent influence of whites) was able to produce a substantial film oeuvre.[17]

His career spanned the silent and sound movie eras and, according to Donald Bogle, although the films were "technically inferior [and] the acting could be dreadful," they were "similar to the Hollywood product [and] resembled the best B pictures of the time." Micheaux, like the eighties maverick black filmmaker Spike Lee, displayed an eclecticism that often moved beyond the usual concerns of race movies. Although he dutifully produced Negro uplift movies such as *Birthright* (1924) and engaged the popular theme of passing for white in *God's Step-children* (1938), Micheaux also ventured into terrain that was alien to most race movies. His controversial *Within Our Gate* (1920) drama-tized an "anti-Semitic lynching," *The Symbol of the Unconquered* (1921) focused on the terrorism of the Ku Klux Klan, and *Murder in Harlem* (1935) dealt with legal injustices and the threat of lynching that arose when a black man was accused of killing a white secretary. With-out timidity, he often "filmed the unnameable, arcane, disturbing things that set black against black," among them intraracial color prejudice and the deleterious influence of the numbers racket on black communi-ties.[18]

Generally, like other black filmmakers of the period, Micheaux avoided focusing on the humorous depiction of Negroes. He concen-trated on the problems and concerns of the black middle class and largely avoided the rural buffoons and clowns that dominated Holly-wood's depiction of blacks. According to Lorenzo Tucker, "He didn't lean toward comedy and didn't go much for dialect." Still, there was a small white audience that frequented race movies, and Micheaux was aware of their expectations as well as the black common man's fondness for the ethnic humor that dominated the black stage circuit. Moreover, he was not above appealing to those audiences; "he cleverly inserted into almost all his films raunchy cabaret scenes that he knew would appeal to whites."[19]

That impulse led him to include moments of unabashed minstrelsy in his films. *Ten Minutes to Live* (1932), for example, a movie set in a nightclub, includes a rare appearance of blackface actors in Micheaux movies. Introduced as George and Gabby, two clownishly attired come-dians (their ill-fitting clothes a brazen parody of the rural Negro's at-tempt to affect urban decorum) appear as part of a variety act and, although the bit contains a few veiled attacks on racial bigotry, it focuses primarily on time-worn minstrel banter:

> *comic 1:* What you wanna do is stop talkin' 'bout goin' to jail. Uplift yo'self, elevate, be somebody. Follow in the foot-steps a' great men.

comic 2 :   Now what the use of me bein' somebody and elevatin'. What good it's goin' do me, I wanna go somewhere I can eat.

comic 1:   Well, that's all right . . . If you elevate, then you can eat.

comic 2:   I cain' even join the Fresh Air Camp, but dat don't mean nothin' to me now. Gimme less liberty and more food. Got a whole lotta freedom and starvin' to death.

comic 1:   You oughta be satisfied.

comic 2:   I never will forget the words my grandmother use' to tell me when I was a little boy. She use' to hold me on her lap and look into my big blue eyes . . . She push my goldilocks back from my forehead and said, "Son, my darlin' son, where dere's a will dere's a way."

comic 1:   She was right!

comic 2:   I got a will to eat, but I cain' find the way.

comic 1:   Keep on lookin', you'll find it.

comic 2:   But now since you said dat, ah, elevation . . . you know, dat's sumpthin' good. We ought to do that. Get outta the gutter and step on the sidewalk . . .

comic 1:   Now you talkin'.

comic 2:   Follow in the footsteps of great men . . .

comic 1:   Yeah!

comic 2:   Men like Booker T. Washington.

comic 1:   That's a great man.

comic 2:   That's a man whose name is known everywhere.

comic 1:   Yeah!

comic 2:   The chillun knows him. . . . His picture is in de books and papers. Why? Because he was a man that done sumpthin'.

comic 1:   Yeah! What did he do?

comic 2: I don't know. But whatever it was, he done it.

comic 1: Yeah.

comic 2: And look at dat other great man.

comic 1: Who was that?

comic 2: Dat great soldier . . .

comic 1: Who?

comic 2: Frederick Douglass . . . put his gun on his shoulder, walked out onto de battlefield, and said, "Gimme liberty or shoot me" . . .

comic 1: Uh-huh.

comic 2: And dey shot him.

comic 1: What?

comic 2: But there's a man . . .

comic 1: Who?

comic 2: Abraham Lincoln.

comic 1: Dat's a great boy!

comic 2: Now dat's a man that's known everywhere too.

comic 1: Sure dat's . . .

comic 2: He was a man that done sumpthin'.

comic 1: Yeah, dat's the boy that cut down his papa's cherry tree!

comic 2: [Looks at his partner with utter stupefaction.]

In this instance, the choice of performers probably reflects Micheaux's attempt to attract white audiences since, despite its similarity to some classic black comic routines, the comedy is firmly based in a demeaning minstrel mode where humor is derived almost solely from the characters' naïveté and ignorance, particularly about their own racial heroes. A close look at the scene reveals that even the black actors portraying patrons at the cabaret are uncomfortable.[20]

Although other such examples can be found in Micheaux movies, usually they were not so gratuitously heavy-handed. In *Birthright,* for instance, satire at the expense of some backward rural characters is partially justified by their resistance to the returning college-educated hero's attempt to uplift his race. In other films, Micheaux offered some examples of authentic black stage humor that were rarely seen in motion pictures or, in fact, any mainstream outlet.

The surprisingly whimsical *Darktown Revue* (1931), for instance, contrasts scenes depicting a staid, bourgeois Donald Heywood Choir singing such tunes as "Is That Religion?" and "Ain't That a Shame" (not the Fats Domino version) with two classic examples of black ethnic humor. In one scene, the legendary Tim Moore appears with Andrew Tribel in a spirited dialogue involving the big lie, ghosts, and several other comedy standbys:

Tribel: The Island Queen come in dis mornin', let's go down to de levee and see what she brought in.

Moore: Yeah, you can go to dah levee if you wanna. I was down dere yesterday mornin' and got insulted.

Tribel: Who insulted you?

Moore: When dat boat pulled in, outta all of dem folks standin' round on dah levee, the man had to come off the boat and walk up and insult me.

Tribel: How'd he insult you?

Moore: Ask me did I wanna work.

The story takes a different turn here, as Moore explains what happened after he stumbled into a haunted house.

Moore: I was scared to stay in and I was scared to come out. I know there was ghosts in that house.

Tribel: How'd you know it?

Moore: Cause it was chilly in dere. And I thought I'd build me a fire. I looked down into the fireplace and dere was wood and shavin's all ready to be lit! I reached up on dah mantelpiece to get a match. Just as I went to light dah wood and shavin's, dah wood and shavin's disappeared.

Wasn't no wood and they wasn't no shavin's. Live coals burnin' in the grate, red hot!

Tribel: What kinda grate was dat?

Moore: Red hot and steady heatin'. And dat ain't all. I could see dem coals movin' round. All at once dis little kitty come crawlin' out dem hot coals.

Tribel: Outta dah hot coals?

Moore: A little tiny kitty come outta dem hot coals. Turned around and eat some'a dah fire and sit dere and laughed at me, 'ha-ha,' like dat.

Tribel: Boy, I don't blame dat cat for laughin', 'cause dah first time I seen you I like to laugh myself to death.

Moore: And boy, dah cat had on a bathing suit and got up on the edge of dah fire and dived down into dem hot coals and when he come up he had on a tuxedo. And come here talkin' Polish to me.

Tribel: What kinda cat was dat?

Moore: A pole cat, fool!

. . . .

Moore: Boy, dah cat got big as a mule. And turned around and told me to shut up. Then started over where I was. And dat's when it happened.

Tribel: And dat's when what happened?

Moore: Dat's when the window got broke out and dah blind got knocked off.

Tribel: You don't mean to stood up and tell me dat you come through dat window.

Moore: I didn't go around it! All I remember was I started and dah window was in my way. And boy, if I had a missed dat window, dat wall woulda been ruined.

Tribel: How come you leave dat house in such undignified manner? Why didn't you use de doah?

Moore: The doah! You showin' yo' ignorance now.

Tribel: Is I?

Moore: Is you ever been to any school outside de reform school?

Tribel: Yeah.

Moore: Uh-huh. Well, in school did you take up any kinda manual trainin'?

Tribel: Yeah.

Moore: Did you study woodwork?

Tribel: Yeah!

Moore: Well, in yo' studies ah woodwork did you take up windowry or doah-ry?

Tribel: Nah.

Moore: You didn't take dem.

Tribel: Nah.

Moore: But you knows a couple of carpenters and a architect or two.

Tribel: Yeah!

Moore: Well, the next carpenter you see, you ask him and he'll explain to you about doahs. He'll tell you dat a doah was made fo' folks what had a lot a time. But when dat cat spoke to me . . .

Tribel: Yeah.

Moore: . . . by me being punctual, my time dere was up! And right den dah window got well.

Tribel: What you mean, de window got well?

Moore: It got rid of its *pain.*

The film also includes a comic routine rarely seen outside black communities—a parody of a black jacklegged preacher in which the comedian, Amon Davis, reduces the sermon to the most basic element of language, the alphabet. Davis, in top hat, tails, and blackface makeup, drags a podium onto the stage and commences the routine with, "Brothers and sisters, seems as though the congregation is a little bit stiff dis evenin'. Seems as though the contribution box is sadly regressin'. I got a few renouncements to make here dis evenin'." After some familiar folderol about "meetin's at sister Chickenfoot's house," the acceptability of "pints" as a contribution, and such, Amon proceeds to the meat of his routine: "Lookin' down on page two hundred and two-de-two, we find here where it say, A-B-C-D-E-F-G-H-I-J-K, *LMNOP*-Q-R-S-T, UVW-X-Y-Z. Uh-huh, A-B-*C*, D-E-F-G-H-I-J-K, *IJK*, I-J-K, L-M, *LM*, now dere's the question, *LM*. LMNOP! Q-R-S-T-UVWXYZ. Now ain't dat a glorious feeling! I say, A-B-C . . ." With appropriate gestures, exclamations, and punctuations of voice and tonal delivery, Davis presents a dramatic send-up that hilariously captures every nuance of the rural preacher's sermonic presentation.

Difficult to recreate in print, the routine depends almost entirely on intonation and gesticulation to drive home the satire. It is similar to the Richard Pryor "Our Text for Today" routine, in which the comedian delivers the following sermon: "Let us turn our text to . . . dah Book of Wonder, where it say, 'A boy, was born, in Hard Time, Miss'*sippi*. Surrounded by fo' walls . . . that was not pretty! His parents—that's two peoples—give him love, and affection. Just to keep him strong . . . *movin' in the right direction!* Give him just enough! I said, *just enough!* For the Ci-*ty!*'" Pryor's routine also uses a sermonic presentation of nonreligious text, but the earlier bit, by reducing the verbal content to a fundamentally nonsensical recitation of the alphabet, stretches the parody further. It is a revealing example of the type of ethnic comedy that appeared on the stages of black theatres. And while Davis dons blackface makeup and riddles the piece with minstrel-like references and mispronunciations ("sister Chickenfoot" or "a few renouncements today"), the use of a nonsensical, abstract text clearly confirms that the humor is intentional, a performance and not an instance of naïveté or innate idiocy. The bit is a riotous example of a black comedian cleverly pushing his humor beyond the perimeters of the limited areas in which many were forced to work.[21]

The early black filmmaker who, second to Micheaux, most resisted white control of his films was Spencer Williams. Despite being an accomplished comedian and writer (he had performed and written for Paramount's Christie Comedies series and later appeared as Amos on *Amos 'n' Andy*), he usually focused on serious topics in the movies he produced in association with white producer Alfred Sack during the forties. *Juke Joint* (1947), a film that weaves a story of black family life in a small Texas town around a sketchy script featuring slapstick comedy and a generous dose of ethnic stage humor, was an exception. Comedians July Jones and Mantan Moreland appeared with Williams, and at times the film offered examples of the street banter one might have heard at a jocular moment in a black barber shop:

Williams: We're now following the advice of one of the finest men in America, Mr. Horace Greeley. Mr. Greeley said, "Go West, young man, and do yo' best, then come East and spend yo' grease."

Jones: Say, how come I couldn't go East and get my grease, then come back South and hush my mouth.

On another occasion Jones interrupts the solemn ritual of saying grace before a family dinner with, "Thank you, ladies. And if we able, we goin' eat everything that's on this table. And if there's anything left in the pot, bring it out while it's good and hot." Scenes such as these, in a different context, may have seemed self-depreciative, but in a setting dominated by pious, hardworking black folk, the facile street rap of Jones's character seemed merely an amusing interlude. July Jones also teamed up with Williams in *Beale Street Mama* (1946). As the title suggests, the film was a straight-out comic romp and, in the manner of Miller and Lyles and other black comic teams, Jones and Williams reenact many of the trickster and naive sidekick bits that were popular on stage.[22]

As a filmmaker, however, Spencer Williams is better known for his brooding religious fantasy, *Blood of Jesus* (1941), which, despite its technical deficiencies, is considered one of the most affecting depictions of Southern black church life on film. In that movie—as in *Go Down Death* (1944), *Of One Blood* (undated), and *Dirty Gerty From Harlem USA* (1946), his remake of Somerset Maugham's *Rain*—Williams concentrated on moral issues and religious themes. To the extent that they focused on the everyday problems of earnest, hardworking black people, Williams's serious films were more representative of independent race movies made by blacks than his comedies. They reflected the desire to establish a cinema image that countered mainstream depictions of happy-go-lucky musicians and dippy, self-effacing pranksters and Sambos.

African-Americans, however, seldom determined the thematic content of the race movies in which they were involved. The Lincoln Motion Picture Company, Oscar Micheaux, the Douglass Film Company, the Reol Motion Picture Company, Spencer Williams, and a few smaller organizations (most of which produced only one or two films) were exceptions; the producers' ability to leave a personal imprint on their works usually resulted from their sheer tenacity and resolve or from self-financing. Others were not as successful. The raft of race movie companies that emerged in the twenties and nearly all those that surfaced during and after the Depression were completely controlled by whites (who sometimes employed black front men).

Still, this arrangement did facilitate production of some exemplary black genre movies. Among the most accomplished were two films released by the Colored Players Company, *Ten Nights in a Barroom* (1926), which starred Charles Gilpin, and *Scar of Shame* (1928), a film that effectively explored the color caste system among blacks; *The Emperor Jones* (1933), which starred Paul Robeson and was produced independently and directed by Dudley Murphy; *The Spirit of Youth* (1937), a drama about the rise of a young boxer, which starred Joe Louis and Clarence Muse; and *Broken Strings* (1940), a drama about a concert violinist's conflict with his son, which also starred Clarence Muse and was probably the best of the lot.

The success of these movies notwithstanding, the combination of white control and black performers perpetuated the tendency to portray blacks in the established Hollywood mold and frequently gave credence to mainstream comic stereotypes that had little to do with the black community or its authentic inside humor.

Non-black producers, after all, had their own entrenched ideas about what race movies should depict. According to James Murray, the film editor for *Black Creation* magazine, in a 1942 interview Jack and Bert Goldberg (whose Herald Pictures, Hollywood Pictures, and Harlemwood Company controlled much of the race movie industry) claimed, "All [Negroes] know is that they want plenty of singing and dancing or drama depicting Negro life in typical Negro spirit." By 1947, Ted Toddy (whose Toddy Pictures had become a major producer and distributor of black films) insisted that "Negro audiences do not care for the heavy emotional dramas. Their choice in film entertainment is the picture which features light comedy, outdoor adventures, musical comedies with an abundance of singing, dancing, and comedy-romances." These opinions were transformed into cinema reality and largely determined the content of race movies during the forties.[23]

Significantly, despite disdain for the idea of producing genuine dramatic films for black audiences, these filmmakers often presented their comic and musical extravaganzas in the *guise* of drama. The result was a kind of cinema hybrid, black-cast films that pretended to engage real situations but were actually vehicles for the music and comedy that producers assumed were the only entertainment blacks enjoyed. This compromised approach often resulted in films that not only distorted black humor but also trivialized serious aspects of African-American life.

Worst in this regard were black-cast dramatic productions that mimicked formulaic Hollywood genres such as Westerns and gangster movies. Most of these films included black funnymen whose role, as in Hollywood films, was to provide comic relief and validate the heroic or "serious" depiction of the film's stars by acting out traditional coon behavior. Flournoy Miller, Mantan Moreland, Johnny Lee, Nicodemus Stewart, and Willie Best were among the comedians whose parts in these movies, although tempered by the all-black environment, were often reduced to eye-rolling, head-scratching idiocy. As one film historian notes, "The new generation of race movies revived interest in the genre precisely because they were like Hollywood movies"; it could be added that the comedy in these films usually failed for exactly the same reason.[24]

There were, of course, exceptions. As mentioned in chapter 6, Stepin Fetchit's performance in *Miracle in Harlem* (1947)—released by Jack and Bert Goldberg's Herald Pictures—revealed a dimension of the comic's shuffling darky caricature that was rarely seen in his Hollywood vehicles. *Beware* (1946)—from Astor Pictures, a company headed by white Southerner Robert Savini—although *Newsweek* criticized it as "55 minutes of heavy-handed melodrama, inexpertly directed," included songs that captured both Louis Jordan's infectious rhythm and blues beat and his flair for comic lyrics.[25]

Hi-De-Ho (1947)—released by Emmanual Glucksman's All-American Company—was a musical with a gangster subplot. It also included Dusty Fletcher's rendition of the famous "Open the Door, Richard" routine. The bit is much funnier on the screen than on record, because much of its comic appeal depends on Fletcher's riotous slapstick antics. Dressed in top hat, tattered oversized jacket, and the clown's patented floppy shoes, Fletcher literally stumbles about the stage, reeling, falling, and bemoaning his state of total intoxication, "You know, I ain' never drink no whiskey befor' that won't let you go nowhere." The high point,

so to speak, is his near-acrobatic antics with a ladder, which he struggles
to set upright, then climbs to gain entry to his second-story apartment
after vainly trying to rouse his sleeping roommate. Finally, perched
near the top of the unsupported ladder, he reels and sways as he shouts
to his roommate. Just when it seems that he is about to topple over, he
announces, "I"m high as a Georgia pine, but it ain't no use being too
high," and descends. The acrobatics are, of course, complemented by a
running monologue with himself, an unresponsive Richard, and whoever else will listen.

While dramatizing Harlem's bigotry and social decay, *Souls of Sin*
(1949)—released by Alexander Productions before the black filmmaker
William Alexander joined Glucksman's All-American Company—has
its hero engage in some pointedly satirical social commentary. For
example, when a friend says, "I'll be back as soon as I find a job,"
without a hitch, he quips, "Come back anyway."[26]

There are numerous instances of this type of authentic black American humor buried in the crevices of the hastily produced, often shoddy
race movies released in the thirties and forties. In fact, the comic
interludes probably represented the films' most rewarding moments.
As most serious critics agree, the dramatic aspects of the films, usually
hopelessly skewed, were their weakest component. Even when adequately scripted and well acted, the films had an eerie, chimerical
quality about them—a quality that I experienced firsthand as a youth.

I got my first glimpse of race films as an adolescent in Ohio during
the fifties. The movies were shown in my hometown's only black theatre
(the Regent, which, due to its abundance of vermin, we sardonically
dubbed "the Rat Show") and, except for the rare presence of one
of the down-and-out whites who through some obviously disastrous
circumstances had become habitués of the "colored" section of town,
played to an entirely black audience. Although the films offered a certain camaraderie and welcomed external verification of our existence—
which was absent when viewing Rock Hudson or Doris Day features—
it was nearly impossible to reconcile with reality the fantastic charade
of black performers acting out a scenario quite obviously based on a
white world in which non-black problems and non-black reactions to
those problems predominated.

Most reputedly serious films from non-black producers of race
movies during the forties had simply substituted blacks for whites in
adaptations of well-trodden, non-black melodramatic situations. Consequently, the emotional rhythms were seldom correct, the assumed pri-

orities were off-key, and underlying motivations were, at best, alien. It was one thing, for instance, to accept an environment composed entirely of Negro cowboys, but quite another to swallow that even in that world heroes such as Herb Jeffries rode white horses and mouthed the same corny dialogue as Buck Jones or Roy Rogers. And although white producers may have insisted that love scenes mimic Clark Gable seducing Greta Garbo or Jean Harlow, rote imitation by black performers usually elicited muffled laughter or loudly voiced, often obscene, protestations; the Hollywood notion of romantic seduction had nothing whatsoever to do with the erotic rap used in black communities. To the majority of the working-class audience that frequented the black theatre (bourgeois Negroes would rather have attended a Ku Klux Klan meeting), such romanticism was dismissed as lame. The answer to contemporary critics and later historians who pose questions about "whether the laughs muffled inner tears of despair or whether some scenes deserved a horse laugh" is emphatically the latter.[27]

Moreover, as a northerner raised in a partially integrated community in which non-blacks were present everywhere except in one's home or a few social clubs, cabarets, and, on some occasions, theatres, the spectacle of a parallel, exclusively Negro society that duplicated manners and mores which we privately ridiculed was, in itself, laughable. Black genre movies that religiously reenacted Hollywood melodramatic scenarios (fantasies even in white middle-class society) inevitably sacrificed the cynicism, irony, and double-edged perception that, for better or worse, still largely defined black life. As a result, for me, most of my peers, and seemingly most others in the audience, they delineated a fanciful, distorted world. They were curios representing a harmless, perhaps less demeaning kind of minstrelsy and were funny in a manner their creators probably did not contemplate. The humor derived from their implicit misconceptions often eclipsed the calculated comedy provided by their comedians. But whether accidental or designed, the response echoing through that dilapidated picture show was more often than not spirited catcalls and heedless, often caustic, but always riotous laughter. Humor held sway.

Even the best of the period's independent black companies sometimes reverted to standard darky types to provide levity. Million Dollar Productions—formed in the mid-thirties by black actor, dancer, and longtime Apollo Theatre emcee Ralph Cooper, black stage actor George Randol, and Hollywood producers Harry and Leo Popkin— released a number of movies that, overall, were well-intentioned, serious, and technically superior to most films by their competitors. Among them were *Dark Manhattan* (1937), one of the first black gangster movies; *The Duke Is Tops* (1938), the romantic musical in which Lena Horne made her movie debut; *Reform School* (1939), a drama about a mother's problems with a troublesome child; *Am I Guilty?* (1940), in which Ralph Cooper portrayed an altruistic doctor who gets involved with ghetto hoodlums; and *One Dark Night* (1942), which featured Mantan Moreland in one of his rare dramatic roles. These and other Million Dollar films generally avoided blatant coonery and farce; in fact, they were sometimes criticized for moving too far in the opposite direction. A *Variety* review of *Am I Guilty?* for example, claimed that, "In endeavoring to get away from the usual obvious Negro comedy style, it risks being too high-brow." The writer went on to suggest that whereas "the comparatively sophisticated audience of Harlem" enjoyed the film, "poorly-educated Negroes of the South" might prefer to see low comedy.[28]

On several other occasions, Million Dollar Productions did not shun the obvious or expected. Such comedians as Pigmeat Markham, Nicodemus Stewart, and Mantan Moreland were regularly called on to provide some familiarly uninspired buffoonery that had no hint of either sophistication or black origins.

Most companies producing black movies were even less concerned with avoiding comic stereotypes. Jed Buell, who, according to Thomas Cripps, "exploited any gullible audience—religious pietists, Negroes, even midgets," turned out a score of mostly mediocre films in the thirties and forties. He initiated the black Western genre with *Harlem on the Prairie* (1937); the film starred Herb Jeffries as a singing cowboy and featured Mantan Moreland and Flournoy Miller doing their scared coons bit—with a dark cave substituted for the usual haunted house. In 1940, Buell teamed with Ted Toddy to form Dixie National Pictures and released such films as *Mr. Washington Goes to Town* (1940) with Moreland and Miller, and a sequel, *Lucky Ghosts* (1941), in which Eddie Anderson joined the comic duo. The former was flailed by the black press, and the latter, as the title suggests, was yet another in the series of comic, scary darky farces.

A raft of these predictable quickies was turned out in the late thirties and the forties by white directors and producers such as Buell, Jack and Bert Goldberg, Ted Toddy, Robert Savini, Bud Pollard, Alfred Sack, and Richard Kahn, who produced three more black Westerns—*Bronze Buckeroo* (1939), *Harlem Rides the Range* (1939), and *Two Gun Man from Harlem* (1940)—which also starred Jeffries and cast Flournoy Miller and Spencer Williams in roles as comic sidekicks or cooks. Pigmeat Markham, John "Rastus" Murray, Stepin Fetchit, Sam McDaniel, Eddie Green, Johnny Lee, and many other comedians as well appeared as comic foils used in many instances exactly as black comics were in mainstream movies.

The most genuine instances of black comedy in race films emerged in revues or entertainment showcases. Produced for distribution in theatres within black communities and most often ignored by white audiences and critics, these shorts and features represent the only unadulterated record of the humor of many of the finest black ethnic comedians.

Although the short films usually concentrated on music, some did feature prominent comedians. A widely distributed outtake from *Hi-De-Ho* featured the Dusty Fletcher "Open the Door, Richard" routine. Stepin Fetchit was called on to portray the unresponsive roommate in Robert Savini's *Richard's Answer*, which was also released in the late forties. The comic's Laziest Man in the World act was perfect for the role. Fetchit, appearing in nightshirt and sleeping cap in this ten-minute short, had merely to stay in character and deliver a monologue that approximated his stage routine:

> I was laying here dreamin' everybody was tryin' to wake me up. . . . Why I have such a dream like that? I ain' botherin' nobody, just tendin' to my own business, doin' nothin', restin' up . . .

With Earl Bostic and his orchestra providing a catchy musical background and singer Flores Marmon attempting to persuade Fetchit to get out of bed and open the door with seductive overtures over the telephone, the comic dialogue escalates. A drowsy Fetchit asks, "Who's that on that phone? My roommate's downstairs knocking, tell'um I hear'um, Jones. Rave all he wanna, but tell'um I'm sure. I ain' goin' open that door." Then questions Marmon, "What size hair is you got? I sorta recognize yo' voice but yo' breath sound like you been eatin' a onion." Finally, the exhausted Fetchit hangs up the phone and, lying down again, announces, "Right now, I'mo finish a little nap I started week befo' last. I ain' goin' open that door."[29]

In a similar manner, Pigmeat Markham appeared in some short films that were essentially recreations of his stage act. *One Big Mistake* (1940), for instance, was a "featurette" based on a slapstick routine that, according to Markham, he reworked for the camera. In this bit, the straightman approaches three comedians and offers them some advice on how to treat a woman. Two of the comics try the suggested tactic and return to announce that the advice works: "It sure does work—you gotta treat 'em rough and make 'em like it." Markham's girlfriend is not so easily manipulated. When he approaches her, she says, "Boy, who the devil do you think you're talkin' to?" Then, in his words, "she knocks me down and beats me and kicks me all over the set." After the straightman returns and reminds him that he was supposed to make her like it, the browbeaten Markham says, "I can treat her rough—but I'll be doggone if I can make her *like* it." The skit was little more than an average sample of the vaudeville or burlesque theatre humor of the period, but it did display Markham's comic talent in a more or less uncompromised fashion.[30]

Markham's screen appearances, however, were at best checkered. Later in the forties, he and John "Rastus" Murray also appeared in a series of Toddy Pictures features that awkwardly grafted coon clichés onto makeshift melodramatic scenarios. In the comic mystery *Fight That Ghost* (1946), for instance, the comic duo literally run through walls trying to escape the imaginary spooks pursuing them. This movie, like *Bronze Buckeroo, Lucky Ghosts,* and a raft of mainstream Hollywood films spotlighting frightened black comics, clearly illustrates the difference between the artful telling of a ghost story—as seen in Bert Williams's stage routine or Tim Moore's appearance in Micheaux's *Darktown Revue*—and the slapstick reenactment of the scared coon scenario. Not coincidentally, when similar scenes were enacted by white comedians—Abbott and Costello, for example—one member of the comic team usually resisted the humorously rendered but nevertheless craven urge to headlong flight. With few exceptions, black comedians were uniformly portrayed as being innately fainthearted. Comedy, in these instances, was merely an affirmation of the mainstream conception of African-American racial identity.

The most unadulterated comedy emerged in race movies that showcased black entertainers with little impediment from hackneyed plots borrowed from mainstream movies. Without the need to shape their humor around familiar social roles, black comedians had license to present current stage comedy with less distortion. The routines featured in Oscar Micheaux's *Darktown Revue* are appropriate examples. Even in these instances, however, filmmakers, whether white or black, as well as comedians were intent upon presenting the most socially acceptable face of black humor. The overriding theme of assimilation shaped the mass media presentation of African-American humor during the thirties, forties, and early fifties. Therefore, much of the cynicism and nearly all off-color barbs were excluded from motion pictures— even race films. The result was an emphasis on light, slapstick comedy that deliberately avoided both controversy and the kind of risqué suggestiveness frequently heard on race records.

Big Timers (1946), an Astor Pictures/All-American Pictures release starring Stepin Fetchit and Moms Mabley, was among the first of these films. While Fetchit was free to exhibit more of the wit and trickster aspect of his darky caricature, the more cynical side of Mabley's humor (by this time, a central part of her stage act) was noticeably absent.

Two years later, Josh Binney directed two All-American Pictures releases, *Killer Diller* and *Boarding House Blues,* that were even less restricted by plot or storyline. *Killer Diller* strung a succession of musical and comedy routines on a thin plot involving a magician whose disappearing act goes haywire and disrupts performances at an all-black theatre. The skeletal plot allowed Binney to shoot most of the film in a theatre before a black audience. Dusty Fletcher stars as the inept magician and is supported by a cast that includes Moms Mabley, Butterfly McQueen, George Wiltshire (longtime straightman for Fletcher and Pigmeat Markham), Nat King Cole, and Andy Kirk and his orchestra. Fletcher is rambunctious and mildly suggestive as he performs a few set pieces with McQueen, but Moms Mabley is curiously disengaged here, uncharacteristically having to prod the live audience for laughter. Although its inane, Keystone Kops–inspired chase scenes are distracting, the movie manages to capture some of the tenor of a live stage show.

Boarding House Blues was also an entertainment showcase and cast Mabley as a kind of house mother to a group of struggling entertainers who are about to be evicted by a greedy landlord. Humor is more prominent in this film as Mabley, although her material is still restricted, finds room to display a bit of the cynicism that marked her comedy. In addition, Dusty Fletcher does some turns on his drunk routine; a stuttering Johnny Lee displays a comic side not shown as Calhoun on *Amos 'n' Andy*; and John "Spider Bruce" Mason (the originator of the "Open the Door, Richard" bit) offers a burlesque routine in which he outwits and shames a rival for the attention of a beautiful woman. The finale—an impromptu show by the tenants—not only raises enough money to fend off the landlord but justifies another round of comedy sketches.

By the mid-fifties, as the push for assimilation reached its peak and the very idea of race films loomed as regressive, Studio Films produced some of the last movies made for theatres in black communities. *Jazz Festival* (1954) was a variety showcase presenting the top jazz artists of the day; it was followed by *Rock 'n' Roll Revue* and *Rhythm and Blues Revue,* both released in 1955. These films eliminated any pretense of plot and simply presented an array of black musical and comic entertainers on stage at various Harlem theatres. Apollo Theatre emcee and comedian Willie Bryant introduced the acts and engaged in some between-performance banter. In addition to musicians such as Ruth Brown, Nat King Cole, Count Basie, Duke Ellington, Sarah Vaughan, Dinah Washington, Cab Calloway, Joe Turner, and Lionel Hampton, the films featured comic acts by Leonard Reed, Mantan Moreland, and Nipsey Russell.[31]

Moreland and Russell offered a variety of standard stage routines in these films, including the "Indefinite Talk" bit, and Moreland displayed a comic range that was far more expansive than the eye-rolling buffoonery that he perfected in Hollywood films. Bryant, in brief routines with Honi Coles and Cholly Atkins, Leonard Reed, Nipsey Russell, and even the surprisingly funny Dizzy Gillespie, was an accomplished straightman. Finally, while these variety showcases captured the tenor of black stage shows, striving for decorum, they sacrificed much of the earthiness of the humor.

In fact, race films generally avoided the risqué elements of black humor as well as its more biting satirical overtones. It was genuine black stage comedy all right, but it was selectively chosen. Although their targeted market was black, most producers of race films were unwilling to risk bringing more controversial elements of African-American humor to the screen. Much of what they might have filmed, in any case, would not have gotten past the censors. By the late forties and early fifties, black public humor—at least on stage—had begun reflecting the cynicism and frankness that characterized black street humor. Mainstream America was not prepared for that type of assault on its morality and national character, as such comedians as Lenny Bruce and, to a lesser extent, Redd Foxx would soon discover.

It was no accident that Foxx, Slappy White, and other comics whose material was more aggressively double-edged did not appear in black genre entertainment revues; nor that Moms Mabley was so obviously disengaged in *Killer Diller,* since her usual routines were much too indelicate to be filmed. The choice of Mantan Moreland (whose vaudeville and Hollywood movie experience had prepared him for moderating his humor) and Nipsy Russell (who, according to Jack Schiffman, son of former Apollo Theatre owner Frank Schiffman, along with Bill Cosby "is the least ethnic of all black comics") perfectly suited the desired aim of these films. Moreland and Russell were both outstanding comedians and, so long as Russell avoided the social satire that he displayed on stage, they provided acceptably inoffensive humor.

Still, black genre films left a rare visual record of some genuinely funny performances by Butterbeans and Susie, Willie Bryant, Leonard Reed, George Wiltshire, Dusty Fletcher, John "Spider Bruce" Mason, John "Rastus" Murray, Pigmeat Markham, and many others. Moreover, the films presented such comic performers as Stepin Fetchit, Mantan Moreland, Flournoy Miller, Tim Moore, and Moms Mabley—to name a few—in a darker but, ironically, more revealing light than that in which they were seen in Hollywood movies or later on television.

Ultimately, race records provided a less sanitized sample of early twentieth-century black humor than did black genre films. The recording industry was not subjected to the rigid censorship imposed on motion pictures. Although often banned on radio, comedy routines and songs presented on phonograph records could reflect risqué or earthy aspects of black humor that were taboo in films. From such recordings as Bessie Smith's "Need a Little Sugar in My Bowl" ("Need a little hot dog between my roll. . . . Move your finger, drop somethin' in my bowl") and Speckled Red's "Dirty Dozens," on to such rhythm and blues recordings as Bull Moose Jackson's "I Want a Bow-Legged Woman" or Hank Ballard's "Work With Me Annie" and "Annie Had a Baby" ("Can't work no more"), race records regularly tapped a suggestive, bawdy aspect of black humor that was suppressed in motion pictures.[32]

Nowhere is that clearer than on the raft of so-called "blue" recordings that Redd Foxx made. Foxx was first recorded by black record company owner Dootsie Williams in the early fifties. Although Williams branched out to rhythm and blues recordings (the Penguins' "Earth Angel" was released on his Doontone label), his line of risqué party and comedy records by Foxx, Ruby Ray Moore, Hattie Noel, and others remained the company's mainstay. Foxx was the company's star performer, and his bawdy underground or race record comedy had made him famous in black communities long before Sanford's junkyard became one of television's most popular domiciles. By the seventies, Ruby Ray Moore was recording some of the most explicit and bawdy toasts and ballads from the fringe world of black hustlers and pimps; they went far beyond Foxx's records. Those early records offer a sample of the mostly risqué and often satirical comedy that many African-Americans sampled when mainstream America, enthralled with the likes of "Uncle Miltie," considered such humor scandalous.[33]

Foxx pulled few punches, spicing his stage routines and records with double-entendres and focusing on the scatological and sexual in the placid fifties when the mere mention of sex was considered outrageous: "What's the difference between a pickpocket and a peeping Tom?" one of his less explicit gags asks. "A pickpocket snatches watches."

Although off-color jokes, many of the locker room variety, peppered Foxx's humor, he also leveled his comedy at more serious matters. On the poverty during the Depression, he quipped, "My father said, 'The garbage man is here,' and my mother said, 'Ask him to leave a couple of bags.'" He also gibed about racial bigotry at a time when most comedians assiduously sidestepped the issue:

> My great, great grandfather, Redd Foxx the first, was one of the first black politicians in Mississippi. He ran for the border . . . and made it!

> See, blacks have had white folks fooled for years with one word—*boss.* "Well, good night, boss," "Yes sir, boss." Boss spelled backward is double-S, O-B, and that's two of 'em. That's right, "Good night, you son of a bitch, you."[34]

The Redd Foxx albums, usually kept in the back of record collections, beyond sight of "polite" Negro company, were seldom mentioned at racially mixed gatherings. An underground source of uncensored black humor, these early recorded examples of comic routines and monologues popular in black cabarets and the black stage circuit were among the first of their kind to be made available to the general public. Although at the time of their release they were considered more contraband than mere race records, the albums were as essentially connected to the core or unassimilated black community as were the original Okeh releases of the twenties. The only other place that African-Americans might turn to see or hear public performances that matched them in authenticity was on stage at black nightclubs, cabarets, or segregated theatres on the "chitlin' circuit." Those were the public arenas where black humor flourished with the least distortion. Generally, however, as Sidney Poitier suggested, non-black America had still seen only a caricature of authentic black humor.

9.

---●●●●●●●●●●●●●●●●●●●●●●●●●●●---

THE THEATRE OWNERS

BOOKING ASSOCIATION

AND THE APOLLO

THEATRE . . .

changing the joke and

slipping the yoke

15

PIGMEAT MARKHAM

16

MOMS MABLEY

PEOPLE ALWAYS ENJOYED THE LOW-STYLE COMEDY OF THEIR HERITAGE. IT WAS THE SAME WITH THE BLACKFACE COMEDIAN; HE NOT ONLY MADE PEOPLE LAUGH AT HIM AND HIS PEOPLE, HE ALSO MADE FUN OF OTHER RACES AND NATIONALITIES.

—SAMMY DAVIS, JR.

MY UNCLE WAS A COMIC TOO. MY UNCLE WAS A PART OF A TEAM. HE WAS AROUND DURING THE OLD DAYS. . . . YOU KNOW WHEN THE TEAMS HAD NAMES LIKE OFF AND ON . . . UP AND DOWN AND UNDER AND OVER AND UNDER AND STOP AND GO. MY UNCLE BELONGED TO A COMEDY TEAM CALLED WELL ENOUGH AND BAD ENOUGH. AND, UH, THEY WERE DOING ALL RIGHT. THEN BAD ENOUGH GOT MARRIED. MY UNCLE STARTED WORKING ALONE. . . . HE WAS DOING WELL ENOUGH.

—FLIP WILSON

THERE IS A TRADITION AT THE APOLLO THEATRE THAT HAS BEEN BUILT UP OVER THE YEARS. IT'S CALLED BORROWING FROM THE BEST. YOU SEE THE APOLLO THEATRE IS UPTOWN. BUT MANY PERFORMERS FROM DOWNTOWN WOULD COME UPTOWN TO SIT IN THIS THEATRE AND COPY DOWN WHAT THE UPTOWN PEOPLE WERE SAYING SO THEY COULD TAKE IT DOWNTOWN. SO THAT MANY OF THE FAMOUS COMICS WOULD COME AND SIT RIGHT WHERE YOU ALL ARE—WELL, NOT REALLY—MOSTLY IN THE BACK, BECAUSE THEY HAD PAPER AND PENCIL AND THEY WOULD COPY DOWN WHAT THE UPTOWN PERSON WAS SAYING AND THEN TAKE IT DOWNTOWN. MANY DANCERS, CHOREOGRAPHERS, CAME UPTOWN TO COPY DOWN WHAT THEY SAW UPTOWN AND TAKE IT DOWNTOWN WHERE PEOPLE THOUGHT IT WAS NEW AND INVENTIVE AND THEY HAD CREATED IT DOWNTOWN. BUT THEY HADN'T! THEY SAW IT UPTOWN AND KEPT IT QUIET ABOUT WHAT PART OF TOWN THEY SAW IT AROUND WHEN THEY WROTE IT DOWN.

—BILL COSBY[1]

I

While white producers or directors nearly always selected and determined the comedy heard on race records and seen in black movies, black performers on stage had more leeway in shaping the content of their acts. It was standard procedure to modify or shift emphasis in stage acts to suit the tastes of specific audiences. Within the limits of a particular repertoire, routines could be subtly altered and gags took on the more or less bawdy or assertive tone established by the crowd.

Generally, black acts that were popular or successful enough to move into the mainstream—Broadway shows, big-time vaudeville (the Keith and Orpheum circuits), or, later, Hollywood films and cabarets catering to white or mixed audiences—were most constricted in the type of entertainment they presented. They were usually pressured to present whitewashed versions of their music and, in comedy, to affirm basic racial stereotypes ("come black") and eliminate overt social satire.

By the late nineteenth century, however, black performers had found an outlet for stage humor that was less restricted. In shows traveling the rural South and Midwest and playing primarily before black audiences, like the so-called "jig shows" that followed large carnivals and circuses, black comics still appeared in blackface and offered many of the same minstrel-like routines seen in mixed arenas. But there was less emphasis on "playing the fool" or coming black, and gags about segregation and injustice often took on a different tenor.

As more black entertainers emerged and black audiences swelled, mainstream resistance to socializing with blacks as well as the lure of a profitable enterprise prompted businessmen to organize a theatre circuit that both showcased these footloose performers and catered to the black masses who followed them. In 1907, F. A. Barrasso, a Memphis-based Italian businessman who owned several theatres in the South, founded the Theatre Owners Booking Association. The TOBA expanded rapidly and, at its peak in the twenties, included more than forty theatres throughout the country. The TOBA and several smaller theatrical circuits—one started in 1913 by Sherman S. Dudley, a black comedian and former minstrel—provided an extensive network of theatres in which the rapidly expanding circle of black entertainers could be showcased. Among the better-known outlets were the Palace in Memphis, the Lyric in New Orleans, the Royal in Baltimore, the Howard in Washington, D.C., the Regal and Monogram in Chicago, the Standard and Earle in Philadelphia, and the Lincoln and Lafayette in Harlem. Most of the prestigious urban theatres were owned by whites, but except when a small section was roped off for non-blacks, the audiences were consistently Negro. There were also many smaller theatres, among them the Globe in St. Louis, the Bijou in Nashville, the Lincoln in Kansas City, and the Douglas in Macon, Georgia. The tour also included stops in cities such as Birmingham, Shreveport, Louisville, Richmond, Atlanta, Dallas, Houston, Cincinnati, Cleveland, Pittsburgh, and Detroit.[2]

The TOBA booked individual acts or complete companies such as "Silas Green from New Orleans" or "Gonzelle White and Her Jazz Band"; engagements ranged from one-nighters to week-long stints. In one sense, the TOBA was a godsend for struggling black performers; it created a tour that offered bookings for extended periods and eliminated the desperate search for the next engagement that plagued all but the top acts. And since the association could effectively determine which artists were playing specific theatres, it partially offset the sometimes unethical dealings of small-time theatre owners who were known to withhold payment or cancel bookings at whim.

Still, there were drawbacks. Theatre owners did not pay traveling expenses, so many artists avoided schedules involving long-distance travel; marginally paid, minor acts barely broke even on those tours. And many of the "white-run theatres provided pretty squalid working conditions," Giles Oakley writes in *The Devil's Music: A History of the Blues.* "In some, artists would dress underneath the stage behind thin partitions, come out through the orchestra pit and climb precariously up a ladder, hoping to get on stage before the lights came up." Ethel Waters recalled in her autobiography, *His Eyes Are on the Sparrow:* "Of all the rinky-dink dumps I played, nothing was worse than the Monogram Theatre in Chicago." It had paper-thin walls and was near the El, so "you stopped singing—or telling a joke—every time a train passed," then continued when the noise died down. "You dressed away downstairs with the stoker," where you had to stoop over to get into costume, "then you came up to the stage on a ladder that looked like those on the old-time slave ships."[3]

Perhaps most distressing, the circuit included extensive travel in the South, where blacks, and particularly black entertainers, were not welcomed by the town fathers. Engagements often required traveling hundreds of miles by bus through towns displaying signs that warned, "No Niggers Allowed!" Finding sleeping accommodations was always difficult; segregated restaurants and diners often meant traveling miles out of the way to eat or, worse, simply going hungry.

Some Southern theatres were owned or managed by unscrupulous, outspoken racists who, while profiting from African-American performers and patrons, displayed outright contempt for Negroes. Charles P. Bailey, owner of Atlanta's 81 Decatur Street Theatre, was one of many. Described by Ethel Waters as a "tough-bitten old Georgia cracker," Bailey was one of the most powerful men in Atlanta during the teens and twenties and, with the help of local police, ran his theatre like an antebellum plantation. According to Waters, he often harassed female performers; after an argument, he beat Bessie Smith and had her thrown in jail. During a heated disagreement about working conditions, Waters responded to one of Bailey's outbursts ("No Yankee nigger bitch is telling me how to run my theatre") with, "You and no other cracker sonofabitch can tell me what to do." Leaving her fee and many of her costumes behind, Waters had to sneak far enough out of town by horse and buggy to get to an out-of-the-way railroad station where she could buy a ticket to leave Atlanta and escape Bailey's fury.[4]

Many towns also had curfews for blacks, which meant that overnight travel involved breaching local laws. Working in those towns often required obtaining a pass in order to leave the theatre after a performance. Atlanta was one of the cities that banned blacks from the streets after certain hours and, as Waters's experience indicates, Bailey and other theatre owners used the law to control performers. Moreover, as in many other areas of the South, Atlanta whites were not pleased to see "their Nigras" leaving town. Doll Thomas, a minstrel show performer and later a projectionist at the Apollo Theatre, recalled an early experience in Atlanta. Having witnessed the humiliation of a fellow performer who had attempted to enter the front door of the theatre, Thomas decided it was time to go: "A week later," he recalled, "I went to the railroad station, put my money down and said, 'Give me a ticket to New York.' That red-faced cracker looked at me and said, 'Ain't no niggers leavin' here. We don't allow them out.' That man refused, absolutely refused, to sell me a ticket."[5]

Soon, to many black entertainers, the acronym TOBA became widely known simply as "Tough on Black Asses."

Still, TOBA looms as one of the most important chapters in African-American entertainment history. It provided the principal stage for the transition from minstrelsy's rigidly maintained stereotypes to a performance style that more accurately reflected the majority tastes of the black community. Just as, later, Apollo Theatre audiences were known to be demanding and impatient, TOBA circuit audiences were outspoken and inhospitable to acts that either were lackluster or strayed too far from preferred black performance style. There was no hook to drag inept performers off the stage, not even (as on Amateur Night at the Apollo) a Porto Rico or Executioner to rush out and escort bungling acts off when the boos reached a crescendo. But audiences would greet unpopular acts with derisive catcalls, invective, and an occasional flying missile. That was usually enough to tighten up a performer's act. Moreover, in addition to providing an exacting training ground for the best of the black performers—Bill Robinson, Bessie Smith, Stepin Fetchit, Ethel Waters, Eddie Anderson, Count Basie, and Sammy Davis, Jr., to name a few—for most others, it was practically the *only* outlet.

This was particularly true for comedians. Mainstream America was unprepared to accept black humor that did not clearly mirror minstrelsy's coon images, and middle-class African-Americans, struggling to establish themselves as serious members of the society, zealously resisted any humorous portrayals of blacks.

Still, the insistent condemnation of black comedians by the black middle class established a skewed, negative view of early stage humor that, in retrospect, is simply not justified. Admittedly, most comics who stepped up from medicine and tent shows to the TOBA circuit had not eliminated all traces of the buffoonish stage Negro. Initially, nearly all of them still appeared in burnt-cork makeup, in acts that varied only slightly from routines established in minstrelsy. Like black musicians of the period, they were absorbing accepted mainstream forms (often, distorted versions of their own humor) and infusing those stage exaggerations with the real-life humor they experienced every day in the their own community.

For many, African-American humor, like music, was deeply embedded in the routine activities of daily life. It was part of a matrix of attitudes and behavior that extolled storytelling, individual one-upmanship, verbal play, and the ability to transcend mundane circumstances with spirited jesting. That humor was, no doubt, regularly seen then, as it is now, in the camaradarie displayed at barber shops and lodge meetings, the ritualized repartee of signifying, or the spontaneous quips that enliven all but the most sedate bourgeois interactions between blacks. Bringing it to the stage required not only subtly altering images established by minstrelsy's dim-witted stage Negro but also absorbing standard theatrical comic elements (slapstick, burlesque show blackout routines, and vaudeville gags) and molding them into cohesive stage routines that had some basis in real life.

Generally, the themes explored on stage had nothing to do with non-black, mainstream existence—either imitation of it or reaction to it. Black comedians, like blues artists, primarily focused on the immediate problems of their own day-to-day existence—friendships, finances, marital and sexual relationships, the pleasures of eating and drinking. In a rigidly segregated society, whites were largely extraneous to their existence and, consequently, were absent from their humor. When non-blacks did emerge as components in the humor, it was usually in regard to either violent confrontations (such as the period's rampant lynchings) or instances of white greed and deception; these experiences were usually treated with the utmost discretion. Early twentieth-century black humor was the creation of the black common man who, even more than the small, gradually expanding Negro middle class, was rigorously excluded from mainstream society.

So it is not surprising that the stage comedy that flourished on the TOBA circuit was unnoticed by the mainstream and frowned upon by bourgeois blacks. Middle-class Negroes, embarrassed as much by the comic antics of their lower-class brethren as by the earthiness of the blues, disparaged both as demeaning to the race, but under certain conditions, they would attend. During the twenties, for example, the Howard Theatre in Washington admitted only light-skinned, presumably middle-class Negroes to select Sunday night performances, prompting some entertainers to boycott the shows. Mostly, however, the black masses (and a small coterie of white comedians and musicians who observed and usurped the best of the material for their own acts) were the only consistently enthusiastic followers.

TOBA, with its all-black audiences and often shabby, ill-kept theatres, was the perfect incubator for a new form of black stage comedy. "The comedian was the most important part of the show," according to Redd Foxx and Norma Miller, "so the show with the best comic was usually the most successful." And the comedy style that evolved in this all-black context was shaped as much by the common folks, on whose experiences it was largely based, as it was by the performers. The ever-present monitoring by African-Americans who were firmly steeped in black folk culture assured that the comedy did not become overly burdened with cosmetic, show-biz rigmarole, and the shabby theatres in which it was presented must have further reminded its practitioners of the repressed condition of its underclass creators. During the teens, twenties, and early thirties, the style matured, moving closer to a genuine reflection of its roots and establishing a theatrical foundation on which comedians such as Slappy White, Redd Foxx, Nipsy Russell, Timmie Rogers, Flip Wilson, and Richard Pryor would eventually build their stage humor.[6]

II

- - - - - - - - - -

An essential part of that foundation was the classic comic routines created on the TOBA circuit. Although one or more comedians inevitably claimed credit for developing the routines, in most instances their origin is as obscure as many of the now-forgotten performers who contributed to their slow evolution. John "Spider Bruce" Mason's "Open the Door, Richard" and Miller and Lyles's "Indefinite Talk" bits were extremely popular among black audiences, but Pigmeat Markham's "Here Come de Judge" routine is best known because of its exposure on *Rowan and Martin's Laugh In* during the late sixties. Although some insist that it surfaced in the early days of TOBA, Markham contends that "De Judge" evolved out of a routine that originated at Harlem's Alhambra Theatre in 1928, in which he appeared as a magistrate. "Negroes in the audience loved it," Markham wrote, "probably because the judge, the pompous oppressor of the Negro in so many Southern towns, was being taken down a peg by a Negro comedian. . . . I got the idea that I could turn the character into a full act." And so he did. As performed by Markham, the routine nearly always started with another comic announcing Markham's entrance: "Hear ye, hear ye, court is in session and here come de judge. Here come de judge, here come de judge . . ." In *Amateur Night at the Apollo*, Ralph Cooper claimed credit for the bit ("Pigmeat became famous for that routine, written by yours truly") and offered a more elaborate version of the introduction:

Hear ye, hear ye the Court of Swing
Is now about ready to do its thing.
Don't want no tears, don't want no jive,
Above all things, don't want no lies.
Our judge is hip, his boots are tall
He'll judge you jack, big or small.
So fall in line, his stuff is sweet,
Peace, brothers, here's Judge Pigmeat.

Pigmeat would then enter to a chorus of "Here come de judge, here come de judge . . ." and convene his farcical court. He sometimes began with, "The judge is higher'n a Gawgia pine! Everybody's gonna do some time this mawnin' " or, when more ornery, "The judge is mean dis mawnin', I'm goin' start by givin' myself thirty days—next case!" This was followed by one of several blackout bits featuring different comedians brought before the judge. One of the more popular turns on this routine followed Pigmeat's anouncement that everybody would do some time:

Lawyer: Your honor, that's not fair! I object!

Judge: *Object!* You object! You all the time comin' in here and objectin' me outa decisions. Why man, I got all these years in my book and somebody's gotta do 'em! Ain't gonna be me! Where's your first client . . . he's *guilty!*

Client: Judge, please, don't you remember me? I'm the man who introduced you to your wife!

Judge: Introduced me to my wife? *Life* . . . you sonofagun!

Whatever the origin of this routine, ultimately Pigmeat Markham established it as his own. As he wrote in his autobiography, "I added little bits and pieces down through the years—and new jokes all the time, but the format is always the same." It became one of the most popular comedy routines on the TOBA tour and at the Apollo Theatre.[7]

Nearly as popular was the "Go Ahead and Sing" routine, which, according to Redd Foxx and Norma Miller, was developed by Henry Drake and John "Rastus" Murray in 1925. There were many adaptations by mainstream comedians, including a version involving a street vendor and his partner that surfaced in an Abbott and Costello film during the forties. In the Drake and Murray original, two men decide to earn some money by having one sing on a street corner while the other collects money from pedestrians. When the first comic begins, however, a cop approaches and tells him he can't sing in the area. The singer's partner immediately intercedes, questioning the policeman's authority, but the singer assures the cop that he will stop. When the policeman leaves, the partner tells his friend, "We've got a right to stand here and sing too. Ain't no flatfoot gonna tell us what to do. You go ahead and sing. When he comes back I'll talk to him." The singer starts in again, and the cop storms back:

Cop: Wait a minute. Didn't I tell you not to sing on this corner?

Singer: Yes, I know, officer, but my partner said it was all right.

Cop: I don't care what your partner said. I said you can't sing here. This is the last time I'm gonna tell you. If I have to come back here again, I'm gonna take this billy and put it upside your head. Then I'm gonna take you to jail!

As the cop walks away, the singer's partner yells, "You ain't gonna hit me in my head!" The policeman returns and begins beating the singer over the head, stopping only when the singer pleads for mercy. But as the cop turns to walk away again, the partner says, "You got a lot of nerve, hitting a citizen. You ain't gonna hit me no more." The partner continues agitating and signifying as the cop beats the singer off the stage and the lights go down. It was an exaggerated, comic interpretation of the familiar street gimmick of putting someone else "in a trick" by signifying on a third party (perhaps best seen in the folk ballad, "The Signifying Monkey") and never failed to bring howls from the audience.[8]

Comedians on the TOBA circuit, like most funnymen of the period, did not communicate directly with their audience; on Keith's vaudeville circuit, for example, performers were explicitly told not to address anyone in the audience. Stand-up comedy and its unmediated dialogue with audiences, although it was foreshadowed by minstrel show stump speeches and the monologues of humorists such as Bert Williams and Will Rogers, did not become the principal form of stage humor until after the Depression.

Most black comedy avoided direct interaction until the fifties. In *Yes I Can*, Sammy Davis, Jr., pointed out the limitations of that approach. "Most Negro performers work in a cubicle," he wrote. "They'd run on, sing twelve songs, dance, and do jokes—but not to people. The jokes weren't done like Milton Berle was doing them, to the audience, they were done between the men on stage, as if they didn't have the right to communicate with the people out front." The persistence of that approach, even after mainstream comedians such as Fred Allen, Jack Benny, and Milton Berle began experimenting with direct monologue humor, reflected black comics' second-class status both on and off stage.[9]

They were aware that, for many non-blacks, their comic antics on stage were a true reflection of Negro behavior. A black performer who demanded a personal response would have transgressed a boundary by suggesting an equality intolerable to most non-blacks. Still, on the TOBA circuit, a few black comedians did adopt the stand-up approach; despite their popularity among black patrons and the acclaim of their peers, they were shunned by white bookers and generally unknown outside black cabarets and theatres.

Leonard Reed and Willie Bryant, both of whom frequently worked the Apollo, were two of the earliest. Reed, who started in show business as a Charleston dancer, was part of a team called Pen and Ink in the twenties, played the TOBA circuit with the Whitman Sisters show, worked with Bryant in a comedy act called Feet and Brains in the thirties, and later created a comedy act with boxing champ Joe Louis. Although he began doing stand-up in the musical comedy *Hot and Sweet* in the thirties, his comedy routines depended as much on slapstick and dance as on verbal wit. Bryant, a perennial favorite as an Apollo emcee and comedian, was called "the mayor of Harlem" at one time, and because of his funny rap was "Brains" in the Reed-Bryant team. Along with Reed and Timmie Rogers, he appeared on a short-lived television show in the late forties and hosted a series of variety showcase films released in the fifties. Although Reed and Joe Louis took their act to Las Vegas after the champ retired and both Reed and Bryant were well known in black entertainment circles, neither rose to mainstream stardom.

Many performers who saw him insist that Allen Drew was the best of the early black stand-up comedians and among the best in all of show business. According to Honi Coles, he played black clubs from the late twenties to the fifties, and Leonard Reed claims that "he didn't work theatres because his material was too blue." He was known as "the black Milton Berle" and, according to Coles, was "one of the best one-line comics that ever lived. He'd come on with a cigar in his hand and go right into the gags. He was so fast you laughed three gags later, you know, you're still catching up with him. All the white comics, including Berle, came uptown to see him. He was the fastest comic alive. . . . But in the forties he went back home to Chicago and finally became a policeman. He couldn't make any money."[10]

Drew's predicament provides a clue to the nature of black comedy both on and off the TOBA circuit. It basically adhered to entrenched vaudeville and burlesque formats, presenting skits, brief blackout bits, and situational humor in which two or more comics (nearly always in blackface) worked and reworked established routines. Consequently, most black circuit comedians worked in virtual anonymity. Many routines were more famous than the comedians who performed them.

In addition to established situational routines (such as "Here Come de Judge" or "Open the Door, Richard"), most often comedians worked in pairs and established a dialogue involving rapid responses to each other's patter, as in the "Indefinite Talk" routine. Comics walked onto the stage, chatting with one another, allowing audiences to overhear their routines. This setup characterized almost all of the early black circuit humor. A typical example is the following Tim Moore and Andrew Tribel routine:

Moore: Boy, you remember dah other night when the rain come up.

Tribel: Yeah.

Moore: Boy, dat rain was a wang, wasn't it?

Tribel: Oh man!

Moore: Well, I was comin' by that house—me an' another Hawaiian boy—and, ah we was walkin' along. Then I didn't wanna get wet. . . . So I said, "I'm goin' in here and get me a room." So I walked up dere. I thought somebody was livin' in dah house.

Tribel: Did you?

Moore: When I got up on dah porch, I went to ring dah bell. . . . Fore I could touch dah bell, dah bell rung by itself and I ain't had no finger on it.

Tribel: De bell rung and you ain't never touched it?

Moore: Ain't touched it.

Tribel: Ah . . . dat's mag-i-nation.

Moore: Dat's what you say. Boy, dat house is haunted! There's a gang of ghost hang out down dere. Boy! And I went to put my hand on the knob to open dah do'h. Fore I could touch dah knob, dah knob turned by itself. And dah do'h flew open and nobody home. What kinda do'h was that!

Tribel: I can explain dat. Maybe dah wind blowed it open.

Moore: Boy, dere's always a solution to every problem. You win the first point in dah debate. The wind coulda blowed dat do'h open.

Tribel: Dah wind blowed it open!

Moore: Yeah but dere ain't no wind turned that knob![11]

An early variation on this theme emerged in husband and wife teams who combined the comic patter with dance. One of the most successful acts in the teens was the husband and wife team of Stringbeans and Sweetie May. According to the historians Marshall and Jean Stearns, "They played only Negro theatres and their act was created of, by, and for Negroes." One performance at the Glove Theatre in Jacksonville, Florida, opened with Sweetie May sashaying onto the stage in a sexy gown and singing a blues tune as she deftly performed the Buck and Wing, one of the popular dances of the time. Then Stringbeans emerged wearing clownish attire and, as was popular among city dandies on and off stage, sporting a large diamond in one of his front teeth. "The force of his presence [was] so powerful that the audience fell silent." After reeling off a tale about duping a gullible white policeman, Stringbeans moved to the piano and began one of the blues songs that usually initiated their comic verbal sparring:

**Listen no-good womens
Stop kickin' us men aroun'
Cause us men gonna be your iceberg
And send you sinkin' down.**

As the routine continues, Stringbeans alternately comes on as an arrogant dandy or a servile, pleading "Monkey Man" (a henpecked husband, in blues jargon), wrenching laughter from both characterizations even as he occasionally adds some acute social observations:

**White folks got all the money
Colored got all the signs
Signs won't buy you nothin'
Folks, you better change your mind.**

Combining song, suggestive dance, and acerbic patter, the bit offered a ritualized comic portrayal of some prominent themes in black male-female relationships. Finally, having toyed humorously with some heavily laden, essentially black emotional issues, the pair always reached a kind of affectionate accommodation. It was one of the most popular acts on the TOBA tour.[12]

Butterbeans and Susie, a comedy team that had performed with Stringbeans and Sweetie May, ultimately inherited their routine and became one of the most enduring black stage acts. Jodie Edwards started as a singer and dancer in 1910 and met his partner, Susie Hawthorne, in 1916 when she was part of the chorus of the *Smart Set* show; they were married on stage the next year and developed a song and dance act later. During the early twenties, after "Stringbeans" (his real name is variously given as Butler May and Budd LeMay) died, a promoter advised Edwards to adopt his funny costume and take the name "Butterbeans."

Edwards took his advice, and the team of Butterbeans and Susie was born. Shifting their emphasis to comedy, Butterbeans appeared on stage in tight pants, a bowler hat, and oversized shoes that were in marked contrast to Susie's more stylish gowns. They usually began their act with a duet. Then, after she sang a blues tune, they might join in a cakewalk and begin the comic patter. Like Stringbeans and Sweetie May, their humor often revolved around marital relationships. One of their most popular routines—based on a song so ribald that it was spurned by Okeh Records even though Columbia Records released Bessie Smith's version in 1933—was Susie's rendition of "I Want a Hot Dog for My Roll." Susie, in her usual flirtatious manner, belted out the lyrics: "I want a hot dog without bread you see. 'Cause I carry my bread with me. . . . I want it hot, I don't want it cold. I want it so it fit my roll." And while dancing suggestively, Butterbeans would add such quips as, "My dog's never cold! Here's a dog that long and lean." The double-entendres continued as Susie sang, "I sure will be disgusted, if I don't get my mustard. . . . Don't want no excuse, it's got to have a lot of juice."

Humorous send-ups of marital squabbles were also a part of their act, and they would often punctuate their song and dance routines with snappy quips and lighthearted signifying. One of their funniest and most popular songs, in fact, was "A Married Man's a Fool if He Thinks His Wife Don't Love Nobody but Him." And in another bit, Susie would warn the preening Butterbeans that he was about to be drafted and, while he was gone, she might "leave him for a high yaller." He answers, "If I come home and found you out, baby, you don't live here no more. . . . A ground hog will deliver your mail. There'll be flowers and you won't smell 'em on the day you change your name, baby." The verbal sniping was always in good fun, however, and inevitably the act ended on a humorous note. Susie would sing a more conciliatory tune, and Butterbeans always concluded the act with his hilarious comic dance "the Heebie Jeebies" (sometimes called "the Itch"). As James Cross ("Stump" of Stump and Stumpy) described the dance, "He kept his hands in his pockets and looked like he was itching to death, and when he took his hands out of his pockets and started to scratch all around the beat, the audience flipped."[13]

Despite the often racy material, their act was among the most beloved on the circuit. There was, ironically, something ingenuous and warm about it. The mock hostility and cutting quips aside, Susie was a plumpish, disarmingly attractive woman who exuded charm, and Butterbeans, even when most truculent and loud, projected an aura of cheerfulness and affection. The humorous stage spats were inevitably seen as mock squabbles.

Many of the most popular stage skits used material with strong sexual overtones. Dewey Markham, in fact, acquired his stage name from such an act when he joined the Gonzelle White show in the mid-twenties and eventually replaced Crackshot Hackley as the number-one comic. "Pigmeat," a term with clear sexual connotations in blues lyrics, was the name of a character in the show. Markham played the part and, at the end of the skit, shouted, "I'm Sweet Papa Pigmeat. I got the Jordan River in my hips, and the women is raving to be baptized." The name stuck; as Markham later said, "Pigmeat was my ticket to fame."[14]

In addition to his famous slapstick routines, Markham had a number of spicy burlesque theatre bits that he regularly performed. In one routine, he shows up at a cheap hotel with a beautiful showgirl and asks for a room. The clerk tells him that he must be married to get a room there. A sleazy preacher (Markham's partner, Johnny Lee Long) happens by and Markham quickly asks him to perform a ceremony. Brimming with anticipation, Pigmeat and his "wife" go off to their room. After they leave, a policeman enters, accuses the preacher of being a con man, and arrests him. The snooty clerk immediately calls the newlyweds back to the desk, where they appear in nightclothes:

Clerk: You two have to get your clothes and get out of here. You ain't married!

Pigmeat: Not married! But didn't the reverend just marry us?

Clerk:	He was no reverend, just an old confidence man. The cop just took him away.
Girl:	Then you mean we're not married?
Clerk:	No, and you've got to get out!
Pigmeat:	Well, it's too damn late now! C'mon gal!

Frustrated, but beyond being denied, Pigmeat rushes his "wife" off the stage.[15]

Another of the familiar suggestive routines performed on the circuit was a hospital bit in which Spider Bruce Mason often appeared. Mason —who Honi Coles insisted was, along with Dusty Fletcher, "the funniest of the Apollo Theatre comedians in the early days"—was the originator of "Open the Door, Richard" but, despite recognition by his peers, remained one of the most underrated of all the TOBA funnymen. Working in blackface in the hospital routine, Mason plays an expectant father pacing up and down the corridor outside the maternity ward. The sound of a crying child is heard and, moments afterward, a nurse and an extremely light-skinned doctor come out with two bundles. The nurse shouts, "Twins, your wife has given birth to twins." Anxiously, Mason rushes over and looks at the babies, then steps back as he sees something that disturbs him.

Mason:	How come one of them is so black and the other is so light?
Doctor:	That's just the way they was born. Must come from the father.
Mason:	Yeah, well I don't think I'm gonna pay that bill for $200 I just got.
Doctor:	Here's my half. . . . [Blackout][16]

This type of burlesque-style humor appeared frequently on the TOBA tour. In many instances, the comedians who played the parts were interchangeable. Not only were such featured comics as Markham, Mason, Crackshot Hackley, Dusty Fletcher, Leonard Reed, and Tim Moore called upon to perform the bits, but often band members, singers, and dancers were enlisted. Comedy may have been king in

TOBA shows, but the throne was not restricted purely to comic royalty. "Somehow or another, dancers always always got into the sketches, because they needed bodies," Honi Coles recalled. "You were either a messenger or some other minor character. That's how we learned comedy, filling in during the skits. Eventually, a little of that comedy technique rubs off on you. At one point, a laugh was more important to me than getting a big hand on a dance step."[17]

Although Coles remained a featured tap dancer, he appeared in a comedy act with Bert Howell for a time, and the Coles and Atkins team often spiced their slick dance routine with comic patter. Others who started as dancers ultimately became full-time comedians. Legendary stars Stepin Fetchit, Eddie "Rochester" Anderson, and Bill "Bojangles" Robinson, for instance, all danced on the TOBA circuit before emerging as comedians in motion pictures and on radio and television. Similarly, black circuit funnymen such as Leonard Reed, Willie Bryant, and Dusty Fletcher started out as dancers and used dance extensively in their comedy routines. In fact, Pigmeat Markham claimed that he invented Truckin', a comical dance that became a craze in Harlem during the thirties. And Moms Mabley's shuffle was a popular part of her comedy act long before Muhammad Ali brought his own version to the boxing ring. On the TOBA tour, music and dance were nearly always intricately connected to comedy.

Still, amid these stock routines and variety show embellishments, many acts developed distinctive bits that were purely comic. Boots Hope, for instance, worked in a venerable black comic tradition and was known as one of the TOBA's funniest storytellers or "liars." According to Count Basie, "He could get out there and lie his butt off. . . . When he got going on something that was really just outrageous any way you tried to look at it, he always used to interrupt himself and look right at the audience with his eyes wide open and say . . . 'I ain't lying. I ain't lying.' " Pigmeat Markham, in addition to his "Here Come de Judge" routine, was known for a "scared darky" bit that was set in a graveyard. Dusty Fletcher's stage character was nearly always inebriated, and his trademark line ("Yeah, it's me, and I'm *drunk* again!") introduced a variety of routines. And Jackie Mabley, when she became known as Moms, traded on the portrayal of a slightly lecherous older woman who regularly quipped, "An old man can't do nothing for me but bring me a message from a young one."[18]

Comedy teams, of course, dominated the TOBA, and as Flip Wilson suggested in this chapter's epigraph, the names were often as offbeat as the acts themselves. Step and Fetchit, Pete and Repeat, Moss and Frye, Chuck and Chuckles, Pen and Ink, Stump and Stumpy, Midnight and Daybreak, Buck and Bubbles, Crackshot and Hunter, and Pot, Pans, and Skillet are just a few of the more colorfully named acts. Most of them worked some version of the city slicker and underdog tandem pioneered by Flournoy Miller and Aubrey Lyles, but many had their own signature routines that became famous on the circuit. Moss and Frye, for instance, had a bit they called "Dumb Talk," which featured a barrage of nonsensical, rapid-fire patter. Leonard Reed and Joe Louis featured a unique slapstick boxing routine. Examples are obviously too numerous to mention here, but *The Redd Foxx Encyclopedia of Black Humor* lists over a dozen classic stage bits, and other sources suggest dozens more.[19]

Overall, TOBA humor was characterized by its reliance on situational comedy. Whether single acts, teams, or skits involving three or more players, TOBA acts—with such rare exceptions as Allen Drew, Willie Bryant, or Moms Mabley—spurned monologues or stand-up comedy. Comedians worked within familiar (if sometimes farfetched) dramatic scenarios. It was an approach favored by most of the period's funny-men.

Comedy was also the central attraction in mainstream vaudeville, which was at the height of its popularity during the teens and twenties. Comedy on the TOBA circuit included little or no direct social or political commentary, whereas a few mainstream comedians—most notably Will Rogers—made it their specialty. Reportedly, one of Rogers's earliest departures from his silent cowboy roping act was the offhand comment, "Swingin' a rope's all right—if your neck ain't in it." The audience's response prompted Rogers to add more dialogue and, in years to come, he increasingly spiced his monologues with topical references. Much of his material was based on items from newspapers, and politicians were his favorite targets. When asked if he would run for public office, he commented: "There's already too many comedians in Washington. Competition would be too keen for me." His disarming, rural demeanor and homespun delivery apparently deflected criticism of the cutting satire underlying his humorous observations and, at the height of his career, even his principal targets were admirers.[20]

As one might expect, however, popular black comedians rarely addressed political issues directly. It simply would not have been tolerated. Although the black-inspired characters presented by white interpreters on the *Amos 'n' Andy* radio show regularly commented comically on politics (racial issues, on the other hand, were scrupulously avoided), real black comedians carefully shunned references to the larger society. In an era when anti-Negro sentiment and lynching were at their peak, publicly discarding the mask of naïveté, revealing the aggressive aspects of their humor, and openly challenging tacit assumptions about the nature of black comedy (indeed, about black *nature*) on a circuit that not only regularly toured the deep South but also played theatres owned by outspoken racists would have been suicidal.

Although the classic bits and routines that have been recorded and passed along have few political references, one suspects that, like traveling bluesmen, TOBA comedians occasionally slanted their material for specific audiences and used alternative lines and extemporaneous remarks to reflect the black community's more assertive off-stage humor. While it is innocuous when compared to more recent barbs about the racist nature of the judicial system—among them, Richard Pryor's quip, "I went down there looking for justice, and that's what I found . . . Just Us"—Pigmeat Markham's "Here Come de Judge" routine was one of the more poignant bits of social satire seen on the TOBA circuit.[21]

The absence of social criticism and political satire is largely responsible for the characterization of TOBA as simple or unsophisticated by many critics. Curiously, some black comedians have bolstered that evaluation with their own assessments of African-American humor. Flournoy Miller, for example, just prior to the Broadway opening of his *Shuffle Along of 1933*, offered the following opinion in William Randolph Hearst's *New York American:*

The simplicities of life translated into terms of the human frailties make for the best humor. Which, in a way, explains why the Negro has such a remarkable sense of the comic. . . . And the reason I say the Negro excels in humor because of the simplicities of life is not because the Negro cannot understand humor we characterize as subtle, but because by nature he is unaffected. His problems, his habits and his perspective are confined strictly to his own race. This, too, holds true of the Caucasian race, most of whom lead simple lives. That is why both races laugh at horseplay and slapstick. I maintain, however, that the Negro has a much better developed sense of humor in simplicities than his white brethren because he has not graduated to the more subtle types of comedy.

Revealingly, the journalist conducting this interview qualified Miller's remarks with the caveat, "Miller . . . knows Negro humor. And knows, too, the kind of Negro humor Caucasian audiences appreciate best."[22]

Despite Miller's immense contribution to the development of a stage humor that broke away from minstrel buffoonery, the concept of black humor expressed above seems firmly mired in a mainstream view of Negro life. It is perhaps not surprising when one considers that Miller made his most important creative efforts early in his career, in the teens and twenties, when he and Aubrey Lyles fashioned original comic routines that were widely imitated. Lyles died in 1932 and, afterward, Miller was often simply rehashing comic ideas that had been fresh a decade before. In addition, Miller had left the TOBA circuit and the all-black audiences that originally inspired his performances. Increasingly, he worked on the mainstream vaudeville and Broadway stage or in Hollywood motion pictures as a writer and performer; his notions of what black audiences preferred in comedy and of the simplistic nature of black life were no doubt heavily influenced by that experience.

In fact, with the exception of a few extraordinary comedians such as Will Rogers, Bert Williams, and W. C. Fields, mainstream vaudeville humor was as "simplistic," as dependent on horseplay and slapstick, as was TOBA humor. Joe E. Brown, Jimmy Durante, Abbott and Costello, and even Eddie Cantor relied on physical or low comedy techniques similar to those seen at black circuit theatres such as the Howard, Monogram, and Lafayette. In this context, Miller's assessment provided a comforting message, one that incidentally cast the kind of bland frivolity that *Shuffle Along of 1933* presented in a more favorable light. But if anyone had looked beyond the stage and screen and assessed the humor that, by this time, was appearing in literature as well as on the streets, the superficiality of Miller's remarks would have been revealed.

Miller was correct, however, in observing that, as far as stage humor was concerned, the problems, habits, and perspectives revealed by blacks were "confined strictly to [their] own race." That limitation realistically mirrored the actual predicament of the average Negro during the twenties. The overriding concern was survival and establishing an economic foothold. Despite the Harlem Renaissance's much ballyhooed Negrophilia, for most blacks access to mainstream society was limited to jobs as menials, and appealing to whites for relief was seen largely as a futile endeavor. Common black folks were effectively excluded from the mainstream world and, despite the clamor created by intellectual and bourgeois blacks, generally ignored the white world as long as its activities did not directly affect them. They focused on their own segregated communities and frequently dismissed other concerns with the simple remark, "That's white folks' affairs." Comedy routines on the TOBA focused on that reality while avoiding underlying resentments.

But with the stock market crash of 1929, "white folks' affairs" suddenly intruded in black life. In one sense, the poverty and deprivation that consumed the majority of Americans during the Depression were old hat to many African-Americans. As blues singer Georgia Tom ironically quipped, "I don't feel as depressed, for I didn't have a thing to start with." But, as the situation worsened, and whites were first in line to receive state and local assistance, racial antagonism increased in some quarters. Still, despite cases of terrorism and intimidation when blacks demanded their share of public assistance—and such widely publicized incidents as the Scottsboro case—in many instances the catastrophe brought white and black America closer together. In the South, for example, some biracial tenant farmer unions were formed, and President Roosevelt's New Deal policies, according to some historians, "marked a real turning point in the trends of American race relations." Soup lines were seldom segregated and, even when they were, an underlying sense of common distress eradicated much of the pretense of racial superiority. The Ku Klux Klan, whose terrorism and popularity had soared in the twenties, "became transformed into a largely social organization." Downtrodden, hungry whites begged in Harlem, the South Side in Chicago, and on Memphis's Beale Street as readily as blacks; "Brother, can you spare a dime?" was, most often, a colorless refrain.[23]

Repercussions in the entertainment world were also immediately felt. Big-time vaudeville, already severely strained by network radio and the introduction of sound movies, expired; diminishing patronage compelled theatre owners to close or eliminate more expensive live entertainment and turn to motion pictures. In 1932, New York City's Palace Theatre, the jewel of mainstream vaudeville, closed its doors. Black circuit vaudeville had succumbed even earlier. Black entrepreneur Sherman S. Dudley was forced to sell his theatres and booking agency in 1929. And within the next three years, although some theatres remained open, the TOBA network fell into ruin.

The nation reeled as it experienced its most severe test since the Civil War. African-Americans, devastated more than any other segment of society, joined with others in seeking a political solution to the problem. Black participation in the election of Franklin D. Roosevelt marked the end of African America's regressive allegiance to the party of Lincoln and reflected an assertive attitude toward political participation that would continue escalating until the Civil Rights movement and voter registration drives of the sixties.

But the Depression also unleashed a long-smoldering resentment and militancy that blacks had previously suppressed. In 1935, after reports that a black youth had been killed by a white merchant for allegedly stealing a knife, Harlem citizens went on a rampage. The main targets were the white-owned stores dotting Seventh Avenue and 125th Street. When the violence and looting subsided, two hundred stores had been wrecked. It was probably the first black-initiated riot in American history since Emancipation and marked a distinct shift away from a predominantly passive acceptance of mainstream oppression. As Ralph Cooper noted, "The so-called riots helped end the grand illusion that Harlem was full of happy-go-lucky blacks too busy singin' and dancin' and struttin' to want a slice of the American pie." The hardships of the Depression had elicited an unmistakably aggressive reaction to social injustices; the tolerance threshold had been reached and, increasingly, black diffidence and indirect expression of discontent would give way to overt disdain and outspoken criticism of racial inequities and white pretense of fair treatment.[24]

As entertainers struggled to find work in cabarets, motion pictures, and those theatres still showcasing black acts, comedians began reflecting the black community's more assertive mood.

III

With the closing of many deep South theatres on the TOBA circuit, urban theatres in the North assumed even more importance for black performers. And Harlem, already the mecca of black American entertainment, became even more eminent. Naturally, the struggle for control of this potentially rich enterprise was intense but, by the mid-thirties, Frank Schiffman and the Apollo Theatre had emerged as the pinnacle of black variety entertainment on stage.

The Apollo, however, was not initially Harlem's premier showplace. There were nearly a dozen theatres in Harlem during the teens, most of which did not admit blacks. The major theatres on Seventh Avenue and 125th Street were for whites only. The Crescent and Lincoln, both on 135th Street between Lenox and Fifth avenues, and later the

Lafayette at Seventh Avenue and 132nd Street, allowed black patrons. By the twenties, as the so-called Black Belt spread, theatres such as the Alhambra opened their balconies to black patrons but continued reserving the orchestra section for whites. (The Lafayette was the first of Harlem's major showplaces to allow blacks unrestricted access.)[25]

Even as other theatres relaxed their policies, the Lafayette (called the Uptown Palace) remained Harlem's most prestigious showplace during the twenties. At first the Lafayette offered a wide variety of entertainment, including productions of classic plays by Shakespeare and others that featured the Lafayette Players, a black troupe headed by famed actor Charles Gilpin. It also featured headline performers such as Bill Robinson, Louis Armstrong, and Buck and Bubbles. When Frank Schiffman and Leo Brecher took over in 1925, they began presenting vaudeville-like stage shows with chorus girls, orchestra, and variety acts. Despite protests by blacks who wanted a serious, legitimate theatre, the shows were a popular success. Schiffman would eventually use the new format at the Apollo, but first he faced some tough competition from an unexpected source.

Known as a shrewd, voracious businessman, Schiffman had driven out several competitors, including the Alhambra, by 1931. When newly elected Mayor Fiorello La Guardia began pressuring owners to close burlesque houses in 1933, several of the 125th Street burlesque and variety houses were forced out of business. In January 1934, however, Sidney Cohen and Morris Sussman opened the original 125th Street Apollo Theatre in what had been Hurtig and Seamon's Burlesque. They promised "the finest theatre in Harlem." The new theatre, located on Harlem's central thoroughfare between Seventh and Eighth Avenues, quickly cut into the Lafayette's profits. In June, Schiffman responded by moving his operation from 132nd Street to the Harlem Opera House, also on 125th Street. After a nearly year-long battle involving machinations worthy of international espionage, the owners realized they were cutting their own throats; two theatres presenting essentially the same entertainment, often the same performers on alternate weeks, could not function profitably within a stone's throw of each other. A deal was made, the theatres merged, and in May 1935, Frank Schiffman emerged as the manager and half owner of the Apollo Theatre, which changed its billing to "The Only Stage Show in Harlem."

Schiffman was a controversial figure in black entertainment. Admired and respected by some, scorned and excoriated by others, he was rarely viewed neutrally. His Machiavellian approach to business is a matter of record, and most would admit that he was an unrepentant shark in business matters. He quickly eliminated his competitors and for decades eradicated all serious competition, which earned him the grudging esteem of other showmen. Among performers, however, the estimate was not glowing. Of his knowledge of black acts, John Bubbles said, "Only thing he knew was how to get people as cheap as he could, and work them as long as he could." And John Hammond, a record producer and friend, flatly declared, "Frank had no artistic taste at all." Even so, with ironclad control and a hands-on approach that had him personally evaluate nearly every act that played the theatre, he fashioned what even his detractors admit was the most illustrious showplace for black entertainment ever to arise in Harlem or anyplace else.[26]

The early Apollo shows were vaudeville or variety presentations with big bands, a chorus line, comedians, dancers, and featured acts, including all of the top performers of the era—Duke Ellington, Cab Calloway, Count Basie, Louis Armstrong, Stepin Fetchit, Bessie Smith, Fats Waller, Lena Horne, Bill Robinson, Noble Sissle, Ella Fitzgerald, and more.

The legendary Apollo Amateur Night—which included renowned early successes such as Ella Fitzgerald and Billy Eckstine and, later, curious failures such as Roy Hamilton and Luther Van Dross, who was booed off the stage (one wonders whether the audience was not wearing blackface on those nights)—was also a key factor in the theatre's popularity. Ralph Cooper had inaugurated the shows shortly after Cohen and Sussman opened the Apollo in 1934. Interest grew steadily, and by the time Schiffman took over the theatre, Amateur Night was as much a part of Apollo allure as were its big-name acts. Despite a well-publicized rift between Schiffman and Cooper, who had left Schiffman's Lafayette to join the new Apollo, Amateur Night continued with Cooper as emcee. In later years, Willie Bryant, Leonard Reed, and others would host this weekly extravaganza.

Comedians were not usually featured acts during the early years, although Stepin Fetchit and Pigmeat Markham did occasionally headline shows. Nevertheless, comedy was a pervasive element in the theatre's mystique. The emcees regularly engaged in lighthearted banter with the band and performers—Willie Bryant might draw Dizzy Gillespie into a comical exchange, or Leonard Reed might trade jibes with dancer Honi Coles—and comedians such as Moms Mabley would offer impromptu lines that broke up the audience: "Count [Basie], I sure would like to know what that drummer is doin' after the show." As with all aspects of the shows, Schiffman exerted palpable control. According to Honi Coles, "Schiffman wouldn't allow the word 'damn' on the stage. If a comic came out and said, 'damn,' he'd tell them, 'You'll have to take that out.' He'd go downstairs and listen to rehearsals and, if something came up that he didn't like, he'd say, 'You can't do that, can't do that in *this* theatre.' That was it. Hell and damn were not allowed."[27]

Restrictions were relaxed when Schiffman's sons, Bobby and Jack, assumed control of the theatre in later years. At the outset, however, comedy on the Apollo stage lost some of the earthiness displayed on the TOBA tour, but not enough, apparently, to satisfy the more conservative forces in the community. A Harlem journalist, concerned about the image of Negroes presented to visitors from downtown, wrote, "I shudder as I think of the impression he must take back downtown with him. . . . When the comedy remains absolutely in the sewer and seldom ever rises to the level of the gutter, I wonder how many of what kind of people will be content to have it reflect their lives, thoughts and actions to the outside world?"[28]

His was, of course, a familiar complaint—one which, again, was more focused on what non-blacks thought of the entertainment presented than on its actual content. It was based, perhaps justifiably, on the blackface makeup that Apollo comedians still inexplicably wore, but also, quite obsessively and self-consciously, on the assumption that for non-blacks the antics of those blackface jesters represented the *real* character of all blacks. What these critics ignored was that much humor, as one theorist noted, by its very nature forces us to "drop the mask we have composed into the features of our decent, cautious selves . . . strips man of his breeches." For most middle-class black observers, laughter derived from candid lampooning of the foibles of lower-class black life was unacceptable. They were, after all, idealistically dedicated to eventual assimilation through uplifting the race and projecting an image of unfaltering propriety. Overcautiously monitoring the negative impression some whites may have drawn from black humor, they ignored not only the double-edged irony embedded in such routines as Pigmeat Markham's "Here Come de Judge," but also the positive benefits for African-American audiences. Laughter, as Henri Bergson noted, is often a "distancing" factor, and most blacks viewing the low, roustabout comedy presented on the Apollo stage no doubt experienced the transcendence or "disassociation from the object of laughter" commonly resulting from such comedy.[29]

As stage comedy developed, however, even as many Apollo comics continued in the tradition of TOBA humor, some of its more blatant buffoonery was gradually being mediated. Despite the Schiffmans' penchant for clean humor and black bourgeois disapproval, the Apollo audience—many of whom presumably had taken part in the riot of 1935—began demanding less veiled expression of actual black sentiments regarding the larger society. More and more often, they received it.

The change occurred within a rather unique setting. Perhaps the most remarkable aspect of Apollo Theatre comedy during the thirties and forties was its ensemble company makeup. According to Honi Coles, there were a dozen or so comedians who were, in effect, regulars. In addition to perennial favorites Pigmeat Markham, Mantan Moreland, Dusty Fletcher, Tim Moore, and John "Spider Bruce" Mason, there were those who doubled as emcees, including Ralph Cooper, Willie Bryant, and Leonard Reed. Then there was a raft of such talented second-tier comics and straightpeople as John "Ashcan" LaRue, Johnny Lee Long, Jimmy Baskette, Eddie Green, Sandy Burns, George Wiltshire, Edna Mae Harris, Crackshot Hackley, Spo-Dee-O-Dee, Monte Hawley, John "Rastus" Murray, and Vivian Harris. All of these performers contributed to the scores of sketches and skits, many developed on the TOBA circuit, that became the hallmark of Apollo comedy.

But even as old routines were rehashed, the inbred situational skits increasingly began to take on a different tone. Although tame in comparison to the assertiveness and derisive wit heard decades later in the stand-up comedy of Dick Gregory and Richard Pryor, Apollo comedians were beginning to infuse their humor with perceptions and jokes reflecting the more aggressive mood of the Depression-besieged black masses.

An early example of topical humor cited in Jack Schiffman's *Harlem Heyday* involved Patterson and Jackson, a dance-comedy team billed variously as "640 lbs. of humor" or "two tons of fun." Here, instead of the usual focus on food, sex, or money, African-Americans' flexibility in dealing with Southern racism is the subject of the joke:

Got on the train in Tampa, Florida, on the way to New York. Conductor came around, said, "Give me your ticket, boy." Gave him my ticket, he punched it and gave it back. Came around again in Richmond, Virginia, said, "Give me your ticket, boy." Gave him my ticket; punched it and gave it back. In the Lincoln Tunnel on the way into New York City, conductor came around and said, "Give me your ticket, boy." Turned around to him and said, "Who the hell you callin' boy?"

Presumably, the elder Schiffman was not in attendance that night but, according to his son Jack, the bit "brought roars of laughter and sometimes a standing ovation."[30]

In many instances, the show's emcee (who, unlike most of the other comedians, did address the audience directly) had the greatest opportunity to insert more poignant, socially relevant commentary. Some, particularly the glib Willie Bryant and later Nipsey Russell with his trademark line, "The natives are restless," did so frequently.

Even Butterbeans and Susie occasionally widened the range of their down-home mockery and aimed barbs at targets broader than the vacillations of black domestic life. In Ted Fox's *Showtime at the Apollo*, bandleader Andy Kirk recalled one of their Apollo routines:

Susie: I'm ready to go down South.

Butterbeans: I ain't goin' with you, Sue.

Susie: Why ain't you goin' with me, Butter?

Butterbeans: 'Cause there's too many ups down South.

Susie: What you mean "ups," Butter?

Butterbeans: Well, early in the mornin' you got to wake up. Then you got to get up. Then you got to go out and on the farm, and if you didn't do the work like the boss said, the boss would beat you up.[31]

Another theme that emerged with more regularity was the prickly issue of color prejudice within the African-American community. In one such instance, two comedians spy a voluptuous young woman standing with her back to both them and the audience. They trade quips about how fine she is and how she must be either a "high yaller" or a "tan." Their exuberance escalates and they become even more profuse in their compliments and certain that the woman is at least a "tan." Finally, they make a wager and try to get her attention. When she turns around, they see that she is black as coal. The audience would inevitably roar with delight.

The comic who most successfully and frequently combined the emerging mood of assertiveness and increased worldliness with traditional black stage motifs in the thirties and forties was Jackie "Moms" Mabley. Born in North Carolina in 1897, Mabley grew up in Cleveland and, by the time she was sixteen, had become a stage performer. Although she began as a dancer and singer, she dabbled in comedy almost from the beginning. During the twenties, while she was performing on the TOBA circuit in Dallas, Butterbeans and Susie saw her act and helped her get better billings. Like most TOBA comics, she appeared primarily in skits with other performers at first. But Mabley was one of the earliest black comics who turned to monologue humor; by the thirties, although she was not yet billed as "Moms," she had begun appearing in oversized clodhoppers, tattered gingham dresses, and oddball hats, and affecting the persona of a sage, down-to-earth, older woman. Early on, she sometimes abandoned the character and, in 1933, even had a minor role in the movie *The Emperor Jones*. She also appeared at Connie's Inn, in several Broadway shows (at least one of which also starred Harlem Renaissance writer Zora Neale Hurston), and was a regular on the black cabaret circuit, where her more ribald material was much appreciated. Essentially, however, Mabley's stage character was set; soon she would be headlined as "Moms."

The journey from a fourteen-dollar-a-week performer on the TOBA tour to top billing at the Apollo was not easy. Despite comediennes such as Fanny Brice, Belle Barth, Jean Stafford, and Mae West, traditionally there has been an uneasy accommodation to women in comedy. Even those women who did breach the gender line in mainstream stage comedy often had to endure public opprobrium; they were regularly shunted into stereotypical roles as mannish or dumb, or as virtual harlots. On the TOBA circuit, access was not quite as difficult, but it posed similar problems.[32]

As was common on the black circuit, blues singers often engaged in a kind of extemporaneous humor involving call and response with the members of the band or full-time comedians. The riotous quips with which Fats Waller punctuates Ada Brown's rendition of "That Ain't Right" in the film *Stormy Weather* provide an example of this long-standing tradition. As a result, some of the earliest black comediennes were blues singers who expanded their roles and became regulars in the comedy bits. Lillie May Glover (known as "Big Mama Blues") was one of the earliest of these converts. As she recalled, "I made me some red plaid overalls and bought me a white shirt at the Salvation Army. I taken those white tennis shoes and put some plaid in them, and I put the tennies on the wrong foot. Then I got in front of the looking glass and locked the door and talked to myself to say what I was going to say." There is no record of exactly what she said, but Big Mama did apparently appear as a comic in the olio segment of some tent shows during the mid-teens. Women such as Sweetie May and Susie, who teamed with male partners, were much more successful.[33]

Mabley, although she was a competent dancer and vocalist, was not a true blues singer, so while still in her twenties, she devised an offbeat gimmick for presenting her comedy routine. She assumed the character of an elderly earth mother. The guise provided the buffer or intermediary necessary to quell resistance to a woman doing a single comic routine. As she later recalled, the character "was like my granny, the most beautiful woman I ever knew. . . . She was so gentle, but she kept her children in line, best believe that." Still, even though she was the first comedienne to appear as a single at the Apollo and played the theatre regularly from the thirties to the sixties, according to Jack Schiffman, "the star billing was not hers" until near the end of her career, when she graduated to ten thousand dollars per week.[34]

But Mabley's brand of suggestive, often irreverent humor had made her a favorite during the thirties. She often worked with Pigmeat Markham, Dusty Fletcher, and even Stepin Fetchit in the early years, but she was at her best alone—with just a microphone and what one journalist described as "an outfit Phyllis Diller might wear if she was black."

She would do her famous shuffle, sing some comical parody of a popular song, tell stories, or just stand there, and the audience would howl. The stories most often focused on some folksy experience she shared with the audience or the obsessive quest for a young man, a gambit that became her trademark. In her slow, Southern drawl, she often trailed off into a litany of epicurean gratification: "They shipped me some meat, you understand what I me-e-ean. They shipped me some neckbones with a whole lot of meat on it. Not like the neckbones you get up here. When they say neckbones, they mean neck *bones* . . . nothin' on 'em but bones. Baby, I had the meat on, I put it on with a pot of cabba-a-age . . . and I made some crackling bread . . ." The crowd, totally identifying with Mabley's reveries and relishing the imagined orgy of soul food, would howl in appreciation. Mabley was brilliant at establishing a mood of comforting affiliation with her audience; on stage she could literally become the grandmother that most everyone knew at one time or another. But she could also shift abruptly, tossing a suggestive aside to a band member or returning to her riper retorts: "I can't do nothin' with an old man, 'cause he can't do nothin' with himself." Such lines anticipated the assertive sexual humor unveiled by female stand-up comics in the eighties, when comediennes commonly offered retorts such as, "Why don't you come up and see me sometime? Come on Wednesday, that's amateur night." Like Mae West, Mabley comically undercut male sexual prowess at a time when such disrespect was regarded as mutinous. "A woman is a woman until the day she dies," she once quipped, "but a man's a man only as long as he can."[35]

Mabley also was one of the pioneers of social satire at the Apollo. One of her most popular stories concerned two bank robbers, one white and the other black, who killed three bank tellers and two policemen and wounded a bystander. When they are sentenced to be hanged, the white man becomes overwhelmed with terror. "I don't want to be hung. I don't want to be hung," he pleads. "Oh man, we done killed up all them people and you talk about you don't want to be hung. . . . They gonna hang you, so why don't you face it like a man?" The white man replied, "That's easy for you to say, you're used to it."

Southern racism was a frequent target of her satire, and in a monologue about the dangers of performing in the South, she quipped, "Now they want me to go to New Orleans. . . . It'll be Old Orleans 'fore I get down there. The Greyhound ain't goin' take me down there and the bloodhounds run me back, I'll tell you that." Another bit involved her experiences driving through the South. "I was on my way down to Miami . . . I mean *They*-ami. I was ridin' along in my Cadillac, you know, goin' through one of them little towns in South Carolina. Pass through a red light. One of them big cops come runnin' over to me, say, 'Hey woman, don't you know you went through a red light.' I say, 'Yeah, I know I went through a red light.' 'Well, what did you do that for?' I said 'Cause I seen all you white folks goin' on the green light . . . I thought the red light was for us!' "

By the forties, she was experimenting with a bit involving telephone calls to celebrities, which would later include satiric conversations with presidents Eisenhower, Kennedy, and Johnson and their families. She would also muse about her visits to the White House. During the fifties, for example, she joked about her amity with President Eisenhower and the First Lady: "I was standin' on the White House lawn, talkin' to Ike the other day. Me an' him an' Adam Clayton Powell an' Governor Faubus an' Bo Diddley an' Big Maybelle. . . . I asked Ike a simple question. I said, 'Listen, boy . . .' " Her ability to move easily from folksy homilies to ribald double entendres and on to social and political satire was remarkable. Perhaps more than any of the other early Apollo comics, she foreshadowed the shift to direct social commentary and stand-up comic techniques that would define humor by the late fifties.

Along with the gradual emergence of a broader social outlook in comedy, the Apollo era witnessed the last gasp of blackface stage makeup. Most African-Americans seemed already to have disassociated themselves from the derisive caricature presented by corked-up comics. Laughing at those caricatures implied no more condemnation of self than did non-black audiences' acceptance of the imbecilic antics and outlandish appearance of such mainstream comedians as the Three Stooges or Joe E. Brown. Moreover, there was a tradition within the black community that sanctioned and, in fact, encouraged the mocking of simpleminded or miscreant behavior.

As Zora Neale Hurston points out in her autobiography, *Dust Tracks on a Road,* the reproach "Dat's just like a nigger!" and the mirth generated by so-called "monkey stories"—in which "the Negro, sometimes symbolized by the monkey, and sometimes named outright, ran off with the wrong understanding of what he had seen or heard"—were common among blacks in her rural Southern hometown. These instances of blacks exaggerating and ridiculing the ineptitude of other blacks were puzzling and unsettling to her as a child—primarily because they were at odds with the glorified view of Negroes so often fervently expressed by preachers and orators. Ultimately, Hurston realized that *both* impulses were legitimate expressions of the African-American character. As she wrote, "I could see that what looked like ridicule was really the Negro poking a little fun at himself. At the same time, just like other people, hoping and wishing he was just what the orators said he was."[36]

Many other blacks had come to the same conclusion, so black stage comedians' insistent pillorying of the foibles of Negro life was not seen as unusual or outrageous. And blackface makeup (for Negro audiences) probably lessened any actual racial connotations that might have been drawn, since that bizarre, lifeless mask served to create an aura of fantasy and move the stage characters outside the boundaries of real life. It might even have been interpreted in a positive manner, since the act of poking fun at oneself is universally thought to reflect a healthy skepticism about one's self-importance and, in most homogeneous social situations, functions as a humanizing influence. In African societies, for instance, ridicule songs served to chastise and curb anti-social behavior.

In America, however, with its accumulation of myths and specious theories of Anglo-Saxon superiority, self-mockery among blacks had come to signify affirmation of racial inferiority to whites and some of the black middle class. This ubiquitous shadow haunted nearly every joke black Americans told about themselves—no matter how frivolous the intent or mild and jocular the reprimand. The natural inclination of humorous expression, which nearly always focuses on differences and contradictions, was perverted by context more than anything else. In troublesome periods like the Depression, when reality intercedes most harshly and the instinct in most communities is to draw together, humor that focuses almost exclusively on inner-community rifts and derision begins to pale. Among African-Americans, burnt-cork makeup, the most visible component of black stage humor, was the most obvious point of attack.

As minstrelsy declined and America's obsession with watching stage darkies (whether white or black) waned, black performers increasingly faced all-black audiences. In that context, visual illusion, the fabricated image of blackness, became less important than the content and style of the comic performances. Gradually, burnt cork assumed the primarily cosmetic role that it had at the outset. Although it still may have provided an element of theatrical fantasy, it no longer functioned as a crucial visual embellishment of a loathsome stereotype, as it had in white minstrelsy. The burnt cork makeup worn by Pigmeat Markham or Dusty Fletcher was less consciously distorted and repugnant than that of early Negro minstrels such as Billy Kersands or Ernest Hogan.

Even though some comedians abandoned blackface while working on the TOBA circuit, the practice persisted, and most comics continued corking up on the "chitlin' circuit" and the Apollo stage during the thirties. Its use, however, seemed more a matter of habit than an intentional symbolic gesture. For many comedians, blackface, like the sketches and skits that dominated black circuit stage humor, had become a kind of safety valve, a gimmick that distanced the performer from the performance and obscured the direct line of communication that stand-up would eventually demand. Many regarded the burnt cork as no more than a theatrical device, a stage illusion with little more meaning than spotlights, sound effects, or the ludicrous costumes worn by comedians on mainstream and black circuit stages.

The truth, however, was that blackface had taken on a deeper psychological meaning for common black folks in the audience as well as for the dickty or middle-class Negroes who protested most vociferously.

By the mid-thirties, pressure to put an end to blackface was building from organizations such as the NAACP. As protests mounted, even diehard comedians dropped the darky facade. One of the last to do so was Pigmeat Markham, who had corked up since his stage debut as a minstrel, through his years on the TOBA circuit with partner Johnny Lee Long, and on to his ensemble and single routines at the Apollo. For Markham, blackface makeup served the same purpose as the greasepaint and bulbous false nose worn by circus clowns: it not only functioned objectively as a humorous mask but also worked subjectively to permit Markham to step outside of himself and into a stage character. He felt naked without it and was anxious about abandoning it. The story of when and how Markham was finally convinced to discard cork makeup has several versions. Both Ralph Cooper and Bardu Ali, a promoter and manager, claim to have been instrumental in the change and offer different versions, but what is certain is that, by the mid-forties, Markham was appearing au naturel, revealing a complexion that, according to some, was darker than the burnt cork. Another seasoned comic, Crackshot Hackley, continued blacking up until the early fifties, and may have been the last of the popular black circuit comedians to do so. By that time, however, few objected, since it was such an obvious anomaly. African-American stage humor was rapidly changing —not only cosmetically but also in terms of its candor and its range of subjects.

By the late forties, Nipsey Russell was stirring interest at the Baby Grand, which was also on 125th Street, little more than a block away from the Apollo. As emcee and house comedian, he was doing a stand-up bit that eschewed dialect humor and included the comic poems that would bring him nationwide attention on *The Jack Paar Show*. Redd Foxx and Slappy White had teamed up and were presenting an act that stretched the bounds of black circuit comedy in terms of topicality and assertiveness. They opened with: "I'm Redd." "I'm White." "You're kidding." Timmie Rogers, who had been part of a comedy-dance team called Freddie and Timmie in the early forties, abandoned the loud zoot suits that he and his partner had worn and donned a tuxedo in the mid-forties. It was the first time a black comedian appeared on stage in formal dress. A few years later, his dignified approach to comedy and popular catchphrase, "Oh yeah," would enable him to crack downtown clubs and theatres. Dick Gregory, who in the sixties would revolutionize stage comedy with unbleached satirical monologues that ripped the cover off African-Americans' true feelings about racism, was still in a

St. Louis high school. As the skinniest kid on his block, Gregory was temporarily honing his glib retorts and piercing wit on the streets, where his knack for signifying not only kept the bullies off his back but kept everybody else in stitches.

African-American stage comedy's isolation in tent shows, black cabarets, "chitlin' circuit" theatres, and more renowned showplaces such as the Apollo was coming to an end. The late forties and early fifties saw a brief upsurge of mainstream interest in the classic ethnic humor developed in those closed quarters: Pigmeat Markham, Moms Mabley, and a few others got some abbreviated exposure. Most others were ignored except, of course, by non-black comedians. Pirating jokes or routines— a common occurrence in mainstream stage humor—was even more prevalent when black performers' material was concerned. Comedians from downtown reportedly visited Apollo midnight shows regularly, accompanied by secretaries with steno pads. Milton Berle, of course, was known for his larcenous ways, and Pigmeat Markham insisted that he remembered Berle as "this little white cat hardly out of knee pants" who "showed up with his scratch pad and pencil and started copying down every word I said." He also claimed that Joey Adams once met him downtown and told a bystander, "Here's a man I ought to give half my salary to. I stole my first act from him at the Apollo." And, according to Stump and Stumpy, Dean Martin and Jerry Lewis borrowed freely from their act and once actually offered to pay them for the material.[37]

These forays into black theatres and clubs by non-black comedians belie the frequently advanced claim that black circuit comedy was too vulgar and inept for mainstream consumption. Despite its numerous critics or its lack of exposure, the comedy developed on the stages of the TOBA and "chitlin' " circuits and at the Apollo from the teens to the early fifties represents a classic era in black American humor.

Perhaps the most popular and recognizable character to emerge from this era was the high-spirited city slicker. Usually teamed with a less pretentious, more dutifully honest straightman whose cautious approach proved more prudent, this ebullient comic staple became the centerpiece in black stage comedy. On the TOBA and "chitlin' " circuits and at the Apollo Theatre, its most riotous interpreters were Tim Moore (who later brought the character to television as Kingfish), John Mason, and Pigmeat Markham. With subtle variations, each put their distinctive comedic stamp on the type. Bombastic, irrepressible, and bigger than life, the character strode through black circuit stage routines like a jovial version of folklore hero John Henry, flashing his infectious smile and outrageous schemes at whoever would look or listen. Although his schemes were seldom successful—in fact, in most instances they backfired and ended in total disaster—he was never deterred. It was his indefatigable nature and recourse to an undissipated pool of energy or enthusiasm that braced his comic posture with an underlying note of practical philosophy and realism. For underneath the surface failures, his resoluteness and refusal to be beaten down by the unassailable forces massed against him reflected an abiding belief shared by most African-American audiences. His courage and perseverance in the face of defeat, even his whimsical acceptance of that defeat, mirrored blacks' determination to press forward even in the most inhospitable circumstances.

The city slicker thereby delineates the most prominent characteristic of black stage comedy. The comedy was almost always reality-bound. Prior to the thirties, it adhered fundamentally to circumstances outside the realm of mainstream concern. It represented the humorous extension of Booker T. Washington's maxim, "Cast down your buckets where you are." Critics would assail this focus on the down-to-earth reality of black life and its resultant comical emphasis on "low-down" or "common" pursuits. But, after all, those perimeters were imposed by a society mired in a Jim Crow mentality. As one historian notes, "By keeping blacks barred from middle class literate culture America forced them back upon the resources of their folk tradition. . . . Blacks had to develop their artistry and style *below* [mainstream] cultural standards." The stage comedy of the first half of the twentieth century is a rich example of the use of black folkways.[38]

Long after the Depression had practically compelled African-Americans to abandon their acquiescent relationship to the white world and adopt a more assertive posture, when their public humor had begun reflecting the previously concealed discontent, one of the black stage's most resilient comedians spoke out about the difference between TOBA humor and the more assertive stand-up comics who had taken center stage.

"Comedy," Pigmeat Markham said, "is a big field. And there's room enough for everybody. But me, I'm a situational comic, and I never wanted to be anything else. My laughs grow out of the situation, while the stand-up gets his out of what he says.

"But what does he get? Giggles. The situation comic gets a *belly laugh* every time. Listen to Mort Sahl, say, and then listen to Red Skelton. Then you'll see what I mean. Man, I could never work for giggles."[39]

Traditional black stage humor centered on a broad, bawdy, rambunctious, knock-'em-down comedy style that reflected a rough-hewn, blues-saturated African-American culture that disregarded the decorum, restraints, and self-conscious cleverness of mainstream humor. The rush to disavow that traditional humor in the fifties and sixties often placed its practitioners in a defensive position. Pigmeat Markham, while acknowledging the effectiveness of later comics who openly attacked America's racism, explained the origins of his comic style and asked a penetrating question: "I was born and raised black," he wrote. "I learned my comedy from black comedians. The earliest skits I did on a stage or under a tent were invented by black men. The audiences I learned to please, all those years in small towns and in big cities, they were mostly black, too. . . . White people aren't tuned to my act at all. . . . They don't dig the slang, they have trouble following my accent, they don't even get the point of some of the jokes." He asked his detractors, "Who kept our people together in the real bad days so that they could survive long enough to be able to march on Washington later—during those depression days when home relief was nothing, when the rats were even huge-er and hungrier, when a sense of humor was all we had to feed on?"[40]

Markham's remarks point out the essential nature of TOBA and Apollo Theatre humor—its cloistered origins—and suggest both its underlying historical significance for blacks and the reason it was so popular. By the mid-fifties, however, the push toward assimilation and equality, and the insistent emphasis on the similarities of black and white culture had nearly rendered the old, inbred humor obsolete. But when the walls of segregation began to crumble, the new breed black comics took a turn that shocked many. As if testing the sincerity of mainstream America's grudging relaxation of rigid racist policies, they turned to a more biting humor. The pent-up resentment and anger, which had been largely excised from public humor before, was unleashed in scathing monologues by comedians such as Nipsey Russell, Godfrey Cambridge, and, most incisively, Dick Gregory.

Curiously, this acrimonious wit took some critics by surprise—for instance, Steve Allen, a notable humorist and usually a perceptive observer of the comedy scene. In his book *Funny People*, which notes society's reluctance to "permit the emergence" of witty or intellectual black comedians of the calibre of Bob Hope or Mort Sahl before the sixties, Allen goes on to argue that, "with few exceptions," blacks had not progessed enough to produce "philosophical" humorists. What produced the new-breed African-American comedians was the civil rights movement and that, he argues, was accomplished because "whites, by 1960, had become civilized enough to *grant* the black man freedom to indulge in biting social commentary."[41]

Despite the disclaimer "with few exceptions," Allen suggests that stage comedians such as Bert Williams, Allen Drew, Willie Bryant, Moms Mabley, Nipsey Russell, and Redd Foxx did not exist. In fact, African-American humor had a tradition of caustic wit and biting social commentary. It was not created out of whole cloth. The critical and disdainful edge of black humor foreshadowed on the stage by Moms Mabley and openly expressed by the new breed of stand-up comics represented nothing more than a shift in emphasis in the *public* display of black humor. That edge had been present since slavery.

One needed only to drop in at almost any black barber shop, house party, or gutbucket cabaret, or to read black writers from the Harlem Renaissance to the sixties, or to peruse the folktales, toasts, and humorous stories that, by the forties, were being collected and anthologized. The emerging humor of the late fifties and sixties was not really new at all. It was simply that when the gate to equal opportunity was cracked just a bit, the truth slipped out.

10.

LITERARY REFLECTIONS OF

AFRICAN-AMERICAN

HUMOR . . . *depictions of*

things unseen

17

O-D-2

GODFREY CAMBRIDGE AND RAYMOND ST. JACQUES
IN *COTTON COMES TO HARLEM*

"THAT MOONSHINE YOU HAD'LL TAKE CARE O' EVERYTHING. JES' GIVE IT ANOTHER HOUR TO WORK AND YOU'LL BE BLIND AS A BALTIMO' ALLEY." "TROUBLE WITH YOU," SAID BUBBER, " IS, YOU' IGNORANT. YOU' DUMB. THE INSIDE O' YO' HEAD IS ALL BLACK."

"LIKE THE OUTSIDE O' YOURN."

"IS YOU BY ANY CHANCE ALLUDIN' TO ME?"

"I AIN'T ALLUDIN' TO THAT POLICEMAN OVER YONDER."

"LUCKY FOR YOU HE IS OVER YONDER, ELSE YOU WOULDN'T BE ALLUDIN' AT ALL."

—RUDOLPH FISHER (*The Conjure-Man Dies*)

A READY EYE FOR HUMAN FOIBLE MAY HAVE BEEN LANGSTON HUGHES' GREATEST GIFT. . . . HIS LAUGHTER DID NOT PILLORY A VICTIM. IT ONLY SURROUNDED ITS TARGET WITH MIRTH THAT WAS AFFECTIONATE AND FULL OF UNDERSTANDING EVEN WHEN IT TOOK FULL NOTE OF MANKIND'S TENDENCY TO ERR.

—BLYDEN JACKSON

YOU GET A COUPLE OF PREACHERS, THE NEXT STEP IS TO HAVE A BUNCH A HONKY SOCIAL WORKERS. NEXT THING YOU KNOW THEY DONE FIXED THE STREET, PUT IN NEW SEWERS, BUILT A NEW SCHOOL, AN' RAISED THE TAXES. THERE GOES THE DAMN NEIGHBORHOOD.

—DAVID BRADLEY (*South Street*)[1]

I

Until the late 1960s, the vast majority of Americans were unaware of black literature. Black writers' works were generally destined for obscurity, dismissed as "special interest" titles. Even when the mainstream took notice, those exposed to African-American literature in which genuine humor was abundant were often predisposed toward finding angry protest tracts, thereby missing the humor. In 1952, for example, the *Yale Review*'s critic extolled the "brooding, bitter tone" of Ralph Ellison's *Invisible Man* but lumped it with other "crude" and "overearnest" works that had "little or no humor." However myopic it may now seem, the critic's reading of Ellison is partially explained by the absence of precedent for humor in African-American writing. Few early black writers chose comedy as their principal mode of expression.[2]

At first glance, this avoidance seems peculiar, since intimate involvement with contradiction and chaos often leads to a heightened comic sensibility, and America's racial arrangements were among its most absurdly contradictory features. On the other hand, it is not so surprising considering the restrictions that pioneer African-American writers faced. Foremost among them is the fact that the earliest black writers were totally dependent on white-owned publishing outlets. Non-blacks determined not only when their writing would appear in print but also, to a great extent, the nature of the work published.

Nonetheless, some black Americans had begun to switch from an essentially oral expressive mode to a written one as early as the eighteenth century. The first poem attributed to an African-American was Lucy Terry's "Bars Fight" (circa 1746) and, shortly afterward, poems by Jupiter Hammon and Phyllis Wheatley were published. Slave narratives constitute the earliest published prose writing and also date back to the mid-1700s. No lengthy fiction by African-Americans appeared until the mid-nineteenth-century publication of William Wells Brown's *Clotel, or, The President's Daughter* (London, 1853) and Harriet Wilson's *Our Nig; or Sketches from the Life of a Free Black* (1859). From these floundering beginnings in antebellum America, African-American literature evolved to produce poets such as Langston Hughes, Gwendolyn Brooks, and Amiri Baraka; essayists such as W. E. B. Du Bois and James Baldwin; and novelists such as Jean Toomer, Richard Wright, Ralph Ellison, Toni Morrison, Ishmael Reed, and John Edgar Wideman.[3]

Slave autobiographies, as Henry Louis Gates notes in *The Slave's Narratives: Texts and Contexts,* constituted "the most fully sustained beginnings of the Afro-American narrative tradition" and became invaluable as primary sources describing the texture, detail, and "complex workings" of slavery from the slaves' viewpoint. But they were written by former slaves who were generally versed only in the rudiments of narrative technique and their use was primarily political—both to delineate the excesses of master-slave relationships and to affirm "the common humanity and intellectual capacities that persons of African descent shared with Europeans and Americans"—so humor or satire was rare. The abolitionists who initially encouraged and published the narratives were interested in graphic descriptions of the evils of slavery. As James Olney writes in "I Was Born: Slave Narratives, Their Status as Autobiography and as Literature," when abolitionists "invited an ex-slave to tell his story [and] subsequently sponsored the appearance of that story in print, they had certain clear expectations, well understood by themselves and well understood by the ex-slaves too, about the proper content to be observed, the proper theme to be developed, and the proper form to be followed."[4]

Moreover, while humor may be, as George Meredith and other theorists have suggested, "the ultimate civilizer" and perfect antidote for hubris, wrongheadedness, and pretension, it is also an outlet for sublimated aggression. It implicitly suggests an equality or even superiority that most abolitionists were unwilling to accept from blacks. Although they abhorred the institution of slavery, few perceived blacks as their equals. The peculiar institution may have been odious, but its victims were primarily seen as docile and dependent, like Harriet Beecher Stowe's Uncle Tom, worthy of support and sympathy but nonetheless inferior. The poems of slaves such as Phyllis Wheatley and Jupiter Hammon, for example, were noticeably restrained. As slaves, they were obviously not permitted to express negative or satirical attitudes about their plight. Like concert pianist Blind Tom, they were treated as prodigies, curiosities, or anomalies and encouraged to extol the virtues of their position and mimic the somber, romantic sentiments of their non-black contemporaries. Even if an incipient African-American wit capable of writing in the manner of Jonathan Swift had surfaced, it is unlikely that white abolitionists would have encouraged scathing ridicule of their Southern brethren as New World Yahoos.

This is not to say that slave narratives did not *relate* numerous examples of humorous folktales and encounters between masters and slaves. In fact—while many non-black *interpretations* of blacks' comical nature had been printed—slave autobiographies had, at least by the nineteenth century, begun providing the first written record of genuine African-American humor. Except in rare instances, however, it is not in the literary execution but in the powerful recollected detail of these autobiographies that the humor resides.

For instance, the tale in which the slave Pompey induces his master to admit that he was not a noble lion but a jackass (see chapter 1) was related in Peter Randolph's *From Slave Cabin to Pulpit* (Boston, 1855). Gilbert Osofsky's *Puttin' on Ole Massa* and Charles H. Nichols's essay "The Slave Narrator and the Picaresque Mode" are among sources that recount other humorous anecdotes found in the autobiographies of former slaves. They vary from the irreverent to the innocuous and reflect bondsmen's contempt for and resistance to slavery's debasement, their wit and subterfuge, as well as their prevailing folkways and superstitions. But, as Nichols points out, although slave narratives share some features of picaresque satires such as *Tom Jones* and *Candide* ("exaggeration, innuendo, mistaken identity and ridicule"), "the slave narrative is rarely comic." Still, Osofsky observes, "Ingenuity, deception, courage, and aggressive humor also pervade the stories."

The best of these narratives smoothly translate the slaves' oral tradition to print and are spiced with examples of folk humor and wit, which would be repeated and amplified in tales collected by folklorists well into the twentieth century.[5]

Moreover, by the nineteenth century, autobiographies by ex-slaves such as William Wells Brown and Frederick Douglass would move beyond the limits of conventional slave narratives. Instead of merely recounting humorous or satirical tales, they began displaying an ironic resonance in their own writing. Douglass, as most critics and historians have confirmed, "was an extraordinary man and an altogether exceptional writer," and his prose, although basically polemical in nature, was not without irony and other humorous narrative devices.[6]

African-Americans did not assume any control over published works either about them or by them until the nineteenth century. The United States' first black newspaper, *Freedom's Journal*—begun by John Russwurm, America's second black college graduate, and the Reverend Samuel Cornish—did not surface until 1827 in New York City. Under its new name, *Rights of All*, the newspaper initially published "Appeal to the Colored Citizens of the World," the militant anti-slavery tract written by David Walker, which, when published in pamphlet form as *Walker's Appeal* in 1829, proved too assertive for most white Americans and was denounced by both pro- and anti-slavery factions. ("A reward of one thousand dollars was offered for Walker if dead, ten thousand dollars if he was delivered alive to the South.") Several dozen more independent black newspapers emerged before the Civil War, among them *The North Star*, edited by Frederick Douglass.[7]

The emergence of black newspapers in antebellum America, however, did not lead to an upsurge in humorous writing by black journalists comparable to that found in the white press. In effect, black writers restricted themselves, choosing to focus on abolishing human bondage and selecting polemics and moral persuasion as their means of expression. Journalists usually adopted a grave or somber tone—simultaneously attacking pro-slavery arguments and attempting to demonstrate that African-Americans were not the irresponsible, frivolous souls portrayed in minstrelsy, Southern mythology, and the growing number of comic, fictional tales of black life. From the outset, then, the form of African-American writing was significantly influenced by blacks' reaction to the larger society's stereotypical views. This reflexive or reactionary tendency largely dominated black journalism as well as other forms of African-American writing until the twenties and the Harlem Renaissance.

Such mid-nineteenth-century novels as William Wells Brown's *Clotel* and Martin Delaney's uncompleted *Blake, or the Huts of America* (1859) were fashioned after Stowe's *Uncle Tom's Cabin* and crudely followed its melodramatic excesses. Although loosely structured around the life of its heroine, the supposed mulatto daughter of President Thomas Jefferson, *Clotel* is basically a series of vignettes demonstrating the barbarity of slavery. Still, there is some comedy when Brown relates tales of the shams and deceptions slaves used to escape or avoid punishment. And although it is heavy-handed, Brown's portrait of the wholesale miscegenation that occurred during slavery is ironic—especially when he depicts instances in which even whites were powerless to prevent their own slightly tainted relatives from being sold into slavery and prostitution. There are also a few examples of what may be the first use of satirical slave folk rhymes in American fiction. At one point, when a master has his slaves step forward to show a visitor how contented they are, Jack, the "most witty slave on the farm," offers the following toast:

> The big bee flies high,
> The little bee makes the honey;
> The black folks makes the cotton,
> And the white folks gets the money.

On another occasion Brown has two white characters overhear the slaves "mourning" the death of their master in song:

> We'll no more be roused by the blowing of his horn,
>   Our backs no longer he will score;
> He no more will feed us cotton-seeds and corn;
>   For his reign of oppression now is o'er.
> He no more will hang our children on the tree,
>   To be ate by the carrion crow;
> He no longer will send our wives to Tennessee;
>   For he's gone where the slaveholders go.[8]

Brown's use of humor and satire in this novel, however, is spare. Although a good writer with an eye for detail, he was so intent on contesting southerners' idyllic view of slavery that he too often veered toward creating a transparent anti-slavery document. Delaney's *Blake*, the characters of which seem even more indebted to Harriet Beecher Stowe, is also so intently focused on offsetting myths about the benign nature of slavery that it succumbs to the pitfall of creating a cast of entirely virtuous black characters who are pitted against evil white slaveholders. It differs from *Uncle Tom's Cabin* in that it is "much more concerned with the slaves than with white characters," and stresses "the spirit of discontent and revolt in even the ordinary fieldhand," but it also readily abandons plot and character to embrace polemics. And unlike Brown's *Clotel*, the dramatization of the struggle between right and wrong is seldom relieved by humor or satire.[9]

The point, however, is not to dismiss such works but to note the extraliterary influences that greatly shaped early black writing. It is remarkable that these writers, who had been forced surreptitiously to gain the rudimentary tools of literacy, were able to produce books at all.

Black poets were also initially pressured to address abolitionist issues, counter the ongoing dissemination of negative caricatures of African-Americans by whites, or avoid writing about black life altogether and turn to so-called "universal" themes. Nineteenth-century poets such as George Moses Horton and Frances Ellen Harper usually focused on anti-slavery themes; Harper's "The Slave Auction" is among the best of the antebellum poems.

By the turn of the century, Paul Laurence Dunbar, the first nationally recognized black poet, had emerged. Dunbar preferred his standard English poems, and those works included some of the best poems written by early black American writers. But his popularity was based primarily on dialect verse. Compared to works by whites writing in Negro dialect (a trend that peaked during this period) his poems were less distorted. Some, like "When Malindy Sings," are perfectly pitched and capture the vitality, joy, and humor of black common folks better than most of his contemporaries:

> Fiddlin' man jes' stop his fiddlin',
>   Lay his fiddle on de she'f;
> Mockin'-bird quit tryin' to whistle,
>   'Cause he jes' so shamed hisse'f.
> Folks a-playin' on de banjo
>   Draps dey fingahs on de strings—

Bless yo' soul—fu'gits to move em,
When Malindy sings.

But whether by choice or pressure from publishers, many of his poems mirrored characterizations common in the works of plantation-tradition writers. The humor was most often derived from comical dialect voices, and Dunbar's fictional slaves were prone to deliver such lines as, "Tell Marse Linkum for to take his freedom back." Much of his popularity was derived from portraying blacks in the minstrel mode. White editors and readers expected it and—although he once remarked that being restricted to dialect poetry was like writing "jingles in broken English"—he continued to do so throughout his career.[10]

Some other pre–Harlem Renaissance poets, including George Marion McClellan and William Stanley Braithwaite, generally avoided both dialect and African-American themes. Braithwaite, although some consider his romantic, ivory-tower approach passionless, was one of the best of the early black poets. But he had no abiding interest in satire or humor as significant features of his work.

At the end of the nineteenth century, with slavery no longer an issue and a small African-American middle class emerging, black fiction began to reflect the trends that would largely define it for the next half century.

II

Frances Harper's *Iola Leroy* (1892) and J. McHenry Jones's *Hearts of Gold* (1896) were among the earliest examples of accommodationist or apologist fiction, a genre that extolled the virtues of decent blacks and appealed to America's sense of justice in race relations. In contrast was Sutton Griggs's *Imperium in Imperio* (1899), an example of nationalistic or militant fiction in which the separatist hero plots a takeover of Texas, and *The Hindered Hand* (1905), which the critic Addison Gayle, Jr., describes as "one man's attempt to combat the malicious propaganda of his time." Both creative strains were reactions to post-Reconstruction oppression and the derogatory portrait of Negroes presented by white writers. The propagandistic intent of most of these works is clear, but ultimately they were no more tendentious than the works to which they reacted. Still, they were generally less art than entreatment, and as such usually floundered in melodramatic and rhetorical excess.[11]

In mainstream literature of the early twentieth century, humor was widespread, and much of it employed the traditional figure of the wise fool or the common man. By this time, however, the image of the ordinary black man had been appropriated by mainstream culture and presented as a genuine fool—a common man without common sense. The image of the craven, irresponsible, ignorant Negro buffoon was by then a national symbol. Only a literary wizard could have overcome the social and political obstacles of the time and supplanted that image with one of a wise, black American Socrates. Most early twentieth-century black writers simply avoided humor as a literary technique and followed W. E. B. Du Bois's suggestion to abandon the comic depiction of Negroes.

But there were also more subtle reasons for African-American writers to eschew humor. The post-Reconstruction era's stepped-up repression had deflated much of the optimism and expectations blacks had felt after Emancipation. Black Americans had to define themselves in a chaotic climate in which the professed ideals of the nation and its social reality were diametrically opposed. Many of the most educated and vocal members of the race (the emerging middle class) were from the relatively small group of formerly free Negroes and were at least half white. Miscegenation, as *Clotel* suggested, was far more common than society wished to acknowledge. And many of the progeny of those typically clandestine interminglings were unwilling to accept society's arbitrary racial division.[12]

They sought a classification based on education and cultural achievement—not merely on race or, more precisely, the discernible appearance of "color." At the turn of the century, they were still jockeying for position on the social ladder. Strong appeals for a closing of ranks among all those identified as Negroes did not occur until the teens. The "unreconciled strivings" and anxious observance of self "through the eyes of others" of which Du Bois wrote derived, at least partially, from the black elite's identification with mainstream America and desire to distance itself from the black masses. Their self-appraisal was reflected in the apologist or accommodationist camp of writers as well as in the lack of an outpouring of humor based on racial polarization.

Although the ability to observe one's self with some degree of detachment is most often a prerequisite for humor, the comic impulse rarely co-exists with hesitancy, passivity, and self-consciousness. It is an "art of the bravado personality," as one critic noted. Even when it arises out of an underlying sense of insecurity, it issues most effectively from an *assumed* position of eminence and self-assurance based on some real or imagined trait such as physical prowess, social status, or intellectual or moral superiority. Whether stoked by irreverence or self-righteousness, as with satirists such as H. L. Mencken and Jonathan Swift, or nourished by worldliness or the underdog's eye for contradiction and pretension, as with, say, George Bernard Shaw and Will Rogers, humor reflects an aggressive thrust or ascendancy. It may assume the guise of modesty and self-effacement, as with comics such as Steven Wright and Woody Allen, but even then, at minimum, it still extols and celebrates the perspicuity of that viewpoint. Perhaps most important, humor is seldom neutral; someone or something is nearly always the object of ridicule, the butt of the joke.

America at the turn of the century, however, did not offer black writers the kind of popular support and security that usually girds political or social satire. Without that support, the assertiveness and self-assuredness required for a humorous posture could not easily develop among African-American writers.

Charles Waddell Chesnutt was one of the few early twentieth-century African-American writers who made humor a prominent element in his fiction. Generally, his short stories far outstrip his novels in literary merit and, perhaps not coincidentally, he used a comic approach less sparingly in those stories. The tales collected in *The Conjure Woman* (1899), for instance, revolve around Chesnutt's Uncle Julius, a character who bears some surface resemblance to Joel Chandler Harris's Uncle Remus but is actually a sly trickster whose obsequiousness masks his efforts on behalf of other slaves. And *The Wife of His Youth* (1899), also a collection of sketches and stories, includes one of Chesnutt's most bitingly humorous tales.

In "The Passing of Grandison," a plantation patriarch's son attempts to win the hand of Charity, the young woman whom he is courting, by demonstrating his boldness and independence—traits he decides to display by freeing one of his father's slaves. Dick Owens convinces his father that he needs a servant for a trip to the North, then sets off to Boston with the intention of simply allowing the slave to wander off. His companion is Grandison, an elderly servant whose "wise subordination and loyal dependence" is unquestioned and who, according to the patriarch, is "too fond of good eating to risk losing his regular meals."

In a hilarious comic turnabout, Chesnutt recounts the young master's attempt to first allow Grandison to escape by his own initiative. He gives him money and leaves him alone for long periods, then introduces him to abolitionists. But Grandison spurns the opportunities and, instead, repudiates the abolitionists and the free Negroes that he meets: "Dey're diffe'ent f'm de niggers down ou' way. Dey 'lows dey're free, but dey ain' got sense 'nuff ter know dey ain' half as well off as dey would be down Souf, whar dey'd be 'preciated." Finally, at wit's end, Owens takes the slave to Canada and simply abandons him. Owens returns to the South alone and, although his father is outraged at the loss of his chattel, marries Charity. Shortly after the marriage, however, a ragged, weary Grandison makes his way back home. Ecstatic at Grandison's return, the patriarch lionizes his "faithful nigger" and rewards him for his escape from the loathsome abolitionists by giving him special concessions and making his life a "slave's dream come true." Three weeks later the slaveholder discovers that Grandison is again missing. This time, however, the slave's wife, mother, father, brothers, and sister are gone also. The tale ends as the elder Owens stands on the shore of Lake Erie shaking his fist as Grandison and his family wave from a steamboat headed for Canada.[13]

"The Passing of Grandison" combines broad comedy, wily deception, and ironic understatement. Chesnutt revealed a similar comic sensibility in many of his other tales, often reversing the popular use of dialect so that it reflected blacks' ingenuity rather than confirming their assumed ignorance. The novelist and critic John Edgar Wideman notes that "Black speech in the form of Negro dialect entered American literature as a curiosity, a comic interlude, a short-hand for perpetuating myths and prejudices about Black people." Wideman underscores Chesnutt's successful use of the African-American oral tradition with its double meanings, tonal definitions, and capacity to "talk behind a victim's back while looking him in the face." The story Wideman analyzes, "A Deep Sleeper," features Uncle Julius and revolves around the trickster theme. The narrator's recounting of a tale told by Uncle Julius corroborates white expectations about Negro behavior on the surface but actually buys time for Uncle Julius and his cohorts to accomplish their own ends. As in "The Passing of Grandison," the tale employs ironic comic inversion, reversing the traditional derogatory use of black dialect to give its black characters the last laugh.[14]

Few contemporary black writers used dialect and ironic humor as effectively or subtly as Chesnutt. Irony was most often turned to a tragic or, occasionally, a tragicomic end.

In novels about "passing" or crossing the color line, for example, irony appears repeatedly, but usually as a device to garner sympathy for mixed-blood protagonists seeking their proper place in society; it was seldom employed to ridicule the inherent absurdity of the system that perpetuated the irrational black-white schism and societal pretense. Protagonists who appeared white but either knew or found out about their Negro backgrounds were inevitably portrayed as serious souls who accepted social custom as fixed reality.

"Tragedy accepts the flaw in the world as it is," the critic Wylie Sypher writes, "then ventures to find nobility in 'the inexorable march of actual situations.'" In many early black novels, Negro blood becomes a tragic flaw that ultimately consumes and destroys its near-white possessors. Unlike the comic hero, who "quickly changes one mask for another" and is capable of playing various roles with gusto, these piteous mulattoes are unable to escape their fate; they accept their "misfortune and . . . responsibility with a stoic face." No trickster mulattoes emerged in these stories, no semi-black Falstaff who could move unrestrictedly in both worlds, thumbing his nose at the underlying idiocy of the static racial concept. Characters in these novels are devoid of a comic vision, a heightened consciousness of the "duplicity of existence." Instead, somber melancholy marked a raft of "tragic mulatto" novels in which the disillusioned hero or heroine, like William Wells Brown's Clotel, usually perished. Brown's *Clotel*, Harper's *Iola Leroy*, and Chesnutt's *The House behind the Cedars* (1900) are early examples of the genre, but the theme remained popular in fiction by blacks and whites well into the twentieth century.[15]

The Autobiography of an Ex-Colored Man (1912) was one of the few novels that treated the passing theme with some humor and ironic distance. Its author, James Weldon Johnson (who, as noted before, had collaborated with his brother Rosamund in writing theatrical comedies), disclosed his intent when, in the first paragraph, he had the nameless first-person narrator announce: "I know that I am playing with fire, and I feel the thrill which accompanies that most fascinating pastime; and, back of it all, I think I find a sort of savage and diabolical desire to gather up all the little tragedies of my life, and turn them into a practical joke on society." At one point, after the protagonist has infiltrated white society, he comments: "when I returned to my room after an enjoyable evening, I laughed heartily over what struck me as the capital joke I was playing."[16]

Johnson's approach, however, was not typical. Most African-American writers treated the ironic circumstances of black life humorlessly. W. E. B. Du Bois's *The Souls of Black Folk*, for instance, includes "Of the Coming of John," a story dealing with a young black college student's return to his rural Georgia hometown. Before his departure, John was a source of pride to the black community. He was even liked by white folks, although they insisted college would "spoil him" and thought of John basically as "good-natured and respectful . . . a fine plough-hand." After he comes back, "Every step he made offended some one." His education has left him out of touch with family and former friends, and his uppity bearing angers whites. The situation is rife with ironic implications, but it is turned to what Blyden Jackson calls "uneasy laughter"—"the wry reaction of the ironist" that suffuses nearly all black literature. Instead of exploring the comic nuances of the character's predicament ("the alternative to tragic self-annihilation"), Du Bois focused on tragic defeat. He opted for a fictional approach that demands "a law of necessity or destiny" within whose confines "the hero is given to sacrifice or death." As the tale ends, John is a forlorn, alienated figure facing "the coiling twisted rope."[17]

"Of the Coming of John" is a typical example of the direction that the small group of "serious" early black writers took in depicting the black experience prior to the 1920s. Their desire to be taken seriously generally precluded the use of humor as a central literary technique. The "talented tenth" writers' overwhelming choice of tragedy over humor or comedy made perfect sense given their goal of clearly dramatizing the disastrous consequences of racism—the human misery that it inevitably provoked. Tragedy is a " 'closed' form of art, with a single, fixed, and contained meaning." Somehow it shows "what 'must' happen, even while there comes a shock of unsurmised disaster." In contrast, comedy is more complex and, often, less exacting; it embraces contradiction, chaos, and the irrational. It penetrates the surface, our civilized masks, and reveals the prodigal and absurd. As Pirandello suggested, it notes the contradictions between the body and its shadow.[18]

But ironically, the "talented tenth" writers' insistence on tragic portrayal not only further separated their work from the laughter and more humanized existence experienced by most black Americans but, by casting blacks solely in the role of victims, in some ways affirmed the authenticity or, at least, the efficacy of the belief in racial destiny they struggled to eradicate.

A more satirical approach might have more vividly revealed the inherent absurdity of America's racial arrangements. But an upsurge of such writing would not occur until African-American writers abandoned their stiff, middle-class formality and more honestly embraced the perspective and folk humor of the black masses.

III
∙-∙-∙-∙-∙-∙-∙

In the twenties, middle-class apologists—for whom the popular "primitive" stereotype of the period was as reprehensible as the ignorant darky image of earlier times—continued producing works depicting staunch bourgeois types who exemplified traditional values and the Protestant Ethic. A few others adopted the satirical spirit of such mainstream writers as H. L. Mencken and Sinclair Lewis and evoked the underlying vitality and sense of impiousness and irony that most often had been suggested only in literary portraits of free-spirited, urban blacks. In effect, they abandoned exaggerated, surface caricature but retained the cynical disregard for mainstream priorities; they also increasingly turned to black folk humor and satire as expressive tools in their literary works.

James Weldon Johnson, an admirer of H. L. Mencken, reflected the shift in his *New York Age* column in 1922 when he wrote that some aspects of the race question were "so absurd that they cannot be effectively treated except in a satirical manner." He was not the first black writer to advocate a satirical response to bigotry or, in fact, to use satire in attacking the blatant contradictions between slavery or Jim Crowism and democracy. There were some examples in slave narratives (notably in the Frederick Douglass autobiographies) and in anti-slavery pamphlets.[19]

For instance, in his famous *Appeal*, published in 1829, David Walker referred to a South Carolina newspaper that juxtaposed an article claiming the Turks were "the most barbarous people in the world" and excoriating them for treating the Greeks "more like brutes than human beings" with notices promoting the sale of African-Americans and offering rewards for the return of runaways. "It is really so *funny* to hear Southerners and Westerners of this country talk about *barbarity*," Walker wrote, "that it is positively enough to make a man smile." By the early twentieth century, cartoons and editorials in black newspapers regularly used satire in emphasizing the irreconcilability of America's racial policy and its humanitarian pretensions. In 1918, for example, Robert S. Abbott, the editor of *The Chicago Defender*, wrote in Swiftian fashion, "Who knows but there may be such a thing as a refined mob, composed of 'colonels,' 'Southern aristocracy' and the ever present 'best citizens'? Who knows, after seeing their work, that they have improved on the art of torture practised in savage life and made it more fiendish?"[20]

Johnson, however, was advocating the use of satire and humor not only in expository works but also in poetry, drama, and fiction. Although there were exceptions (Langston Hughes and Countee Cullen among them), the black poets of the twenties did not produce an abundance of humorous verse. Novelists responded to Johnson's exhortations more favorably. The Harlem Renaissance ultimately produced the first notable African-American writers to employ humor as a central element in their work. Their politics differed widely, but before the Renaissance ground to a halt in the thirties, three satirists and two significant folk humorists had emerged.

George Schuyler was the most prominent satirist as well as the most controversial of the Renaissance writers. He, too, was an admirer of Mencken, who encouraged him to satirize whites as well as blacks; while Mencken was editor (1924–1933), Schuyler appeared more frequently in *American Mercury* than any other contributor. Like his mentor, he was a versatile iconoclast whose barbed wit found a vast array of targets. In his column for *The Pittsburgh Courier* and articles for *The Messenger* and *American Mercury*, he expectedly satirized "Nordics" and the "United Snakes" in articles such as "Our White Folks," "Blessed Are the Sons of Ham," and "Our Greatest Gift to America"; the recurring theme in these articles was the inherent idiocy of race as a tenable social concept and white America's unlimited ability to delude itself. Since he debunked the entire concept of race, he also pilloried the notion of "black art" and ridiculed black nationalists and racial apologists. The logical extension of his unbending view of race as total myth would, by the fifties, cast him as a right-wing outsider whose opposition to liberal social programs and the civil rights movement isolated him from the central drift of African-American thought.[21]

Schuyler's two novels, *Slaves Today* and *Black No More* (both published in 1931), reflect his basic intellectual and satirical concerns. The former targets the Republic of Liberia, skewering the political and social order established by Negroes from America. Its theme, as one critic describes it, is that, with regard to "cruelty and exploitation, repression and oppression, Blacks are one with whites throughout the world." There are some amusing comic turns to the satire in this work, but the novel is so heavy-handed and Schuyler's depiction of the black leaders' villainy so unrelenting, that satire lapses into farce, burlesque, and bludgeoning realism. As another critic notes, the leaders of the country are portrayed as if they had "taken a correspondence course in civic government from the Imperial Wizard of the Ku Klux Klan. . . . They project the very irrationality of evil itself." [22]

Black No More is a more balanced and humorous sample of Schuyler's satire. Set in America, the tale concerns the discovery of a process that turns blacks into Caucasians in three days, and comically details the social effects of the mass transformation. It is an occasion for Schuyler to lampoon racial bigotry, false racial pride, and a raft of scarcely veiled race leaders, both black and white. A white supremacy organization is led by the Reverend Henry Givens, "who had finished the eighth grade in a one-room country school" but holds his flock spellbound with explanations of "the laws of heredity" and other scientific subjects. A Garvey-like character named Santop Licorice is the leader of a back-to-Africa movement but owns a fleet of ships that "had never been to Africa, had never had but one cargo and that, being gin, was half consumed by the unpaid and thirsty crew before the vessel was saved by the Coast Guard." And the Du Bois–like Dr. Shakespeare Agamemnon Beard writes editorials for "*The Dilemma* denouncing the Caucasians whom he secretly admired and lauding the greatness of the Negroes whom he alternately pitied and despised." It is a direct salvo aimed at the myth of race and all those who (from Schuyler's perspective) profit by it. Fittingly, at the conclusion, it is discovered that the Negroes who have undergone the Black No More treatment are a shade lighter than regular Caucasians; whiteness becomes the measure of inferiority and the insanity continues. [23]

Despite his absolute rejection of race as a legitimate social concept and the ensuing criticism of his work, George Schuyler established himself as the leading black satirist (a *racial* label, by the way, that he would have emphatically rejected). His rational and objective view of the racial problem placed him at the outer edge of what can be called African-American humor, but his lively deflation of the assumptions that issued from advocates of both sides of the racial myth give him a unique standing as a black satirist.

The most relevant criticism of Schuyler's work concerned his dismissal of actual cultural differences that accrued from segregation and the entrenched belief in race. In articles such as "Negro Art Hokum," Schuyler leaned toward arguing that there were no cultural differences between blacks and whites; that underlying belief may well account for the near absence of African-American folk humor in his works. Other writers of the period avoided that exclusion; consequently, their work was buoyed by a richer, as well as less pristine and intellectual, humor.

Wallace Thurman and Rudolph Fisher were the other two prominent black satirists of the period. In both *The Blacker the Berry* (1929) and *Infants of the Spring* (1930), Thurman turned his sardonic wit inward, toward the black community. The title of his first novel is based on the folk saying "The blacker the berry, the sweeter the juice," and indicates the direction the tale takes. Through the frustration and exploitation of Emma Lou, the novel's beautiful, intelligent, but dark-skinned heroine, Thurman enacts a bitterly satiric exposé of blacks' hypocrisy regarding color prejudice among themselves. Although the humor is low-key, it is a refreshing antidote to the tragic mulatto theme. In *Infants of the Spring*, Thurman, like Schuyler, turned his barbs toward his fellow Renaissance artists. His scathing description of the bohemian gatherings at "Niggerati Manor" is punctuated by satiric portraits of actual Renaissance figures, who fare no better than Dr. Beard and Mr. Licorice in Schuyler's novel. Overall, Thurman's satire is grim in the extreme and representative of *black* humor more in the generic literary sense than in the racial one. The thrust of both novels is tragic rather than comic. Again, like Schuyler, as an elitist and intellectual, Thurman was only faintly concerned with the folksy but richly transcendent humor of the black masses.

In *The Walls of Jericho* (1928) and *The Conjure-Man Dies* (1932), Rudolph Fisher moved closer to incorporating the rhythms and tone of black street humor. The critic Addison Gayle, Jr., concludes that "of the Renaissance writers . . . he is the comic novelist, a forerunner of Ralph Ellison and Ishmael Reed." Fisher's *The Conjure-Man Dies* is recognized as the first detective story by an African-American author and, like Fisher's earlier novel, is infused with the language and comic spirit of the ordinary blacks who frequent barber shops, juke joints, and poolrooms. There is a touch of romantic primitivism in this novel, but unlike the exaggerated, carefree exotics who appeared in many Renaissance novels, most of Fisher's folks are genuine people whose concerns go beyond dance, drink, and sex. The plot is centered on the investigation of a murder in Harlem and features two of Fisher's most amusing comic characters—Jinx Jenkins and Bubber Brown. "The antics of Jinx and Bubber are first-rate slapstick," Sterling Brown observes, "and though traces of Octavus Roy Cohen appear, most of the comedy is close to Harlem side-walks."[24]

Jinx and Bubber had also appeared in *The Walls of Jericho*, Fisher's most expansive and successfully balanced satire of Harlem life. Here they join a cast of characters ranging from Harlem's "dickties," or upper crust, to the patrons of Patmore's Pool Parlor, "where you met real regular guys and rubbed elbows with authority." Among the regular guys are Jinx and Bubber, furniture movers who spice the tale with a barrage of street raps, jargon, and gibes. Although they are funny and speak in black urban dialect, Fisher seldom loses sight of their humanity. They are neither over-antic coons nor dim-witted darkies. Instead, their bantering and signifying provide a glimpse of a humorous spirit grounded in a realistic street perspective that acknowledges blacks' peripheral status in the white world but concentrates on the tangible enjoyment of their present position.

"Fays don' see no diference 'tween dicky shines and any other kind o' shines," Bubber tells Jinx. "One jig in danger is ev'y jig in danger." A moment later, after Jinx comes close to "slipping into the dozens," they are nearly ready to fight. But despite being egged on by the crowd, the two friends settle their differences when Jinx assures Bubber, "Ain' nobody studyin' yo' family." In this exchange, and elsewhere in the novel, Fisher integrates the folk wisdom of ordinary blacks with their fondness for jest and verbal play. He was one of the first African-American authors to portray the humor of the common, urban black man without distorting it with a veneer of insistent self-ridicule or an infusion of romantic guff about noble primitives and flight into a world of sensuous music, drink, and dark passions.[25]

Fisher was most notably a satirist, however, and *The Walls of Jericho* intertwines portraits of lower-class blacks with ironic and satirical observations of Harlem during the twenties. There is a devastating depiction of the white philanthropist Miss Agatha Cramp, who "had been devoting her life to mankind," but had regarded Negroes as "rather ugly but serviceable fixtures." Her black maid's beauty produces an epiphany, after which "the startling possibility occurred to her that Negroes might be mankind, too." There are also satiric portraits of a General Improvement Association (NAACP) ball, of impressionable whites who come uptown "to see the niggers," and of Harlem's black elite. Among the latter is Fred Merrit, one of the first trickster mulattoes to emerge in American fiction. Although "downright rabid . . . on things racial," he passes back and forth over the color line, using his access to buy property in a segregated neighborhood or, in a more ironic vein, to twit the gullible Miss Cramp, who is convinced he is white: "Nobody laughs at the miseries of life like the Negro," he tells her. "He accepts things, not with resignation but with amusement. . . . How could you wound a fellow who simply laughed? How could you be sure what he was laughing at? Himself? Maybe. But I know I'd begin to think he might be laughing at *me*."[26]

In that and similar passages, Fisher explored the areas of put-on and sham that are the natural consequences of America's absurd racial posture, and therefore the special province of African-American humor. Merrit—as lawyer, black man, white man, imposter, and ultimately trickster and race man—was the embodiment of this absurdity. Along with Jinx and Bubber, he symbolized the humor and assertiveness of the New Negro in a manner that was not seen or heard in movies or the theatre, on records or radio, or in the works of other Renaissance writers. *The Walls of Jericho* provides a genuine look at authentic African-American humor long before it reached the mainstream.

Fisher "was the first Negro to write social comedy," and *The Walls of Jericho* was the most resonant and revealing comic novel produced by a Renaissance writer. He was—if not in fact, at least in the opinion of Langston Hughes—also "the wittiest of these new Negroes of Harlem, [his] tongue was flavored with the sharpest and saltiest humor." Still, he fell short of Zora Neale Hurston and Hughes in bringing genuine folk humor to black literature.[27]

IV

Technically, Hurston was not a Renaissance writer, since her first novel, *Jonah's Gourd Vine*, was not published until 1934, after the movement had ended. But she arrived in New York in 1925, published her first short story in *Opportunity* that same year, and, by the late twenties, had become an accepted member of Harlem's coterie of writers. Her ability as a raconteur was legendary, and she was considered one of the most amusing and eccentric members of the literary circle she dubbed "the Niggerati." As Sweetie May Carr, she was among the bohemian crowd lampooned by Wallace Thurman in *Infants of the Spring*.

Hurston was a collector of folklore as well as an actress and writer. Tales collected in the South from 1928 to 1930 were published in *Mules and Men* (1935) and, later, she continued her research in Jamaica, Haiti, and the Bahamas. Some, like the poet and critic Larry Neal, maintain that "she made her most significant contribution to black literature in the field of folklorist research," but others put more weight on her fiction. Hurston's biographer, Robert Hemenway, for example, calls *Their Eyes Were Watching God* (1937) "one of the lesser-known masterpieces of American literature." Another critic aptly observes that, in *Their Eyes Were Watching God,* "Hurston the creative artist and Hurston the folklorist were perfectly united."[28]

Hurston's fiction is rife with examples of the humor and lore that she heard as a child in Florida and later went back to record. Unlike most Renaissance and Depression-era black writers, who focused on the urban scene, Hurston's venue is the pastoral South; her fiction usually centers on the rural Negro who, as she put it, "glories in his own ways" and "likes his own things best." *Jonah's Gourd Vine* and, especially, *Their Eyes Were Watching God* offer a rich catalogue of the manners and humor of those rural types and, with portraits of genuine black people who have not severed their connection to the soil or their rural heritage, effortlessly shatter the stereotypes of buffoonish, subhuman Sambos and Toms proffered by plantation-school writers.[29]

Her approach riled some African-American writers and critics, mostly those who for political purposes sought to emphasize either the new, urban Negro's achievements or racism's destructive consequences. Richard Wright, for example, accused Hurston of pandering to mainstream America's taste for "minstrel" Negroes in a review of *Their Eyes Were Watching God,* and Sterling Brown complained that *Mules and Men* lacked "bitterness" and had "only a bit of grumbling about hard work, or a few slave anecdotes that turn the tables on old master." Hurston, however, was more interested in a celebration of the joys of rural life, of the positive, textured lives that blacks had fashioned within the limited niche they had carved for themselves.[30]

Her approach allowed for expression of a natural brand of black wit and humor that was generally neither overly defensive nor reactionary. In *Jonah's Gourd Vine,* the humor is muted. Characters signify and trade quips such as, "Whuss de news?" "Oh de white folks is still in de lead." And there are severals rich examples of old-fashioned braggadocio and lying:

> "Yeah man, dat's de way it 'tis—niggers think up eve'ything good and de white folks steal it from us. Dass right. Nigger invented de train. White man seen it and run right off and made him one jes' lak it and told eve'ybody he thought it up. Same way wid 'lectwicity."

Their Eyes Were Watching God is more profusely laced with folk humor and, in the indomitable Janie and her carefree lover, Teacake,

Hurston created her most enduring female character and most imposing folk figure. Teacake, as one critic notes, is the "incarnation of the
folk culture." Before it ends in tragedy, their relationship affords Hurston a solid platform for depicting a mother lode of folk sentiment and
comedy that, in large measure, makes this her best novel.[31]

Langston Hughes, like Hurston, concentrated on fictional characters
drawn almost exclusively from the ranks of ordinary black folks. And
although they were more often northerners, few mirrored the exoticism
of the Renaissance's romantic primitives; instead they were working-
class people who reflected both the hardships and joys of everyday
experience. Hughes's dedication to depicting ordinary folks and his
continuing interest in black American folklore would ultimately confirm
him as the Renaissance's leading humorist.

"It is almost surely in the novel *Not Without Laughter*," one critic
wrote, "that the comedy of the Renaissance reached its apogee." The
claim is arguable, since in that novel Hughes neither equaled Schuyler
or Thurman as a satirist nor matched Fisher's ability to integrate comedy in the novel form. *Not Without Laughter* (1930), however, in its
attempt to show how laughter mediates the hardships of African-American life, not only offers numerous genuine examples of black humor
but also shows how the comic spirit may function as a unifying element
in black communities. Set in a small Kansas town during the Depression, Hughes's only novel is filled with the tall tales, lies, and verbal
play of its folksy characters. From the rambling slavery tales of Uncle
Dan ("the world's champeen liar") to Aunt Hager's quips about "white
folks" ("They's good as far as they can see—but when it comes to po'
niggers, they just can't see far"), Hughes evokes a real picture of small-
town, Midwestern African-American humor. Although his knack for
comedy is apparent here and in some of the stories collected in *The
Ways of White Folks* (1934), it was not until 1943, when Jesse B. Simple
first appeared in his *Chicago Defender* column, that Hughes confirmed
himself as one of America's foremost humorists.[32]

Hughes's "newspaper sketches of Jesse B. Semple [*sic*], an unlettered
but philosophical Harlemite (just be simple)," according to the critic
Robert Bone, "are among his finest literary creations." They were also
unquestionably his finest works of humor. As Arna Bontemps, a fellow
Renaissance writer and Hughes's close friend, wrote, "Here was a Harlem peasant, a Lenox Avenue ne'er-do-well, spouting the folk lore of
the city streets. . . . I had the feeling this was the freshest, most stimu-
lating feature Negro journalism had produced in our generation." But

Simple (as he was known in the sketches) was not confined only to Hughes's newspaper column; the stories were collected in several anthologies, and the character was featured in the play *Simply Heavenly* (1953). He was Hughes's most popular fictional creation and, during the forties and fifties, Simple's exploits and witty commentary on subjects ranging from food and drink to social relations, women, and racial issues were topics of discussion at black gatherings throughout America.[33]

He was Hughes's conception of the black Everyman, the embodiment of an average African-American who, for the most part, had not been depicted in the works of black or white writers. (Rudolph Fisher was one of a few notable exceptions.) Simple was not exceptional in any discernible way; he was neither a tragic mulatto nor an alienated intellectual, neither a noble savage nor a brutalized casualty of ghetto life. To that extent, he was comparable to Zora Neale Hurston's idea of the average Negro who "glories in his ways." He had no use for Negroes who were "ashamed to like watermelon" or passed for "non-chitterling eaters." Disturbed by a woman who was so embarrassed over buying a watermelon that she had the clerk wrap it before she left the store, Simple asserts, "I would eat one before the Queen of England" and he would "give the Queen a slice." As a transplanted Virginian, he differed from Hurston's characters in that his rural roots were partially cloaked with a patina of urban hipness. He represented the common, urban black man who confronted America's social constraints with a no-nonsense approach and wry wit that did not deny his second-class status but neither meekly accepted it nor allowed it to poison the joys of his personal life. As one critic writes, "Hughes never succumbed to the monstrous error of arguing that, because race prejudice is itself monstrous, it has made Negroes monstrous." Therefore, Simple emerged both as a fictional embodiment of African-Americans' realistically grounded, if obliquely expressed, humor and as a testament to Hughes's "faith in human nature" and "the soundness of his affirmations about Negroes, America, and humanity in general."[34]

The Simple tales usually involved conversations between Hughes's folk hero and the nameless acquaintance who not only was the first-person narrator of the sketches but represented the pretensions and conventional thinking of the black middle class. Although the sketches frequently dwelt on Simple's enjoyment of ordinary pleasures in the black community (beautiful black women, soul food, rent parties, jazz) or his contretemps and arguments with other blacks—particularly his girlfriend, Joyce—much of the satire evolved from his observations of the race problem. Hughes once called the character his "social protest mouthpiece" and one of the narrator's regular complaints to Simple was, "You can't discuss any subject at all without bringing in color." In their exchanges, Simple's forthright or *simple* assessment of the situation at hand was contrasted with the narrator's more evasive, accommodationist views. As Charles A. Watkins points out in "Simple: The Alter Ego of Langston Hughes," Jesse B. Simple represented not only the natural, ordinary black man but also "the authentic unassimilated black." His unadorned street dialect and unwavering acceptance of his outcast position in American society made him a kind of Socratic clown with an adversarial relationship to both the narrator and white society. Just as with traditional characters who donned the mask of the fool, his wise observations and comments unmasked the pretensions and follies of his opponents.[35]

In "Race Relations," for instance, Simple tackled the sensitive issue of miscegenation when he complained that race relations committees were missing the point by concentrating exclusively on voting rights and job security. "I always thought *relations* meant being related," he says. "But I don't hear nobody speaking about us being kinfolks." When the narrator suggests that equal rights have nothing to do with the "touchy" subject of intermarriage, which angers the South, Simple insists that they do and asserts that the South has done more "relating" than anybody else. "I keep telling you, race relations have nothing to do with that kind of relating," the narrator protests. But Simple insists:

> "If they don't . . . they are not relations."
> "What you say is entirely beside the point."
> "The point must have been moved then," Simple said.
> "Absurd. . . . We are not talking about the same thing at all," I said patiently. "I am talking about fair employment, and you are talking about . . . "
> "Race relations," said Simple.

In "Dear Mr. Butts," an unemployed Simple complains to the narrator about "Negro leaders" who "ain't lived in Harlem in ten years" but consistently write about how great democracy is. Then he reads a letter he has written to one of the black spokesmen, Mr. Butts. It reads, in part:

Now, all this later part of your article is hanging onto your *but*. You start off talking about how great American democracy is, then you but all over the place. In fact, the *but* end of your see-saw is so far down on the ground I do not believe the other end can ever pull it up. . . . Dear Butts, I am glad to read that you writ an article in *The New York Times*, but also sometime I wish you would write one in the colored papers and let me know how to get out from behind all these buts that are staring me in the face. . . . I will not take but for an answer.[36]

Jesse B. Simple established Langston Hughes as one of America's foremost humorists and escalated his popularity as a writer immeasurably. Moreover, Simple's folk wit offered an authentic mirror of black humor (both inwardly and outwardly directed) for more than two decades. They were decades of turbulent transition for the nation and for African-Americans and their humor. During much of the period, mainstream America still clung to the illusion that Rochester, Amos and Andy, and Beulah, with their ever-sanguine hospitality, reflected the true spirit of African-American comedy. It was a self-delusion that would come to an abrupt end as the civil rights movement turned violent in the sixties. Simple, too, would be undermined by the sixties' black militancy. In his newspaper column of August 16, 1963, Hughes published a letter from an irate, if misled, Harlem resident who called Simple an "Uncle Tom" and questioned why Hughes "perpetuated the stupid, ignorant offensive character." Two years later Hughes would abandon the Simple stories, explaining that "the racial climate has gotten so complicated and bitter that cheerful and ironic humor is less understandable to many people."[37]

African-American folk humor, despite its undeniable value in helping its creators overcome the burdens of slavery and segregation and its resonant, if muted, assertive thrust, was still considered an impediment to black political advancement. Most activists publicly called for harsher, more belligerent, and less conciliatory forms of expression. As the letter from the irate Harlemite suggests, some blacks were simply embarrassed by Simple's lack of sophistication and the lingering veneer of rural idiosyncrasies. It was a shortsighted, reflex response similar to the reaction twenty-six years later when *Mule Bone*—a "Comedy of Negro Life" on which Hughes and Zora Neale Hurston collaborated in 1930—was staged for the first time in 1991. On that occasion, too, critics and pundits debated the merits and pitfalls of authentically presenting certain unvarnished aspects of black humor in public forums.

"Are we still trying to figure out what is real about ourselves that we know about that [is] too dangerous to say it in public?" the novelist and playwright Ntozake Shange asked at a Lincoln Center gathering of critics, directors, actors, and writers. The critic Henry Louis Gates, Jr., was more pointed when he disapprovingly suggested that "many black Americans still feel that their precarious political and social condition within American society warrants a guarded attitude toward the way images of their culture are projected" even when "the work of two of the greatest writers in the tradition" is the focus of discussion. As Gates noted with regard to Hughes and Hurston's depiction of the rural characters who gather at Joe Clark's Eatonville, Florida, country store, the problem most often centers on fear of "what white people might think." Even if such concerns are acknowledged, with Hughes's Jesse B. Simple—a character whose political stance and racial identity seem unquestionably *correct*—the criticism and the obsession with creating a serious public image of black life appear to have reached new heights of irrationality.[38]

The self-censorship issue notwithstanding, Langston Hughes (along with Zora Neale Hurston) emerged among America's most estimable folk humorists. Although that recognition is not readily forthcoming from mainstream sources (Hughes, for instance, is curiously absent from the *Dictionary of Literary Biography* volume on American Humorists), his Simple tales provided some of the most authentic examples of African-American humor in literature prior to the seventies. But Hughes's career spanned several eras in black literary history and, from the publication of *Not Without Laughter* in 1930 to the demise of Simple in 1965, there were other advancements in the use of humor in African-American literature.

V

By the late thirties, the exoticism and satire of the Harlem Renaissance had been eclipsed by a naturalist tradition popularized by such mainstream writers as John Dos Passos, John Steinbeck, and Theodore Dreiser. William Attaway and Ann Petry were among the black writers who adopted the naturalist approach, but the most acclaimed was Richard Wright. His novel *Native Son* (1940) and autobiography, *Black Boy* (1945), are considered American classics. Although Wright determinedly depicted the grimly realistic side of black ghetto life and was sometimes guilty of narrowly focusing on the monstrous casualties that Hughes avoided, his fiction also includes numerous genuine examples of African-American ghetto humor.

For example, in *Native Son* Wright occasionally used bitter humorous exchanges between his characters to portray the gradual alienation of Bigger Thomas, his most beleaguered and violent character. After Bigger tells Gus, a poolhall buddy, that he wants to be a pilot, the following discussion ensues:

> "If you wasn't black and if you had some money and if they'd let you go to that aviation school, you *could* fly a plane," Gus said. . . .
>
> "It's funny how the white folks treat us, ain't it?"
>
> "It better be funny," Gus said.
>
> "Maybe they right in not wanting us to fly," Bigger said. " 'Cause if I took a plane up I'd take a couple of bombs along and drop 'em sure as hell. . . . "
>
> "God'll let you fly when He give you wings up in heaven," Gus said.

The posthumously published *Lawd Today* (1963) is filled with examples of signifying and ironic verbal play in which racial oppression is openly joked about:

> "Even when you's dead, they tell you where to go."
>
> "Lawd today! Jim Crow *graveyards!*"
>
> "Ain't *that* a bitch!"
>
> "Who in the hell can a *dead* black man hurt?"
>
> "Maybe a black spirit'll rape a white spirit."
>
> "Aw, nigger, hush!"
>
> "Hohohoho!"
>
> . . . .
>
> "They don't allow no *white* hen to lay no *black* eggs, or *black* hens to lay no *white* eggs. . . . Hohoho!"
>
> "They make the colored folks dye the sheets on their beds *black!* Hahaha!"
>
> "They kill a *black* cow if she gives white milk. . . . Hehehe!"
>
> "Nigger, hush! Hahaha!"[39]

Chester Himes, like Wright, initially adopted the realistic approach of the period. Although he had written crime stories in the thirties, his first two novels were "serious" naturalist works. (In 1970, critic and novelist John A. Williams called him "the single greatest naturalistic American writer living today.") The hero of *If He Hollers Let Him Go* (1945)—Bob Jones, a middle-class black man who migrates from Ohio to the West Coast to find work in a defense plant during World War II —was described by one thin-skinned critic as a character who made "Bigger Thomas seem well adjusted by comparison." His second novel, *Lonely Crusade* (1947), a less fragmented extension of the same theme, also set in California, was about a more cynical labor organizer who fights against bigoted unions and the Communist Party. The cool critical response to *Lonely Crusade* led Himes to leave the United States and, eventually, alter his fictional approach.[40]

A more ironic bent began surfacing in his writing. By the late fifties, Himes, as Rudolph Fisher had done in *The Conjure-Man Dies,* turned to detective stories spiked with satire and comedy culled from their Harlem settings. Himes's sardonic black detectives, Coffin Ed Johnson and Grave Digger Jones, were introduced in *A Rage in Harlem* (1964) and appeared in a series of novels (all save one initially published in France). These books, as a puckishly acerbic Ishmael Reed has written, were "dismissed by 'jerks' as potboilers," but were actually colorfully scathing social satires.[41]

In *Blind Man with a Pistol* (1969), Coffin Ed and Grave Digger attempt to unravel a bizarre murder case that threatens to rend a chaotic Harlem community. Farce and satire are intermixed with slapstick mayhem, comedy snippets (such as a shaggy dog tale from Dusty Fletcher's Apollo Theatre routine), and Himes's darkly comical portraits of a host of outrageous minor characters. There is, for example, General Ham, a black Messianic figure who tells his followers:

"I ain't a race leader neither. . . . Does I look like I can race? That's the trouble with you so-called Negroes. You're always looking for a race leader. The only place to race whitey is on the cinder track. We beats him there all right, but that's all."

But Himes's black detectives, through their pungent observations, provide the real edge. Questioned by their white superior about who was responsible for starting a Harlem riot, they explain:

"I take it you've discovered who started the riot," Anderson said.

"We knew who it was all along," Grave Digger said.

"It's just nothing we can do to him," Coffin Ed echoed.

"Why not, for God's sake?"

"He's dead," Coffin Ed said.

"Who?"

"Lincoln," Grave Digger said.

"He hadn't ought to have freed us if he didn't want to make provisions to feed us," Coffin Ed said. "Anyone could have told him that."[42]

Many mainstream critics were put off by Himes's satire and irreverent social views. But his blasphemous humor—especially in the Coffin Ed and Grave Digger's tales—had an authentic source in black vernacular culture. Himes was depicting aspects and attitudes gleaned from the grim, often outlandish, world of Harlem street life. His work often mirrored the bitter underside of the traditional Sambo and coon humor that ruled in the domain of mainstream comedy.

Himes's most piquant novelistic explorations of African-American humor were not published in America until the sixties, however, and by that time the novel that most eloquently and exhaustively employed black humor had been available for a decade. Ralph Ellison's *Invisible Man* (1952) is not only far more textured and resonant than Himes's work but is among the best American novels ever written. Volumes have been written analyzing its form and structure as well as its use of African-American humor and aspects of the blues idiom. It has also justifiably attained mythical status as a superb comic novel and is generally assumed to embody what Henry James and Constance Rourke called *the* American joke—the comic images created by America's frantic search for a national identity that has been a preoccupation ever since the first colonists, severed from their past and forced to confront an uncertain future, landed on these shores. Ellison writes that this search "gave Americans an ironic awareness of the joke that always lies between appearance and reality, between the discontinuity of social tradition and that sense of the past which clings to the mind." *Invisible Man* is framed by this essentially comic perception. Its nameless protagonist's pursuit of his own identity leads him ever deeper into the realm of contradictions and the absurd, into that fluid, undefined space where the comic spirit rules—where as one critic has noted, "critical self-consciousness" emphasizes the "discrepancy between subjective vision and objective appearance."[43]

Beyond these wider literary considerations and of more immediate concern in terms of revealing previously veiled aspects of black American culture is Ellison's specific use of African-American folk humor. "Classical literature, fairy tales, early novels, works by Freud, Marx, Eliot, Wright, Malraux, Hemingway, Faulkner—all provide allusions in *Invisible Man*," the critic Robert O'Meally observes, and "black in-jokes reverberate throughout this novel." Many were so obscure or so weighted by social taboo that they were either overlooked or became a source of embarrassment to critics. "Ellison brilliantly exploits [the] tension over black/white humor," O'Meally notes. Ellison himself confirmed the nature of that tension in comments about early responses to the novel: "By the time I finished the book," he said, "I had white friends, sensitive readers, people who knew much of the world's literature, reading my novel . . . and reacting as if it were in utter bad taste for a white reader to laugh at a black character in a ridiculous situation." The double-edged nature of African-American humor was still a mystery to most white readers, and the appearance of Negro jokes in a *serious* novel presented a dilemma to them as well as to many black intellectuals who similarly assumed that such jokes were inherently demeaning or anticipated that non-blacks would consider them so. Despite this reaction, Ellison assertively weaved that humor into the fabric of his novel and, ultimately, helped revise those stubbornly wrong-headed notions.[44]

Farce, slapstick comedy, racial jokes (aimed at both blacks and whites), puns, folktales, minstrel jokes, broad satire, and subtle wit are all interwoven with the sustaining theme of self-discovery, transcendence, and triumph through the acceptance of absurdity that defines the comic spirit. The novel's ironic direction is foreshadowed early in chapter 1, when the narrator's grandfather, thought to be "the meekest of men," counsels from his deathbed:

> "Son, after I'm gone I want you to keep up the good fight. I never told you, but our life is a war and I have been a traitor all my born days, a spy in the enemy's country ever since I give up my gun back in the Reconstruction. Live with your head in the lion's mouth. I want you to overcome 'em with yeses, undermine 'em with grins, agree 'em to death and destruction, let 'em swoller you till they vomit or bust wide open."

The guileless protagonist's puzzlement over this advice largely determines the course of his bizarre, picaresque journey to self-discovery
and the corresponding symbolic historical excursion through blacks'
American experience. His naïveté and inability to discern the difference
between appearance and reality, to recognize societal masks or, when
necessary, to adopt one, places him in an "absurdly disjointed space"
where the comic and grotesque are sovereign. Consequently, his journey is not only an often painful rite of initiation into the society's
labyrinthine racial arrangements ("the way things are and the way
they're supposed to be," as Dr. Bledsoe, the maniacal black college
president advises him) but also a hilarious romp in which the various
comic guises that define those arrangements are unveiled.[45]

Before he achieves self-revelation or enlightenment, the protagonist
is literally cast as the straightman or dupe in the American joke. His
highly praised graduation address on "humility" is rewarded with an
invitation to repeat the speech before a gathering of white citizens but,
in addition, he is asked to participate in a "battle royal," a melee in
which black youths are urged to pummel themselves into unconscious-
ness to amuse white spectators who shout invectives such as "Sambo"
and "nigger." At college, his earnest efforts to accommodate Norton,
the white philanthropist, lead to a scandalous confession by Trueblood,
an incestuous black sharecropper, mayhem at the Golden Day bar,
and, finally, his expulsion by Dr. Bledsoe, who berates him: "Why, the
dumbest black bastard in the cotton patch knows that the only way to
please a white man is to tell him a lie! What kind of education are
you getting around here?" Bledsoe sends him off with seven letters of
recommendation, whose contents, in effect, echo a disturbing sequence
in a dream the protagonist has had in which a letter in his briefcase
reads, "Keep This Nigger-Boy Running." As the narrator's journey continues, he haplessly lurches through comically revealing encounters
with employers, the Brotherhood or Communist Party, black and white
women, black militants, and other bizarre types who emerge as caricatures of the various guises worn by the inhabitants of America's racial
nightmare.[46]

The solution to the narrator's dilemma is insinuated throughout his
journey as Ellison reveals his own high regard for vernacular culture
and suggests that it is an antidote or palliative to his protagonist's confusion as well as a guideline for his triumph and survival. In these instances, *Invisible Man* is most revealing in its use of African-American
humor. The advice offered by his grandfather and similar counsel given

the hero by a veteran first encountered at the Golden Day ("Play the game, but don't believe in it") suggest that the tactical folk approach of duplicity and recourse to a comic mask is the key to unraveling the mystery. The hero's trek toward self-discovery is fueled by his escalating awareness of the meaning and deeper significance of folk rhymes, blues lyrics, snippets of black comic routines, and such inside jokes as the paint factory slogan, "If It's Optic White, It's the Right White," which recalls a jingle from childhood:

> If you're white, you're right,
> If you're brown, stick around,
> If you're black, get back.[47]

As the narrator advances toward self-awareness, he begins to accept both himself and the culture he formerly disparaged. Admitting that he "no longer felt ashamed of the things [he] loved," he can laughingly claim, "I Yam what I am!" Later, at a Brotherhood meeting, a drunken heckler demands that he sing a spiritual or a work song:

> Like this: '*Ah went to Atlanta—nevah been there befo'*,' he sang, his arms held out from his body like a penguin's wings, glass in one hand, cigar in the other. '*White man sleep in a feather bed, Nigguh sleep on the flo'* . . . Ha! Ha! How about it Brother? . . . Come on, brother, git hot! Go Down Moses,' he bellowed.

Embarrassed more by the others' eyeballing than by the drunk's remarks ("Why was everyone staring at me as though I were responsible?"), the narrator defends the drunk's behavior. Then:

> Suddenly I was laughing hysterically. 'He hit me in the face,' I wheezed. 'He hit me in the face with a yard of chitterlings! . . . He threw a hog maw. . . . He's high as a Georgia pine.'

His amused response to "the outrageous example of racial chauvinism" initially baffles the white onlookers, but they ultimately join him. Later, he wonders, "Shouldn't there be some way for us to be asked to sing? Shouldn't the short man have the right to make a mistake without his motives being considered consciously or unconsciously malicious?"[48]

This defense of ethnic humor forecasts views that Ellison would later express more directly. "When Americans can no longer laugh at one another, then they have to fight with one another," he said in 1971. Humor "tends to make us identify with the one laughed at despite ourselves. . . . It's a humanizing factor." In fact, overall, the narrator's experience can be seen as a bildungsroman or journey to self-awareness and humanization through perception and acceptance not only of the spirit of African-American humor but also of the comic spirit itself. Progressively, he learns to deal with the absurdity surrounding him. He acquires a resiliency that eludes "serious" souls trapped by the limitations of appearances—the way things are, or seem to be—and allows him finally to answer societal perfidy with a spontaneous creativity. As Robert O'Meally points out, Ellison's hero echoes Kenneth Burke's observation about the "comic frame," which allows man to "transcend occasions when he has been tricked or cheated." "The comic perspective," writes O'Meally, "permits one to be . . . optimistically poised to respond effectively." Viewing the world through a comic frame, Ellison's narrator can "nurture his own life, taking all things, however absurdly baffling, as they come."[49]

That perception so dominates *Invisible Man* that even when it veers toward the tragicomic, as in the depiction of Tod Clifton, it is relieved by satire or burlesque. Clifton, a black member of the Brotherhood, drops out after his motives—indeed, his black identity—are questioned by a nationalist; later, he reappears on a midtown street selling Sambo dolls:

> "He'll keep you entertained. He'll make you weep sweet
> Tears from laughing.
> Shake him, shake him, you cannot break him
> For he's Sambo, the dancing, Sambo, the prancing,
> Sambo, the entrancing, Sambo Boogie Woogie paper doll."

While the narrator watches, Tod is approached by a policeman (he "had an itching finger and an eager ear for a word that rhymed with 'trigger' "), and when their verbal dispute escalates to violence, Tod is shot and killed. This apparent affirmation of the tragedy and powerlessness of black life and the insignificance of black death, however, is transformed by the narrator's ironic and comic eulogy. While he despairs over Clifton's death, the event is described as "a comic-book killing, on a comic-book street in a comic-book town on a comic-book day in a comic-book world" and punctuated with a turn on a black verbal riff ("When they call you *nigger* to make a rhyme with *trigger* it makes the gun backfire"). A decade or so later, Dick Gregory would use a different turn on the wordplay as a comeback to racist hecklers: "You hear what that guy just called me? Roy Rogers' horse. He called me Trigger!" With a similar spirit and intent, Gregory would entitle his 1964 autobiography *Nigger*.[50]

Ellison's remarkable novel—with its embrace of the comic spirit and elaborate use of black folk humor—was an embarrassment to many whites, as well as to those blacks who still fretted over revealing supposed backward examples of African-American folk wit. In 1952, most American fiction still adhered to the romanticism and naturalism established earlier in the century. The modern fantasists and fabulists who, as critic Robert Scholes notes, would "turn the materials of satire and protest into comedy" had not arrived in force, and Ellison's novel "was one of the earliest in the postwar period to fuse realism and surrealism, jokes and blues, in the form of an ironic picaresque." Later in the decade, many mainstream writers would venture into farce, symbolism, and fantasy, but, for the most part, black novelists continued in a realistic vein until the emergence of Ishmael Reed in the late sixties.[51]

Charles Wright's second novel, *The Wig* (1966), was a notable exception. Called the "first certified Negro black humorist" by *New York Times* critic Victor Navasky, Wright had made his initial foray into darkly humorous fiction in 1963 with *The Messenger,* a novel that depicted its hero stumbling through a series of absurd situations initiated by his role as a courier. With *The Wig,* however, Wright delved more intimately into the world of African America's hidden aspirations and frailties, that clandestine, potentially embarrassing province where the confusion between black identity and American identity often surfaces in its most absurd and comic form. Set in the sixties—when dashikis, Afros, and other external affirmations of the *natural* self measured nationalist identity and acceptance of an African heritage—Wright's novel concerns a black man who is determined to be accepted in the "Great Society." Lester Jefferson, who in previous attempts to "get over" masqueraded as an Arab, finally discovers the solution to his problem. After a drugstore clerk tells him, "With this, you may become whatever you desire," Lester returns home with a jar of "Silky Smooth Hair Relaxer," convinced that, after its transforming effect, "the black clouds would soon recede," that he might "shake his head triumphantly like any white boy."[52]

Appropriately coiffed or conked, and confidently proclaiming, "I *am* an American," Lester begins his assault on the Great Society. What follows is a series of bizarre comic episodes in which Lester's identity crisis and the absurdity of America's racial policies are submitted to riotous ridicule. In one of his first encounters, Lester meets a black woman who is attracted to him but, assuming he is not black, insists upon being paid: "No finance, no romance." He then meets a Stepin Fetchit–like former movie star, who tells of being invited to the White House where congressmen sang "He's a Jolly Good Nigger" and gave him a gold-plated medal carved with the figure of a naked black man hanging from a rope. Later, he meets a militant nationalist, Tom, who despite groveling and "bowing and rolling his eyes" at his job, calls Lester an "infidel" and almost kills him when he sees what he has done to his hair. The incidents continue and Lester realizes that, despite his being accepted as a non-black, his new "wig" is not producing the desired results. After a black psychic or hoodoo queen warns that he "is on the road to self-destruction" and tells him, "You may find the way, *despite* The Wig," Lester reluctantly shaves his head.[53]

Realistic depictions of characters who slip in and out of social masks are interwoven with fantasy and farce in Wright's comic world. As Frances S. Foster contends in "Charles Wright: Black Black Humorist," *The Wig* shares many of the qualities of the black humor literary genre. Lester, for instance, describes his father's death in the deadpan style of a Kurt Vonnegut: "My father had learned to read and write extremely well at the age of thirty-six. He died while printing the letter Z for me." And other shocking incidents are depicted with similar aloofness and treated as little more than jokes. A white policeman, for example, who is just "doing his duty" helps a black mother discipline a child who does not want to go to a segregated school by slamming his nightstick against the child's head and killing him.[54]

These instances of the genre of black humor, however, both overlap and are intermixed with African-American humor. For example, the black humor tack of perceiving societal contradiction as a joke is not far removed from the African-American community's stoic perception of racist absurdity as humorous. Moreover, the basic premise of the novel derives from one of the key defining sources of African-American humor—the tension between the trickster's ploy of using masked behavior, a charade, as a pragmatic means of dealing with racism and the covert perception that such behavior betrays one's heritage. Wright's novel comically treats this tension on a surface or cosmetic level. But in its vernacular use, "wig" not only means "hair" but also "mind or mental state" (as in "wigged out" or crazy). *The Wig*, then, can also be seen as a comic exploration of the premise that, to be accepted in mainstream society, African-Americans must alter their behavior and sever their spiritual association with black culture.

Charles Wright's fiction not only reflected much of the genuine spirit and content of black American humor but also demonstrated its connection to mainstream anti-establishment humor. He was a vastly underrated novelist who, at the time his work appeared, was exploring virgin territories for black writers.

Still, some other works published in the mid-sixties included genuine examples of African-American humor. John Oliver Killens's impious Army recruit, Scotty, for example, is "the most memorable character" in his second novel, *And Then We Heard the Thunder* (1962), primarily because his comic antics and bizarre behavior are appropriate responses to "the madness of the black soldier's situation" during World War II. Scotty is given to such proclamations as "a cracker is a mama-jabbing motherhuncher" and considers himself a "fieldhand" in the military's plantation-like hierarchy; he goes about subverting Army routine in much the same manner that slaves diagnosed as having *dysaesthesia Aethiopica* broke, wasted, and destroyed everything they handled in the antebellum South.

Scotty's challenging of the military's segregated policies and satirical reactions to irrational racist strictures reveal the comic irony of the black soldier's situation. "Naw, we don't like it," he roars at one point. "Here you goddamn people 'bout to send us somewhere south of west-hell to do your dying and you have the goddamn nerve to build a canteen in pissing distance from our tents and dare us to put our foot inside." His forthright street approach and irreverent wit spur the novel's denouement and graphically depict how insightful black protest may be (and often is) couched in the most profane and hyperbolic gibes. In 1970 Killens would move even more boldly toward satire and the comic mode with his riotous *The Cotillion*, a novel which, as Addison Gayle, Jr., writes, "verges upon the tragic and the comic" and focuses "upon the black community, upon the pretensions and illusions of its inhabitants."[55]

VI
- - - - - - - - -

By the early seventies—largely through the mass media exposure of comedians such as Dick Gregory, Bill Cosby, Flip Wilson, Redd Foxx, and a still-reserved Richard Pryor—black comedy had taken one large step out of its ghetto confinement to make a small dent in America's consciousness. Even the overwhelming majority of mainstream Americans, who were unfamiliar with the works of Chesnutt, Schuyler, Fisher, Hurston, Hughes, Himes, and Ellison, or blind to the satire and comic thrust of their work, began suspecting that their revered Beulahs and Snowballs, their coon and Sambo figures, discarded their masks in private and reveled in a different kind of humor. The mystery surrounding African-Americans' persistent, often disconcerting, laughter was increasingly being unraveled on prime-time television in full view of non-black audiences primed on Uncle Remus, racial ventriloquy, tar-faced, goggle-eyed knickknacks, and rotund, beamingly complacent servants.

Not surprisingly, more black authors began reflecting the comic resonance, uninhibited self-assurance, and assertively impudent tone of those stage wits and clowns. Although James Baldwin, the sixties' best-known black writer, generally eschewed the comic, others enthusiastically embraced it. A raft of poets, for instance, abandoned the more polite satire and measured, European cadences of their forerunners and adopted an explosive, street-based expressive voice. Combining such African-American comic devices as puns, tall tales, and braggadocio with blues and jazz rhythms and an often militantly iconoclastic approach, they aggressively pilloried mainstream American politics and culture, and, in the spirit of the popular song that most ardently echoed the tenor of the era (James Brown's "Say It Loud, I'm Black and I'm Proud"), exuberantly celebrated black life. Their voices ranged from strident to nuanced, from cynically revolutionary to satirically conciliatory. Among the most successful were Larry Neal, David Henderson, Sonia Sanchez, Quincy Troupe, Sarah Webster Fabio, Mari Evans, A. B. Spellman, Jay Wright, Carolyn Rogers, Don L. Lee, June Jordan, Ishmael Reed, and Nikki Giovanni.

Another, Amiri Baraka (formerly LeRoi Jones) employed a sardonic approach that variously skewered black bourgeoisie apathy, white racism, and white cultural imperialism, in his poetry as well as in his plays, essays, and fiction. Baraka is "a master of comic modes," Charles H. Nichols contends, "of mirror-and-mask effects, irony, sarcasm, and paradox." A prolific commentator on black music and culture, Baraka made lavish use of the vernacular idiom in his creative satiric works. Humor in his poetry often took the form of scathing sarcasm, as in "Three Modes of History and Culture":

> . . . The Party of Insane
> Hope. I've come from there too. Where the dead told lies
> about clever social justice. Burning coffins voted
> and staggered through cold white sheets listening
> to Willkie or Wallace or Dewey through the dead face
> of Lincoln. Come from there, and belched it out.

In his play *Dutchman* (1964), the mocking, signifying exchanges between Lula and Clay offer insight into the seething but often comic vicissitudes of interracial encounters of the period. Throughout his work, there is an attention to incongruity and a knack for creating arch juxtapositions that not only mirror the slickest street raps and putdowns but also enliven them with the selective imagery of a poet. In the Harlem evoked in his short story collection *Tales* (1968), one may encounter "various freaks up and down the street. Like black blondes or niggers with good jobs." And a character can, with sly irony, brag, "I was always hip. I mean, I knew about Brooks Brothers when I was 10." Glib and observant, Baraka's satire is rooted in an intense awareness of those persistently absurd aspects of American life that have fueled African-Americans' comic perception since slavery.[56]

Poet, essayist, and novelist Ishmael Reed began exploring the comic in an even more expansive and caustic manner in the sixties. Like Baraka and other contemporaries, Reed targeted the assumed priority of Western ideology, as well as black bourgeois mimicry of those ideals in literature, politics, and mass culture. ("My main job," he wrote, "was to humble Judeo-Christian culture.") But unlike Baraka, in whose work satire and humor were essentially used to heighten and punctuate a primarily rational dissection of Western hegemony, in his fiction Reed created an imaginative world that not only ridiculed the icons and tenets of Western culture but evoked the Dionysian rites or festivals to which Aristotle traced the comic spirit. More precisely—since Reed would likely disavow any significant connection between his art and ancient Greece, and has argued that his work presents figures modeled on "African art"—his work evokes what he calls "Neo-Hoodoo," whose source is the nihilist African *loa* or spirit Guede and whose center is "the drum the anhk and the Dance." However one defines the creative source of Reed's imagination, there is little doubt about its mordant comic thrust. Reed's novels place the reader squarely in that turbulent domain where societal masks are ripped away, pretensions and conceits are challenged and ridiculed, and upheaval and chaos—"the priority of disordered life"—are exalted while tyrannical order is exposed as oppressive and demeaning. As such, they cut to the center of the comic province and reflect a dominant aspect of African-American humor— its cynical apprehension of mainstream American culture and insistent embracing of a more spontaneous, fluid, and jocular approach to daily life. According to Reed, in the sixties, "black writers started going back to the folklore and that's where the humor is. The punchlines and nuances of Afro-American humor go back to that tradition—humor is more third world than Western and Christian."[57]

Reed's first novel, The *Free-Lance Pallbearers* (1967), was, on one level, an allegory in which the hero, Bukka Doopeybuk, attempts to gain access to the throne of power in the land of Harry Sam—a country ruled by a dictator of the same name. A parody of the Horatio Alger success story, the novel follows Bukka (a naive hospital orderly) as he grapples his way to the top. But Harry Sam is dominated by corruption and madness, which in Reed's fictional construct is characterized by one central symbol: excrement. Harry Sam (or Uncle Sam) is ruler of an anally oriented society; he is also a cannibal whose throne is a toilet on which he sits for extended periods of time. Sewage backs up throughout the land and Bukka, who spends his days emptying bedpans, has a relative who "once kissed Calvin Coolidge's ass" and an intellectual mentor, U2 Polyglot, who shoves a pile of dung around with his nose to test a literary theory about Kafka's "Metamorphosis." "The languages of advertising, of politics, of scholarship, of bureaucracy, of medicine, and of religion are specifically shown to be forms of human waste," the critic Keith E. Byerman argues. To another critic, the novel has, "at different times, a nightmarish fantasy, a Kafkaesque absurdity, the horrible prophesy of some new version of 1984, the violence, squalor, and realism of ghetto life." Moreover, it is also a black satirist's darkly comic imaginative rendering of a dismissive view of America and the American dream commonly held by ordinary blacks in the sixties— that it was "full of shit."[58]

Reed continued his assault on Western culture and tradition in *Yellow Back Radio Broke Down* (1969). Advertised as the first "Hoodoo Western," it was, like its predecessor, a parody of a popular literary genre. Its black cowboy hero, the Loop Garoo Kid (possibly a takeoff on Lash LaRue, one of Hollywood's few Western stars who wore black), is a folk hero in the "bad nigger" mold who sets out to destroy the prevailing religious, social, and political order. But he is also a root-doctor or conjure man ("born with a caul over his face and ghost lobes on his ears") who employs the power of hoodoo to humiliate, outwit, or destroy his adversaries. The struggle between hoodoo culture and Western ideology also dominates Reed's third novel, *Mumbo Jumbo* (1972). Here the hero is Papa LaBas, a New Orleans Houngan who, during the roaring twenties, attempts to discover the source of Jes Grew, the mysterious "psychic plague" that is sweeping the nation. Like African-American syncopated music, or jazz, Jes Grew has spread from New Orleans to Chicago and, along the way, amassed a following in whom the spirit of nihilism, a passionate desire to dance, and the uninhibited pursuit of pleasure have immediately surfaced. It has also attracted an array of determined opponents. A Southern congressman in the novel clearly voices the nature of their opposition: "Jes Grew is the boll weevil eating away at the fabric of our forms our techniques our aesthetic integrity."[59]

In *Mumbo Jumbo,* Jes Grew (whether it is seen as jazz or the spirit of the Harlem Renaissance, as critics have variously suggested), represents the hoodoo or spirited African-American equation in Reed's lexicon of values. As in his previous two novels, it is set against the conservative, controlling influence of Western culture. But while this tension framed Reed's satirical approach in his early novels, it never totally defined it. There is a freewheeling, almost frenetically inspired mischievousness in Reed's work that transcends most critical definitions. His novels are montages in which historical fact, actual people, and literary or media-created fictional characters are combined with parody, farce, jokes, folklore, street vernacular, and outrageous imaginative leaps to lampoon an assortment of people, concepts, and institutions. In the manner of H. L. Mencken and George Schuyler (whom Reed admired), nearly anything that Reed finds regressive, spiritually confining, or inhumane becomes a target for his scatter-gun wit. Like the hero of *Yellow Back Radio Broke Down,* Reed often seems to be "scatting arbitrarily, using forms of this and adding his own. . . . blowing like that celebrated musician Charles Yardbird Parker—improvising as he goes along."[60]

The Free-Lance Pallbearers, for example, besides skewering the spiritual and political underpinnings of Harry Sam's domain, pillories artists who have "prostituted their art for 'hoola hoops'" and signifies about the literary works of, among others, T. S. Eliot and Ralph Ellison "as though they were cultural detritus." *Yellow Back Radio Broke Down* not only unleashes the hoodoo-inspired Loop Garoo Kid on the forces of repression but also satirizes the Pope and parodies Black Aesthetic advocates through Bo Shmo (the leader of a "neo-realist gang" who writes "suffering books" about his neighborhood and warns the "crazy dada nigger" hero that they "can't afford the luxury of individualism gumming up our rustling"). In addition, the novel is rife with puns (a voyeuristic congressman is described as having "groucho marxed into the room") and humor that, like Flip Wilson's stand-up routines, uses cultural and historical displacement for comic effect: the Pope's suggestion that Loop's men can be lured away with "a bottle of cheap dirty wine, 2 stagecoach tickets and a rolled-up 10 dollar bill" is reminiscent of Wilson's Christopher Columbus routine in which the supplies for Chris's voyage include "two pair of fatigues, some shades, two chicken sandwiches, three cans of Vienna sausages, five cases of Scotch, a small Seven-Up, and a new rag to tie his head with."[61]

In addition to its satirical portrait of the conflict between Jes Grew and its antagonists—the Atonists (dedicated to the "glorification of Western culture") and the affiliated Wallflower Organization (whose creed is "Lord, if I can't dance, No one will")—*Mumbo Jumbo* includes some riotous parodies of Harlem Renaissance types and actual figures. Warren Harding and Irene Castle (a popular dancer in the twenties) appear as themselves and become involved in a conspiracy to stamp out Jes Grew. Carl Van Vechten is parodied as Hinkle Von Vampton, a Wallflower member who infiltrates the Harlem community to manipulate its artists and destroy the movement. Abdul Hamid is a black Muslim whose allegiance to Allah puts him at odds with Jes Grew ("Cut out this dancing and carrying on, fulfilling base carnal appetites") and ultimately leads him to betray it. The narrative is spiced throughout with Reed's impious wisecracks and sly puns.[62]

Like Charles Wright's *The Wig*, Ishmael Reed's fiction reflects the "spirit of playfulness" displayed by the fabulators or mainstream black humorists of the sixties and seventies, who turned "the materials of satire and protest into comedy" even as they massed a "sardonic, scatological, parodistic assault upon the elements of . . . Western culture." But unlike the work of most of those writers, his satire and humor are girded by a prevailing faith in the spontaneous wit and diversity of black folk culture. The Bad Nigger hero of *Yellow Back Radio Broke Down* and the root-doctor protagonist of *Mumbo Jumbo* would be joined in subsequent novels by characters based on such folk heroes as Brer Rabbit and John Henry; even comic stereotypes such as Amos and Andy appear and become grist for Reed's satiric mill. The jive talk and vernacular speech and jokes that dice his work are obviously drawn from black folk humor, but so, too, are many of the clever puns that combine street smarts and allusions based on current or historical events. It does not detract from Reed's fictional innovation to suggest that much of his humor flows from the same source that inspired such black armchair or barber shop philosophers as Crow, a lean spokesman from my hometown. (*Tall like pine, black like crow, talk mo' shit than a radio.*) During the fifties I overheard him dismiss politics and the effectiveness of voting by asserting: "*Tru*-man was a boldface liar, and Eisen-*hour* weren't worth a minute to us. Don't seem to me like we been asked to nar' one a they parties."[63]

During the late sixties and early seventies, as African-American humor was being ungagged on the mainstream stage, Reed was the most adventurous of the raft of black writers who aggressively incorporated comedy into their fictional works. Humor suddenly emerged as one of the principal elements in African-American literature. Examples vary from the lyrical folk humor of Albert Murray's blues-saturated *Train Whistle Guitar* (1974), set in Alabama during the 1920s, to the surrealistic intensity of Barry Beckham's *Runner Mack* (1972), an allegorical tale in which a black baseball player's struggle to infiltrate the Major League (mainstream society) is impeded by a series of bizarre, tragicomic mishaps. If one novel were chosen, however, to represent the comic amplitude displayed in the rush of fiction published during this period, it would be Cecil Brown's *The Loves and Lives of Mr. Jiveass Nigger* (1969).

Brown's first novel was a picaresque bildungsroman that charted the exploits of George Washington (its lustful trickster hero) from his rural Southern upbringing, through an Ivy League education and a sojourn in Copenhagen, to self-revelation and return to America. His view of the world—"all is jive and vexation of the spirit. . . . Jive, it's all jive"— echoes a cynicism and sense of absurdity expressed in works by Ellison, Reed, and Charles Wright, and leads to the seductions, artful conniving, and inveterate lying that provide most of the comedy. Brown weaves folklore—for instance, an exaggerated retelling of the tale in which the slave John slaps his master's wife to prove how *bad* he is—and comic but often bitter exchanges between the sexes into this tale as he satirizes the sexual conquests that promise to confirm our identities but ultimately only obscure and mask them. The novel forecasts a concern with the comic spirit that would lead Brown to screenwriting (he co-authored Richard Pryor's *Which Way Is Up?*) and a second novel, *Days Without Weather* (1983), which deals specifically with the fate of a black comedian in Hollywood and anticipates many of the themes aired in Robert Townsend's satirical film depiction of blacks in mainstream movies, *Hollywood Shuffle* (1989).[64]

By the late seventies and early eighties, farce, folklore, fantasy, myth, and rich examples of the ironic, comic perception that distinguishes many ordinary African-Americans' world view had become staples in black literature. Ishmael Reed continued his hoodoo aesthetic in novels such as *Flight to Canada* (1976) and *The Terrible Twos* (1982); acceptance of folk humor and wisdom was a prominent theme in many of the stories in Toni Cade Bambara's *Gorilla My Love* (1972); satire and fantasy enlivened George Cain's nightmarish depiction of a junkie's travails in *Blueschild Baby* (1973); David Bradley's *South Street* (1975), a novel "finely tuned on the edge of comic thrusts and bitter reality," used burlesque and satire to evoke the vitality of ghetto life; Gayl Jones explored myth, madness, and the destructive edges of humor in *Eva's Man* (1976) and her collected short stories, *White Rat* (1977); Al Young etched memorable portraits of common black folks whose warm senses of humor abetted their day-to-day struggle to survive in *Sitting Pretty* (1977) and *Ask Me Now* (1980); and in *Song of Solomon* (1977) and *Tar Baby* (1981), Toni Morrison lyrically evoked aspects of black myth and folklore that nurtured her characters and allowed them to surmount earth-bound deprivations. These black writers, and others too numerous to mention, wrote fiction that affirmed the preeminence of an African-American comic spirit that had been too long distorted or denied. Their work not only reflects an abiding appreciation of the earlier efforts of writers such as Schuyler, Fisher, Hughes, Hurston, and Ellison but also demonstrates that "subtle faith in the humanizing value of laughter."[65]

Finally, the vernacular rhythms, folk ironies, and satiric, comic riffs that embroidered or sometimes defined African-American literary humor often mirrored specific examples of black folklore and comedy whose source was the street humor of ordinary black folks. Writers frequently heightened the comic notes—investing them with resonances from European literature and folklore or assuming the double-edged spirit of African-American wit themselves and imaginatively amplifying them—but their works also regularly incorporated many examples intact. In the latter instances, they functioned as a window to a comic vision that, like the prophetic hero of Ralph Ellison's novel, was largely invisible because of America's preconceived notion of black life.

Given the oversights of many critics, it is not surprising that ordinary readers often overlooked black literature's comic resonance. Still, for those interested, African-American folklore, a prime source of yesterday's street humor, might also have provided lavish examples of the real thing.

11.

···

FOLKLORE AND STREET

HUMOR . . . *"if you*

grinnin', you in 'em"

18

JACK JOHNSON

TO MOST CAUCASIANS THE NOTION OF JOKES BY NEGROES LAMPOONING WHITES COMES SOMEWHAT AS A SURPRISE. YET AS AN ACTUALITY SUCH HUMOR MAY OUT-DATE ITS WHITE COUNTERPART.

—JOHN H. BURMA

YOU KNOW, THE GREATEST NEGRO HUMOR IS IN THE NEGRO HOME, NOT ON THE STAGE. WHEN IT COMES TO *OUR* HUMOR, THE WHITE MAN IS OUR GREATEST CLOWN.

—DICK GREGORY

NIGGERS JUST HAVE A WAY OF TELLING YOU STUFF AND NOT TELLING YOU STUFF. MARTIANS WOULD HAVE A DIFFICULT TIME WITH NIGGERS. THEY BE TRANSLATING WORDS, SAYING A WHOLE LOT OF THINGS UNDERNEATH YOU, ALL AROUND YOU . . . THAT'S OUR COMEDY.

—RICHARD PRYOR[1]

I

Authentic folktales, ballads, and toasts collected and published by folklorists both documented an important part of African-American oral history and provided the most accurate and revealing *mainstream* exposure of black street humor up until the mid-twentieth century. A few of these collections (most notably Zora Neale Hurston's *Mules and Men*) went beyond mere enumeration of isolated tales and described the circumstances in which they were repeated. With regard to humor, those collections are the most informative, since they document the organic interplay among the participants, revealing the introductory remarks, audience responses, and digressive commentary that accompanied the tales. This textured depiction not only more clearly exposed the "front stage" humorous direction of the tales but also unmasked their real-life application—their underlying or "background" function as moral instructives and coded expressions of outrage at actual grievances.[2]

Still, printed descriptions rarely capture the complexity of any oral humor. The grass-roots outpourings of tales, proverbs, and jokes offer the most legitimate examples of any group's distinctive humorous expression. The problem, as anthropologist and folklorist Alan Dundes notes, is "that the very nature of esoteric humor is such as to make it extremely difficult for anyone outside the culture even to collect texts, much less understand them."[3]

The task was made more formidable by African-Americans' continued suspicion of white Americans' motives, and the consequent widespread use of secrecy, subterfuge, and a mask of accommodation when dealing with whites. Despite these evasions, select examples of black folk humor began surfacing on stage (through minstrelsy) and in literature quite early in American life. Usually these humorous tidbits represented what Ralph Ellison called "prefabricated Negroes ... superimposed upon the Negro community." But even when not willfully distorted or misinterpreted, the material typically adopted by non-black performers and writers and established in popular culture was selected because it offered surface confirmation of stereotypes cherished by whites. In *Laughing on the Outside: The Intelligent White Reader's Guide to Negro Tales and Humor,* Philip Sterling writes, "Negroes' stories about themselves are one of the original sources of the derogatory anti-Negro stereotype which has flourished for 150 years."[4]

True enough, but from Stepin Fetchit's "World's Laziest Man" caricature and Mantan Moreland's fleet-footed exits when facing danger to the near-libelous verbal sparring between black males and females on sitcoms in the seventies and eighties, the mainstream media have most often missed the point of black-inspired humor by presenting it out of context. African-Americans' humor, like that of other ethnic groups, varies widely, ranging from rural to urban and lower-class to middle-class; it includes social satire and ridicule of those outside the group as well as self-critical lampooning of its own members. Focus on the last of these and a disinclination or inability to discern its often double-edged or ironic nature partially accounts for the preponderance of negative humor that appeared in mainstream literature and theatres.

Even when African-American entertainers and writers began presenting their own versions of black folk humor, however, there were major barriers. The blunt, often profane street vernacular in which folk humor was frequently couched, often an integral part of the style and meaning of the tales or jokes presented, was not tolerated in popular culture before the 1960s. And in an attempt to project a positive image in mainstream culture, the black middle class imposed further obstacles by publicly denouncing theatrical or literary humor that, although genuine, depicted blacks in a seemingly unflattering manner or exposed supposedly backward or unrefined customs to outside scrutiny.

In addition, most critical social or racial commentary was to a certain extent internally restrained by the entertainer's observance of ritual and sense of propriety regarding the use of ridicule. Within the black community, verbal ridicule was an accepted, indeed an expected activity. When extended outside one's immediate circle in that community, however, it was usually seen as a direct challenge or prelude to violence.

External restraints on discarding the mask of naïveté and accommodation and revealing the satirical underside of black humor were even more clear-cut. Performers who overstepped the vague line between acceptable comedy and ridicule of white society, or even attained a level of celebrity considered too grandiose for a Negro, exposed themselves to physical reprisal. W. C. Handy's report of the need to assume a servile, minstrel-like posture even off stage in many cities; Williams and Walker's unfortunate meeting with the group of redneck ruffians who stripped them and ran them out of a Southern town; and the incendiary exhortations to get Ernest Hogan, Williams and Walker, and Cole and Johnson during the New York City riots of 1900—all demonstrate the life-threatening encounters that frequently awaited Negro entertainers or any African-American who overstepped the bounds of society's unyielding stereotypes.

So it is small wonder that black comedians were cautious in expanding the range and thrust of their routines. They probably took note of the tagline to a familiar story concerning the reaction of an integrated group of workers to an attractive young white woman who walks past. A Negro murmurs, "Lawd, will I ever?" A white worker who overhears him says, "No, nigger, never." Undeterred, the Negro says, "Long as there's life, there's hope." To which the white worker responds, "*Yes, and long as there's a nigger, there's a rope.*"

Within the black community, however, humor was free of these externally imposed restrictions. It sometimes focused on actual, negative situations that were part of day-to-day reality—the above joke, for example, is attributed to blacks—but inside black humor was more often assertively pro-black. Most often it simply ignored whites. In fact, contrary to social scientists such as Gunnar Myrdal, who insisted that most Negro humor was reactive (shaped by a desire to please whites or avoid punishment), or others who claimed Negroes were humorous only in a naive or unintended sense, humor was (and still is) as prominent and richly expressive a part of black cultural life as music.

Yet humor seldom reveals itself to objective anthropological or sociological inquiry. Humor is founded on contradiction and, as Freud pointed out, by its very nature represents an upsurge of unconscious, often repressed, motives and desires. It distorts the rational and evades most logical decoding and is often amusing because, as Langston Hughes suggested, it *is* what it *is not*. Moreover, its intended meaning can be switched instantly by subtle shifts in the jester's intent. When it is viewed in the context of African-American culture—which has been described by some as "double-edged, indirect and ambivalent" and not yielding "meaningful answers to the positivist who is preoccupied with surface phenomena"—humor becomes even more difficult to define. Moreover, up until the sixties, most blacks resisted divulging anything even remotely significant about the nature of their private humor to whites or even black outsiders. The Richard Pryor epigraph at the beginning of this chapter alludes to the kind of obfuscation likely to be encountered by outsiders. In the introduction to *Mules and Men* (1935), Zora Neale Hurston described the reasons for and method of this evasiveness: "The white man is always trying to know into somebody else's business. All right, I'll set something outside the door of my mind for him to play with and handle. He can read my writing but he sho' can't read my mind. Then I'll say my say and sing my song."[5]

The pitfalls notwithstanding, by 1881 Joel Chandler Harris had made inroads with the retelling of animal tales collected from Georgia slaves in *Uncle Remus: His Songs and Sayings*. Despite his disavowal of the tales' underlying satire and subsequent debates over whether they had an African source, he had introduced and memorialized a body of genuine folk humor. Harris, as one commentator suggests, may have "fitted the hate-imbued folk materials into a framework, a white man's framework, of love" in order to make them more palatable to mainstream readers, but he also initiated a still-expanding interest in black folklore.[6]

By the twentieth century, folk collectors had discovered the slave tales of John and his master—"a spate of tales" that, according to the folklorist Richard M. Dorson, "provides the most engaging theme in American Negro folklore." Like the animal stories introduced by Harris, the John and Old Master tales reflect the trickster motif. These tales never matched the popularity of the Remus tales for mainstream audiences, however; the portrayal of a slave outsmarting his master was simply not acceptable to most non-blacks. According to one folklorist, John's adventures remain among "the least discussed [stories] in American Negro folklore."[7]

By the 1920s, a few African-Americans entered the field. Arthur Huff Fauset and Zora Neale Hurston, among the first, were followed by J.

Mason Brewer and Daryl Cumber Dance. Their emergence "marks the first time when the story lore of Afro-Americans in the United States was collected in a manner that might place the lore in the context of the people's everyday lives." In fact, Hurston was one of the few collectors to have lived in the community in which she gathered her material; she depicted not only the folktales but also the living environment and actual circumstances in which they were related. *Mules and Men* documented Hurston's return to her Eatonville, Florida, hometown and her interactions with a raft of colorful locals, including Bubber Mimms, Sack Daddy, Johnnie Mae, and Big Sweet. The tales told by these and other characters present a wide range of rural African-American folk humor. There are examples of the rhymes, legends, songs, and animal and John or Jack tales that are found in most collections of black folklore; but here, instead of being arranged categorically and given a detached anthropological cast, they emerge as aspects of the day-to-day amusement of the people who retell them. Like the songs and banter that usually precede or accompany them, they are revealed as an integral part of black rural life.[8]

Initially, Hurston encouraged the outpouring of tales by sponsoring "lying contests." Once she was accepted, however, the stories flowed at social gatherings as easily as the homemade spirits consumed by the "liars." John tales were most popular. "Ah love to hear about Ole Massa and John. John sho was one smart nigger," one informant said, and the collection is filled with traditional tales in which the folk hero either intentionally outwits his master or accidentally gains the upper hand. In one story Ole Massa has decided to hang the uppity John, but John tells another slave to climb to the top of the tree and light a match each time he hears John ask to "let it lightnin'." When Massa takes John to the tree, John asks to pray before he dies. So John says, "O Lord . . . if you're gointer destroy Ole Massa tonight, with his wife and chillun and everything he got, lemme see it lightnin'." The other slave lights a match and Ole Massa says, "John, don't pray no more." But John repeats the prayer, and again, the other slave lights a match. After the third time: "Ole Massa started to run. He gave John his freedom and a heap of land and stock. He run so fast that it took a express train running at the rate of ninety miles an hour and six months to bring him back, and that's how niggers got they freedom today."

In another, John convinces Massa that he can tell fortunes. When they stop at a neighboring plantation, Ole Massa mentions John's talent. The other plantation owner says, "Dat nigger can't tell no fortunes. I bet my plantation and all my niggers against yours dat he can't tell no fortunes." John's Massa accepts the bet and, the next day, they return. Meanwhile, the neighboring plantation owner had gone out and caught a coon and "had a big old iron wash-pot turned down over it."

> Ole Massa brought John out and tole him, say: "John, if you tell what's under dat wash pot Ah'll make you independently rich. If you don't, Ah'm goin' kill you because you'll make me lose my plantation and everything I got."
>
> John walked 'round and 'round dat pot but he couldn't git de least inklin' of what was underneath it. Drops of sweat as big as yo' fist was rollin' off John. At last he give up and said: "Well, you got de old coon at last."
>
> When John said dat, Ole Massa jumped in de air and cracked his heels twice befo' he hit de ground. De man that was bettin' against Ole Massa fell to his knees wid de cold sweat pourin' off him. Ole Massa said: "John, you done won another plantation fo' me. That's a coon under that pot sho 'nuff."
>
> So he gave John a new suit of clothes and a saddle horse. And John quit tellin' fortunes after that.[9]

Numerous other John tales—including one in which John takes on mythical status and proves that he is "de king of de world" by physically besting a grizzly bear and a lion—are interspersed with trickster animal stories, tales about creation and the origins of specific animals, stories of flagrantly ignorant slaves and bogus preachers (often followed by the maxim: "My race but not my taste"), and tales of superhuman feats by legendary blacks such as Big Sixteen (who was banished from "Heben" because he "was too powerful"). Among the latter is a story about three men vying for the hand of a beautiful young girl. The girl's father cannot decide which is the best suitor, so he says, "Y'all be here tomorrow mornin' at daybreak and we'll have a contest and de one dat can do de quickest trick kin have de girl." As the story goes, the winner "took his high-powered rifle and went out into de woods about seben or eight miles until he spied a deer. He took aim and fired. Then he run home, run round behind de house and set his gun down and then run back out in de woods and caught de deer and held 'im till de bullet hit 'im."[10]

In Hurston's collection, such imaginative descriptive comments as

"Ah been strugglin' in Yo' moral vineyard, but Ah ain't gathered no grapes" or "De sun was so hot till a grindstone melted and run off in de shade to cool off" amplify the humor, as do asides such as "Well, as long as you don't see no man wid they mouth cut up and down, you know they'll all lie jus' like de rest of us" or "Hurry up so somebody else kin plough up literary and lay-by some alphabets." Perhaps most revealing, the interchanges usually take the form of topping or capping the other participants. A round of quips about how hot it is, for example, progresses from "it was so hot till we saw old stumps and logs crawlin' off in de shade" to "it was so hot till two cakes of ice left the ice house and went down the street and fainted." When the commentary turns to stories about the biggest mosquitoes, jibes escalate from "a mosquito come along and et up de cow and was ringin' de bell for de calf" to "Dat wasn't no full grown mosquito" and the tale of mosquitoes that sang like "bull alligators" and "screwed off dem short bills, reached back in they hip-pockets and took out they long bills and screwed 'em on and come right on through dem blankets and got us." Often, when the competition heated, the sessions veered into bouts of good-natured signifying and verbal sniping, such as, "You so black till they have to throw a sheet over yo' head so de sun kin rise every mornin'. Ah know yo' ma cried when she seen *you*."[11]

Because these tales were usually presented with thematic continuity, Hurston's method also frequently clarified the humorous intent of the stories. Not surprisingly, folktales taken out of context and analyzed in isolation often prove puzzling to readers and analyst alike.

In the essay "Negro Humor: John and Old Marster," for example, the folklorist Harry Oster recounts a story in which John is tricked by his master. In the tale, John's "marster," after discovering that John prays under an oak tree every day, puts his two sons in the tree with a sack of stones. When John prays, "Give me religion, Lord, give me religion. . . . Drop something on my head, let me feel it," one of the boys drops a stone on his head. And when John implores, "Drop a little harder," the boy drops "a great big old stone" and knocks John out:

> When Old John come back to, he said, "Look."
> He looked up in the air, he said, "Jesus, that the way you got to give me religion? Knock me out? Take your religion on back to heaven. I'm gonna stay down here and do the best I can do. Please, now."

Oster classifies the tale as one in which the Negro "is the ridiculous butt of a joke" and asks, "Why do Negroes laugh at this story which makes one of them appear such a fool, the butt of Old Marster's sadistic joke at the expense of John's literal faith in God's intervention in his affairs?" He speculates that the story may be funny to blacks because most people "enjoy laughing at the idiocies of an inferior member of their group" and, paraphrasing Thomas Hobbes, suggests that the humor may arise from "a sudden happy fulfillment of their own need for a sense of superiority." He also considers that the tale may direct "elements of sophisticated satire against the old-fashioned stereotype of the naive Negro who is gullible enough to have an intense religious faith" and may be the product of "the creative intelligence of a sophisticated, cynical observer."[12]

Had the tale been placed in context and the storyteller's point of reference been made clear, such speculation may not have been necessary. The story is more likely connected to a strain of cynicism regarding Christianity that surfaced early in African-Americans' slavery experience. Numerous instances of slaves' resistance to accepting a white God are found in slave narratives and in the writings of slaveholders. Charles Eliot's *The New England History, II* (1857), for example, included the following anecdote:

> **One of my Reverend ancestors found his Negro Cuff bowing and mumbling before a rough God, that he had made out of stone. "What's this, Cuff?" he said sharply. Cuff at last answered, "White man steal nigger; nigger no like white man's God. Cuff make his own God and den he know 'em."**

And in the 1920s, after intensive fieldwork among rural Southern blacks, sociologist Newbell Niles Puckett wrote, albeit patronizingly, that "race pride hangs pictures of heaven, dusky with black angels, in many lowly Negro cabins, and buys Bibles containing pictures of these same angels."[13]

The folktale analyzed by Oster—similar to a tale, recorded in *Mules and Men,* that concludes with the slave awakening to say, "Lawd, I ast you to kill all de white folks, can't you tell a white man from a nigger?" —is more likely a satiric expression of a not insignificant suspicion among blacks that white Christianity is a hoax. If so, it has some affinity with the type of double-edged wit found in the familiar "Where do Negroes hang out around here?" joke, and although John's gullibility may contribute to the humor, the story is funny because of its affirmation of white hypocrisy and its indirect lampooning of Christianity. It corresponds to mainstream black or gallows humor, which turned the most appalling circumstances into comedy. (In Hurston's collection the story appears within a sequence of tales that satirize white America's devious use of religion and focus on the difference between appearance and reality in spiritual encounters.)[14]

Hurston's collection avoids much of the speculation about why Negroes laugh at specific tales, since the intent of many stories is spelled out in conversations that precede them. Broadly, the tales can be categorized as trickster tales, in which John or Brer Rabbit usually triumph through their own wit; etiologic or "how it happened" tales, which display the narrator's cleverness at embellishing or concocting stories about the origins of various things, including heaven, hell, and the world, as well as specific animals and races; tales that poke fun at such Negro peccadilloes as laziness or ignorance; tales that humorously exaggerate the physical prowess of blacks; and outright lies, which depend on the narrator's wit, imagination, and storytelling ability in creating far-fetched, circuitous accounts of everyday events.

Noticeably absent from the collection, however, are examples of hostility or bitter satire. That omission led Sterling Brown to write that the "picture is too pastoral, with only a bit of grumbling about hard work, or a few slave anecdotes that turn the tables on old master." There are, in fact, numerous stories of slaves turning the tables and outwitting Ole Massa, but no examples of the more aggressive "Bad Nigger" tales that by the late twenties had begun to emerge in blacks' urban folklore and humor. The rural setting of *Mules and Men* partially explains the omission. Still, Hurston, who had lived in New York City, was doubtless aware of them; their absence gives her book a parochial, localized cast.[15]

On the other hand, the folktales that Hurston collected in rural Eatonville clearly demonstrate that much African-American humor was neither overly concerned with or excessively focused on the mainstream white world. Except for slave stories, the tales offered by Hurston's informants concentrate primarily on the insular black world in which they lived. Although folk collections from other rural areas offer similar material, none evokes the competitive tenor and the unique manner in which the Negro "farthest down" expresses himself or spreads "his own junk in his own way" more vividly than *Mules and Men*.

I I

Zora Neale Hurston's vivid documentation of the combative nature of much black verbal wordplay illuminates one of the central components of African-American humor—signifying, ranking, or (currently) *dissin'*. Intricately connected to that popular strain of humorous expression is a maxim that simply warns, "If you grinnin', you in 'em." Now, undoubtedly, some non-black researchers have occasionally wandered into a sepia juke joint or cabaret, a down-home black barber shop or country store, and found themselves in the midst of one of those verbal duels. If they were not greeted by the icy silence that often descended in such situations, they might have been exposed to some particularly cutting barb or "insult" and perchance cracked a smile. Then, whether they knew it or not, they would likely have found themselves at least tangentially embroiled in a round of double-edged ranking in which the players used language that went underneath, betwixt, and all around the interlopers. The humor was there, sharp as a razor; it's just that for a long time some white folks didn't know they had been cut and nobody bothered to tell them. Fortunately, there were exceptions.

Among them was the folklorist and ethnographer Roger D. Abrahams, who, in "Joking: The Training of the Man of Words in Talking Broad," writes that joking "is one of the key behavioral manifestations" among black youth. He classifies the African and African-American oral tradition in two specific categories: "broad talk," which emphasizes joking and license, includes signifying and mother-rhyming (the dozens), and brings the "vernacular into stylized use, in the form of wit, repartee, and direct slander"; and "formal" or "sweet" talk, which focuses on "eloquence and manners through the use of formal standard English." Abrahams's essay outlines the ritualized indoctrination of black youth in the use of the vernacular and suggests the extent of its widespread acceptance as a traditional source of expression. The broad talker "is licensed to play the fool or clown" and, in that capacity, he may portray the "high as low" and reveal the virtuous "as lecherous and dishonest charlatans."[16]

By the 1980s and 1990s, this oral tradition regularly surfaced in somewhat sanitized versions, on such television programs as *The Arsenio Hall Show*, *The Fresh Prince of Bel Air*, and even the curiously cross-cultural cartoon series, *The Simpsons*, and was seen in its natural state in almost any black school yard, pool hall, cabaret, or bar. It has been an essential part of African-American culture since the outset, when Europeans observed and became confounded by their slaves' seemingly jovial temperaments and unrestrained laughter. And from the beginning, one of its most prominent features has been an irreverent tone aimed at the high and mighty in order to pillory such pretentiousness as vanity and arrogance both in whites and "uppity" or "siditty" blacks.

Shuckin' and jivin', talkin' and testifyin', dippin' and grippin', slappin' and cappin', or simply dissin' are all vernacular descriptions for African-American inner-community verbal play. Although each term has a slightly different meaning depending upon who uses it and where (a derivative of the culture's elastic nature), they all refer generally to verbal exchanges corresponding to Abrahams's "broad talk." They describe the core verbal interaction that defines one of the fundamental attributes of African-American humor.

As the Hurston collection and its lying contests reveal, the play is most often couched as a challenge, an invitation to spar and compete. In *Die Nigger, Die!* H. Rap Brown wrote, "There'd be sometimes 40 or 50 dudes standing around and the winner was determined by the way they responded to what you said. If they fell all over each other laughing, then you knew you'd scored. It was a bad scene for the dude that was getting humiliated." Brown was writing about the most intensely charged verbal confrontations, the dozens; the situation, however, was not markedly altered if the repartee was confined to signifying or just telling a story—testifying.[17]

When I was a teenager in Ohio, for instance, getting to high school required a mile walk with other students that inevitably involved a continuous round of signifying. Anything from one's physical features or clothes to his personal habits or intellect would be unmercifully ridiculed and, depending on who was most aggressive at a given time, nearly everyone had his turn in the barrel. If you were unfortunate enough to have become the victim, you might arrive at school reduced to tears. But, usually, they were tears of laughter, since the entire interchange transpired within the context of a group of relatively close friends. It was a daily ritual, which was usually confined to putting down or ranking a specific person in the group, but if someone's derisive acuity reached a more cutting level, it could easily slip into the dozens and offer thematic progressions like the following:

A: Jim, you so ugly you got to sneak up on the dark.

B: Yeah, well, man, you so dark you ain' seen daylight in ten years.

A: Don't say nothin' about darkness, now, 'cause you the only dude I know can cast a shadow on coal.

Whereupon "Jim" might shift and respond:

B: Yeah, well you better ask yo' momma about that. She sho' love my nightstick.

That, in turn, might start a round of sexually explicit, patterned mother-rhyming:

A: Fucked yo' momma on the refrigerator, copped some ice, said, "See you later." . . . Seen yo' sister in the movie show, she ain' too smart, but she sho' can blow . . .[18]

Hostile overtones aside, among friends this kind of repartee was usually carried out in the spirit of good-natured teasing. It was ritualized play. When confined to friends and familiar circumstances, it was viewed, much like a basketball or baseball game, as competitive sport. (In fact, just as in professional sports today, "talking trash" was a regular part of nearly every football or basketball game.) If, however, one of the limitations were ignored—say, someone appeared with his girlfriend and his manhood was questioned—the game could escalate into hostility and violence. As H. Rap Brown noted, this daily routine also complemented the formal education received in class: "We exercised our minds by playing the dozens. . . . We learned what white folks called verbal skills."[19]

Beyond establishing a framework for jokes, this combative verbal play repeatedly utilized linguistic devices that in themselves helped to shape private black humor. Geneva Smitherman is among the folklorists and linguists who have categorized the most prominent of these devices. A large part of her book *Talkin and Testifyin* is devoted to a classification of African-American modes of discourse. Among them are call and response, signification, and narrative sequencing. She also lists specific qualities or rhetorical devices, including exaggerated language, mimicry, proverbial statements, punning, image-making, braggadocio, and indirection. The approaches and specific devices enumerated by Smitherman, although they are neither exclusive to blacks nor exhaustive of linguistic techniques used by blacks, provide a basic inventory of the structures that largely define private African-American humor.[20]

In fact, since they were easily perceived, derivations of popular rhetorical devices frequently appeared in early Negro stage humor. A studied adaptation of call and response (the spontaneous interaction of speaker and audience, perhaps most familiar in the interaction between minister and congregation in black churches), for example, was widely used in minstrelsy when the endmen's carping asides provided counterpoint to the interlocutor's pompous speeches; it also appeared in the continuous banter between Tambo and Bones. The humorous interplay with which Stringbeans, Butterbeans, and Fats Waller punctuated the lyrics of blues tunes sung by female vocalists provided some of the funniest and most imitated instances of its use. "I got the blues," a vocalist might wail, and a band member would shoot back, "That ain't the worst you gonna get, baby." The most recognizable and, perhaps, most creative use in a practiced routine, however, was in Miller and Lyles's "Indefinite Talk" bit, in which the call and response device—carried to its comical extreme—became both the form and content of the comedy. Here the humor derives totally from exaggeration of the rhetorical ploy as the two comedians anticipate one another's thoughts and jive their way through a series of nonsensical, rapid-fire retorts:

Comic 1: Yeah, I bet on that horse and the rascal didn't come in until . . .

Comic 2: Was he that far behind?

Comic 1: Yeah!

Comic 2: Who was the jockey ridin' him?

Comic 1: A jockey by the name of . . .

Comic 2: He can't ride!

Signifying or verbal insult, in one form or another, has appeared in stage humor since minstrelsy and can be traced through vaudeville to the present—from W. C. Fields or Butterbeans and Susie to Don Rickles or the late Redd Foxx. It was just as prominent in mainstream humor as it was in black circuit comedy, and remains so today. What is usually missing on stage, however, is the indirection it often assumes in private humorous wordplay among blacks. A bit of that nuance is apparent in a remark that a customer in a predominantly black bar made to an uppity employee: "Man, why don't you put that broom down, you know you don't know nothin' 'bout no machinery."

Narrative sequencing (a storytelling technique involving spontaneous diversion and nearly stream-of-consciousness meandering) is also a widely used stage device. Monologists such as Will Rogers or Moms Mabley, who spoke directly to audiences, used it frequently, but it was also an essential component in the acts of many comic teams who were ostensibly speaking to each other. The Tim Moore and Andrew Tribel routine described earlier, for instance, exploits the technique to the fullest as Moore rambles through a dialogue that begins with some perceptions about the value of work, wanders into a fantasy about ghosts or haunts who inexplicably change shapes, then ends with some pragmatic observations about time, carpentry, and the nature of fear.

In fact, that routine is also a model of the other modes of African-American discourse mentioned by Smitherman and of nearly all the expressive devices common to black grass-roots verbal expression and humor. Call and response occurs throughout as Tribel's interjections both exhort and amplify Moore's commentary. Both comedians use mild insults to make their points, as when Tribel says, "Boy, I don't blame that cat for laughin', 'cause dah first time I seen you I like to laugh myself to death," or when Moore says, "You showin' yo' ignorance now." Exaggerated language occurs with Moore's coining of the words *windowry* and *doah-ry*; braggadocio in his suggestion that if not for the window, he would have exited through the wall; mimicry in his imitation of the cat; indirection in the circuitous course through schooling, carpentry, and the advantages of punctuality that he takes to explain his quick departure; and, of course, punning in the pole cat reference and the concluding joke—"My time dere was up! And right den dah window got well." "What you mean, de window got well?" "It got rid of its *pain*."

Overall, the Moore-Tribel bit is a rich example of the comic use to which verbal attributes common to private discourse among blacks may be put; it demonstrates how those attributes, when creatively combined, can produce humorous scenarios that are observably black-oriented. As detractors of this type of inbred ethnic humor would quickly point out, however, while the structural apparatus and cleverness of black verbal play are abundantly represented, the thematic focus of the routine remains mired in stereotypes that not only avoid challenging but also affirm negative mainstream perceptions of African-Americans —in this instance, cravenness, an abhorrence of work, and a superstitious belief in ghosts. Unfortunately, most stage or public performances mirrored a similarly one-dimensional projection of black humor even when they exploited genuine techniques of inner-community discourse and comedy.

The stage acts of comics such as Moore, Butterbeans and Susie, Miller and Lyles, Dusty Fletcher, Moms Mabley, and Pigmeat Markham brought surface elements of private black humor into the theatre and, in many instances, a sense of the wily perception and ironic wit that informed the folkways of its creators. But they rarely ventured into the depiction of African America's most outrageous folklore type, the legendary "Bad Nigger," even though the type frequently appeared in aggressive, off-stage jokes and was, along with the wily Brer Rabbit and the slave John, a preeminent folk hero.

Mainstream portrayals of humorous Negroes, of course, also avoided the type. After all, the aggressive black man who refused to bow or back down from confrontations with whites had been seen as mainstream society's worst nightmare since slavery, and by the early twentieth century, that image had been indelibly etched in the public mind by Thomas Dixon, D. W. Griffith, and others. In mainstream culture, uppity blacks were villains, a threat to the status quo; they were seldom treated humorously. When they were, the contradictory inner logic of humor immediately revealed the effort as a charade. White minstrels, for example, regularly pilloried the Negro city slicker or dandy through their depiction of Zip Coon or Jim Dandy, an extravagant, motley-dressed pretender to urbane worldliness. But the very process of burlesquing this urban hustler entailed portraying him as an imposter; humor was derived from casting him as the stereotypically loud, venal, depraved, and, ultimately, simple-minded "nigra" who futilely aspired to an independence reserved for whites. He was, finally, only Sambo in the nineteenth-century version of a zoot suit.

Although, before the sixties, these characters rarely reached the stage, muted, less aggressive versions of this urban type were found in black stage comedy sketches that typically featured a city slicker preying on a rural underdog. Such teams as Miller and Lyles modified the standard minstrel portrayal—eliminating much of the foolish affectation and comic pretentiousness—but still undercut the strength of the character by having the underdog outwit his typically more physically imposing and sophisticated urban adversary. Brer Rabbit, in other words, consistently emerged victorious.

Other comedians, while portraying a closer likeness of the type than early minstrels, wrung laughter from their ability to deflect hostilities from themselves and maintain their tough, haughty posture as someone else suffered the consequences of their actions. Drake and Murray's "Go Ahead and Sing" bit, in which one comic goads his partner into defying a policeman, was an example. Some even reverted to portrayals approximating the minstrel stereotype, revealing the Bad Nigger as craven and, despite his vociferousness, totally ineffective against societal dominance and control. One of Stump and Stumpy's popular Apollo Theatre skits offered an example. The sketch opened with them laughing and rollicking in a Northern night club; soon Stumpy spies a menacing, light-skinned waiter or bouncer standing behind them. Stump notices his friend's distress and says, "What's wrong, man? You up North now, let's have a ball." He continues his loud, aggressive behavior as Stumpy cowers in his seat. Finally, Stump looks around and sees the bouncer. Puffing himself up, he shouts to Stumpy, "Straighten that fool out, man. Straighten that fool out!" He is hardly finished when the bouncer pounces on him and beats him to the floor. As Roger D. Abrahams observes, when the tables are turned on the trickster or Bad Nigger, when he himself is duped or defeated, "his exploits are nothing less than clownish and his mask is that of the noodle, the simpleton."[21]

Most often, however, stage facsimiles of the Bad Nigger were confined to all-black settings and mythical opponents or depicted a character who turned his anger against himself and other blacks, reflecting Abrahams's portrait of the "hard-hero" who, "frustrated in his attempts to strike back at white society . . . turns his anger inward." This surfacing of black aggressiveness in comedy skits occurred frequently in the acts of the male-female comedy teams who worked the TOBA. In his act with Susie, for instance, Butterbeans often satirized the Bad Nigger's aggressiveness. In one skit he claimed, "I'd fight all the animals in the jungle or even in the zoo, I'd grab a lion and smack his face and tear a tiger in two! . . . If that ain't love, it'll have to do." But the belligerence was exposed as a sham when Susie asked, "Till when, till when?" and Butterbeans replied, "Until another *fool* come along." On other occasions his hostility was turned toward Susie: "I'd whip your head every time you breathe; rough treatment is exactly what you need." But Butterbeans' comic assertiveness was always mediated by the couple's affection for one another; all Susie needed to do was smile and his hostility vanished. This was not necessarily the case with dancer-comedian "Two-Story Tom," who built his act around lampooning the Bad Nigger's treatment of women. In one of his typically threatening forays, he proclaimed, "When I start after you, you'll run so fast you'll cut out a new street."[22]

Despite the avoidance, distortion, and restriction of targets that characterized portrayals of the Bad Nigger on stage, the type represented a source of pride for most blacks. In a serious vein, many stories circulated about slaves and freedmen who put their lives on the line rather than capitulate to societal emasculation.

As a child, I heard my grandmother tell numerous tales about fiercely determined black men and women who directly resisted white oppression during slavery and shortly afterward. Most, as she quickly admitted, had paid with their lives, but there were also dozens of tales about those who defiantly resisted and either escaped to the North or, by sheer tenacity and refusal to submit, won the respect of whites and carved out a stable life. The latter, of course, were rare, and their ability to survive often depended on some connection with a powerful white family—based either on clandestine lineage or their ability to curry favor in those quarters by affecting a more docile or dependent presence.

Examples of these stories also appear frequently in slave narratives. In *Lay My Burden Down: A Folk History of Slavery*, for example, B. A. Botkin relates a tale about one Leonard Allen and another slave. In describing them, Botkin's informant said, "If the devil hisself had come and shook a stick at them, they'd hit him back." As the story goes, on the day the plantation master returned from the Civil War, he heard Allen's sarcastic remark: "Look at that goddamn soldier. He fighting to keep us niggers from being free." When he was ordered to approach his master, who had picked up a gun, "Leonard opened his shirt and stood there like a big black giant, sneering at Old Marse." The informant fled but emphatically recalled how he later saw the ex-slave "laying on the ground with that bloody hole in his chest and that sneer on his black mouth."[23]

William H. Wiggins, who comments on the Leonard Allen tale in the article "Jack Johnson as Bad Nigger: The Folklore of His Life," recalls that his father had related stories about similarly intransigent or bellicose blacks in the early 1900s. One involved a black carpenter in Georgia who, while working on another job, finally told an insistent and surly white man that, if he couldn't wait for some work to be done, he could take his business elsewhere. The prospective customer, infuriated at being dismissed by a Negro, kicked the carpenter in the seat of his pants. The carpenter gathered his tools and left without saying a word. Shortly afterward, he returned, pulled out a gun, and killed the white man. After hiding out until nightfall, the carpenter and his family escaped to Chicago.[24]

These tales of ordinary black folks, most often recounted in hushed voices far from earshot of non-black listeners, no doubt contributed to the Bad Nigger legend. Other defiant blacks—including slave insurrectionists Nat Turner and Gabriel Prosser, sports hero Jack Johnson, and such notorious figures as Morris Slater, who, after killing a white policeman and escaping in a railroad car, was mythologized as Railroad Bill—were probably the source of mythical, superhuman, Bad Nigger figures such as Stackolee (or Staggerlee), Shine, and, to a lesser extent, John Henry. (As Zora Neale Hurston has pointed out, John Henry "occupies the same place in Negro folk-lore that Casey Jones does in white lore.") Equally bold individuals were the basis for the raft of lesser-known stories involving African-American aggressiveness or defiance that circulated almost exclusively within black circles.[25]

One tale involves a black man who faces a white judge in court after having kicked a "white man's behind":

Judge: John, what is this about you kicking someone?

John: Well, Captum, what would you do if someone called you a black son of bitch?

Judge: Well, John, nobody will ever call me that.

John: Well, Captum, spose they call you the kind of son of bitch you is?

Judge: Give him 30 days.

In some versions, the last line is omitted.[26]

Contrary to popular thought, race-conscious jokes such as these, many of which openly expressed resistance to segregation, along with a rich body of humor that assertively expressed pride in black lifestyles without reference to whites or pridefully exalted the achievements and triumphs of black folk, were a significant part of inner-community African-American humor long before Dick Gregory and others brought them to mainstream audiences. In fact, as we shall see, many of the jokes told by such sixties stand-up comedians as Gregory, Redd Foxx, Richard Pryor, and others came directly from the streets. The explosion of assertive black satire unleashed in America's popular culture during the sixties did not represent the sudden emergence of a new, militant perception or recently acquired penchant for ethnic chauvinism; instead, it was more a public unveiling of a covert or privately held sardonic view of America that many common black folks had held for decades. Initially, the newly public humor barely scraped the surface of the unflinchingly graphic urban ballads, toasts, and street humor that folklorist Daryl Cumber Dance has described as "blatantly hostile, sadistic, and obscene."[27]

III

On one level, so-called Bad Niggers were merely African-Americans who, long before the sixties' Civil Rights movement, refused to participate in the elaborate hoax that had defined American racial relationships and stood up for their rights as citizens. They insisted upon being treated as equals, rejected traditional obsequious postures when interacting with whites, and refused to adopt trickery and deception as a means to desired ends because those strategies superficially appeared to affirm inherent white superiority. In effect, they stepped outside or shattered the covert racial pact that the critic Robert E. Hemenway aptly calls a "ritual of self-delusion" in which both blacks and whites participated. Broadly speaking, from slavery to at least the 1950s, the rigid structure of racial oppression forced blacks to face a dilemma: Either accede to segregationist policies and outwardly accept inferior social status, or, risking harsh reprisals, defy the white hierarchy and demand the rights and respect accorded non-black Americans.

Naturally, there were infinite gradations in each of these choices. Accommodationists, for instance, included proper, middle-class blacks, who salvaged some respect and gained a degree of acceptance by conforming to white norms of behavior and thought; tricksters or fabulists, who, whether adopting the posture of a middle-class Negro or that of a docile Negro sycophant, used subterfuge and deceit to undermine the racist structure; and those blacks who accepted the stigma of inferiority as reality and capitulated to their lowly status. Bad Niggers were distinguished by their belligerence; they either extended their defiance to white society and its symbols of authority or confined it to the black community. Although those who did the latter commanded a certain respect or, at least, grudging deference, admiration was mostly reserved for those who stood firm against white oppression.

Under slavery's absolute tyranny and violent suppression, resistance was most effectively expressed indirectly through subterfuge, and as black folklore and humor indicate, such tricksters as the slave John were as much admired as leaders of slave rebellions. But after Emancipation, as direct resistance to white dominance assumed less risk, the physical strength and courage of Bad Niggers who defied white society increasingly established them among black America's foremost heroes. At the same time, institutionalized racism and Jim Crow laws ensured that African-Americans who insisted upon the fair treatment normally accorded non-black Americans would frequently run afoul of the law. Bad Niggers, then, particularly those who challenged rigid, strictly enforced customs about Negroes' proper behavior and place, were regarded as criminals by mainstream society. (Ironically—although the Bad Nigger of folklore fame is invariably masculine and women are usually regarded as adversaries—from a broader perspective, Rosa Parks, whose refusal to accommodate a Montgomery, Alabama, segregated-seating policy symbolically sparked the sixties' Civil Rights movement, looms as one of the most socially effective representatives of the type.)

Defiant blacks continued to assume more heroic status in real life as well as in African-American folklore and humor. As they did, the mythical Bad Nigger gradually assumed more outrageous, anti-social, and violent proportions. For example, despite his superhuman physical prowess, John Henry was a comparatively conventional folk hero. Alan Dundes suggests that the legend's near-instant popularity among mainstream whites shortly after it surfaced at the turn of the century derived partially from the hero's benign nature—the fact that he does not challenge white sovereignty. The steel-driving man's victory is over a machine, and, since he dies and receives no recompense for his efforts, Dundes suggests that the "legend encapsulates the evils of exploitation." There were, however, more belligerent black folk heroes on the horizon who would bring a new, disdainfully satiric dimension to African-American humor. Their attitude was, as Saunders Redding describes it, "not only truly exuberant, but incorrigibly irreverent, showing a decided lack of respect for most of those values—thrift, industry, honesty, continence, gentility—so loftily enshrined in the hierarchies of American values."[28]

Eventually, according to the folklorist Roger D. Abrahams, in "urban Negro lore" the trickster's "amoral," "strongly aggressive," but indirect approach was "replaced by the vicious badman who carries out his aggression quite overtly. Drinkers, sadists, wenchers, the Great Mac-Daddy, Davie Winston, Railroad Bill, and Aaron Harris break the law of the whites and are energetically described as 'the baddest man in the whole world' or as 'mean enough and bad to whip his mammy and shoot his daddy.' " Some, like boxing champion Jack Johnson, were real people whose flamboyant lives inspired legends. Others, like the mythical Shine, whom novelist Ishmael Reed has called "black America's Ulysses" and critic and poet Larry Neal lionized in the essay "And Shine Swam On," were imaginative creations whose superhuman exploits expressed the pent-up rage and bitterness of the black masses as well as their sardonic view of mainstream society. "Because of his experience in this country," psychologists William H. Grier and Price M. Cobbs contend, "every black man harbors a potential bad nigger inside of him."[29]

In his essay on Jack Johnson as Bad Nigger, William H. Wiggins, Jr., shows how Johnson's lifestyle reflected four principal characteristics of the Bad Nigger: disregard for life and death; pride in sexual virility; extravagance in dress and possessions; and an "insatiable love of having a good time." Indeed, Johnson's accomplishments in the ring and his prodigious lifestyle outside it provide numerous examples of basic traits attributed to the Bad Nigger, including scorn for the basic beliefs of middle-class white society. He stirred black pride and initiated a search for a "Great White Hope" by becoming the first black heavyweight champion and openly mocking hypocritical mainstream values. (In the sixties, Muhammad Ali revitalized that search with his incendiary banter, outspoken anti-war stance, and conversion to the Black Muslim faith.) Johnson was much more controversial, however; his romantic conquests and his flaunting of taboos against consorting with white women also inspired a still-popular euphemism for the male genitalia ("Johnson") and, according to some, prompted passage of the Mann Act and numerous state laws against interracial marriage. In addition, he inspired some boastful and humorous oral narratives:

The Yankees hold the play
The white man pull the trigger;
But it makes no difference what the white man say,
The world champion's still a nigger.[30]

Johnson's real-life accomplishments, irreverent style, and bravado were the stuff of legend, but his exploits pale when compared to mythical counterparts who, like Great MacDaddy, could boast: "I've got a tombstone disposition, a graveyard mind./ I know I'm a bad motherfucker, that's why I don't mind dying." And the ballad of Stackolee, with its familiar opening lines, "Back in '32 when times were hard,/ He had a Colt .45 and a marked deck of cards," presented a character whose violent disposition and sexual appetite became the prototype of the legend. In one unexpurgated rendition, Stackolee narrates:

I walked through water and I walked through mud,
Come on a little hole-in-the-wall, they call the "Bucket of Blood."
I walked in and asked the bartender, "Dig, chief, can I get
    something to eat?"
He threw me a stale glass of water and flung me a fucked-up
    piece of meat.
I said, "Raise, motherfucker, do you know who I am?"
He said, "Frankly, motherfucker, I just don't give a damn."
I knowed right then that chickenshit was dead.
I threw a thirty-eight shell through his motherfucking head.

In milder versions, such as the one found in the *Book of Negro Folklore*, edited by Langston Hughes and Arna Bontemps, profanity is eliminated and sexual references are expressed metaphorically. Therefore, when Stackolee arrives in hell:

He said, "Devil, devil, put your fork up on the shelf
'Cause I'm gonna run this devilish place myself."
There came a rumbling on the earth and a tumbling on the ground
That bad son-of-a-gun, Stackolee, was turning hell all around.

        .   .   .   .

Meanwhile, Stackolee went with the devil's wife and with his
    girlfriend too,
Winked at the devil and said, "I'll go with you."
The devil turned around to hit him a lick.
Stackolee knocked him down with a big black stick.
Now, to end this story, so I heard tell,
Stackolee, all by himself, is running hell.[31]

The ballad "Shine" (whose date of origin is somewhere between 1912 and 1920, according to Alan Dundes) also has been told in expurgated form. As its alternate title, "The Sinking of the Titanic," suggests, the tale concerns the exploits of a lone black man on that ill-fated voyage. In some polite renditions, the story begins:

> It was 1912 when the awful news got around
> That the great Titanic was sinking down.
> Shine came running up on deck, told the Captain, "Please,
> The water in the boiler room is up to my knees."
>
> Captain said, "Take your black self on back down there!
> I got a hundred-fifty pumps to keep the boiler room clear."
> Shine went back in the hole, started shovelling coal,
> Singing, "Lord, have mercy, Lord, have mercy on my soul!"

and continues with Shine's escape:

> The old Titanic was beginning to sink.
> Shine pulled off his clothes and jumped in the brink.
> He said, "Little fish, big fish, and shark fishes, too,
> Get out of my way because I'm coming through."
>
> Captain on bridge hollered, "Shine, Shine, save poor me,
> And I'll make you rich as any man can be."
> Shine said, "There's more gold on land than there is on sea."
> And he swimmed on.

In its concluding lines, this version reflects its fifties origin: "When all them white folks went to heaven,/Shine was in Sugar Ray's Bar drinking Seagram's Seven."[32]

But "Shine," in the street version that most African-Americans are familiar with even if they avoid repeating it in polite company, is a much more profane and sardonic tale. In one version, after the captain tells Shine to return to the boiler room:

> Shine said, "That may be true because you carrying a load."
> Says, "I'm gon' take my chances in jumping overboard."
> Captain say, "Now, Shine, oh, Shine, don't be no fool and don't
>   be no clown."
> Say, "Anybody go overboard is bound to drown."

Shine say, "You may have them pumps and they better work fast,"
Say, " 'cause I'm going overboard when that water reach my ass."

Shine's scorning of passengers' pleas for help is also expressed more graphically:

All the millionaires looked around at Shine, say, "Now, Shine, oh
    Shine, save poor me";
Say, "We'll make you wealthier than one Shine can be."
Shine say, "You hate my color and you hate my race":
Say, "Jump overboard and give those sharks a chase."
And everybody on board realized they *had* to die.
But Shine could swim and Shine could *float*.
And Shine could throw his ass like a motorboat.
Say Shine hit the water with a hell of a splash.
And everybody wondered if that Black sonovabitch could last.
Say the Devil looked up from hell and grinned,
Say, "He's a *black, swimming motherfucker*. I think he's gon' come
    in."

Other versions are more explicit, depicting Shine's obscene dismissals of pregnant women and children who ask for help:

She say, "Shine, Shine, *please* save poor me;
I'll name this *kid* after thee."
Shine say, "*Bitch*, you went and got knocked up, that's fine,
But you got to hit this water just like old Shine."

Or:

She said, "Shine, Shine, save poor me,
My little baby has a papa to see!"
Shine said, "You round here lookin' like a pregnant pup.
Go find that motherfucker who knocked your ass up."

Shine's rebuke of an infant is just as cold:

After a bit, Shine met up with a baby. The baby was cryin'.
Shine said, "Baby, baby, please don't cry.
All y'all little motherfuckers got a time to die."

He said, "You got eight little fingers and two little thumbs,
And your black ass goes when the wagon comes."[33]

Unlike Stackolee, John Henry, or most other heroes of black toasts and ballads, Shine nearly always survives his exploits. And some analysts have suggested that he symbolizes African-Americans' plight in America (the Titanic) where they are relegated to inferior positions and denied equality; as the ship sinks, however, they are called on for help. Shine's rejection of those pleas mirrors the militant blacks' contempt for white America's hypocrisy and its symbols of middle-class esteem.

In most instances, however, the Bad Nigger's rebellion does not reflect social consciousness as much as a total abrogation of social responsibility, affirmation of ego, and an insatiable pursuit of physical challenges and good times. Violence, drugs, the domination of women, and the exploitation of normal working class people are often substituted for restrictive mainstream ethics and the inferior status derived from adherence to middle-class values. A typical example is "The Hustler":

The name of the game is to beat the lame,
Take a woman and make her live in shame.

It makes no difference how much she scream or holler,
'Cause dope is my heaven and my God the almighty dollar.

I, the Hustler, swear by God
I would kill Pope Paul if pressed too hard.

I would squash out Bobby and do Jackie harm
And for one goddamn dollar would break her arm.

I, the hustler, kick ass morning, noon, and night,
I would challenge Cassius and Liston to a fight.

.   .   .   .

I, the Hustler, can make Fred Astaire dance and Sinatra croon,
And would make the Supreme Court eat shit from a spoon.

Another Bad Nigger, Dolemite, even as a baby possessed the mythical powers, glib rap, and contempt for authority that defines his breed:

At the age of one he drinking whiskey and gin.
At the age of two he was eating the *bottles* they came in.

Now Dolemite had a uncle they called Sudden Death
That killed a *dozen* motherfuckers from the smell o' his breath.
So Dolemite's aunt tol' his uncle how he was treatin' his ma and
    pa.
He say, "Lemme go and check this little bad motherfucker fo' he
    go too far."
So one *cold*, dark *December* night his uncle came broking in on
    Dolemite.
He said, "Dolemite, you better straighten up and treat your
    mother right,
'Cause if you keep on with your dirty mistreatin'
I'm gon' whip your ass till your heart stop beatin'."
Dolemite was sittin' on in the living room floor playin',
He say, "Uncle, I see your lips going up and down,
But I don't hear a motherfuckin' sound."[34]

Reflecting mainstream abhorrence of the Bad Nigger type, the toast concludes, after Dolemite dies, with:

And the preacher said [solemn tone], "Ashes to ashes,
And dust to dust, I'm GLAD this BA-AD motherfucker
Called Dolemite is no longer with us."

Violent, anti-social animal types are also found in urban toasts and occasionally reflect the same values as such badmen as Honky-Tonk Bud, Stackolee, and Pimping Sam. Instead of Brer Rabbit, however, the monkey (who in many rural stories is a numbskull type) most often assumes the role of the badman and emerges triumphantly. In "The Monkey and the Coon," for instance, a dapper monkey hustles a coon in pool and, after some quick sleight of hand, also wins in cards; "The Pool-Shooting Monkey" relates a similar tale.[35]

But "The Signifying Monkey" (sometimes called "The Elephant, the Lion, and the Monkey") is probably the best known of these stories. Oscar Brown, Jr., recorded a laundered version to jazz accompaniment in the sixties, and polite renditions can be found in many folklore collections. Although there are versions in which the lion triumphs, usually the monkey makes a fool of the King of the Jungle. The toast often begins with:

Said the Monkey to Lion, one bright, sunny day.
"There's a bad motherfucker livin' down yo' way.
You take that sucker to be yo' friend,
But the way he talks about yo' mamma is a goddamn sin.
Talks about yo' daddy and yo' sister, too,
Matter of fact, he don't show too much respect fo' you."
Now, the Lion took off like a bat outta hell,
Bananas split open and coconuts fell.
Lion found the Elephant sittin' under a tree,
Say, "Now, motherfucker, you belong to me."
Elephant looked outta the corner of his eyes,
Say, "Go on, motherfucker, play with somebody yo' size."
But the Lion wouldn't listen, and he made a pass.
The Elephant kicked him dead in his ass.

. . . .

Now they fought all night and they fought all day.
Don't know how the Lion ever got away.
He crawled back through the jungle, more dead than alive,
And that's when the Monkey started that signifying jive.
Say, "Hey Mr. Lion, you didn't fare too well,
Seem to me, you caught *all* the hell.
You look like a ho' with the seven-year-itch,
And you s'pose to be King of the Jungle, ain't that a bitch.
Now, motherfucker, don't you dare roar,
'Cause I'll jump down and kick yo' ass some more."
But the Monkey got frantic, started jumpin' up and down.
His foot missed the limb, he fell dead on the ground.
Like a bolt of lightnin' and a streak of heat,
The Lion was on with all fo' feet.
Monkey looked up with tears in his eyes,
Say, "Please, Mr. Lion, I apologize.
But, if you let me get my balls out the sand
I'll fight yo' ass like a natural man."
Say, "If you jump back like a good man should,
I'll bounce yo' ass all over these woods."
Lion stepped back and was ready to fight,
But the Monkey jumped up and was clean outta sight.
And I heard him explain as he went out of view,
"Tell yo' momma and yo' daddy, too,
Signifying Monkey made a fool outta you."[36]

"The Signifying Monkey" is one of the most popular and well known black folk ballads; with minor modification, it can be enjoyed in even polite company. It is also among the funniest and invariably elicits gales of laughter from listeners. Although this version of the tale has more in common with trickster animal tales than it does with typical Bad Nigger toasts and ballads, it does echo themes common to those more blasphemous tales: physical and verbal challenge, an abundant use of street language, and a contemptuous view of traditional symbols of authority, in this instance, the King of the Jungle, whose wit and physical potency are ridiculed. In addition to advocating a more defiant and assertive posture, the story, like the Bad Nigger toasts, clearly celebrates another fundamental characteristic of black folk humor—boasting or lying.

As Thomas Kochman points out in *Black and White Styles in Conflict*, extravagant boasting or self-aggrandizement is not only an accepted form of behavior among African-Americans but also "is a source of humor . . . a form of verbal entertainment." Conversely, according to Kochman, in ordinary circumstances the practice is frowned upon by most white Americans. The disparity is similar to the difference in black and white attitudes regarding "hotdogging" or flaunting one's accomplishments in sports, which was mentioned earlier. Of course, exaggeration and boasting are familiar aspects of both Euro-American and African-American folk humor. Outlaws, brawlers, and braggarts, for example, are readily found in the frontier humor of Daniel Boone and Davy Crockett, the picaresque exploits of Simon Suggs, or the tales of Mark Twain; boastful exaggeration was a prominent element in the ethnic humor of various groups during the nineteenth and early twentieth century. But although it still survives in some isolated pockets, America's melting pot syndrome worked to eliminate or diminish enthusiastic expression of folk humor within most groups.[37]

Black Americans, however, were largely excluded from the pot. Losing their hyphenated ethnic label or escaping the opprobrium associated with slanderous racial epithets by simply becoming *Americans*, as most other ethnic groups had, was virtually impossible. Cast as pariahs or outcasts in mainstream culture and left to develop a culture outside the norm, they maintained many of their folkways. And that alternate folk culture was not strictly confined to the lower classes.

In the introduction to *Shuckin' and Jivin': Folklore from Contemporary Black Americans*, for instance, Daryl Cumber Dance explains that the folktales included were collected from "the completely uneducated and illiterate to the most highly educated, from some of Virginia's poorest, most obscure, and most inconspicuous Black citizens, to some of Virginia's most affluent and most prominent Blacks." The educational and class variety found among his informants reflects the extent to which folk humor permeates African-American life. Such traditional folktales as the John and Old Master stories as well as many of the "obscene" tales from contemporary black folklore are as well known to black professionals as they are to the street folks who created them. Away from their offices and out of earshot of white colleagues, middle-class blacks often spice their conversations with tidbits from those tales or, more importantly, adopt both the patois and the tales' implicit satiric humor in their leisure joking and bantering. With few exceptions (the followers of certain fundamentalist religious sects among them), blacks have probably retained their traditional folkways (and folk humor) more than most other Americans.[38]

The expressive attributes most highly esteemed in the black folk tradition—the verbal acuity and spontaneous wit displayed in signi-fying, boasting, and storytelling or "lying"—also characterize black American humor. Another characteristic of that humor is the near ab-sence of what is usually defined as a joke—the progression from setup to punchline that *The Comic Encyclopedia* describes as "a brief single incident, a comic tale stripped of all non-essential detail. It begins with a situation, has no middle, and ends with a surprise, an unexpected twist." ("I hear your husband tried to get a government job. What is he doing now?" "Nothing. He got the job.") Repetition of such gags or even repeated recitation of one-liners ("He had to fire his secretary; his wife considered her a security risk") is rarely witnessed at black rap sessions or social gatherings.[39]

One-line rejoinders to greetings—"What's happening?" or "How you living?" "White folks still ahead" or "Livin' large!"—often occur, but although these responses are likely to evoke a laugh in black circles, the humor is not derived from the typical joke process. It flows from the participants' commonly held satiric view of the world and themselves. Humor in those instances is not based on unexpected twists or reversals; on the contrary, it is derived from an acknowledgment of the shared ironic attitude underlying the quip. Quick rejoinders or clever quips are admired, however, when they are spontaneous reactions to real situa-tions and humorously underscore an alternate view. They are often a form of signifying, and the put-down can be devastating. An example occurred in the film *Do the Right Thing* when the glib Sweet Dick dismisses a character who is attempting to organize a boycott of the neighborhood pizza shop with the quip: "What you ought'a do is boycott that goddamn barber that fucked up your head."

When it involves turning the quip to a new, inventive end, repetition of familiar one-liners is sometimes esteemed. A conversation between two men and a woman overheard at a New York bar, for instance, revealed a clever turnabout of this sort. The original folktale, popularized in a Richard Pryor routine during the seventies, concerned two men standing on a bridge and comparing the length of their penises while urinating; one says, "Damn, the water's cold," and his friend replies, "Yeah, and it's *deep*, too!" The response was put to an altogether different use in that Manhattan bar. After one of the men went on too long with a rap about how much money he had, the woman sarcastically snapped, "Fool, if money was air, you'd have to borrow an oxygen tank to breathe." Bent with laughter, the other man said, "Damn, home boy, that's cold." Without missing a beat, the woman quipped, "Yeah, and it's deep, too," which caused all three to break into spasms of laughter. Their spontaneous banter, which not only involved signifying and one-upmanship but also inventively refocused the punchline from a traditional folktale with which they were all familiar (in this case heightening the original put-down, since the woman indirectly suggested that she was as much a man as her would-be admirer), was a perfect example of spontaneous reshaping of familiar folk wit.

Most often, reflecting what Geneva Smitherman labeled "narrative sequencing," jokes are either embedded in longer stories with the "nonessential detail" that is stripped away in traditional joke telling assuming a larger role, or the joke is redirected toward an unsuspected target. Inventiveness or spontaneity and the ability to leave one's personal stamp on the story are prized much more than the simple recounting of a familiar gag.

During social gatherings, for example, whenever I have heard the joke about the black stranger who arrives in a small Southern town and asks where Negroes hang out, the storyteller invariably embellished it with a wealth of detail that (depending on his skill) was not only funny in itself but also enhanced the punchline. A Harlem barber shop raconteur began almost apologetically with, "Y'all done heard the story of that Chicago boy who got off the bus in Lynchburgh and made the mistake o' askin' some cracker where dah niggers was, right? Well, lemme tell you how that stuff really went down. See, I was on dat bus myself." As he told it, the three- or four-minute tale involved an aunt of his who happened to be at the depot, digressed through a nearly fatal attempt to use the bus station men's room, which was for whites only, and finally turned on the naive Chicago visitor's asking a local sheriff for directions. "That's when that redneck constable told dat fool, 'Well, the last ones I saw was in dat tree over yonder, boy. If I was you, I'd get my ass back on dat bus, and I mean *waaaay* back!' "

Similarly, when I've heard the tale of the black man who sees a white woman pass by and wonders aloud, "Oh, Lord, will I ever?" it is seldom isolated and presented as *just* a joke. Typically it is embroidered with details about the woman's appearance or the black man's background and often enhanced by references to topical events that occurred during the time the incident was supposed to have happened. In one version, the speaker spiced the tale with, "You know, it was back there in the time when Jack Johnson was regularly crossing the line, nigger musta thought he was the heavyweight *cham-peen* or sumpthin, so he say, 'Yeah, boss, long as dere's life, dere's hope.' White boy told 'im, 'Uh huh, and where dere's a nigger, dere's a rope.' Dat's when the boy forgot all about boxing gloves and white women folks."

In both of the above instances, the tales were told by Northern black men who normally spoke without heavy Southern dialects. They were known as accomplished storytellers, however, and easily mimicked the rural patois. The jokes embedded in their stories were finally only a small part of the humor, which was primarily derived from their nuanced telling and the subtle addition of imaginative detail that expanded the elemental joke, placing it in a specific time and suggesting the attitudes that shaped its underlying irony. Not everyone participating in rap or bull sessions, of course, is a consummate storyteller. Novice or untutored jesters who eliminate textured detail that might enhance a particular joke or tale often find that, instead of the tale itself, their inept telling of the story becomes the source of humor. In a predominantly black bar in Ohio, I once heard a more respected, older storyteller interrupt a younger man midway through a tale, saying, "That ain't shit, fool. You *Bob Hopin'* the damn story. Shut up, and let me tell it like it was!"

These examples, like the "lying contests" and other forms of black jesting described in Hurston's *Mules and Men,* demonstrate that the straightforward recitation of gags or jokes is frequently subordinated to other expressive techniques in African-American humor. The competitive emphasis in black verbal play and signifying, the value attributed to spontaneous wit and placing one's own individual stamp on a humorous tale, and the fondness for embellishment of detail and the evocative or dramatic recreation of characters all contribute to the uniqueness of African-American humor.

Its mode of expression aside, however, African-American humor is, as Saunders Redding wrote, primarily based on the "ironic perception of the difference between appearance and reality"; included in that perception is the unavoidable discernment of pretense derived from contrasting the nation's democratic rhetoric with blacks' own experience of being largely excluded from the American dream or national fantasy. Therefore, blacks' humor is most often not predicated on fabricated scenarios intended merely to entertain or *symbolically* to expose absurdity; instead, since black life in America is rife with examples of such absurdity, much black humor derives from a candid, unflinching view of everyday life. To some extent, mainstream America's social reality *is* African America's humor, a fact that no doubt prompted Dick Gregory's sardonic claim that "the white man is our greatest clown."[40]

The irony of receiving flagrantly inequitable treatment in a society that boasts of its democratic heritage has been a main source of black humor from slavery:

> We raise de wheat,
> Dey gib us de corn;
> We bake de bread,
> Dey gib us de cruss;
> We sif de meal,
> De gib us de huss.

to Richard Pryor's quip about the contemporary legal system:

> You go down there lookin' for justice, and that's what you find,
> Just-Us.

Although non-blacks often are confounded as to why such material is funny, for blacks merely verbalizing these obvious ironies has remained not only an indictment of white perfidy and hypocrisy but also a source of contemptuous amusement. That aspect of the African-American humorous sensibility marks the place where it most clearly overlaps black literary humor, which turns the materials of tragedy, protest, and satire into outright comedy.

The grounding in reality of most African-American humor is not confined to satire aimed at non-blacks, however; since the core perspective is on the disparity between appearance and reality, blacks are also targets and, frequently, are lampooned as vigorously as non-blacks. Slaves' stories often ridiculed ignorance and putting on airs among their own members, and reserved the most pointed satire for those who (as in the tale of the slave whose prayers are answered by stones thrown at him by his master's son) were duped by slaveholders' trickery. Later, in the rural South, numbskull tales in which the monkey's ineptitude is mocked coexisted with trickster stories in which the crafty monkey outwitted his opponents. And although urban folktales often mirrored a new militancy among blacks and, as with Bad Nigger stories, forecast the aggressiveness of the sixties, they still offered many instances of inner-directed satire.

Whether aimed at the follies of black or white Americans, however, the most conspicuous characteristic of African-American humor is its insistent impious thrust. Never fully accepted by mainstream society, most blacks never subscribed to the popular American notion that, essentially, humor was only a playful diversion or innocuous entertainment, one that only occasionally referred to pertinent real-life situations. Following in the "libelist" tradition of the African source from which it was partially derived, most African-American humor—like that of mainstream society's satirist and ironist—is bitingly satirical. Initially, as was dictated, the satire was often veiled and presented indirectly. But gradually, during the twentieth century, the folk humor emerging from many young blacks became more direct, hostile, and intentionally obscene. "Frustrated and disillusioned by the hypocrisy, the insanities, and the horrors they view daily in American government and society," Daryl Cumber Dance writes, "their bitter pessimism finds expression in perverse and sardonic tales, which have their bases in some of the veiled attacks in earlier narratives." Still, throughout its evolution, the humor has remained an integral part of the day-to-day routine or lifestyle of the black community. It functions as an outlet for grievances and a vehicle for critical expression, and even as it amuses or entertains, most always reflects an underlying ironic vision shared by most African-Americans.[41]

As its prominent appearance in work songs, blues, rhythm and blues, and rap suggests, black folk humor is closely associated with African-American music. It also shares many of the attributes normally associated with the creation of that music. One reason traditional jokes do not assume greater importance among blacks is that improvisation is as much esteemed in black humor as it is in music. As in blues tunes, folktales are commonly changed, their details altered, to give them a personal twist that fits the style of the storyteller or the priorities of a particular setting. While traditional urban ballads such as "Shine" or "The Signifying Monkey" are appreciated when related unaltered and such long raps as the H. Rap Brown monologue mentioned earlier are admired, the highest regard is reserved for spontaneous wit and inventiveness. Therefore, traditional tales and ballads have infinite variations; in verbal dueling or signifying, the most elaborate or devastating rap, after being heard once, can be *cut* or *dissed* with a clever, situationally oriented, obviously improvised retort.

In most African-American humor, visual and auditory nuances play an important role as well. "One thing that may be exclusive to black humor," singer and comedian Robert Guillaume contends, "is the compendium of looks, facial expressions, and silences that we developed at one time because we couldn't say anything to anybody. If you did, you knew you might be lynched, because there was no way to fashion a statement that would reveal the anger, frustration and bitterness. We developed a whole style with the mouth and eyebrows and even body language . . . what I call mumbling on the face . . . that's the source of much of our humor."[42]

Add to this physical style the crucial role that tonal semantics play in most African-American discourse, and the difficulty of accurately conveying in print the meaning of a humorous exchange between blacks becomes clearer. From its inception, African-American discourse was intended to communicate while confounding and defying access to outsiders who insisted upon rigid denotative interpretation. Nearly every word or phrase had multiple meanings; correct interpretation required familiarity with tonal changes and subtle shifts in facial expression. Although this double-edged discourse gradually diminished in import after Emancipation, it was by no means eliminated. (That most audiences needed interpreters to decipher the lexicon of terms employed by rap artists during the eighties and nineties reflects its currency.) It is particularly pervasive in humor, where tone of voice can determine the difference between mockery and praise or insult and good-natured jesting.

So, despite their invaluable literal presentation of oral tales and anecdotes, folklore collections could not convey the full resonance of folk or street humor. Many cryptic folktales might well have been appended with the old adage, "You had to be there." For non-blacks, however, being accepted there was unlikely, even to those who might have been interested. It was left to professional black comedians to unveil the broad spectrum of African-American humor for a wider audience—to bring black folk humor to the stage, to enliven its exuberant celebration of life, as well as to unmask its darker, clandestine satire.

By the 1950s, the process had begun in black theatres and clubs. Redd Foxx and Moms Mabley were among the first comics methodically and successfully to tap this source. Mabley continually drew on folk sources for her down-home brand of humor and, in fact, some of her routines were built entirely around black folklore. For example, in the monologue recounted earlier, quips about *"They*-ami" as opposed to *"Mi*-ami" and seeing "all you white folks goin' on the green light" so "I thought the red light was for us" are taken directly from familiar folktales. That they are associated more with Mabley than with their folk sources is a tribute to her talent and a reminder that folk humor is most vividly conveyed aurally and visually.

The early efforts of Foxx and Mabley were crucial in bringing elements of authentic folk wit and satire to a wider audience. Still, the performer who could transfer the full range of this rich body of humor to the stage had not appeared.

12.

THE NEW COMICS . . . *what*

you see is what you get

19
DICK GREGORY

20
FLIP WILSON

I

During the early fifties America's mainstream comedy scene was as
segregated as Woolworth's luncheon counter in Selma, Alabama. And
the humor that audiences were being spoonfed was generally what one
might expect to find in a five-and-dime eatery. It reflected tastes shaped
by the "dominant tradition of Anglo-American culture, which since the
eighteenth century has believed that humor is intrinsically good-
natured, trivial, and kindly."[2]

Radio and television comedians, as well as comedy acts appearing at
more prestigious nightclubs and theatres, adhered to a policy of chaste
humor that neither challenged the status quo nor questioned traditional
values; acts flourished by, as humorist and author Tony Hendra puts it,
"kneading the public into a pleasant stupor." That policy would survive
well into the sixties. (The Smothers Brothers, whose 1967 television
show initially attracted huge audiences but was canceled in 1969 when
their "cheerful dopey banter" was revealed as a mask for some impious
wit, were told that they were "incompetent to make social comment.")
Tight restrictions on both the presence and the roles of women and
blacks would also continue. In *Women in Comedy*, Linda Martin and

Kerry Segrave claim that the forties and fifties "marked the lowest ebb for female comics in terms of the images they projected" and media critic David Marc observes that after "the cancellations of *Amos 'n' Andy* and *Beulah* in 1953 . . . no sitcoms concerning black Americans appeared on the air at all for fifteen years. . . . Domestic situation comedy narrative was thoroughly dominated by professional, college-educated WASPs."[3]

The veneer of middle-class propriety and ethnic homogeneity did not, of course, reflect a genuine portrait either of American society or of its humor. Beneath the surface of the Eisenhower era were signs of unrest; darker, more profane and cynical impulses were stirring. On the most serious domestic level, they would escalate into a full-fledged social revolution in which African-Americans and women would challenge the nation's white male power structure. In comedy, those impulses would be nurtured on the street and in burlesque theatres, coffeehouses, ethnic nightclubs, and an assortment of unsavory, obscure dives until they gradually surfaced and began to dominate mainstream humor in the sixties. As in the struggle for equal rights, however, there was formidable opposition to the rise of this irreverent, underground humor.

Most small, mainstream club owners adhered to many of the same prohibitions observed on radio, television, the legitimate stage, and at the nation's posh night spots. They avoided controversy and insisted that the comedy be kept clean. "If one did a line considered 'blue,' he was told not to, by fellows who inspired easy listening," Phil Berger recounts in *The Last Laugh*. Since race was a controversial issue, it was rarely mentioned, and black comedians, who might have brought up the subject, were seldom seen.[4]

Nonetheless, two comics emerged in the early fifties who challenged the system and opened the way for more dissonant voices. In 1953, Mort Sahl began doing a stand-up act at the hungry i in San Francisco. By 1956, he had been featured in *Playboy* magazine's monthly interview column and, by the sixties, was being compared to Will Rogers. Lenny Bruce started his stage career earlier but struggled in strip joints and dives until, like Sahl, he gained a following at a club in San Francisco's hip North Beach area in 1957. Although he became a cult figure and, ultimately, a legend, during his lifetime Bruce never achieved the mainstream acceptance, let alone reverence, accorded Sahl.

Sahl, as Tony Hendra points out, "came from nowhere, out of left field, with no warnings and few antecedents." He was, frankly, an oddity as a stand-up comedian; his rigorous pillorying of official governmental inconsistencies and incompetence seemed connected more to literary satire than to the stage. Avoiding the theatrical persona traditionally used to convey political humor (the wise fool), he introduced a more studious and assertive posture. Consequently, comparisons to Will Rogers were quickly rejected: "Rogers assumed the role of the yokel who questioned the common sense of the educated men managing the country, while [Sahl] was an educated man questioning the sense—if there was any—of the yokels in government." Sahl's humor was not only caustic and satiric but also aggressively intellectual. He was interested in ideas and concepts at a time when nearly all his peers were still wringing laughs from baggy pants, slapstick antics, and tired mother-in-law jokes; he was the first recognized comedian to reject the fifties' insistent conformity.[5]

"The relevance Mort Sahl initiated," in Phil Berger's view, "Lenny [Bruce] jazzed up. He talked about sex, drugs, religions, show business, race and politics—but with a head-rattling angle, a mix of whirling words and ideas that sometimes crashed through to small revelations." While Sahl, much like an impassioned Ivy League professor, disturbed and sometimes enlightened with a collision of ideas, Bruce often shocked by inundating his audience's complaisant assumptions about propriety and decorum with candid references to taboo subjects, outlandish images, scatological impressions, and profane language. Sahl once asserted that "the ultimate taboo is not against racial jokes or off-color jokes but against intellectual content." But the authorities' relentless harassment of Bruce, after he focused his act on the implicit contradictions of the era's fundamentalist outlook and brought his satire to respectable rooms, suggests that Bruce's earthy approach cut deeper and rankled much more than Sahl's rational raillery.[6]

In a sense, Bruce was a glib, hyper, Jewish embodiment of Norman Mailer's "white Negro." He had worked the sleazy dives or "toilets," as he and Redd Foxx called them, and, like Foxx, had been banished from the worst of them for daring to describe their excremental ambience in plain English. Lured by the danger and excitement of night life, he hung out with jazz musicians, hustlers, and strippers, immersing himself in a world of booze, drugs, and sex. He seemed obsessed with living on the edge, testing both his audience's and his own tolerance.

Bruce's frenetic delivery had the explosiveness and boldness of bebop, a jazz movement that intentionally thumbed its nose at mainstream traditions and expectations. His audience, as Steve Allen points out in *Funny People* (1981), "consisted of adult jazz musicians, night-club employers . . . and 'hip' people generally in the mid-thirties bracket." He not only worked the clubs but was also an habitué of the mostly dingy, offbeat joints in which that music was spawned. Along with "Lord" Buckley (a true eccentric who was even more infatuated with the dark side of the jazz world than Bruce and called his comic use of jive language "hipsomatic") and, later, Steve Allen (who told fairy tales in jive talk), Bruce was among the first of the white comedians to incorporate black vernacular speech and jazz jargon into his routine without intentional ridicule. But Allen's use of hip vernacular was principally whimsical, and Buckley's—despite having satiric overtones—was primarily a syntactical gimmick that complemented his lordly presence and further distinguished him from the "straights" or "squares" in the audience. In the fifties, Buckley's most famous routine involved the story of Jesus Christ, whom he described as "the Naz":

> But I'm gonna put a cat on you was the sweetest gaaaaawwwwn-est wailingest cat that ever stomped on this sweet-swingin' sphere. And they call this hyar cat . . . THE NAZ.

The approach had infinite variations; the Gettysburg address, for example, was transformed to:

> Four big hits and seven licks ago, our before-daddies swung forth upon this sweet groovy land a swingin', stompin', jumpin', blowin', wailin' new nation, hip to the cool groove of liberty and solid-scent with the ace lick that all the studs, chicks, cats and kitties, red white or blue, is created level in front.

Still, as Berger observes, it was "more a high-flying elocutionary lick than a comic one." Buckley's "appeal was limited," as another journalist notes. "He was too abstract for the masses; he was not an iconoclast of popular culture, as Bruce was." Moreover, Bruce had absorbed the reflexes and spontaneous adaptiveness that Mailer attributed to the black lifestyle, combined it with the intellectual disposition and facile delivery of a New York Jew, and produced a satirical comic sensibility that, as events would demonstrate, threatened middle-class America more than any comic act it had ever seen.[7]

Critics have also commented on the jazz influence in Sahl's comedy, suggesting that his clever dissections of the rationale supporting sanctioned absurdity were delivered with jazz-like verbal riffs. But despite his introducing comedy to some jazz clubs and appearing in concert with Dave Brubeck and others, the measured, controlled cadences of Sahl's humor had little to do with the volatile energy of bebop musicians like Charlie Parker or even the otherworldly coolness of Miles Davis; it was also far removed from the rhythms and spirit of black American humor. A gangling figure in slacks and Ivy League cashmere sweaters, Sahl adhered stylistically to Western intellectual conventions even as he skewered American political figures and practices. His ready acceptance by mainstream critics and even the politicians he lampooned—he wrote for John F. Kennedy during the 1960 election campaign and established a tentative relationship with the Camelot entourage—suggests that the disparity between his viewpoint and that of the military-industrial complex he satirized was one of degree and not of a fundamental nature. (For political humor and satiric commentary more thoroughly steeped in the rhythms and accents of black jazz, one might better turn to the dialogues and comic riffs offered by Gil Scot Heron in the seventies.) Instead, like Brubeck (who, according to former *New York Times* jazz critic John S. Wilson, opened the door to the "intellectual approach to jazz"), Sahl's wit was guided more by a modulated, cerebral tempo and initially appealed to a white college audience.[8]

Sahl and Bruce were to comedy what such novelists as Ralph Ellison, Kurt Vonnegut (*Player Piano*, 1952), and Joseph Heller (*Catch-22*, 1955) and beat poets Lawrence Ferlinghetti and Allen Ginsberg were to the literature; they reintroduced a satiric alternative to the fifties' shallow optimism and foreshadowed the social criticism that dominated the sixties. Their satire targeted the injustice, repression, and bureaucratic corruption lying beneath Madison Avenue's image of a prosperous, contented, suburban haven. Satirically echoing the cynicism and ironic perceptions of those Americans who would be defined by Michael Harrington's *The Other America* in 1962, they challenged the status quo and, as Woody Allen said of Mort Sahl in 1963, "made the country receptive to a kind of comedy it was not used to hearing." Both helped pave the way for the upsurge of underground comedy —variously called "sick," "gross," "anti-establishment," "gallows," or "black" humor—that would emerge in the sixties and flourish in the seventies.[9]

As Tony Hendra documents in *Going Too Far* (1987)—a chronicle of the "rise and demise" of this brand of irreverent humor—Sahl and Bruce were followed on the mainstream stage by such improvisation groups as Second City and The Committee; such television shows as *The Smothers Brothers Comedy Hour* and *Saturday Night Live*; and such individual performers as Shelley Berman, Bob Newhart, George Carlin, Woody Allen, and John Belushi. But in its irreverence and underground or anti-establishent sentiments, the genre called black humor is also closely aligned with a significant strain of African-American humor. As Ralph Ellison and other commentators have noted, no group is more intimately familiar with the absurd nature of America's social arrangements than are African-Americans. So as black humor made significant inroads into mainstream comedy, a previously suppressed satirical aspect of black American comedy began to gain currency.

Bruce's satirical viewpoint reflected a broader social displacement and alienation than did Sahl's. His comic assault on the intrinsic absurdity of race relations, religious practices, police tyranny, and hypocrisy concerning sex and drugs cut to the core of America's social contradictions. Moreover, he delivered his satirical thrusts in a hip, impious style that was clearly removed from polite middle-class society. Mirroring the street wit of the black musicians and night people with whom he associated, it smacked of a profane contempt that was both alien and frightening to mainstream America. Ridiculing political malfeasance and ineptitude was a touchy matter, but it had precedents in literary satire dating back to the Colonial period. Comically strafing those closely guarded, personal prejudices and assumptions on which the majority population's identity rested was blasphemy of a different, more terrifying order—particularly as it was accomplished in a manner reflecting the dark rhythms and impromptu, off-color language of a segment of society whose struggle for acceptance, even as Bruce performed, was being thwarted at every turn.

The changes Bruce effected in mainstream comedy—without diminishing the overriding uniqueness or "genius" that even his critics acknowledged—parallel Elvis Presley's impact on popular music. Just as Presley, whom the critic Nelson George has called a "symbol of white Negroism," took on the phrasing and performance style of black R & B and gospel singers, Bruce adopted aspects of the style and language of black hipsters and musicians. Unlike blackface minstrels, whose corked-up appearance and vernacular speech often disguised an essentially non-black or anti-black spirit, Bruce, in some of his material, conveyed a comic *attitude* reflecting prominent aspects of genuine black American humor. He adopted the swagger and assertive impiety of the black hipster in many of his routines and, more than any previous comedian on the mainstream stage, he evoked an iconoclasm and irreverence that mirrored the tempo and thrust of black street humor.[10]

Combining his own sensitivity and philosophical approach with the satiric profanity of the toasts created by black hipsters, hustlers, and pimps, he unveiled the blasphemous, often obscene perceptions of African-American humor at its least assimilated levels. Only a few black comedians—among them, Allen Drew and Redd Foxx—were drawing on this underground source. Their audiences, however, were primarily black; consequently, their impious gibes were not threatening to mainstream America. As with race records, a degree of irreverence and perceived vulgarity could be tolerated as long as the assumed depravity was carefully hidden from non-black audiences. Bruce broke this tacit accord by bringing hip black street perceptions into an integrated setting and legitimizing them with a reasoned, philosophical presentation that might appeal to whites. Even more than rock 'n' roll—the popularization of African-American rhythm and blues, which was considered a critical assault on traditional American values—Bruce's humor was viewed as a dire threat to white America.

From the mid-fifties until he died in 1966, Bruce was hounded by police. Arrested and jailed on several occasions, he saw his career brought to a virtual halt, and, according to some accounts, near-crazed, he overdosed on heroin in 1966. His persecution, ostracism, and ultimate martyrdom reflect the repressive nature of the era with regard to alternative ideas, comedy, and maintenance of the racial status quo. Still, Bruce's bold venture into hip, counterculture comedy set the stage for the mainstream emergence of African-American comedians who, though less insistently and inflexibly, were flirting with the same taboos. "Lenny paved the way for all of us," Redd Foxx said in the sixties. After another comic agreed that Bruce was a "real hero," Foxx added, "But you got to remember one thing: Heroes ain't born; they're cornered."[11]

For several reasons, however, African-American comedians did not surface immediately. Most black entertainers in the fifties played exclusively to black audiences. Those who did successfully cross over to become popular attractions on the mainstream stage were usually musical performers, like Nat King Cole or Sammy Davis, Jr., whose non-abrasive styles were easily accepted by white audiences. Ed Sullivan, who stubbornly resisted advice to ignore black entertainers, occasionally even showcased old-time comedians such as Pigmeat Markham, but for most white Americans, black comedians were practically nonexistent.

African-Americans, of course, knew better; comedy was as much a part of black life as the rhythm and blues and jazz sounds that blared from nearly every store or bar in black neighborhoods. Although they chuckled at the likes of Jack Benny, Rochester, Milton Berle, and the Three Stooges, they saved their belly laughs for Pigmeat and Moms, Foxx and White, such teams as Stump and Stumpy and Butterbeans and Susie, and the local wits, liars, and storytellers who could be found in barber shops, bars, and after-hours joints or at street corner and front porch gatherings in every black community in America.

The black comics were out there, and they were funny, even though you usually needed a ghetto guide to find them. The most successful were booked into Harlem's Apollo Theatre and a small group of associated showplaces in Chicago, Detroit, Cincinnati, Baltimore, Washington, D.C., and Philadelphia. Others, the newcomers and the old-timers in decline, appeared along with jazz groups, blues bands and vocalists, tap dance acts, and upstart doo-wop groups on the chitlin' circuit—the cabarets, nightclubs, and small theatres strewn across the country that catered almost exclusively to black patrons, although most were owned by whites, some of whom had suspicious connections with shadowy underworld types. It was in these sometimes expensively decorated but usually boisterous, get-down cabarets and honky-tonks that most black comedians honed their skills in the fifties.

On the West Coast there was the Cotton Club and Oasis in Los Angeles and Slim Jenkins in Oakland. New York City had the Palm Café, Club Barron, and Small's Paradise; Philadelphia had the Media AA Club; and Baltimore had the Club Astoria. In the Midwest, on the Black Belt nightclub circuit, there was the Faust Club and Jordan Chambers's Riviera in St. Louis; the Ritz Lounge and Rum Boogie in Chicago; the Club Morocco in Louisville, Kentucky; the Baby Grand in Detroit, and the Music Box and Club 100 in Cleveland. In these and a thousand other similar spots in major cities and smaller towns across the country, the transformation in black comedy began. Often doubling as M.C.'s and sandwiched between funky organ trios or larger ryhthm and blues dance bands and floor shows featuring exotic dancers and bluesy singers, black performers were initiating a less restricted brand of African-American stage comedy.

The audiences were often raucous crowds who liked their comedy blunt and broad, and they got what they expected. Moms Mabley, for example, answered charges by media executives that her humor was too blue for television by saying: "It's you and others in your position who keep me working where I have to use that kind of material." Although the comedy seldom matched the explicit expressive levels heard in hustlers' toasts and ballads, by the late fifties profane denunciations of white bigotry and graphic sexual jokes were commmon in chitlin' circuit showplaces—particularly the numerous gutbucket cabarets "where good Negro folks would never venture and stepping on a brother's Florsheims has meant hospitalization."[12]

Before they were accepted in integrated clubs, television, and motion pictures, Mabley and Redd Foxx thrived in these joints. Mabley, of course, had worked similar clubs on the TOBA circuit and, after its demise in the thirties, moved on to chitlin' circuit clubs. In Los Angeles, Foxx worked as a dishwasher in the Alabam before gaining a reputation as a blue comic elsewhere, then returned to the club as a stand-up act. Nipsey Russell showcased his articulate brand of whimsy and social commentary at the Baby Grand in Harlem. As a stand-up comic, Slappy White toured many of the circuit's theatres and clubs with Dinah Washington and could be found at the Riviera and Faust clubs in St. Louis during a period when Foxx, LaWanda Page, and a young Richard Pryor were also booked into the latter.

According to jazz pianist Junior Mance, Allen Drew—a black pioneer of racy, rapid-fire one-liners whom many considered "quicker than [Milton] Berle or [Henny] Youngman"—was a regular at the Ritz Lounge and the Club DeLisa on Chicago's South Side. Mance (who toured with the Dinah Washington Show while White was the comedian) also affirms the tale that George Kirby began as a busboy or janitor at the Club DeLisa but, because his comic impersonations were more entertaining than many of the acts on stage, was asked to fill in one night. He never looked back. Dick Gregory worked Chicago's Esquire Show Lounge and Roberts Show Club and, in the late fifties, watched such big-time acts as Count Basie, Sammy Davis, Jr., and the fast-rising Nipsey Russell perform at the latter. Roberts Show Club was the "biggest Negro club in America" and featured "Red Saunders' big house band and an eight-girl chorus line." Richard Pryor, in his *Live on Sunset* concert film, gave one of the circuit's smaller clubs some dubious publicity when he related a comic anecdote allegedly based on his attempt to get his salary from the recalcitrant owners (Lebanese, not Italian as suggested in the comedy routine) of the Casablanca in Youngstown, Ohio, by pulling a toy pistol on them. In that same club —which featured exotic dancers, female impersonators, and R & B bands like Big Boogie D—a frustrated Pryor reportedly screamed to a hostile audience, "Hey, yall can boo me now. But in a couple of years I'm gonna be a star, and you dumb niggers will still be sittin' here!"[13]

The destiny of the audience is undocumented but, at least in part, Pryor was right about himself. Less than five years later, he made his first appearance on a nationally televised variety show.

Throughout the country, in thousands of black cabarets—as obscure as the Casablanca or as prominent as Roberts Show Club—old-guard comics and young, fast-rising wits such as Gregory, Pryor, and Flip Wilson performed in virtual anonymity during the fifties and early sixties. In varying degrees, their acts began reflecting the more militant attitudes of their segregated patrons and began to echo much of the satire and scathing humor of the streets. As quiet as it was kept, a nucleus of genuine African-American stage comedy was being shaped. By the late sixties, the exposure of the more biting humor of Sahl and Bruce and the Civil Rights movement's escalated push for equal opportunity had helped bring this underground humor to the mainstream stage.

II

Timmie Rogers, Nipsey Russell, and Slappy White were among the first black comedians to do stand-up comedy on stage before predominantly white audiences. As trailblazers, they not only absorbed many of the rejections and embarrassments visited on those who explore new territory but also pioneered many of the adjustments black comedians were forced to make in order to amuse non-black patrons.

Rogers began his stage career as a child and was a vaudeville performer as a teenager during the thirties; he appeared in *Blackbirds of 1936* along with stars such as Tim Moore, Peg Leg Bates, and the Nicholas Brothers. In the mid-forties, he pioneered a crucial change in the stage image of African-American comedians by abandoning the traditional clownish attire and donning a tuxedo for his act. He also altered his material. A singer, dancer, and songwriter, Rogers began lacing his song and dance routines with a monologue and "social satire" that was, as he put it, "strictly political and other side of the coin" when playing to white patrons. At the time, however, many owners and audiences were not ready for the shift. The first time he introduced the formal attire and revamped act, the owner of the Los Angeles Clover Club fired him on the spot.

Rogers was facing a problem that all of the emerging black comedians would encounter: how to adapt their humor, with all of its inside racial references, to present it successfully to an integrated audience. Despite the setback at the Clover Club, he stuck with his new approach. Rogers explained that before white audiences, "I used sophisticated material that they already knew about. In the forties, blacks weren't into that, there was no television so we just knew about our uptown humor. What makes a black person laugh, a white person may not understand. A black comedian can say, 'Shut up fool!' and black folks will laugh their butts off. Downtown that wouldn't even get a chuckle." Rogers's flexibility and persistence paid off. Smooth dancing, clever songs, mildly upbraiding social satire, combined with his bubbling personality (reflected in the infectious catchphrase "Ohh . . . yeah!" which punctuated almost all of his jokes) had made him one of America's most successful black comics by the fifties. In fact, he became the first comedian to headline a show at the Apollo Theatre in 1957, where he introduced new variations on his "If I Were President" routine, in which familiar mother-in-law jokes were enlivened by a political setting:

President: Now, Momma, you can't talk to me like that, I am the President of the United States.

Mother-in-law: Yeah, another one of your temporary jobs. In four years, you'll be back on the street again.

A few years later, while most African-American comics were still playing black rooms, he was working such downtown clubs as Café Society.[14]

Slappy White, whom Jack Schiffman (son of former Apollo Theatre owner Frank Schiffman) described as "one of the most intelligent, careful comics in show business," began in a knockabout comedy act called the Two Zephyrs. Later, teamed with Willie Lewis and then Redd Foxx, he moved from visual or physical comedy to dialogue humor. In the early fifties he began working as a single act. Although White continued playing chitlin' circuit clubs and theatres, he also appeared before predominantly white audiences as part of the Dinah Washington show in Las Vegas and other clubs and theatres across the country. Little of the Two Zephyrs' slapstick routines or the risqué material developed during his partnership with Foxx was transferable to appearances before non-black crowds. (White recalled that he and Foxx had bombed before a white audience at the Palace Theatre in New York in the early fifties.) But White, cited as the "father of the integrated joke" by some writers, was an inventive comedian and quickly adapted to the new circumstances. He began using topical humor that, despite having considerable bite, was acceptable to many white audiences:

> Mayor Daley did a nice thing to elevate the dignity of a black family in Chicago. He moved them from a $100 a month apartment to one that rented for $300 so they could be closer to the welfare office.

"I don't tell racial jokes to offend anyone," he would later explain. "I try to create a little humor so that all people can laugh."[15]

Still, as with Rogers, he encountered considerable resistance. In one of White's earliest stand-up appearances in Miami Beach during the mid-fifties, a white producer insisted that he drop his monologue and pretend to be a porter. White complied for a few performances, playing to small audiences, then reinserted his own material and was kept on. In subsequent years, his tact and ability subtly to weave social satire into broad humor would permit him to become one of the first black comics to work the Catskills' resort hotels; later, he successfully teamed with white comedian Steve Rossi. Both as a comic writer and a pioneer cross-over performer, White played an important role in black American comedy's rise to mainstream recognition.[16]

Due to his frequent television appearances on talk and game shows in the seventies and eighties, Nipsey Russell is probably more recognizable to most Americans than either Rogers or White. But he also started out on the chitlin' circuit in the forties and, between stints at the Baby Grand, continued traveling the circuit in the fifties and sixties. Like Rogers, however, Russell began shaping a more "respectable" and assertively intellectual comic image early in his career. He also abandoned the traditional buffoonish garb and, except for a raffish porkpie hat, appeared in conventional business clothing. A graduate of the University of Cincinnati, Russell leaned toward topical wit and sardonic social observations. During one performance at the Baby Grand in the early sixties, he held up a photograph of some aspiring astronauts and said, "Not a Mau Mau among them." Later, on the subject of integration, he observed, "A seat on the top deck don't mean a thing if the ship is sinking." An articulate social satirist, Russell, more than any other black comic during the fifties, challenged his audience's verbal acuity. His use of multi-syllabic language prompted Timmie Rogers to warn him against using "too many words that your audience didn't understand." Bristling, challenging, defiantly confident, Russell pushed black comedians a step closer to popular acceptance by reclothing the impious vernacular wit of the streets in proper, middle-class language. By the sixties, audiences at his Baby Grand performances were increasingly integrated.[17]

Subsequently, Russell became a frequent guest on Jack Paar's *Tonight Show* and, like Slappy White, was booked into the Concord Hotel in the Catskills. His ability spontaneously to produce funny rhyming couplets led to his being called the "Poet Laureate of Comedy," and he inevitably introduced catchy topical jingles when he appeared on such TV quiz shows as *Hollywood Squares*. His humor frequently centered on racial absurdities, as in the tale of an African delegate who stops at a Maryland restaurant and is told that they don't serve blacks. "But I'm the African delegate from Ghana," the delegate proudly asserts. "Well, you ain't *Ghana* eat here," the waitress replies. Russell's humor, however, was not confined to black issues; he prided himself on the universality of his material and insisted that he did not want to be considered a "black comic." Much of his humor focused on broader topics and offered general observations, as in his famous quip: "America is the only place in the world where you can work in an Arab home in a Scandinavian neighborhood and find a Puerto Rican baby eating matzo balls with chopsticks."[18]

Although, through his frequent television appearances, Russell attained more prominence than Rogers or White, none of these excellent comedians received the national exposure they might have. In the fifties, mainstream America's tolerance for black comics was, at best, spotty. (By the sixties, Dick Gregory would temporarily eclipse all competitors as he was catapulted to the top of the heap.)

George Kirby, more a song and dance man and master impressionist than a stand-up monologuist, was the only African-American comic entertainer to achieve national recognition in the fifties. After being discovered at the Club DeLisa in 1947, he became a regular guest on television variety and talk shows and played some of the best rooms in the country, breaking down long-standing racial barriers. His career was halted when he spent two years at the United States Public Service Hospital in Lexington, Kentucky, for treatment of his drug addiction. Released in 1960, he began a comeback but never achieved the stardom promised by his fifties' accomplishments.

Rogers, White, Russell (despite his reluctance to be pigeonholed as a black comic), and Kirby made the first significant moves toward bringing a new image of African-American comedy to a national audience. The temper of the times, however, assured that, before the comics reached mass, mainstream audiences, much of the edge in their humor was blunted. While all four comics intentionally abandoned the dialect jokes, buffoonish costumes, and obsequious postures associated with the old-time comedians, white owners and media executives made sure that they also toned down the explicit language, sexual references, and bluntly assertive racial and social satire that had begun to emerge on the chitlin' circuit.

Initially, in front of white audiences, there were clear restraints on the role of the freewheeling jester commenting with impunity on whatever struck his fancy. Pianist Junior Mance recalled, for instance, that Slappy White frequently addressed his gibes to audience members. During a Las Vegas engagement with the Dinah Washington Show in the mid-fifties, when the "cigar-chomping" manager of the room they were working began nervously pacing the floor each time White started his act, White targeted him. After a few performances, the manager, irritated by the mild jokes at his expense, approached White and told him he was through. White had overstepped the tacit agreement that black comedians avoid wisecracks or insolent quips to white customers (let alone managers of clubs). There were, of course, limits on every comedian's material, but for black comics in the fifties the restraints often had a distinctly racial cast. White stayed with the show in this instance, but only because Dinah Washington insisted that if he left, the rest of the act would also leave.[19]

Nearly all of the African-American stand-up comedians who began working in white or integrated clubs in the fifties had similar experiences. They were forced to walk a tightrope. They represented the frontline in the mainstream emergence of genuine African-American humor, and they were aware of the discretion required. Moms Mabley and Redd Foxx, by adhering to the blunter and more irreverent humor of the black masses, assured that they would be bypassed initially. But the discreet entry of Rogers, White, Kirby, and Russell into the world of mainstream stand-up comedy had begun breaking down the barriers; by the end of the decade black comedians were no longer arbitrarily eliminated from consideration for bookings before white audiences. By the sixties, as these pioneers advanced their careers, a group of younger, less inhibited, and even more assertive African-American comedians were preparing their acts.

Formidable obstacles remained. For some of those who honed their comic skills on the chitlin' circuit, aiming their humor at exclusively black audiences, a full-scale revamping of their style and material was required. As Timmie Rogers points out, white audiences could not be expected to understand undiluted African-American humor. It was not necessarily, as Rogers claimed, that the material had to become more "sophisticated," however; instead, it had to be stripped of jargon and inner-community referents that were meaningless or puzzling to outsiders. Actually, much black humor had to be simplified or decoded for non-black audiences. The maze of double or reverse meanings, code words and gestures, stealth, and intentional obfuscation that since slavery had shaped and informed the discourse and humor of most African-Americans had to be translated into literal terms and symbols that were recognizable to outsiders.

Inevitably, something was lost in the translation, since in many instances, the ambivalent manner in which a humorous remark was couched was itself the essence of the humor. Moms Mabley's familiar opening—"Hi, children. How y'all doin' tonight? . . . Yeah, *I know!* I know how y'all feel. Moms is tired, too"—for example, was not just a folksy greeting. It drew applause and laughter from black audiences because of a shared recognition of its underlying irony and *indirect* criticism of American racial bigotry. To white audiences in the forties and fifties, however, it was probably unfathomable. (By the seventies, Richard Pryor could elicit laughter or at least squirmish acknowledgment from mixed crowds by expressing the sentiment candidly: "How long? How l-o-o-n-n-n-g? *How long,* will this bullshit go on?")

Beyond the problems of mechanics—vernacular speech, circuitous delivery, and cryptic referents—an even larger impediment loomed: the interpersonal dynamic between the comedian and the audience. As Sigmund Freud pointed out, although the "comic process" needs only two elements (the comedian and the person or thing that is the object of the humor), external affirmation of the success of that process or "joke-work" lies with a third party—the listener or audience. According to Freud, "Some degree of benevolence or a kind of neutrality, an absence of any factor that could provoke feelings opposed to the purpose of the joke, is an indispensable condition if the third person is to collaborate in the completion of the process of making a joke." Somehow, then, African-American comedians had to defuse the racial hostility and entrenched "us" versus "them" syndrome that characterized traditional black-white relationships in America. As Lily Tomlin noted about stage comedy in general, "the best material . . . makes a comment without ridiculing and includes everyone in the comment." The audience had to be included in the joking process to the extent that a shared viewpoint regarding the object of the joke was established. An "integrated joke" is finally one in which, momentarily at least, black comic and white audience function in an equitable "we" relationship—one that not only shatters the image of the naive Negro stage comic but also includes non-blacks in the humor—instead of, as in much black circuit comedy, excluding whites by either focusing on inside humor or making them the object of the joke. In the fifties and sixties, this was no small order for black comics.[20]

One of the first to overcome these obstacles and rise to national prominence was Dick Gregory, who as a wiry, quick-witted, twenty-eight-year-old upstart was catapulted to fame shortly after appearing at Chicago's Playboy Club in January 1961. Gregory had been raised by his mother in a St. Louis slum; with the aid of an athletic scholarship, he attended Southern Illinois University before deciding to pursue a career on the stage. In the late fifties, he worked small black clubs like Chicago's Esquire Lounge as emcee and comedian for ten dollars a night and, by 1960, had worked up to the more imposing Roberts Show Club. But Gregory was an ambitious and methodical comedian; even while he played black clubs in the Chicago area he began fashioning a strategy for the future when he would perform "where the bread was, in the big white clubs."

Gregory had watched Nipsey Russell "slay" the mostly white audience (most of whom were making "their first trip to the South Side of Chicago") who turned out for his appearance with Sammy Davis, Jr., at Roberts Show Club in 1960. But he had also watched Russell present the same routine downtown, in a white club, as part of an audition for the American Guild of Variety Artists, where he "died." Gregory concluded that the white listener was so nervous in a black environment that "anything the comic says to relieve his tension will absolutely knock him out." When "comfortable and secure" on their own turf, however, white audiences felt no compunction to laugh at "racial material that they didn't want to hear." The solution, for Gregory, was thoughtfully calculated: "I've got to go up there as an individual first, a Negro second. I've got to be a colored funny man, not a funny colored man. I've got to act like a star who isn't sorry for himself—that way, they can't feel sorry for me. I've got to make jokes about myself, before I can make jokes about them and their society."[21]

Using this general framework, Gregory conceived of a rapid-paced act ("Hit them fast, before they can think"):

Just my luck, bought a suit with two pair of pants today . . . burnt a hole in the jacket.

Then a joke about the Civil Rights movement and a request to buy a lifetime membership in the NAACP:

Told them I'd pay a week at a time. Hell of a thing to buy a lifetime membership, wake up one morning and find the country's been integrated.

A pause, then more misdirection:

Wouldn't it be a hell of a thing if all this was burnt cork and you people were being tolerant for nothing?

"Now you've got them. No bitterness, no Tomming. . . . Now you can settle down and talk about anything you want."[22]

Gregory carefully examined the curious relationship between a black jokester whose material, in part, targets white racism and white audiences whom the comic is supposed to amuse. He realized that the psychological baggage—anxiety, guilt, subliminal anger, and hate—was boundless and potentially disastrous. Hecklers, for example, were a problem for stand-up comics in the best circumstances, but they loomed as a much greater threat in integrated settings. They had to be quieted and, of course, there were many standard rejoinders for black audiences: "I wouldn't come on your job and knock the mop outta your hand," Flip Wilson might say at the Apollo. More bitingly, one might use Timmie Rogers's "Shut up, fool!" or Richard Pryor's ultimate equalizer, "What about yo' momma?" But while these or the more devastating retorts employed by Redd Foxx worked with black audiences, at the time they were impractical for white crowds. There was too great a chance of turning the room against you, severing the tentative bond that a comic must establish with an audience.

For Gregory the answer was, again, diversion: deflect the hostility and potential insult, make a joke of it. He even prepared for the maximum affront—the drunk who calls you a "nigger." "You hear what that guy called me? Roy Rogers' horse. He called me Trigger." Or he would explain that his contract stipulated that he got fifty dollars every time someone shouted the word and request that "everybody in the room please stand up and yell nigger."[23]

When he was unexpectedly called to replace Professor Irwin Corey at the Playboy Club in January 1961, Gregory had already tested his approach in small, working-class white clubs. He was prepared and, although the manager suggested he postpone his appearance because the club was hosting a convention for a group of Southern businessmen, Gregory insisted that it was not a problem. He later admitted, "the audience fought me with dirty, little, insulting statements," but by the end of the evening he had a room filled with converts:

> Good evening, ladies and gentlemen. I understand there are a good many Southerners in the room tonight. I know the South very well. I spent twenty years there one night. . . .
>
> It's dangerous for me to go back. You see, when I drink, I think I'm Polish. One night I got so drunk I moved out of my own neighborhood. . . .
>
> Last time I was down South I walked into this restaurant, and this white waitress came up to me and said: "We don't serve colored people here."
>
> I said: "That's all right, I don't eat colored people. Bring me a whole fried chicken."
>
> About that time these three cousins come in, you know the ones I mean, Klu, Kluck, and Klan, and they say: "Boy, we're givin' you fair warnin'. Anything you do to that chicken, we're gonna do to you." About then the waitress brought me my chicken. "Remember, boy, anything you do to that chicken, we're gonna do to you." So I put down my knife and fork, and I picked up that chicken, and I kissed it.

Gregory's Playboy Club date was a sensation; his contract was quickly extended from a few weeks to three years. Within a year of his debut, he was a national celebrity. After a *Time* magazine reporter saw his act and wrote an article, appearances on the *Jack Paar* and *David Susskind* television shows followed, then a recording contract and bookings in the best rooms. By December of 1962, a *Newsweek* story would report: "From the moment he was booked into the Playboy Club . . . Jim Crow was dead in the joke world." Success at one crucial booking had snatched him from relative obscurity and thrust him into the limelight.

Gregory had vaulted ahead of a large field of more experienced African-American comedians and become the first black comic superstar since Bert Williams and Stepin Fetchit; simultaneously, he had opened the floodgates for a raft of previously ignored black comedians.[24]

Although older black comics benefited from Gregory's overnight acceptance, they were also startled and perplexed. His material, after all, was not radically innovative. As mentioned in chapter 11, some of the jokes he told were common currency in black communities. (In a more pointed street version of the joke about the racists who tell a black man, "anything you do to that chicken, we're gonna do to you," the black man kisses the chicken's ass.) And like most comedians, he had picked up lines from other funnymen and reworked them to fit his routine. In fact, Timmie Rogers, Slappy White, and Nipsey Russell, who had ventured into non-black clubs while he was still in college, felt that he had "pirated some of their best lines." According to Nat Hentoff, when Gregory opened at the Blue Angel in New York in 1961, they sat at a front row table with a tape recorder. "The angry trio did tape Gregory's act, watching him with undisguised disdain all the while. 'We wanted to find out,' Slappy White wrote Gregory a few days later, 'which of our material not to use any more.' "[25]

Parts of Gregory's material may have been familiar to black audiences, but few white Americans had heard anyone talk so candidly about race. His appraisal of the psychological dynamics of black-white interactions had served him well. The careful, moderately assertive approach he adopted, in retrospect, was perfectly suited for mainstream audiences who, either out of guilt or sincere concern, were prepared to be chided about racism even though they might have balked at scornful lampooning or outright ridicule. Gregory had devised a stand-up persona that cast him as a patient, self-assured ironist, capable of dispensing witticisms about racial relationships with cool detachment. His monologues mirrored the bitingly satiric perceptions of the most alienated segment of black America but, because they were delivered deftly and without rancor, were not perceived as obloquy. Sophisticated, aloof, and seemingly observing from a viewpoint of amused neutrality, he was able to introduce into integrated settings a racial satire that, while more aggressive than that of his predecessors, was clearly more palatable to white Americans.

In part, his method—much like that of Rogers, White, and, especially, Nipsey Russell—involved discarding the clownish appearance, dialect speech, and inside (Negro) jokes that might characterize him as a black comedian and distance him from mainstream audiences. He also avoided the candid sexual material on which Redd Foxx and Moms Mabley traded. "If you use blue material," he wrote in *Nigger*, "you slip back into being that Negro stereotype comic." It was not until later in his career that he introduced mildly suggestive jokes, such as the one about the white suburbanite who sees a Negro cutting the lawn of the previously vacant house next door and asks, "What do you get for doing yardwork?" The Negro answers: "I get to sleep with the lady of the house. You need any help?"[26]

In effect, Gregory avoided most of the superficial mannerisms and traditional subjects that overtly defined old-time African-American humor, concentrating on the irony and satire that undergirded it. While partly a concession to mainstream entertainment style, this modification allowed him to focus more intently on the humorous depiction of racial inequities that were not only his central concern but also had been a significant subject of black American comedy since slavery.

Still, that adaptability does not entirely explain how Gregory outstripped more experienced comedians and quickly assumed the mantle of America's leading black comedian in the sixties. Perhaps, of course, he was simply a far more talented comedian than his rivals, but despite his sharp wit, some critics question his ability as a pure comic. "Gregory is more a mechanic than a spontaneously creative comedian," Nat Hentoff wrote. "He would probably be decimated in an ab-lib duel with Redd Foxx, Moms Mabley or Nipsey Russell."[27]

Ironically, the timing of Gregory's emergence suggests that his *inexperience* in working the black comedy circuit may have hastened his ascendancy. The sixties were volatile times in which social and interpersonal racial relations were rapidly shifting. Television viewers were being besieged by violent images of racial confrontations in the South. The contradictions between segregation and democracy were forcing many Americans to reexamine their moral stance and question their personal convictions about race and equality more candidly than at any other time in American history. Since African-American entertainers were among the most visible representatives of the black community, for many Americans they assumed a disproportionately significant role in this process. Moreover, stand-up comedy was changing the way that comedians related to their audiences.

"Without the protection of the formal mask of narrative drama, without a song, a dance, or any other intermediary composition that creates distance between performer and performance . . . the stand-up come-

dian addresses an audience as a naked self," the media critic David
Marc notes. "The exposure of the stand-up comic to public judgment is
extraordinarily raw and personal." For black comedians working white
rooms, the increased importance placed on a comic's personal acceptance was diametrically opposed to the traditional roles assumed by
black entertainers and white audiences in America.[28]

Public acknowledgment or sanction of personal relationships between blacks and whites had been fiercely resisted for over two hundred
years. From the early twentieth-century black minstrels, who wore their
ragged stage costumes even when off stage to avoid harassment by
whites, through the disturbances caused by release of *Darktown Jubilee*
(1914), in which Bert Williams appeared without blackface in top hat
and tails, on to the riots caused by non-black females' over-enthusiastic
displays of affection for such performers as Nat King Cole and Cab
Calloway, the insistence on depersonalized relations between black performers and white audiences had been zealously enforced. Specifically
with regard to comedy, white audiences had traditionally laughed *at*
black comics, not *with* them.

Dick Gregory emerged at a time not only when the distance between
comedians and audiences was being erased but also when the established public barriers between whites and blacks were being challenged
at lunch counters and flaunted through integrated freedom rides. Many
mainstream Americans, shaken by blacks' intensifying push for equal
rights, were primed for a satirical African-American voice that mirrored
the moral and ethical candor displayed by such Civil Rights leaders as
Martin Luther King, Jr. Some, able to empathize with blacks' frustration and impatience, were even receptive to the assertiveness of a Malcolm X. Few, even among the most virulent racists, could still be
amused and comforted by the servile postures and diffident tricksterism
of the old-time Negro stage comedians when evening news shows
broadcast pictures of thousands of blacks (formerly perceived as Uncle
Toms and Sambos) braving fire hoses, police dogs, rabid mobs, and
brutal sheriffs in a struggle for equal rights. The sham was over—both
in the streets and on stage. And Gregory, more a candid satirist than an
entertaining funnyman, appeared at exactly the right time.

Although such comedians as Rogers, White, Kirby, and Russell pioneered the transition from classic, black stage humor (with its traditional
costumes, dialect, and indirect satire) to more forthright and dignified
comic presentation on mainstream stages, they had worked the black

circuits for years. Despite having abandoned the prominent stereotypes associated with that humor, most retained some subtle residual mannerisms: a passively slumped shoulder while delivering a punchline, an overly exaggerated widening of the eyes, or an apprehensive glance in search of approval from non-black crowds.

Gregory had been interested in topical humor from the start of his career. Although he played black clubs where the patrons insisted on blue humor, he had resisted, weaving topical jokes into more risqué material and often annoying owners and customers. For a brief period in 1959, he even opened his own club, the Apex in Robbins, Illinois, in which he could concentrate on the social satire that he preferred. Unlike his precursors, he had not been thoroughly groomed in black circuit stage humor, which requires, among other things, that one be a funnyman or jester in the traditional sense. Less hampered by the baggage of traditional Negro stage images, he more easily assumed the cockier, more self-confident approach of the social satirist. In a sense, Gregory was to most of his black forerunners what Mort Sahl was to Milton Berle and other non-black vaudeville comics.

Gregory, as Sahl had earlier, realized that the social climate had shifted enough to make his brand of satire palatable to a larger audience. In addition, he had also squarely faced the problem of whites' stereotyped view of black performers. As he points out in his autobiography, black comics encountered white audiences who either hated them or felt sorry for them because they were Negroes. The former were usually unreachable and the latter, in terms of laughter, were unreliable. "They can't respect someone they pity, and eventually they'll stop laughing," Gregory observed. African-American comedians had to dispel the pity with self-assurance; they had to project a cocksure, dauntless image that erased lingering suspicions of inferiority and clearly engaged their audience on an equal basis. It was not necessary that they told racial jokes or focused on social satire, but it was essential that they dislodge all traces of the minstrel image of the servile, slowwitted Sambo, which had hounded them like a shadow for over a century.[29]

Clever, witty, deeply committed to social revolution in the streets, and practically untutored in the evasive, indirect humor of the black stage, Gregory was perfectly equipped for the challenge. Initially, he moderated his commentary. Shortly after his appearance before the largely Southern audience at the Playboy Club, for instance, a critic wrote, "He is cautious and deft, and never deeply cutting or openly aggressive." Once he had gained a foothold, however, Gregory's social satire assumed more acerbic overtones.[30]

From the outset, his cleverness and sense of irony were apparent: "I sat at a lunch counter for nine months. They finally integrated and didn't have what I wanted." Indirection and sarcasm were soon replaced by jibes aimed at more specific targets. On America and racism he quipped:

I'm really for Abraham Lincoln. If it hadn't been for Abe, I'd still be on the open market. . . . You know the definition of a Southern moderate. That's a cat that'll lynch you from a low tree.

Or:

What a country! Where else could I have to ride in the back of the bus, live in the worst neighborhoods, go to the worst schools, eat in the worst restaurants—and average $5,000 a week just talking about it.

White American arrogance was pilloried:

You gotta say this for whites, their self-confidence knows no bounds. Who else could go to a small island in the South Pacific, where there's no crime, poverty, unemployment, war, or worry— and call it a "primitive society."

The political process and African-American disdain for its inherent hypocrisy was targeted as well:

The President is willing to give Lockheed $250 million. . . . When it comes to giving welfare layouts to black folks, so many legislators say, "They ought to learn to pull themselves up by their own bootstraps." So I sent the president of Lockheed Aircraft a telegram. . . . "Why don't you learn to pick yourself up by your own landing gear?" I just can't understand Lockheed asking for all that welfare money and they don't even have any illegitimate planes!

Or:

Reagan is "Nigger" spelled backwards. Imagine, we got a backwards nigger running California.

Fully aware of his link with comedy's new straight-talking social satirists, at the end of his act Gregory would often quip: "If I've done anything to upset you, maybe it's what I'm here for. Lenny Bruce shakes up the Puritans; Mort Sahl, the conservatives; and me—almost everybody."[31]

By the mid-sixties, as he became more involved in the Civil Rights movement, Gregory's humor became more caustic and bitter. He also became more of a political and human rights advocate than a humorist. His commitment to political activism forced him to cancel concerts and club dates and, gradually, comedy became a secondary enterprise. In 1967, he said that he viewed himself "as a social commentator who uses humor to interpret the needs and wants of Negroes to the white community, rather than as a comedian who happens to deal in topical social material." By that time, however, his lasting impact was readily apparent. As Redd Foxx asserted in 1967, "a new brand of Negro comic" had surfaced. "He's clever, poised, informed and tells it like it is." Gregory's influence on this newly emerging type was enormous. "He established a new voice, a new sound for black comics and satirists," which was, Tony Hendra notes, "not aggressive so much as non-ingratiating, less challenging than unapologetic, and therefore more real and more confident." Gregory's more "real" humor was not, of course, new to black Americans, but it was a revelation to its new white audience. By introducing it to the public, he opened the mainstream stage for many older black comedians as well as a new group of younger ones who waited anxiously in the wings.[32]

III

Among them were Bill Cosby, who was enrolled at Temple University and worked as a part-time bartender and substitute comedian at a bar in his native Philadelphia; Godfrey Cambridge, an actor who had worked his way from small parts in Off-Broadway shows to an Obie Award–winning performance in Jean Genet's *The Blacks* (1961) and a major role in Ossie Davis's *Purlie Victorious* (1961) and was just beginning to test his stand-up comedy act as an emcee for rock 'n' roll shows; Flip

Wilson, who was establishing himself as a regular at the Apollo after seven years of working small black clubs and dives throughout the country; and Richard Pryor, who was still struggling to create his comic stage persona in chitlin' circuit clubs in the Midwest. There were others, of course, but, these four young black comedians, along with veterans Redd Foxx and Moms Mabley, would soon inherit the throne vacated when Gregory turned to politics and, in little more than a decade, totally alter white America's conception of African-American humor.

Cosby was the first to gain national recognition; in fact, his rise to stardom can be aptly described as meteoric. He left college in 1962 and came to New York's Greenwich Village, where he worked at the Gaslight and Cafe Wha?. "Cosby was a natural," Phil Berger writes in *The Last Laugh*. "No beginner's kinks in his style. He was the flimflam man from the start." The comic Adam Keefe, who worked the Village coffeehouses during the early sixties, remembers him as "supercool. . . . It was like he'd already made it." Bright, charming, and supremely self-assured, Cosby was able quickly to establish a rapport with the mostly white audiences in Village cafés. Although at the outset he told some jokes and included some racial material, he was essentially a folksy monologuist who related stories with comic turns and ironic insights. Soon the straight-out jokes (setup, misdirection, and punchline) and racial references were eliminated. "In my monologues, the humor itself goes straight down the middle," Cosby said of his style, meaning that his biblical parodies and tales of childhood and family ties focus on experiences familiar to nearly all audiences.[33]

In a sense, Cosby's presentation of an essentially colorless comedy routine was revolutionary. No previous African-American comedian had attempted or been allowed to step so boldly into this non-racial territory before non-black audiences. Traditionally, the few black comedians who were booked into white clubs or theatres were expected to present familiar ethnic comedy, heavily laden with dialect, that corroborated the image of naive humor established during minstrelsy. Only a decade earlier, black comics had been passed over or fired because they were not "Negro" enough. Transition comics Timmie Rogers and Slappy White had adjusted their routines, incorporating some topical and non-racial material, but there was still an aura of the traditional black circuit style about their acts. Even so, Rogers recalled several occasions when he was dismissed and bluntly told that he "was doing a white man's act." Times had changed, however, and, since the more acerbic *Negro* humor of Nipsey Russell and Dick Gregory had surfaced, Cosby's insistently non-racial humor was now preferred by many whites. It was an ironic turn of events since, in projecting an image of a hip, intelligent black man who had moved beyond racial concerns, Cosby was quietly asserting that there was no difference between the races—a suggestion of equality that previously would have been instantly silenced. Moreover, he had the temerity to joke openly about it. "One morning I woke up and looked in the mirror. There was a freckle and it just got bigger and bigger," he quipped early in his career.[34]

But the implicit assertiveness of Cosby's approach was overlooked. Instead, audiences responded to the apparently non-radical tenor of his whimsically exaggerated tales and ironic perceptions of everyday experiences. Whether intended or not, Cosby's outward congeniality was crucial to his quick ascendancy. At a time when racial confrontations were escalating in the streets, his relaxed, chatty style and surface image of a clean-cut, sanguine black man was the antithesis of the menacing figures on the street. And mainstream America, though it could abide the slashing satiric wit and more easily perceived anger of a Dick Gregory, seems to have been consoled by the playful brilliance of Cosby's approach. His first television appearance on *The Tonight Show*, in 1963, was a hit, and during that same year, *Newsweek* ran an article applauding the promising young Negro comedian. In rapid succession, a record contract and more substantial bookings followed. Cosby was rising quickly and, by 1965, was recruited to co-star with Robert Culp in *I Spy* (1965), the first non-comic TV series to star a black male. He had become a full-fledged superstar.

Despite critical rumblings about the non-threatening or non-racial character of his humor—criticisms advanced in the sixties to explain his overnight success and rehashed in the eighties to criticize the "unrealistic" portrayals of *The Cosby Show*'s Huxtable family—and aside from his being the most financially successful black humorist, Bill Cosby is clearly among the best African-American comedians. "I did racial material, what I called guilt material, when I started out in the Village," Cosby said on *The Arsenio Hall Show* in 1991. But he insisted that it didn't work for him. It did not fit his comic temperament. As a performer, Cosby was more comfortable with humor that cut through color boundaries and dealt with situations which, as Redd Foxx wrote, "let you see that being black is no different from being white or brown or whatever color."[35]

The children in his stories, for instance, have almost no uniquely black or ghetto aspects to their personalities. Although listeners know they are black, Fat Albert, Dumb Donald, and Weird Harold are appealing because they humorously recall childhood experiences, attitudes, and revelations that are familiar to nearly everyone. Cosby presents them with vivid pictorial resonance and comical sound effects that bring them to life and make his audience identify with them:

> Everytime you hit Harold with a snowball in the face—BLOP!—he always says the same thing, says [in whining, childish voice]: "Hey man, whatcha wanna hit me in the face with a snowball for, man." You know, and I just wanna laugh—"aha-ha-ha-ha." So I'm waiting for him and I got this light, fluffy snowball, you know, ready to hit him. And that's the rules of the game. You cannot hit a kid in the face with a slush ball. Slush ball has ice and water and gunk all in it, you know. You cannot drop it in his open galoshes either, 'cause it sends him home.

His classic Noah routine, like the comical biblical bits that David Steinberg presented in the seventies, wrings humor from the literal presentation of essentially bizarre or supernatural events—not, as in Flip Wilson or Richard Pryor routines, from the imposition of a black perspective on the material. Pryor, for example, describes an encounter with God as follows: "I knew it was the voice of God for it came from without a dark alleyway as only the voice of God can come. However, I did not venture down that dark alley-*way*. For it might *not have been* the voice of God, but two niggers with a baseball bat." Noah, as depicted in Cosby's routine, is ethnically nondescript; he is an Everyman. When the Lord calls, Noah responds:

> "Who is that?"
> "It's the Lord, Noah."
> "R-i-i-ight . . . Where are you? What do you want? I've been good."
> "I want you to build an ark."
> "R-i-i-ight . . . What's an ark?"
> "Get some wood. Build it, 300 cubits by 80 cubits by 40 cubits."
> "R-i-i-ight . . . What's a cubit? Let's see, I used to know what a cubit was."
> "Well, don't worry about that, Noah. And when you get that done, get out into the world and collect all of the animals in the world by twos, male and female, and put them into the ark."

"R-i-i-ght . . . Who is this really? What's goin' on? How come you want me to do all these weird things?"

"I'm going to destroy the world."

"Ri-i-i-ght . . . Am I on *Candid Camera?* How're you gonna do it?"

"I'm gonna make it rain 4,000 days and drown them right out!"

"Ri-i-i-ght . . . Listen, do this and you'll save water. Let it rain for 40 days and 40 nights and wait for the sewers to back up!"

"*Ri-i-i-ght!*"

Later:

"I'm sick and tired of all this. I've had enough of this stuff. I been working all day, working days and days . . ."

"Noah, how long can you tread water?" . . .

"The whole neighborhood's out there laughing at me. They're all having a grand time at good old Noah, there. I went out and got my best friend, Larry! I said, 'Larry, listen, I been talkin' to the Lord.' Larry said, 'Oh really!' I said, 'Yeah, yeah! Listen, Lord, Larry . . . Larry, Lord.' . . . I hear 'em all up there laughing at me. You know, I'm the only guy in this neighborhood with an ark. People around here laughing, picket signs, walkin' up and down. I'm sick and tired of this stuff."

In *Funny People,* Steve Allen claims that "Bill Cosby is nothing less than the most gifted monologist of our time"; he also suggested that Cosby reflected "the child that still lives within us, the Thurber-ish innocence in a dangerous world." It is an apt description, since Cosby's disarming, non-ethnic narrative voice recalls that guileless perception of the world that we all shared prior to indocrination into a complex, splintered society in which arbitrary racial distinctions prevail.[36]

Although Cosby has occasionally ventured into satire that lampoons religious and racial bias (in his one-man television special, *I'm a Bigot,* for example), he has generally maintained his colorless brand of humor. Notwithstanding scorn for his approach from supposed militant black spokesmen, it not only reflects the sentiments of a large segment of the African-American community but also mirrors an important part of black Americans' humorous tradition.

Cosby's accentuation of the similarities between blacks and whites is an indirect assault on the illusory tenets that support racial bias. He demonstrates in each performance that racial differences are only skin deep and that, regardless of color, we all respond to life's everyday problems with similar emotions. And just as it was a distortion to assume that African-American humor was primarily self-ridiculing or without any rancor, it is also shortsighted to assume that authentic black humor is obsessively focused on racial inequities and white repression. As James Baldwin pointed out, Aunt Jemima and Uncle Tom had a life of their own, independent of mainstream society but rich in humor and a joy in living. Cosby presents that strain of black humor with dignity and hilarity.

Moreover, even though Cosby's routines are usually without racial references, when presenting adult material in nightclubs or in Las Vegas, he infuses his delivery with a subtle undercurrent of African-American style. One critic has called him "the Art Tatum of comedy," and indeed, his hip, vernacular speech and circuitous development of comic themes parallels the musician's approach to jazz. Cosby may have excised the earthier, down-home blues and raucous rhythm and blues associations that traditionally colored black humor, but he replaced them with the sophisticated, nuanced shades of progressive jazz. In essence, his comedy is less funky than the central strain of African-American humor. But from his early days in Greenwich Village to his role as head of the Huxtable family on *The Cosby Show*, he has presented a modified version of a black comic staple—the glib and irrepressible raconteur or liar—in a manner that cuts across all racial barriers.[37]

Godfrey Cambridge was the next black comedian to gain national prominence. He surfaced as a dramatic and comic actor in the early sixties but did not attain celebrity status as a stand-up comedian until after Bill Cosby's emergence. Although Cambridge credited Gregory with opening the door—"before Dick came in, a Negro comedian couldn't get arrested"—in some ways his comic style can be seen as a synthesis of the approaches taken by Cosby and Gregory.[38]

Although he was born in Harlem, as a youth Cambridge was sent to Nova Scotia, Canada, where he lived with his grandparents and attended elementary school. In the late forties, he moved to a nearly all-white neighborhood in Queens, New York, where he attended high school. "All my life I ignored being colored," he said later. "I never felt racial prejudice because I was the only Negro. . . . It's terrible for someone to reach the age of twenty-one and realize he's a Negro." When the revelation hit home, Cambridge was a premedical student at

Hofstra College. Prompted by the emerging Civil Rights movement and a desire to escape his closeted academic life and come to grips with his racial identity, Cambridge left college and began pursuing a career in show business. By the early sixties, although he was gaining a reputation as an actor, his real interest had shifted to stand-up comedy. And, largely because of his sheltered upbringing, he had an unusual approach.

"I came from a very religious family," he told a reporter, "and the only place you could see any Black comics was in nightclubs and theatres and my folks wouldn't allow me to go there." As a result, the earliest influences on his humor were not black comedians but radio and television stars such as Jack Benny, Fred Allen, and Jack Carter. The chitlin' circuit influenced his comic sensibility very little. Educated and articulate, in his delivery Cambridge projected a non-ethnic image similar to Bill Cosby's. On stage, he chatted with his audiences, immediately establishing a rapport as an equal. Then, using his acting background, he presented comic scenarios based on his observations of everyday interactions between people—reenacting all the parts. Cambridge did not avoid racial issues, however; he was a brilliant satirist and, although he did not concentrate on them, the contradictions and absurdities of bigotry often entered into his expansive social satire.[39]

His act often began with his running onto the stage and opening with: "I hope you noticed how I rushed up here. We do have to do that to change our image. No more shuffle after the revolution. We gotta be agile." The suggestion was clearly that a new, equal status had already been fixed. The monologues that followed ranged from ironic quips about the Civil Rights movement that echoed Gregory's style:

> Right now, it's not a question of getting served at the counter. It's a matter of eating too much. I never got served before, but now I have to eat at all the restaurants. The food is so good and I'm eating so well that I can't sing *We Shall Overcome*, I have to burp it.

to such non-racial observations as his comment about the problems of urban living:

> "Share in community activities," they say. The walls [of my apartment] are so thin, you can't help share in community activities. . . . I didn't know going to the bathroom was a social experience.

One of his favorite stories concerned two airplane travelers—one black and the other white. At first, the white man objects to sitting next to a Negro but, when the aircraft experiences turbulence, fear overrides his bigotry and the two passengers commiserate with one another. As the the plane flails in the air and seems near crashing, the white passenger abandons all traces of his assumed superiority; it appears that mutual adversity has erased the racial barrier. When the plane lands safely, however, the white man resumes his contemptuous attitude. The annoyed Negro snaps, "Then give me back my hand and get the hell off my lap."

Another story lightly prodded the formal, surface congeniality that hastily evolved between middle-class blacks and whites as the struggle for equal rights escalated on the streets. Cambridge described the interaction between himself and a white man waiting for an elevator:

> He was dressed just like I was, with an attaché case too. You know, they copy everything we do. After the doors of the elevator opened, we accidentally bumped into each other. He leaped aside and said, "After you. As a responsible member of the white community, I wouldn't want to set a spark to that smoldering resentment that's been harbored in the Negro community for over a hundred years." I leaped aside and said, "No, no, after you because as a responsible member of the Negro community, I recognize the danger of offending old friends in the white community and at the same time driving others into the waiting arms of extremists on both sides."

Woven between these longer stories, his routines also featured terse, ironic observations gleaned from his personal experiences. Some touched on racial matters: "Do you realize the amount of havoc a Negro couple can cause just by walking down the street on a Sunday morning with a copy of *The New York Times* real-estate section under the man's arm?"[40]

Cambridge, however, used racial material selectively. "If I would do just racial material, I would go out of my cotton-picking mind," he said. "If something happens to me and it's in a Black context, then fine. But I don't feel I have to use my race." When he did focus on the racial problem, he rarely pushed satire to the acerbic levels reached by Dick Gregory. Often, in fact, he blunted the racial edge of his routines by occasionally turning his satire to black attitudes: "Don't they know a Negro is not afraid of bricks, and bombs, and burning crosses? He's afraid another Negro is going to move in [to the neighborhood]. . . . Most people try to run away from their ethnic groups. This way to the melting pot. Let's melt!" It was this subtle mixture of racial and non-racial material, as well as Cambridge's candid assessment of absurdity, wherever he found it, that distinguished his humor. "It's anything, man; anything that fits the moment," he said. "What I do is take the truth and twist it. Or I take something which is untrue . . . and take it to such ridiculous proportions that you see how absurd it really is. I'll take a situation and stretch it until it cannot really hold any truth anymore. When I talk about alimony its not just Black people's alimony."[41]

Cambridge's unique wit and ecumenical approach to satiric targets had catapulted him to stardom by the late sixties. Before long—based on his performances in Melvin Van Peebles's *Watermelon Man* (1970) and Ossie Davis's *Cotton Comes to Harlem* (1970), a film adaptation of Chester Himes's novel—he was recognized as an exceptional actor as well. His career was cut short in 1978, however, when he died of a heart attack while filming *Victory at Entebbe,* a film in which he was to play the deposed Ugandan president Idi Amin. Cambridge was a major comic talent—according to Apollo Theatre director Bobby Schiffman, "the best black comedian in the business"—as well as a key figure in the evolution of African-American humor for the general public.[42]

Certainly, he was instrumental in cracking the virtual blackout of African-American stand-up comics on national television and in main-stream nightclubs and theatres in the fifties and sixties. As early as 1965, *Time* magazine had confirmed the breakthrough in an article citing Cambridge as "one of the country's four most celebrated Negro come-dians" (Russell, Gregory, and Cosby were the others). Their ascendancy owed much to the new mood that the Civil Rights movement had spurred in the nation. Gregory wryly underscored the phenomenon when he quipped that "there aren't enough of us to go around." Soon, he said in a routine, "I expect to see a Hertz Rent-A-Negro." Moreover, as Gregory ironically observed, recognition was no longer reserved for light-complexioned Negroes only: "Now they want the blackest faces they can find, and they put them all up in the front of the office." The expansiveness of this trend and the justification for Gregory's sardonic remarks were highlighted two years later when President Lyndon John-son explained his choice of Civil Rights activist and NAACP lawyer

Thurgood Marshall for the Supreme Court over a less controversial black man by saying, "Son, when I appoint a nigger to the court, I want everyone to know he's a nigger."[43]

Despite an increasingly liberal climate, club owners, television executives, and theatre managers were not as bold or audacious as the President in the mid-sixties. The black comedians they initially selected to appear before mixed audiences were not representative of the central strain of African-American humor. Although the six comedians who pioneered cross-over comedy during the previous decade were definitely not candidates for tragic mulatto roles, they had either eliminated most *outward* characteristics of black circuit humor or had come to the stage without prolonged experience in that arena. In fact, there was a distinct intellectual cast to their comedy; all except Rogers and White had attended college. They were far removed from both the old-style knockabout humor of Pigmeat Markham and Dusty Fletcher and the franker and more risqué cabaret humor of Redd Foxx and Moms Mabley.

Each, in his own fashion, was innovative. Rogers cast aside the image of the stereotypical clown and demonstrated "that Negro comedians can be both zany and dignified." White, who more than the others retained identifiable black circuit mannerisms, still fashioned a stand-up routine that made his winding stories and visual comedy accessible to mixed audiences. Russell added extemporaneous jingles, clever retorts, and direct social commentary to an act that had been molded on the chitlin' circuit, spicing his jest with acerbic wit. Gregory completely abandoned the traditional pose of the stage clown and, like Mort Sahl, substituted irony, satire, and an incisive intellectual approach that elicited as much insight and revelation as carefree laughter. Cosby brashly excised all racial identity, demanding, in effect, that the audience engage him as an equal as he offered his unique brand of sophisticated whimsy. And Cambridge combined oppositional satire with an elusively playful image which, although more obviously black than Cosby's, still insistently forced his audience to identify *with* him instead of, as with Gregory, in contrast to him.[44]

In negotiating the shift from black to integrated audiences, each of these pioneers had, in varying degrees, either toned down or discarded the demeanor and style, the distinctive folk voice of African-American humor. The most cynical explanation is that promoters, club owners, and theatre managers arbitrarily promoted those African-American comedians whose performance styles deviated least from the mainstream

norm. This consideration undoubtedly influenced managers and bookers, since the entertainment world, like other forms of American enterprise, is seldom revolutionary or adventurous in its marketing approach.
During the fifties and sixties, avoiding traditional black stage comedy
must have seemed prudent, for despite subtle shifts in the mainstream
perception of blacks, most white Americans were still struggling with a
stereotypical view of African-Americans as either childish and naive or
uncouth and threatening. Given the increasing assertiveness of civil
rights activists and blacks' criticism of television shows such as *Beulah*
and *Amos 'n' Andy,* non-blacks were uneasy about laughing at traditional black stage acts that on the surface smacked of Tomism and
toadying. On the other hand, despite the guilt factor, they were wary of
comedians who kindled a menacing vision of dark, visceral impulses
(sex, violence, and vengeance). Americans were looking for comedians
who, much as the Motown sound bridged the gap between the turbulence and raw sensuality of rhythm and blues and the pallid romanticism of mainstream popular music, presented black humor in a more
palatable form.

Moreover, from a black perspective, before the emergence of the
Black Power movement in 1966, the Civil Rights struggle was clearly
aimed at assimilation; its underlying ideals encouraged a melting of
blacks into the larger society, a merging of black and white cultures,
and an accentuation of the similarities between the races. From a purely
practical viewpoint, much of the undiluted humor of the streets and
the chitlin' circuit was either inaccessible or too candidly ribald for
mainstream taste. In 1965, Dick Gregory acklnowledged that "little
things I knew as a Negro couldn't be used until the public discovered
them. They know about most of them now."[45]

Actually, Gregory's comment was premature; America still had been
exposed only to selective aspects of the African-American humorous
tradition. The popularity of anti-establishment humor was rapidly escalating, however, and a series of shattering political and social events
would soon intensify the mood and militancy of American blacks and
hasten the emergence of a less self-consciously tempered, even blacker
form of African-American comedy.

IV

Quietly, a less sanitized and intellectually oriented but equally aggressive form of black humor actually had begun surfacing at about the

same time that Dick Gregory appeared at the Playboy Club. Moms Mabley and Redd Foxx were excluded from the initial upsurge of African-American comedy, but even as other comics gained access to national television appearances and bookings at premiere white showplaces, they had begun their gradual climb to mainstream acceptance.

As with Gregory, the Playboy Club provided the stage for one of Mabley's earliest mainstream appearances. Reflecting the philosophy of its parent magazine, the club not only encouraged social satire with an anti-establishment bent (Mort Sahl and, later, George Carlin were often booked) but also welcomed comedy with a slightly blue tint. Consequently, after Gregory's success, Mabley was booked into the Chicago club in August 1961. Her matronly, offbeat appearance and down-home ruminations about politics and the Civil Rights movement, and her fondness for younger men, were perfectly suited to the club's racy image. Mabley rolled off spicy double entendres and homely witticisms as uninhibitedly as she had in gutbucket clubs:

> My slogan is if it don't fit don't force it. In other words, if you can't make it, don't fake it. Let somebody else take it. . . . I'd rather pay a young man's way from here to California than to tell an old man the distance. . . . Don't get me wrong, it ain't no disgrace to come from the South. But it's a disgrace to go back down there.

Like Gregory, she was an immediate hit. That engagement, along with the success of her first two comedy albums, helped her to vault out of the confines of black circuit cabarets. Her bookings improved, and in 1967, Mabley made her first TV appearance on the special, *A Time for Laughter,* produced by Harry Belafonte. Before her death in 1975, she had gained national recognition through guest spots on TV shows hosted by Bill Cosby, the Smothers Brothers, and Flip Wilson.

Foxx had also moved onto the periphery of mainstream comedy by 1960, the year he made his first important appearance as a single act in a white club at the Crescendo in Hollywood. When Russell, Gregory, Cosby, and Cambridge were making headlines a few years later, Foxx was working at New York's Basin Street East. In that non-black setting, he had to temper the blue material used on his albums. But while restricted from using some of his favorite routines, he demonstrated why comedian Leonard Reed has said, "take away Redd's filth, take away his dirt [and] and he's the best natural comedian around today."

His monologue segued easily from such innocent jokes as one about a streetwise kid:

> There was kid went into a candy store, said, "Mister, how much are those candy bars?" The fellow said, "They're two for a quarter." Kid says, "Well, how much for one?" Fellow said, "Fifteen cents." He said, "Well, give me the *other* one."

to more ethnic material, which he cleaned up for some audiences:

> I've just composed a love song, it's called "I love you darling, if you never have any cash money in your pocket book during your entire life in this world. But I *won't* be with you, darling . . . if you never have any cash money in your pocket book during your entire life in this world or anywhere else you might go with nothing. Cause I don't need nobody to help me do bad. I can starve to death by myself, sugar. So try and forget me. But always remember I love you more than any woman I've ever known in my life, 'cause that night I went up to your house and got drunk you didn't mess with none of the money that was left in my wallet 'cause you must have known, *deep down in your heart*, if I'd a come to and found some of my hard earned money gone, I'd a went home and got a two-by-four that I been soaking in motor oil since 1953. And I'd a came back searching for you, and if I found you anywhere on earth with any of the money in your bag, I'd a took my greasy two-by-four, knowing that it would not break, bend, or splinter, and try to cave your skull in with it . . . cha-cha-cha."[46]

Unlike Lenny Bruce, whose act suffered when stripped of profanity and who had made some disastrous television appearances, Foxx could be funny while limiting the risqué aspect of his humor and retaining its ethnic quality. Despite his reputation as a blue comic, he made his first television appearance, in 1964, on *Today* with Hugh Downs; soon afterward he appeared on *The Tonight Show* with Johnny Carson. He was beginning to get the national exposure that he sought, but he still preferred nightclubs and Las Vegas bookings, where he could use explicit material. "There was always the question, should Redd Foxx clean up his act?" he wrote in his *Encyclopedia of Black Humor*. "I actually did it a couple of times. I started to believe all that crap about how it would keep me off the mass media. But . . . I hated the thought that I was selling out." Although he made some concessions for his television appearances, for the most part Foxx stuck with X-rated routines during the sixties. "It's human, it's honest," he asserted during an interview. "It's adult—I don't perform for youngsters. If you don't have an adult mind, get the hell out."[47]

Considering Foxx's proven ability to temper the scatological and sexual overtones of his comedy when necessary, in retrospect the niggling over the offensiveness of his nightclub act appears to be something of a diversion. The underlying reason for his inability to crack the high-paying white clubs was more likely his relentlessly aggressive stage image. Unlike the other comedians who broke into mainstream comedy during the sixties, Foxx delivered his humor in an unmistakably black voice—one that echoed a pride and belligerence that was associated with more militant factions of the African-American community. Even when joking, Foxx had something of the combative aura of his old friend, Malcolm X, about him. He was not only capable of the kind of shocking and profane comic insights that had made Lenny Bruce unacceptable, but his comedy sometimes verged on the type of insult humor that Don Rickles would make fashionable in the seventies. Because he was black, however, that posture was more threatening and, to most mainstream audiences, totally unacceptable. Compared to the image of college-educated, assimilable blacks that Cosby, Cambridge, and Russell projected, Foxx conjured up visions of insolence and independence more reminiscent of black folklore's Bad Nigger. Of the sixties comics, only Gregory challenged in a similar manner, but since his defiance was intellectual, it triggered a cerebral response. Foxx elicited a gut reaction. His sly expressions, swaggering demeanor, and rapid-fire gags and put-downs in many ways were separated only by a hairline from images of the fast-talking, pompous, razor-toting black man that mainstream America had traditionally feared. Moreover, he boldly accentuated his underlying attitude with a litany of jokes that often cut much deeper than the funny bones of his audiences:

> To those of you who applauded, I want you to know I appreciate it. To those of you who didn't, I hope your dog dies.

> White people, quit moving around the country like a bunch of damned gypsies. Wherever you are, we'll be there.

> They say Negroes carry knives. That's a lie. My brother has been carrying an ice pick for years.

> I don't have to be up here entertaining you. I could be in an alley
> with a blackjack waiting for one of you suckers.

Not surprisingly, America was not ready, in the mid-sixties, for this
type of direct assault on its subconscious fears and lingering prejudices.
As Godfrey Cambridge noted: "A comedian is in many ways a historian.
He reflects the times and the mood of the country and the world."
Foxx's unacceptability—as well as the embrace of comedians who projected a less truculent, more polite middle-class demeanor—reflected
more the limits of white tolerance for African-American belligerence
than the individual talents of the comedians involved.[48]

From 1963 to 1968, however, historical events radically shifted the
nation's conception of what was and was not belligerent. Beginning
with the assassinations of President John F. Kennedy and Civil Rights
leader Medgar Evers in 1963, the country experienced an era of political and racial turmoil that rivaled the social upheaval of the Civil War.
Race riots, violent anti–Vietnam War protests, Stokely Carmichael's
call for Black Power, the March on Washington, the assassinations of
Malcolm X, Robert Kennedy, and Martin Luther King, Jr., all stretched
the nation's concept of radicalism. By the seventies, Redd Foxx's brand
of blunt, confrontational humor was no longer considered extreme.
There was hardly a murmur of protest in 1972 when Foxx debuted as
an eccentric, irascible, and lovable old junk dealer, Fred Sanford, on
Norman Lear's *Sanford and Son* (1972–77, NBC).

In scarcely seven years, Foxx had moved from virtual pariah status
with TV executives to a leading role in what soon was one of the most
popular sitcoms on the air. Despite the fact that he had laundered
his blistering language for TV censors, he maintained much of the
belligerence that marked his stage act. Quips such as "I ain't going in
there with that ugly old white woman" or retorts such as "Yeah, white!"
when a policeman asks what color some robbers were, echoed the
defiance and cockiness of Foxx's stand-up routine. Along with *The Flip
Wilson Show*, which debuted in 1970, the series also provided the first
glimpse of traditional, black circuit comedy seen on television since *The
Amos 'n' Andy Show*. Although some scripts were inane and there were
complaints from blacks about the lack of African-American writers, the
input of Foxx, such regulars as the obstreperous LaWanda Page (who
played Aunt Esther), such guests as Slappy White, and, occasionally,
such black writers as Richard Pryor and Paul Mooney, guaranteed that
the show consistently offered humor with a distinctive black voice. It

quickly catapulted Foxx to national recognition. Critics of its lack of political relevance notwithstanding, *Sanford and Son* demonstrated that a black sitcom could be funny while most often avoiding denigrative stereotypes.[49]

Foxx was not the first African-American comedian with a distinctively black style to attain national prominence, however; earlier, when still struggling himself, he had helped launch the career of a friend and fellow comic. In 1965, during one of his early appearances on the *Tonight* show, Johnny Carson had asked him who was the funniest comedian around. Foxx's reply was, "Flip Wilson." Shortly afterward, Wilson appeared on Carson's show and instantly became a favorite on the *Tonight* show as well as such other talk and variety shows as the *Today* show, *Rowan and Martin's Laugh-In,* and the *Ed Sullivan, Mike Douglas,* and *Merv Griffin* shows. By the early seventies, he had become America's most popular comedian.[50]

Clerow "Flip" Wilson grew up in Jersey City and, after dropping out of high school, joined the Air Force, where he dabbled in comedy. Shortly after being discharged in 1954, he determined that his future was on the stage and began working in small clubs on the West Coast. During the late fifties, he traveled across the country working black circuit joints, many like the East St. Louis club that LaWanda Page described as "the kind of place where if you ain't home by nine o'clock at night you can be declared *legally* dead. [Everybody] walked around with knives in there. You better had one, too—knife or gun or something!" Wilson survived and, around 1960, he graduated to the chitlin' circuit theatre tour. He had been thoroughly initiated into the hard life and the demands of working the rough, unsavory night spots on the black comedy circuit. Like Redd Foxx and countless others before him, he had learned to satisfy those demands.[51]

"I got a special feeling working before black audiences," he said during an interview in the late seventies. "I worked at a higher energy level when I was working in those little black clubs where people came in at the end of the week with about $20 and wanted to have a good time. You gotta get their attention, hold their interest. And to do that it takes a certain talent—you gotta work hard, keep the energy up." Sometimes holding the audience's interest in chitlin' circuit clubs or even the Apollo Theatre was not so easy. Wilson illustrated the point in an anecdote about an Apollo appearance that he related to Jack Schiffman:

A few minutes later I start to tell this junkie story, when a gal on the right side of the balcony hollers. "God damn! Another junkie bit. Why the hell do I always have to hear that?" I turned my head toward her, when from the left I heard—"Bitch! Shut up and let the man tell the story, sheeeit!"

"How come every time I come in the damned place I gotta listen to that shit?" comes the lady's voice from balcony right.

"Bitch, now shut up and let the man talk," comes from the left again. Well, I'm just standing there looking from left to right as all this is goin' on. Ain't had time to tell half the story myself.

"Damn it all to hell," starts the gal on the right when the voice from balcony left booms out once more, "Bitch! If you don't shut up and let the man talk, I'm gonna come over there and throw you the hell over the balcony."

Wilson's overall approach to comedy was partially shaped by experiences in this type of uninhibited, boisterous atmosphere. But although his comedy retained the energy and spirit of these lively, down-to-earth black showplaces, he generally avoided the profanity and (except for sly double entendres) the explicit sexual jokes associated with them. Therefore, unlike many of the black circuit comics who stepped into the national limelight before him, he did not have to alter his style seriously to be accepted when he appeared on national television or before integrated audiences. (The junkie jokes were the only noticeable deletions from his early routines.) Although his comedy was steeped in language and attitudes molded by his own background and experiences common to the all-black crowds he had played to for years, he could present it in practically undiluted fashion to any audience. "It's easier working before white audiences," Wilson said, "because you can use more finesse and subtleties. It's not more fun . . . but I discovered I didn't have to drain myself. I could get the humor across with the inflection, the voice thing, not the entire body energy."[52]

In addition, his easier access in the late sixties was facilitated by the older comedians who had struggled to break down barriers. Rogers, White, Russell, Gregory, Foxx, and Mabley had made tremendous inroads; Cosby and Cambridge had demonstrated that comedy could be essentially colorless. The public was, quite simply, beginning to become accustomed to black comics. Still, Wilson's enthusiastic celebration of black style was unique when he emerged; in one sense it was a throwback to the old ethnic comedy of the Negro stage clown, but Wilson managed to present it in a new, more dignified and assertive style, giving it universal appeal. Timing, an un-self-conscious affection for African-American mannerisms and culture, a meticulous, studious approach to comedy, and a captivating personality were all, in part, responsible for his success.

Foremost was his personality. "Infectious!" is how Jack Schiffman described his boyish charm, and a *Time* magazine cover story asserted that "he puts his material over gently, through sheer likability." Richard Pryor once told him that "you're the only performer that I've ever seen who goes on the stage and the audience hopes that *you* like them." Wilson's beguiling style helped him establish an immediate rapport with his audience and prepared them for his sudden shifts from light, whimsical material to more satirical pieces.[53]

Glowing with an ingenuous smile, he sometimes announced:

> Generally, when a comic's getting under way they begin with their best stories. Then, once they've gained the audience's confidence, they drop the bomb—the bad story. I feel the audience knows every comic has bad stories. So why sneak 'em in on them. . . . It's my new policy to do my worst story first. Let the audience relax. It's a rotten story.

Then he might relate one of his many shaggy dog tales, such as the story of Roman Herman, who, after finding a unique berry, becomes the toast of ancient Rome. He becomes a wealthy man, marries, and gives his berry to his new wife. Then two guys with spears show up at Herman's door and ask, "You the guy with the berry?" Herman says, "That's my wife's berry. . . . You come to praise her berry?" "No," one of them says, "we came to seize her berry, not to praise it." Or Wilson might tell the story of the old-time comic who was part of the team called Well Enough and Bad Enough, a tale which winds circuitously through some zany asides and, after the comic has been assaulted by a hotel clerk, ends in a courtroom scene. When the assailant is sentenced, he asks, "How come you being so hard on me?" And the judge says, " 'Cause I'm trying to teach you to leave Well Enough alone."

With a mischievous glint lighting his eyes, he could then shift abruptly and, without a wrinkle, move to more pointedly satirical material like his "Confidential Report" bit:

Visualize a very modest residential area. A fellow driving through the area pulls up in front of a very nice home there. Takes out his attaché case, walks up to the house, knocks on the door. A man answers the door. Fellow says, "Good afternoon, sir. I'm conducting a confidential survey. I'd like to inquire as to whether your wife would object to her daughter marrying a Negro." Fellow says, "I don't know, she's upstairs. Just a minute, I'll ask her. Hey, Ethel, would you mind if our daughter married a Negro?" Ethel's reply [in high-pitched voice of Geraldine] is: "She can marry anybody she wants."

Or his brilliant "Cowboys and Colored People" routine, which begins:

The Indians aren't ready yet. . . . Do you want to build a fifty thousand dollar home and have some guy build a wigwam next to it? I'm not against Indians, now. I don't want anyone to leave here feeling I'm against Indians. There have been Indians I've admired. Guys I've looked up to. Fellows who in my mind didn't let the fact that they were Indians hold them back. They were aggressive, they went out and asserted that aggressiveness and made a name for themselves. Guys like Tonto, Little Beaver, those guys . . .

Wilson's diligent approach to comedy was reflected in the "Cowboys and Colored People" bit and his famous "Christopher Columbus" routine ("Chris goin' find Ray Charles"), which took seven years to develop. It could be seen as well in his storytelling technique—his use of casual observations and clever asides to embellish a story. "Anything can be funny," he once said. "When I look at something I see it six or seven different ways." And that unique perception is apparent in the quips that dot his tales. "You couldn't get a bet on the Christians in the arena. Christians had a great coach but the team was shaky." Or, "He waited until 'bout four that morning. . . . That's a good time to sneak, four in the morning, 'cause anyone you run into, they're sneaking too." Since Wilson did not tell jokes or depend on a stream of one-liners like most comics, this anecdotal flair was an essential part of his comedy.[54]

From the perspective of African-American humor, however, his greatest contribution was the introduction of a distinct black voice to mainstream comedy. Wilson has said, "I'm not a black comic. . . . Funny is not a color. Funny just is, that's all. Being black is only good from the time you get from the curtain to the micophone." Journalists echoed that view when they claimed his humor "was without a shred of racial rancor." But Wilson also said, "Being black, my culture is what I know best. I was just expressing that—it's real, it's what we all know. I'd bring different facets of black culture to the act, trying to expand consciousness. I was telling an American story, and I think people understood it."[55]

In addition, Wilson admits that the turning point in his career came after a white friend had given him some blunt advice:

> He said, "Look, I think you've got a lot to express but you're inhibiting yourself . . . well, because you're a nigger. But I want you to understand why I said that. I think black people are too self-conscious about having been slaves. All people have been slaves and nobody has come back faster than black people. Nobody has the warmth and inner spiritual beauty that black people have." He said, "Now, I'm a Jew, and we were in ghettoes and we had to find a way to free ourselves. The point is, it's over!" He said, "Damn what anybody thinks of you. Say what you have to say, and help open up somebody else's eyes. You can do it, and don't think one minute about being black. . . . I'm amazed at black people, yet they spend all that time feeling sorry for themselves."
>
> Right then, I realized something. So I said, "Yeah!" That's when I realized how interesting being black is. I said to myself, "Okay. They waiting to see a nigger who's afraid or shy. No way, niggers is fun. Niggers is good!" We came back and said, "Hey, I ain't mad. Screw it! Look at the Indian, he can never come back." I decided to enjoy myself—be myself. What I try to express is real. It's what I know, I'm not tricking anybody. This is the way we are as people, we have desires, the urge to conquer, to hunt, to survive. That's what I do on stage, now. I hunt hearts![56]

According to Wilson, that revelation helped turn his career around and allowed him to reflect an uninhibited celebration of black life in his humor. Ultimately, that un-self-conscious approach—which echoes Zora Neale Hurston's observation that the "average Negro glories in his ways"—most distinguished Wilson's comedy. His frank reflections of typical black attitudes and flamboyant use of the timbre and resonances of black street language gave his routines a distinctly black voice that (until Redd Foxx, Moms Mabley, and Richard Pryor gained national recognition) was unique among the cross-over black comedians of the fifties and sixties.

That quality was most obviously seen in Wilson's tack of imposing an African-American perspective on historical events and in the characters he created. The humor and subtle satire in his Christopher Columbus and David and Goliath routines, for instance, stem from viewing past events with the double-edged irony of an African-American. Queen Isabelle Johnson's excitement over the prospect of Chris's finding Ray Charles and the reaction of the "fine little *West* Indian girl" who greets the ship at the shore—"We don't wanna be discovered. You cain' discover nobody if they don't wanna be discovered. You better discover your ass away from here"—not only celebrated black culture but also pointed out the conceited absurdity of claiming to discover a country that is already occupied.

It was in his humorous characters, however, that Wilson most assertively advanced a black comic voice. The Reverend Leroy, the playboy Freddie Johnson, and especially Geraldine, the irrepressible black woman, provided humorous but basically positive caricatures of authentic African-American types whom white humorists had usually grotesquely distorted and black stage comics had until then rendered self-consciously and tentatively in integrated settings. Wilson's enthusiasm and unflinching affection for his characters allowed most audiences to transcend the associations established by similar but far more derogatory caricatures in the past. His infectious spirit and bold interpretation helped legitimize the public presentation of humorous material that previously had been an embarrassment to many blacks. Its source was near to the core of genuine African-American humor, since it was based on those inner-community interactions in which gibing, jesting, and verbal play are enjoyed without regard to outside judgments or evaluations.

There were criticisms, of course, particularly when Wilson became, in 1970, the first black comedian successfully to host a weekly television variety show. Wilson's Reverend Leroy and his Church of What's Happening Now was a source of irritation for the black clergy. And Geraldine, with her popular catchphrases—"The devil made me do it," "Watch out, honey! Don't touch me!" and "What you see is what you get"—was attacked as a throwback to Sapphire of *Amos 'n' Andy* infamy.

Naturally, Wilson did not agree with the criticism. Referring to the television show, he said, "they didn't need a black man to try and be white." As the narrative voice in his routines, he maintained that he reflected the image of a "serious" black man. "It was the characters who joked and were funny, and most people knew they were just characters."

> With the characters I created, I was showing different faces of blacks. They expressed my values. . . . Geraldine, for instance, was created because many times when I was working the black clubs [white] guys would come over and say, "Hey, can you get me a girl?" I took offense, you know. I realized black guys wouldn't go into a white club and say, "Can you get me a girl?" I wanted Geraldine to show pride in herself, and dedication to her man. You know, she'd say, "Watch out! You can look if you want to, but don't touch nothin', sucker." I made her flashy, and she was not that refined. But at that time women's lib was coming in, so she was strong and her love for Killer was honest. I got the feeling, the inspiration for her and my other characters from blacks . . . people I grew up with and people in the audience when I was starting out. I always admired the freedom that girls had when I was working and they'd be down in front of the stage. When they saw something they really liked—just for a minute—they'd let themselves go. You know, the way they move, and they'd say, "Whooee!" And for a second they'd be free. Those people gave me inspiration. . . . My humor reflects all of that.[57]

Audience response supported Wilson's claims, for *The Flip Wilson Show* was television's premiere variety show for several years and remained on the air until 1977. The old bugaboo of the proper image for blacks in the public eye had risen again, but this time the voices of dissent had not been as loud.

By the early seventies, Wilson was the nation's favorite comic. A *Time* magazine cover story compared him to other comedians: "[He] does not have the slashing wit of a Lenny Bruce, the angry bite of a Dick Gregory, the satirical punch of a Godfrey Cambridge, or the intellectual edge of a Bill Cosby. His approach is at once older and newer than the others." It was an incisive judgment, since Wilson had successfully invested his characters with the broad, boisterous humor of older black circuit comedy and combined their portrayal with the more assertive, intellectual thrust of the new stand-up comics.[58]

The comedians who broke into mainstream comedy earlier in the

fifties and sixties revolutionized black stage humor by revealing a satirical aspect of African-American comedy that previously had been reserved for the black community. But whether because of their personal
styles or a desire to avoid old stereotypes, they had, in accentuating that
satirical element, muted or eliminated the distinct style of the street
humor from which most of them drew. They candidly revealed the
acerbic bite and discontent that was veiled or indirectly expressed in
most black humor but suppressed the exuberance and joy that was
equally essential to it. Flip Wilson maintained some of the satire and,
through his rambunctious characters and ebullient style, reinserted the
external flourishes, the black voice. His temperament dictated that he
express it in one of its more playful or whimsical guises, but his efforts
paved the way for the emergence of other comics. The door separating
genuine African-American humor from mainstream exposure had been
opened a bit further; by the mid-seventies, Richard Pryor would tear
down that door and remove the hinges.

13.

━━━━━━━━━━━━━━━━━━━━━

PRYOR AND THEREAFTER

. . . on the real side

RICHARD PRYOR

[RICHARD PRYOR] IS THE GROUNDBREAKER. . . . FOR MOST OF US HE WAS THE INSPIRATION TO GET INTO COMEDY AND ALSO SHOWED US THAT YOU CAN BE BLACK AND HAVE A *BLACK VOICE* AND BE SUCCESSFUL.

—KEENAN IVORY WAYANS

IF [CHARLIE CHAPLIN] HAD FOUND THE STREET LANGUAGE TO MATCH HIS LOW-LIFE, TRAMP MOVEMENTS, HE MIGHT HAVE BEEN SOMETHING LIKE RICHARD PRYOR, WHO'S ALL OF A PIECE —A MASTER OF LYRICAL OBSCENITY. PRYOR IS THE ONLY GREAT POET SATIRIST AMONG OUR COMICS.

—PAULINE KAEL

PRYOR IS CERTAIN OF ONE THING. HE IS PROUDLY, ASSERTIVELY A NIGGER, THE FIRST COMEDIAN TO SPEAK IN THE RAW, BRUTAL, BUT OFTEN WILDLY HILARIOUS LANGUAGE OF THE STREETS.

—

TIME MAGAZINE[1]

I

In 1963, when Richard Pryor decided to abandon the Midwestern chitlin' circuit tour and take a shot at New York City and the "big time," a tentative but innovative rapprochement had been established between white audiences and a select group of black comedians. The transitional comics of the fifties (Rogers, White, Kirby, and Russell) had made inroads and, in varying degrees, Dick Gregory, Bill Cosby, and Godfrey Cambridge all had bridged the racial impasse. "Every joke calls for a public of its own and laughing at the same jokes is evidence of far-reaching psychical conformity," Sigmund Freud wrote; these comedians had discovered that elusive common ground on which many blacks and whites in the sixties could share laughter and humor. It was a crucial breakthrough, not only in the public expression of genuine African-American humor, but also in forthright communication between the races; still, the process of interracial joking on stage was being enacted within relatively restricted terrain.[2]

The area staked out by these pioneers, the grounds on which they initially found acceptance, had a distinctly intellectual cast. This was an ironic, perhaps even startling development, since white America's traditional perception of Negroes as naive or childlike and simple— which effectively denied recognition of any deliberate ridicule or satire

—had been one of the key impediments to acknowledging black humor. Steve Allen suggests as much when he argues that "our society would not permit the emergence of black comedians who were the equivalent of Bob Hope, much less any that were the equivalent of Lenny Bruce or Mort Sahl." Jack Schiffman's explanation of why the "efforts of black comics were rejected as 'unworthy' of attention, for years and years," was even more incisive:

> The principal reason, I believe, is that comedy is a more intellectual art than say dance, which is directed toward our visual senses, or music, which *may* be enjoyed intellectually, but *must* be enjoyed aurally, emotionally, sensually. Comedy has to be thought about to be understood at all. . . . Its appeal is to ideas rather than feelings or even images. In my judgment, according comedy its due place would have required an acknowledgment by white America that blacks did, in fact, possess intelligence and the ability to think. It would have required a tacit admission that all the slander about a lack of black intelligence was false.

Despite his narrow definition of comedy (for instance, much slapstick comedy arguably does *not* require an intellectual response), Schiffman's remarks are insightful.[3]

From the period of slavery (when Frederick Douglass and others wrote of the advantages accruing to those slaves who presented themselves as happy or slow-witted and the perils faced by those who appeared sullen or impudent) to the mid-twentieth century, so-called "smart niggers" were deemed uppity and impudent—a distinction that often resulted in physical reprisal or, at the least, ostracism and the loss of white favor. Racial relationships in America had largely been shaped by the tacit accord that dictated that blacks avoid challenging white intellectual superiority. It was an arrangement that not only permeated everyday interracial exchanges but molded black comic routines on stage. African-American comedians were accepted as clowns and jesters but were expected to avoid satire and social commentary—the comedy of ideas.

Given this tradition, the breakthrough of black intellectual comedians was truly remarkable. Despite their assertiveness and frequent skewering of America's inequitable racial arrangements, however, their comedy routines were couched in a non-ethnic mainstream voice or presented with a polite, tranquil veneer that belied any notion of deepseated unrest or hidden fury. It was a far cry from the traditional stage Negro's guise of duplicitous idiocy, but it still lacked the stylistic flourish and raw, razor-sharp edge that characterized much black street humor. As Dick Gregory's mounting bitterness and increasingly more biting humor confirmed, much of the early softening of his satire had simply been the price of acceptance. His early circumspection no more reflected his actual attitude than stoic imperturbability reflected Jackie Robinson's true feelings in the face of threats and racial insults when he broke the color line in major league baseball in 1947.

Nevertheless, these early sixties comics established the model by which other aspiring cross-over black comedians would be judged. For the brash and ambitious Richard Pryor, that model was as constricting as a proper, elegantly-made British shoe that was several sizes too small.

Before arriving in New York, Pryor had shown the unpredictable side of his nature on several occasions; his outbursts—whether inspired by personal demons or his intolerance of societal hypocrisy—would soon become legendary. As a teenager in the Army, he had several violent run-ins with fellow enlistees. He had been jailed for thirty-five days in Pittsburgh after being convicted on assault and battery charges brought by his girlfriend. And his fulminations in a Youngstown, Ohio, nightclub had not only revealed his determined ambition and short fuse but also (as many of his personal debacles would in the future) provided a rich source of material for his comedy act. Pryor (nineteen or twenty years old at the time) confronted the allegedly mob-connected owners of the club after a female singer had come to him in tears complaining that they had refused to pay her. More than twenty years later, in his concert film *Live on Sunset Strip* (1982), Pryor transformed that confrontation into a hilarious comic routine:

> I had a *cap* pistol! You know, them blank starter pistols. I busted into the office with the motherfucker talkin' 'bout, "All right! Gimme the money, motherfucker!" Doing my best black shit, you know [mugging, grimacing] . . . that shit usually scare whitey to death. And these motherfuckers didn't do nothin'. I'm sure that those men are sitting in that office today, laughing. . . . He just started laughing, "haa-haa-haa-hahaa, this fucking kid . . . haa-haa-hahaa. Hey, Tony! Come here—*stickup!* haa-haa-hahaa. This fucking kid, come here. He's got a pair of *gagoozees* on him. . . . Hey, you want a little *ca-zee-aroni*. Hey, Paulo, fix him a little . . . put some *shroo-gee* on it. Fry it up, they like fried food." . . . They

paid everybody off, let everybody go. Kept me—like a pet. . . .
"You got a way home, you want us to give you a ride . . . haa-haa-
hahaa."

Pryor ended the routine with a bit of disturbing but typically candid
dark humor:

Don't go out with the Mafia, 'cause you can't buy 'em dinner. . . .
If you say, "Let me buy tonight"—"Hey, kid, let me tell you
something. We're crime, and crime don't pay."

Pryor's turbulent personal life—his inflammatory public outbursts,
his chaotic relations with women, his drug use, brawls, and run-ins with
the law—have been thoroughly documented in a raft of books and
articles. Since many of these public transgressions and personal set-
backs have surfaced in his comedy, many commentators have suggested
that there is an intricate connection between his erratic personal behavior and his comedy act; analysts (from colleagues to journalists) typically
assume that his humor is either inspired or impeded by his alleged
instability and mercurial mood shifts. Rarely has the age-old temptation
to connect genius with neurosis been more overindulged. Few comedians have been subjected to the type of pseudopsychological, ad homi-
nem interpretations that mark discussions of Pryor's life and work.

Paul Schraeder—Pryor's director on *Blue Collar* (1978)—for example, claimed, "Richard's an enigma in that he's totally tortured by inherent contradictions in his personality. . . . The more successful he is in
the white world, the more resentful he becomes, the more afraid that
he is not black enough." In the view of the writer William Brashler,
Pryor "was a man torn between his resentment of being black—and
what it means to be black in this country—and his desire to be big, the
biggest in a white-oriented, white-run industry." Burt Reynolds said,
"Richard is capable of bringing genuine punishment upon himself. He
seeks it out because like all of us he wonders if he deserves success . . .
he's frightened."

"He's a person of supreme intelligence—you can see that by his
material, by his insights. But because he formally has only a ninth-grade
education, *he* believes he's not bright," Pryor's former manager and
attorney, David Franklin, has said. Sally Hanson, a costume designer
and friend, speculates that Pryor's "well-spring of humor" comes from
"pain. He had, you know, a really rough upbringing—such a painful

childhood that the only survival was humor." And Steve Allen contends that "as so often seems to be the case, his comic genius is balanced by —perhaps even inseparable from—a pattern of erratic behavior and social irresponsibility that consistently gets him into trouble."[4]

Clearly Pryor has inspired much unsubstantiated conjecture about the basis of his sometimes bizarre behavior and the connection between pain or eccentricity and comic genius. (As Pryor might have quipped some years ago, If hard times and pain made good comedians, every nigger in America would be a superstar.) The suggestion that the tone and content of Pryor's humor is derived from his natural comic ability, offered by the comedian Dan Aykroyd, seems more accurate than most other theories: "If you're born with it, if it's in the chemistry, in the blood, no matter what happens you're going to try and see the worst possible world situation as a humorous one. . . . He has just always been a satirist, a wit, a caustic. This is the way his mind and soul work." Theories concerning the inspiration of Pryor's humor aside, there is little doubt that his stark adolescent experiences set him apart from such early sixties black comedians as Russell, Gregory, Cosby, and Cambridge.[5]

Although some facts vary in specific recountings by Pryor, the basic details of his background have been confirmed. His grandmother, Marie, ran a string of whorehouses in Peoria, Illinois, that catered to locals as well as transients, including the entertainers and vaudeville performers who passed through Peoria, a lively stop on both the mainstream and black vaudeville circuit during the thirties and forties. (The old show business expression "Will it play in Peoria?" reflects the city's previous stature as a show town.) Marie's son, Leroy, eventually entered the family business and married Gertrude Thomas, one of the prostitutes, after she became pregnant by him. Their son, Richard, was born in 1940 and, like the rest of his family, lived in one of the brothels.

Still, both Pryor's grandmother and mother insisted that he attend church and worked to instill in the boy middle-class values that would permit him to better himself. "My parents were honest," he said. "They had great dignity. My mother taught me about being decent." But the illicit sexuality and often violent reality of brothel life were also part of Pryor's daily routine. He described it as "fantasylike. . . . It was an adventure, it was two worlds." Indeed, the clash of experiences— watching his mother and other prostitutes entertain customers through transoms on the brothel doors and listening to earnest entreaties by his grandmother and mother to develop proper values—exposed the young

Pryor to a chilling dilemma. Although he may have reconciled this moral paradox as long as he remained in an insular world presided over by his grandmother's loving reassurances, the outside world soon intervened. When he was six, his grandmother enrolled him in a Catholic school, but when school authorities discovered the nature of the family business, he was quickly expelled. The real world's estimate of Pryor's exotic homelife was indelibly imprinted. "To experience corruption and dignity in such intimate proximity," a *Newsweek* journalist wrote, "explains a lot about the contradictions of Pryor's life and art."[6]

In addition to the extreme circumstances of his family's involvement in prostitution, like nearly every other African-American of his generation, as a youth Pryor soon discovered that to much of the outside world he was a member of a despised minority. The word "nigger" and his pariah status in mainstream society became realities for him shortly after he began attending public school. To the supersensitive Pryor, it was a devastating revelation.

Like many successful comedians, however, Pryor had demonstrated a knack for comedy at an early age. He was a practical joker and the class cutup during his adolescence. A frail, skinny kid, he soon began using his "quick wit" and "belligerent humor" to ingratiate himself with bigger, more violent teenagers in neighborhood street gangs and gain a measure of status among his peers. The ploy worked on the street; Pryor "was usually successful at smart-alecking his way out of trouble." But although his antic behavior and assertive repartee delighted his classmates, they were disruptive in classrooms and contributed to his estrangement from teachers and eventual abandonment of formal education. Before leaving school in the ninth grade, however, Pryor had two educational experiences that helped to shape his future.[7]

In the sixth grade, one teacher agreed to let the twelve-year-old Pryor entertain his classmates for ten minutes once a week if he cut down on classroom disturbances and got to school on time every day. Pryor took up the challenge and began developing material for his weekly performances. The arrangement not only temporarily ignited his interest in school but no doubt also contributed to his confidence as a performer. A year later, he met Juliette Whittaker, a drama major who, after graduation from the University of Iowa, came to Peoria to direct the Carver Community Center. She took special interest in Pryor, whom she later called "a fourteen-year-old genius," and convinced him to join the drama group. Although he would quit the group when he was sixteen, Pryor later recalled that his experience on stage at the Carver Center and Whittaker's support were crucial events in his development as an entertainer.[8]

By the time Pryor arrived in New York City in 1963, he had worked odd jobs around Peoria, fathered a child, married, served two years in the Army, and spent several years on the black club circuit. The experiences that set him apart from his college-educated black contemporaries were in place, even though he had not developed the resolve and technique to exploit them fully. Still, his raw talent prevailed. Working such Greenwich Village clubs as the Cafe Wha?, Pryor freely copied the styles of other black comedians—particularly Bill Cosby, of whom he said, "This nigger's doin' what I'm fixin' to do." Within a year, he was being described as a rising young star, and critics at *Variety* were commenting on his "avant garde viewpoint," "healthy instinct for irreverence," and "feel for expression."[9]

Pryor was moving up quickly, but he had developed neither the style nor the comic material that would ultimately establish him as America's number-one comedian; he was still working in the shadow of Cosby and Gregory. Although he acknowledged that he was "probably the worst joke teller in the whole world" and had turned more to stories in which he assumed the parts of different characters, before white audiences he shied away from the more profane ghetto voices that often appeared in his act before black crowds and eventually would dominate his work. The choice was partly his own—a lack of confidence in his ability to make those characters acceptable to whites. As Paul Rovin noted in *Richard Pryor: Black and Blue,* Pryor "viewed the Cosby style as the road to success." A chorus of advisers also encouraged him to take that path. One agent, for example, told him, "Don't mention the fact that you're a 'nigger.' . . . Be the kind of colored guy we'd like to have over to our house. Now, I'd introduce *Bill* [Cosby] to my mother, but a guy like you . . ." Bill Grundfest, owner of the Comedy Cellar in New York, accentuated the point when he said, "In those days, if [Pryor] hadn't done what we would consider not whitewashed material, 'Oreo' material, he never would have gotten to square one. . . . Compromise was a necessity of the times." Pryor recalled that "they were gonna help me be *nothing* as best they could."[10]

Still, he compromised. Within a year of his arrival in New York, he branched out to other Village clubs and soon was booked into a few of the Catskills resort hotels. Pegged as another non-racial comic, the next Bill Cosby, in 1964 he made his first television appearance on Rudy Vallee's *On Broadway Tonight.* There was little of the poise and swagger associated with vintage Pryor on that night. The rail-thin twenty-three-year-old was diffident and hesitant, clapping anxiously at his own jokes and nervously seguing with "Wait, I got more to tell you" or a deferential "Thank you." His narrative voice was pure white bread and, except for a hillbilly type, so were the characters. After announcing that he was from Peoria, he opened with:

> When I was young I used to think my people didn't like me because they used to send me to the store for bread and then they'd move.

Then, after a physical routine about the perils of opening a can of evaporated milk with a butcher knife and a quick impression of a spastic Jerry Lewis:

> I watch a lot of advertising on television commercials, really funny, like the woman—"Honey, I got a giant in my washer!" "Yeah, well it better be gone before I get home."

followed by a little dark humor:

> My favorite commercial, a kid in bed, and they get real dramatic, right. They play it up real big. A kid's laying in bed. [In deep, sonorous voice] "Nine fifteen—Tommy Jones can't sleep!" And they cut to Tommy Jones—"Aaggghhh! Mommy, I can't breathe!" His mommy comes rushing in, "Good, it's working."

The concluding segment of the act begins with the nasal voice of the hillbilly character that would become a permanent part of Pryor's repertoire:

> I heard a knock on the door. I said to my wife, "There's a knock on the door." My wife said, "That's pecul-yar, we ain't got no door."

When the character confronts an intruder who enters the house, Pryor's voice switches to a facsimile of Bill Cosby's rapid-fire Everyman accent:

> I grabbed *thee* crook . . . that was *thee* wrong move. He-threw-me-down-I-got-up-he-knocked-me-down-I-got-up-he-kicked-me-

down-I-got-up-he-said-get-up, I-said-ha-haaa. Then my wife threw him across the furniture, she-slapped-me-the-police-came-she-beat-them-up-they-took-her-away . . . me and the crook livin' happily ever after.

Although the material is innocuous compared to his later routines, Pryor made it funny. He had not yet developed his masterful use of body language and facial expressions, but there was a skittish energy to his performance, a youthful exuberance and vulnerability that was disarming. He offered, in his words, "white bread humor," which was often juvenile, but perfect for television in the mid-sixties. Soon, Pryor was appearing on Johnny Carson's *Tonight Show* and the *Ed Sullivan* and *Merv Griffin* shows. His career was taking off, and bookings were being offered in uptown New York clubs as well as in Las Vegas. But even as his star rose, he was having second thoughts about the nature of his act.

Pryor was becoming not only disenchanted with constant comparisons to Cosby but also annoyed with club owners, agents, and advisers who insisted he refrain from using street language and adding more biting racial material to his act. In 1966 and 1967, despite resistance, he began developing and using more ethnic material; some of it would appear on his first album, *Richard Pryor* (1969). Although not nearly as trenchant as the routines he would present in the seventies, his "Super Nigger" bit is a good example of this transitional material:

I always thought, why they never have a black hero. I always wanted to go to the movies and see a black hero. I figured out maybe someday on television they'll have it, man. . . . Look, up in the sky! It's a crow. It's a bat. No, it's Super Nigger. Able to leap tall buildings with a single bound; faster than a bowl of chitlin's. . . . We find Super Nigger with his X-ray vision that enables him to see through everything, except whitey. . . . We find Super Nigger disguised as Clark Washington, mild mannered custodian of the *Daily Planet*, shuffling into Perry White's office:

"Hey, man, I'm quittin', baby!"

"Great Caesar's ghost, I can't talk to you now."

"Talk to *me*, Jack, 'cause I'm ready to quit, man. I've had it up to here, you dig. Tired of doin' them halls, every time I finish, Lois Lane and them come slippin' and slidin' down through there and

I have to do it over again. You dig it, baby. I'm through . . . *fire me!*"

"I can't talk to you now. The warehouse is on fire."

"What warehouse?"

"Warehouse 86."

"Damn, that's where I got my stash. . . . This looks like a job for Super Nigger."

Pryor also introduced his "Black Ben" routine, which was set in a Southern prison and called "Prison Play" on his first album. In it, a redneck guard objects to the theme of a play about to be presented by an acting group (a Southern white girl falling in love with a slave), until he is reassured that "the nigger gets killed." Bits such as "Smells," an irreverent toast to funkiness, began to assume the shape and rhythmic pace, if not the satirical content, of his later material:

Deodorants are dangerous, man. Did you ever read on the deodor-ant can? . . . They say, "Caution, contents highly inflammable, may explode." I don't know about you people, but I don't want nothin' under my arm that's goin' explode. 'Cause you could be walkin' down the street, you know . . . [sound of explosion]

"What the hell's the matter with him?" [in hillbilly voice] "I don't know. . . . He don't smell, though."

In other routines, he started drawing directly on black community attitudes—frequently in a less than positive vein.

Used to be some beautiful black men would come through the neighborhood dressed in African shit, really nice shit. And they be . . . "Peace, love, black is beautiful, remember the essence of life, we are a people of the universe, life is beautiful." My parents would go, "That nigger crazy."

In these bits, Pryor began introducing more street types and observa-tions, mirroring the inflections and intonations of black street patois. He also refined the intricate interplay between his narrative voice and his characters, moving closer to a comedy style that *Rolling Stone* would call "a new type of realistic theater." The non-ethnic facade and debt to Cosby and others were fading.[11]

The metamorphosis had been partly expedited by his work at Budd

Friedman's Improvisation Comedy Club in midtown Manhattan. Opened in 1963 as a coffeehouse and hangout for Broadway performers, with the old Village spots turning to rock formats, the Improv was transformed into a comedy club in 1965. The ambience was casual and informal and, according to Friedman, "it was one of the hippest places in town." Pryor was a frequent visitor and tried out some of his more authentic material before white or mixed audiences there. He was apparently very much at ease in this loose atmosphere. On one occasion, while a female singer was performing, Pryor paraded before the stage nude accept for shoes and a hat. The incident caused no great furor but did prompt Friedman's wife to comment: "Well, there goes another myth." More importantly, Pryor was able to experiment with both a blacker comic voice and improvisational, character-based vignettes that combined comedy with pathos and drama. "The concept of story theatre" appeared early at the Improv, Friedman says, "when Dave Astor, Ron Carey, and Richard did an act together. Dave would recite a story and Richard and Ron would act it out."[12]

Despite the comparative freedom of the Improv and the introduction of new, more genuinely black material, pressure to present the staid routines that had initially made him popular still rankled. Even fulfillment of his lifelong dream, his first movie role—a small part in *The Busy Body* (1966), in which Godfrey Cambridge also appeared—failed to satisfy Pryor's thirst for creative expansion. "I made a lot of money being Bill Cosby," he said, "but I was hiding my personality. I just wanted to be in show business so bad I didn't care how. It started bothering me later because I was being successful at it. I was being a robot comic . . . repeating the same lines, getting the same laughs for the same jokes. The repetition was killing me." Pryor's frustration surfaced dramatically when he "went crazy," "cracked up," or had what he described as a "nervous breakdown" on stage at a Las Vegas hotel. That public repudiation of the middle-of-the-road, robot comic image dramatically hastened the emergence of the real Richard Pryor.[13]

I I

The details and actual date of the Las Vegas debacle differ in many of Pryor's accounts of the incident. According to John A. Williams and Dennis Williams in *If I Stop I'll Die: The Comedy and Tragedy of Richard Pryor*, the date varies from 1969 to 1971 and some accounts have Pryor simply walking off the stage while others claim that he said,

"What the fuck am I doing here? I'm not going to do this anymore," then stripped, ran into the casino, leaped onto a table, and screamed, "Black Jack." Paul Rovin describes two incidents at the Aladdin Hotel in Las Vegas—one in 1967, during which Pryor stripped, and another in 1970, when he quietly walked off the stage. But John and Dennis Williams insist that there was but one confrontation at the Aladdin and that it occurred in September 1967; their account is attributed to author Claude Brown, and they suggest that he received his information from, among others, Bill Cosby. According to them, Pryor was performing for a group of "Very Special People" who had brought members of their family to the show. When Pryor (who, according to Brown, may have been "high and-or undergoing some metamorphosis") stripped or harangued the audience with obscenities or otherwise insulted the "Very Special People," he was "wrestled offstage or through a panel or off the blackjack table . . . whatever. Pryor's ass belonged to the Very Special People."

The Williamses report that Cosby and other entertainers intervened, pleading for a "reversion of sentence" and that, finally, it was Cosby's entreaties that saved Pryor's life. "The Very Special People reversed their decision, shoved the jittering, out-of-it Pryor into Cosby's arms. 'Okay,' Brown says they told Cos, 'You can have him, but if he crosses the state line again, nobody'll ever see him.'" [14]

John and Dennis Williams's version of the Aladdin Hotel incident may or may not be accurate. According to Cecil Brown, for example, Claude Brown did not know Pryor until he introduced them at Berkeley more than two years after the 1967 Aladdin incident. But, although Pryor's Las Vegas debacle is shrouded with mystery, rumors of sinister threats from the "Special People," and a veil of contradictory reports, clearly Pryor was undergoing a major crisis involving his comic identity during the years 1966–70. Suppressing what he later called his "natural material" was apparently taking a personal toll: his antic behavior continued and he had several run-ins with the law. [15]

Increasingly, he seemed determined to abandon the whitewashed, "respectable" comedy that had initially made him successful and couch his act in a voice that echoed black street humor. In some ways, his decision mirrored the revelation that led Flip Wilson to overcome self-consciousness and embarrassment at negative assessments of his ethnic heritage and exclaim, "Niggers is fun," accentuating how "interesting being black is." Ignoring advice given by the agent who told him to avoid mentioning that he was a "nigger," Pryor began aggressively using the term to describe all blacks, as he incorporated the voices and stories of the lower-class black working people and hustlers he had known in Peoria and on the black club circuit into his act.

Fed up with the restrictions of comic appearances on television, he failed to show up for an *Ed Sullivan* booking. He moved to Los Angeles in 1966 to concentrate on films and club dates. In addition to *The Busy Body,* he had small roles in *Wild in the Streets* (1968), *The Green Berets* (1968), and *The Phynx* (1970), none of which were memorable. But in his nightclub appearances, he experimented with a comic style that was revolutionary and shocking to mainstream audiences. At first, the response was less than encouraging. White audiences often reacted with embarrassment and baffled silence. Even some of the hippest African-Americans were initially puzzled and offended. For example, Paul Rovin recounts, "to prove to his managers and himself that there was an audience for this kind of material [Pryor] did a show in Los Angeles, to which he invited local black disc jockeys. They hated him, taking particular offense at his frequent use of the word *nigger.*"[16]

In 1970 Pryor went underground. Since he had recently split up with his third wife and was thousands of dollars in debt, his flight from celebrity may have been inspired by personal problems. It also may have been prompted by the inhospitable reaction to his new material and threats by some club managers to cancel his engagements unless he reverted to the old routines. Or, as some contend, Pryor may have been blacklisted because of the Aladdin Hotel incident. Pryor's own accounts of this period are evasive and contradictory. Whatever the immediate cause, he gathered his belongings from his Los Angeles apartment and moved north to Berkeley.

It was in that center of student protest, radical thought, and academic freedom that he earnestly set about developing a more authentic black voice for his comedy routines. Out of the spotlight, the disconsolate comedian reportedly began the rigorous self-evaluation and transformation that allowed him openly to embrace the street humor, folklore, and downtrodden but wise characters that would soon distinguish his act. Removed from the influence of entertainment professionals who had charted him on a safe, middle-of-the-road course, Pryor began to examine African-American history and to see himself and his humor in the larger context of ethnic pride. His personal evolution was aided immensely by a new group of acquaintances—such bright, young black writers and intellectuals as Ishmael Reed, Cecil Brown, Al Young, Claude Brown, and David Henderson, some of whom were experiment-

ing with black folklore, street humor, and gallows humor in their own
literary works.

The interaction between these college-educated writers and the brilliant upstart comic no doubt was mutually beneficial. Despite frustration with his career, Pryor was a successful, nationally known
entertainer who had established a foothold, however precarious, in
show business. His success in the cutthroat commercial world was appreciated by writers who were struggling to achieve national prominence. Pryor, on the other hand, could not have helped being
impressed by accredited intellectuals who nevertheless shared his affection and enthusiasm for the humor and lifestyles of common black
folks.

As Jim Haskins observes in *Richard Pryor: A Man and His Madness,*
"in the liberal atmosphere of Berkeley [Pryor] found support for his
refusal to do colorless material." Inspired by his literary friends, Pryor
began reading such material as the collected speeches of Malcolm X,
whom he came to regard as "someone who thinks like I do." He also
began concentrating on writing new material and, perhaps influenced
by Ishmael Reed's "Hoodoo Western" *Yellow Back Radio Broke Down,*
began a script for a cowboy movie, which he called *Black Stranger.*
That script led to Pryor's later efforts as a co-writer with Mel Brooks
and others on *Blazing Saddles* (1974). Primarily, however, Pryor intensified his firsthand research of the ghetto types who would people his
routines in the future. "He began remembering the people he knew
here [in Peoria]—the drunks, the braggarts, the bullies—and he started
working with that," said his old Peoria friend Juliette Whittaker. "He
went to the ghetto and started watching people." Haunting the hip bars
and clubs in Oakland, San Francisco, and Berkeley, he studied the
crowds, then returned to his apartment and taped his impressions of
the people he had seen. When he had worked out a routine based on
his research, he tried it out in one of the local clubs, such as Basin
Street West in San Francisco or Mandrakes in Berkeley.[17]

The novelist Cecil Brown met Pryor at Mandrakes after a friend told
him, "There's a comedian down there who's crazier than you." Impressed by Pryor's "free association and stream-of-consciousness" approach
to comedy, Brown became one of the comic's closest Bay Area friends.
They began a collaborative writing association that ultimately produced
Which Way Is Up (1977) and several other unfilmed scripts. Brown
also introduced Pryor to Berkeley's coterie of black writers, and that
group formed an early version of the much-publicized Hollywood

"Black Pack," which emerged in the late eighties and included Eddie Murphy, Robert Townsend, Keenan Ivory Wayans, and other comedians and writers.

In addition to the writers, according to Brown, the Berkeley clique included a few lesser-known but even grittier ghetto personalities. Among them were Reverend Banks, "a kind of preacher type from the deep South who was full of folklore," and "a felon who we ran into—he was a funny dude, just got out of prison." They partied together and often rapped well into the night, exchanging stories and ideas. "Richard was pulling material from all of us," Brown said. "He would listen to tales . . . like one night somebody mentioned how his father had told him to 'get that bass outta yo' voice' . . . and soon it would appear in Richard's act. He would add to it, shape it, and next day he'd use it."[18]

Pryor's Berkeley retreat ultimately proved to be a source of genuine inspiration. By 1971, confident at least of the direction in which he wanted to take his humor, he returned to Los Angeles. Although he was still testing nuances of his revamped approach in small clubs, it was apparent that a new, rejuvenated Richard Pryor had surfaced. In fact, shortly after Pryor's return to Los Angeles, Cosby caught his act and later recalled, "I was in the audience when Richard took on a whole new persona—his own. Richard killed the Bill Cosby in his act, made people hate it. Then he worked on them, doing pure Pryor, and it was the most astonishing metamorphosis I have ever seen. He was magnificent."[19]

Indeed, Pryor's startling transformation, his switch to the candid presentation of character-based comedy derived from aspects of black culture, language, and humor that—at least, on the stage—had been previously ignored or methodically excised, was simply dumbfounding to many audiences. Its first significant exposure outside of small clubs filled with ultra-hip devotees came with the release of the album *Craps (After Hours)*, which was recorded live before a predominantly black crowd at the Redd Foxx Club in Hollywood and released in February 1971. Although still raw, that performance is the earliest recorded example of the new Richard Pryor. On it the timid, hesitant references to racial topics are gone. Instead, Pryor boldly employs racial topics, touching on subjects such as police harassment of blacks and the differences in sexual attitudes between the races; using an after-hours club called Hank's as the setting, he unleashes a galaxy of street characters (prostitutes, pimps, con men) who authentically mirror the bottom rung of ghetto life. Although it is now considered one of Pryor's best albums, initially record sales were dismal. Even the black audiences for whom it was intended—people nurtured on the frequently scatological, explicitly sexually material heard on Redd Foxx's recordings— ignored it at first.

And when Pryor first introduced the new routines to integrated mainstream audiences, he was often greeted with stunned silence or uneasy, embarrassed chuckles. Much of this material was tested at the Improv in New York City. His September 1971 appearance before a relatively hip crowd was taped and later released as *Live and Smokin'*, a video film that demonstrated the expanded creative possibilities of his new approach as well as its hazards. By then the processed hair was gone, replaced by an Afro, and his vulnerable, boyish appearance was veiled by a goatee and mustache, which gave him a raffish, militant look that was often reflected in the material. He opened with:

> Yeah, I'm really nervous 'cause I ain't had no cocaine all day. . . . I imagine a lot of yall will be leavin' during my shit. . . . I hope I'm funny and shit, you know, 'cause just to be a nigger standin' up here saying nothin' ain't shit.

The noticeably fidgety Pryor then plunged into a routine that included material introduced on his *Craps* album as well as rough versions of some brilliant bits that would appear on his best-selling mid-seventies albums.

> I never wanted to be white. . . . No, I always wanted to be somethin' different, you know, than a nigger, 'cause niggers had it so rough. I tried to be a black cat with neat hair. I thought that was the problem—the hair. I say, "If my hair was straight, then whitey'd dig me." So I got a process . . . *wrong!* . . . You be Puerto Rican with a process. In the Midwest Puerto Ricans was famous. Not like New York. No, 'cause they got a lot of Puerto Ricans. They got like three in the whole Midwest. I was one of them. . . . I was jivin'. . . . I was a nigger for 23 years. I gave it up, no room for advancement.

These subjective jibes at the burdens and perils of being an African-American got mild laughs, as did Pryor's wino and old philosopher tales, which often turned on the contrast between black-white language and behavior:

I'm one of the first coloreds, man, in the F.B.I. That's right, J. Edgar Hoover appointed me personally, girl. Wanted somebody on the railroad to watch the Mexicans. That's right, 'cause couldn't nobody in the Bureau at that particular time speak Mexican talk. And they hired me. I could understand Mexican, 'cause I hear 'em talkin' I say, "What you say, motherfucker?" They tell me!

When Pryor's wit turned outward, lampooning mainstream white attitudes, the laughter subsided noticeably.

I remember tricks used to come through our neighborhood. That's where I first met white people. They come down through my neighborhood to help the economy. Nice white dudes though . . . "Hello, little boy, is your mother home? I'd like a blow job." I wonder what would happen if niggers go through white neighborhoods doin' that, "Hey, man, is yo' momma home? Tell the bitch we wanna fuck."

Ain't no niggers goin' to the moon, you know that. First of all, ain' no niggers qualified, so you all tell us. . . . Niggers was hip they'd help yall get to the moon. "Hey, man, let's organize and help these white motherfuckers get to the moon, so they leave us alone."

When Pryor became more ever irreverent, turning his satire toward religion or sex with white women, the audience lapsed into an embarrassed silence that was occasionally punctuated by hostile murmurings. A bit about "Jesus' momma's" alleged virginity brought disgruntled ohs and ahs, as did an offhand comment in his Dracula routine: "You expect Dracula to jump out at you at any second. If he did, I'd a held the cross up, 'cause he's allergic to bullshit."

His comments on interracial sex, however, elicited the most negative responses. The quip, "I like white women. . . . I could be a revolutionary but I like white women with big titties," was greeted with cold silence, as were his comments about President Nixon's daughter: "Tricia Nixon can't give her pussy away. Even the Secret Service men . . . 'Ah, naw . . . I gotta wash the car.' " When he added that the most important part of being a Negro was "fucking white girls," there was a distinctly hostile buzz. Some people left, prompting Pryor to say, "I hate to see folks leave when I be talkin'. I hope yall get raped by black folks with clap, and ain't nothin' worst than the black clap." After launching into his wino and junkie routine—the best and most well-received part of his act that night—Pryor concluded with a bit about Martin Luther King, Jr., which ended with: "I been to the mountain top, too, and what did I see? Mo' white folks with guns."[20]

It was a new, unadulterated, brutally realistic Richard Pryor. He had clearly adopted what he called a "character-heavy" approach to comedy that would be called, among other things, "the theatre of the routine." It was basically comedy without jokes, a combination of ironic observations and realistic portrayals of mainstream society's outcasts and marginal people that elicited pathos as well as the humorous release that comes from recognition of another human being's foibles. As Pryor explained, "I . . . take the emotion to a peak and then level it off . . . with a nice laugh." But although his soon-to-be-legendary characters were in place and his language and delivery had assumed the unmistakable tenor of black street humor, there was still some hesitancy and ambiguity in Pryor's narrative voice when he abandoned his characters and spoke as himself. His anxious glances about the room after he launched his most scathing satirical lines or emerged from the portrayal of some blasphemous ghetto character may have derived, as he suggested, from his nervousness because the show was being filmed. But it probably also resulted from his awareness that he was not only participating in the introduction of a relatively new style of comic performance but initiating a crucial breakthrough in African-American stage humor as well.[21]

The racial satire in his humor was not new; Dick Gregory, Godfrey Cambridge, and, to a lesser extent, Moms Mabley and Redd Foxx had introduced similar material to white audiences. But with the possible exception of Flip Wilson, Pryor's disclosure of previously closely guarded comic referents, racially based attitudes, and cultural eccentricities that were often "embarrassments to the black middle class and stereotypes in the minds of most whites" was untried on the mainstream stage. Pryor was not only challenging traditional show business assumptions about the viability of ungentrified black material and an unmoderated black voice but also breaking with blacks' long-standing tradition of subterfuge and concealment of inner-community customs. So it was not surprising that, at the outset, he occasionally pulled back.[22]

Nor was it surprising that, in the early seventies, he chose to hone his act in black clubs and theatres. As the Improv date demonstrated, white audiences often failed to recognize the subtle indirection in Pryor's delivery (the way African-Americans "say a whole lot of things underneath you, all around you," as he put it) and were bewildered by some language and cultural references that were routine in black circles; he paused in disbelief several times, for example, when the crowd seemed puzzled by subjects that for most blacks were ordinary currency. Although, like Flip Wilson, he insisted that black crowds were tougher to please, he understood that to enhance or even maintain his authentic edge, it was necessary to direct his act at an African-American sensibility. So while he played hipper, integrated spots such as the Improv during this period, he concentrated on showplaces with nearly exclusive black audiences. He appeared in black theatres and clubs in large cities such as Washington, Chicago, and Detroit, and, of course, at Harlem's Apollo Theatre. But even in those citadels of inbred African-American entertainment, where tolerance for off-color humor was high, the reception was not always positive; many customers were offended by what Jack Schiffman refers to as Pryor's "pure and unadulterated vulgarity." Bobby Schiffman, manager of the Apollo during those years, recalls that "he was dirty, and there were possibly a lot of people who walked. But Richie was before his time."[23]

Still, despite offending some people, Pryor was slowly building a grass-roots following among African-Americans, particularly those under thirty-five, who were increasingly rejecting the traditional black middle-class tactic of de-emphasizing cultural differences between the races and embracing the Black Power stratagem, which, besides its political agenda, encouraged an assertive flaunting of ethnic behavior that had been disapprovingly associated with the black masses and self-consciously suppressed. Militant new voices—the Black Panthers and Stokely Carmichael, among others—reflected a shift in the African-American mood, so Pryor's switch to an outspoken black voice occurred at precisely the right time. His early seventies concert tour created a solid foundation of black followers.

At the same time, he was making significant inroads in mainstream entertainment, both behind the scene and in front of the camera. He wrote for the Flip Wilson and Redd Foxx shows and worked as a co-star and co-writer on Lily Tomlin's two 1973 television specials. He won an Emmy for his writing contribution to *Lily*, the second of those shows, which was honored as Outstanding Comedy-Variety Special. Although disappointed at being passed over for the lead role of the black cowboy in *Blazing Saddles* (1974), he won awards from both the American Academy of Humor and the Writers' Guild of America as a co-writer of the movie. Pryor's most notable film role during this time was his supporting part as Piano Man in Motown's *Lady Sings the Blues* (1972), where he subtly invested the basically dramatic part with tidbits from his comedy routines and, some critics insisted, deserved an Oscar nomination. He also appeared in such less-publicized films as *Wattstax* (1972), *Some Call It Loving* (1973), *Dynamite Chicken* (1973), *The Mack* (1973), and *Hit* (1973); he had a cameo role in the Bill Cosby–Sidney Poitier hit *Uptown Saturday Night* (1974). Despite this exposure, Pryor had not yet found the vehicle that would elevate him to the status of either a mainstream film or a comic star.

On stage, however, his popularity was growing. African-Americans flocked to see his insistently black humor but, as Pryor put it, "It was human humor, too. And human beings were liking it. I'd get confused to see more and more whites in the audience. What was happening was that they were saying, 'Hey, we're people. We enjoy something good.'" When his comedy album *That Nigger's Crazy* was released in 1974, it surprised record industry executives with its appeal to young whites as well as blacks. It went gold and won the Grammy Award for Best Comedy Recording of the year. The album was followed in 1975 by . . . *Is It Something I Said?*, which also went gold and won another Grammy.[24]

Those albums, featuring material developed and polished on his concert tour and recorded before predominantly black audiences, present a much more poised comedian. Pryor had eliminated some of the raw edges heard on the *Craps* album, moving from characters to narrative voice with much more finesse, and showed little of the hesitancy or anxiety seen in the *Live and Smokin'* Improv appearance. *That Nigger's Crazy*, in fact, contains the best recorded performances of some of Pryor's most memorable routines.

Focusing primarily on humorous insights derived from the difference between black and white social customs, he moves easily from contrasting views of popular films:

> Yall seen *The Exorcist?* It's a story about the devil . . . gets into this 12-year-old girl. Devil's a *low* motherfucker, Jack. See, there wouldn't a been a movie it had been niggers in it. Movie would'a been about seven minutes long. "*Hellooooo* [in the eerie, rasping voice of the movie's possessed child] . . . Good-bye!"

to explorations of how male-female relationships differ in black and white communities:

White men and women, they seldom ever have fistfights. They be goin' intellectual hurtin' each other . . . so they say. White woman say some funny shit to her man, "Your dick is short and you can't even screw." And the white dude go, "Uh, we'll discuss it tomorrow." You say that shit to a nigger, you got a fight, "Bitch, is you *crazy* . . ."

Occasionally, the contrasts veer into more pertinent social issues:

Police live in yall's neighborhood. . . . "Hello, Officer Timson, going bowling tonight? Yes, ah, nice Pinto you have, ha-ha-ha." Niggers don't know 'em like that. See, white folks get a ticket they pull over . . . "Hey, officer, yes, glad to be of help . . . cheerio!" Niggers got to be talkin' 'bout, "I am reaching into my pocket for my license, 'cause I don't want to be no motherfuckin' accident."

More often, Pryor stays on a lighter level and highlights the disparity between the usually controlled behavior of whites and the more robust and spontaneous interactions of blacks. A black family's rowdy table manners, for instance, is contrasted with the exaggeratedly stilted etiquette of a sedate white family:

Pass the potatoes . . . thank you, darling. Can I have a bit of that sauce? How are the kids coming along with their studies? Think we'll be having sexual intercourse this evening? We're not, oh, what the heck.

This album also contains the best recorded performance (video or audio) of Pryor's legendary "Dracula" and "Wino and Junkie" routines as well as many of the signature one-line quips and observations that became code words to his admirers. Two of the most famous are a man's response to a woman's claim that she can't have sex because of her period ("Bitch, you goin' bleed to death") and another man's desperate plea when he is unable to get aroused ("Oh, God! Lord, don't let her know . . . just let it stay heavy if not hard"). Others range from the comparatively innocent, "Better lay off that narcotic, nigger, that shit done made you null and void" or "Could you exorcize this motherfucker to Cleveland or some place," to the more profane, "This bitch was fine, pops. I ain' lyin'. Bitch was so fine, I wanted to suck her daddy's dick."

These routines showcased Pryor's range and, perhaps, explained his growing popularity among white audiences. He often focused on social issues reflecting African-Americans' inequitable treatment, but he did not avoid touchy issues within the black community. Both his fearlessness and the ecumenical nature of his humor were demonstrated, for example, by a comment about interracial relationships that was greeted by boos and catcalls and nearly caused his audience to turn on him:

Don't ever marry a white woman in California. A lot of you sisters probably sayin', "Don't marry a white woman anywhere, nigger. Shit! Why should you be happy?" . . . Sisters look at you like you killed your momma when you go out with a white woman. And you can't laugh that shit off, either.

Aware of the limits to which he could push the crowd, even if he did not always confine himself to them, Pryor deftly acknowledged that some of his material might be stretching the boundaries of good taste for even an admiring audience: "I see some older people in the audience look at me and say, 'Uh-uh-uh, boy, you ought to be shame of yo'self.'"

A year later, on the . . . *Is It Something I Said?* album, Pryor continued his comic exploration of the differences between black and white culture and social customs. One bit begins with: "White folks date different than we do" and proceeds as Pryor satirizes whites' pretended disinterest in sex ("Good night, dear . . . been a pleasure being with you") and blacks' obsession with it ("Nigger spend thirty-four dollars . . . somebody givin' up somethin'"). Another monologue compares white churches, which are "too scary" and have "pictures of Jesus hanging around lookin' at your ass," with a black church in which people "get down" and the preacher's text is "The Book of Wonder," which turns out to be the lyrics of Stevie Wonder's "Living for the City."

This album, however, contains more pointed racial satire than his previous records. Pryor opens with: "Good God, boy, a lot of niggers here today. . . . Some white folks, too. Look a here! You motherfuckers come in bunch. 'Stick with me. Don't worry about a thing. Just come on.' Shortage of white people lately. I don't seen no whites folks no more. Yall stop fucking?" On the trend of whites adopting Vietnamese children, Pryor remarks, "People in Mississippi, white folks in Georgia . . . adoptin' babies. Shit goin' last for about a year. Then that racism goin' come out. 'Goddamn! What the hell we got here, Margo? Ain't his eyes ever goin' round out? Look like one of the neighborhood coons.'" And, on the influx of Vietnamese in general: "We the motherfuckers got to give up the jobs for 'em. . . . Got all the Vietnamese in the Army camps and shit, takin' tests and stuff, learnin' how to say 'nigger'—so they can be good citizens." In a routine about the courts, Pryor remarks, "I went to jail for income tax evasion, right, you know I didn't know a motherfuckin' thing about no taxes. I told the judge, said, 'Your honor, I forgot, you know.' He said, 'You-remember-next-year, nigger.' . . . They give niggers time like it's lunch down there. You go down there lookin' for justice, that's what you find, *just us!*" [25]

As in most of his performances, the comedy on the album is wide-ranging, with Pryor caustically launching into subjects as varied as the sexual contretemps between men and women, jail, President Nixon, and the curious turns of a man's ego when his woman leaves him. Moreover, balancing the numerous urban street types that dominated his black characters, Pryor introduces his down-home raconteur, Mudbone, whose oblique satire and rambling riffs about the old days allowed Pryor to bolster his performances with examples of traditional folktales and rural wit.

With these mid-seventies albums, Pryor had more or less set the perimeters of his humor and won over a hard-core African-American following as well as a scattering of hip, young white devotees. His status as a cult star was affirmed by an invitation to appear as guest host on *Saturday Night Live* in December 1975. With the 1976 release of a new album, *Bicentennial Nigger*, and the movie *Silver Streak* (in which Pryor co-starred with Gene Wilder and stole the film), and the debut of his own television show in 1977, Pryor was fast becoming a cross-over star.

Still, there was resistance in some quarters. It is considered a classic now, but *The Richard Pryor Show* lasted less than two months (September to October 1977) on television. Besides its mediocre ratings, NBC honchos were rankled by its blunt, irreverent satire, and when Pryor resisted moderating his approach, the show's fate was sealed. During the same period, in addition to Redd Foxx in *Sanford and Son*, the black sitcoms *What's Happening!!* (ABC, 1976–79), *The Jeffersons* (CBS, 1975–85) with Sherman Hemsley, and *Good Times* (CBS, 1974–79) with Jimmy Walker were thriving. Each, in its own way, spotlighted the more acceptable ethnic humor that Flip Wilson had popularized on TV. In fact, Walker, with his mugging, physical comedy, and rousing exclamation, "Dyn-o-*mite!*" had become one of the most popular comedians on television. His role as J.J., however, was one of the reasons that some critics labeled the seventies sitcoms "the New Minstrelsy." Only Foxx as Sanford, Hemsley as the feisty but larcenous businessman George Jefferson, and Marla Gibbs as the Jeffersons' caustic housekeeper consistently brought real bite to their roles. None, however, came close to the raucous satire of Pryor's show; it was simply ahead of its time.

Still, by the time *Richard Pryor Live in Concert* (his first filmed concert performance distributed in theatres) was released in 1979, Pryor had not only become one of Hollywood's most sought-after movie stars but was also considered the nation's most creative funnyman. Playwright Neil Simon, for example, called him "the most brilliant comic in America. There's no one funnier or more perceptive." With his ascendancy and exposure, for the first time authentic African-American humor appeared in the mass media.

III

Volatile yet vulnerable, crass but sensitive, streetwise and cocky but somehow still diffident and anxious, Richard Pryor emerged at the right time and brought with him the incredible array of dramatic and comic talent needed fully to introduce and popularize that unique, previously concealed or rejected part of African-American humor that thrived in the lowest, most unassimilated portion of the black community. As Redd Foxx and others have pointed out, before the sixties Pryor would probably have been banned from every club or theatre in America. But America was being coerced into honestly confronting the hypocrisy of its past racial arrangements; the time for the surfacing of black American humor, which had surreptitiously mocked those arrangements since slavery, had arrived. In the end, however, it was Pryor's finely tuned sensibilities and theatrical genius that brought it to the stage and expedited its acceptance.

The content of Pryor's comedy was not new. Perhaps more than any other popular comedian, he depended on perceptions and stories taken from real-life characters and brought to stage practically unaltered. Often, his routines were enriched by black folk humor, for example the tale of the contest between two friends related by Mudbone:

Ah, that nigger could tell lies. That's how we became friends, see. He tell a lie, I tell a lie, see, and we compliment each other's lies.

He make me laugh all day long, bless his soul. He told me this lie one time, told me 'bout the niggers with the big dicks, see. Yall ever heard it? The niggers had the biggest dicks in the world, and they were trying to find a place where they could have their contest, see. And they wasn't no freaks, didn't want everybody lookin'. . . . They was walking around lookin' for a secret place. So they walked across the Golden Gate Bridge and the nigger seen that water and make him want to piss, see. Boy say, "Man, I got to take a leak." He pulled out his thing and was pissing. The other nigger pulled his out, took a piss. One nigger say, "Goddamn! This water cold." The other nigger say, "Yeah, and it's deep, too."

Although amplified by Pryor's perfectly pitched delivery through the character of Mudbone, it is a familiar folk story. Similar tales involve contests where scales are used. One involved Sam, the sweeper in a Southern general store, who after he *outweighs* his white opponents and wins the bet, returns home to his wife with the prize money.

Wife: How'd you win all this money?

Sam: Uh, uh, we had a contest.

Wife: What kinda contest was it?

Sam: It was a duh, uh, uh, a dick-weighing contest.

Wife: You mean you done won all this money showin' yo' dick?

Sam: Uh, I only showed half of it.

As Langston Hughes wrote, "In the category of bawdy joke there are hundreds illustrating the prevalent folk belief in the amorous powers of the Negro male."[26]

Even more than from traditional folklore and folktales, Pryor drew from current street humor and the ordinary folkways and attitudes of the people he grew up with and, later, met in urban nightclubs and bars. Unlike many collectors of black folk humor (who, as mentioned earlier, searched primarily for jokes, tales, and other verbal examples of humor), Pryor was aware that much African-American humor is joke-free, attitudinal, and frequently visual. What he apparently gleaned from his own childhood experience and from observing pimps, con men, hustlers, and other denizens of ghetto clubs and after-hours joints was that their indigenous humor was distinguished from most main-stream comedy by its overriding dependence on style in language (cryptic and often profane) and delivery, as well as its close-to-the-bone adherence to real human situations.

Pryor's comedy, in many ways, reflected the aspect of his father's personality that he most admired. Leroy Pryor, as the comedian said in one routine, was a man who was sometimes "so scary . . . I'd piss on myself" when he called. But Pryor also said, "My father was devastatingly funny and would tell the truth even if you didn't want to hear it." On stage, he illustrated his father's "brutally honest" nature by dramatizing his behavior at Pryor's stepmother's funeral on "one of the coldest days in the history of Peoria." According to Pryor, he said, "It get any colder out here they goin' have to bury the bitch by herself. . . . The *dirt* . . . get to the part with the dirt! Shit it's cold. Yeah, baby, I love you but, shit, it's cold out here." The routine, which is greeted with rolls of laughter from blacks and whites on *Richard Pryor: Live in Concert,* is a representative example of Pryor's humor both in its origin and comic technique. It includes nothing that ordinarily would be considered a joke. Instead, Pryor realistically reenacts an actual incident that from a polite, mainstream perspective was probably perceived as humorous because it was shocking and, for many blacks, was funny because it truthfully mirrored an amusing and offbeat but nevertheless common, down-to-earth aspect of black lower-class life. "I be listening to dudes talking, all over," Pryor said, "in whorehouses and places. Everybody be talking the same kind of talk. No matter what city you go to, it's the same feeling, a universal feeling. That's what they be laughing at, themselves. They see themselves when I do a character."[27]

The mannerisms and expressions of common black folk provided the material for most of his routines after 1971. Bubba (a dude who "could not tell a joke" but was so intimidating that everyone laughed anyway) and Oilwell ("I don't take no ass whuppin's, and don't know nothin' about being unconscious . . . you got to *kiilll* me") were based on "Bad Nigger" types from his childhood. Besides his father, Pryor's grandmother was a rich comic source. She was realistically portrayed as the kind of harsh but loving matriarch who was the cornerstone of many African-American families in the fifties and sixties; she inspired Pryor's brilliant bit about being punished as a child:

My grandmother is the lady used to discipline me, you know, beat my ass. Anyone here remember them switches? Right, you used to have to get 'em off the tree yourself and take the leaves, like that. I see them trees today, I will kill one of them motherfuckers. . . . My grandmother say, "Boy, go get me somethin' to beat yo' ass with" . . . and you know you couldn't come back with no little switch, right, 'cause if you did she go out and get the tree and beat yo' ass with it. . . . Then, she fix you up, "Come here, baby. Now see, you shouldn't done that, goddamn it. I told ya not to—just sit still, now. And next time you do it, I goin' tear your ass up again."

Another routine documented her initially hysterical reaction at discovering Pryor using cocaine, as well as his panic and her practical folk response:

"Momma, don't do that shit. I'm throwin' the shit out. Sixteen hundred dollars' worth of shit down the drain. . . ." She found out how much it cost, she say, "You dumb motherfucker. You could'a sold that shit back to the man you bought it from. I told you that shit make you ignorant."

Other tales of the peripheral inhabitants of the ghetto netherworld were similarly based on actual interactions or observation. Pryor obviously shaped and embellished the material as necessary, but as Bill Cosby noted, "Richard Pryor is the only comedian that I know of today who has captured the total character of the ghetto." His routines sometimes verged on dramatic readings of real ghetto behavior, exposing its follies and the stoic acceptance of day-to-day inequities and hardships; humor emerged from the pathos, tensions, and subtle ironies attending that behavior.[28]

Given that he drew his comedy from the largely untapped reservoir of African-American street humor familiar to most blacks, Pryor's genius did not reside so much in the creation of his material as in its presentation. By the end of the seventies, he was at the top of his form. He had refined his physical gestures and facial expressions so much that he could indicate a shift in character or mood without saying a word; mime had become an essential part of his comic repertoire. "I couldn't do it just by doing the words of the person," he told James McPherson. "I have to *be* that person. I *see* that man in my mind and go with him." He also had begun amplifying his routines by more frequently giving voices to animals and inanimate objects, a tack that enriched his performances with a resonance that transcended race. The theatrical style was novel to many non-blacks and they were able more easily to appreciate and identify with his less direct expression of ethnicity. Many African-Americans were aware, however, that the technique was part of a black vocal style that, on occasion, required that the "voice be used not so much for informational as deliberate, textural purposes." Routines in which dogs, monkeys, pipes, or automobiles spoke in black voices called forth images of antebellum animal tales and the oral techniques of black storytellers or "liars," in whose stories, as Roger D. Abrahams has noted, "voice modifications and imitations become comic devices to build up dramatic interest."[29]

By this time, Pryor's narrative voice had lost all traces of hesitancy. In his "Killing My Car" routine, for example, in a matter of seconds he moves back and forth from his own narrative voice to anthropomorphic portrayal of various inanimate objects without the slightest hitch:

> It seemed fair to kill my car to me, right, 'cause my wife was goin' leave my ass, you know. I say, "Not in this motherfucker you ain't. Uh-uh, no Lawd . . . if you leave me you be drivin' them Hush Puppies you got on. 'Cause I'm gone kill this motherfucker here." And I had one of them big ole magnums. You know that noise they make when you shoot somethin'. I shot it, "Phew-whoom!" Tire say, "Aahhh-aaahhhh." It got good to me, I shot another one, "Bwoooom! . . . Uuhhh-aaahhhhh." And that vodka I was drinkin' said, "Go head, shoot somethin' else." I shot the motor, motor fell out the motherfucker, right. The motor say, "Fuck it!" Then the police came . . . I went into the house. Cause they got magnums, too. And they don't shoot cars, they shoot nig-*gars*.

By 1978, Pryor had put every facet of his stage act together. He had also proven himself as an actor. In 1976, besides *Silver Streak*, he had supporting roles in *Car Wash* and *The Bingo Long Traveling All-Stars and Motor Kings*. Those films were followed by starring roles in *Which Way Is Up?* (1977), *Greased Lightning* (1977), *Blue Collar* (1978), *California Suite* (1978) and *The Wiz* (1978). With his status as a bankable Hollywood draw firmly in place, he again turned to the concert stage. "I had a chance to do what I really love," he told *Rolling Stone* reporter David Felton. "I just had to go out and work, that's all I know, and get in touch with my people again." After about four months of preparation, he was on the road again. The 1978 tour featured his most polished work to date; excerpts from the concerts were released on the album *Wanted, Richard Pryor Live and In Concert* (1979). More significantly, since Pryor was increasingly using his acting ability and emphasizing visual embodiment of his characters to maximize the comic effect, he agreed to allow a concert to be filmed for the first time since 1971. In January 1979, at the Terrace Theatre in Long Beach, California, the performance that would be released as *Richard Pryor: Live in Concert* (1979) was filmed. In the estimate of many critics, it was Pryor's finest comedy performance.

Certainly, that movie presents a smoother, more expansive and poised Richard Pryor than had been seen or heard earlier in the decade. Most noticeably, he ventures more into mime and vocal impersonation of animals, objects, even parts of his own body. In fact, although no written account can convey the near-magical physical transformations that enhanced Pryor's mimicry, those theatrical vignettes produced some of the movie's most remarkable moments.

In his account of hunting with his father as a child, for example, he recreates the sounds and atmosphere of the woods with eerie accuracy and, in one of the film's many high points, brilliantly mimics the tremulous anxiety of a deer drinking water. Comic portraits of his squirrel monkeys, his guard dogs, and his next-door neighbor's vicious German shepherd are just as arresting. In each instance, Pryor not only gives voice to the animals but also assumes their physical appearance. Pryor's face, for example, melts into an expression of concern and confusion when, as the German shepherd, he looks up and says, "What'sa matter, Rich?" but quickly switches to an expression of inconsolable grief when, as himself, he mutters, "My monkeys died." He effortlessly alternates viewpoints:

> "Say what! Your monkeys died. Ain't that a bitch. You mean the monkeys used to be in the trees, they *died?*"
> Say, "Yeah, they died."
> Say, "Shit . . . I was goin' eat them, too. Don't linger on that shit too long, you know—it'a fuck wit'ya."
> Say, "I'll try."
> "Yeah, you take care."
> Then he went back and jumped over the fence and just before he jumped, he looked back at me and said, "Now, you know I'm goin' be chasin' you again tomorrow."

The most riveting and funny anthropomorphic bit in the performance, however, focuses on an unlikely subject for a comedy routine —the heart attack Pryor had experienced some years earlier. Again, depicting both his own actions and comments as well as those of a vindictive heart speaking in the fierce, irreverent tones of a ghetto authority figure, Pryor produced a comic mini-drama that far exceeded the boundaries of ordinary stage comedy.

I was walkin' in the front yard, I was just walkin' along and somethin' say:

"Don't breathe!"

[looking from side to side and pressing his fist into his chest] "Huh?"

Say "You heard me, motherfucker, I said don't *breathe!*"

[wincing in pain as he twists his fist into his chest] "Okay, I-won't-breathe-I-won't-breathe-I-won't breathe."

"Then shut the fuck *up!*"

"Okay, okay, I'll shut up. Don't-kill-me-don't-kill-me-don't-kill-me . . ."

"Get on one knee and *prove it!*"

Dropping to one knee, Pryor shrieks, "I'm-on-one-knee-I'm-on-one-knee, don't-kill-me-don't-kill-me . . ." The relentless interchange continues as Pryor, writhing and gasping for air after collapsing on the stage, is excoriated for "eatin' all that *pork*" and ignoring the fact that black people are susceptible to high blood pressure.

Then Pryor sits up, shifting back to his normal voice: "You be thinkin' about shit like that when you think you gonna die. . . . You put in an emergency call to God, too, right?" After Pryor reenacts an abortive call to God, the voice of his heart intrudes again: "Was you tryin' to talk to God behind my back?" When Pryor nervously shakes his head and mumbles, "No, I wasn't," he is flung back down on the stage as his heart bellows, "You's a lyin' mother*fucker!* You was." The routine concludes with: "I woke up in a ambulance, right? And there wasn't nothin' but white people starin' at me. I say, 'Ain't this a bitch. I done died and wound up in the wrong motherfuckin' heaven. Now, I gotta listen to Lawrence Welk the rest of my days.' "

This is classic Pryor, a perfect illustration of his taking the audience to the "peak of emotion" and topping it off with "a nice laugh."

The concert marked a departure in that Pryor avoided most of the

ghetto street types that had peopled his earlier work. Instead, he focused primarily on personal experiences—his parents, children, and
friends, even his pets and health. Later, he said he had been "purging"
himself, "facing them demons and wiping 'em out."[30]

Still, there were occasional striking references to differences between
black and white culture, as in the concluding line of the heart attack
routine or another bit that contrasted racial behavior at funerals or his
comment about the Doberman pinschers policemen sometimes use:
"They fast, too. . . . They catch the average white boy." Some of the
most caustic material surfaced during the opening, when Pryor toyed
with the audience, saying, "The fun part for me is when white people
come back after intermission and find out niggers done stole their
seats." Here Pryor switched to the effete, nasal voice he adopted for
his portrayals of middle-class whites: "Uh, uh, weren't we sitting here,
dear?" "Yes, we were sitting right there." Then, shifting to a deeper,
more threatening tone: "Well, you ain't sittin' here *now*, motherfucker!" A later bit about the Los Angeles police accidentally killing
a black man with their "choke hold" was just as biting: "Ah, shit, he
broke. Can you break a nigger? Is it okay? Let's check the manual. . . .
Yep, page eight, you can break a nigger. Right there, see."

Overall, however, the audience enjoyed a mellower, more subtle
Pryor. He seemed less intent on shocking or focusing on racial contrasts
and more concerned with including blacks and whites in the humor—
finding a common ground. Finally, although the concert was steeped in
genuine African-American humor and delivered in a predominantly
black voice, it was a concert that only Richard Pryor with his acting
ability and uncanny knack for mimicry and mime could have successfully performed. He had taken the humor of the streets, black America's
presumedly "low" comedy—with much of its vulgarity, profanity, explicit sexuality, and unvarnished satirical perception—and, without losing any of its intensity, turned it into high art. Quips and perceptions
that had been brought to the stage almost unaltered and presented with
a defiant attitude at the beginning of the decade were now delivered
with less overt hostility. He had devised a tactic that allowed him both
to express the satirical thrust of black street humor and to expose
the human ironies and frailties that lay beneath it. His genius was to
demonstrate its universality.

With *Live in Concert*, in fact, he had shown that nearly undiluted
African-American street humor—much of it expressed in vernacular
language and little of it cloaked by middle-class propriety—could ap-

peal to all audiences, regardless of race. Pryor had tapped the broader, human source of his ethnic comedy, and even mainstream critics raved. *Newsweek* called the concert "the peak of Pryor's art . . . one of the funniest movies ever made." A critic for *The New York Times* wrote: "Prowling the stage impishly, slipping effortlessly from one hilarious impersonation to the next, [Pryor] radiates an intensity that isn't often visible in even his very best feature-length acting performances." David Felton wrote in *Rolling Stone* that, while he regretted the absence of familiar characters such as Pryor's "preachers, drunks and junkies, and . . . Mudbone," the "performance is more unified and more personal. . . . He doesn't just tell us about the stuff, like most comedians, telling jokes. He brings it to life and exposes its soul." And *New Yorker* critic Pauline Kael declared the film "a consummation of his years as an entertainer . . . one of the greatest performances we'd ever seen or ever would see."[31]

Pryor's breakthrough and increased appeal to mainstream white audiences partially derived from the selection of material for the *Live* concert. Focus on his personal life (family and friends, celebrities and show business associates) and the consequent absence of characters unique to ghetto street life allowed non-blacks to identify more readily with the humor. Moreover, as the concert demonstrated, Pryor's brutally honest presentation of African-American humor extended beyond authentic portrayal of blacks' language, candid engagement of taboo subjects such as sex, and emphasis of African-Americans' comic view of whites; it also exposed blacks' comic view of themselves. Like Zora Neale Hurston, Pryor was aware of the many-faceted nature of genuine black humor and did not insist that it always reflected positive race consciousness; his scathing wit lampooned mainstream arrogance, insecurities, and racism, but also attacked the infirmities and pretenses of black life.

Pryor's cockiness and assertiveness was balanced by an introspection and vulnerability that permitted him to jest not only about the less manly or commendable aspects of his own personality but also about the less militant or exemplary aspects of black life in general. Earlier quips such as, "I seen't a Chinese man have two sticks like this and a bowl of food, didn't drop a got-damn speck. Nigger lose three pounds of food wid' a knife and fork"; the warning a black character gives to extraterrestrial beings when they arrive on earth ("Better get yo' ass away from 'round here, you done landed on Mr. Gilmore's property"); or his "Why should you be happy" jibe regarding relationships with white women reflected his willingness to satirize blacks. In the *Live* concert, although he echoed earlier tales of blacks' physical and sexual prowess, he undercut those rigid macho posturings with less guarded admissions. At one point he said, "If somebody pulled a knife on you, and you can't pull out nothin' but a hand with some skin on it, your intelligence ought'a tell you to—*run!* . . . and teach yo' old lady how to run so you don't have to go back after her ass." After describing how some blacks boast, "I can fuck eight, nine hours, Jack," he quipped, "You some lyin' motherfuckers. . . . I can make love for about *three minutes.* I do about three minutes of serious fuckin', then I need eight hours' sleep . . . and a bowl of Wheaties." His honest display of vulnerability transcended race, permitting nearly everyone to identify with him.

Such middle-class white Americans as an editor at a Manhattan cocktail party and a salesman at a Youngstown, Ohio, motel bar talked about his "ability to strip away pretense" and "the way he cuts right through the bullshit to make you laugh at yourself." A hip, young female bartender from Manhattan said, "He was the first black comedian doing ethnic material that I had ever been exposed to. Even though some people thought they were obscene, we were including Pryor one-liners in almost every conversation." And a prim Staten Island housewife commented: "We had all listened to Bill Cosby growing up, but that was extremely tame and could be listened to in your mother's house with the doors open. Then along came Pryor, speaking the way we only spoke among ourselves and about things we wouldn't dare. . . . His jokes were risqué and a welcome break from the silliness of George Carlin and Robert Klein. Pryor was outrageous and angry and willing to put himself into his material, often to the extent of being the butt of the joke."[32]

Pryor gave substance to types that were outcasts even in the ghetto. And despite the comical cast that he often gave them, overall there was an aura of truth about his characters. It was not accidental. "People react because they know exactly what I mean," he said in one interview. "Art is the ability to tell the truth, especially about oneself." On another occasion, he added, "I think there's a thin line between being a Tom on them people and seeing them as human beings. When I do the people I have to do it true. If I can't do it, I'll stop right in the middle rather than pervert it and turn it into Tomism. There's a thin line between to laugh *with* and to laugh *at.*" Pryor rarely crossed that line. Consequently, for many blacks, his humor afforded a cathartic experience, a public purging of embarrassments and frustrations built up over decades of concealing real attitudes and cultural preferences, suppressing customs that largely defined existence for them. For those African-Americans who, like myself, were of his generation, Pryor's exuberant portrayal of humorous but real black folks inspired a release similar to what Flip Wilson must have felt when he was struck by the revelation that "Niggers is fun!"[33]

Many younger blacks, even those from middle-class backgrounds, had similar reactions. In *If I Stop I'll Die*, Dennis Williams, who attended college in the seventies, wrote, "It gave brothers like me who had done little time in the streets a new, hip way of expressing ourselves, and a license to do so. . . . Triumph, struggle, despair? It was all there. . . . He was telling 'them' off and taking them to school even as he taught and entertained us. And he didn't give a damn what anybody thought."[34]

But Pryor's comedy went beyond merely giving substance and external validation to the attitudes and perceptions of ghetto types. Ultimately, it humanized them, made them as memorable and indelible as the creations of some of our best novelists. As Steve Allen points out, there is a sense in which "Pryor is much closer to literature than to traditional nightclub or concert comedy." And because of his irreverent approach, the literature that his comedy most closely mirrors is that found in black humor fiction by writers like John Barth, Charles Wright, Thomas Berger, Bruce Jay Friedman, and Ishmael Reed—fiction that, according to one analyst, "seems to have little respect for the values and patterns of thought, feeling, and behavior that have kept Anglo-American culture stable and effective, have provided a basis of equilibrium for society and the individual."[35]

In fact, Pryor's comic contrasts of black and white behavior directly lampooned the hypocrisy and pretense of many Anglo-American social and cultural patterns and often depicted them as fatuous and obtuse. Early quips (such as "If my hair was straight, then whitey'd dig me. So I got a process . . . *wrong!*") humorously alluded to a societal alienation and identity crisis that is common in black humor as a literary genre and, more specifically, echoed the same comically abortive effort to be accepted in America's "Great Society" that Charles Wright explored in *The Wig*. Pryor's "Wino and Junkie" routine, especially the wino's poignant concluding rejoinder ("You don't know how to deal with the white man, that's yo' problem. I know how to deal with 'em. . . . That's why I'm in the position I'm in today"), also clearly suggests the darker undertones and ironies, the stultifying dilemmas that connect his comedy to the genre of black humor.

That connection, however, seemingly derived more from Pryor's dogged presentation of authentic black folk and street humor than from any effort to simulate literary fabulists. As mentioned earlier, there are numerous similarities between the circumstances that inspired literary black humor (alienation from an irrational, impersonal society) and those that inspired much African-American humor (ostracism from mainstream society and its irrational racial arrangements). But not all African-American humor is so pessimistic or angst-ridden. Compared to the typical hero in black humor fiction, who finds that his "suffering is immedicable" and whose "attempt to locate an alternative to his condition only confronts him more starkly with the formlessness responsible for it," blacks could more easily identify the cause of their ostracism. So while there are many examples of African-American humor in which the joke turns on a stoic acceptance of the seemingly irresolvable nature of racism ("Where do black folks hang out . . . ?"), many others either aggressively pinpoint the source (non-blacks) and find comic relief in ridiculing it or, avoiding the issue altogether, turn to non-racial themes. Pryor reflected these less torturous aspects of African-American comedy just as authentically.[36]

In fact, in many ways, Pryor's comic repertoire comprised a practical inventory of those central elements that, taken together, distinguish African-American humor from other ethnic varieties. One such element is the frequently off-color vernacular speech of black common folks. By revealing its underlying meaning, emphasizing its implicit emotive significance, Pryor transformed it from mere vulgarity to a resonant expression of a world view that is insistently down-to-earth and bluntly realistic. His language mirrored the explicit obscenity and hyperbole of urban street folks and, alternately, the subtle, guileful misdirection of rural blacks. In each instance, his voice was perfectly pitched, laden with satiric undertones and defiance.

Naturally, his approach was scorned by some. But Pryor insisted, "There is no such thing as profanity in what I do. I talk to people in their own words." Still—as social scientists William Labov, Paul Cohen, Clarence Robins, and John Lewis point out in "Toasts," a linguistic study of street lore—African-American street vernacular defies "the values of middle-class society in respect to language: in [its] use of taboo words and . . . scorn for sentimental and abstract verbiage." It does not, however, "reject the esthetic values of poetry," and others looked beyond the surface vulgarity. The critic Pauline Kael hailed Pryor as a "master of lyrical obscenity."[37]

In addition, Pryor's performances were enhanced by his body language. By insinuating the wary, slump-shouldered, but stoic posture of rural types or the hip, swaggering, crotch-grabbing, head-bopping urban black persona into the public forum without ridicule or condescension, Pryor forced recognition of African-American types that society had either burlesqued or vigorously spurned.

Aside from the linguistic and physical mannerisms that defined his comic approach, Pryor, more than any previous comic, mirrored the full range of African-American humor. Dick Gregory had exposed the wit and acerbic social commentary that often infuses black humor. Bill Cosby had advanced the art of storytelling or "lying" in his act. And while introducing upbeat comic characters steeped in black street lore, Flip Wilson had revealed not only blacks' pride in their folkways but also the exuberance and joy of much black humor. Pryor incorporated all of these attributes and, thereby, completely unmasked the complex matrix of pride, self-mockery, blunt confrontation of reality, double-edged irony, satiric wit, assertive defiance, poetic obscenity, and verbal acuity that finally define the elusive entity that may be called African-American humor.

It was nothing short of revolutionary. Pryor had finally integrated style and substance. He was the first African-American stand-up comedian to speak candidly and successfully to integrated audiences the way black people joked among themselves when most critical of America.

It was a revolution that perhaps only Pryor, with his unusual background and astonishing array of dramatic and comic skills could have accomplished. For although African-Americans' folk humor is essentially shaped by their African heritage and a shared ironic vision derived from their American experience, its expressive forms are diverse. By enlivening all of those voices—from the self-effacing trickery of the slave John, to the articulate, satiric wit of Dick Gregory, to the desecratory hyperbole of the legendary Shine—Pryor asserted himself as an authentic embodiment of the black comic spirit. Only Bert Williams before him (in a restricted, oblique manner) had neared such a consummate representation of African-American humor. If Bert Williams was, as some claim, the finest American comedian of his time, then Pryor had inherited that mantle. Without doubt, he changed America's attitude about black folk humor, lifting it from obscurity and establishing it as a preeminent form of humorous expression.

By the eighties, the American comedy scene was undergoing a period of tremendous expansion. The popularity of stand-up comedy had reached new heights, and comedy clubs were surfacing not only in New York, Los Angeles, and other large cities, but also in small towns across the country. Pryor's ascendancy, which had effected a literal emancipation of African-American humor, combined with the flood of new outlets for performers, opened opportunities for a raft of new, young talents. Although Pryor starred in two more excellent concert films—*Live on Sunset Strip* (1982) and *Here and Now* (1983)—and several less commendable standard movies, his career declined as the result of a near-fatal accident and failing health. His influence, however, as attested by the comic stars who gathered for a September 1991 tribute, was firmly entrenched.

Eddie Murphy was the first of the bright young wits to emerge. In 1982 one journalist reported: "Not since Richard Pryor has a black comic played so dauntlessly—and so adroitly—with racial, and racist, stereotypes." By 1985, along with Pryor and Bill Cosby, he had become one of America's leading cross-over stars. In fact, by age twenty-three Murphy had assumed Pryor's spot as the top black comic. *Newsweek* called him the "hottest star in the Hollywood heavens, the closest anybody gets to a sure thing in box-office terms." Typically, he was unreserved in his praise of Pryor. In his first filmed concert, *Delirious* (1983, HBO), he demonstrated how much Pyor had affected his comic style. The performance was liberally diced with material that recalled earlier Pryor routines.[38]

A bit about *The Amityville Horror* in which Murphy contrasts the cinema image of whites' apparent obliviousness to clear warnings of imminent danger with blacks' instant recognition, for example, is but a heartbeat away from Pryor's lampooning of *The Exorcist*. Murphy also occasionally lapses into a Pryor-like nasal impersonation of an average American white man. Still, he is much more than a Pryor clone in the film. His own brand of cocksure, irreverent comedy is also evident. A master at comic mimicry, he burlesques such celebrities as Bill Cosby, Mr. T, Elvis Presley, James Brown, Michael Jackson, and Stevie Wonder with caricatures that, though often cruel (Luther Van Dross, for

instance, is described as a "big Kentucky Fried Chicken–eatin' motherfucker"), are almost unerringly accurate as impersonations. And a
monologue about his father conveys an uproarious sense of the distinctive attributes of the working-class black family.

The young Murphy did not display the subtly textured resonance
of Pryor's humor, but, perhaps, that was asking too much. Murphy
represented a new, youthful African-American comic voice—one inspired by the audaciousness of Shine but unapprised of the subtle
manipulation of tricksters like John the slave. And if he sometimes
teetered on the brink of excess—stentorian and superficial profanity,
crass indulgence in bravado, homophobia, and sexism—his usually outrageous parodies were often perfectly conceived and executed.

Many characters that he introduced on *Saturday Night Live* during
his 1981–84 stint remain memorable. Among them were Mr. Robinson
(a takeoff on the *Mister Rogers' Neighborhood* children's show), Tyrone
Green (a racist black author), and Velvet Jones, the pimp who hawked
his book *How to Be a Ho:* "Are you a female high-school dropout
between the ages of sixteen and twenty-five? Are you tired o' lying
around in bed all day with nothin' to do. Well, you need never get up
again, because in six short weeks I can train you to be a high-payin' ho.
. . . Fifteen hundred dollars a week without ever leavin' the comforts of
yo' own bedroom." Some bits also boldly touched on political issues
that most comics avoided. In one, imitating Jesse Jackson, Murphy
appeared with a doo-wop backup group and couched an apology to
Jews in the song, "Don't Let Me Down, Hymie Town":

I was yo' one and only
Until I read the news.
Now, I'm sad and lonely,
Since I put down the Jews.
We have so much in common,
'Cause we both been so oppressed.
We both have big noses,
And gold chains on our chests.

Don't let me down
(I'm begging you, please).
Don't let me down
(I'm down on my knees).
Don't let me down, Hymie Town.

While not exactly traditional political satire, the routine demonstrated Murphy's willingness to lampoon any individual or group.

Murphy's boyish charm and audacious approach, as affirmed by the television comedy special *A Laugh, A Tear*, made him the "comedian of the eighties." On television and in a series of movies—including *48 Hours* (1982), *Trading Places* (1983), *Beverly Hills Cop* (1984), *Raw* (1987), *Beverly Hills Cop II* (1987), and *Harlem Nights* (1989)—he flaunted an irrepressible, macho comic image that reflected the brazen impiousness of a brash, hip-hop culture epitomized by "gangsta" rappers who, as Henry Louis Gates has said, "take the white Western culture's worst fear of black men and make a game of it."[39]

The eighties also saw the rise of Whoopi Goldberg, a comedienne whose television special *Fontaine . . . Why Am I Straight?* presented an array of characters that subtly fused comedy and drama. An Oscar-winning actress as well as a stand-up comic, Goldberg demonstrated a comic range that rivaled Pryor's in a riveting performance featuring such characters as the intellectual junkie Fontaine, a naive West Indian maid, and a black child who fantasizes about having straight hair. In that special, Goldberg proved that she could be as blasphemous as Murphy, but her humor spotlighted social and political satire as well as straightout parody.

Among others who made their marks in the eighties and early nineties were Arsenio Hall, Robert Townsend, Marsha Warfield, Keenan Ivory Wayans, George Wallace, Chris Rock, Sinbad, Damon Wayans, and Martin Lawrence. The extraordinary range represented by these comics was matched by such theatrical presentations as Joseph Papp's production of *The Colored Museum* (1985) and Lincoln Center's presentation of Langston Hughes and Zora Neale Hurston's *Mule Bone* (1991) and the television debut of shows ranging from the subtle humor of *Frank's Place* (CBS, 1987–88) and *The Cosby Show* (CBS, 1984–91) to the outrageous parody of *In Living Color* (Fox, 1990) or the in-your-face mayhem of Russell Simmons's *Def Comedy Jam* (HBO, 1992).

Pryor's ground-breaking unveiling of genuine African-American folk humor had led to an explosion of more authentic black comedy in nearly every media outlet. By the nineties, it was not unusual to see guests on *The Arsenio Hall Show* engaging in verbal banter, even outright signifying, that two decades ago might have only been heard at black social gatherings. On one show, for instance, Will Smith (star of *The Fresh Prince of Bel Air*, NBC, 1990) and Hall engaged in a lively round of mother-rhyming at another comic's expense:

Smith: His momma's so dumb she tried to cook a TV dinner on the television set . . . tried to change channels.

Hall: I saw his momma at Super Cuts, and when she sat down get a haircut she opened her shirt.

Smith: His momma so bald, when she go to sleep at night her head keep slippin' off the pillow.

On a less frivolous note, *In Living Color* frequently featured parodies and satirical routines with a more cutting edge. The show's brightest comic, Damon Wayans, for instance, portrayed a homeless but militant derelict who in one skit aggressively imposes himself on middle-class society. When he appears at an Army recruiting center in his usual slovenly and disheveled state and announces, "I'm here to be all I can be," the staff scatter in disgust. As the brash and pugnacious black clown Homey, Wayans regularly ridiculed middle-class ideals and satirized the image of a cheerful, kindly clown. During a puppet show in one episode, Homey berates a figure named Mr. Establishment for "trying to hold me down and structure society so Homey ends up in jail." In another skit, he allows some ad men to think he has abandoned his militancy and joined the establishment—until he gets the opportunity to see *The Man*. Then, shouting "You can't buy Homey," he proceeds to attack him verbally and physically.

African-American humor had arrived in mainstream America not only in force but also with a healthy variety that reflected nearly all of its many facets. In addition to entertainment, for the observant it offered what George Meredith called "thoughtful laughter" and provided a needed and valuable insight. The comic spirit, Meredith wrote in "An Essay on Comedy," lingers "overhead," and when it sees mankind "self-deceived, or hoodwinked, given to run riot in idolatries, drifting into vanities, congregating in absurdities, planning short-sightedly, plotting dementedly . . . whenever they offend sound reason, fair justice; are false in humility or mined with conceit [it] casts an oblique light on them, followed by volleys of silvery laughter."[40]

The laughter that accompanies a similar vision has echoed throughout black life from nearly the inception of slavery, through Washington Irving's observance of "obstreperous peals of broad-mouthed laughter" in the nineteenth century, and on to the present. But, misconstrued or ignored, it was either labeled as naive, Sambo-like Tom-foolery or silenced and relegated to the society's darkest and most inconspicuous corners. By the eighties, displayed center stage and often in prime time without distortion, its meaning had become obvious to nearly everyone.

Since African-Americans have been inescapably engaged with the absurdity of America's racial arrangements for centuries, survival and sanity dictated that they adopt a comic view of society. As Ralph Ellison put it, because of "knowing the reality of a society that had the power to treat you as though you were actually inferior, but knowing within yourself that you were not, you were thrown into a position in which you were either going to develop a sense of humor or . . . die of frustration, of a sense of the irrational."[41]

With the growing popularity of comedy in general, that initially enforced viewpoint, along with other satirical perspectives, is being more widely disseminated. Ultimately, the skepticism and self-scrutiny implicit in embracing of the comic vision may help to heal the wounds of a nation groomed on racism, sexism, and the easy acceptance of denigrative stereotypes—those offenses to "sound reason" and "fair justice" that Meredith mentions. The critic Wylie Sypher suggests as much: "The perception of the self as comic touches the quick; and honest self-inspection must bring a sense of the comical. This kind of awareness is an initiation into the civilized condition; it lightens the burden of selfishness, cools the heat of the ego, makes us impressionable by others." And Meredith was as optimistic when he wrote that comedy is the "ultimate civilizer."[42]

Comedy, of course, can be distorted; when used to deny others' humanity or to inflate and justify our own vanities, it belies the lofty ideals of the comic spirit, which is derived from common-sense perception and honest engagement of reality. The foregoing survey has offered numerous examples of humor being put to less laudable purposes. The key lies with individuals who are able to laugh at *themselves* as well as others. "No society is in good health without laughing at itself quietly and privately," an astute critic wrote. "No character is sound without self-scrutiny." And the comic vision assures that those who embrace it maintain vigilance on themselves even as they satirize the hypocrisy and follies of others.[43]

Most African-Americans, as W. E. B. Du Bois and Ellison noted, have been compelled to view themselves through the eyes of others—to engage in intensive, critical self-observation. They have also scrutinized other Americans and examined the contradictions that erode their claims of superiority. Black American humor is finally based on those perceptions. It is the shared ironic vision of a group who, in seeking to establish their place as Americans, have skeptically viewed the gap between appearances and reality and have often found contradiction and absurdity.

Still, categorically defining African-American humor is tricky. As I mentioned at the outset, no one yet has definitively described humor in general. Since black humor is doubly masked—that is, it often pretends to be naive or cloaks its satire in a mask of innocence—it presents an especially knotty problem.

Luigi Pirandello's metaphor of body and shadow looms as the most fitting and enlightening definition. African-Americans have been cast as a shadow-like presence in America since their arrival in the seventeenth century. From a mainstream perspective, they have been insistently portrayed as outsiders attempting to duplicate the customs and behavior of European-Americans and ridiculed for not succeeding. That portrayal not only has surfaced in social theory and conceptual analyses of blacks but also was enforced as social reality and perpetuated by media depictions of cultural icons (for instance, the Negro Caruso, the black Lenny Bruce). Moreover, in a curiously ironic turn, it has surfaced in popular entertainment, where even as non-blacks obviously imitated blacks, they struggled to give the impression that the mimicry was reversed.

Although Thomas D. Rice, one of the earliest Ethiopian delineators, had initially based his act on his impression of a Negro stable hand, he performed a "shadow dance" in which a black child, after emerging from a gunny sack that Rice carried over his shoulder, would imitate his every move. In the early twentieth century, Ted Lewis used a similar act: a black performer would follow him about the stage, duplicating and sometimes comically exaggerating his movements, as he played "Me and My Shadow." In a more sardonic vein, the surfacing of a joke based on the hero of a 1950s radio show, *The Shadow* ("Who knows what evil lurks in the hearts of men? The Shadow *do!*"), in the seventies, reflected America's continued fascination with casting African-Americans in shadow imagery.

The imagery also has folk and literary roots and has spawned serious psychological inquiry. The shadow or double, the critic and humorologist Stanley Trachtenberg contends, "brings to consciousness the unacceptable desires of the ego . . . [and] characteristically takes the form of

opposition between a social self and a repressed instinctual impulse.
. . . The double invites comic treatment." Here again, the similarity
between the shadow image and blacks' assigned social position as both
a comic symbol and an embodiment of America's uninhibited, immoral
instincts reaffirms African-Americans' symbolic status as a shadowy
presence in America.[44]

If we accept African-Americans' role as a shadow presence in
America, along with Pirandello's explanation of the comic interaction
between shadow and body—"it [the shadow] stretches this much or
grows that much fatter, as if to make fun of the body, which all this
time does not concern itself with the shadow or its size"—a striking
and vividly revealing image emerges.[45]

African-American humor can be seen as a shadowy comic vision that
satirizes and humanizes America's main body. As Pirandello suggested,
it variously stretches and turns, creating grotesque apparitions or comic
shades that reflect the perfidy and concealed desires of the mainstream.
Sometimes, as at high noon, it may coincide perfectly with the main
body, demonstrating a convergence of humor and social aspirations. But
usually it veers to this side or the other, twisting wildly and ridiculing a
mainstream that vainly attempts to legitimize its rigid and often absurd
pretense of decorum and propriety. The black humorist's oblique light
is not aimed at mainstream America alone, however; it is also directed
at African-Americans and focuses on their follies as well.

For most of America's past, the main body has been more or less
unmindful of its own comical disfiguration. But from the slaves' animal
tales and Old John trickster tales, Bert Williams's comic pathos, Stepin
Fetchit's willful lethargy, Shine's outrageous exploits, and the rolling
eyes and quick exits of cinema clowns like Mantan Moreland and Willie
Best; through Moms and Pigmeat's ribaldry and down-home spoofing,
Butterbeans and Susie's domestic shadow boxing, the Signifying Monkey's wily bombast, Kingfish's shenanigans, and the innovations of
Rogers, Russell, White, and Foxx; on to Gregory's wit, Cosby's charm,
Wilson's effervescence, Reed and Ellison's pointed satire, and the ge-
nius of Richard Pryor, black America's comic vision has consistently
focused on the mainstream as well as on itself.

In the seventies, released from the dark, inconspicuous corners
where its imagery was hidden and obscured, black humor assumed a
more prominent role in America's social satire. Now, with its newfound
exposure, it is perhaps more bold and belligerent. But not surprising, it
still thrives on irony, as all comedy is inclined to. As Langston Hughes

suggested, humor boomerangs; things are often funny because we don't know we're laughing at ourselves.

African-American humor, after all, still sardonically amplifies the seventies' vernacular joke: "Who knows what evil lurks in the hearts of men?"

Indeed, "the Shadow do" . . . and has for some time.

In order to avoid repetition, the references included here—unless otherwise stipulated—are keyed to the bibliography that follows this section. If an author has more than one source listed in the bibliography, the specific title referred to is indicated.

INTRODUCTION

1. *Tuesday* magazine, September 1966, 4; from Godfrey Cambridge, "A Lot of Laughs, A Lot of Changes," 361.
2. Allen, 221–22.
3. Rubin, 3–15. "The Great American Joke," Rubin's introductory essay to his volume—which contends that the "verbal incongruity" between the formal, higher ideals of democracy and the "informal language of everyday life" and ordinary people is "emblematic of the nature and the problem of democracy"—persuasively documents the importance of humor in understanding the growth and development of American democracy.

PROLOGUE: *Black Humor*

1. Spalding, 428; quotation from Langston Hughes, *Book of Negro Folklore* (Dodd, Mead, 1966). Freud, 181–85. Sypher, 242.
2. Boskin, 66; quotation from Washington Irving, *Knickerbocker's History of New York* (New York: Capricorn Books, 1965), 103–4.
3. Courlander, *Negro Folk Music, U.S.A.*, 81–82; quotation from *New York Times* correspondent Frederick Olmsted, "Journey in the Seaboard Slave States," in *The Slave States Before the Civil War*, edited by Harvey Wish, 114–15.
4. Boskin, 66; quotation from James Fenimore Cooper, *Satanstow: or the Littlepage Manuscripts: A Tale of the Colony* (New York: Burgess, Stringer, 1845), vol. 1, 65, 70.
5. Myrdal, 960–61.
6. Ellison, *Going to the Territory*, 190. Ellison's essay, "The Extravagance of Laughter," is a remarkably textured and probing riff on, among other things, the relationship of black laughter and comedy to self-identity, social roles, and the larger society.
7. Foxx and Miller, 94; quotation from an interview with Sammy Davis, Jr., by the authors.
8. Holland, 44–45.

9. Holland, 52. Schutz, 27, 31.

10. *The New York Times,* Aug. 28, 1979, Virginia Adams, "The Anatomy of a Joke—Studies Take Serious Look."

11. Holland, 66–67.

12. Kittredge, 227; from *Love's Labour Lost,* act V, scene II. Freud, 140–58. In "The Motive of Jokes—Jokes as Social Process," Freud argues that a "joke-work" is dependent on two elements (the comic and the person or thing which is the object of the humor) but that a third element (the listener) may or may not affirm the supposed humor. Holland, 173; Holland writes that "amusement, like beauty, is in the eyes of the beholder."

13. Du Bois, W. E. B., *The Souls of Black Folk,* 45.

14. Holland, 25.

15. Ellison, *Shadow and Act,* 131–32.

16. Ellison, *Shadow and Act,* 276–77.

17. Novak and Waldoks, *The Big Book of Jewish Humor,* xiii, xiv.

18. Brewer, 318–19.

19. Bert A. Williams and Alex Rogers, "Nobody" (Marks Music Corp., *BMI.*

20. Richard Pryor, live performance, Madison Square Garden, circa 1975.

21. Freud, 185; Gregory, *Nigger,* 132.

22. Freud, 111–12. Novak and Waldoks, *The Big Book of Jewish Humor,* xv–xvi. Wertheim, 132; quotation from Martin Grotjahn, *Beyond Laughter* (New York: 1957), 22.

23. Huggins, 257–61.

24. Boskin, 223. Curiously, near the end of his study, Boskin also acknowledges that collections of authentic black humor published in the 1960s had revealed its "complexity and power," even astonishing such humorists as Ogden Nash. This outpouring of previously veiled material, he writes, "echoed as a chorus of militancy in humor. Afro-Americans defied, indeed, taunted whites to enter into the sanctuaries of laughter. . . . People who had once been jived in private now found themselves the butt of jokes from the stage and on television. Jokes that had been confined to the inner reaches of the black community had made their way into white society." (220–21) The existence of this "private" humor from the black community does not significantly alter Boskin's appraisal of the impact of the negative Sambo stereotypes on blacks *before* their discovery in the sixties, however—a point on which this study wholeheartedly disagrees.

25. Spalding, 51; post-slavery tale from *The Atlanta Constitution* (June 13, 1867), 67.

26. Schechter, 33.

27. Boskin, 58, 60. Freud, 184.

28. Baldwin, 68. "American Humor," an address by Ralph Ellison, Oklahoma State University, April 1970.

29. Freud, 195–96.

30. Richard Wright, *Black Boy,* 203–4.

31. John H. Johnson, 42.

32. Hurston, *Mules and Men,* xxiii; from the introduction by Robert E. Hemenway.

33. Cunard, 28; quotation from "Characteristics of Negro Expression" by Zora Neale Hurston (1933).

34. Sartre, 95. Fanon, 116. Du Bois, *The Souls of Black Folk,* 47.

35. Hughes and Bontemps, 71.

36. Moms Mabley, live performance, Apollo Theatre, circa 1962.
37. Philip Sterling, 18; from the introduction, "Escape into Pride and Dignity," by Saunders Redding.
38. Interview with Robert Guillaume in Los Angeles, Jan. 1980.
39. Pasteur and Toldson, 180.
40. Sypher, 65; quotation from Henri Bergson, "Laughter."

PART ONE

CHAPTER ONE: *Slavery*

1. Douglass, *My Bondage and My Freedom*, 252–53. Herskovits, 960; quotation from W. D. Weatherford and Charles S. Johnson, *Race Relations* (1934), 284. *Tuesday* magazine, Sept. 1965, 4; quotation from Godfrey Cambridge, "A Lot of Laughs, A Lot of Changes."
2. Davidson, *Africa: History of a Continent*, 214.
3. Joyner, xxi.
4. Devere and Vollmer, 106.
5. Stuckey, 7.
6. Devere and Vollmer, 103.
7. Klein, 12.
8. Davidson, 217.
9. Davidson, *Africa: History of a Continent*, 222.
10. Weinstein and Gatell, 102–4, from Stanley M. Elkins, "Slavery and the Negro Personality," an excerpt from his book, *Slavery: A Problem in American Institutional and Intellectual Life* (Chicago: University of Chicago Press, 1968), and 135, from "Through the Prism of Folklore: The Black Ethos in Slavery," by Sterling Stuckey, an essay that originally appeared in the *Massachusetts Review*, vol. IX, no. 3 (Summer 1968). The Stuckey essay expounds a view of the still-debated question of how the majority of blacks reacted to the ordeal of slavery that is shared by this author: "Those historians who, for example, point to the dependency complex which slavery engendered in many Afro-Americans offer us an important insight into one of the most harmful effects of that institution upon its victims. That slavery caused not a few bondsmen to question their worth as human beings—this much, I believe, we can posit with certitude. We can also safely assume that such self-doubt would rend one's sense of humanity, establishing an uneasy balance between affirming and negating aspects of one's being. What is at issue is not whether American slavery was harmful to slaves but whether, in their struggle to control self-lacerating tendencies, the scales were tipped toward a despair so consuming that most slaves, in time, became reduced to the level of 'Sambos.' . . . My thesis, which rests on an examination of folk songs and tales, is that slaves were able to fashion a life style and set of values—an ethos—which prevented them from being imprisoned altogether by the definitions which the larger society sought to impose."
11. Genovese, 610; quotation from James Pope-Hennessy, *Sins of the Fathers*, 134–35.
12. Takaki, 118–19. The author provides a revealing discussion of slaveholders' "need for Sambo," their vigorous construction of a "Sambo-making machine," and slaves' resistance to such efforts (117–22). Perhaps not coinci-

dentally, masks were key elements in the religious and celebratory rituals of many West African societies. Masks were often the reliquaries of divine powers and so were constructed in exactingly expressive modes—beautiful, terrifying, or appeasing—in order to attract chosen spirits to inhabit them. Once the spirit was attracted, for the duration of the ceremony, the wearer was thought to be possessed. Speaking with a different voice and moving with a different gait, he or she was thought to have effectively experienced a transformation from the human to the divine. Although several commentators have used the mask metaphor to describe the behavior of African captives during slavery (see Goldstein, 157–58, "Survival Techniques of Black Americans" by W. M. Phillips, Jr., for example), there has been little attempt to establish a psychological connection between the ritual masks of Africa and the adoption of a social mask to survive in the Americas. See Bleakley, Introduction, unpaged, and Huet and Paudrat, 14–17, for more on the functions and meaning of African tribal masks.

13. Nye, 227–28; Takaki, 119.
14. Lester, *To Be a Slave*, 99; quotation from Frederick Olmsted, *Journey in the Seaboard Slave States* (New York: Dix and Edwards, 1856).
15. Sterling, Philip, 157, 207. These tales appear in numerous collections of African-American folktales and vary slightly depending on the collector's source.
16. Folk saying that appears in slightly different variations in numerous sources, including slave songs and blues lyrics. See Lester, *To Be a Slave*, 101, for an example.
17. Ostendorf, 5–6.
18. Stuckey, 24.
19. Meier and Rudwick, 3–4.
20. See Fitzhugh, 199–203, on "Negro Slavery," for a representative example of pro-slavery rhetoric; and Fredrickson, 91–96, for an explication of Evrie's "peculiarly radical conception of white democracy" and his contention that *all* white men were superior to blacks, white miscreants being simply the consequence of moral lassitude, while blacks are inherently inferior. Also see Fredrickson, 75–82, for a discussion of Nott's "scientific" proof that the Negro was not of the same biological species as whites.
21. Herskovits, 3; quotation from "The Conflict and Fusion of Cultures with Special Reference to the Negro," *Journal of American History*, vol. 4, no. 116 (1919).
22. Myrdal, 928.
23. Myrdal, 784.
24. See Ellison, *Shadow and Act*, 303–17, "An American Dilemma: A Review," for a balanced evaluation that both acknowledges the study's many accomplishments and criticizes its assumptions about the reflective or reactionary nature of African-American life and culture as well as the limitations imposed by its implicit political intent.
25. Ostendorf, 3; quotation from E. Franklin Frazier, "Tradition and Patterns of Negro Family in the United States," in *Race and Culture Contracts*, E. B. Reuter, ed. (New York, 1934). Even earlier, Frazier had written: "Many of those who criticize the Negro for selecting certain values out of American life overlook the fact that the primary struggle on his part has been to acquire a culture. In spite of the efforts of those who would have him dig up his African past, the Negro is a stranger to African culture." Quoted by Cruse,

154, from "La Bourgeoisie Noire," *Modern Quarterly*, vol. 5 (1928–30), 78–84. For more on the disagreement between Herskovits and Frazier, see *Nation*, Jan. 27, 1940, and Feb. 14, 1942, where the authors review each other's books.

26. Bontemps, 215. Johnson, in addition to his many achievements as a scholar and educator, was the founder of the National Urban League's influential journal *Opportunity*, which published works of many of the Harlem Renaissance writers.

27. Weinstein and Gatell, 92–116. Also see Meier and Rudwick, 69, for comments on Elkins's appraisal of the "Sambo stereotype" in the context of his overall view of the "dehumanizing quality of slavery" in the United States. See Kochman, *Black and White Styles in Conflict*, 8, for quotation from Daniel Patrick Moynihan and Nathan Glazer, *Beyond the Melting Pot* (Cambridge, 1963): "The Negro is only an American and nothing else. He has no values or culture to guard and protect."

28. Myrdal, notes to chapter 35, 1394. Ostendorf, 5.

29. Harper and Stepto, 256; quotation from "Africa, Slavery, and the Roots of Contemporary Black Culture," by Mary F. Berry and John W. Blassingame.

30. Meier and Rudwick, 18. Thompson, *Flash of the Spirit*, 132–41. Thompson also demonstrates that the "bottle trees" of some Southern black communities are derived from Kongo tribal practices (142–45) and that certain building techniques common among American blacks are derivative of the construction practices of the African Mande civilization (197–206). Stuckey, 22–23, 12.

31. Thompson, *African Art in Motion*, 148.

32. Keil, 15–16.

33. The term *Sambo*, according to some sources, is derived from the African Mande civilization and means "to disgrace," but the *Oxford English Dictionary* gives its derivation as eighteenth-century Spanish, meaning the offspring of a Negro and mulatto. It appeared in 1833 in the title of a mock sermon satirizing blacks and religion, *Sambo's Address to His Bred'ren* (see Dennison, 41–45), and, by the mid-nineteenth century, became the most commonly used derogatory term for blacks among white Americans. Boskin, 61; quotation from *Retrospectives on America, 1797–1811*, by John Bernard, 126–35 (New York: Harper and Row, 1887). Bernard, an English comedian, calling Negroes "the happiest race he had ever seen," compared them to the "lower Irish," who have "the same confusion of ideas and difficulty of clear expression."

34. Douglass, *My Bondage and My Freedom*, 97. Brown, Davis, and Lee, 716; quotation from *Twelve Years a Slave: The Narrative of Solomon Northrup* (1853).

35. Abrahams and Szwed, 388–89; quotation from *Travels in the United States of America and Canada* by John Finch (London, 1833), 237–38.

36. Abrahams and Szwed, 399; quotation from Joseph H. Ingraham, *The Sunny South; or, The Southerner at Home* (Philadelphia, 1860), 104–8.

37. Hughes and Meltzer, 7, source unspecified.

38. Boskin, 54.

39. Malapropism—deliberately misusing words for comic effect—is not listed as a comic device in Evan Esar's *The Comic Encyclopedia*, but blackface minstrels, vaudeville comedians, and some twentieth-century black comedians frequently employed the device in their acts. Malapropism was com-

monly used by such nineteenth-century comic writers as Artemus Ward and others of the misspeller school of humor, and it was a staple of the humorous dialogue in acts such as the *Amos 'n' Andy* radio and television shows. For some contemporary comedians, such as Norm Crosby and Professor Irwin Corey, it remains the central element in their routines. Redfern, 159; Julian Franklin observed, "The pun is the power-unit that drives, and that has driven British humour," in *Which Witch?*, xi, quoted by Redfern, 157.

40. Rubin, 81–82; quotation from Cecil D. Eby, "Yankee Humor." Also see Rourke, 18–32; Blair, 38–62, and Trachtenberg, 592–96, for more on Yankee humor.

41. Rubin, 104, 9–10, from James M. Cox's essay "Humor of the Old Southwest" and Rubin's Introduction. Blair, 311; quotation from Johnson J. Hooper, *Some Adventures of Simon Suggs* (1872 edition), "Simon Becomes a Captain." See Spiller *et al.*, 728–45; Blair, 62–101; and Trachtenberg, 587–622, for succinct overviews of frontier or Old Southwest humor of this period.

42. Rubin, 128–33, from "The Misspellers," by Brom Weber. Holton, 102–5. Scruggs, 10–11; quotation from *Publishers Weekly* 96, Sept. 20, 1919, advertisement for Dodd Mead. Cohen's writing was usually focused on burlesque presentations of black Southern types. His work is obviously in the minstrel show vein—ridicule of black caricatures by comparison to bourgeois standards—and clearly illustrates the connections among American rural humor, minstrel shows, and the misspellers.

43. Material available on Richard Pryor, *Wanted: Richard Pryor Live in Concert* (Warner Brothers Records, 1978).

44. Billington places the appearance of the Fool in the thirteenth century and traces its presence through Chaucer, Shakespeare, the appearance of Jack Pudding, Harlequin, and the clown, then onto more recent American incarnations such as Hollywood silent screen comedians. Billington includes neither antebellum American blacks nor black-faced entertainers or the so-called Ethiopian Delineators who appeared later in this tradition. But the insistent perception of black slaves as comic and, in the nineteenth century, the appearance of blackface comedians in minstrelsy appear to be instances of the refurbishing by white Americans of their traditional European culture with an ebony cloak to enhance its appeal to the average citizen, who sought a folk-based culture.

45. Redfern, 162–63; quotation from *Comedy High and Low* by Maurice Charney (New York: Oxford University Press, 1978). Redfern, 33; quotation from *Society Against the State* by P. Clastres (New York: Urizen, 1972).

46. During the first half of the twentieth century, many social scientists questioned the existence of wit, humor, and wordplay in Africa. See Myrdal, 960. According to Myrdal, "The good humor that is associated with the Negro's emotionalism is the outcome, not only of the attempt to enjoy life to its fullest, but of stark fear of the white man. Much of the humor that the Negro displays before the white man in the South is akin to that manufactured satisfaction with their miserable lot which the conquered people of Europe are now forced to display before their German conquerors. . . . In a similar manner, the Negro slave developed a cleverness in language which is akin to the 'bright sayings' of children. Like the 'Negro laugh,' he [sic] found that a clever remark amused the white man and often staved off punishment or brought rewards. Charles S. Johnson adds: "The humor of the Negro has been regarded as one of his native characteristics. It is, indeed, one of the

useful contributions of the race to the grim struggle of Americans for progress and wealth. This humor has enlivened the public and private stage, the joke columns of the press, and countless after-dinner speeches. . . . Since the native African is not a very humorous person, it seems most likely that this quality of humor was developed in slavery." Weatherford and Johnson, *Race Relations* (1934).

47. Fabre, 4. Epstein, 5–6; quotations from John A. Atkins, *A Voyage to Guinea, Brasil, and the West-Indies, in His Majesty's Ships, the Swallow and Weymouth* (London: printed for C. Ward and R. Chandler, 1735), 53. Epstein comments that "this improvised 'blame or praise' was to be transported to the Americas, becoming a standard feature of festive singing on holidays and of all kinds of worksongs from corn songs in Kentucky to Calypso songs in Trinidad."

48. Schechter, 13. Gorer, 39, 37.

49. Kochman, *Rappin' and Stylin' Out,* 217–18; quotation from Roger D. Abrahams, "Joking: The Training of the Man of Words in Talking Broad" (1972). Some social scientists have suggested that the practice of mother-rhyming is called the dozens in the United States because of the enforced breakdown of the black family structure during slavery and the fact that dozens of black women were available to white masters and overseers. In fact, overseers' "punishment" of female slaves often took the form of sexual abuse: see Jacqueline Jones, 19–24, and Giddings, 35–38, for more on sexual exploitation of black women slaves.

Until the 1990s, the dozens were a bit too earthy for most public performances. But such comedians as Richard Pryor and Redd Foxx occasionally used this put-down tactic as a means of silencing hecklers in the audience. In fact, Foxx directly flirted with the device when he employed an audience participation bit in which he asked someone near ringside if he was married, then, if the answer was yes, inquired as to whether he had any children. If the answer was again yes, Foxx quipped: "Sir, you're a motherfucker!" The impact of signifying on humor is, of course, readily seen from minstrelsy through the stand-up comedy routines of such 1980s comics as Foxx, Pryor, Sam Kinison, and Don Rickles, such 1990s stand-ups such as Martin Lawrence, and in contemporary show business celebrity roasts, where it has been elevated to ritual status.

Rawson, v–vi. The dozens, incidentally, have a historical connection to customs regularly practiced in ancient Greece, where within the context of sanctioned "play," bystanders or outsiders were mocked or insulted, or in England, where *flyting* or the impromptu exchange of invective was common. According to W. H. Auden, *flyting* was once a "studied literary art" whose "comic effect arises from the contradiction between the insulting nature of what is said, which appears to indicate a passionate relation of hostility and aggression, and the calculated skill of verbal invention." From "Notes on the Comic," in *The Dyer's Hand and Other Essays* (London, 1963).

50. Samuel Charters, 17.

51. Charters, p. 13; quotation from *Green's Collection of Voyages* (London, 1745).

52. Vollmer and Devere, 18–20; source of Mylene Remy quotation unspecified. Bebey, 26; see also 24–26, where Bebey writes that the "West African *griot* is a troubador, the counterpart of the European minstrel."

53. Gutman, 70. The author cites instances of slaves using song and music to sanction others: the former slave Priscilla McCollough, for example, explained that "in Africa when a girl dohn act jis lak day should, deh drum uh out uh town. . . . Sometimes wen dey bad, deh put um on duh banjo. Dat was in dis country. . . . When dey play dat night, dey sing bout dat girl and deh tell all bout uh. Das puttin on duh banjo." Douglass, *My Bondage and My Freedom*, 99, 98.

54. Freud, 182–86. Freud provides some insight into the dynamics of this shift of emphasis—as well as into slaves' motives for "playing dumb" even when they had gained some facility with English—in a discussion of the difference between naive comedy and jokes. He contends that naive comedy arises when a person (the source of the comic remark) displays no inhibition about the comic incongruity or exaggeration on which the humor is based because it is not conceptually possible for him to do so. "It is a condition for the naive's producing its effect that we should know that the person concerned does not possess the inhibition; otherwise we call him not naive but impudent." The naive, for Freud, occurs more frequently among children and uneducated or childish adults. Jokes, in contrast, require that the speaker "has intended to make a joke"—that he is *suspending* inhibition and is aware of the comic thrust of his remarks. Accordingly, the speaker is often cognizant of the implicit assertiveness and aggressiveness of his humor. Perhaps as important, jokes also require that the listener is aware of the speaker's intent; otherwise a joke may be inaccurately interpreted as an instance of naïveté—in which case, ironically, it is the listener who assumes the naive role instead of the speaker.

   Myrdal also recognized pretense among Negroes. He observed that "in addition to all this actual ignorance, there is a good deal of pretended ignorance on the part of the Negro. . . . To volunteer information is often a sure way of being regarded as 'uppity' by whites. . . . They act humble, which also gives them an air of dumbness," 960.

55. Osborne, 39. Osborne writes: "Thus developed one of the many contradictions in the white view of Negroes that ever would torment the South. It was believed with equal conviction that Negroes were docile by nature and therefore in no need of freedom, and at the same time intractable by nature and therefore a danger to society if they were freed." Titon, 228; quotation from the *Encyclopedia Britannica* (11th, 12th, and 13th editions), under the entry *Negro*.

56. Cohen, 107; from Charles H. Nichols, "Comic Modes in Black America (A Ramble through Afro-American Humor)." Nichols cites *From Slave Cabin to Pulpit* (Boston: J. H. Earle, 1893), a slave narrative by Peter Randolph, as the source of the Pompey tale.

57. Kochman, *Rappin' and Stylin' Out*, 179, 177, 183; from David Dalby, "The African Element in American English," an essay on African linguistic survivals that includes a list of over eighty Americanisms traced to African sources.

58. Dundes, 490; from Russell Ames, "Protest and Irony in Negro Folksong." Foxx and Miller, 4.

59. Smitherman, 104–18, 99–100, 97–99. The author provides a detailed analysis of the linguistic devices mentioned in the text, as well as other examples of black speech patterns, such as "braggadocio," "narrative sequencing," and "love rapping," 73–166.

60. Weinstein and Gatell, 118–33; see "Resistance to Slavery," an essay in which

George M. Fredrickson and Christopher Lasch provide a concise, balanced appraisal of various forms of slave resistance, considering Kenneth Stampp's position ("Slave resistance, whether bold and persistent or mild and sporadic, created for all slaveholders a serious problem of discipline") as well as that of historians like Stanley M. Elkins who subscribe to the "contented slave" theory. See Giddings, 44–45, for comments on instances of infanticide.

61. Brewer, 314, 320, 322, 321.
62. Spalding, 332.
63. Spalding, 338.
64. Ostendorf, 37.
65. Trachtenberg, 193; from an article on Harris by R. Bruce Bickley, Jr., Joel Chandler Harris, 3, 23.
66. Joel Chandler Harris, 4, 9, 12. Dundes, 527; quotation from "Uncle Remus and the Malevolent Rabbit," by Bernard Wolfe, reprinted from *Commentary*, vol. 8 (1949), 31–41. Also see Lester, *The Tales of Uncle Remus*, xiv–xvi, for more on Harris's possible motives; Lester's contemporary versions of these fables also provide an interesting comparison to earlier versions.
67. Hughes and Meltzer, 33–37. Henson's memoir, *Truth Stranger Than Fiction: Father Henson's Story of His Own Life* (New York: Corinth Books, 1962), which was first published in 1858 with an introduction by Harriet Beecher Stowe, documents his capitulation to the slaveholder's viewpoint during bondage. Excerpts from Henson's autobiography may be found in Lester, *To Be a Slave*, 93–98.
68. Fredrickson, 110–29; the author discusses Stowe's works as well as other examples of romantic racialism, demonstrating how this movement, which began as an attempt to prove the inherent worth of blacks, became a propaganda tool that was eventually used against them.
69. Downs, 44–48; Downs asserts that "the legendary life of Aesop is held by scholars to be entirely apocryphal" and engages the question of whether Aesop "was a wholly mythical person." He concludes that "Aesop, or someone like him, was the first to collect, retell in concise, easy-to-remember style, and disseminate widely for moral instruction previously existing fables, doubtless adding a few of his own." Others, however, noting that the tales attributed to Aesop were preserved primarily through the works of Phaedrus, an Athenian freedman, and Babrius, the son of Roman emperor Alexander Severus, have suggested that the source is actually the Ethiopian fabulist Lokman, who is described as "deformed, of a black complexion, with thick lips and splay feet." Also see Hughes and Bontemps, viii, and Spalding, 4–6.
70. Trachtenberg, 601; quotation from *The Rise and Fall of American Humor* (1968) by Jesse Bier appears in Sandy Cohen's article on the humor of the South and Southwest. Also see Hughes and Bontemps, viii–ix.
71. Joyner, 172.
72. Joyner, 180.
73. Joel Chandler Harris, 29–30.
74. Joyner, 181–82.
75. See Joel Chandler Harris, 80–84, for the "Tortoise and Hare" tale; see Joyner, 180–83, for more on Partridge tales.
76. Joyner, 183.
77. Hughes and Bontemps, 67–68.
78. Joyner, 185, 187. The tale of John's feigned death, "The One 'Bout John,"

from WPA manuscript; "Strong Man John" from WPA manuscript, Type 1612, Motif K 1961.

79. Locke, *The Negro and His Music*, 19–20. Citing W. E. B. Du Bois's comments on "The Sorrow Songs" in this early but still pertinent essay on black music (1936), Locke observes that only "since 1900 has the profundity and true folk character of the spirituals been gradually discovered and recognized. . . . Underneath broken words, childish imagery, peasant simplicity, was an epic intensity and a tragic depth of religious emotion."

80. Epstein, 186; quotations from *The Valley of Shenandoah; or, Memoirs of the Graysons* by George Tucker (New York: C. Wiley, 1824), 116–18, and *The History of the General Council and General Assembly of the Leeward Islands* by Clement Caine (printed by R. Cable, 1804), 110–11.

81. Courlander, *Negro Folk Music, U.S.A.*, 89.

82. Courlander, *Negro Folk Music, U.S.A.*, 117, 89. Brewer, 198, 187.

83. Dundes, 489–90; from Russell Ames, "Protest and Irony in Negro Folksong" (lyrics from Lawrence Gellert's "Me and My Captain").

84. Spalding, 40.

CHAPTER TWO: *Minstrelsy*

1. Dennison, 49–51, 142; "Jim Crow" by Thomas Dartsmouth Rice was initially published in New York by E. Riley in 1829. Lyrics of "Going Ober de Mountain" from *Lady's Musical Library Extra: Music of the Ethiopian Serenaders, Nine Songs and a Set of Cotillions* (Philadelphia, 1845). Ostendorf, 80–81.

2. LeRoi Jones, *Blues People;* see 100, 170, and 122 for more commentary on Whiteman, Goodman, and Presley.

3. Dennison, 8–9; quotation on fitness from *Pennsylvania Gazette*, April 16, 1767.

4. Rourke, 79–80. Forrest's costumer and "personal slave," a black actor named Andrew Jackson "Dummy" Allen, adds an interesting footnote to the development of minstrelsy. Allen was an eccentric character who was known to exaggerate and distort his accomplishments, but if his claims are to be taken seriously, he appeared as a page in a 1786 production of *Romeo and Juliet.* On that basis he advertised himself as the "oldest living actor" and the "Father of the American Stage." Besides his association with Forrest, he apparently led a flamboyant life as an actor, restaurateur, and costumer until his death in 1853. For more on Allen, see Wittke, 13–16.

5. Dennison, 505; quotation from *Yankee Theatre: The Image of America on the Stage, 1825–1850,* by Francis Hodges (University of Texas Press, 1964), 19–21, 505–18. Rourke, 79–80.

6. Dennison, 36–40. Hamm, 117.

7. Wittke, 16–18.

8. Toll, 18.

9. Rourke, 82.

10. Ronald L. Davis, 209.

11. Foxx and Miller, 14.

12. Rourke, 81.

13. Toll, 30; the Virginia Minstrels' assertion that they were the originators of minstrelsy was challenged by some other troupes. E. P. Christy of the

Christy Minstrels, for example, had his claim as originator of the minstrel format endorsed by the Supreme Court of New York. Also see Dennison, 88.

14. Toll, 36.
15. Dennison, 27–86; there is still debate about the originators of much minstrel music. The claims of Dan Emmett and many other "composers" of the period have been challenged by musicologists and scholars, and Dennison examines these claims. Toll, 31. Wittke, 211–13.
16. Hamm, 131–36. See Toll, 36–38, for more on this development in minstrelsy.
17. Schechter, 56–57.
18. Toll, 53; quotation from "Early History of Negro Minstrelsy," by T. Alston Brown, *New York Clipper*, May–Aug. 1913.
19. Foxx and Miller, 18–19; variations of this much-repeated quip, as well as many other now-familiar jokes, were the staples of interlocutor-endman humor.
20. Wittke, 159–65; jokes from Frank Dumont, *The Whitmark Amateur Minstrel Guide and Burnt Cork Encyclopedia* (New York, 1899), and *George Christy's Essence of Old Kentucky* (New York, 1864). Wittke comments that "when reduced to cold type [many of these jokes] must strike the reader of today [1930] as rather futile or far-fetched attempts at comedy," 160. For more on the original content of minstrel shows, see Wittke, chapter 4, "The Technique of the American Minstrel Show," 135–209.
21. Esar, 245.
22. Fletcher, 37–38.
23. Toll, 55.
24. Toll, 73–76, 97.
25. Dennison, 154; lyrics from the *Negro-Forget-Me-Not-Songster*, 86.
26. See Dennison, 171–80, for parodies of *Uncle Tom's Cabin* in minstrel songs.
27. For a detailed description of antebellum minstrelsy, see Dennison, 27–244; Esar, 87, 244–45, 389, 475–76; Foxx and Miller, 12–20; Huggins, 244–301; Toll, 25–133; Wittke, 41–134; Jackson, 155–64.
28. Schechter, 46–49; quotation from "an anonymous collector of minstrel speeches."
29. Erenberg, 67–68.
30. Toll, 139–42, 145. Another significant change in minstrelsy was the appearance of several all-female minstrel troupes in the early 1870s. According to Toll, they performed "the basic minstrel show supplemented with special attractions of their own." The major attraction of female minstrel shows was the presentation of scantily clad women, according to many observers; those shows are considered the forerunner of modern-day "girlie shows."
31. Toll, 145; the first quotation is Toll's paraphrasing of Haverly; the latter is from the playbill of Haverly's United Mastodon Minstrels, 1878.
32. Wittke, 135.
33. Toll, 149–52, 155.
34. Wittke, 110–11.
35. Boskin, 85–93.
36. Ostendorf, 73; quotation from *Mark Twain's Autobiography* (1924), chapter 12. Rourke, 99, 94–95.
37. Ostendorf, 75.
38. Huggins, 253–57.

39. Fletcher, 57–58.
40. Handy, 44, 47–51.
41. Handy, 43.

CHAPTER THREE: *Black Minstrelsy to Vaudeville*

1. Handy, 33. Schechter, 56. Baldwin, 68, from "Many Thousands Gone."
2. Hughes and Meltzer, 40–45.
3. Southern, 103–4, 106–7, 246–47.
4. Ostendorf, 77.
5. Wittke, 17–18; Southern, 93–94.
6. Foxx and Miller, 16–17.
7. Epstein; see 141–44 for further description of juba patting. Also see Oliver, 20–25.
8. Oliver, 120–24. After citing various descriptions of slave dances by European observers in which the term "jig" is used, Epstein concludes: "The writers of the above reports were either English or Irish men who presumably could recognize English or Irish jigs when they saw them. Not one contemporary witness has associated the Negro jig with jigs known in the British Isles, although they used the same word for both, leading to unfortunate ambiguity," 122.
9. Foxx and Miller, 16. Toll, 43.
10. Stearns, 46; Dickens quotation from *American Notes,* vol. 1 (London: Cahpaman and Hall, 1842), 218. Also see Epstein, 142–43, and Ostendorf, 78, 80.
11. Toll, 197–98. Southern, 95.
12. Toll, 198–99.
13. Toll, 202–4.
14. Toll, 205; quotations from *The Clipper,* Aug. 7, 1880, July 19, 1879, and June 26, 1880.
15. Toll, 209–11.
16. Southern, 229–30. Toll, 211–12. Also see Foxx and Miller, 22–38, for more on black troupes. The authors contend that Lew Johnson began his first troupe in 1864.
17. Sampson, 59–60. Wittke, 130.
18. Toll, 213–15. Southern, 229–30.
19. Ostendorf, 84; quotation from *They All Played Ragtime,* by Rudi Blesh, revised edition (New York, 1971), 84–85.
20. Fletcher, 62–65.
21. Fletcher, 61. In *Black Dance,* Edward Thorpe contends that both the Buck and Wing and Virginia Essence were black folk dances that originated during slavery. Dancers would imitate the strutting movements of a courting pigeon or cock in the Buck and Wing, while the Virginia Essence involved intricate shuffling steps that gave the impression of gliding across the floor. He credits Dan Bryant with bringing the Essence to the minstrel stage and agrees that it was a forerunner of the soft shoe. See Thorpe, 26–27, 46–49.
22. Southern, 237–38. Fletcher, 62–63. Handy, 17.
23. Fletcher, 62–65.
24. Fletcher, 79–90.
25. Southern, 237. Dennison, 260–61. Hamm, 274–77.

26. Al Rose, 48.
27. James Weldon Johnson, *Black Manhattan*, 90.
28. Fletcher, 67–76, Lucas quotation, 69–70.
29. For more on Lucas's career and the early development of black musical shows, see Fletcher, 67–76; Toll, 217–18; Huggins, 274–76; Foxx and Miller, 30–31.
30. Dennison, 261–62.
31. Sampson, 397–401, 376.
32. Sampson, 375–77.
33. Toll, 200–201; quotations from *The Clipper*, Oct. 21, 1865, and *The Whig* (Troy, N.J.) quoted in *The Clipper*, Dec. 30, 1865.
34. Theodore B. Wilson, 63.
35. William Loren Katz, 7–9.
36. William Loren Katz, 7.
37. Huggins, 259–60.
38. Fletcher, 62. Toll, 226–27.
39. Toll, 226–27.
40. Ashe, 43–57.
41. Toll, 256–57; quotation from *The Clipper*, March 7, 1891.
42. See Gilbert, 61–85 ("Racial Comics of the Eighties") for more on Irish, German, and Jewish comedy of the 1880s. Oliver, *Songsters and Saints*, 107.
43. Osofsky, *Puttin' on Ole Massa*, 46.
44. Osofsky, *Puttin' on Ole Massa*, 46–47. Old John tales from Richard Dorson, *Negro Folktales in Michigan*, and John Q. Anderson, "Old John and the Master," *Southern Folklore Quarterly*, vol. 25 (1961), 195.
45. Smythe, 687; from "Black Influences in the American Theater: Part I," by Langston Hughes.

PART TWO

CHAPTER FOUR: *Vaudeville and Early Twentieth-Century Black Humor*

1. Dennison, 427. Words and music for "It's Getting Dark on Old Broadway" by Louis A. Hirsch, Gene Buck, and Dave Stamper (New York: Harms, 1922). Ann Charters, 105. Sampson, 76.
2. Nash, 30; quotation from G. S. Dickerman, "The Drift to the Cities," *Atlantic Monthly*, 112 (Sept. 1913), 349–53.
3. Sinkler, 243; quotation from the President's speech to Illinois delegation, July 25, 1888, published in Charles Hedges's compilation of Harrison's speeches (New York: 1892). Osofsky, *Harlem—The Making of a Ghetto*, 21–22. The author, basing his remarks on documentation by Ida B. Wells (*A Red Record: Tabulated Statistics and Alleged Causes of Lynching in the United States*) and others, writes that "there were more Negroes lynched, burned, tortured and defranchised in the late eighties, nineties and first decade of the twentieth century than at any other time in our history." Novak and Waldoks, *The Big Book of American Humor*, 235, from "The Civil War: A Nation Pokes Itself in the Eyeball."
4. *Negro History Bulletin*, June 1951, 205–6; quotations from *The New York Times*, editorial, July 13, 1910; news article, July 12, 1910, 14; news article,

Feb. 14, 1913, 5; "Nuggets," July 23, 1901, 6, taken from the *Philadelphia Press;* "Nuggets," Aug. 10, 1902, 6, taken from the *Kansas City Star.*

5. *Negro History Bulletin,* June 1951, 205.
6. Osofsky, *Harlem—The Making of a Ghetto,* 10–12; quotation from Charles Dickens, *American Notes* (London, 1900), 102–5.
7. James Weldon Johnson, *Black Manhattan,* 127. Osofsky, *Harlem—The Making of a Ghetto,* 46–52; quotation from *The New York Times,* Aug. 16, 1900, and Aug. 24, 1900.
8. Low and Clift, 232. Also see Smythe, 50–51, for more on race riots in early twentieth-century America.
9. Sampson. 78–79.
10. Fletcher, 105.
11. Erenberg, 148–53; the author argues that the changes in social dance were "part of a growing social and cultural ferment as men and women turned to greater intimacy in social and sexual relations and a single standard of sexual relations." Anderson, 180; H. L. Mencken quotation from an editorial in *The American Mercury,* n.d.
12. Jasen and Tichenor, 14–15; Dennison, 350–51.
13. Dennison, 357; lyrics from John Queen's "Got Your Habits On."
14. Fletcher, 138–39.
15. Fletcher, 138. Jasen and Tichenor, 8–13.
16. Hamm, 317–21. Bullock, 118; quotation from J. Rosamond Johnson, "Why They Call American Music Ragtime," *The Colored American* 15 (January 1909), 636–39. Erenberg, 152. Oakley, 31–32; quotation by Rupert Hughes (1899) from R. Blesh and H. James, *They All Played Ragtime* (1960), 103–4.
17. LeRoi Jones, 110–11.
18. Sampson, 62; quotation about McIntosh's act from the *Indianapolis Freeman,* July 3, 1897.
19. Sampson, 63–64. James Weldon Johnson, 99. Also see Southern, 296–97.
20. Sampson, 66; quotation from the *Indianapolis Freeman,* March 30, 1901. Dennison, 362–63.
21. Southern, 295.
22. Spellman, 98–99. Sampson, 100–1; account of the origin of *Silas Green from New Orleans* and quotation from an article by J. Homer Tutt, the *Baltimore Afro-American,* Aug. 15, 1936.
23. Oliver, *Songsters and Saints,* 63–66.
24. Oliver, *Songsters and Saints,* 63, 277; quotation from Arthur F. Raper, *Prelude to Peasantry* (New York: Atheneum, 1968), 392–94.
25. Stein, 100; quotation from Hartley Davis, *Everybody's Magazine* vol. 13 (Aug. 1905), 231–40.
26. Sampson, 71. James Weldon Johnson, *Black Manhattan,* 108–9, 114–15.
27. Patterson, *Anthology of the American Negro in the Theatre,* 55; quotation from Will Marion Cook, "Clorindy, the Origin of the Cakewalk," 1944.
28. Sampson, 134; quotation from the *Brooklyn Eagle,* n.d.
29. Hughes, *The Big Sea,* 223.
30. *The New York Herald Tribune,* May 24, 1921. Phyllis Rose, 53; quotation from Alan Dale, *The New York American.* For more on *Shuffle Along,* see Al Rose, 69–83; Thorpe, 74–77; Southern, 427–28; Foxx and Miller, 59–61; Sampson, 113–14; Fletcher, 201–6; Huggins, 288–90.
31. Gilbert, 284.

32. Kochman, *Black and White Styles in Conflict*, 130.

33. Kochman, *Black and White Styles in Conflict*, 130.

34. Patterson, *Anthology of the American Negro in the Theatre*, 30–31; quotation from Jesse Fauset, "The Gift of Laughter," 1925. Huggins, 259.

35. James Weldon Johnson, *Black Manhattan*, 98.

36. Sampson, 111–14.

37. Foxx and Miller, 69.

38. Ann Charters, 105. Example of Williams's stage dialect from the manuscript "Anecdotes, Jokes, Axioms, Proverbs, Funs and Puns compiled, some constructed; some reconstructed. All 'spade footed' for Bert Williams by Alex Rogers," July 4, 1918, New York Public Library, Schomburg Center for Research in Black Culture, 100.

39. Ann Charters, 132–33.

40. Gilbert, 285–86.

41. *American Magazine*, January 1918, article by Bert Williams; from Bert Williams file, New York Public Library for the Performing Arts.

42. "Anecdotes, Jokes, Axioms," etc., Schomburg Collection, 53, 77. Lawrence Gellert, "Bert Williams: Philosophical Tid-bits Gleaned from His Songs and Stories," an unpublished Works Projects Administration Research Paper, n.d., 8.

43. "Anecdotes, Jokes, Axioms," etc., Schomburg Collection, 113. Lawrence Gellert, "Bert Williams: Philosophical Tid-bits," etc., 2.

44. Gilbert, 286.

45. Sampson, 134; quotation from the *Brooklyn Eagle*, n.d. "The Negro in American Culture," a Research Memorandum prepared by Sterling A. Brown (Carnegie-Myrdal Study), New York, 1940; Ziegfeld quotation from chapter 2, "Negroes in Song and Dance," 31. Newspaper article by Eddie Cantor, New York, April 15, 1922, publication unspecified; from Bert Williams file, New York Public Library for the Performing Arts.

CHAPTER FIVE: *Hollywood's Silent Years*

1. Brownlow and Kobal, 54. Cripps, *Slow Fade to Black*, 29. Null, 7.

2. Panati, 222–25. Brownlow and Kobal, 28.

3. Schickel, 117–18.

4. See Maltin for an analysis of early film comics. See Brownlow and Kobal, 142–55, for more on silent screen comedies.

5. Fletcher, 121–22.

6. Klotman, 261, 378, 130, 89, 425. Robbins and Ragan, 62. Bogle, *Toms, Coons, Mulattoes, Mammies, and Bucks*, 8. Cripps, *Slow Fade to Black*, 22.

7. Cripps, *Slow Fade to Black*, 25, 14.

8. Hampton, 28–29. Joseph McBride, "Stepin Fetchit Talks Back," *Film Quarterly*, Summer 1971, 22.

9. Pratt, 132; quotation from W. Stephen Bush, "The Social Use of Moving Pictures," *The Motion Picture World*, vol. 12, No. 4, April 27, 1912, 305–6.

10. Frederickson, 280–81; quotation from *The Leopard's Spots*, 33 and *passim.* Also see Schickel, 267–302, for more on Dixon's propagandistic intent in promoting *Birth of a Nation*; quotation, 268–70. Holton, 100; quotation from Thomas Dixon, *The Clansman* (New York: A. Wessels, 1907), 250.

11. Schickel, 268–70.

12. Schickel, 293–302; Trotter quotation from Stephen R. Fox, *The Guardian of Boston* (Atheneum, 1970), 192–97, 189. Brownlow and Kobal, 62–65.

13. Brownlow and Kobal, 64–65. Cripps, *Black Film as Genre*, 15. The Ku Klux Klan demonstrations in Atlanta were also inspired by the Leo Frank rape case. Frank, a Brooklyn Jew, had been accused and convicted of raping a thirteen-year-old Atlantan; when the governor of Georgia commuted the sentence to life imprisonment on June 21, 1915, Frank was abducted from the state prison and lynched. Later evidence suggested that he was innocent. See Steve Oney, "The Lynching of Leo Frank," *Esquire*, September 1985, 90–104.

14. Schickel, 276–77; quotation from Louis Sherwin, *The Evening Globe* (New York), March 4, 1915, and *The New York Times*, March 4, 1915. Brownlow and Kobal, 62. Robert Henderson, 156–59. Cripps, *Slow Fade to Black*, 29.

15. Campbell, 12; also see his chapter 1, "The Growth of the Mythology," 3–32.

16. Cripps, *Slow Fade to Black*, 257; quotation from *Variety*, May 31, 1931, 6.

17. Sklar, *Movie-Made America*, 67. Cripps, *Slow Fade to Black*, 10–11; quotation from Terry Ramsaye, *A Million and One Nights* (New York, 1926, 1964), 303.

18. Bogle, *Toms, Coons, Mulattoes, Mammies, and Bucks*, 101–2. Robbins and Ragan, 62–63. Cripps, *Slow Fade to Black*, 407. Halliwell, 561.

19. Scenes from *Fish* and *A Natural Born Gambler*, Biograph, 1916. Cripps, *Slow Fade to Black*, 134. Also see Cripps, *Black Film As Genre*, 20–21.

20. Brown, Sterling, *The Negro in American Fiction*, 1–3; Brown's categories included the "comical" and "happy-hearted Negro," the "brute," the "wretched freedman," and the "quaint" or exotic Negro.

21. Null, 8; source of quotation unspecified. Clip from *Off to Bloomingdale Asylum* shown in documentary film *Black Shadows on a Silver Screen*, Post-News Week Station, Inc., 1975.

22. Bogle, *Toms, Coons, Mulattoes, Mammies, and Bucks*, 9.

23. Brownlow and Kobal, 56. Null, 8. Bogle, *Toms, Coons, Mulattoes, Mammies, and Bucks*, 8. Campbell, 35.

24. Halliwell, 561. Patterson, *Anthology of the American Negro in the Theatre*, 231; quotation from Carlton Moss, "The Negro in American Film," 1964. Klotman, 91.

Chapter Six: *The New Negro: Harlem and Hollywood*

1. Sklar, *The Plastic Age*, 187; quotation from Charles S. Johnson, "The Black Migration Northward." Joseph McBride, "Stepin Fetchit Talks Back," *Film Quarterly* (Summer 1971), 22. Scene from *The Smiling Ghost*, Warner Brothers, 1941.

2. McBride, *Film Quarterly*, Summer 1971, 26. Interview with Matt Robinson, December 1990.

3. David Levering Lewis, 13; source of quotation unspecified.

4. Scruggs, 53; Mencken quotations from "The Land of the Free," *Smart Set*, vol. 65 (May 1921), 138–39, and "The Curse of Prejudice," *Smart Set*, vol. 69 (September 1922), 144. Sklar, *The Plastic Age*, 1.

5. James Weldon Johnson, *Along This Way*, 341–42.

6. David Levering Lewis, 88–118.

7. Osofsky, *Harlem—The Making of a Ghetto*, 181; quotation from Alain Locke and Lothrop Stoddard, "Should the Negro Be Encouraged to Cultural Equality?" *Forum*, vol. 78 (Oct. 1927), 508. See Mariann Russell, *Melvin B. Tolson's Harlem Gallery*, for more on William Pickens's *The New Negro: His Political, Civil and Mental States and Related Essays* (New York: Neale, 1916).

8. Anderson, 168–80.

9. Ostendorf, 84–85; quotation from Carl Van Vechten, *In the Garrett* (New York, 1919), 312. Anderson, 142. Osofsky, *Harlem—The Making of a Ghetto*, 185; quotation from "The Slumming Hostess," *The New York Age*, Nov. 6, 1926. James Weldon Johnson, *Along This Way*, 328.

10. Erenberg, 254–55.

11. Cripps, *Slow Fade to Black*, 218, 220. In response to a letter from Foster, James Weldon Johnson wrote: "I myself have noticed that their voices record much better than white voices"; quotation from Johnson correspondence (Aug. 15, 1929) in James Weldon Johnson Memorial Collection, Beineke Library, Yale. In correspondence with George P. Johnson, Foster claimed, "tests proved one great outstanding fact—the low mellow voice of the Negro was ideally suited for the pictures"; quotation from George P. Johnson Collection, n.d., Special Collections, UCLA.

12. Mordden, 4–9. Oberfist, 83; also see Oberfist, 60–188, for more on Jolson's pre-Hollywood or minstrel career.

13. Mordden, 24.

14. Patterson, *Anthology of the American Negro in the Theatre*, 249; quotation from Peter Noble, "The Coming of the Sound Film." Noble also includes critical appraisals of *Hearts in Dixie*, *The Green Pastures*, *Gone with the Wind*, and other movies in this essay. Bogle, *Blacks in American Film and Television*, 103.

15. Furnas, 429–30. Cripps, *Slow Fade to Black*, 259–60. Patterson, *Anthology of the American Negro in the Theatre*, 258; quotation from Peter Noble, "The Coming of the Sound Film."

16. Nichols, 36–37. Rampersad, 368; quotation from Langston Hughes Papers (June 25, 1951), James Weldon Johnson Collection.

17. Scene from *Check and Double Check*, Video Treasures, 1986. Cripps, *Slow Fade to Black*, 106; quotation from the *Amsterdam News*, Aug. 13, 1930.

18. Maltin and Bann, 18, 277–78, 273–74.

19. Maltin and Bann, 263–64, 277.

20. Maltin and Bann, 138, 134.

21. Bogle, *Toms, Coons, Mulattoes, Mammies, and Bucks*, 23.

22. Maltin and Bann, 32, 12.

23. See Maltin and Bann for a synopsis of *Our Gang* films and for an analytical and historical examination of the series and its stars.

24. Klotman, 87. Cripps, *Slow Fade to Black*, 135–37.

25. Bogle, *Toms, Coons, Mulattoes, Mammies, and Bucks*, 23. Maltin and Bann, 116.

26. Holton, 102–3.

27. Carl Van Vechten, 223.

28. Scruggs, 10; quotation from *Publishers Weekly* 94 (August 3, 1918), cover, and *Publishers Weekly* 96 (September 20, 1919).

29. Fletcher, 122–23.

30. Cripps, *Slow Fade to Black*, 181. Klotman, 129.

31. Scruggs, 10–11.
32. Klotman, 180–81. Cripps, *Slow Fade to Black*, 224–27.
33. Holton, 104.
34. Scene from *Brown Gravy* (1929); included in *That's Black Entertainment*, Skyline Entertainment, 1986.
35. Klotman, 187, 367, 347. Cripps, *Slow Fade to Black*, 222–24.
36. Markham and Levinson, unpaged; the book details Markham's show business career.
37. Bogle, *Blacks in American Film and Television*, 388; quotation from *Variety*, n.d.
38. Matt Robinson, "Stepin Fetchit, Why Do They Call You Stepin Fetchit?" unpublished manuscript, 1979, 9.
39. Cripps, *Slow Fade to Black*, 225–26.
40. Foxx and Miller, 65–66; quotation from Mark Hellinger, *Chicago Daily Mirror* (October 1930). Smythe, 687; quotation from Langston Hughes, "Black Influences in the American Theatre: Part I," 1966.
41. Sampson, 407.
42. Fletcher, 290–91, 297.
43. Fletcher, 289–90. Foxx and Miller, 88.
44. Scenes from *The Little Colonel*, Twentieth Century–Fox, 1935.
45. Fletcher, 291. Buckley, 121.
46. Taped interview with Honi Coles, Aug. 1979.
47. Maltin and Bann, 278. Cripps, *Slow Fade to Black*, 130; Madame Sul-te-Wan quotation from a taped interview with Thomas Cripps.
48. Cripps, *Slow Fade to Black*, 103–4.
49. Klotman, 36, 532. Cripps, *Slow Fade to Black*, 103, 243–44.
50. McKee and Chisenhall, 48; quotation from an interview with Rufus Thomas, Oct. 9, 1973.
51. Cripps, *Slow Fade to Black*, 96.
52. Cripps, *Slow Fade to Black*, 112.
53. Bogle, *Blacks in American Film and Television*, 415–16. Scene from *Alice Adams*, MGM, 1935. Cripps, *Slow Fade to Black*, 303–4; quotation from *The New York Times*, Aug. 16, 1935.
54. Scenes from *Affectionately Yours*, Warner Brothers, 1941, and *China Seas*, MGM, 1935. Cripps, *Slow Fade to Black*, 351–52; source of quotation unspecified.
55. Cripps, *Slow Fade to Black*, 361; quotation from *Time*, Dec. 25, 1939, 30–32.
56. Cripps, *Slow Fade to Black*, 106–8; Best quotation from George P. Johnson Collection, UCLA.
57. Klotman, 523. Scene from *Cabin in the Sky*, MGM, 1943. Scene from *The Smiling Ghost*, Warner Brothers, 1941.
58. Scenes from *Pride of the Bluegrass*, Warner Brothers, 1937. Cripps, *Slow Fade to Black*, 354.
59. Klotman, 49. Bogle, *Toms, Coons, Mulattoes, Mammies, and Bucks*, 134.
60. Scene from *Ready, Willing, and Unable*, shown in *A Laugh, A Tear*, a television special produced by S. I. Communications, 1990.
61. Lawrence Gellert, "Bert Williams: Philosophical Tid-bits Gleaned From His Songs and Stories," unpublished Works Project Administration Research

Paper, n.d., 8, New York Public Library, Schomburg Center for Research in Black Culture. William McFerrin Stowe, Jr., "Damned Funny: The Tragedy of Bert Williams," *Journal of Popular Culture*, vol. 10, no. 1, Summer 1976, 5.

62. Cooper, 127–28.

63. Matt Robinson, "Stepin Fetchit, Why Do They Call You Stepin Fetchit?" unpublished manuscript, 1979, 9. Delmarie Cobb and Antoinette Marsh, "The Father of Black Movies," *Black Star*, December 1978, 33–35.

64. Taped interview with Matt Robinson, November 1979.

65. Radio interview, Stepin Fetchit with Warren Bolt, Clinton, Iowa, Spring 1967.

66. Bogle, *Toms, Coons, Mulattoes, Mammies, and Bucks*, 38; source of quotation unspecified. Cripps, *Slow Fade to Black*, 285; quotation from Howe, "Steppin's High-Colored Past," 123–24.

67. Bogle, *Blacks in American Film and Television*, 389; source of Robert Benchley quote not specified. Cripps, *Slow Fade to Black*, 285. Patterson, *Anthology of the American Negro in the Theatre*, 28; from Peter Noble, "The Coming of Film."

68. Maltin, 11–20. Bryan B. and Frances N. Sterling, 2.

69. Wertheim, 74; quotation from Gulf radio broadcast, April 14, 1935, by Will Rogers. Bryan B. and Frances N. Sterling, 147, 153–54; quotations from reviews in *The New York Times* (October 12, 1934, and January 19, 1935) and *The New York World-Telegraph* (January 19, 1935). Rogers quotation from Robert Easton, "Humor of the American Indian," in *The American Indian: Selected Readings from Mankind Magazine* (Los Angeles: Mankind Publishing, 1970), 183.

70. Lamparski, 194.

71. *The New York Times*, July 7, 1951. Cripps, *Slow Fade to Black*, 184–85; John Ford's comment from an interview, Spring 1970.

72. "Where Are They Now?" *Newsweek*, November 20, 1967.

73. Scene from *Stand Up and Cheer*, Fox Films, 1934.

74. *The Daily Worker*, May 28, 1945; quotations from interview in *The Baltimore Afro-American*, Stepin Fetchit with Michael Carter, May 1945. *Ebony*, February 1952.

75. Review by Bosley Crowther, *The New York Times*, May 10, 1952.

76. Taped interview with Honi Coles, August 1979.

77. Radio interview, Stepin Fetchit with Warren Bolt, Clinton, Iowa, Spring 1967. *Newsweek*, November 20, 1967.

78. "Stepin Fetchit Calls His Image Progressive," *The New York Times*, July 24, 1968, July 21, 1970.

79. *The New York Times*, July 21, 1970. Matt Robinson, "Stepin Fetchit, Why Do They Call You Stepin Fetchit?" unpublished manuscript, 13.

80. Cooper, 124.

81. Scenes from *Miracle in Harlem*, Screen Guild Productions, 1948.

82. Ellison, *Invisible Man*, 151–53.

83. Sypher, 228–29; Sypher uses the term "shrewd humility" to describe Socrates' indirect and deferential approach to the "so-called 'wise' men of Athens." Grier and Cobbs, *The Jesus Bag*, 24–25.

84. Carol Deck, "Flip Wilson," *Soul Illustrated*, 1969 (month unknown), 65.

85. Scenes from *Stormy Weather*, Twentieth Century–Fox, 1943. Also see Vance, 171–72.

86. Mordden, 177. Ellison, *Shadow and Act*, 280–81.

CHAPTER SEVEN: *Radio and Early Television*

1. Heide and Gilman, 32. Wertheim, 152–53; dialogue from *The Jell-O Program*, vol. 7, script #38 (June 20, 1937), 6. Miller and Nowak, 361–62.

2. Faith, 83; quotation from Morella, Epstein, and Clark, *The Amazing Careers of Bob Hope* (New York, 1973).

3. Wertheim, 5–7. Esar, 310–11.

4. Vance, 97–98, 111–13. Collier, 89–90. MacDonald, *Don't Touch That Dial!*, 329–30.

5. Al Rose, 108. MacDonald, *Don't Touch That Dial!*, 335, 359. Low and Clift, 273.

6. Dunning, 63, 187–88, 551–52. Wertheim, 26–28. MacDonald, *Don't Touch That Dial!*, 344.

7. Rich Correll outlined the creation of Sam and Henry in *Amos 'n' Andy: Anatomy of a Controversy*, a television special that was syndicated in the late seventies. Foxx and Miller, 56–62.

8. Wertheim, 24, 29–30. Pomerance, 159–62.

9. O'Connor, 67; quotation from Arthur Frank Wertheim, "The Rise and Fall of Milton Berle." Ted Poston, "Halfway to 100 Years of Negro Humor," *New York Post*, April 1, 1967. Faith, 88–89. Rovin, 53, 41.

10. Pomerance, 159–60. Ely, 23. Wertheim, 18–19, 24–25.

11. Dunning, 33.

12. Wertheim, 37–39. 52–53. Dunning, 32–33.

13. Al Rose, 108. "Amos 'n' Andy on Television," *Ebony*, May 1951, 24. Dunning, 33. Furnas, 119. Wertheim, 55, 39–40; article on colloquial speech, "Amos 'n' Andy Dialect Rules Wherever Groups Congregate," appeared in Norfolk (Va.) *Pilot*, April 27, 1930.

14. Wertheim, 47, 44, 48; editorial comment from "Lessons from Amos 'n' Andy," Everett (Washington) *News*, February 21, 1930, and "The Seven O'Clock Calm," McKeesport (Pa.) *News*, March 14, 1930.

15. Dunning, 34.

16. MacDonald, *Don't Touch That Dial!*, 343; quotation from *The Amos 'n' Andy Show*, CBS radio, n.d.

17. MacDonald, *Don't Touch That Dial!*, 329, 331, 351.

18. Dunning, 251.

19. Wertheim, 151–52.

20. Wertheim, 152; quotation from *The Jell-O Program*, vol. 7, script # 38 (March 28, 1937), 10–11, Jack Benny Collection, UCLA.

21. MacDonald, *Don't Touch That Dial!*, 336–37; quotation from *The Jack Benny Show*, April 3, 1938. Wertheim, 153–55; quotations from *The Jell-O Program*, April 12, 1942, 9, Doheny Library, USC, and the Los Angeles *Sentinel*, February 1950.

22. Wertheim, 153–54; quotation from *The Jell-O Program*, vol. 7, script # 38 (June 20, 1937), 12–13, Jack Benny Collection, UCLA. Scene from *The Jack Benny Program*, CBS Television, 1954.

23. Wertheim, 154.

24. Bogle, *Blacks in American Film and Television*, 145–46; quotation from *The New York Times*, n.d. Wertheim, 155.

25. Markham and Levinson, unpaged, chapter 10.

26. Pomerance, 143–44. MacDonald, *Don't Touch That Dial!*, 331.

27. Sammy Davis, Jr., and Boyar, *Yes I Can*, 104–5.

28. MacDonald, *Don't Touch That Dial!*, 344–45.

29. Marx, 136–37.

30. Paley, 231–33.

31. Dunning, 218–23, 507–9, 415–16, 9–11, 198–99. Marx, 199–211. Faith, 224, 227–29. Wertheim, 384, 380–95.

32. George, 11–12, 49–50. Oakley, 220–23; Stackhouse quotation from interview with Jim O'Neal, *Living Blues* (No. 17, Summer 1974). McKee and Chisenhall, 247–49.

33. Quotation from *Rock 'n' Roll: The Early Years*, Archive Films, 1984. Shaw, xxiv; "Good Rockin' Tonight" was written and performed by bluesman Roy Brown but was a hit rhythm and blues release for Harris on King records in 1948.

34. George, 41–43; source of quotation unspecified. McKee and Chisenhall, 93. Also see Redd, 25–42, for more on the development, influence, and resistance to race records and rhythm and blues.

35. George, p. 41. Shaw, 27, xxiv; Speckled Red's "The Dirty Dozens" (1929) was recorded for Brunswick Records and was followed by "The Dirty Dozens, No. 2," in 1930. Scene from *Rock 'n' Roll: The Early Years*, Archive Film, 1984.

36. George, 42–43.

37. O'Connor, 36–37; from Thomas Cripps, "Amos 'n' Andy and the Debate over American Racial Integration." MacDonald, *Don't Touch That Dial!*, 354–55, 359–62.

38. Panati, 226. Paley, 216.

39. Dunning, 543–44, 305–6.

40. Paley, 217.

41. Markham and Levinson, unpaged, chapter 9.

42. "Can TV Crack the Color Line?" *Ebony*, vol. 6, May 1951, 62.

43. Foxx and Miller, 132. McNeil, 746. Bogle, *Blacks in American Film and Television*, 235.

44. Charles and Ritz, 98–99. Redd, 59–60; quotation from *Playboy*, vol. 17 (March 1970), 68.

45. "Out of the Mouths of Pro's," *Soul Illustrated*, 1969 (month unknown), 18.

46. Miller and Nowak, 6–7, 21–29.

47. Miller and Nowak, 6; Norman Mailer quotation from John Montgomery, *The Fifties* (London, 1965), title page.

48. Kearns, 302, 305; quotations from Norman Mailer, "The White Negro," 1957.

49. O'Connor, xvii–xx.

50. O'Connor, 37–38; quotation from Thomas Cripps, "Amos 'n' Andy and the Debate Over American Racial Integration"; *Ebony* magazine quotation from "Can TV Crack the Color Line?", May 1951, 58.

51. Bogle, *Blacks in American Film and Television*, 259.

52. Scenes from *Beulah*, ABC Television, 1951.

53. "Amos 'n' Andy on Television," *Ebony*, May 1951, 21. O'Connor, 33; quotation from Cripps, "Amos 'n' Andy . . ."

54. Paley, 232.
55. O'Connor, 44; quotation from Cripps, "Amos 'n' Andy . . ."
56. "Requiem for the Kingfish," *Ebony,* July 1959, 57–64. Bogle, *Blacks in American Films and Television,* 425–26.
57. Waldon, 183–84.
58. These and subsequent scenes or quotations from *Amos 'n' Andy* are from *The Amos 'n' Andy Show,* CBS television, 1951–53.
59. Martin and Segrave, 205.
60. Low and Clift, 104.
61. Quotations from *Amos 'n' Andy: An Anatomy of a Controversy,* a syndicated television special, circa 1975.
62. *Channels,* April/May 1981, 56; from Mel Watkins, "Beyond the Pale."
63. *Channels,* April/May 1981, 58; from Mel Watkins, "Beyond the Pale."

PART THREE

CHAPTER EIGHT: *Race Records and Black Films*

1. James Murray, 14. Sackheim, 398; quotation from "The Dirty Dozens," by Speckled Red. Allen Morrison, "Negro Humor: An Answer to Anguish," *Ebony,* May 1967, 100; quotation from *A Time for Laughter,* ABC television, 1967.
2. John H. Johnson, 42.
3. Dennison, 354–57
4. Oliver, *Songsters and Saints,* 93–94.
5. Southern, 303–5, 365–67. Oliver, *Songsters and Saints,* 8–11, 2. Titon, 207.
6. Oliver, *Songsters and Saints,* 100–104. Some lyrics of "Good Old Turnip Greens," as in many recorded songs of the period, appear in other folk songs; the lines "White man goes to college/Negro to the fields," for example, can be found in a different context in Lawrence Gellert's collection "Negro Songs of Protest," which appeared in *New Masses* in 1932, and in Nancy Cunard's *Negro.* There the lines are followed by "White man learn to read an' write/Nigger axe to wiel'/Well it makes no diff'rence how you make out yo' time/White folks sure to bring de nigger out behin'."
7. Walton, 34. Albert Murray, *Stomping the Blues,* 45, 51.
8. Sackheim, 254; lyrics from "Judge Harsh Blues" by Furry Lewis. Oliver, *Blues Fell This Morning,* 128–30; lyrics from Speckled Red, "The Dirty Dozens" (recorded on Brunswick 7116, 1929), and "The Dirty Dozens, No. 2" (recorded on Brunswick 7151, 1930).
9. Oliver, *Songsters and Saints,* 108.
10. Jim O'Neal, liner notes to *Laughing at the Blues: Redd Foxx and Dusty Fletcher* (Savoy Jazz, SJL 1181); quotation from *Blues and Rhythm,* March 1986.
11. Monologues from "Open the Door, Richard" and "Mad Hour" (recorded on Savoy Jazz, SJL 1181).
12. Monologue from "Shopping for Clothes" (originally entitled "Clothesline"), written by Kent "Boogaloo" Harris (Atlantic Records, 1960).
13. Walton, 35–36; Hesse quotation from *Steppenwolf* (New York: Bantam, 1969), 43.

14.   Redd, 39–40; quotations from Jimmy Kennedy, *Variety*, vol. 198 (March 9, 1955), 49, and from *Newsweek*, April 23, 1956, 32.
15.   James Murray, 7.
16.   Bogle, *Toms, Coons, Mulattoes, Mammies, and Bucks*, 111; source of Tucker quotation unspecified. Cripps, *Black Film as Genre*, 26.
17.   Author interview with Honi Coles, August 1979. See Bogle, *Toms, Coons, Mulattoes, Mammies, and Bucks*, 109–16, for an excellent synopsis of Micheaux's career; also Cripps, *Black Film as Genre*, 26–30, 41–42, and *Slow Fade to Black*, 342–46.
18.   Bogle, *Toms, Coons, Mulattoes, Mammies, and Bucks*, 115, and *Blacks in American Film and Television*, 422. Cripps, *Black Film as Genre*, 27.
19.   James Murray, 10; source of Tucker quotation unspecified.
20.   Dialogue from *Ten Minutes to Live*, Micheaux Films, 1932.
21.   Stage routines seen in *Darktown Revue*, Micheaux Films, 1931. Richard Pryor routine available on *Richard Pryor . . . Is It Something I Said?* (Reprise REP2285, 1975).
22.   Scenes from *Juke Joint*, Alfred Sack, 1947.
23.   James Murray, 12, 14; source of quotations unspecified.
24.   Cripps, *Black Film as Genre*, 41.
25.   *Newsweek*, July 8, 1946, 85.
26.   Scene from *Hi-De-Ho*, All-American Films, 1947. Scene from *Souls of Sin*, Alexander Productions, 1949.
27.   Cripps, *Slow Fade to Black*, 342.
28.   *The Duke Is Tops* has also been released as *Bronze Venus*, and *One Dark Night* as *Night Club Girl*. Cripps, *Slow Fade to Black*, 342; quotation from *Variety*, October 2, 1940, 25.
29.   Scenes from *Richard's Answer*, Robert Savini, circa 1949.
30.   Markham and Levinson, unpaged, chapter 10.
31.   Redd, 47; the author quotes *Billboard* (Oct. 8, 1955) on the filming and promotion of *Rock 'n' Roll Revue*.
32.   Bessie Smith, "Need a Little Sugar in My Bowl" (Columbia, 14634-D, Nov. 20, 1931).
33.   Liner notes, *Naughties but Goodies*, Redd Foxx (Dooto Records, Comedy Series, DTL-838, 1965). Shaw, 268.
34.   First Redd Foxx routine available on *Naughties but Goodies* (Dooto Records, Comedy Series, DTL-838, 1965).

CHAPTER NINE: *The Theatre Owners Booking Association and the Apollo Theatre*

1.   Foxx and Miller, 91; quotation from an interview with Sammy Davis, Jr., n.d. Flip Wilson routine from live performance at Apollo Theatre, 1966. Bill Cosby quotation from *Motown at the Apollo Twentieth Anniversary*, NBC, 1985.
2.   McKee and Chisenhall, 15. Oakley, 104–5. Basie, 85–106. See Sampson, 39–48, for more on Sherman S. Dudley and his black theatre circuit. During the twenties, Dudley owned several theatres in Washington, D.C., and booked acts into twenty-eight theatres. At the onset of the Depression in 1929, he sold his theatres and booking agency to a white-owned corporation.

3. Oakley, 104. Waters, 77.
4. Waters, 164–70.
5. Schiffman, 44.
6. Foxx and Miller, 72.
7. Markham and Levinson, unpaged, chapter 9. Ralph Cooper, 114–16. Live performance at the Apollo Theatre, circa 1960.
8. Foxx and Miller, 76–78.
9. Davis and Boyar, *Yes I Can,* 105.
10. Interview with Honi Coles, August 1979. Schiffman, 224.
11. Scene from *Darktown Revue,* Michaeux Films, 1931.
12. Marshall and Jean Stearns, "Frontiers of Humor: American Vernacular Dance," *Southern Folklore Quarterly,* vol. 30, 1966, 228–29. Also see Waters, 88–89.
13. Sampson, 350–52. "Butterbeans and Susie," *Ebony,* April 1952, 57–63. Fox, 92. Stearns, "Frontiers of Humor," *Southern Folklore Quarterly,* vol. 30, 1966, 230–31.
14. Basie, 98. Markham and Levinson, unpaged, chapter 8.
15. Fox, 93–95.
16. Schiffman, 221.
17. Interview with Honi Coles, August 1979.
18. Basie, 98–99.
19. Foxx and Miller, 72–98. Schiffman, 215–37. Fox, 91–97.
20. Cahn, 54–55. Maltin, 113–20.
21. The Richard Pryor "Just Us" retort is credited to writer/comedian Paul Mooney on the album *Richard Pryor . . . Is It Something I Said?* (Reprise REP2285, 1975).
22. *The New York American,* December 25, 1932.
23. Oakley, 163; Georgia Tom comment from BBC interview, 1976. Meier and Rudwick, 238. William Loren Katz, 121.
24. Low and Clift, 236. Cooper, 59.
25. Anderson, 110–11.
26. Fox, 29.
27. Interview with Honi Coles, September 1979.
28. Fox, 91; source and author of quotation unspecified.
29. Sypher, 208. Moses, 19; the author is paraphrasing commentary by Bergson in *Laughter* (New York: Macmillan, 1921).
30. Schiffman, 225.
31. Fox, 92.
32. A 1909 newspaper article echoed the prevailing estimate of female comics when it proclaimed, "measured by the ordinary standards of humor [women are] as comical as a crutch. . . . A woman is made to be loved and fondled . . . and certainly she was not made to be laughed at." As late as 1962, a *Mademoiselle* article would proclaim, "a woman who really makes one laugh is about as easy to find as a pauper taking his Sunday brunch in the Edwardian Room." See Martin and Segrave, 13–17, 100–106: news article source unspecified; Sarel Eimerl quotation from *Mademoiselle,* November 1962.
33. McKee and Chisenhall, 147–48.
34. Martin and Segrave, 289; source of quotation unspecified. Shiffman, 119.
35. Charles E. Jones, "Moms," *Soul Illustrated,* 1969 (month unknown), 27. Fox, 97. Martin and Segrave, 289. Barreca, 157–58.
36. Hurston, *Dust Tracks on a Road,* 221, 224.

37. Ted Poston, "Halfway to 100 Years of Negro Humor," *New York Post,* April 1, 1967. Fox, 183.
38. Ostendorf, 77.
39. Poston, "Halfway to 100 Years of Negro Humor."
40. Markham and Levinson, unpaged, chapter 3. Poston, "Halfway to 100 Years of Negro Humor."
41. Allen, 221–22.

CHAPTER TEN: *Literary Reflections of African-American Humor*

1.   Fisher, *The Conjure-Man Dies,* 32. Rubin, 295; from Blyden Jackson, "The Harlem Renaissance." Bradley, 208.
2.   O'Meally, 11; quotations from James Yaffe, "Outstanding Novels," *Yale Review,* 41, Summer 1952.
3.   Low and Clift, 519, 793. Brown, Davis, and Lee, 694. Osofsky, *Puttin' on Ole Massa,* 408–9.
4.   Gates and Davis, x, xii, 1, 126.
5.   Osofsky, *Puttin' on Ole Massa,* 21–24, 30. Gates and Davis, 266–81; from Charles H. Nichols, "The Slave Narrators and the Picaresque Mode: Archetypes for Modern Black Personae."
6.   Gates and Davis, 135; quotation from James Olney, "I Was born: Slave Narratives, Their Status as Autobiography and Literature."
7.   Dann, 16, 20. David Walker, v–vii; quotation from the preface by William Loren Katz.
8.   William Wells Brown, 138, 149–50.
9.   Brown, Sterling, *The Negro in American Fiction,* 40. Brown, Davis, and Lee, 139.
10. Brown, Sterling, *Negro Poetry and Drama,* 32–36. Hughes and Bontemps, *The Poetry of the Negro,* 37. Low and Clift, 520; from Donald B. Gibson's essay on poetry.
11. Gayle, 69.
12. Sowell, 122–27. In seventeenth-century Virginia, for instance, "between one-fourth and one-third of children born to white unwed mothers were mulatto."
13. Chesnutt, *The Wife of His Youth,* 177–79, 185.
14. Gates and Davis, 167, 173; from John Edgar Wideman, "Charles Chesnutt and the W.P.A. Narratives: The Oral and Literate Roots of Afro-American Literature."
15. Sypher, 246, 232, 221.
16. James Weldon Johnson, *The Autobiography of an Ex-Colored Man,* 3, 197.
17. Du Bois, *The Souls of Black Folk,* 246, 258, 263. Rubin, 299; from Blyden Jackson, "The Harlem Renaissance." Moses, 19. Sypher, 218.
18. Sypher, 218–19.
19. James Weldon Johnson, "Satire as a Weapon," *The New York Age,* October 14, 1922.
20. David Walker, 23. Scruggs, 55; from an editorial in *The Chicago Defender,* March 2, 1918.
21. Scruggs, 72–73, 77.
22. Gayle, 104. Scruggs, 137.

23. Schuyler, 113, 103, 89.
24. Gayle, 135. Brown, Sterling, *Negro Poetry and Drama*, 135.
25. Fisher, *The Walls of Jericho*, 5, 8, 14.
26. Fisher, *The Walls of Jericho*, 60–61, 73, 36, 121–22.
27. Brown, Davis, and Lee, 142. Hughes, *The Big Sea*, 240.
28. Watkins, 20; from Larry Neal, "Eatonville's Zora Neale Hurston: A Profile." Alice Walker, 16; from the introduction by Mary Helen Washington.
29. Cunard, 28; from Zora Neale Hurston, "Characteristics of Negro Expression."
30. Alice Walker, 17–18; Wright's review ("Between Laughter and Tears") appeared in *New Masses*, October 5, 1937. Sterling Brown, 160–61.
31. Hurston, *Jonah's Gourd Vine*, 87, 233. Bone, 30.
32. Rubin, 302; from Blyden Jackson, "The Harlem Renaissance." Hughes, *Not Without Laughter*, 254, 69.
33. Bone, 75. Nichols, 269; from a letter, dated December 8, 1949, from Hughes to Bontemps in which Hughes reminds Bontemps of his "original" comments about Simple at the time of the publication of *Simple Speaks His Mind* (New York: Simon and Schuster, 1950).
34. Hughes, *The Langston Hughes Reader*, 198; quotations from "Fancy Free," which appeared in *Simple Takes a Wife* (New York: Simon and Schuster, 1953). Blyden Jackson, 79–80.
35. Charles A. Watkins, "Simple: The Alter Ego of Langston Hughes," *The Black Scholar*, June 1971, 19, 25. Hughes, *The Langston Hughes Reader*, 220.
36. Hughes, *The Langston Hughes Reader*, 193–94; 210–11; quotations from "Race Relations" and "Dear Mr. Butts," which appeared respectively in *Simple Speaks His Mind* and *Simple Takes a Wife*.
37. Berry, 324–26.
38. Henry Louis Gates, Jr., "Why the 'Mule Bone' Debate Goes On," *The New York Times*, February 10, 1991.
39. Richard Wright, *Native Son*, 20, and *Lawd Today*, 176–77. Also see Smitherman, 121–28, for more examples of signifying in the novels of Wright and Chester Himes.
40. Williams and Harris, 27; from John A. Williams, "My Man Himes: An Interview With Chester Himes." Bone, 158.
41. Reed, *Shrovetide in Old New Orleans*, 96; from the essay "Chester Himes: Writer," which appeared originally in *Black World*, March 1972. *A Rage in Harlem* was initially published as *La Reine des Pommes* (1957) by Serie Noire-Gallimard and won the *Prix du Roman Policier* in 1958. It was also published as *For Love of Imabelle* by Gold Medal Books in 1959.
42. Himes, *Blind Man with a Pistol*, 72, 135, 76.
43. Ellison *Shadow and Act*, 53. Moses, 31.
44. O'Meally, *New Essays on "Invisible Man*," 10–12; Ellison quotation from "American Humor," an address which appeared in Elwyn E. Breaux, "Comic Elements in Selected Prose of James Baldwin, Ralph Ellison, and Langston Hughes," unpublished thesis, Fisk University, 1971. Also see Hersey, 151–59; Earl H. Rovit, "Ralph Ellison and the American Comic Tradition."
45. Ellison, *Invisible Man*, 13–14, 109. O'Meally, 15.
46. Ellison, *Invisible Man*, 14–25, 41–52, 57–75, 107.
47. Ellison, *Invisible Man*, 118, 165.

48. Ellison, *Invisible Man,* 201, 236–39.
49. From "American Humor," an address by Ralph Ellison (Oklahoma State University, April 11, 1970). O'Meally, 18.
50. Ellison, *Invisible Man,* 326, 345–46. Rovin, 43.
51. Scholes, 41. Spiller et. al., 1467.
52. Victor Navasky, *The New York Times Book Review,* February 27, 1966. Charles Wright, 3–4, 6–7.
53. Charles Wright, 33, 47, 92.
54. Frances S. Foster, "Charles Wright: Black Black Humorist," *CLA Journal,* September 1971, 44–53. Charles Wright, 21, 162–63.
55. Killens, xv, 85, 215. Gayle, 269.
56. Cohen, 116; from Charles H. Nichols, "Comic Modes in Black America (A Ramble Through Afro-American Humor)." LeRoi Jones, *Black Magic,* 4, and *Tales,* 100, 11.
57. Reed, *Shrovetide in Old New Orleans,* 133, and *Conjure,* 22–23. Byerman, Keith E., 217, 237. Interview with Ishmael Reed, May 1979.
58. Byerman, 219; also see 219–21. Cohen, 120; from Nichols, "Comic Modes in Black America."
59. Reed, *Yellow Back Radio Broke Down,* 9, and *Mumbo Jumbo,* 17.
60. Reed, *Yellow Back Radio Broke Down,* 154.
61. Cohen, 121; Nichols, "Comic Modes in Black America." Byerman, 219–20. Reed, *Yellow Back Radio Broke Down,* 149–55, 114–17, 34–36, 118, 155.
62. Reed, *Mumbo Jumbo,* 57, 65, 34.
63. Scholes, 41. Rubin, 366; from Brom Weber, "The Mode of 'Black Humor.'" Byerman, 237.
64. Cecil Brown, *The Life and Loves of Mr. Jiveass Nigger,* 14, 60–65.
65. Mel Watkins, "Old Winos, New Bottles," review, *The New York Times,* October 4, 1975. Scholes, 41.

CHAPTER ELEVEN: *Folklore and Street Humor*

1. Dundes, 624; quotation from John H. Burma, "Humor as a Technique of Race Conflict" (reprinted from *American Sociological Review,* vol. 2, 1946, 710–15). *Show Business Illustrated,* October 10, 1961, 94; Gregory quotation from Nat Hentoff, "Goodbye Mistah Bones." *The New York Times Magazine,* April 27, 1975, 40; from James McPherson, "The New Comic Style of Richard Pryor."
2. Ostendorf, 34–37.
3. Dundes, 611.
4. Ellison, *Shadow and Act,* 123. Philip Sterling, 23.
5. Spalding, 428; Langston Hughes reference based on quotation from *The Book of Negro Folklore* (New York: Dodd, Mead, 1966). Ostendorf, 5–6. Hurston, *Mules and Men,* 4–5.
6. Dundes, 531; from Bernard Wolfe, "Uncle Remus and the Malevolent Rabbit."
7. Dundes, 550; from Harry Oster, "Negro Humor: John and Old Marster"; Dorson remark quoted from *Negro Folk in Michigan* (Cambridge, Mass.: 1956), 49.
8. Abrahams, xx.
9. Hurston, *Mules and Men,* 75, 87–90.

10.   Hurston, *Mules and Men*, 82, 42–43.
11.   Hurston, *Mules and Men*, 24, 22, 93, 107–8, 31.
12.   Dundes, 552–53: from Oster, "Negro Humor."
13.   Charles Eliot, *The New England History, II* (New York: Charles Scribner's, 1857), 180. Puckett, 5.
14.   Hurston, *Mules and Men*, 96–97. Scholes, 41.
15.   Sterling Brown, 160–61.
16.   Kochman, *Rappin' and Stylin' Out*, 221, 219, 235; quotations from Roger D. Abrahams, "Joking: The Training of the Man of Words in Talking Broad."
17.   H. Rap Brown, 26.
18.   Discussion and interview with former high school classmates, March 1991.
19.   H. Rap Brown, 26, 29.
20.   Smitherman, 94–149.
21.   A descriptive version of this routine appears in Stearns, "Frontiers of Humor," *Southern Folklore Quarterly*, vol. 30, September 1966, 233. Coffin, 171; from Roger D. Abrahams, "Trickster, the Outrageous Hero."
22.   Chrisman and Hare, 54; from William H. Wiggins, "Jack Johnson as Bad Nigger: The Folklore of His Life" (Wiggins refers to Roger D. Abrahams's article, "Some Varieties of Heroes in America," which originally appeared in *Journal of the Folklore Institute*, vol. 3, 1966, 35). *Southern Folklore Quarterly*, vol. 30, September 1966, 231–32; from Stearns, "Frontiers of Humor."
23.   Chrisman and Hare, 55–56; from Wiggins, "Jack Johnson as Bad Nigger."
24.   Chrisman and Hare, 56.
25.   Hurston, *Mules and Men*, 5.
26.   See Philip Sterling, 81, for alternate example.
27.   Dance, xix.
28.   Dundes, 561–62; from editor's notes to "The Steel-Drivin' Man," by Leon R. Harris. Philip Sterling, 18; from the introduction, "Escape Into Pride and Dignity," by Saunders Redding.
29.   Coffin, 172; from Abrahams, "Trickster." Interview with Ishmael Reed, San Francisco, May 1979. Grier and Cobbs, *Black Rage*, 65.
30.   Chrisman and Hare, 54, 157–58, 67. In his *Pittsburgh Courier* column (June 22, 1946), George Schuyler wrote that laws preventing the "transportation of women over state lines for allegedly immoral purposes" were passed to stop Johnson; in *Black Odyssey*, Roi Ottley contends that Johnson's marriages to white women prompted the passage of laws against intermarriage in Wisconsin, Iowa, Kansas, Colorado, Minnesota, New Jersey, Michigan, and New York. Johnson oral narrative from J. Mason Brewer, *Worser Days and Better Times* (Chicago, 1965).
31.   Dance, 224. Abrahams, 238. Hughes and Bontemps, 362–63.
32.   Dundes, 334; from editor's notes to "Toasts," by William Labov, Paul Cohen, Clarence Robins, and John Lewis. Hughes and Bontemps, 366–67; Hughes wrote that this polite version of the story was heard in Harlem in 1956.
33.   Dance, 215–16; Dance's collected tales came from sources who either had lived in Virginia or were still living there when they were recorded; the version of "Shine" quoted in the text was recorded in Washington, D.C., in 1970 and was provided by an informant who had lived in Richmond. For more examples of toasts and ballads that mirror the Bad Nigger theme, see Roger D. Abrahams, *Deep Down in the Jungle* (Chicago, 1970).
34.   Wepman, Newman, and Binderman, 156–57; collected in 1966 from a

prison inmate. Dance, 230–32; from "Dolemite," collected at Virginia State Penitentiary, December 2, 1974.

35. See Dance, 236–37, for a version of "The Monkey and the Coon," and Wepman, Newman, and Binderman, 30–34, for a text of "The Pool-Shooting Monkey."
36. Collected from a Washington, D.C., resident, September 1990. The informant was in his late forties; his version approximates one I heard as a teenager.
37. Kochman, *Black and White Styles in Conflict*, 63, 70.
38. Dance, xix.
39. Esar, 406.
40. Philip Sterling, 17; from the introduction by Saunders Redding.
41. Dance, xix.
42. Interview with Robert Guillaume, Los Angeles, 1980.

Chapter Twelve: *The New Comics*

1. *Tuesday*, September 1965, 7; from Godfrey Cambridge, "A Lot of Laughs, A Lot of Changes." Foxx and Miller, 178. Interview with Flip Wilson in Malibu, November 1979.
2. Rubin, 362; quotation from Brom Weber, "The Mode of Black Humor."
3. Hendra, 3, 205. Martin and Segrave, 203. Marc, 178.
4. Berger, 7.
5. Hendra, 31, 35.
6. Berger, 79. Hendra, 35; Sahl quotation from *The New York Times* (December 1958).
7. Allen, 79. Berger, 60–61. Rovin, 49.
8. Wilson, 76–77; the liner notes for the Brubeck Octet's first recording in 1950 contained an explanation of the group's aim; according to saxophonist John Desmond, their music contained "the vigor and force of *simply* jazz, the harmonic complexities of Bartok and Milhaud, the form (and much of the dignity) of Bach, and at times the lyrical romanticism of Rachmaninoff" [italics mine].
9. Hendra, 39: source of Woody Allen quotation unspecified.
10. George, 65. Robbins and Ragan, 20.
11. Price, 77.
12. *Show Business Illustrated*, Oct. 17, 1961, 94; from Nat Hentoff, "Goodbye Mistah Bones." Williams and Harris, *Amistad 2*, 24; from Mel Watkins, "The Lyrics of James Brown."
13. Price, 41. Haskins, *Richard Pryor*, 32. Interviews with Junior Mance (February 1991) and Honi Coles (August 1979). Gregory, *Nigger*, 129–30. Interview with Richard Bright, former member of house band at the Casablanca, March 1991.
14. Telephone conversation with Timmie Rogers, January 1991.
15. Schiffman, 229. Williams and Williams, 3. Foxx and Miller, 171.
16. *Show Business Illustrated*, Hentoff, 89.
17. *Show Business Illustrated*, Hentoff, 88. Telephone conversation with Timmie Rogers, Jan. 1991.
18. Foxx and Miller, 164, 166. Schiffman, 228.
19. Interview with Junior Mance, February 1991.

20. Freud, 144–45. Rovin, 75; source of Lily Tomlin quotation unspecified.
21. Gregory, *Nigger,* 130–33.
22. Gregory, *Nigger,* 132.
23. Gregory, *Nigger,* 134–35.
24. Gregory, *Nigger,* 144. Hendra, 156; quotation from *Newsweek,* n.d.
25. *Show Business Illustrated,* Hentoff, 90.
26. Gregory, *Nigger,* 132.
27. *Show Business Illustrated,* Hentoff, 94.
28. Marc, 13–14.
29. Gregory, *Nigger,* 131–32.
30. *Show Business Illustrated,* Hentoff, 94.
31. Berger, 119. Hendra, 157, 160. Foxx and Miller, 178–80. Gregory, *Dick Gregory's Political Primer,* 5, 227. Schechter, 189.
32. *The Wall Street Journal,* December 4, 1967; from David Garino, "Comic with a Cause." *Ebony,* May 1967, 104; from "Negro Humor: An Answer to Anguish," by Allan Morrison. Hendra, 160.
33. Berger, 129. Adler, 11; source of Cosby quotation unspecified.
34. *Ebony,* January 1951, 40.
35. Foxx and Miller, 191.
36. Allen, 119, 123.
37. Allen, 117.
38. Schechter, 192.
39. Low and Clift, 13. Schechter, 191. *Soul Illustrated,* 1969 (month unknown), 63; from Walter Burrell, "What It Means to Be Godfrey Cambridge."
40. *Time,* February 1965, 94. Schechter, 192–94.
41. Schechter, 192–93. *Soul Illustrated,* Burrell, 46.
42. Schiffman, 227.
43. *Time,* February 1965, 94. *The New York Times,* July 21, 1991, Section 7, 29; from Nicholas Lemann's review of *Lone Star Rising: Lyndon Johnson and His Times, 1908–1960,* by Robert Balleck.
44. *Ebony,* January 1951, 39.
45. *Time,* February 1965, 94.
46. *Show Business Illustrated,* Hentoff, 69. Leonard Reed quotation from *A Laugh, A Tear,* a television special produced by S. I. Communications, Inc., 1990.
47. *Sepia,* June 1972, 44; from Robert Bennett, "How Redd Foxx Went From Blue Jokes to Black." Fox, 279–80. Foxx and Miller, 244. Foxx interview from television special *A Laugh, A Tear.*
48. Schechter, 196–97. *Soul Illustrated,* Burrell, 65.
49. *Sepia,* June 1972, Bennett, 41.
50. *Time,* Jan. 31, 1972, 59; from "When You're Hot, You're Hot."
51. Interview with Flip Wilson, November 1979. Haskins, *Richard Pryor,* 25; source of LaWanda Page quotation unspecified.
52. Interview with Flip Wilson, Nov. 1979. Schiffman, 235.
53. Schiffman, 234. *Time,* Jan. 31, 1972, 56. Interview with Flip Wilson, Nov. 1979.
54. Interview with Flip Wilson, Nov. 1979.
55. Interview with Flip Wilson, Nov. 1979. *The New York Times,* 1968 (clipping from New York Public Library file on Flip Wilson, date unavailable), section D, 27; from Tom Burke, "It Pays to Be Flip."
56. Interview with Flip Wilson, Nov. 1979.

57. Interview with Flip Wilson, Nov. 1979.
58. *Time*, Jan. 31, 1972, 57.

CHAPTER THIRTEEN : *Pryor and Thereafter*

1. Keenan Ivory Wayans quotation from *A Laugh, A Tear,* a television special produced by S. I. Communications, 1990. *The New Yorker,* April 5, 1982, 184; from a review of *Richard Pryor Live on Sunset Strip* by Pauline Kael. Robbins and Ragan, 53; date of *Time* quotation unspecified.
2. Freud, 151.
3. Allen, 221. Schiffman, 235–36.
4. Robbins and Ragan, 116, 119. Williams and Williams, 51; quotation from *Playboy* article (December 1979) by William Brashler. *Rolling Stone,* July 24, 1980, 14; from David Felton, "Pryor's Inferno, A Great Comic's Tragic Life." Rovin, 189. Allen, 231.
5. Robbins and Ragan, 117.
6. *Newsweek,* May 3, 1982, "Richard Pryor, Bustin' Loose," 50. Rovin, 14. Haskins, *Richard Pryor,* 8.
7. Rovin, 19–20.
8. Haskins, *Richard Pryor,* 11, 15–21. Rovin, 33.
9. Williams and Williams, 39. Rovin, 55; date of *Variety* article unspecified.
10. *Newsweek,* May 3, 1982, 52. Rovin, 54–55.
11. *The New York Times Magazine,* April 27, 1975, 20; from James McPherson, "The New Comic Style of Richard Pryor."
12. Interview with Budd Friedman in Los Angeles, Nov. 1969.
13. Rovin, 68; source of Pryor quotation unspecified.
14. Williams and Williams, 53–57.
15. Telephone interview with Cecil Brown, July 1991.
16. Rovin, 75.
17. Haskins, *Richard Pryor,* 62–63. Rovin, 80–81; source of Pryor quotation unspecified.
18. Interview with Cecil Brown, Jan. 1991.
19. Williams and Williams, 48; source and date of Cosby quotation unspecified.
20. Material from Richard Pryor's September 1971 Improv appearance is available on the video *Live and Smokin'* (1981).
21. Rovin, 58; source of Pryor quotation unspecified.
22. *The New York Times Magazine,* April 27, 1975, McPherson, 22.
23. Schiffman, 231. Fox, 277.
24. Rovin, 100; source of Pryor quotation unspecified.
25. Versions of the above routines can be found on *That Nigger's Crazy* (Reprise REP2287, 1974) and *Richard Pryor . . . Is It Something I Said?* (Reprise REP2285, 1975).
26. Dundes, 652; Sam tale from Paulette Cross, "Jokes and Black Consciousness: A Collection with Interviews," reprinted from *Folklore Forum,* vol. 2., no. 6 (Nov. 1969). *The Negro Digest,* June 1951, 24; from Langston Hughes, "Jokes Negroes Tell on Themselves."
27. Haskins, *Richard Pryor,* 7; source of Pryor quotation unspecified. *The New York Times Magazine,* April 27, 1975, McPherson, 32.
28. *The New York Times Magazine,* April 27, 1975, McPherson, 20. Williams and Williams, 12; source and exact date of Cosby quotation unspecified.

29. *The New York Times Magazine,* April 27, 1975, McPherson. 22. Abrahams, 25–26.
30. *Rolling Stone,* May 3, 1979, 52; from David Felton, "Richard Pryor's (Portrait of the Godhead as a Young Dog)."
31. *Newsweek,* May 3, 1982, 48. Rovin, 177; date of *New York Times* quotation unspecified. *Rolling Stone,* May 3, 1979, Felton, 50–52. *The New Yorker,* April 5, 1982, Kael, 184–85.
32. From interviews conducted 1983 through 1989 in various parts of the United States.
33. *Encore American and Worldwide News,* November 24, 1975, 28; from Frederick D. Murphy, "Richard Pryor: Teetering on Jest, Living by His Wit." *The New York Times Magazine,* April 27, 1975, McPherson, 22.
34. Williams and Williams, 215–16.
35. Allen, 227. Rubin, 362; from Brom Weber, "The Mode of 'Black Humor.' "
36. Cohen, 46; from Stanley Trachtenberg, "Berger and Barth: The Comedy of Decomposition."
37. *Encore American and Worldwide News,* November 24, 1975, Murphy, 28. Dundes, 336; from William Labov, Paul Cohen, Clarence Robins, and John Lewis, "Toasts." *The New Yorker,* April 5, 1982, from a review by Pauline Kael.
38. *The SoHo News,* Feb. 2, 1982, 12; from Michael Shore, "Eddie Murphy Reignites Black Comedy." *Newsweek,* Jan. 7, 1985; from "Crazy Eddie."
39. *The New York Times,* June 17, 1990; Gates quotation from Jan Pereles, "Rap: Slick, Violent, Nasty and, Maybe, Hopeful."
40. Sypher, 47–48; from George Meredith, "An Essay on Comedy."
41. From "American Humor," an address given by Ralph Ellison at Oklahoma State University, April 11, 1970.
42. Sypher, 252.
43. Sypher, 252.
44. Cohen, 52–53; from Trachtenberg, "Berger and Barth."
45. Holland, 25.

Much has been made of African America's cultural impact on American society—the influence of black music in particular—but neither the rich expansiveness of African-American humor nor its contribution to America's comic heritage has been appropriately documented.

Two noteworthy exceptions are *The Redd Foxx Encyclopedia of Black Humor* (1977) by Redd Foxx and Norma Miller and *The History of Negro Humor in America* (1970) by William Schechter. The Foxx and Miller *Encyclopedia*, as the title suggests, is primarily an informative catalogue of comedians and jokes, but it does contain insightful, albeit brief, expositions on the nature of black humor and on its origins. Moreover, since the authors are themselves comedians and have the advantage of intimate familiarity with the often closed world of performers, there is an air of subjective authenticity about it. There is perhaps no finer reference to the various styles and routines of professional black comics. Schechter's *History* of black humor is broader in scope theoretically but less detailed and much less illuminating regarding the stylistic texture or actual content of black humor. The author, for instance, devotes only thirty-five pages to the period between minstrelsy and the 1960s—a time during which privately and in the relatively isolated confines of segregated road shows and variety houses, black comedy blossomed so extensively that the period may reasonably be called the classic age of African-American humor. Consequently, although Schechter's book encompasses the development of black humor from Africa to the sixties, in essence it is more an outline than a fleshed-out study. Needless to say, however, both of these volumes have been extremely helpful in the preparation of *On the Real Side*.

Cultural historians Donald Bogle, Thomas Cripps, J. Fred MacDonald, Henry T. Sampson, Robert C. Toll, Arthur Frank Wertheim, and others have produced studies of minstrelsy, motion pictures, radio, and television that, while not directly focused on comedy, provide revealing documentation of the ascent of African-American humor.

In addition, there have been numerous publications of collections of black folklore and humor since the 1960s. Many of these anthologies contain some description and analysis of the original materials assembled, and in some instances provide useful explanations of their derivation as well as their social significance; even when they have not provided specific sources or in-depth commentary, many have indicated where such information might be found. Folklorists and scholars J. Mason Brewer, Roger D. Abrahams, Langston Hughes, Zora Neale Hurston, and Sterling A. Brown, among many others, have provided essential research and commentary without which this or any other examination of the subject would be impossible. References to their works are made throughout this book.

NONFICTION

Abrahams, Roger D. *Afro-American Folktales: Stories from Black Traditions in the New World.* New York: Pantheon, 1985.

Abrahams, Roger D., and John F. Szwed, ed. *After Africa.* New Haven: Yale University Press, 1983.

Adler, Bill. *The Cosby Wit: His Life and Humor.* New York: Critic's Choice Paperbacks, 1986.

Allen, Steve. *Funny People.* New York: Stein and Day, 1981.

Anderson, Jervis. *This Was Harlem: A Cultural Portrait, 1900–1950.* New York: Farrar, Straus and Giroux, 1982.

Arce, Hector. *Groucho.* New York: G. P. Putnam's Sons, 1979.

Ashe, Arthur R., Jr. *A Hard Road to Glory: A History of the African-American Athlete 1619–1918.* New York: Amistad/Warner Books, 1988.

Baldwin, James. *The Price of the Ticket: Collected Nonfiction 1948–1985.* New York: St. Martin's Press, Marek, 1985.

Barreca, Regina. *They Used to Call Me Snow White . . . But I Drifted.* New York: Viking, 1991.

Basie, Count, with Albert Murray. *Good Morning Blues: The Autobiography of Count Basie.* New York: Random House, 1985.

Bebey, Francis. *African Music: A People's Art.* New York: Lawrence Hill, 1975.

Berger, Phil. *The Last Laugh: The World of Stand-Up Comics.* New York: Ballantine Books, 1976.

Bermel, Albert. *Farce: The Comprehensive and Definitive Account of One of the World's Funniest Art Forms.* New York: Touchstone Books, 1982.

Berry, Faith. *Langston Hughes: Before and Beyond Harlem*. New York: Lawrence Hill, 1983.

Billington, Sandra. *The Social History of the Fool*. New York: St. Martin's Press, 1984.

Blair, Walter. *Native American Humor*. New York: Chandler Publishing, 1960.

Bleakley, Robert. *African Masks*. New York: St. Martin's Press, 1978.

Bogle, Donald. *Blacks in American Films and Television: An Illustrated Encyclopedia*. New York: Fireside Books, 1989.

Bogle, Donald. *Toms, Coons, Mulattoes, Mammies, and Bucks: An Interpretive History of Blacks in American Films*. New York: Viking Press, 1973.

Bone, Robert. *The Negro Novel in America*. Rev. ed. New Haven: Yale University Press, 1970.

Bontemps, Arna. *The Harlem Renaissance Remembered: Essays Edited with a Memoir by Arna Bontemps*. New York: Dodd, Mead, 1984.

Boskin, Joseph. *Sambo: The Rise and Demise of an American Jester*. New York: Oxford University Press, 1986.

Brewer, J. Mason. *American Negro Folklore*. Chicago: Quadrangle Books, 1968.

Brown, Claude. *Manchild in the Promised Land*. New York: Signet, 1966.

Brown, H. Rap. *Die Nigger Die!* New York: Dial Press, 1969.

Brown, Jim, with Steve Delsohn. *Out of Bounds*. New York: Zebra Books, 1989.

Brown, Karl. *Adventures with D. W. Griffith*. Edited and with an introduction by Kevin Brownlow. New York: Farrar, Straus and Giroux, 1973.

Brown, Sterling. *"Negro Poetry and Drama" and "The Negro in American Fiction."* New York: Atheneum, 1969.

Brown, Sterling A., Arthur P. Davis, and Ulysses Lee, ed. *The Negro Caravan*. New York: Arno Press and The New York Times, 1969.

Brownlow, Kevin, and John Kobal. *Hollywood: The Pioneers*. New York: Alfred A. Knopf, 1979.

Buckley, Gail Lumet. *The Hornes: An American Family*. New York: Alfred A. Knopf, 1986.

Bullock, Penelope L. *The Afro-American Periodical Press 1838–1909*. Baton Rouge, La.: Louisiana State University Press, 1981.

Burns, George. *George Burns: The Third Time Around*. New York: G. P. Putnam's Sons, 1980.

Byerman, Keith E. *Fingering the Jagged Grain: Tradition and Form in Recent Black Fiction.* Athens, Ga.: University of Georgia Press, 1985.

Cahn, William and Rhoda. *The Great American Comedy Scene.* New York: Julian Messner, 1978.

Campbell, Edward D. C., Jr. *The Celluloid South: Hollywood and the Southern Myth.* Knoxville: University of Tennessee Press, 1981.

Chambers, Bradford. *Chronicles of Black Protest.* New York: Mentor, 1969.

Charles, Ray, and David Ritz. *Brother Ray: Ray Charles' Own Story.* New York: Dial Press, 1978.

Charters, Ann. *Nobody: The Story of Bert Williams.* New York: Macmillan, 1969.

Charters, Samuel. *The Roots of the Blues: An African Search.* Boston: Marion Boyars, 1981.

Chrisman, Robert, and Nathan Hare, eds. *Contemporary Black Thought: The Best From The Black Scholar.* New York: Bobbs-Merrill, 1973.

Clark, William Bedford, and W. Craig Turner, eds. *Critical Essays on American Humor.* Boston: G. K. Hall, 1984.

Clarkson, Atelia, and Gilbert B. Cross. *World Folktales: A Scribner Resource Collection.* New York: Charles Scribner's Sons, 1980.

Coffin, Tristam Potter. *Our Living Conditions: An Introduction to American Folklore.* New York: Basic Books, 1968.

Cohen, Sarah Blacher, ed. *Comic Relief: Humor in Contemporary American Literature.* Chicago: University of Illinois Press, 1978.

Collier, James Lincoln. *Louis Armstrong: An American Genius.* New York: Oxford University Press, 1983.

Cook, Michael J. *Afro-American Literature in the Twentieth Century.* New Haven: Yale University Press, 1984.

Cooper, Ralph, with Steve Dougherty. *Amateur Night at the Apollo: Ralph Cooper Presents Five Decades of Great Entertainment.* New York: HarperCollins, 1990.

Costello, Mark, and David Foster Wallace. *Signifying Rappers: Rap and Race in the Urban Present.* New York: Ecco Press, 1990.

Courlander, Harold. *Negro Folk Music, U.S.A.* New York: Columbia University Press, 1970.

Courlander, Harold. *A Treasury of Afro-American Folklore.* New York: Crown, 1976.

Cox, Samuel S. *Why We Laugh.* New York: Benjamin Blom, 1969.

Cripps, Thomas. *Black Film as Genre.* Bloomington, Ind.: Indiana University Press, 1978.

Cripps, Thomas. *Slow Fade to Black: The Negro in American Film, 1900–1942.* New York: Oxford University Press, 1977.

Cruse, Harold. *The Crisis of the Negro Intellectual.* New York: William Morrow, 1967.

Cunard, Nancy. *Negro: An Anthology Collected and Edited by Nancy Cunard.* New York: Frederick Unger, 1970.

Dance, Daryl Cumber. *Shuckin' and Jivin': Folklore from Contemporary Black Americans.* Bloomington, Ind.: Indiana University Press, 1978.

Dann, Martin E., ed. *The Black Press: 1827–1890.* New York: G. P. Putnam's Sons, 1971.

Davidson, Basil. *Africa: History of a Continent.* New York: Macmillan, 1972.

Davidson, Basil. *The African Genius: An Introduction to African Social and Cultural History.* Boston: Atlantic Monthly Press, 1970.

Davis, Ronald L. *A History of Music in American Life.* Vol. 1, *The Formative Years, 1620–1865.* Malabar, Fla.: Robert Krieger, 1982.

Davis, Sammy, Jr., and Jane and Burt Boyar. *Why Me? The Sammy Davis, Jr. Story.* New York: Warner Books, 1990.

Davis, Sammy, Jr., and Jane and Burt Boyar. *Yes I Can: The Story of Sammy Davis, Jr.* New York: Noonday Press/Farrar, Straus and Giroux, 1990.

Dennison, Sam. *Scandalize My Name: Black Imagery in American Popular Music.* New York: Garland Publishing, 1982.

Devere, John, and Jurgen Vollmer. *Black Genesis: African Roots.* New York: St. Martin's Press, 1980.

Dorson, Richard M. *American Folklore.* Chicago: University of Chicago Press, 1959.

Dorson, Richard M. *Handbook of American Folklore.* Bloomington: Indiana University Press, 1983.

Douglass, Frederick. *The Life and Times of Frederick Douglass: Written by Himself.* Secaucus, N.J.: Citadel Press (Facsimile Edition), 1983.

Douglass, Frederick. *My Bondage and My Freedom.* New York: Arno Press and The New York Times, 1969.

Downs, Robert B. *Books That Changed the World.* Chicago: American Library Association, 1978.

Du Bois, W. E. B. *The Souls of Black Folk.* New York: Signet, 1969.

Du Bois, W. E. B. *The Suppression of the African Slave Trade to the United States of America 1638–1870.* New York: Schocken Books, 1969.

Dundes, Alan, ed. *Mother Wit from the Laughing Barrel.* Jackson, Miss.: University Press of Mississippi, 1990.

Dunning, John. *Tune in Yesterday: The Ultimate Encyclopedia of Old-Time Radio 1925–1976.* New York: Prentice-Hall, 1976.

Ellison, Ralph. *Going to the Territory.* New York: Random House, 1986.

Ellison, Ralph. *Shadow and Act.* New York: Random House, 1964.

Ely, Melvin Patrick. *The Adventures of Amos 'n' Andy: A Social History of an American Phenomenon.* New York: Macmillan, The Free Press, 1991.

Epstein, Dena J. *Sinful Tunes and Spirituals: Black Folk Music to the Civil War.* Chicago: University of Illinois Press, 1977.

Erenberg, Lewis A. *Steppin' Out: New York Nightlife and the Transformation of American Culture, 1890–1930.* Westport, Conn.: Greenwood Press, 1981.

Esar, Evan. *The Comic Encyclopedia.* New York: Doubleday, 1978.

Fabre, Geneviève. *Drumbeats, Masks, and Metaphor: Contemporary Afro-American Theatre.* Cambridge, Mass.: Harvard University Press, 1983.

Faith, William Robert. *Bob Hope: A Life in Comedy.* New York: G. P. Putnam's Sons, 1982.

Fanon, Frantz. *Black Skin, White Masks.* New York: Grove Press, 1967.

Fitzhugh, George. *Cannibals All! or, Slaves Without Masters.* Cambridge, Mass.: Harvard University Press, Belknap Press, 1960.

Fletcher, Tom. *100 Years of the Negro in Show Business.* New York: Burdge, 1954.

Forma, Warren. *They Were Ragtime.* New York: Grosset and Dunlap, 1976.

Fox, Ted. *Showtime at the Apollo.* New York: Holt, Rinehart and Winston, 1983.

Foxx, Redd, and Norma Miller. *The Redd Foxx Encyclopedia of Black Humor.* Pasadena, Calif.: Ward Ritchie Press, 1977.

Franklin, Joe. *Joe Franklin's Encyclopedia of Comedians.* New York: Bell Publishing, 1985.

Fredrickson, George M. *The Black Image in the White Mind: The*

Debate on Afro-American Character and Destiny, 1817–1914. New York: Harper and Row, 1971.

Freud, Sigmund. *Jokes and Their Relation to the Unconscious.* Edited and translated by James Strachey. New York: W. W. Norton, 1963.

Furnas, J. C. *Stormy Weather: Crosslights on the Nineteen Thirties: An Informal Social History of the United States 1929–1941.* New York: G. P. Putnam's Sons, 1977.

Gates, Henry Louis, and Charles T. Davis, eds. *The Slave's Narrative: Texts and Contexts.* New York: Oxford University Press, 1984.

Gayle, Addison, Jr. *The Way of the New World.* New York: Doubleday, 1975.

Genovese, Eugene D. *Roll, Jordan, Roll: The World the Slaves Made.* New York: Random House, Vintage Books, 1976.

George, Nelson. *The Death of Rhythm and Blues.* New York: E. P. Dutton, Obelisk, 1988.

Giddings, Paula. *When and Where I Enter: The Impact of Black Women on Race and Sex in America.* New York: William Morrow, 1984.

Gilbert, Douglas. *American Vaudeville: Its Life and Times.* New York: Dover, 1963.

Gitler, Ira. *Swing to Bebop: An Oral History of the Transition in Jazz in the 1940s.* New York: Oxford University Press, 1985.

Goldstein, Rhoda L., ed. *Black Life and Culture in the United States.* New York: Thomas Y. Crowell, 1971.

Gordon, William S. *Recollections of the Old Quarter.* Freeport, N.Y.: Books for Libraries Press, 1972.

Gorer, Geoffrey. *Africa Dances: A Book About West African Negroes.* New York: W. W. Norton, 1962.

Gregory, Dick. *Dick Gregory's Political Primer.* Edited by James R. McGraw. New York: Harper and Row, 1972.

Gregory, Dick, with Robert Lipsyte. *Nigger: An Autobiography.* New York: Washington Square Press, 1986.

Grier, William H., and Price M. Cobbs. *Black Rage.* New York: Basic Books, 1968.

Grier, William H., and Price M. Cobbs. *The Jesus Bag.* New York: McGraw-Hill, 1971.

Grimsted, David, ed. *Notions of the Americans 1820–1860.* "The American Culture" series. New York: George Braziller, 1970.

Gurewitch, Morton. *Comedy: The Irrational Vision.* Ithaca, N.Y.: Cornell University Press, 1975.

Gutman, Herbert G. *The Black Family in Slavery and Freedom, 1750–1925.* New York: Pantheon, 1976.

Gwaltney, John Langston. *Drylongso: A Self-Portrait of Black America.* New York: Random House, 1980.

Halliwell, Leslie. *The Filmgoer's Companion.* 4th Ed. New York: Hill and Wang, 1974.

Hamm, Charles. *Yesterdays: Popular Song in America.* New York: W. W. Norton, 1979.

Hampton, Lionel, with James Haskins. *Hamp: An Autobiography.* New York: Warner Books, Amistad Books, 1990.

Handy, W. C. *Father of the Blues: An Autobiography.* New York: Da Capo Press, 1961.

Harper, Michael S., and Robert B. Stepto. *Chant of Saints: A Gathering of Afro-American Literature, Art, and Scholarship.* Chicago: University of Illinois Press, 1979.

Harris, Middleton, with Morris Levitt, Roger Furman, and Ernest Smith. *The Black Book.* New York: Random House, 1974.

Haskins, Jim. *The Cotton Club.* New York: Random House, 1977.

Haskins, Jim. *Richard Pryor: A Man and His Madness, A Biography.* New York: Beaufort Books, 1984.

Heide, Robert, and John Gilman. *Dime-Store Dream Parade: Popular Culture 1925–1955.* New York: E. P. Dutton, 1979.

Henderson, Robert M. *D. W. Griffith: His Life and Work.* New York: Oxford University Press, 1972.

Henderson, Stephen. *Understanding the New Black Poetry: Black Speech and Black Music as Poetic References.* New York: William Morrow, 1973.

Hendra, Tony. *Going Too Far.* New York: Doubleday, Dolphin, 1987.

Hersey, John, ed. *Ralph Ellison: A Collection of Critical Essays.* Englewood Cliffs, N.J.: Prentice-Hall, 1974.

Herskovits, Melville J. *The Myth of the Negro Past.* New York: Beacon Press, 1958.

Holland, Norman N. *Laughing: A Psychology of Humor.* Ithaca, N.Y.: Cornell University Press, 1982.

Holton, Sylvia Wallace. *Down Home and Uptown: The Representation of Black Speech in American Fiction.* Cranbury, N.J.: Fairleigh Dickinson University Press, 1964.

Huet, Michel, and Jean-Louis Paudrat. *The Dance, Art and Ritual of Africa.* New York: Pantheon, 1978.

Huggins, Nathan. *Harlem Renaissance*. New York: Oxford University Press, 1971.

Hughes, Langston. *The Big Sea: An Autobiography*. New York: Alfred A. Knopf, 1940.

Hughes, Langston. *The Langston Hughes Reader*. New York: George Braziller, 1958.

Hughes, Langston, and Arna Bontemps. *Book of Negro Folklore*. New York: Dodd Mead, Apollo Editions, 1958.

Hughes, Langston, and Arna Bontemps, eds. *The Poetry of the Negro 1746–1970*. New York: Doubleday, 1970.

Hughes, Langston, and Milton Meltzer. *Black Magic: A Pictorial History of the Negro in American Entertainment*. Englewood Cliffs, N.J.: Prentice-Hall, 1967.

Hurston, Zora Neale. *Dust Tracks on a Road: An Autobiography*. 2nd ed. Chicago: University of Chicago Press, 1984.

Hurston, Zora Neale. *Mules and Men*. Bloomington, Ind.: Indiana University Press, 1978.

Jackson, Blyden. *The Waiting Years: Essays on American Negro Literature*. Baton Rouge, La.: Louisiana State University Press, 1976.

Jasen, David A., and Jay Tichenor. *Rags and Ragtime: A Musical History*. New York: Seabury Press, 1978.

Johnson, James Weldon. *Along This Way: The Autobiography of James Weldon Johnson*. New York: Viking Press, 1933.

Johnson, James Weldon. *Black Manhattan*. New York: Atheneum, 1968.

Johnson, John H. *Succeeding against All Odds*. New York: Warner, Amistad, 1989.

Jones, Jacqueline. *Labor of Love, Labor of Sorrow: Black Women, Work and the Family, From Slavery to the Present*. New York: Vintage Books, 1986.

Jones, LeRoi (Amiri Baraka). *Blues People: Negro Music in White America*. New York: William Morrow, 1963.

Joyner, Charles. *Down by the Riverside: A South Carolina Slave Community*. Chicago: University of Illinois Press, 1984.

Kael, Pauline. *Hooked*. New York: E. P. Dutton, William Abrahams, 1985.

Kael, Pauline. *State of the Art*. New York: E. P. Dutton, William Abrahams, 1983.

Katz, Bernard. *The Social Implications of Early Negro Music in the*

United States. New York: Arno Press and The New York Times, 1969.

Katz, William Loren. *The Invisible Empire*. Seattle, Wash.: Open Hand Publishing, 1986.

Kearns, Francis E. *Black Identity: A Thematic Reader*. New York: Holt, Rinehart and Winston, 1970.

Keil, Charles. *Urban Blues*. Chicago: University of Chicago Press, 1966.

Kittredge, George Lyman, ed. *The Complete Works of William Shakespeare*. New York: Grolier, 1958.

Klein, Herbert. *African Slavery in Latin America and the Caribbean*. New York: Oxford University Press, 1986.

Klotman, Phyllis Rauch. *Frame by Frame: A Black Filmography*. Bloomington, Ind.: Indiana University Press, 1979.

Kochman, Thomas. *Black and White Styles in Conflict*. Chicago: University of Chicago Press, 1981.

Kochman, Thomas, ed. *Rappin' and Stylin' Out: Communication in Urban Black America*. Chicago: University of Illinois Press, 1972.

Lamparski, Richard. *Whatever Became Of . . .* New York: Crown, 1967.

Lester, Julius. *To Be a Slave*. New York: Scholastic, 1968.

Lewis, David Levering. *When Harlem Was in Vogue*. New York: Alfred A. Knopf, 1981.

Lewis, Marlo and Mina Bess. *Prime Time*. New York: St. Martin's Press, 1979.

Locke, Alain. *"The Negro and His Music"* and *"Negro Art: Past and Present."* New York: Arno Press and The New York Times, 1969.

Locke, Alain, ed. *The New Negro*. New York, Atheneum, 1968.

Lovell, John, Jr. *Black Song: The Forge and the Flame*. New York: Macmillan, 1972.

Low, W. A., and Virgil A. Clift, eds. *Encyclopedia of Black America*. New York: McGraw-Hill, 1981.

MacDonald, J. Fred. *Black and White TV: Afro-Americans in Television Since 1948*. Chicago: Nelson Hall, 1983.

MacDonald, J. Fred. *Don't Touch That Dial!* Chicago: Nelson Hall, 1981.

Maltin, Leonard. *The Great Movie Comedians: From Charlie Chaplin to Woody Allen*. New York: Crown, 1978.

Maltin, Leonard, and Richard W. Bann. *Our Gang: The Life and Times of the Little Rascals*. New York: Crown, 1977.

Maquet, Jacques. *Africanity: The Cultural Unity of Black Africa*. New York: Oxford University Press, 1972.

Marc, David. *Comic Visions: Television Comedy and American Culture*. Boston: Unwin Hyman, 1989.

Martin, Linda, and Kerry Segrave. *Women in Comedy*. Secaucus, N.J.: Citadel Press, 1986.

Marx, Arthur. *Red Skelton*. New York: E. P. Dutton, 1979.

Markham, Pigmeat, and Bill Levinson. *Here Come the Judge*. New York: Paperback Library, 1969.

McKee, Margaret, and Fred Chisenhall. *Beale Black and Blue: Life and Music on America's Main Street*. Baton Rouge, La.: Louisiana State University Press, 1981.

McNeil, Alex. *Total Television: A Comprehensive Guide to Programming from 1948–1980*. New York: Penguin Books, 1980.

Meier, August, and Elliot Rudwick. *From Plantation to Ghetto*. Rev. ed. New York: Hill and Wang, 1970.

Miller, Douglas T., and Marion Nowak. *The Fifties: The Way We Really Were*. New York: Doubleday, 1977.

Mingus, Charles. *Beneath the Underdog*. New York: Alfred A. Knopf, 1971.

Mitchell, Loften. *Black Drama: The Story of the American Negro in the Theatre*. New York: Hawthorne Books, 1967.

Mordden, Ethan. *The Hollywood Musical*. New York: St. Martin's Press, 1981.

Moses, Joseph. *The Novelist as Comedian: George Meredith and the Ironic Sensibility*. New York: Schocken Books, 1983.

Mphahlele, Ezekiel. *The African Image*. New York: Praeger, 1974.

Murray, Albert. *The Omni-Americans: New Perspectives on Black Experience and American Culture*. New York: Outerbridge and Dienstfrey, 1970.

Murray, Albert. *Stomping the Blues*. New York: McGraw-Hill, 1976.

Murray, James. *To Find an Image: Black Films from Uncle Tom to Superfly*. New York: Bobbs-Merrill, 1974.

Myrdal, Gunnar. *An American Dilemma: The Negro Problem and Modern Democracy*. New York: Pantheon, 1972.

Nash, Roderick, ed. *The Call of the Wild: 1900–1916*. "The American Culture" series. New York: George Braziller, 1970.

Nichols, Charles H., ed. *Arna Bontemps–Langston Hughes Letters: 1925–1967*. New York: Dodd, Mead, 1980.

Novak, William, and Moshe Waldoks, eds. *The Big Book of American*

Humor: The Best of the Past 25 Years. New York: Harper Perennial, 1990.

Novak, William, and Moshe Waldoks, eds. *The Big Book of Jewish Humor.* New York: Harper and Row, 1981.

Null, Gary. *Black Hollywood: The Negro in Motion Pictures.* New York: Citadel Press/First Carol Publishing, 1975.

Nye, Russel B. *Society and Culture in America: 1830–1860.* New York: Harper and Row, 1974.

Oakley, Giles. *The Devil's Music: A History of the Blues.* New York: Taplinger, 1977.

Oberfirst, Robert. *Al Jolson: You Ain't Heard Nothing Yet!* New York: A. S. Barnes, 1980.

O'Connor, John E., ed. *American History/ American Television: Interpreting the Video Past.* Foreword by Erik Barnouw. New York: Frederick Unger, 1983.

Oliver, Paul. *Blues Fell This Morning: The Meaning of the Blues.* New York: Horizon Press, 1960.

Oliver, Paul. *Songsters and Saints: Vocal Traditions on Race Records.* New York: Cambridge University Press, 1984.

O'Meally, Robert. *The Craft of Ralph Ellison.* Cambridge, Mass.: Harvard University Press, 1980.

O'Meally, Robert, ed. *New Essays on "Invisible Man,"* New York, Cambridge University Press, 1988.

Osborne, John, and the Editors of Time-Life Books. *The Old South: Alabama, Florida, Georgia, Mississippi, South Carolina.* New York: Time-Life Books, 1968.

Osofsky, Gilbert. *Harlem—The Making of a Ghetto: Negro New York, 1890–1930.* New York: Harper & Row, 1963.

Osofsky, Gilbert, ed. *Puttin' on Ole Massa: The Slave Narratives of Henry Bibb, William Wells Brown, and Solomon Northup.* New York: Harper and Row, 1969.

Ostendorf, Berndt. *Black Literature in White America.* Totowa, N.J.: Barnes and Noble Books, 1982.

Paley, William S. *As It Happened: A Memoir.* New York: Doubleday, 1979.

Panati, Charles. *The Browser's Book of Beginnings: Origins of Everything Under (and Including) the Sun.* New York: Houghton Mifflin, 1984.

Pasteur, Alfred B., and Ivory L. Toldson. *Roots of Soul: The Psychology of Black Expressiveness.* New York: Doubleday, Anchor, 1982.

Patterson, Lindsay. *Black Theatre: A Twentieth-Century Collection of the Work of Its Best Playwrights*. New York: New American Library, 1971.

Patterson, Lindsay, ed. *Anthology of the American Negro in the Theatre: A Critical Approach*. "The International Library of Negro Life" series. New York: Publishers Company, 1968.

Perrett, Geoffrey. *America in the Twenties*. New York: Simon and Schuster, 1982.

Pomerance, Alan. *Repeal of the Blues*. Secaucus, N.J.: Citadel Press, 1988.

Pratt, George C. *Spellbound in Darkness: A History of Silent Film*. Greenwich, Conn.: New York Graphic Society, 1973.

Price, Joe X. *Redd Foxx, B.S. (Before Sanford)*. Chicago: Contemporary Books, 1979.

Pryse, Marjorie, and Hortense J. Spillers, eds. *Conjuring: Black Women, Fiction and Literary Tradition*. Bloomington, Ind.: Indiana University Press, 1985.

Puckett, Newbell Niles. *The Magic and Folk Beliefs of the Southern Negro*. New York: Dover, 1969.

Rampersad, Arnold. *The Life of Langston Hughes*. Vol. 1, *1902–1941, I Too Sing America*. New York: Oxford University Press, 1986.

Rawson, Claude, ed. *English Satire and the Satiric Tradition*. New York: Basil Blackwell, 1984.

Redd, Lawrence N. *Rock Is Rhythm and Blues: (The Impact of Mass Media)*. New York: Michigan State University Press, 1974.

Redfern, Walter. *Puns*. New York: Basil Blackwell, 1984.

Reed, Ishmael. *Shrovetide in Old New Orleans*. New York: Doubleday, 1978.

Robbins, Fred, and David Ragan. *Richard Pryor: This Cat's Got Nine Lives*. New York: G. P. Putnam's, Delilah Books, 1982.

Rose, Al. *Hubie Blake*. New York: Schirmer Books, 1979.

Rose, Phyllis. *Jazz Cleopatra: Josephine Baker in Her Time*. New York: Doubleday, 1989.

Rourke, Constance. *American Humor: A Study of the National Character*. New York: Harcourt Brace Jovanovich, Harvest, 1931.

Rovin, Jeff. *Richard Pryor: Black and White*. New York: Bantam, 1984.

Rubin, Louis D., Jr., ed. *The Comic Imagination in American Literature*. New Brunswick, N.J.: Rutgers University Press, 1973.

Sackheim, Eric. *The Blues Line: A Collection of Blues Lyrics From Leadbelly to Muddy Waters*. New York: Schirmer Books, 1975.

Sampson, Henry T. *Blacks in Blackface: A Sourcebook on Early Black Musical Shows.* Metuchen, N.J.: Scarecrow Press, 1980.

Sartre, Jean-Paul. *Anti-Semite and Jew.* New York: Schocken Books, 1965.

Schechter, William. *The History of Negro Humor in America.* New York: Fleet Press, 1970.

Schickel, Richard. *D. W. Griffith: An American Life.* New York: Simon and Schuster, 1984.

Schiffman, Jack. *Harlem Heyday.* Buffalo, N.Y.: Prometheus Books, 1984.

Scholes, Robert. *The Fabulators.* New York: Oxford University Press, 1967.

Schutz, Charles E. *Political Humor: From Aristophanes to Sam Ervin.* Cranberry, N.J.: Fairleigh Dickinson University, 1977.

Scruggs, Charles. *The Sage in Harlem: H. L. Mencken and the Black Writers of the 1920's.* Baltimore, Md.: Johns Hopkins University Press, 1984.

Shaw, Arnold. *Honkers and Shouters.* New York: Macmillan, 1978.

Shore, Sammy. *The Warm-Up: The Autobiography of a Number Two Man.* New York: William Morrow, 1984.

Sidran, Ben. *Black Talk.* New York: Holt, Rinehart and Winston, 1971.

Sinkler, George. *The Racial Attitudes of American Presidents: From Abraham Lincoln to Theodore Roosevelt.* New York: Doubleday, 1971.

Sklar, Robert. *Movie-Made America: How the Movies Changed American Life.* New York: Random House, 1975.

Sklar, Robert, ed. *The Plastic Age: 1917–1930.* "The American Culture" series. New York: George Braziller, 1970.

Smitherman, Geneva. *Talkin and Testifyin: The Language of Black America.* Boston: Houghton Mifflin, 1977.

Smythe, Mabel M., ed. *The Black American Reference Book.* Englewood Cliffs, N.J.: Prentice-Hall, 1976.

Southern, Eileen. *The Music of Black Americans: A History.* 2nd edition. New York: W. W. Norton, 1983.

Sowell, Thomas. *The Economics and Politics of Race: An International Perspective.* New York: William Morrow, 1983.

Soyinka, Wole. *Ake: The Years of Childhood.* New York: Random House, 1981.

Soyinka, Wole. *Myth, Literature, and the African World.* New York: Cambridge University Press, 1976.

Spalding, Henry D. *Encyclopedia of Black Folklore and Humor.* Middle Village, N.Y.: Jonathan David, 1972.

Spellman, A. B. *Black Music: Four Lives.* New York: Schocken, 1970.

Spiller, Robert E., Willard Thorp, Thomas H. Johnson, Henry Seidel Canby, Richard M. Ludwig, and William M. Gibson. *Literary History of the United States: History.* 4th ed., rev. New York: Macmillan, 1974.

Stearns, Marshall and Jean. *Jazz Dance: The Story of American Vernacular Dance.* New York: Macmillan, 1968.

Stein, Charles W., ed. *American Vaudeville: As Seen By Its Contemporaries.* New York: Alfred A. Knopf, 1984.

Sterling, Bryan B. and Frances N. *Will Rogers in Hollywood: An Illustrated History of the Film Career of America's Favorite Humorist.* New York: Crown, 1984.

Sterling, Philip. *Laughing on the Outside: The Intelligent White Reader's Guide to Negro Tales and Humor.* New York: Grosset and Dunlap, 1965.

Stuckey, Sterling. *Slave Culture: Nationalist Theory and the Foundation of Black America.* New York: Oxford University Press, 1987.

Sypher, Wylie, ed. *Comedy: "An Essay on Comedy," by George Meredith, and "Laughter," by Henri Bergson.* Baltimore, Md.: Johns Hopkins University Press, 1980.

Takaki, Ronald T. *Iron Cages: Race and Culture in Nineteenth-Century America.* New York: Alfred A. Knopf, 1979.

Thompson, Robert Farris. *African Art in Motion.* Berkeley, Calif.: University of California Press, 1973.

Thompson, Robert Farris. *Flash of the Spirit: African and Afro-American Art and Philosophy.* New York: Random House, 1983.

Thorpe, Edward. *Black Dance.* Woodstock, N.Y.: Overlook Press, 1990.

Titon, Jeff Todd. *Early Downhome Blues.* Chicago: University of Illinois Press, 1977.

Toll, Robert C. *Blacking Up: The Minstrel Show in Nineteenth-Century America.* New York: Oxford University Press, 1974.

Trachtenberg, Stanley, ed. *American Humorists, 1800–1950.* Detroit: Gale Research Company, A Bruccoli Clark Book, 1982.

Travis, Dempsey J. *An Autobiography of Black Jazz.* Chicago: The Urban Research Institute, 1983.

Vance, Joel. *Fats Waller: His Life and Times.* New York: Berkley Medallion Books, 1979.

Waldon, Vince. *Classic Sitcoms: A Celebration of the Best in Prime-Time Comedy*. New York: Macmillan, 1987.

Walker, Alice, ed. *I Love Myself, When I Am Laughing . . . And Then Again When I Am Looking Mean and Impressive: A Zora Neale Hurston Reader*. New York: Feminist Press, 1979.

Walker, David. *Walker's Appeal*. New York: Arno Press and The New York Times, 1969.

Walton, Ortiz M. *Music: Black, White and Blue. A Sociological Survey of the Use and Misuse of Afro-American Music*. New York: William Morrow, 1972.

Waterman, Christopher Alan. *Juju: A Social History and Ethnography of an African Popular Music*. Chicago: University of Chicago, 1990.

Waters, Ethel, with Charles Samuels. *His Eye Is on the Sparrow: An Autobiography*. New York: Pyramid Books, 1972.

Watkins, Mel, ed. *Black Review No. 2*. New York: William Morrow, 1972.

Weinstein, Allen, and Frank Otto Gatell, eds. *American Negro Slavery: A Modern Reader*. 2nd ed. New York: Oxford University Press, 1973.

Wepman, Dennis, Ronald B. Newman, and Murray B. Binderman, eds. *The Life: The Lore and Folk Poetry of the Black Hustler*. Philadelphia: University of Pennsylvania Press, 1976.

Wertheim, Arthur Frank. *Radio Comedy*. New York: Oxford University Press, 1979.

Wilkerson, Tichi, and Marcia Borie. *The Hollywood Reporter: The Golden Years*. New York: Coward-McCann, 1984.

Williams, John A., and Charles F. Harris, eds. *Amistad 1* and *2*. New York: Random House, 1970 and 1971.

Williams, John A. and Dennis A. *If I Stop I'll Die; The Comedy and Tragedy of Richard Pryor*. New York: Thunder's Mouth Press, 1991.

Wilson, John S. *Jazz: The Transition Years, 1940–1960*. New York: Appleton-Century-Crofts, 1966.

Wilson, Theodore B. *The Black Codes of the South*. Tuscaloosa, Ala.: University of Alabama Press, 1966.

Wittke, Carl. *Tambo and Bones*. Westport, Conn.: Greenwood Press, 1968.

Wood, Gordon S. *The Rising Glory of America, 1760–1820*. New York: George Braziller, 1971.

Wright, Richard. *Black Boy*. New York: Perennial Classic, 1966.

Ziff, Larzer. *The American 1890's: Life and Times of a Lost Generation*. New York: Viking Press, 1966.

FICTION

Beckham, Barry. *Runner Mack*, Washington, D.C.: Howard University Press, 1983.

Bradley, David. *South Street*. Signature Edition. New York: Charles Scribner's Sons, 1986.

Brown, Cecil. *Days without Weather*, New York: Farrar, Straus and Giroux, 1983.

Brown, Cecil. *The Life and Loves of Mr. Jiveass Nigger*. New York: Farrar, Straus and Giroux, 1969.

Brown, William Wells. *Clotel, or the President's Daughter*. New York: Arno Press and The New York Times, 1969.

Chesnutt, Charles W. *The Conjure Woman*. Ann Arbor, Mich.: University of Michigan Press, 1969.

Chesnutt, Charles W. *The Wife of His Youth*. Ann Arbor, Mich.: University of Michigan Press, 1968.

Ellison, Ralph. *Invisible Man*. Thirtieth anniversary edition. Random House, 1982.

Fisher, Rudolph. *The Conjure-Man Dies*. New York: Arno Press and The New York Times, 1971.

Fisher, Rudolph. *The Walls of Jericho*. New York: Arno Press and The New York Times, 1969.

Gaines, Ernest J. *A Gathering of Old Men*. New York: Knopf, 1983.

Harris, Joel Chandler. *Uncle Remus: His Songs and Sayings. The Folklore of the Old Plantation*. Atlanta, Ga.: Cherokee Publishing, 1981.

Himes, Chester. *Black on Black: Baby Sister and Selected Writings*. New York: Doubleday, 1973.

Himes, Chester. *Blind Man with a Pistol*. New York: Vintage Books, 1989.

Hughes, Langston. *Not without Laughter*. New York: Macmillan, Collier, 1970.

Hughes, Langston. *The Ways of White Folks*. New York: Alfred A. Knopf, 1934.

Hughes, Langston, and Zora Neale Hurston. *Mule Bone: A Comedy of Negro Life*. New York: Simon and Schuster, 1990.

Hurston, Zora Neale. *Jonah's Gourd Vine*. New York: J. B. Lippincott, 1971.

Hurston, Zora Neale. *Moses, Man of the Mountain.* Chicago: University of Illinois Press, 1984.

Hurston, Zora Neale. *Their Eyes Were Watching God.* New York: Harper and Row, Perennial Library, 1990.

Johnson, James Weldon. *The Autobiography of an Ex-Colored Man.* Garden City, N. Y.: Knopf, Garden City Publishing, 1927.

Jones, LeRoi. *Black Magic: Collected Poetry, 1961–1967.* New York: Bobbs-Merrill, 1969.

Jones, LeRoi. *Tales.* New York: Grove Press, 1967.

Kelley, William Melvin. *Dancers on the Shore.* Washington, D.C.: Howard University Press, 1984.

Killens, John Oliver. *And Then We Heard the Thunder.* Washington, D.C.: Howard University Press, 1983.

Lester, Julius. *The Tales of Uncle Remus: The Adventures of Brer Rabbit.* New York: Dial Books, 1987.

Morrison, Toni. *Song of Solomon.* New York: Knopf, 1977.

Morrison, Toni. *Tar Baby.* Knopf, 1981.

Murray, Albert. *Train Whistle Guitar.* New York: McGraw-Hill, 1974.

Reed, Ishmael. *Conjure: Selected Poems, 1963–1970.* Amherst, Mass.: University of Massachusetts Press, 1972.

Reed, Ishmael. *Mumbo Jumbo.* New York: Doubleday, 1972.

Reed, Ishmael. *Yellow Back Radio Broke Down.* New York: Doubleday, 1969.

Schuyler, George. *Black No More.* College Park, Maryland: McGrath Publishing, 1969.

Stowe, Harriet Beecher. *Uncle Tom's Cabin or Life Among the Lowly.* New York: Signet, 1966.

Van Vechten, Carl. *Nigger Heaven.* New York: Harper, 1971.

Wright, Charles. *The Wig.* New York: Farrar, Straus and Giroux, 1966.

Wright, Richard. *Lawd Today.* New York: Avon Books, 1963.

Wright, Richard. *Native Son.* New York: Perennial Classics, 1966.

Young, Al. *Ask Me Now.* New York: McGraw-Hill, 1980.